The
United Lutheran Church
in America, 1918–1962

E. Theodore Bachmann
with Mercia Brenne Bachmann
edited by Paul Rorem

Fortress Press
Minneapolis

The United Lutheran Church in America, 1918-1962

Cover design by David Meyer
Book design by Ann Terman Olson
Cover photos: Frederick H. Knubel, ELCA Archives, Chicago, Photograph
Collection, JYH00631; Franklin Clark Fry, ELCA Archives, Chicago, Franklin
Clark Fry Papers, PA 97.

Library of Congress Cataloging-in-Publication Data

Bachmann, E. Theodore (Ernest Theodore)
      The United Lutheran Church in America, 1918-1962 / E. Theodore
   Bachmann ; with Mercia Brenne Bachmann ; edited by Paul Rorem.
         p.   cm.
      Includes bibliographical references and index.
      ISBN 0-8006-2925-6 (alk. paper)
      1. United Lutheran Church in America—History.   I. Bachmann,
   Mercia Brenne.   II. Rorem, Paul.   III. Title.
   BX8048.B33   1997
   284.1'335'09—dc21   97-20819
                                                               CIP

The paper used in this publication meets the minimum requirements of
American National Standard for Information Sciences—Permanence of Paper
for Printed Library Materials. ANSI Z329.48.1984.

Manufactured in the U.S.A.

00   99   98   97   1   2   3   4   5   6   7   8   9   10

CONTENTS

WORKS FREQUENTLY CITED

A. R. Wentz, *Basic History* = Wentz, Abdel Ross. *A Basic History of Lutheranism in America*, rev. ed. Philadelphia: Muhlenberg Press, 1964 [1955].

A. R. Wentz, *Gettysburg Seminary Record* = Wentz, Abdel Ross, ed. *Gettysburg Lutheran Theological Seminary, Volume 2, Alumni Record*. Harrisburg, Pennsylvania: Evangelical Press, 1964.

A. R. Wentz, *Lutheran Church* = Wentz, Abdel Ross. *The Lutheran Church in American History*, 2nd ed. Philadelphia: United Lutheran Publication House, 1933.

Bachmann, *Lutheran Churches* = Bachmann, E. Theodore and Mercia Brenne Bachmann. *Lutheran Churches in the World*. Minneapolis, Minnesota: Augsburg, 1989.

F. K. Wentz, *Lutherans in Concert* = Wentz, Frederick K. *Lutherans in Concert: The Story of the National Lutheran Council, 1918-1966*. Minneapolis, Minnesota: Augsburg, 1968.

Gilbert, *Commitment to Unity* = Gilbert, W. Kent. *Commitment to Unity: A History of the Lutheran Church in America*. Philadelphia: Fortress Press, 1988.

Jacobs, *History* = Jacobs, Henry Eyster. *A History of the Evangelical Lutheran Church in the United States*. New York: The Christian Literature, 1893.

Kaufmann, *Philadelphia Seminary Record* = Kaufmann, John A., ed. *Biographical Record of the Lutheran Theological Seminary at Philadelphia, 1864-1962*. Philadelphia: The Lutheran Theological Seminary, 1964.

Mr. Protestant = *Mr. Protestant: An Informal Biography of Franklin Clark Fry*. Philadelphia: The Board of Publication of the United Lutheran Church in America, 1960.

Nelson, *Lutherans in North America* = Nelson, E. Clifford, and associates. *The Lutherans in North America*. Philadelphia: Fortress Press, 1980 [1975].

NOTES = The Personal Notebooks of the Rev. E. Theodore Bachmann. To be deposited in the Archives of the Evangelical Lutheran Church in America. Chicago, Illinois. (Cited by volume and page number; e.g. NOTES 365:60.)

Palette = *Franklin Clark Fry: A Palette for a Portrait*, ed. Robert H. Fischer, Supplementary Number of *The Lutheran Quarterly*, vol. 24 (1972).

R. C. Wolf, *Documents* = Wolf, Richard C. *Documents in Lutheran Unity in America*. Philadelphia: Fortress Press, 1966.

Tappert, *Philadelphia Seminary History* = Tappert, Theodore G., *History of the Lutheran Theological Seminary at Philadelphia, 1864-1964*. Philadelphia: The Lutheran Theological Seminary at Philadelphia, 1964.

ULCA *Minutes* = *Minutes of the Biennial Conventions of the United Lutheran Church in America*, 1918-1962.

ULCA *Year Book* = *Yearbook of the United Lutheran Church in America*, various eds. Philadelphia: The United Lutheran Publication House.

FOREWORD

by H. George Anderson

The Evangelical Lutheran Church in America has a big family tree. The stories of most of its predecessor bodies have been told, but up to now one important branch has been missing. This volume fills that void.

The United Lutheran Church in America (1918-1962) was the largest of the "grandparent" bodies of the ELCA. Its forty-four years spanned the time from the end of the first World War, through depression and a second war, to the growth years of the 1950s. Its own birth out of the merger of three earlier Lutheran traditions made it an eager participant in the ecumenical movement and in Lutheran efforts toward unity. In 1962 those efforts produced the Lutheran Church in America, and the ULCA provided that body with its first president, Franklin Clark Fry.

The ULCA was not so much a union as a reunion. It traced its origins back to the first waves of immigration to America, when Lutherans settled in colonies along the east coast and gradually moved westward with other land-hungry pioneers. These scattered believers gathered into local synods, and the synods eventually formed a loose union called the General Synod. During the Civil War the General Synod lost its southern members to a movement that later called itself the United Synod, South. Another split, this time over theological issues, resulted in the formation of a third group, the General Council. It was these three groups, stimulated by the celebration of the four hundredth anniversary of the Reformation in 1917, that organized themselves into the United Lutheran Church.

The structure of the ULCA reflected its origin from many synods rather than from one national entity. Synods varied in their liturgical practices and in their historic connections to overseas mission fields. Institutions like colleges and seminaries relied on synodical loyalties. This manifold character required deliberate efforts toward cooperation, and the experience of the ULCA in creating and maintaining unity was one of the gifts that it brought to subsequent Lutheran mergers.

Here the story of the ULCA is told by a historian who witnessed many of its key events. As a child E. Theodore Bachmann watched a reenactment of Luther posting his ninety-five theses during the anniversary celebrations of 1917. He later became a pastor and leader in the ULCA. For the rest of his life he helped to create the history that he has recorded here. Because of his personal involvement in the events he describes, he has been able to offer details and perspectives that ordinary historical research seldom can provide.

As readers we can all be grateful that Dr. Bachmann took on this task at a time in life when many others would have been too weary. We can be doubly grateful that, when he did not live to complete the manuscript, his helpmate of fifty-four years, Mercia Brenne Bachmann, agreed to carry the project through to publication. In this effort she has been joined by Paul Rorem, Benjamin B. Warfield Professor of Ecclesiastical History at Princeton Theological Seminary. Their contribution is not only evidence of their love and respect for Ted Bachmann but also of their own gifts as faithful interpreters of Lutheran history.

H. George Anderson
Presiding Bishop
Evangelical Lutheran Church in America

PREFACE

by Mercia Brenne Bachmann

On the last day of my husband's temporal life he expressed his deep regrets and sorrow that he had not been able to finish the history of the United Lutheran Church in America. When I assured him that I would try to finish the story, he mentioned the names of a few friends who might be able and willing to help. Those were expressions of love for each other and for our Lord's church.

In 1985 when the Lutheran Church in America was anticipating a merger with the American Lutheran Church and the Association of Evangelical Lutheran Churches to form the Evangelical Lutheran Church in America, Fortress Press commissioned W. Kent Gilbert to write the LCA's twenty-five-year history. Fortunately, three of the four churches that had formed the LCA had their histories already written. But there was no complete history of the ULCA, the oldest and largest of the four bodies. Its account had been given only in parts in various general American Lutheran histories like that of A. R. Wentz and E. Clifford Nelson. This left an enormous gap in the historiography of Lutheranism in North America.

Since almost a quarter of a century had elapsed from the time the ULCA became part of the LCA in 1962, the number of historians who had experienced all or most of the forty-four-year life of the ULCA was greatly diminished, or they were past their prime. Nevertheless, Fortress did turn to E. Theodore Bachmann. He was then seventy-five years of age and busy with a number of important unfinished projects. When urged to accept the commission, he did so with my approval and with the understanding that there would be no time pressure.

The Fortress officials realized that their chosen author had an unusually broad view of the ULCA. He grew up in a ULCA parsonage. His father was the pastor and director of the Deaconess Community in Philadelphia, with wide responsibilities for the work of deaconesses in numerous congregations and institutions throughout the ULCA. The senior Bachmann was also a delegate to the ULCA organizing convention in 1918, where he was elected to the Board of Inner Mission and became its first president, with influence in shaping the ULCA's social ministry. Supplementing this environment, the young son was enrolled in the Sunday school at Messiah, "The Friendly Church," where the widely-known Rev. Ross Stover held forth in low-church style as in the former General Synod.

After a Quaker education—Friends' Select, Penn Charter and Haverford College—he had a year at Harvard University studying American History (M.A., 1934). There he experienced the ULCA's concern for students at non-Lutheran colleges and universities by way of the nearby University Lutheran Church. After a summer in Europe where he was confronted with Hitler's National Socialism and the courageous participants of the bitter church conflict (Kirchenkampf) he

E. THEODORE BACHMANN in his study in 1987, the year he began work on the ULCA history. Photo by Mary L. Bachmann, his daughter.

returned home, not to study law as expected but to study theology at the Lutheran Theological Seminary at Philadelphia (1934-37). Postponing ordination, he had another year of study in Germany at Erlangen and Tübingen Universities where there still were outstanding professors resisting Hitler. This was supplemented by ten weeks of study in the Near East, including a long stay in the new Israel and Palestine. While here, a call came from Trinity Church, Pottsville, Pa., a congregation of thirty-two hundred members in the coal country then suffering from the depression of the 1930s. After ordination on June 26, 1938, in the chapel of the Philadelphia Deaconess Motherhouse by the president of the Ministerium of Pennsylvania, the ULCA's oldest synod, he had a fruitful year under the guidance of the able and understanding pastor, the Rev. Emil W. Weber. This began his contribution to and his immense benefits from being a pastor, professor, author, ecumenist, and briefly a bureaucrat in the United Lutheran Church in America.

A leave of absence from this first congregation enabled him to return to Harvard. After finishing residence requirements for a Ph.D., he began two research projects, one on Christian Frederick Heyer, the first American Lutheran missionary to India (1842) and the other on the Missouri Synod, the Lutheran church body about which he knew the least. Both projects required research not only in Cambridge but also in the Midwest. His trip, visiting seminaries, colleges, church offices, social agencies, and congregations, brought him more than expected—a life partner. By the end of the leave he submitted *They Called Him Father* to Muhlenberg Press. It was one of several manuscripts competing for the Rung Prize, for the best book to help the ULCA celebrate in 1942 the one-hundredth anniversary of Heyer's leaving for India and the two hundredth anniversary of Muhlenberg's arrival in America in 1742. The book not only won the prize but was published by Muhlenberg Press. Read by many throughout the church, it created new interest in the ULCA mission in India. It also launched Bachmann on a teaching career. From his second parish experience at St. Stephen's congregation in Wilmington, Delaware, where he was substituting for the Rev. Park Huntington, who was on leave for military service as chaplain, he was called to the reorganized Chicago Lutheran Seminary in Maywood, Illinois (1942-48). There he taught church history and social missions and completed his Ph.D. work at the University of Chicago (1947). During the fifties he was Professor of History and Missions at the relocated Pacific Lutheran Seminary in Berkeley, California.

Meanwhile, he was a frequent delegate to the ULCA's biennial conventions and was elected to the Board of Deaconess Work in 1952. He translated and edited volume 35 on "Word and Sacrament" of *Luther's Works* published by Muhlenberg Press and Concordia Publishing House. Then, in 1961, he was called by the ULCA Board of Higher Education to be Associate Secretary for Theological Education. In this position he established a Continuing Education program for pastors and prepared the way for the Board of Theological Education in the new Lutheran Church in America. While on leave of absence from the Chicago Seminary (1946-47) he strengthened the ULCA's ecumenical relations by serving as the first liaison representative of the World Council of Churches in the Process of Formation to the churches in Germany. Shuttling between Geneva and Germany, he helped to bring the Protestant churches into the ecumenical partnership from which Nazi policy had excluded them. During this year (1947) he also participated in the first Assembly of the Lutheran World Federation in Lund, Sweden, as a delegate of the ULCA. In 1952 his small book, *Epic of Faith*, published by the National Lutheran Council, prepared delegates and visitors of all American Lutheran church bodies for the Second Assembly in Hanover, Germany. He was also an active participant of the Minneapolis Assembly in 1957 and the Helsinki Assembly in 1962.

The author's work with the WCC and his volunteer service visiting Prisoner of War camps in the Chicago area under the International YMCA (1945-46) was noticed by the United States Department of State. In 1948 he was "drafted" to be Chief of Protestant Affairs in the Religious Affairs Branch of the Military Government in Germany. Remembering his past service, German church leaders received him not only as a government official but also as a brother in Christ offering help. This position enabled him to bring a number of well-chosen church leaders from America, Britain, and Scandinavia into Germany to help the churches in their reorientation. Among them was Professor A. R. Wentz from

Gettysburg Seminary who had been so instrumental in working with the German Lutherans in forming the Lutheran World Convention in the 1920s. The Religious Affairs branch also sent numerous students and church leaders to the United States, and the ULCA benefited from this interchange.

Returning to the United States, he may have softened the strained relationship between the Norwegian Lutheran Church of America and the ULCA by filling the great need at Luther Seminary for a guest professor of church history for three semesters (1951-52). During his Berkeley days he supported the ULCA's membership in the National Council of Churches by editing Volumes I and III of the *Churches in Social Welfare* series. An academic year (1959) in Brazil teaching at the Escola Superior de Teologia in São Leopoldo under LWF sponsorship strengthened the ULCA's long sought partnership with the Evangelical Church of the Lutheran Confession.

These experiences helped the author see the ULCA from the viewpoint of others. Choosing the "Rise of Missouri Lutheranism" as the subject of his Ph.D. thesis and spending much time and effort to know and understand the ULCA's critics, he gained a fresh understanding and appreciation of his own beloved church.

With this personal background and the handbook *Lutheran Churches in the World* ready for publication, the author began the project with enthusiasm in 1987, with the intention of completing it by late 1991. Of course it was apparent then that such a book, *The United Lutheran Church Remembered*, would require more than personal recollections and impressions. Untold number of days, weeks, and months were therefore spent researching materials in the Lutheran Seminary libraries of Philadelphia, Gettysburg, and Columbia in South Carolina, and in the Princeton Seminary Library near our home, as well as in the minutes and reports of the ULC biennial conventions. We also spent many days in the ELCA Archives in Chicago. Here we had the excellent support and help of Elizabeth Wittman and her staff. It was my privilege to assist in all these efforts to obtain a clear and—as far as possible—an adequate history. Correspondence of the two presidents, back copies of *The Lutheran*, the ULCA official periodical, as well as other journals and regular releases served to put flesh on skeletal minutes. We gathered far more material than could be used. If the author had not known so much about the ULCA it would not have taken him so long to write its history.

The year 1991 passed and the ULCA story was far from finished. The author had become more and more involved in its lengthy prehistory including the European background for Reformed and Lutheran intermingling. He was also aware of the tremendous need to trace the histories of the various functions of proclamation and service in a church combining differences in polity as well as interpretation of their common heritage.

With these factors in mind, he planned a book of forty chapters. A quick general history would be followed by chapters on various aspects of ULCA development. However, in time he realized that this was entirely too ambitious for what was wanted. The chapters that he finished on the synods, the constitution and theological education have to a certain extent been included in the general history, now reduced to twelve chapters. After the 1918 organizing convention (chapter 1) and a dip back into the prehistory (chapters 2 and 3) the story proceeds in chronological order. It was his aim to write the story in such a way that it would make sense and be of interest to lay members, as well as giving an account that would meet the standards of the best church historians.

Perhaps some readers will think too much space was allotted to the prehistory. To condense 275 years into two short chapters and still give a fair and understandable story requires skill. The author was never satisfied that he had accomplished this, and during the last few weeks of his life he tried again with a new approach. Since this was left unfinished, let it be a challenge to present day historians. Especially needed is a complete history of the General Synod (1820-1918), the oldest and largest of the three bodies forming the ULCA, in order to complete the story of Lutheranism in America. Without apologies I am glad that this past (incomplete as it is) can be shared with all ELCA members, for it now is their history. By merger as in a marriage we gain relatives with a surprising history. However, if there are those who do not want to gain this knowledge, they may skip chapters 2 and 3. In time they may want to return to this early period that is older than our nation.

As I write these last words before the book goes to press, I still wonder why the LCA publication officials chose my husband instead of finding a young historian. An accurate historical document could have been written from minutes, official reports, and periodicals. However, it might have lacked in personalities—note the plural. A church is made up of people. This was very important to the author, as readers will discover. With respect and understanding he described them in detail, limps and all. He also divided the book in such a way that two sections begin with a biography of the elected president. In so doing he had no intention of diminishing the importance of others. Rather it was to stress the fact that during its lifetime, the ULCA had only two presidents. The strength of both was their ability to attract and support creative and capable leaders in the various fields of proclamation and service. Their biographies also illustrate how they were influenced by history as well as how their lives shaped history. It was natural that the author's personal concerns—church body relationships, deaconess and social missions service, and world missions—should receive special attention. Nevertheless, his ability to identify with others plus his historical training prevented these favorite themes from assuming too large a place in the overall story.

Although Fortress Press honored its agreement not to demand a time limit, the author realized that he needed one. In May 1994 we scheduled a visit at Augsburg-Fortress Press in Minneapolis. We were then assigned an editor who would do his part in bringing the book to completion by June of 1996. Unfortunately this editor soon left the publishing house for another position. Nevertheless, we kept working, hoping to meet the deadline. With the author's death in November 1995, this date became an impossibility. But a finished book was still a promise.

Early in 1996, the Rev. Paul Rorem, Professor of Church History at Princeton Theological Seminary, volunteered to serve as editor and arranged for this with Fortress Press. This began a unique working partnership. He set time limits for me to produce one finished chapter after another. Meanwhile, I would review the author's work. Some chapters had been written several times with different slants. So for these there was much choosing or combining. Rorem would then edit the chapter and return it to me for approval. When it was necessary for me to research and compose missing spots, Rorem was great encouragement and support. Yes, there were times when I too had to turn to the well-marked ULCA minutes and reports that the author kept close to his desk. From 1918 to 1944 they were those of his father.

Rorem had the assistance of a very efficient secretary, Judith Attride, who could make sense out of his editorial scrawls and my deteriorating handwriting. He also had the assistance of two Lutheran Ph.D. students, Carolyn Schneider and the Rev. David Lose. They deserve the highest praise for their meticulous checking of footnotes and bibliography.

Various chapters were critically read by Frederick Wentz, James Crumley, Franklin Drewes Fry, and Henry Horn—all ULCA pastors and scholars. Others, such as W. Kent Gilbert, E. Dale Click, Don Houser, and George W. Forell reviewed various sections and made valuable corrections or additions. Sisters Mildred Winter and Louise Burroughs checked the deaconess history in the postscript to chapter 12. Then the entire book was critically read by Robert Fischer, a recognized scholar in American Lutheranism. His numerous questions, corrections, and comments were of immense value in producing an accurate history. Besides, I had encouragement from numerous friends of my husband and others who have for too long awaited this history of the United Lutheran Church in America.

If the author were writing this preface, I am sure that he would have a much longer list of those who should be thanked. Among them would be the committee that had confidence in him, especially Robert W. Endruschat, president of the Board of Publications of the LCA, and Reuben Swanson, LCA secretary. He would also recognize Helen Knubel, National Lutheran Council archivist, and George Harkins, the last ULCA secretary. They could be counted on to know or to find the answer to every question the author had.

Even with all the freely given help, I submit the book for publication with anxiety. Has our editing been fair to the author and to the United Lutheran Church in America? Therefore, I must request all readers to remember that the author, E. Theodore Bachmann, was not permitted to make his final revisions. Yet a few months before his death he began his foreword with these basic words:

"Church history is the story of how the Gospel has fared in the human family over the generations and around the world. Basic to this definition is the work of the Holy Spirit who, in Luther's words, 'calls, gathers, enlightens and sanctifies the whole Christian Church on earth and keeps it in union with Jesus Christ.'"

Mercia Brenne Bachmann
The Author's Helpmate

LIST OF ABBREVIATIONS

ABS =   American Bible Society
AELC =   Association of Evangelical Lutheran Churches
ALC =   American Lutheran Church
BAM =   Board of American Missions
B.D. =   Bachelor of Divinity
BFM =   Board of Foreign Mission
BG =   British Guiana
BHE =   Board of Higher Education
BSM =   Board of Social Missions
CHEY =   Christian Higher Education Year
CLC =   Canadian Lutheran Council
CSBH =   Common Service Book of the Lutheran Church
         with Hymnal
D.D. =   Doctor of Divinity
ELC =   (Norwegian) Evangelical Lutheran Church
ELCA =   Evangelical Lutheran Church in America
ELCIC = Evangelical Lutheran Church in Canada
FCC =   Federal Council of Churches
IMC =   International Missionary Council
IWM =   Interchurch World Movement
JCLU =   Joint Commission on Lutheran Unity
JELC =   Japan Evangelical Lutheran Church
LBW =   Lutheran Book of Worship
LCA =   Lutheran Church in America
LCC =   Lutheran Church of China
LCL =   Lutheran Church of Liberia

LEM =   Lutheran Evangelism Missions
LLA =   Luther League of America
LLM =   Lutheran Laymen's Movement [for Stewardship]
LSAA =   Lutheran Student Association of America
LWA =   Lutheran World Action
LWF =   Lutheran World Federation
LWR =   Lutheran World Relief
NBC =   National Broadcasting Corporation
NCC =   National Council of Churches
NCCCUSA = National Council of the Churches of Christ in
          the United States of America
NLC =   National Lutheran Council
Ph.D. =   Doctor of Philosophy
PLTS =   Pacific Lutheran Theological Seminary
POW =   Prisoner of War
SBH =   Service Book and Hymnal
ULCA =   United Lutheran Church in America
ULCM =   United Lutheran Church Men
ULCW =   United Lutheran Church Women
UN =   United Nations
USO =   United Service Organization
WCC =   World Council of Churches
WCTU =   Women's Christian Temperance Union
WMS =   Women's Missionary Society
YMCA =   Young Men's Christian Association

CHAPTER 1

THE ORGANIZING CONVENTION,
NOVEMBER 1918

NEVER IN LIVING MEMORY HAD CANADA AND THE UNITED STATES been swept by such ecstasy as on that Monday, November 11, 1918. A four-line banner on the front page of *The New York Times* proclaimed.

ARMISTICE SIGNED, END OF THE WAR
BERLIN SEIZED BY REVOLUTIONISTS
NEW CHANCELLOR BEGS FOR ORDER
OUSTED KAISER FLEES TO HOLLAND[1]

Canada had been involved in the Great War from its beginning in August 1914. Reluctantly the United States intervened only after Germany had defeated Russia and was massing its full power on the Western Front. American entry on the side of the Allies, France and Britain mainly, turned the tide.[2] For the defeated it meant the loss of empire and dynasty: first went the Russian Empire and the Romanov dynasty, then the German Hohenzollern, then the Austria-Hungarian and the Hapsburg.

For the victorious the struggle had been to "make the world safe for democracy," in President Wilson's words. A corollary, now to be worked out, was "the right of self-determination of peoples." This was the heady agenda that Americans envisioned and with which Europeans subsequently grappled.[3] At home, in countless families and communities, there was now the prospect of return to "normalcy," and of reunion and demobilization. "Keep the home fires burning . . . till the boys come home," with its haunting melody, approached fulfillment. In local churches and elsewhere hung the service flags honoring the number of young men who had enlisted. For each one there was a blue star on the white field inside the broad red border; for those killed in action, the star was gold.

Four days after the signing of the Armistice, while New York City was still agog with excitement sufficient to eclipse every other interest, the United Lutheran Church in America was being born. Before turning to its organizing convention there are several things worth keeping in mind. First is the broad social scene. A foremost theologian declared that "the great word of our day is organization." He warned that the test of the civilization lay in the fitness of its institutions to respond to the demands made upon them.[4] To meet the needs of the wartime situation, the Federal Council of Churches had issued a balanced statement of principles concerning the war. The council had created the General Wartime Commission of the Churches as an agency through which the government could deal collectively with most of the Protestant denominations.[5] Second, Lutherans were also concerned about confessional identity. In liaison with the Missouri Synod they formed a National Lutheran Commission for Soldiers' and Sailors' Welfare (1917). This led to the formation of the National Lutheran Council in September 1918. The council became the confessional context in which the United Lutheran Church developed.[6]

This author was a seven-year-old at the time of the Armistice. On that day church bells were ringing, factory whistles blowing, streetcar gongs clanging, trucks honking, autos and horse-drawn wagons competing, neighbors and strangers exchanging spontaneously the joy that peace had broken out. A second-grader in a parochial school, I remember marching proudly the mile-long walk to school, and then hearing our teacher, a kindly man of German birth, speak movingly of what it must be like for people on the losing side. On the next day, the 12th, my father, pastor of the Deaconess Motherhouse community in Philadelphia, bade my mother and me his prayerful adieu. He was New York-bound by train, a delegate to the final meeting of the General Council and to the organizing convention of the new church body.[7]

THE BEGINNING

It was Thursday, November 14, 1918, a bright autumn afternoon in Manhattan. Delegates converged at the entrance to the Lutheran Church of the Holy Trinity, at 65th Street and Central Park West. By mid-afternoon 515 out of 558 pastors and laymen, representing forty-five synods in the United States and Canada, had registered. There were some women, but not yet as delegates. Mutual acquaintanceship among the gathered was limited largely to previous association in one or another of the three general bodies about to merge.[8] Of these three the largest number was from the General Synod, whose final convention met that morning at St. James Church, across Central Park, at 73rd Street and Madison Avenue. The smallest number, from the United Synod in the South, had wound up its affairs (begun earlier in Roanoke, Virginia) at the Church of the Advent, on Broadway and 93rd Street. The General Council, numerically not far behind the General Synod, had already held its closing convention here at Holy Trinity, the host church.[9] A select number of guests and groups were also entering, including a class from the Philadelphia Seminary, led by their professor, Charles M. Jacobs. He was eager, as Conrad Bergendoff, one of the students, later recalled, "to have us experience church history in the making."[10]

The first business session began promptly at three-thirty, exulting in the words of the Psalmist, "Great is the Lord, and greatly to be praised in the city of our God, in the mountain of his holiness" (48:1). Thereupon the waiting congregation broke into Martin Luther's invocative hymn, "Come, Holy Spirit, God and Lord," number 146 in the recently completed *Common Service Book and Hymnal*.[11] M. G. G. Scherer, of Columbia, South Carolina, led in prayer, and declared the first meeting of the United Lutheran Church in America opened in the Name of the Father, and of the Son, and of the Holy Ghost.[12]

Preliminaries included a recognition of the twenty-one-member Joint Committee on Ways and Means, whose task it had been to plan the Merger and this organizing convention. The committee's chair, T. E. Schmauk, was elected temporary president of the convention; and William M. Baum (Canajoharie, N.Y.), temporary secretary. Initial requirements were thus met for incorporating the ULCA in New York State, by providing that one of its officers, in this case Baum, be a New Yorker. With a roll call of the synods a whole continent seemed to pass in review. The General Synod constituency included twenty-four synods, the General Council thirteen synods, and the United Synod in the South eight synods. General Synod delegates outnumbered the combined total of the General Council and the United Synod in the South. Anyone with an eye on the upcoming elections, especially for the presidency, could anticipate an interesting outcome.

By a rising vote the delegates adopted a forthright declaration proposed by the Ways and Means Committee on the religious and moral issues facing the nation at home and abroad now that the war had ended and Christians were called upon to strive for a just peace for all. A copy of the declaration was ordered sent to the Associated Press. Meanwhile the Federal Council of Churches, via telegram, was the first religious organization to send greetings to the newborn ULCA.[13] All this was but prologue.

The first religious service of the United Lutheran Church, according to the record, "was an inspiring act of worship of great solemnity and inspiration." That Thursday evening at eight o'clock a capacity throng packed the Church of the Holy Trinity. The celebration of Holy Communion was according to the Common Service whose content adhered to the Church Orders of the Lutheran Reformation and whose language drew on kindred liturgical expression in the Episcopal (Anglican) *Book of Common Prayer*, even as the roots of this liturgy ran back through the Roman Catholic Mass and to the ancient church.

The continuity of Christ's church was affirmed in the reading of the appointed Epistle and Gospel, and in the confession of faith in the words of the Nicene Creed. The hymns that resounded from Holy Trinity's neo-gothic vaults spanned the centuries and drew on the treasures of the recently completed hymnal that accompanied the Common Service. First came that familiar hymn of tenth century Latin origin, "Come, Holy Ghost, Our Souls Inspire"; then, "Hail, Holy, Holy Lord" (a paraphrase of the *Te Deum* by the eighteenth century Independent, Edward Perronet, and set to an old Welsh melody); and, lastly, from the contemporary American scene, "Lord Jesus Christ We Humbly Pray" by Henry Eyster Jacobs.[14] A couplet from this last hymn led into the heart of the

Communion liturgy and summed up the thankfulness of the faithful for the God-given unity in Christ: "One Bread, one Cup, one Body we, United by our life in Thee."

In his sermon Henry Eyster Jacobs, dean of the Philadelphia Seminary and recognized, at the age of seventy-four, as still the foremost among America's Lutheran theologians, looked to the future as he described "The Race Set before Us." The words of his text (Hebrews 12:1-2) were familiar. But the surge of emotion evoked by the news of war's end and by the formation of a united church body gave new power and fresh meaning to the words, "cloud of witnesses," laying aside the encumbering weight and the besetting sin, running the race with patience, and looking to Jesus "who is set down at the right hand of the throne of God." These were exhortations to get up and go.

Dean Jacobs, with his love of history, placed this founding moment in grand perspective. Some excerpts from his half-hour sermon catch the mood of the moment:

> Two hundred and seventy-five years ago, on this island of Manhattan, a group of humble Lutheran laymen were engaged in a valiant struggle, primarily for the right to have their children trained in the Lutheran faith, but, fundamentally, for that religious liberty for which their ancestors had only a century before, battled in The Netherlands, and upon which all true civil liberty rests.[15]

Jacobs continued:

> What country in all the earth, I ask, offers the Lutheran Church what is afforded here? Tell me, you who know the Old World, where has our Church had similar freedom to apply its principles . . . , to frame its own constitution, and determine its own policy?[16]

Yet this enjoyment of privilege brought new obligation:

> The Old World is in ruins. Prostrate Europe, in its exhaustion, looks hither for the means of reconstruction. What is the special contribution that we as American Lutherans can make? . . .[17]

The Jacobs sermon was not a program of action but a summons to faith active in love.

> Here [at home] is our open door for a theology, new in form, but identical in substance with that of the Reformation, in the English language (now the world language) and in terms of modern thought. The call to Repentance, with which Luther awoke the slumbering world, must be sounded forth. . . . Every soul must be taught what sin is and what repentance means. . . . Nor should we fail to make especially clear the doctrine of the Church—the true mean between the two extremes, of a spiritualism that undervalues the Church as an institution, and of a materialism which ignores the Church's spirituality, and finds its unity alone in schemes of outward organization . . . instead of an inflexible fidelity to Holy Scripture.[18]

Touching on many subjects as part of an impending agenda, including unity among Lutherans despite their continuing diversity and the fostering of mutual respect among earnest Christians, Jacobs concluded:

> Let each communicant who here comes to the altar make a new vow and conse-crate himself to the service that is asked. . . . 'Let us run the race set before us, look-ing unto Jesus, the Author and finisher of our faith.' . . . [19]

If the sermon left its imprint, many admitted this gladly, the appearance of the preacher also lodged in memory. It was his crag-like profile, a large head on a stocky frame, as cut on a cameo, that depicted the scholar.[20] We shall meet him again in other contexts.

In the year of the convention Holy Trinity Church was observing its fiftieth anniversary. Its new edifice at 65th Street and Central Park West was dedicated in 1914. Built in neo-gothic style, Holy Trinity's sanctuary reflected the liturgical character of a Lutheranism devoted to the Common Service. For the more than five hundred delegates this was, in the estimation of most, a memorable place to launch the United Lutheran Church in America.[21] However, for the next four days the convention would be meeting in other and larger settings.

The convention had been widely publicized. Experience gained by the Lutheran Bureau, an office based in New York set up initially to publicize the events marking the observances of the Reformation Quadricentennial (1917), prepared the way for the church papers and secular press to pick up the story. The Bureau was led by the imaginative, maverick young Missouri Synod pastor, Otto H. Pannkoke. His associate, Walton H. Greever, Columbia, South Carolina, was at that time also editor of *The American Lutheran Survey*, a weekly with inter-Lutheran coverage published in the South.[22]

In a succession of eight news releases, from October 14 to November 11, the nature and purpose of the merger was explained; its size and extent noted; its policy in higher education set forth; its quest for the right kind of leadership made clear; the extent of Lutheran enterprises in charitable work described; the missionary challenge at home set forth (at the time there were an estimated three million unchurched Lutherans, many of recent immigration, in the United States and Canada); the missionary challenge overseas described (fields in India, Africa, Latin America, and elsewhere).

The eighth and final release spelled out the event itself under the heading, "Great Lutheran Convention to open in New York Tomorrow." Its lead sentence caught the reader's imagination, "Tomorrow, November 12, will begin what has been called the most important convention of Lutherans ever held in America." Focus was on the 12th, not the 14th, because on that Tuesday the General Synod and the General Council would be holding their respective closing conventions. The United Synod in the South meanwhile had already begun its final conven-tion in Roanoke, Virginia, on November 11, prior to relocating and adjourning three days later in New York City. The eighth release also explained why the Ways and Means Committee had chosen New York for the Convention site and not

Pittsburgh. While Pittsburgh was then still regarded as a major gateway to the West, New York was known as the Gateway to America. It was the metropolis of global outreach.[23]

Despite the careful sequence of news releases, the press coverage was modest. The declaration of the Armistice had New York City in a frenzy. *The New York Times*, for example, might otherwise have given the Lutheran event some prominence, for Lutherans were, after the Episcopalians, the next largest Protestant communion in metropolitan New York, but relegated accounts of the convention to inside pages. Space on the front page was preempted by the running accounts of war's end and of the old order in Europe. The Second Reich had collapsed. The Empire of the Hapsburgs had been dismembered and from it independent nations would emerge. For the allies and their American partner in victory immense readjustments captured the news.[24]

Reflecting this exuberant mood, the convention meeting hall, the Auditorium of the Engineering Societies' Building (29 West 39th St., today a drive-up garage), was lavishly draped with the Stars and Stripes. Sessions here as well as the convention's public gatherings held elsewhere were preceded by an enthusiastic singing of the national anthem. The ULCA would have it known that it was a church of patriotism and responsible citizenship, as well as a church of fidelity to the Gospel and to its confessional heritage.[25]

Three Lutheran auxiliaries—women, men and youth—were also meeting. Paralleling the convention, on Friday and Saturday, November 15 and 16, delegates from the Women's Missionary Societies in the three merging bodies filled Holy Trinity Church. There they organized the Women's Missionary Society of the United Lutheran Church in America. The Federal Council of Lutheran Brotherhoods (the men's group) held its fifth convention on Monday, November 11, the very day of the Armistice, including its Wartime Supper (banquet) in the ballroom of the Waldorf Astoria Hotel. This affair was significantly inter-Lutheran.[26] The request of the Luther League of America for recognition by the ULCA was referred to the Committee on Associations of Young People.[27]

BUSINESS SESSIONS

In the format of its business sessions, this convention prefigured others to come, and therefore bears close attention. In the official sessions we can observe, as on a distant screen, the United Church emerging from paper constitution to living structure. Friday morning, November 15, was electric with anticipation. Who would be president of the new church body? Schmauk, the temporary chair, was regarded by many as the logical choice. At age fifty-eight he was a proven leader and a man of vision, fully committed to Christ and His Church. A native of Lancaster, he was a graduate of the University of Pennsylvania and of the Philadelphia Seminary. In the thirty-five years since 1883 he had served but one parish, Salem Church, Lebanon, Pennsylvania. He was active in many capacities: historian, theologian, a life-long devotee of producing scripturally sound and educationally graded Sunday School materials. He was both a member of the seminary board as well as a member of the faculty, for which task he commuted from Lebanon.[28] He was a true pastor-scholar. Schmauk was a big man physically as well as in outgoing friendliness. He never married. A champion of conservative confessional theology, long a critic of the General Synod, he had been re-elected repeatedly to the presidency of the General Council. To many he personified the Ministerium of Pennsylvania. His chairing of the Joint Committee on Ways and Means had given him ample visibility. Reportedly, he would welcome the ULCA presidency.[29] But did he have the votes? Apparently, the Ministerium of Pennsylvania delegates agreed not to support him with their block of votes, which meant that the election was wide open.

The delegates of these three bodies, present and voting already in the first business session, numbered 264 for the General Synod, 170 for the General Council, and 84 for the United Synod in the South. Loyalties, so they said, were not rigid. Even so, simple arithmetic made it clear that if a General Synod candidate showed promise, he would probably take the election. In the custom of those days, outright electioneering was taboo. Church elections were run by ecclesiastical ballot. There was no nominating by committee or from the floor. The first ballot was strictly a silent voting. Each delegate voted as moved by the Spirit. After the first ballot there was no election declared. Nor after the second. Nor after the third when Gettysburg Seminary President Singmaster was near the top. Meanwhile, the work of the convention proceeded. Other matters were treated by rising votes. The fifteen trustees, already proposed by the Ways and Means Committee, and required by state law to be in place in advance of incorporation, were unanimously elected. Likewise, the vote on incorporating the ULCA sailed through without anyone dissenting. Now came the moment to announce the results of the fourth ballot for president. The winner: The Reverend Doctor Frederick Hermann Knubel of New York City.[30] Singmaster had released his votes in favor of Knubel, and the balloting was over. Knubel was apparently added to the General Synod delegation just the day before, replacing Amos John Trover, in anticipation of his candidacy for this post.[31]

Who was this president-elect of the ULCA? Knubel, a native New Yorker and a General Synod man, was ten years younger than Schmauk. In 1896 he had organized the Evangelical Lutheran Church of the Atonement, in upper Manhattan, and had been its pastor ever since. He gained wide recognition during the brief war years as chair of the National Lutheran Commission on Soldiers' and Sailors' Welfare, predecessor to the National Lutheran Council (NLC). From his parish base Knubel was still involved with the welfare of the men in uniform. He had also been instrumental in launching the NLC. Observers pondering the outcome of this election readily made this comparison: Schmauk has distinguished himself in leading the old order; Knubel now has that opportunity with the new order.

The third business session began with brief devotions: prayers by Professor Jacob Fry, the tall, erect eighty-four-year-old homiletician at the Philadelphia

Seminary; a vocal solo by the equally tall and athletic pastor from Ohio, Ross H. Stover (First Church, Wapokaneta); and the spirited singing by the delegates of "The Church's one foundation."[32] For President Knubel his first duty was to appoint "a Nominating Committee to which shall be referred all nominations made by the merging boards." Thus began the process of filling designated positions. All told, there would be 286 slots to be filled by clergy and laity on a dozen boards and nine elective commissions and committees. Most of the preliminary proposing of nominees had already been done by the equivalent units in the three merging bodies. Even so, there was rising anticipation, three days hence, when the results of this manifold elective process would be reported. Then the pattern of partnership would have been transposed from paper to person. The church president would then know specifically the partners with whom he would be working.[33]

Symbolic of continuity, the gavel used at the final convention of the General Synod was presented to Knubel to use at this first convention of the ULCA. The presenter, Victor George Augustine Tressler, a member of the Wittenberg Synod (Ohio), was the last president of the General Synod. The gavel was made of wood gathered from various places of historic interest to Lutherans across the land. It was to be used at this opening convention and then retired. Many of those present were aware that Tressler's own career was as varied as the wood in the gavel. A graduate of Pennsylvania College (Gettysburg) and of McCormick Theological Seminary (Presbyterian, Chicago), his Ph.D. degree was from the University of Leipzig. After a pastorate in San Jose (California) his career thereafter turned academic, with professorships first at Western Seminary (Kansas) and then at Hamma Divinity School (Springfield, Ohio). Tressler made the presentation on behalf of the Lutheran Historical Society. Later the convention elected him to the Executive Board of the ULCA.[34]

The third session then looked back and ahead. As chair of the Joint Committee on Ways and Means, Schmauk presented the eagerly awaited "Historical Report of the Merger." It traced developments toward a uniting of the three general bodies from the 1870s onward. This concise review gave the delegates a panoramic sweep of the terrain traveled by the merging constituencies over nearly five decades.[35] As the Schmauk presentation showed what had been done, Professor Jacob Clutz, secretary of the Joint Committee on Ways and Means, set forth in detail items on which the committee expected convention action. Nearly thirty in number, these items together comprised an agenda that envisioned the diversity of functions the ULCA would have to approve and pursue from the time of its organization onward.

Approval was given for the number and location of boards, for the model constitutions for the several kinds of mission abroad and at home, for a uniform use of Sunday school materials, for a consolidation of church papers, and for a working relationship with the National Lutheran Council. The merging bodies, moreover, received approval to continue as legal entities for the purpose of receiving bequests and winding up other fiscal responsibilities. Appreciation was also expressed to the local committee on arrangements, and so forth. The Ways and Means report was adopted as a whole.[36]

Four other matters rounded out the full afternoon of business. On the second ballot the Rev. M. G. G. (Melanchthon Gideon Grossclose) Scherer, fifty-seven, pastor of St. Andrew's, Charleston (South Carolina) and president of the United Synod in the South, was elected secretary of the ULCA. A North Carolinian by birth, he was a graduate of Roanoke College, Salem (Virginia) and of Southern Seminary, Columbia (South Carolina). In him a thoroughly tested brand of Lutheranism would be brought to a most sensitive function in the new structure.[37] We shall meet him again and more fully, notably in the church's first biennium (chapter 5). Next, the treasurer. On the first ballot E. Clarence Miller was elected. It was he who, reportedly, had used his layman's initiative and been the first one to propose the merger. A well-connected Philadelphia financier, Miller was reckoned among the elite in the church's laity. A gracious gentleman and a committed Christian, he was deeply concerned for good order in the church and for its well-being. As he shared his possessions he was generous almost to a fault. A lifelong member of the Ministerium of Pennsylvania, his election became the former General Council's contribution to the trio of top offices in the ULCA. He had been a friend of Knubel's for some years. His church membership was in St. John's, Melrose Park (outside Philadelphia), an offshoot of old St. John's which, in 1806, had become the first entirely English-speaking Lutheran congregation in America.[38] Happily, as it turned out, Miller would continue as the treasurer of the ULCA for the next quarter century.

Still another election disclosed the names of the twelve men, six clerical and six lay, who would comprise the church's Executive Board. Their responsibility lay in carrying out the decisions of the convention, in company with the three top officers who were members *ex officio*. Three of the Executive Board members were from the South. The one farthest west was in Chicago, where he headed the seminary in Maywood. The other eight were Easterners and from Ohio. Their counsel and supportiveness would be highly valued and often sought by the new president. We shall become better acquainted with them in chapter 5.[39] A fourth item, far reaching in importance, was the convention's action in favor of full ULCA support of the pending appeal of the National Lutheran Council for European relief. Also authorized was the ULCA's active association with other church bodies in the work of the National Lutheran Council.

Here the second day of the convention paused, but only long enough to regroup in the spacious Hotel Astor with hundreds of other confessional kin.[40]

THE GREAT MERGER MEETING

"In the presence of an immense audience," so says the record, "the Public Merger Meeting was held . . . in the Grand Auditorium of the Hotel Astor, Forty-fourth Street and Broadway, on Friday evening, November the 15th, at 8 o'clock."[41] A continuing euphoria over war's end as well as delight over the achieved merger permeated this splendid gathering. To the historically minded this gathering was taking place in a sumptuous hotel named for John Jacob Astor (1763-1848), the immigrant from Waldorf, Wuerttemberg, whose trading ventures were the first to span the continent and to found Astoria (1811) on the Pacific coast.

Meyerbeer's stirring "March of the Prophets" pealed forth from the great organ at whose console sat C. H. H. Booth, organist and choirmaster of New York's Church of the Advent. First to process in were the members of the Joint Committee on Ways and Means, then the New York Committee on Arrangements. Set off were the newly elected officers of the United Lutheran Church in America. Like a victory parade, if seen from the balcony, the contingents of delegates, more than five hundred of them, proceeded to their places. Seniority of founding determined the synodical sequence, from the Pennsylvania Ministerium (1748) to West Virginia (1912). The three merging bodies display a new pattern of solidarity. Presently the entire audience joined in "The Star Spangled Banner." The patriotism of Lutherans was affirmed in and beyond the flag-draped auditorium. The same sentiment was reaffirmed after the benediction with the singing of "America."

For the program proper the stirring hymn "Through The Night Of Doubt And Sorrow, Onward Goes The Pilgrim Band," by the Danish poet B. S. Ingemann, struck the note of confidence and set the tone for what followed. The opening versicles of the Order for Vespers led to the responsive reading of Psalm 46, "God is our refuge and strength" and struck the note of thankfulness. The same sentiment continued through the reading of the Scripture lessons, the prayers and a chorus rendition of the "Gloria" (from the Mass in C Major, an original by Booth, the organist). The concluding hymn, of course, had to be Martin Luther's "A Mighty Fortress." A trio of addresses filled most of the three-hour program. After a welcoming word by a representative of the Governor of New York came presentations by the last presidents of each of the three merging bodies. For the General Synod Victor G. A. Tressler spoke at length, and with hopefulness, on the salient features of Lutheranism. Melanchthon G. G. Scherer was briefer, delineating "the proportions and aims of the United Church" as seen from the South. After the resounding "Gloria" by the augmented choir, Theodore Emanuel Schmauck delivered his swan song for the General Council, the body over which he had presided with distinction for seventeen years. As the correspondent for *The Lutheran* rhapsodized, "Dr. Schmauk put the audience of two thousand in good humor by lifting them occasionally to the stars, sailing through a boundless area of hopes and anticipations in his usual vigorous, buoyant and happy manner."[42]

After greetings from the dean of the New York City pastors (Junius B. Remensnyder, seventy-seven, pastor at St. James) came the long-awaited response from the man who had been presiding, the newly-elected president of the United Lutheran Church, Frederick Hermann Knubel. In the crowded balcony a young woman in a wheelchair was asked by an elderly lady, a stranger, "Do you know this man who is presiding?" With delight she answered, "Yes. He's my father." The young woman was Helen Knubel, then seventeen years of age and making a valiant comeback from the polio which had stricken her two years earlier.[43] President Knubel's brief speech was a reaffirmation of the joy and gratitude surging through the assembled throng. His exact words are not in the record but their gist is remembered. He praised "the contagion of fellowship" pervading this moment in Lutheran history. Like others, he recalled the Psalmist (Ps. 133:1) "Behold how good and how pleasant it is for brethren to dwell together in unity." He repeated that the merging bodies had been lifted by their profound anticipation to a mountain top of vision. From this summit "the world had suddenly become ten-fold larger, and the Lutheran Church's mission and duty in that world had grown immensely."[44]

President Knubel then reminded his hearers that the way down from the mountain and the journey ahead called for hard work and steadfast dedication. He well knew that the euphoria of unity could, in the long pull, lapse into earlier habits of separatism. This would tax even the best of organizational structures. In saying this he voiced the realism of E. Clarence Miller, the treasurer of the new ULCA.[45] As Helen Knubel recalled it, her father was nearly overwhelmed by the prospect of what lay ahead. Privately Knubel visited the runner-up, Schmauk, and assured him that counsel from him, as elder statesman, would be invaluable in days ahead. Helen remembered that her father would have felt relieved if the election had gone the other way. But, as we shall see in later chapters, Knubel was the man for the challenge. Sadly, in less than two years, death took Schmauk, though his influence lived on.

That memorable Friday toward midnight the ornate auditorium stood empty except for a solitary individual or two cherishing impressions of the Great Merger Meeting. The stage was mute. But the view that the speakers had seen from this stage embraced a sea of upturned faces of those on the main floor, above which the people in two-tiered encircling balconies, filled to the last seat, looked down like a cloud of witnesses. From the ceiling at the far end were draped two huge American flags. Their ends were drawn together and formed the backdrop for a large disc of blue on which stood forth a solid white cross. High on a pedestal reaching to the first balcony was a huge bust in white, an idealized image of Martin Luther.[46] Two smaller banners flanked the Stars and Stripes. One bore the Luther emblem: Rose, Heart, and Cross. The other carried an inscription: 21,500,000. This number was a shorthand claim that in the United States and Canada, thanks largely to immigrants and their offspring, the number of nominal Lutherans far exceeded those in the organized churches. This grand total was derived from government census figures which, in those days, still indicated religious preference.[47] As a home missioning challenge this figure was blunt and daunting.

Saturday, November 16, was a comparatively light day on the convention agenda. Its morning business session, the fourth in sequence, was devoted to a variety of procedural and functional matters. Early adjournment allowed for a group picture. The weather was fine and the more than five hundred-man group walked the half-dozen easy blocks from the Engineering Societies' building to the steps of the United States Post Office building on Eighth Avenue, between 32nd and 33rd Streets. They faced the west end of the equally dignified Pennsylvania Railroad Station.[48] For its readers across the continent *The Lutheran* (January 2, 1919) ran a two-page spread of this remarkable assemblage. More than seven decades after the event the discerning elderly viewer can still thrill to identifying some once widely familiar faces. The foursome at the center of the gently arched front row are readily recognizable. Under their high crowned felt hats, from left to right, are: M. G. G. Scherer (secretary), F. H. Knubel (president), T. E. Schmauk (Ways and Means, chair), and E. Clarence Miller (treasurer). Other faces and names could be matched: H. E. Jacobs, hatless and gray haired; his son, C. M. Jacobs, hat on and serious; Augustus Steimle (Church of the Advent), hatless and bald; E. F. Bachmann, hatless and earnest; and so on. It was a carefully planned shot by a good photographer working a panoramic camera.

The Saturday afternoon session turned its attention to legal matters. The convention approved the constitutions of boards and other units, such as were complete. Others were left for the approval of the Executive Board. It received with loud approbation the telegraphed news from Albany announcing that the United Lutheran Church in America had been granted incorporation under the laws of the State of New York. The telegram came from the sharp-minded legal counsel, Marcus W. Hottenstein, Esq., who had served the Joint Ways and Means Committee wisely and well.[49] Thereupon the convention adopted the ULCA Constitution as a whole. The forty-five synods had already debated and approved this constitution earlier in their respective conventions.[50] (A fuller treatment of the constitution's fifteen Articles and By-Laws will be found in chapter 5). E. Clarence Miller, foremost among the lay leaders who urged the speedy formation of the ULCA, pushed hard for the clearest and most durable type of legal instrument. As he saw it, the constitution was to serve the formation of the United Church and to be open to other Lutheran bodies "one with us in faith."[51]

A change of pace from legal matters to global outreach came with the extended greetings from the All-India Lutheran Missionary Society, as read to the convention by the Ohio delegate, E. K. Bell. This society had been formed by Indian initiative during the war years. It merged the General Council Mission based in Rajahmundry and the General Synod Mission based in Guntur, both located in the Telugu speaking Andhra Province. While praising the work of missionary pioneers like Christian Frederick "Father" Heyer, they lamented the decline of support in recent times. Their greeting concluded with a challenge:

> Our appeal to the United Lutheran Church is that her Foreign Mission programme be made on a scale proportionate to her own large constituency in the homeland and to the vastness and urgency of the opportunities that India now presents.

Mention was here also made of the German missions in India whose support from the home base had been cut off by the war. In effect these had become "orphaned missions" urgently requiring help from new sources abroad.[52] On this note of exhortation the business sessions adjourned until Monday.

CELEBRATING THE MERGER IN GREATER NEW YORK

Sunday, November 17, was the day set apart for bringing "the contagion of fellowship" to the people. A select company of pastors among the delegates fanned out across the New York metropolitan area to some seventy congregations. The weather was a handicap. Heavy showers continued through the day and evening. Happily those were the days of neighborhood churches, some twenty-five in Manhattan and the Bronx, thirty-four in Brooklyn, fifteen in Queens, three in Richmond (Staten Island). Across the Hudson the metropolitan area included fourteen ULCA churches, five of which were in Jersey City. Altogether the ULCA congregations in this metropolis exceeded one hundred. They far outnumbered those of the other Lutheran bodies. A large proportion of the members were first and second generation Americans. The others were descendants from earlier times, some from as far back as the beginning of the colonial era. They had been leaders in the transition of Lutheranism into an English-speaking communion.[53] Over the generations New York Lutherans had experienced and survived, often at much cost, chronic bouts over questions of adaptation to ever changing conditions. Therefore it was seen as highly desirable to share the exultant spirit of a uniting church body as widely as possible while the process was under way.[54]

Three Jubilee Mass Meetings, despite the periodic downpours, managed to generate a spirited sense of community. Manhattan's Hippodrome, Brooklyn's Academy of Music, and Jersey City's Orpheum Theater drew large crowds. The cavernous Hippodrome, 43rd to 44th Streets on Sixth Avenue, Manhattan's ten thousand-seat meeting hall, drew about five thousand, the largest of the three rallies. Presiding that afternoon was the venerable Rev. George Unangst Wenner (1844-1934), founder fifty years earlier and still pastor of Christ Church on Manhattan's Lower East Side. At seventy-four he could still project his clear baritone, an ability prerequisite before the age of the public address system. Wenner's dynamic community-mindedness made him a strong advocate of release-time religious education for children in the public schools.[55] The Hippodrome program that afternoon was much to his liking.

After the prelude, an exultant fantasy on "A Mighty Fortress" that displayed the range of the Hippodrome organ, came the national anthem, which the audience sang with fervor. Following the Invocation, the hymn "From Ocean Unto Ocean" (no. 494, *CSBH*) suggested the continental spread of the ULCA. The Psalm, Scripture reading, and Prayer preceded greetings by the presidents of the three merging church bodies. After the offering and organ meditation came three addresses. President Knubel led off with the timely theme, "An Age of Opportunity." The correspondent for *The Lutheran* called Knubel's speech one of his best ever. David Bauslin (Ohio) struck the national note, "Lutheranism and Democracy." Muhlenberg College president, John A. W. Haas, spoke with characteristic animation on "The Message of Lutheranism for a New Age."[56]

That Sunday night, despite the continuing showers, the Brooklyn Academy of Music drew a large audience. Eagerly they heard President Knubel, Schmauk (General Council), Tressler (General Synod), and Kinard (United Synod in the South). This was no stuffy gathering of the faithful, but a responsive audience ready for greater things. "Enthusiastic applause greeted the president of the ULCA" reported *The Lutheran*. A telltale incident marked the occasion, as told in the church press:

> When one of the speakers marched up to President Knubel and delivered the challenge to lead the Church, that where he would go we would follow, if he went over the top [the doughboy term for leaving the trenches and advancing to attack] we would go over the top with him, the audience rose to its feet and thundered applause. That is how Brooklyn feels about this Merger. . . . United we shall go over the top in everything. Watch Brooklyn![57]

There was national pride as well as fervor for the gospel, a kind of Armistice and Merger "hype" that marked much of the convention. Understandably, German-American Lutherans at that moment in time were especially eager to affirm their patriotism. Typically, Schmauk could claim Martin Luther as "the first American," the spiritual forebear of modern democracy as well as of religious liberty. In this vein Knubel declared:

> God has mercifully brought home to us a warning. With comparatively light suffering and losses, He has permitted us to see how the sins of Europe have ruined those nations. Now is the opportunity of the Lutheran Church to stamp its truth upon the waiting world. Up to the present our Church has held aloof, in the background. In the unification so auspiciously begun has come to us an opportunity such as we have never had before. We hold the things for which the world is asking. We have the Gospel which the world needs. We have a distinctive message to the laboring man, whose age this is. We have a message concerning the relation of church and State, a truth concerning democracy. Every age of opportunity is an age of testing the powers and influences that would rule the world. The test that will be placed upon the nation will be the test of our faith in the principles, whether we believe sufficiently in them to live them and to die for them. A similar test is upon the Lutheran Church and all of its members, the test of our faith in the reality of Jesus Christ and His presence with His Church.[58]

In Jersey City's Orpheum Theater still other faithful assembled to celebrate the Merger and experience the "contagion of fellowship." But the theme carried a variation because of the place given to a recognition of the role of the laity in the church. Nine of the city's fifteen Lutheran congregations were affiliated with the General Synod, which perhaps explains why the two featured speakers were both of that body.[59] Otherwise the order of service was the same as the two preceding. John Alden Singmaster, sixty-six, president of Gettysburg Seminary for the past fifteen years, led off. A man of wide experience, he had been on the General Synod Board of Foreign Missions for some two decades, and had served on the Ways and Means Committee preparing for the Merger. It was fitting that at the Orpheum he spoke on "The Church of the Future." Accenting three things in particular, he affirmed the Church's continuity, its unchanging commitment to the great doctrinal teachings, and its manifestation of all this through new leadership faithful to the Bible and active in its missionary task.[60]

Singmaster's approach opened the way for his fellow speaker, John L. Zimmerman, a member of Ohio's Wittenberg Synod. He, too, drew vigorous applause when he extolled the patriotism of Lutherans in America. These were citizens who, during the war effort, had often and unfairly been accused of being "pro-German." They needed to hear again and again that "the Lutheran Church has always been loyal to our country." More than that, lest the ordained clergy take over the church and in this way deny Luther's emphasis on the priesthood of all believers, Zimmerman rallied the lay folk. In the church of the future John Zimmerman saw a rising role for the dedicated men and women and young people in the congregations. He gave emphasis to "the part played by the laymen in bringing on the present Merger."[61]

All three of the Jubilee Mass Meetings as well as the Great Merger Meeting, and at times even the business sessions of the convention, bore a seriousness touched with hyperbole. The hyperbole was the way people felt about the future, particularly at a moment of a fortuitously timed twofold release: from the Great War, and from their own hitherto divided traditions in the church. It would take time to capture the manifold actions in perspective. In his assessment of the biggest of the three Sunday gatherings, a pastor of the New York and New England Synod, became euphoric as he recalled the finale at the Hippodrome. "Then the curtain fell at the conclusion of perhaps the greatest mass meeting of Lutherans since the days of Luther himself and one of the most significant in the history of Protestantism in the New World."[62]

THE IMPORTANCE OF LESSER ITEMS

The last day of the convention, Monday, November 18, saw the Sixth and Seventh Business Sessions cope with a diversified array of items each in some way important for the future. First came a remaining pair of recommendations from the Joint Committee on Ways and Means. Approval was accorded the merging of three church papers into one paper to be known as the official organ of the ULCA with the name, *The Lutheran*. The three terminating papers were the General Council's weekly, *The Lutheran*, The General Synod's *Lutheran Church Work and Observer*, and the United Synod in the South's paper, *The Lutheran Church Visitor*. The consolidated paper would begin publishing in 1919. As it turned out, George W. Sandt, editor of the old *Lutheran* would become editor of the new one.[63] The other Ways and Means recommendation provided for a conference of the Executive Board and the members of all boards elected at the first convention as soon as practicable.[64] We shall see in chapter 5 below how this foresighted arrangement was carried out. Meanwhile, during the morning session the elections to boards and committees were completed.

Other matters were also set in order. The Convention adopted *The Common Service Book and Hymnal* (1917) as the official book of worship of the United Lutheran Church in America. This action provided that no changes in the usage be made without permission. This action would have far reaching effect.[65] On the fiscal side, the budget and apportionment remained unfinished business. The reconciliation of three different fiscal practices, and variations thereof, had posed more of a problem than the committee of five financiers had anticipated. The matter was referred to the Executive Board.[66] The question of ULCA participation in the Federal Council of Churches was also referred. The FCC was manifestly eager to gain a strong Lutheran participation. The General Synod had been one of the charter members of this inter-Protestant association organized in 1908. Its general secretary, Charles S. Macfarland, greeted the convention in person on its last day. Macfarland was warmly thanked. He knew the ambiguity of the ULCA position, basically favorable toward the FCC on the one hand, and cautiously watchful of critical Lutheran church bodies on the other. The latter factor depended on further progress toward a greater Lutheran union.[67]

A succession of other items required attention. Having attained major importance on an inter-Lutheran basis during the war effort, a men's organization was referred to the new Standing Committee on Lutheran Brotherhoods.[68] Publicity and public relations comprised a new field that also called for action. The convention endorsed the continuing services of the Lutheran Bureau, soon to become part of the National Lutheran Council. The bureau had already achieved distinction continent-wide by the quality of its press releases and other information services in connection with the four-hundredth anniversary of the Reformation in 1917 and subsequently the ULCA Merger. As News Bureau of the NLC it would be playing a vital part in the publicizing and interpreting of postwar Lutheran activities at home and overseas.[69] The American Bible Society (1816), with services basic to the outreach of all denominations, greeted the Convention through its representative, W. I. Haven. The delegates reciprocated, noting the admirable extent of ABS wartime services, when this venerable society furnished "the soldiers of America and Europe with millions of copies of the Holy Scriptures in many languages."[70]

The Lutheran missionary outreach overseas had come to the convention's attention in various ways. Especially pointed and practical was Anna Kugler's address to the convention on the last morning. On furlough from India, she was apparently the only woman to address the convention. Hers was the voice of experience. Simply and factually she described the work of medical missions among the people in the Telugu-speaking Andhra Province. Her base of outreach was Guntur, the city where Father Heyer had begun the first missionary work by American Lutherans some seventy-five years earlier. Her own story was one of compassionate pioneering. Anna Kugler was born in suburban Philadelphia. Upon her graduation from the Women's Medical College in that city, she volunteered for missionary work among the women of India. Now, at the convention, she reinforced the already mentioned appeal from the All-India Lutheran Missionary Society and challenged the new ULCA to see and act upon the vision of opportunity for the Gospel in Asia and beyond.[71] The challenge was presently seconded by greetings to the ULCA from Japan. While the United Synod in the South had begun in 1892 to blaze a trail in the Land of the Rising Sun, a searching question remained.[72] How would the new church body follow through on these beginnings? The Augustana Foreign Board also had reaffirmed its agreement (from General Council days) to cooperate with the ULCA in India and the Caribbean.[73]

Drama and emotion surfaced on the last morning of the convention as the ULCA faced its first test of policy. That session throws light on how the church according to its constitution would deal with inherited obligations, particularly in this case with institutions vital to the ongoing mission of the church. The appeal originated with the General Council. It had approved a funding plan for the Pacific Theological Seminary, Seattle, as proposed by the seminary's board and endorsed by the two supporting synods, the Pacific Synod (General Council) and the California Synod (General Synod). The appeal was for "the securing of a two hundred and fifty thousand dollar endowment fund . . . by solicitation from societies and individuals of congregations, and for the obtaining of funds for the erection of buildings." Therefore the General Council had resolved to "recommend the entire plan to the United Lutheran Church with the request for fullest consideration."[74] Westerners and others urged approval by the convention. A great tide of missionary opportunity was rising in the West. *The Lutheran* caught the spark in the appeal, "The crowning fruit of this convention was the vision, and that must be followed now with an enlargement of the heart. A new world is in process."[75] Because this was the first direct appeal to the church and involved an interpretation of the constitution, the convention voted to refer the matter to the Executive Board. This board, in turn, referred it to the Commission of Adjudication, thus giving that court of appeal its first case (see chapter 5).

Should any reader by this time think that the first ULCA convention was preoccupied only with matters internal to church life, two issues then at the forefront of social concern can correct this mistaken impression. One issue on the moral life highlighted the Third Business Session. The presenter was Captain Eugene L. Swan, M.D., representing Secretary of War Newton D. Baker. His linking of spiritual health and moral living came like a ringing challenge to the church. Mustered-out soldiers and sailors, by the hundreds of thousands, would be job hunting. Too many of them were victims of vice and social disease, mainly syphilis. "That is a thing about which we cannot speak, something one mustn't mention," said Captain Swan. He warned against the menace and urged preventive steps. Toward that end the War Department had prepared a motion picture to be shown in small groups. Speaking in the remedial terms of preventive medicine, he held his audience spellbound with his marshaling of facts. President Knubel, in the name of the United Church, "thanked the Secretary of War for the stirring message sent through Captain Swan." By a rising vote the convention resolved: "We pledge the fullest support of the United Lutheran Church in America to the Government of the United States to meet the problems of vice which threaten the physical and spiritual welfare of the boys and girls, the men and women of these United States."[76] Sex-related problems were nothing new to the social ministry, then called Inner Mission, of the church; but it is doubtful that they had ever been accorded such prominence as at this convention.

Temperance, a second issue calling for social action, came near the end of the convention. The Eighteenth Amendment, banning the importation, manufacture, and sale of beverages with an alcohol content of 5 percent or more had been passed by Congress during the War, partly as a conservation measure but mainly under the continuing pressures of the Temperance Movement. Many church-related societies and most prominently the Women's Christian Temperance Union (WCTU) had been involved. In November 1918 the ratification of the Eighteenth Amendment was in process, and was heading toward ratification by January 1919. An East Pennsylvania Synod delegate, the Rev. M. G. Richard, endeavored to get the ULCA into the act. His motion was forthright:

> Resolved, That the United Lutheran Church in America put itself on record favoring temperance legislation, looking toward the elimination of the liquor traffic with the hope and prayer that the National Prohibition amendment may carry in the state legislatures and soon become effective in our nation.

The matter was referred to the Committee on Temperance. This twenty-member unit (fifteen clergy, five lay) was initially chaired by Professor Luther D. Reed, of the Philadelphia Seminary. It would soon (1922) be recognized as the Committee on Moral and Social Welfare, an adjunct unit of the Board of Inner Mission.[77]

Typically, the very last action of the convention dealt with the gathering, care, and conservation of records. Professor Reed, presently to be named archivist of the ULCA, presented the enabling motion, which was adopted:

> Resolved, That the Executive Board be requested to determine and inaugurate a plan for the collection and preservation of original records, charters, agreements, official correspondence, and other documentary material of permanent interest or value pertaining to the United Lutheran Church in America, and the work of its boards, commissions, and important committees.[78]

With this agenda item, crucial for making the ULCA story available to later generations, the convention adjourned. From the *Common Service Book and Hymnal* President Knubel read the concluding lines of the Order for the Closing of Synods, which combined a benediction and an apostolic exhortation to faithfulness in witness and service.[79]

A POSTSCRIPT

Presently the conventioneers resumed their accustomed tasks but now saw them in a new perspective. The example of the Rev. Edwin Heyl Delk comes to mind. An eloquent man of the General Synod, he was pastor of St. Matthew's, a church prominently located near Philadelphia's center city. As one of the best known Lutheran leaders, and ever aware of the General Council majority, for that was Philadelphia's reputation, he cheerfully repeated his contagious slogan: "Merge the best and submerge the rest."[80] It would be a slow process but it worked. To John W. Horine, forty-nine, editor of the South's cherished *Lutheran Church Visitor*, the outcome of the convention brought joy and disappointment. Writing to President Knubel, he felt that the decision to merge the several church papers into a single one, *The Lutheran*, went contrary to an earlier agreement. Happily, his Southern loyalties could soon flourish at the seminary in Columbia (SC), where he would be teaching for the next two decades.

It was typical of John Christoph ("Daddy") Kunzmann, sixty-five, to have his rail journey back to Seattle studded with stopovers. As director of Home Missions in the vast Northwest, he had been active at the convention. Although not a delegate, he rallied support for the Pacific Seminary. For this purpose he found it useful to visit in Philadelphia, Pittsburgh (provisional base of the Home Mission Board), Chicago, Milwaukee, Minneapolis, and St. Paul. Within a year after his return to Seattle he was elected president of "The lone little Sem in the West." The name came from the tuneful ditty with which he closed many a fund-raising speech, at times to the piano accompaniment of a staunch supporter, E. Clarence Miller.[81] In this writer's recollection of returnees from the New York convention there fleets the image of a father, a Ministerium of Pennsylvania delegate. In his spirited way Ernest F. Bachmann, forty-eight, told his deaconess community what the formation of a United Church could foreseeably mean for the work of the sisters and of women in the church at large.

The public notice that would normally have been given so big a merger in the Protestant papers was largely eclipsed by the news and aftermath of the Armistice. Even so, the Episcopal *Churchman* praised the Lutherans (seemingly all of them!) for uniting, and held this up as a worthy example for other denominations to follow. *The Christian Herald* reported, in the words of the knowledgeable H. K. Carroll, that the merger creating the United Lutheran Church in America was more swiftly and smoothly accomplished than any on record.[82] Be that as it may, we now turn to the three prior centuries of Lutheran presence in North America which preceded and produced this merger.

NOTES

1. *The New York Times* November 11, 1918; on microfilm, Princeton Public Library.
2. Good Friday, April 6, 1917.
3. Woodrow Wilson's idealistic "Fourteen Points" for a peace settlement drew Germany to agree to an armistice. The harsh demands of the European victors, however, dispelled the idealism and culminated in the Peace Treaty of Versailles, June 28, 1919. Ironically this was the very chamber, the "Hall of Mirrors," where forty-eight years earlier Bismarck had proclaimed the Second German Reich. By its terms Germany accepted the charge of sole guilt for the war. See Carlton H. J. Hayes, *A Political and Cultural History of Modern Europe*, as summarized in *Columbia Encyclopedia*. (New York: Macmillan Company, 1932) 2: 632-40. (Hereafter cited as *Columbia Encyclopedia*.) Here a reference to what happened next will provide perspective especially for the Lutheran scene. In Germany the Versailles Treaty fueled bitter resentment. The peace settlement was called a "stab in the back." It was made worse by the socialist revolution which overthrew the Kaiser and created a republic. This meant a separation of Church and State. Neither the Kaiser, as King of Prussia, nor any other monarch, like the king of Wuerttemberg, was any longer head of the Protestant Church, *summus episcopus,* in his realm. For Evangelical Christians more so than for Roman Catholics this meant a vacuum of leadership. Under these circumstances America's Lutherans surprised the Germans with their spontaneous aid. This played a reconciling role far beyond expectation. For details, see chapter 5. Even so the process was slow. A decade later at Copenhagen (1929), at the second meeting of the Lutheran World Convention, the German delegates absented themselves from an event commemorating the Versailles Treaty.
4. William Adams Brown, *The Church in America: A Study of the Present Condition and Future Prospects of American Protestantism.* (New York: Macmillan, 1922), 4. (Hereafter cited as Brown, *Church in America.*) See also Sydney E. Ahlstrom, A *Religious History of the American People.* (New Haven and London: Yale University Press, 1972), 883-94. (Hereafter cited as Ahlstrom, *Religious History*).
5. Brown, *Church in America*, 97.
6. Ibid., 102. See chapter 3, below.
7. For the inclination in this volume to accentuate individuals, the author acknowledges an initial indebtedness to his father. Ernest Frederick Bachmann (1870-1954) graduated from the Lutheran Theological Seminary at Philadelphia (Mt. Airy) in 1892. He gathered and served Concordia Church, Buffalo, NY (1892-1906); was pastor at the Mary J. Drexel Home and Philadelphia Motherhouse of Deaconesses (1906-45); and presided over the ULCA Board of Inner Missions (1918-26). From 1901 he was a delegate to the conventions of the General Council, and from 1918 to 1944 a delegate to all ULCA conventions. He was close to President Knubel, to his seminary classmate John A. Morehead, and others. He helped to nurture the international perspectives of the deaconess work, especially in the postwar era (after 1919) when the Philadelphia Motherhouse served as a

center for transmitting relief supplies to deaconess centers in Europe.

8. "The First Assembly of the Delegates of the Three Bodies," *The Lutheran*, November 21, 1918, 5.

9. *Minutes of the First Convention of the United Lutheran Church in America together with Minutes of the Conventions of the General Synod, the General Council and the United Synod Held in Connection with the Merger, November 10-18, 1918*. (Hereafter cited, as in this case, as ULCA *Minutes* 1918).

10. As told the author. See also Byron E. Swanson, "Conrad Bergendoff, The Making of a Lutheran Ecumenist." (Ph.D. diss. Princeton Theological Seminary, 1980), 187.

11. More in Marilyn Kay Stulken, *Hymnal Companion to the Lutheran Book of Worship* (Philadelphia: Fortress Press, 1980), 254-55, hymn No. 163.

12. ULCA *Minutes* 1918: 5.

13. Ibid., 8-10.

14. *Common Service Book of the Lutheran Church with Hymnal* (Philadelphia: Board of Publication of the United Lutheran Church in America, 1918), hymn Nos. 142, 132, 190, respectively. (Hereafter cited as CSBH.)

15. ULCA *Minutes* 1918: 11.

16. Ibid., 14.

17. Ibid., 15.

18. Ibid., 16.

19. Ibid., 19.

20. As etched in the author's memory from meetings a decade and more later.

21. This congregation's founders, well-to-do laymen of conservative bent, had left St. James Church, the foremost English-language Lutheran congregation in Manhattan. Holy Trinity congregation from its outset was a member of the New York Ministerium and the General Council. For over 30 years it had been located on 21st Street between Fifth and Sixth Avenues, but then it followed the movement of population uptown. The pastor of Holy Trinity, Charles J. Smith, was at the time of the convention on temporary duty in Paris. The National Lutheran Commission for Soldiers' and Sailors' Welfare had sent him and Judge Frank M. Riter to survey the needs of Lutheran chaplains and military personnel as well as to form initial contacts with the Lutheran Church of France. George U. Wenner, *The Lutherans of New York, 1648-1918* (New York: The Petersfield Press, 1918), 43. (Hereafter cited as Wenner, *Lutherans of New York*.) *The Lutheran World Almanac and Annual Encyclopedia for 1921*, (New York: The Lutheran Bureau, 1920), 481-82. (Hereafter cited as *Lutheran Almanac for 1921*.)

22. News releases written in advance, Otto H. Pannkoke and Walton H. Greever, eds., Lutheran Bureau, New York. Archives of Cooperative Lutheranism, The Evangelical Lutheran Church in America, Chicago.

23. Ibid.

24. *The New York Times*, 1-20, November 1918.

25. ULCA *Minutes* 1918: 19-20.

26. "Brotherhood Banquet," *The Lutheran*, November 21, 1918, 13.

27. ULCA *Minutes* 1918: 95.

28. John A. Kaufmann, ed., *Biographical Record of the Lutheran Theological Seminary at Philadelphia, 1864-1962* (Philadelphia: The Lutheran Theological Seminary, 1964), 23. (Hereafter cited as Kaufmann, *Philadelphia Seminary Record.*)

29. George W. Sandt, *Theodore Emanuel Schmauk* (Philadelphia: United Lutheran Publication House, 1921), 192-218.

30. ULCA *Minutes* 1918: 36.

31. Gilbert, W. Kent, *Commitment to Unity: A History of the Lutheran Church in America* (Philadelphia: Fortress Press, 1988), 57, note 59. (Hereafter cited as Gilbert, *Commitment to Unity.*)

32. *CSBH*, Hymn 198.

33. ULCA *Minutes* 1918: 37, 97-106.

34. Willard D. Allbeck, *Theology at Wittenberg, 1845-1945.* (Springfield, Ohio: Wittenberg Press, 1945), 117-18. (Hereafter cited as Allbeck, *Wittenberg.*) ULCA *Minutes* 1918: 37.

35. See chapter 3.

36. ULCA *Minutes* 1918: 44-58.

37. *A History of the Lutheran Church in South Carolina* (Columbia, S.C.: The South Carolina Synod of the Lutheran Church in America, 1971), 854-95.

38. ULCA *Minutes* 1918: 43. Also Theodore G. Tappert, *History of the Lutheran Theological Seminary at Philadelphia, 1864-1964)* (Philadelphia: The Lutheran Theological Seminary, 1964), 89. (Hereafter cited as Tappert, *Philadelphia Seminary History.*)

39. ULCA *Minutes* 1918: 58.

40. Ibid.

41. Ibid., 59ff.

42. "The Great Auditorium Meeting," *The Lutheran*, November 21, 1918, 8.

43. Correspondence between Helen Knubel and the author.

44. "Leading Features of the Merger Convention," *The Lutheran*, November 28, 1918, 1.

45. E. Clarence Miller, "Why I Urged the Merger," *The Lutheran*, November 21, 1918, 10.

46. Photograph in *The Lutheran*, November 21, 1918, 5.

47. George Linn Kieffer (1883-1937), outstanding Lutheran statistician, *Lutheran World Almanac for 1921*, 574.

48. ULCA *Minutes* 1918: 61.

49. Ibid., 62.

50. See chapters 3 and 5.

51. ULCA *Minutes* 1918: 62-78.

52. ULCA *Minutes* 1918: 78-79.

53. *The Lutheran Cyclopedia*, Henry Eyster Jacobs and John A.W. Haas, eds., (New York: Charles Scribner's Sons, 1899), v-vi. (Hereafter cited as *Lutheran Cyclopedia.*)

54. Wenner, *Lutherans of New York*, passim, provides data.

55. ULCA *Minutes* 1918: 79-81.

56. M. Luther Canup, "Merger Mass Meeting at the Hippodrome," *The Lutheran*, November 28, 1918, 3. See Chapter 4.

57. S.G. Weiskotten, "The Brooklyn Jubilee Mass Meetings," *The Lutheran*, November 28, 1918, 4.

58. Ibid.

59. ULCA *Minutes* 1918: 81.

60. M. S. Waters, "The Jersey City Merger Meeting," *The Lutheran*, November 28, 1918. 4.

61. Ibid.

62. Canup, "Merger Mass Meeting at the Hippodrome," *The Lutheran*, November 28, 1918, 3.

63. ULCA *Minutes* 1918: 81, 51.

64. Ibid., 55, 81-82.

65. Ibid., 84.

66. Ibid., 87.

67. Ibid., 85.

68. Ibid., 86

69. Ibid., 83.

70. Ibid., 88.

71. Ibid., 86.

72. Ibid., 86, 87.

73. Ibid., 82. See chapter 3.

74. Ibid., 82-83.

75. "Leading Features of the Merger Convention," *The Lutheran*, November 28, 1918, 1.

76. "A Stirring Address," *The Lutheran*, November 21, 1918, 8. ULCA *Minutes* 1918: 43.

77. ULCA *Minutes* 1918: 96; *Minutes of the Third Biennial Convention of the United Lutheran Church in America, Buffalo, N.Y., October 17-25, 1922*, 64. (Hereafter cited as ULCA *Minutes* 1922.

78. ULCA *Minutes* 1918: 96.

79. *CSBH*, Hymn 286.

80. E. H. Delk, a native of Norfolk, Va., graduated from Gettysburg Seminary, Class of 1882. He occupied pastorates in Schohiare, NY, and Hagerstown, MD, before serving in Philadelphia 1902-29. Abdel Ross Wentz, compiler and editor, *Gettysburg Lutheran Theological Seminary*, (Harrisburg, Pennsylvania: Evangelical Press, 1964), Vol. 2, Alumni Record, 94. (Hereafter cited as A.R. Wentz, *Gettysburg Seminary Record*.) Delk's catchy quip was caught up in the author's parental lore.

81. Edwin Bracher, *The First Fifty Years of the Pacific Synod, 1901-1951* (Seattle: The Pacific Synod of the United Lutheran Church in America, 1951), 34-46, esp. 38.

82. As quoted in *The Lutheran Quarterly* 49 (1919), 2.

CHAPTER 2

THE MUHLENBERG TRADITION, TO 1861

L IKE A BARD OF OLD, DEAN HENRY E. JACOBS had recalled for the 1918 conventioneers that moment in time, 275 years earlier, when a few Lutheran folk in
Manhattan were struggling against odds to nourish their faith. The Jacobs'
recital accentuated continuity. From the sixteenth century Reformation to the
sudden emergence of a postwar era he beheld a panorama of four centuries and
a practical contemporary challenge circling the globe. "Church organizations,"
he affirmed, "are rooted in the necessities of Christian faith. Organization cre-
ates no life; but life inevitably leads to organization." At that historic moment
Jacobs reminded his hearers "to be thoroughly identified with all the interests of
this country and not to stand aloof. . . . The name Muhlenberg has left us a brilliant example in both Church and State."[1] Decades later we can still imagine the
thrill animating the 1918 delegates and countless others across the land. The
pieces of the merger, the synods and congregations of a now United Lutheran
Church in America, were at last joined. The twenty-one-member Joint
Committee on Ways and Means had planned and performed superbly. Each of
the forty-five synods had approved the ULCA constitution in advance. The task
was now to grow together.

For the people of 1918, the antecedent developments had already been set
forth in several major books. From Gettysburg had come a popular treatment,
*The Lutherans in America: A Story of Struggle, Progress, Influence and Marvelous
Growth* (1889), by Professor Edmund Jacob Wolf. From Philadelphia there was a
more scholarly tome, *A History of the Evangelical Lutheran Church in the United
States* (1891), by Professor Henry Eyster Jacobs. From Springfield, Ohio, came *A
Brief History of the Lutheran Church in America* (1903 and 1904) by Professor
Juergen L. Neve, in German and then English. All three of these authors endeav-
ored to present an inclusive account of the Lutherans in America, including
Canada. Furthermore, in that pre-war era a widely read book made Americans
aware of themselves as members of a worldwide confessional family: *Lutherans
in All Lands* (1893), by the resourceful John Nicholas Lenker, Home Mission
director in the West. Happily, by the time of the Quadricentennial of the

Reformation, it was possible to see America's Lutherans in a broad context and amid imminent change.

In 1923 Abdel Ross Wentz, at Gettysburg Seminary, published his insightful book, *The Lutheran Church in American History*. A second, revised edition appeared a decade later. In light of the continuity as represented by the ULCA, Wentz prefaced his work with the reminder:

> The position of the Lutheran Church in America rests upon a birthright. It is not an immigrant church that needed to be naturalized after it was transplanted from some European land. It is as old as the American nation and much older than the American Republic. The Lutheran Church in America is an integral and potent part of American Christianity. The people in the Lutheran churches are a constituent and typical element of the American nation.[2]

Further, Wentz pointed out the fruitful parallelism, saying "our Church and our nation were born at the same time, grew up side by side, and developed by similar stages of progress."[3]

In this chapter we need to move rapidly from the seventeenth century to the 1860s. Chapter 3 then carries the story to 1918. The diversity of Europe's Lutheran churches was brought to America by successive stages of newcomers: especially the Dutch, Swedes, Finns, Germans, and Austrians. This required adaptation to a free society and an English-speaking land. All Lutherans coming to North America went through similar experiences, but those who ultimately formed the United Lutheran Church were the first to do so. As such they not only passed through their own often contradictory stages of development, but also were variously appreciated, misunderstood, criticized, or opposed by others. After the initial stories of immigration, the two major factors in the eventual formation of the ULCA were the Muhlenberg heritage and the founding of the General Synod in 1820.

EARLY PLANTINGS

Dutch Lutherans on the Hudson

Lutheran beginnings in the seventeenth century almost failed. New Netherland, a Dutch West India Company venture, was the scene. The Dutch Reformed was the permitted church. The Lutheran minority, mainly German and Scandinavian in origin, was given a hard time, as Dean Jacobs reminded the 1918 New York convention.[4] In old Amsterdam a numerous Lutheran element was tolerated as an exception. These Lutherans kept their interpretation of the Lord's Supper, but in church organization they largely followed the pattern of the Reformed. However, the Lutheran Consistory members were not appointed by the State, but elected, and their support was not from the State but voluntary. In New Amsterdam the local Reformed clergy demanded uniformity. The first Lutheran congregation gathered in 1649 in Fort Orange (Albany). The sole Lutheran pas-

tor sent from Holland, Johannes Gutwasser, was immediately placed under virtual house arrest and sent back within a year (1655-56). The faithful lay folk did
not give up, either at Fort Orange or in Manhattan.

With the capture of New Netherland by the British (1664) the prospects of
the Lutherans improved. The arrival of Jacob Fabritius in 1669 opened a new
era. From Amsterdam, moreover, he appears to have brought a copy of the
Lutheran consistory's constitution, an adaptable form of self-government.[5]
Having married a widow from the Delaware valley, Fabritius, an eccentric from
Transylvania, relocated to Wicaco in 1671 and served the Lutherans of Swedish
descent the rest of his days (1693). But first he installed his successor, Bernard
Arnzius, whose parish was the Hudson valley and whose faithful ministry over
two decades (1671-91) was a long overdue reward for the Lutheran remnant.
Upon his death in 1691 there followed another decade of pastorless persever-
ance.

Swedish Lutherans on the Delaware

New Sweden, first settled in 1638, included parts of today's Pennsylvania and
Delaware. Sweden's colonial bid in the New World had the approval of King
Gustavus Adolphus (d. 1632), and was chartered as New Sweden in 1633. It was
master-minded by Willem Usselinx, who had also planned the New Netherland
venture. Dutch assistance had helped New Sweden get started, and it was the
Dutch Governor Peter Stuyvesant who seized the Swedish colony in 1655 after a
brief seventeen years under the Blue and Gold. The settlers were Swedes and
Finns. Their capital was on Tinicum Island in the Delaware, and their settlements were strung along the river's west bank, from Christina (Wilmington),
and Uppland (Chester) to Wicaco (Philadelphia). Other nationalities moved in,
including Dutch, English, Welsh, and Germans. By the 1690s the descendants of
New Sweden numbered nearly 950.[6]

Under Swedish governance the colonists had been provided with a succession
of pastors. Of them the best known remains John Campanius. His missionary
concern moved him to translate Luther's *Small Catechism* into the language of
the Delaware Indians. After the Dutch takeover no more pastors were sent by the
Church of Sweden, but Lars Lock stayed on until he died in 1688, in Christina.
Like Fabritius in Wicaco, Lock's ministry had been curtailed by the feebleness of
old age. But in the 1680s the scene was changing.

When the English took New Netherland in 1664 and renamed it New York,
they also acquired the later New Jersey and Pennsylvania. By charter the great
expanse of land west of the Delaware River became, in payment of a royal debt
by Charles I, the Proprietary Colony of William Penn. A haven for persecuted
fellow Quakers in the British Isles, Pennsylvania in 1683 began welcoming hard
pressed sectarians—Dunkers, Mennonites, Schwenkfelders and others from
Germany's Rhineland. Germantown, north of the newly laid out Philadelphia,
became an important proof of Penn's experiment in toleration.

In face of the mounting religious diversity the descendants of New Sweden pleaded for Lutheran pastors from Sweden. The enterprising Carl Springer, a recent arrival on the Delaware, begged for

> two Swedish ministers, who are well learned and well exercised in the Holy Scriptures, and who may well defend both themselves and us against all the false teachers and strange sects, by whom we are surrounded, or who may oppose us on account of our true, pure, uncorrupted service to God and the Lutheran religion, which we shall confess before God and all the world.[7]

Also requested were "twelve Bibles, three books of Sermons, forty-two Manuals [of Worship], one hundred Handbooks and Spiritual Meditations, two hundred Catechisms, etc." In reply Sweden's Charles XI, counseled by the Archbishop of Uppsala and Professor Hedberg (later Bishop of Skara), added a third pastor to report on the enterprise. Of the three, Andrew Rudman was their dean. They arrived in 1697 and 1698. They also brought five hundred printed copies of the Campanius translation of the Catechism. Literacy seemed to be on their agenda.

The Swedish Lutheran community revived and built two churches that today are landmarks: Holy Trinity, Wilmington (1699), and Gloria Dei, Philadelphia (1700). Sweden would continue to send pastors, a total of fifty by the time the last one, Nicholas Collin, arrived in 1770. Not long after that, given the language transition to English, most of the descendants of New Sweden had joined the Episcopal Church. Yet, as we shall see, they were of assistance to the Dutch Lutherans in New York and the German Lutherans in Pennsylvania and New Jersey.

Germans in Pennsylvania

German Lutherans of a Pietist strain arrived in Pennsylvania in 1694 and settled near Germantown. About forty in number, they were mainly from Erfurt University, Germany, and had been influenced by the young August Hermann Francke prior to his move to Halle. For them Pennsylvania loomed as a haven from oppressive authorities.[8] Among the newcomers was Daniel Falckner, son of a Lutheran pastor in Saxony. A trip back to Europe in the interests of his group is said to have had the encouragement of the Swedish pastors.

Daniel Falckner's journey accomplished at least three things. First, the Frankfort Land Company, affiliated with the Penn interests, made Daniel its new land agent in place of Francis Daniel Pastorius, the German Quaker (a former Lutheran). The company sought a more rapid sale and settlement of its 26,000 acres purchased earlier from Penn. The change would cost Daniel dearly in terms of his standing in the colony, but it would perpetuate his name on a large tract thereafter called Falckner's Swamp, north of Philadelphia. The record is unclear but the claim has been made that the New Hanover settlement here became the location of the first German Lutheran congregation.[9]

Second, at Halle, site of the new university where Francke had been teaching since its founding in 1691, Daniel paused. Francke and his supporters, like the Lutheran Pietism of Philip Jacob Spener, were at the time building up the schools and orphanage, the Francke Institutions, for which Halle would become famous in missionary circles. Responding to the request of his former teacher at Erfurt, Daniel Falckner wrote detailed answers to over one hundred questions. The resulting book, *Curious Account of Pennsylvania, in Northern America* (1702), helped to arouse interest among prospective emigrants. Third, upon his return journey Daniel Falckner brought his younger brother, Justus. The pair arrived in Philadelphia late in the year 1700. A Halle alumnus, Justus was marking time before seeking ordination. But a hymn he had composed while a student (1699), "Rise you children of salvation," appeared in the Halle Hymnal (Freylinghausen) and remains in American hymnals.[10] His own words challenged him.

Dutch, Swedes, and Germans Cooperate

The Dutch Lutherans in New York, being again pastorless and finding the Amsterdam consistory unable to help, turned in desperation to the Swedish confessional kin on the Delaware. In response Dean Andrew Rudman secured leave from Gloria Dei parish and came to New York with his family. He learned Dutch, served faithfully and remained for over a year. Illness (Yellow Fever) and the loss of a son forced his return to Philadelphia. There he persuaded Justus Falckner to be ordained. In Gloria Dei Church, on November 24, 1703, the first regular ordination of a Lutheran pastor in America took place. As Dean Rudman presided, assisted by the two other Swedish clergy, the solemnity of the service expressed the importance and role of the ordained ministry in Christ's Church. Following the nine scripture passages, the dean concluded with an admonition still ringing today:

> May God give you grace that you may faithfully guard these sayings in your heart. May they be a guide for your conversation, and remind you of your responsibility. May the Word increase your watchfulness, uphold your zeal, and now and forever consecrate you to the service of Heaven.[11]

The worship with its hymns, its versicles and responses, was accompanied by a small organ (said to be the first in the colonies). The pietists from Wissahickon added chanting and instrumental music.

By December 2 Falckner was in New York and soon proved acceptable to the congregation. His parish extended northward to Albany and across the Hudson to Hackensack (East Jersey). In his missionary zeal he gathered many who had strayed. His pastoral concern, his instruction of the young, his reports and writings, as well as his preaching (in acquired Dutch) bore the marks of faithfulness. His ever wider duties, painstakingly recorded, reveal his stature. At the time of his death in 1723, at the age of fifty-one, Falckner was serving fourteen congregations.[12] Some were initially part of the parish. Others he and lay folk had organized. And seven were taken on after the death of a fellow pastor, Joshua Kochertal, who had accompanied the first Palatine Germans arriving in 1708 (see below).

Among Falckner's parishioners were people of various backgrounds. In 1705 he baptized the daughter of Aree van Guinee and his wife Jora, who were African Americans, freed slaves. Having relocated to the Raritan Valley, the Jersey frontier, they brought their infant son to New York in 1708, for baptism by their pastor. But six years later Aree invited Falckner to his Raritan farm for confirmation and the baptism of a grandchild. On the first August Sunday of 1714, an assembled congregation of nearly thirty persons, ten of them African in origin and the rest Palatine German neighbors, comprised what is today New Jersey's oldest Lutheran parish, Zion Church, Oldwick (formerly New Germantown).[13] The growing pains of this congregation, as we shall soon see, would become illustrative of Lutheran organization in America.

The Palatines

The three thousand Rhenish Palatines who arrived in New York in the summer of 1710 represented a new beginning for German Protestantism in America. The Rhenish Palatinate, a region midway down the Rhine valley, extends southward to Swabia (Wuerttemberg) and Baden, and westward to France. The capital of this Palatine region, an assemblage of smallish principalities, was Heidelberg, known also for its university (1386), Germany's oldest. Here in 1518 Luther held forth successfully in a colloquy on the gospel. Yet it was not until 1545 (the year before Luther's death) that the Reformation came to the Palatinate to stay. But it came and stayed as a mix of Lutheran and Reformed influences, with consequences for America.

The Religious Peace of Augsburg (1555), ending the war of the Protestants against Emperor Charles V, granted toleration to territorial princes and Free Cities that had signed the Augsburg Confession, and were therefore Lutheran. The ruler's religion determined the religion of his subjects. The Rhine valley, meanwhile, had continued to funnel Calvinistic doctrine from Switzerland to the Netherlands. The Elector Palatine, Frederick III, personally went the route from Roman Catholic to Lutheran to Reformed. To him Lutheranism had become problematic. Philip Melanchthon, eager to accommodate the Reformed, had modified Article X of the Augsburg Confession which dealt with the Presence of Christ in the Lord's Supper. This revision of 1540 became known as the *Variata*. The *Gnesio* or "genuine" Lutheran theologians insisted on the 1530 version of the Confession, the *Invariata* (Unaltered), as the only legitimate standard. Impatient with this fine-tuning of the theologians, Elector Frederick supported the Melanchthonians.

In 1563 the adoption of the Palatinate Church Order, and with it the Heidelberg Catechism and a Liturgy, "introduced a permanent Reformed tradition to Germany."[14] When reminded that this action could be in violation of the Peace of Augsburg and its accent on the Augsburg Confession, the Elector explained that he and his theologians had no intention of repudiating the German Reformation. Their sole aim was to oppose "the dogmatic orthodoxy of the Gnesio-Lutherans in favor of an evangelical consciousness, previously Melanchthonian, henceforth by necessity Reformed."[15] Nevertheless, the powers of the Elector were such that he could not dictate the confessional choice of the princes whose territories together comprised the Palatinate. Some of them remained Lutheran (ardently so) and others upheld the Reformed faith. Soon the Palatinate became known for the to-and-fro changes between Lutheran and Reformed as determined by the rulers of the local principalities. Immigrants from this area would find it natural to coexist as Lutheran and Reformed in America.

The actual immigration of the Palatines had several causes and stages. Having put the Huguenots to flight, Louis XIV at the end of the seventeenth century ordered a devastation of the Palatinate on France's eastern border. Speyer, Worms, and Mannheim were burned, and the Heidelberg Castle destroyed. The surviving countryside then suffered the coldest winter in memory (1708-09), devastating orchards and vineyards alike. From sheer economic hardship, thousands looked elsewhere. England, the leading Protestant colonial power, received a massive influx from the Palatinate and South Germany. Clotted in and around London, they taxed the resources as well as strained the bounds of hospitality of Queen Anne, last of the Stuarts and an ardent Protestant, with her Lutheran Prince Consort, George of Denmark. Anton Wilhelm Boehme, an alumnus of Halle and one of the three Lutheran pastors in London, played a key role in what happened next.

Since German soldiers made good mercenaries, it was fair to presume that they would make good colonists, even in frontier areas. Projects were devised for them.[16] For the Rhenish Palatines, an advance party, accompanied by Lutheran pastor Joshua Kochertal, had spied out the New York scene in 1708, and also made contact with the local Lutheran pastor, Justus Falckner. Back in London, a resettlement plan for the thousands of Palatines was worked out. Once situated in camps on either side of the Hudson near Newburg (founded by Kochertal's party) the Palatines would begin a tar-making project for the English navy. Proceeds from the tar would pay, so it was thought, for the cost of the transatlantic voyage of the refugees.

Among the three thousand Palatines who arrived in New York in 1710 was John Conrad Weiser from the village of Astaett, south of Stuttgart. Born in 1660, he learned the baker's trade, served his time with the local military and married a local girl.[17] Before the age of fifty he was a widower with a family of fifteen children. Life had become hard. Leaving the youngest with the oldest (already married) and laden with belongings, the Weisers joined up with other emigrants and journeyed down the Rhine to Rotterdam and onward to England, and then America. As with the Kochertal group, this group of three thousand Germans became naturalized subjects of the Queen prior to their setting out for America. The flotilla of ten ships traveled under escort against pirates or French intervention and required about four months under sail from Plymouth to New York.

Accompanying this invasion of newcomers was the new provincial governor, Robert Hunter. To him had been entrusted the project that was expected to make the resettlement of the Palatines a paying proposition. They were thus resettled in camps, eventually villages, some eighty miles north of New York and on both sides of the Hudson. Their task was to fell the pine trees and to make tar, a product essential to the British navy and hitherto imported mainly from Scandinavia. But the Governor knew nothing about tar-making. Neither did the Palatines. The available advice proved incorrect. Development of the process required two years. The tar project failed miserably.

For the Palatines the New York experience had alienated them. The word was soon out, so that after about 1720 the great majority of German immigrants headed directly for Pennsylvania, where Philadelphia became the most heavily patronized port of entry.[18] Some of those who entered through New York remained in their settlements along the Hudson as congregations of Lutherans and Reformed. Amid their abject misery the Lutheran Kochertal and his Reformed associate, Jonathan F. Haeger, ministered heroically. In 1719 Kochertal died, and Justus Falckner assumed the extra burden until his own death four years later.[19] Many moved to the Schoharie Valley, west of Albany, believing this to be their promised Canaan. Here they were served by a vagabond preacher, John van Dieren, an erstwhile tailor from East Prussia and London.[20] The senior Weiser settled in New York's Indian country (later known as "Weisersdorf"), a location in the heart of the Six Nations country, a strategic region where the three big rivers of the East Coast—the Hudson, the Delaware, the Susquehanna—take their rise.[21] Conrad, the junior Weiser, at sixteen was apprenticed to the Mohawk Indians for a couple of years (1712-14). There he learned their sophisticated language, their thoughtways, their sense of justice, their fairness, their religious life, their accent on peace and brotherhood. At first, he was afraid. He was tested, suffered want, shared hard times, and knew that peacefulness could be shattered by the "fire water" of the white man.[22]

Young Conrad Weiser, in 1720, married a fellow Palatine, Anna Eva Feck. The ceremony, writes Conrad, "was performed the 22 November, in My Father's house at schochary," by the Reformed minister Johan Friedrich Heger.[23] Over the next eight years two sons and two daughters were born to the Weisers "at schochary." Then came the big decision to move southwestward along the Susquehanna frontier of Pennsylvania.

It was 1729 when over forty Palatines, encouraged by the Indians, made the laborious move and settled in a promising region not far from today's city of Reading. A creek, the Tulpehocken, gave its name to the settlement and provided access by water to Philadelphia. The Palatines had entered Pennsylvania by the back door and here again had to legitimize their land claim, this time with a friendlier set of authorities. Attuned to the ways of the Mohawks, Weiser became an interpreter and peace-maker between white settlers and Indian nations. The Weiser house in Tulpehocken received callers from both sides. Conrad Weiser remained ready on call to go forth wherever and mediate. Often this was impossible. There was violence. There was shooting and scalping and burning. Whites saw the Indians as terrorists. Indians saw whites as thieves. An outbreak in 1755, during which Tulpehocken was among the raided settlements, severely tested the Quaker policy of non-violence by which the Commonwealth was governed. It also tested the abilities of the man who, since 1730, had served a double role: "Province Interpreter" and, under a title of esteem as given him by Zinzendorf, "Emperor of the Iroquois."[24]

Returning now to the religious scene, what kind of spiritual care was there for these Palatines? First, for the lay folk there was what they had learned by heart: hymns, Bible passages, prayers, and the catechism—Luther's *Small Catechism* for some, the Heidelberg Catechism for the Reformed. A family Bible, with its entries of generations, a hymnal, a book of devotions or even a book of sermons, by Luther or whomever, may have made it across the Atlantic. Even a headlong rush to emigrate could not sever the cords of continuity. But lay folk in the church require pastors whose calling is "to preach the holy Gospel in its purity and who administer the Sacraments according to the Gospel" (Augsburg Confession, VII). For Lutherans and Reformed the requirement for such a public ministry was ordination.

In colonial America ecclesiastically ordained pastors were at a premium and vagabond preachers more plentiful, eager to serve the neglected flocks. After Justus Falckner's death, the Amsterdam Consistory sent William Christopher Berkenmeyer in 1725. He was a talented young theologian from Hamburg where Lutheran orthodoxy prevailed. He brought with him a library and funds for a new church building from friends in Denmark and England as well as Germany. Four years later Trinity Church was dedicated in New York. Berkenmeyer found ten parishes waiting for him, too many for one pastor, and pleaded for assistance. In 1732 Michael Christian Knoll arrived and centered his work in New York City. Berkenmeyer moved to Loonenberg (Athens) to care for the more promising northern parishes. The Hamburg Consistory sent John August Wolf to the Raritan Valley Parish in New Jersey.

By 1741 German settlements extended from New York to Georgia, but most were concentrated in Pennsylvania with extensions into New Jersey, and southward into Maryland, Virginia and the Carolinas. About one half of the German settlers were Lutheran. Here too, impostors traveled from one settlement to another. Credentials were hard to determine. Word of the intense need of pastors for the spiritually hungry settlers reached the homeland. In response a few pastors and theologically trained laymen came to America without calls but with determination to serve. Among them was Anthony J. Henkel (sometimes known as Gerhard) who came with his family in 1717 and served the congregation in New Hanover. At Germantown he organized a congregation and encouraged them to build a church as had been done in New Hanover. Henkel reached out to scattered settlements as far away as Virginia. Tragically, a fall from his horse took his life in 1728. His numerous descendants, many of whom were pastors, helped to lay the foundation for a Lutheran Church in America.

A father and son team, John Casper Stoever Sr. and Jr., arrived in 1728 as "missionaries." The father served in Virginia. Seeing the great need, he went to Europe to raise funds and find pastors and died at sea on his return. The son served fifty years as a roving missionary in Eastern Pennsylvania and beyond. Both Stoevers were ordained by one pastor who thought the spiritual needs so great that he could risk an unconventional ordination.

The stories of these and other early pastors are fascinating and have been well-told.[25] But for the founders of the ULCA, and therefore for us, the father (or patriarch) to follow was H. M. Muhlenberg. His story intersects with one more group of Lutheran immigrants, the Salzburgers.

HENRY MELCHIOR MUHLENBERG

For Lutherans in America the word "United" has a long history, being ever a reminder of a common confessional legacy and a challenge to purposeful partnership. In 1733, 185 years before the formation of the United Lutheran Church in America, three groups of fellow believers in Philadelphia, Providence (Trappe) and New Hanover, Pennsylvania, were moved to call themselves the United Congregations. This happened while John Christian Schulz was their pastor for little more than a year (1732-33), before he and two laymen returned to Europe to recruit pastors and solicit support. Schulz did not return. Time passed, but the call of the United Congregations for a pastor remained.

Finally, and nearly too late, the Lutheran leaders in London and Halle acted on that call. Henry Melchior Muhlenberg was their man. A Hanoverian by birth (Einbeck) and a Göttingen University alumnus, his pastoral experience had included teaching and directing an orphanage linked with the famed Francke Institutions at Halle. August Gotthilf, the younger Francke, had selected him; Michael Ziegenhagen, the German chaplain at the Royal Court in London, had oriented him. His fifteen-week Atlantic crossing included his thirty-first birthday (September 6, 1742) and its trials inflicted the proverbial "sea change." Advised first to visit the Salzburg refugees in Georgia, who were shepherded by the two Halle pastors, Muhlenberg got his first sampling of colonial life.

Georgia, the youngest of the American colonies (1733) was a buffer between the older Carolina colony and the Spanish-held Florida. General Oglethorpe and the newly chartered trustees, in need of settlers, welcomed the Salzburgers who had left their homes in Austria, with some thirty thousand others, rather than convert to Roman Catholicism as demanded by Archbishop Firmian.

The original company of Salzburgers arrived in Georgia in 1734.[26] Ninety-one in number, they settled some twenty-five miles up the Savannah River and named their place Ebenezer: "Hitherto the Lord has helped." Theirs was the toil of clearing the wilderness, tilling the virgin soil, building houses and barns, all with the help of initial assistance from the British stationed in Savannah. Additional contingents of Salzburgers arrived, until in 1741 their settlement totaled more than eleven hundred. For the future of Lutherans in America the

Georgia arrival of two pastors from Halle ushered in a new era. At Ebenezer Israel Christian Gronau (d. 1745) was the teacher and John Martin Bolzius (1703-65) was not only pastor but also chief administrative officer. From March 11, 1734, he held this post until his death thirty-two years later. These two began a line of Halle men, after Falckner, who with Muhlenberg would give colonial Lutheranism the pietism that accompanied its confessional faith. In keeping with their Lutheran pietism, the Salzburgers showed concern for the needy. Already in 1737 when a plague of fever left many children orphans, they built a home for their care. This was the first Protestant orphanage in America and was an example that other denominations followed as well as later Lutherans.

Muhlenberg visited this outpost of Halle pietism first, and returned three decades later to settle a controversy. However, in the fall of 1742, he quickly headed north. The sloop from Charleston nearly sank in the storms of late autumn, but he arrived at Philadelphia, unexpected, on November 25, 1742. He was answering the call of the three United Congregations.

There is no need here for a full study of Muhlenberg and his times, which has been well done.[27] Our task is rather to recall how certain aspects of his career, and the careers of his colleagues and church members, helped to shape the future of the eventually largest Lutheran church body in America. In this respect we can give free play to a sense of wonder that those three United Congregations became the forebears of some 3,473 congregations comprising the ULCA in 1918. Those who formed the ULCA out of three separate church bodies often invoked their common legacy in Muhlenberg as a powerful tool of persuasion and inspiration for merger and mission.

Muhlenberg had been offered a three-year trial period in America, and he remained there the rest of his life, for forty-five years. Those first five weeks at the end of 1742 would have been enough to discourage the faint-hearted. In Philadelphia, he learned upon arrival that most of the German Lutherans had aligned with the visiting patron of the Moravians, who was said to have the church register. But Muhlenberg was a man of faith in action. He rented a horse and accompanied a Lutheran elder who happened to be heading back the thirty-three miles to New Hanover via Providence (Trappe). En route for two days, past Germantown and fording swollen streams, Muhlenberg learned what he could from elder Philip Brandt about people and places. He learned about the sixty-three-year-old John Valentine Kraft (1680-1752), a minister of uncertain credentials who had come in August from Germany's Darmstadt region. Kraft, too, had acted quickly. In all three of the United Congregations he had appointed elders and deacons. He had traveled as far west as Tulpehocken and the Lancaster area, and with John Casper Stoever, the other Lutheran pastor among the Germans, had formed a consistory with claimed powers to ordain.

In New Hanover, the farthest out, Muhlenherg found a pretender named George Schmid in charge. But the congregation's leaders agreed to allow the newcomer to preach, leaving Schmid, the quacksalver, to listen. Thus on the First Sunday in Advent, one year after his farewell sermon in Germany, Muhlenberg preached his first sermon in Pennsylvania and his first in the United Congregations. He had begun to win the people's confidence. Traveling his elongated parish like a horse-borne shuttle, Muhlenberg acquainted himself rapidly. He decided to base himself at Providence, commonly and today called Trappe. On the Second Sunday in Advent he was in Philadelphia, preaching in the morning to a large gathering of German Lutherans in the rented house they shared with their Reformed countrymen. That afternoon, in the Wicaco section near the Delaware, he preached in the Swedish church, Gloria Dei. Peter Koch (Kock), the alert Swedish merchant, had arranged it with his pastor. It was a *de facto* recognition of Muhlenberg's credentials as penned by London's Ziegenhagen.

The Third and Fourth Advent Sundays he spent at Providence. Worship in a barn demonstrated the need for a church building. For Christmas, on a Saturday, Muhlenberg was back in New Hanover. On the Second Christmas Day, accompanied through flooded roads by councilmen, he preached in Providence again, with this difference. Having read his credentials to the lay leaders once more, he secured their agreement, and they signed the statement of acceptance that he had prepared.

Back in Philadelphia for the Third Christmas Day, Muhlenberg secured the acceptance of the elders in that congregation as well. But this was more complicated since Kraft still claimed to be the German Lutheran pastor. At Gloria Dei Church that afternoon Pastor Peter Tranberg, with Swedish thoroughness, was publicly to review the documents of the two contenders. Kraft, however, absented himself. Tranberg read publicly Muhlenberg's authorization by the Rev. Ziegenhagen, his certificate of ordination at Leipzig, his matriculation and certification from Göttingen University, and "the English acceptance signed by the deacons and elders in New Hanover and Providence."[28] Like their counterparts in the two other congregations, the Philadelphians also signed the acceptance. It read in part:

> We testify in God and affirm by Subscription, that we have accepted with a thankful Heart the Rev. Heinrich Melchior Muhlenberg as a lawful called, ordained, and by our Supplications Sent and represent Minister of the Gospel and the Augsburg Confession, by the Reverend Frederick Michael Ziegenhagen his Majestis German Chaplain and member of the Society for promoting Christian Knowledge.[29]

Having only the rented house shared with the Reformed as a place of worship, the German Lutherans gratefully saw their long awaited pastor installed by Pastor Peter Tranberg in the setting of Gloria Dei Church. The call to the United Congregations was thus held intact. Fittingly in the preceding weeks Muhlenberg had refused to consider any dividing of the congregations, as Kraft and others had suggested, without prior consultation with those back in Europe who had sent him.[30] But one last showdown remained.

As self-designated inspector of the Lutheran Church in Pennsylvania, Count von Zinzendorf, with an eye on protocol, had expected Muhlenberg to check in with him upon arrival. Muhlenberg, however, was wary. He already knew of the

Count's multiple interests: the new Moravian communities, the Count's desire to unite the German sects and confessions into one "Church of God in the Spirit," and, aided by the Lutheran Indian agent Conrad Weiser, to promote mission work among the Native Americans. Last, not least, was the question of what Zinzendorf had in mind for the Lutherans, seeing that he had already gained apparent control of the largest of the three United Congregations. Feeling snubbed, the Count nevertheless on December 30 invited Muhlenberg to what became a confrontation.[31] Instead of the two meeting in private the Count received Muhlenberg in a large room. Seated at a small table he was surrounded by a large number of adherents, including disaffected members of the Lutheran congregation. But Muhlenberg was not to be deterred. "My call has been signed and I shall trouble myself no further, but just follow the instructions of my superiors in Europe. If this does not please you, you can settle it with them." Muhlenberg also pointed out with satisfaction that he had been privileged to preach in the Swedish church, a favor of recognition that had been denied the Count.[32] The church register and other items were recovered. On January 1, 1743, the Count left for New York and was soon en route to London. Zinzendorf was gone, Schmid and Kraft were out of the picture, and Muhlenberg was in charge.

The Early Years

By early 1743 the ground had been cleared sufficiently for Muhlenberg to begin his real task. In Philadelphia and Trappe preparations got under way for a Lutheran church building, and for a new school house in New Hanover and Trappe. The new pastor laid emphasis on worship, with preaching in its proper liturgical context. Hymns likewise had their proper place, and the singing benefited from his own musical talent, expressed through a clear tenor voice. When the instrument was available, he played the organ skillfully. In his concern for the rising generation he took part in the church's teaching task. His fondness for and effectiveness with children and young people had already been demonstrated by the way he directed the school and orphanage at Gross Hennersdorf in Saxony. The scene was indeed different in his three-point Pennsylvania parish, but the challenge the same.

Where needed, he exercised pastoral care, conscientiously visiting the sick, the troubled and the bereaved. His two boxes of books, mistakenly left behind in London by the dispatcher, had arrived "by the next boat," as promised. School books, hymnals, Bibles, commentaries, theological works and books of devotion were among them. John Arndt's *True Christianity* was a favorite for nurturing the spiritual life of thoughtful members. Muhlenberg's pastoral acts punctuated his ministry. Prior to the celebration of Holy Communion, members were to announce their intention by seeing the pastor, a good practice for keeping order as well as for retaining some semblance of private confession.[33] Baptisms were frequent and were the pastor's moment to admonish the parents to raise their new child "in the nurture and admonition of the Lord." Marriages were performed legally only by a licensed clergyman or justice of the peace; Muhlenberg's were entered like other pastoral acts into the parish records.

Funerals often rated a fairly full obituary from the pen of the pastor. For Muhlenberg this detour into biography became especially important as a means of acquainting him with his parishioners and their past. These accounts were included in the periodic reports which Muhlenberg sent to "the Reverend Fathers at Halle." It was these "Halle Reports" that, over years, remain as valuable source material on the life of the laity in colonial times. They included not only obituaries but, more importantly, the accounts of the pastor's mission and ministry. These reports, not only by Muhlenberg but also by others of a Halle connection, were reviewed, discussed and commented upon at Halle. This led to a counseling process to-and-fro between the Halle men and their home advisers. Sixteen such reports were published periodically between 1741 and 1786. In edited form the reports were published and distributed in Europe among friends and supporters of the mission work in America. Muhlenberg's correspondence with Ziegenhagen in London and Francke in Halle, as well as with others, developed into a remarkable communications network.[34] For official documents Muhlenberg and his vestrymen devised an ecclesiastical seal. Impressed upon sealing wax, its legend bore the names of the United Congregations of New Hanover, New Providence, and Philadelphia. In the center were three sheaves of wheat enclosed by the sharp edge of a sickle. Above the sheaves is inscribed: "Joh. 4:35-37." ("the fields are already white for harvest . . . one sows, another reaps.") The seal was first used in October 1743.[35]

A building era put the United Congregations on the map. In 1743 at Trappe the decision to build had been taken in January, the cornerstone laid in May, and the unfinished structure used for worship in mid-autumn. Dedicated October 6, 1743 (and completed two years later), it received the name Augustus Church, honoring the memory and work of August Hermann Francke and the benefactors at Halle.[36] The church is still in use and is a historic point of pilgrimage. In New Hanover, meanwhile, the new schoolhouse had been completed. In Philadelphia, belatedly, a suitable site had been purchased and construction begun on what would become St. Michael's Church, dedicated in 1748. Besides, in Germantown, a fourth member of the initially three United Congregations enlarged its facilities in 1746.

Meanwhile Muhlenberg became acquainted with the Palatines settled in Tulpehocken. There he found factional in-fighting between Moravians and Lutherans. The latter had ousted their pastor, John Casper Stoever, and were in need of strong pastoral leadership. Muhlenberg recommended Pastor Tobias Wagner. He no doubt knew of Wagner's grandfather who had been a prominent theological professor and also chancellor at Tübingen University. Wagner, a Tübingen graduate, had with his family accompanied a second group of Württembergers to a colony in Waldoboro, Maine, in 1742. Disappointed with the situation and the climate, they migrated to Pennsylvania. Wagner and his large family needed help.

The field in America was in urgent need of pastors, as Muhlenberg kept on reminding the Reverend Fathers in Halle. He impressed upon them that unless the men sent to America have already been firmly formed in their spiritual life, there is little likelihood of that happening in this country. One could not remind church leaders in Europe too often that conditions are much different over here. In a descriptive phrase that would become his trademark he declared, "the *ecclesia plantanda* [the church that must be planted] is at a very critical juncture here. We need experienced, strong men who will stand in the breach, men who will be able to venture something in great patience and self-denial."[37] Muhlenberg wrote this in his summary of the year 1745, a turning point in his career. It marked the end of his three-year trial period and revealed his determination to stay in America. January had been highlighted by the arrival of his first three assistants from Halle: Peter Brunnholz (already ordained), with two theological students, John Nicholas Kurtz and John Helfrich Schaum.[38]

After Easter that year Muhlenberg married Anna Maria Weiser, third of the eventually fourteen children born to the renowned Indian agent Conrad Weiser and his wife Eve Anna. Tobias Wagner, recently called to Christ Church in Tulpehocken with Muhlenberg's help, had performed the ceremony. Peter Brunnholtz had been the groom's best man and Schaum a witness. At the time Anna Maria was eighteen. Born in Weisersdorf, west of the Schoharie Valley in Upper New York, she had been baptized by William Christopher Berkenmyer, chief pastor of the Lutherans on the Hudson. Of his bride Muhlenberg wrote for the benefit of the Halle Fathers:

> I considered nothing but sincere piety, such as might be convenable both for myself and my work. The Lord also regarded my prayers and granted me a young woman who is pure of heart, pious, simple-hearted, meek, and industrious.[39]

After three months in Philadelphia, the couple made their home at Trappe (Providence), where the foresighted husband had a substantial house under construction.[40] Here pastors and other visitors would stop in, hospitality would be generous, and eventually the seven children who survived infancy would perpetuate the Muhlenberg line with distinction in nation and church. For most of their forty-two years of married life Henry and Anna Maria lived in Trappe.[41]

Besides welcoming his assistants and getting married, in the summer of 1745 Muhlenberg responded to a challenge that would spread his influence with Lutherans in New Jersey and the Hudson Valley. Almost since his arrival in Pennsylvania elders from the parish of small congregations in the Raritan Valley had been importuning him to mediate a struggle between the members and their pastor, John August Wolf. Until then Muhlenberg had been able to put them off on grounds that he had no one to take his place in the United Congregations to allow him even a short absence. Actually the Raritan parish was about as far east of Trappe as Tulpehocken was west. Now newcomers like Brunnholtz could be entrusted with Philadelphia, while Kurtz and Schaum could fill in as teachers or supply briefly where needed. Muhlenberg knew he was needed in Jersey. He came not alone but brought a fellow pastor, Tobias Wagner.

On a previous occasion, in 1735, William C. Berkenmeyer had tried without success to settle the conflict between Wolf and his people. The scene was near the present town of Oldwick, then New Germantown. The congregation, a consolidation of smaller ones, had its roots in the one founded by Pastor Justus Falckner in 1714. As Zion Church it continues to this day, the oldest continuously functioning Lutheran congregation in New Jersey. Without the mediating role of Muhlenberg things might well have fallen apart.

The hearing in July 1745 was held before a justice of the peace. At that time, as earlier, the congregation sought to oust its pastor. Morals charges and general incompatibility had created an impasse. Wolf refused to leave. The congregation refused to pay his salary. Muhlenberg negotiated a "you pay, he'll go" compromise. It worked. The Raritan settlement was a victory for the Halle brand of Lutheranism. The Raritaners begged Muhlenberg to become their pastor. But he offered a more practical alternative. The Raritaners could trust him to be their pastoral superior, or rector, and he would then send them a competent pastoral candidate as vicar.[42]

The Ministerium

Such situations highlighted the need for some common agency to deal with problems common to the growing number of pastors and congregations. Unlike the ready-made church structures and administrations in the old country the accent fell on do-it-yourself in the new country, especially in a commonwealth like Pennsylvania where there was no establishment of religion as in New England (Congregational) or in parts of the South (Anglican). By 1748 a fortunate convergence of developments occasioned the calling together of pastors and representatives of congregations to carry out three acts: to take part in the dedication of the newly completed St. Michael's Church in Philadelphia, to agree on a common order of public worship, and for the pastors to examine and ordain a candidate for the ministry.[43]

The three initial events fit together firmly, like a tripod. The church building, on its rectangular foundation (35 x 70 feet), was the gathering place for the largest congregation in Philadelphia. Much of its membership was transient, redemptioners earning their freedom in a few years and then moving out to the frontier. What they heard and learned at St. Michael's would be remembered. Secondly, how they worshiped God would be recalled in a liturgy already familiar in most of its parts, with admittedly many variations as followed in the homeland. But here the church orders with which the pastors and lay people were familiar harked back to the Reformation era. In fact, Muhlenberg in 1747 had prepared an Agenda or Liturgy which was then agreed upon in the 1748 meeting, each pastor making his own copy of it. It later had an influence on the *Common Service* (1888) and became the standard of worship in English in the ULCA (1918) and in other Lutheran church bodies as well. Thirdly, the ordination of John Nicholas Kurtz was the first of its kind undertaken by a Lutheran synod in America. Forty-five years had passed since the Swedish clergy had ordained Justus Falckner in Gloria Dei Church.

On a Friday in mid-August of 1748, John Nicholas Kurtz arrived from Tulpehocken. There he had been pulpit supply and also teacher. He now checked in with Muhlenberg and received the questions that he was to answer in writing. Saturday, after turning in his replies, he appeared before a panel of examiners that included the pastors Hartwick (Hudson Valley), Handschuh (Lancaster), and Muhlenberg, chair. It was a case of three Halle graduates probing a fourth. A high standard had been set, and the results were gratifying. Sunday morning, the members and the curious gathered around the new church. From the Brunnholtz residence Pastor Muhlenberg led a procession of the principals: the six pastors by twos, and then the thirty-six elders and deacons. "Mr. Muhlenberg consecrated the newly built church," Frederick Handschuh wrote in his diary, "and the consecration was confirmed by a brief prayer by each of the preachers as they knelt about the altar." The sermon by Pastor Handschuh (Lancaster) was followed by Holy Communion, with Hartwick and Handschuh the celebrants. Muhlenberg reported:

> In the afternoon, we again went to the church in procession. Pastor Hartwick preached an edifying sermon. . . . After the sermon [the Swedish] Provost Sandin, Pastors Brunnholtz, Hartwick, Handschuh and I, together with the candidate, Mr. Kurtz, who was to be ordained, took our places about the altar, and three Reformed preachers were witnesses. The delegates from all the congregation again formed a semi-circle, one of us read the formula of ordination, offered prayer at the close, and with the other preachers laid hands upon the candidate, and there-by consecrated him to the holy ministry.[44]

The next day, Monday, August 14, the transactions "mostly concerned only external organization." Bearing in mind that the initially three United Congregations now numbered ten, he continued,

> A twisted cord of many threads will not easily break. There must be unity among us. . . . We are assembled here for this purpose, and, if God will, we shall assemble yearly; this is only a trial and test. We preachers who are here present, not having wandered hither of our own will, but called and necessitated, are bound to give an account to God and our conscience. We stand in connection with our Fathers in Europe. We must provide not only for ourselves, but also for our posterity.[45]

Posterity did take a great interest in this Ministerium, especially when rallying its divided heirs to reunite. The ULCA's mother synod comprised fully one-fourth of the ULCA's total baptized membership in 1918.

Participants in the first Ministerium (1748) had been limited to Halle Pietists plus the Swedish Dean, Sandin. In addition to those in the Philadelphia area there was John Hartwick who, in 1746, had been sent by the Hamburg Consistory to assist Berkenmeyer in New York. Other pastors like Stoever and

Wagner who had come without calls were not invited. For this decision Muhlenberg was duly criticized even by his own father-in-law, Conrad Weiser. Amends were attempted with only partial success. The younger Stoever continued to serve the scattered congregations quite independently until 1763 when he was admitted to the Ministerium. Wagner moved around the Lancaster and Reading area until 1759 when he and his family returned to a village church in Württemberg.[46]

The career of the newly ordained Kurtz is illustrative of future developments. As vicar and then as pastor he served the Tulpehocken parish twenty-four years (1746-1770). He and the members got along well. His support was generous, making even Muhlenberg a bit envious. When there was need of his services elsewhere, as for resolving a conflict in the Germantown congregation (1763-64), the Tulpehockeners released him, albeit reluctantly. As a leader Kurtz gave stability and continuity to the synodical constituency. When Muhlenberg laid down the presidency of the Ministerium in 1770, Kurtz was elected his successor. During the Revolutionary War, the pressures of the times required an instrument of church government in writing. In 1781 Kurtz, with Muhlenberg's son-in-law John Christopher Kunze, produced the Constitution of the Ministerium of the Evangelical Lutheran Church in North America.[47] It solidified the documentary foundations of this, the only organized Lutheran Ministerium in the New World. Kurtz concluded his active ministry with an eighteen-year pastorate in York (1771-89) and then retired to Baltimore where he died in 1794.

By 1781, the number of ministers listed in the new constitution numbered twenty-seven. The congregations were perhaps twice that number, and extended from Pennsylvania into New York and New Jersey, and southward into Maryland, Virginia and North Carolina.[48] Despite the war effort and the virtual cessation of immigration, natural increase showed the number of Lutherans on the increase and their settlement in frontier regions only partially diminished. By this time, Muhlenberg himself was clearly the patriarch, in both ecclesiastical and familial terms. He served parishes throughout, principally in Trappe and Philadelphia, but also for a year in New Jersey and two summers in New York. He mediated conflicts in these areas, and even back in Georgia. His three sons were ordained, and two of four daughters married ministers. Their stories, including son Peter's commitment to the Revolutionary War, are fascinating examples of Americanization.[49]

Lutheran Pietism and the Muhlenberg Tradition

Now that we have had a quick glance at the Lutheran situation in colonial America there are two phrases that should be clarified, for they have been used and will be again. The first is Lutheran Pietism and the second is Muhlenberg tradition.

In Germany, Pietism was a reaction to cold orthodoxy and the spiritual destitution following the Thirty Years War (1618-1648). In 1675, Philip Jacob Spener (1635-1705), known as the father of Lutheran Pietism, wrote an extensive foreword to a new edition of a favored devotional book, *True Christianity* by John Arndt. In this *Pia Desideria* (Pious Desires) Spener laid the basis for a Lutheran Pietism that spread internationally and across church lines despite sharp criticism. Spener emphasized the centrality of a personal religious experience as well as the importance of justification, sanctification and a moral life. He emphasized Bible study and prayer in small groups and encouraged an active participation in social ministry and foreign missions.[50]

The new University at Halle (1694) became the cultural center of Pietism. Here August Herman Francke established the Halle Institutions, which his son Gottlieb August Francke strengthened. It was from here that the first Lutheran missionaries were sent to India in 1705. It was here that Muhlenberg as a young pastor, having returned for a visit, received the call to the United congregations. He was well schooled in pietism. In light of his own experience and conviction, it may rightly be said that Muhlenberg had the authentic piety of a confessional Lutheran.

Since an attempt has been made to clarify Muhlenberg's theological grounding, we can also attempt an understanding of the term "Muhlenberg tradition" that was so proudly and gratefully used when the United Lutheran Church in America was being formed. The Muhlenberg tradition defies definition but yields to description: it is an early stage of adapting a confessional and tradition-rich Lutheran church for survival and growth in an altogether new environment, the English-speaking American scene. Given the diversity of European origins and American conditions, there were bound to be objectors to Muhlenberg's way. But its main features carry a familiar ring to this day: the vision of a united Lutheran church; faithfulness to the Scriptures; justification by faith in Jesus Christ; adherence to the (unaltered) Augsburg Confession; use of Luther's *Small Catechism*; worship in historic liturgical order; piety at the heart of the believer's life; obligation to educate the young; openness to fellow Christians of evangelical persuasion; and, not least, an able, educated, accountable, and ordained ministry.

THE EARLY NATIONAL PERIOD

Although there had been hope, as in the briefly held name, Ministerium of North America, that all, or most, Lutherans could be held together, this hope was bound to disappoint. Language, geography, rural versus urban living, relations with the German Reformed, religious liberty, and the mobility of settlement advancing into the interior, were potent factors in the forming of ever additional synods. When the New York Ministerium was formed in 1786, the mother synod became delimited as the Ministerium of Pennsylvania and Adjacent States. Far to the south, in 1803, the Lutherans in and beyond North Carolina organized their own synod. Beyond the Alleghenies pioneers from Pennsylvania and Virginia began holding their own conferences which in 1818 became the Ohio Synod. By 1820 there were two more, the Tennessee Synod (begun in July) and the Maryland and Virginia Synod (begun in early October).

This early National period of the new United States—for our purposes, the three decades from 1787 to 1817—put Lutheranism to the test. The year 1787, marked by the adoption of the U.S. Constitution and the amendment separating Church and State, also saw the death of Henry Melchior Muhlenberg, leader of Lutherans during the colonial era and later called patriarch of Lutheranism in America. The year 1817 marked the three hundredth anniversary of Martin Luther's initiating the Reformation, an event observed widely on both sides of the Atlantic. In Germany, King Frederick William III took the lead in joining his Protestant subjects, a Lutheran majority and a Reformed minority, into the Evangelical Church of the Old Prussian Union, the cradle of "unionism," which later became such a hot issue among America's Lutherans.

In America, where denominationalism was not strong, the Reformation Tercentenary became a pan Protestant celebration with emphasis on broad evangelical teachings and restraint on distinctive Lutheran doctrines. The New York Synod took the initiative and with the Pennsylvania and North Carolina Synods arranged for simultaneous services on Reformation Day in many places. In New York City a mass rally of five thousand in St. Paul's Episcopal Cathedral featured special music by the Handel-Haydn Society and an address by the local Lutheran Pastor, Frederick Charles Schaeffer, a staunch Lutheran and eloquent bilingual preacher.

During this period when Americans were adjusting to their new freedom and responsibilities, there were conflicting ways of meeting spiritual needs. One was the spread of Rationalism and Deism. The latter was expounded by American leaders such as Jefferson, Madison, and Franklin as well as by universities such as Harvard. Another was revivalism and "New Measures." These were special techniques for bringing individuals through an emotional conversion. Camp grounds, especially on the frontier, were often used for these protracted meetings. Some Lutherans, hungry for the gospel message or out of curiosity, attended in spite of synod admonitions. Lutherans, surrounded by these emphases, were affected and they had their reactions. However, the influences coming from Germany may have had a greater impact.

Broadly speaking, the change in Germany was from Pietism to Rationalism, a common sense Enlightenment. Universities like Halle, once the stronghold of Pietism, had become advocates of a religion of reason. Although emigration to America had slowed to a trickle, the need for pastors in the new nation drew representatives of neology as well as their publications, to these shores. An example was the so-called North Carolina Catechism (1788) of 254 pages, prepared by John Caspar Velthusen, professor at the University of Helmstedt. The New York area was the most affected by the new trend. An example was Frederick Henry Quitman (1760-1832) who arrived in New York in 1795 to fill a vacancy in the Hudson Valley. Elected president of the New York Ministerium in 1807, he served for eighteen years. At Halle he had been influenced by Professor Semler, the father of German Rationalism. Although he was accused of unitarianism and rationalism, his theological spectrum was probably more that of biblical supernaturalism expounded by Gottlieb Christian Storr of the Old Tübingen School. It maintained that both reason and revelation were authoritative. Quitman was a leader in providing English hymnals and catechisms to the rapidly changing climate. His revised Lutheran Catechism was published in 1804 and 1814.[51]

Besides theological differences, the Lutherans faced other problems. Chief among them was the language question. In 1792 the Ministerium of Pennsylvania added German to its title. Although Muhlenberg had used whatever language the people understood best, be it German, Dutch or English, some of those who followed were not so wise. An example was Justus Henry Helmuth (1745-1825), pastor of Zion and St. Michael's in Philadelphia. His influence was great throughout the synod. His eloquent preaching stirred souls to a living faith without "New Measure" techniques. He was also a designated tutor to prepare much needed pastors for service in America. Yet he believed that the only way to preserve the Lutheran heritage was through the German language. In protest, General Peter Muhlenberg, son of the Patriarch, led a group that founded St. John's English-speaking congregation in 1806.[52]

Helmuth and one of his students, John George Schmucker, edited the German *Evangelisches Magazin* meant for all Germans regardless of denomination. It advocated German schools so that children could learn to read hymns, prayers and the catechism. This emphasis on the German language strengthened the already close relationship between Lutheran and German Reformed. Both churches supported the *Magazin,* and both were using a Union Hymnal and both cooperated in managing Franklin College at Lancaster where a joint seminary was in the planning stage. In many places in rural Pennsylvania, as in the Palatinate in Germany, a common church building encouraged union. The same tendencies were apparent in the North Carolina Synod. In New York the trend was toward a union with the Episcopal Church. Like Muhlenberg himself, the New York Synod made it a policy not to organize an English-using Lutheran congregation if an Anglican (Episcopal) church was nearby.

Although large scale immigration from Germany had virtually halted during the fifty years following the outbreak of the War of Independence in 1776, so had the supply of university trained pastors. However, the number of Lutherans grew steadily by natural increase. They like other Americans kept pace with the advancing frontier. The pastoral care of these pioneers was hard to supply. The Synods tried by sending "traveling missionaries" to remote areas who made the rounds preaching, baptizing, and showing concern.

Well-qualified pastors designated by the synods had faithfully been taking ministerial candidates into their homes for tutorial education, sometimes under the auspices of Hartwick Seminary founded in 1797. This was not enough. The need for a local seminary was widely recognized. Finally in New York the Hartwick Academy was opened in 1815 made possible by a legacy of Johann Christoph Hartwick, one of the Halle pastors who with Muhlenberg had formed the Ministerium in 1748. Although he had been sent to New York to work with the staunchly orthodox and capable Berkenmeyer, Hartwick, the pietist, never settled long in any one place but showed special interest and concern for the American Indians. From them he bought large tracts of land. According to his will, the proceeds were to go for an institution to train missionaries for the Indians. The curriculum of the Academy was general, but there was a professor of theology, E. T. Hazelius. Being in a remote area near Cooperstown and not under Synodical jurisdiction, it had its problems. But it was a beginning that encouraged others.[53]

On the frontier, meanwhile, a far more confessional Lutheranism was seeking to assert itself during this National period. Using New Market, Virginia, as a base, Paul Henkel (1754-1825) unfolded his memorable career as an itinerant home missionary and teacher. A third generation American, he was firmly Lutheran. He was also ably bilingual, and an author. He published Luther's *Small Catechism* in German and in English and hymn books in both languages, a popular work on Baptism and also other subjects. These works appeared early in the 1800s. Largely at his initiative, the North Carolina Synod was organized (1803); fifteen years later, the Ohio Synod (1818). The latter was in effect an offshoot of the Pennsylvania Ministerium and a convergence, beyond the Appalachians, of eastern and southern Lutherans in the new West. Four of Paul Henkel's sons became Lutheran ministers; the fifth a physician and owner of a printing press in New Market. When the North Carolina Synod's Lutheran commitment seemed too vague, six pastors (three of them Henkels) met in Green County, Tennessee, at Solomon's Church on Cover Creek and, with nineteen lay representatives from nine congregations, organized the Tennessee Synod in July of 1820. Its confessional basis was expressly indicated: the Unaltered Augsburg Confession. Some called it the Henkel Synod. In due course the Henkel Press, in New Market, published the first English translation of the Book of Concord (all the official Lutheran Confessions), the first edition in 1851, the revised, in 1854.[54]

The General Synod

In view of this process of dispersion and the variety of problems facing Lutherans in America, the Ministerium of Pennsylvania in 1818 proposed, as the North Carolina Synod had done earlier, that an inclusive General Synod be formed. A general body of this type was deemed essential to the survival of Lutheranism in North America. The Evangelical Lutheran General Synod of the United States of America, so named in its constitution, was organized on October 22, 1820, in Hagerstown, Maryland. Four synods were represented: the Ministerium of Pennsylvania (1748); the Ministerium of New York (1786); the North Carolina Synod (1803), and the Maryland and Virginia Synod (1820).

Before tracing the development of the General Synod—and some severe jolts lay immediately ahead—let us join the gathered company in 1820 at Hagerstown and acquaint ourselves with these early bearers of the "Muhlenberg tradition." They were meeting in the wake of the Reformation's three hundredth anniversary, in 1817. Politically and religiously it was the "era of good feeling." John George Schmucker, the General Synod's first president, and others were eager to recover and advance the unity that Muhlenberg and his colleagues had begun to fashion in Philadelphia more than seventy years earlier. In fact, their actual meeting in Hagerstown, instead of in Philadelphia or Baltimore, told a tale of the changing times. Here they were in the picturesque Cumberland Valley of Maryland, not far from the Potomac, and on a route that for generations had been followed by settlers moving southward from Pennsylvania into the Great Valley of Virginia and beyond. Hagerstown represented convergence from North, South, East, and West. The absence of representatives from the new self-declared Ohio Synod (1818), and from the Tennessee Synod (1820), the break-away from North Carolina, cast a pall of disappointment over the General Synodists. But the absence raised a basic question that overarched the tyranny of distance and expressed what would become a chronic unease in many quarters about a Lutheran confessional identity. To be sure, such an identity was assumed in the General Synod's new constitution and spelled out in its title and implied in its purpose, but there was no naming of the Lutheran Confessions, just as many synods had not named them. In part, some said, this was to make membership in the association more palatable to advocates of union with the Reformed as in the new Prussian Union.

The men who gathered in Hagerstown represented not only the frugal rural folk or those making their way in the cities and towns but also others, clerical colleagues. Some of them had been trained in German universities, some, in America. These were men of the "middle period," between the death of Muhlenberg and the Reformation's three hundredth anniversary. Academically as well as intellectually they had found a welcome in other fields besides theology. Nor were there absent from Lutheran ranks honorary doctorates from Harvard, Columbia, and Pennsylvania.

While Episcopalians, Presbyterians, and others were firming up their ecclesial structures, were the Lutherans allowing theirs to decline? The men at Hagerstown in 1820, persuaded that this was indeed the case among the Lutherans, were seeking to make amends. To sum up, the men gathered in Hagerstown were not without a spiritual heritage and living tradition. Yet amid change and in relative isolation from confessional kin, not only in old Europe but also in vast America, there remained much ground to be gained and regained. The preamble of the General Synod Constitution thus seems to inject high determination into the task at hand, declaring:

> JESUS CHRIST, the Supreme Head of His Church, having prescribed no special Regulations concerning the Church government, and every sectional portion of the Church being left at full liberty to make such regulations to that effect, as may be most adapted to its situation and circumstances, therefore—Relying upon God our Father, in the name of our Lord Jesus Christ, and under the guidance and direction of the Holy Spirit in the Word of God—for the promotion of the prac-

tice of Brotherly Love, to the furtherance of Christian Concord, to the first establishment and continuance of the Unity of the Spirit in the bond of Peace . . . adopt the following fundamental articles, viz.

(Signed) Daniel Kurtz, chairman

H. A. Muhlenberg, secretary[55]

At Hagerstown the four synods adopted a constitution that all but New York had accepted by the 1821 meeting in Frederick, Maryland. It was not until 1836 that New York resumed relationship. Already in 1823, the Ministerium of Pennsylvania withdrew, claiming second thoughts and pressured by congregations who feared the General Synod would interfere with the proposed union with the Reformed. In spite of these enormous odds, the General Synod prevailed and grew. We are still awaiting an in-depth history and appraisal of the General Synod and its impact on the ELCA today. As of now the best is the narrative in *A Basic History of Lutherans in America* by A. R. Wentz, revised in 1964 with the assistance of his son, Frederick K. Wentz. Their account gives us a feel for the development of special interest societies, so prominent in the early nineteenth century, and their gradual inclusion into General Synod boards that blossomed later in the United Lutheran Church in America. Here we shall introduce a few prominent leaders and also touch on some issues that gave concern to Lutherans both within and without the General Synod. Certainly the Synod was a great promoter of certain aspects of the Muhlenberg tradition: warmth of heart and a breadth of spirit and a genius for practical affairs that gave vitality to the church.

From its founding the synod included a remarkable father-and-son team: John George Schmucker (1771-1853) and Samuel Simon Schmucker (1799-1873). The father, brought by his parents from Wuerttemberg in 1785, prepared at the University of Pennsylvania and learned theology under two experienced Philadelphia pastors. A parish pastor in Hagerstown, and later in York, he was several times president of the Ministerium of Pennsylvania until, in protest to that body's withdrawal from the General Synod, he founded the West Pennsylvania Synod (1825) and made it a firm supporter of the General Synod and its institutions. An author and a man of conciliatory spirit, he represented the best of the post-Muhlenberg generation. During the early National Era, when there were few immigrant pastors, his sound ministry filled an urgent need.

The later illustrious son, Samuel Simon, grew up in Hagerstown, then trained in Philadelphia at the university and, like his father, was tutored in theology. Young Schmucker spent two years (1818-20) in the warmly evangelical Presbyterian Seminary in Princeton. There he found friends of other Protestant denominations as well. The experience made him a convinced yet generous-minded Lutheran. Upon graduating he resolved to strive for three objectives: to found a Lutheran theological seminary, to found a non-denominational college, and to translate from the German a reliable textbook in theology. Within a dozen years he had accomplished all three objectives. For several decades, S. S. Schmucker led the General Synod. He wrote the organic documents and influenced its policies. In 1823 when the Ministerium withdrew, Schmucker rallied the other synods to advance an educated ministry in their midst. In 1826 Gettysburg Seminary was founded and he became its first professor. He encouraged support from the synods and their members and sent Benjamin Kurtz, grandson of the Kurtz ordained in 1748, to Europe to solicit funds and books for the library. The Seminary was founded on the basis that in German and English the "fundamental doctrines of the Sacred Scriptures as contained in the Augsburg Confession" shall be taught.[56] This explicit naming of the central Lutheran document represented a confessional commitment beyond the Pennsylvania Ministerium's 1792 constitution and beyond the General Synod's official constitution of 1820. At this time, early in his career, Schmucker was leading a movement toward more explicit confessional identity.

Schmucker looked with favor on the founding of Southern Seminary (1830) and encouraged the formation of Wittenberg (Hamma) as an English-speaking Lutheran venture in 1845. A born teacher, a skilled organizer, and a constant advocate of Christian unity, he committed Gettysburg Seminary to reaffirming the role of the Augsburg Confession among Lutherans, even though, as we shall see, he might take liberties with it. Interdenominationally, later leaders honored him as one of the pioneers of the Evangelical Alliance formed in London in 1846, where he was an important participant. They also point to Schmucker as one of the first proponents of what years later (1908) became the Federal Council of Churches. Schmucker was an abolitionist, almost with the fervor of a Congregationalist. Schmucker's home in Gettysburg, on Seminary Ridge, was said to be a stop on the "underground railroad" for fugitive slaves, a charge for which he paid a price when Confederate soldiers looted his home during the battle.

One of the early graduates (1842) of Gettysburg Seminary was William Alfred Passavant (1821-1894). After a short period in Baltimore, where he served a mission and assisted Benjamin Kurtz in editing *The Lutheran Observer*, he accepted a call to Pittsburgh. The practice initiated by the Ministerium of Pennsylvania in 1803 to send pastors westward on missionary journeys—a tactic continued after 1825 by the West Pennsylvania Synod (whose territory lay west of the Susquehanna River)—drew resident pastors onto the scene.[57] So, for example, C. F. Heyer, the later "Father" Heyer, the first American Lutheran missionary overseas (India, 1842), in 1837 led in organizing First English Lutheran Church in Pittsburgh.[58] Presently, Heyer, fluently bilingual, organized two German Lutheran congregations, one on either side of the Allegheny River. In population the German Reformed had preceded the Lutherans, and were oriented more to straight Calvinism, perhaps influenced by the Scotch Irish Presbyterians rather than the Palatine union of Reformed and Lutheran. In this context Lutheranism grew apace and organized. By 1845 about one hundred congregations and preaching places had sprung up among Lutherans around Pittsburgh. On practical grounds the Allegheny Synod emerged out of a portion of the West Pennsylvania Synod in 1842. Three years later came the Pittsburgh Synod. It was largely the work of eight pastors of whom William Alfred

Passavant, in his mid-twenties, was the youngest and the most intense advocate of missions.

It is exciting to ponder what made Pittsburgh "the Missionary Synod." Not only did the synod from the outset engage its own home missioner, albeit at starvation salary, but also it adopted on June 2, 1846, a "Missionary Constitution" that provided for a missionary president, a missionary committee, a missionary superintendent, and guidelines for governing, supporting, and expanding the work. Young Passavant, the dynamo for these developments, had like-minded partners among the pastors and laity. When his physician prescribed a sea voyage as a cure for overwork, Passavant spent the summer of 1846 in Europe. En route, in Halifax, he discovered the forgotten Lutherans in Nova Scotia, the nucleus of the future Nova Scotia Synod. In London, where his Gettysburg professor, Samuel S. Schmucker, played a significant part in the formation of the international Evangelical Alliance (1846), Passavant made ecumenical contacts, including one that took him to Germany. In Kaiserswerth he familiarized himself with the work initiated a decade earlier by Theodor Fliedner, under whose direction the ancient Church's office of deaconess was being revived and, by its communal life, was giving women a new role of service in the Church. The outcome of this visit: Fliedner himself, in 1849, personally escorted four Kaiserswerth deaconesses to Pittsburgh. There they served as the nursing staff of the first Protestant hospital in America, founded by the zealous Passavant.[59]

Passavant's trip to Europe was timely in that it acquainted him with the homeland of emigrants to America as well as with the Inner Mission over there, which could be helpful in America. The orphanages and hospitals Passavant founded ranged from Boston to Chicago and beyond, drawing upon an ever-widening array of donors. Beginning in 1848, his church paper *The Missionary* appeared monthly and was "Devoted to the work of Inner, Home & Foreign Missions in the American Lutheran Church." With a readership far beyond the Pittsburgh Synod this paper rendered an enormous service not only in marshaling help for those in need but also welcoming newcomers and acquainting old timers with their growing number of Scandinavian, German, and other confessional kin. Seeing the need for a well educated laity and an able ordained ministry, he played a leading part in the founding of Thiel College and the Chicago Lutheran Theological Seminary. In overseas missions his special interest was India, and the work begun there by Father Heyer in 1842. One of Passavant's closest associates in home missions was Gottlieb Bassler. A man eight years Passavant's senior, and a key member of the Pittsburgh Synod Mission Committee, Bassler followed up Passavant's earlier contact with Nova Scotia and focused the synod's attention on Ontario. Bassler's visitation in that province during the summer of 1849 laid the basis for the later organization of the Canada Synod (1861).[60] As to Pittsburgh's relation to other synods, it enjoyed advantages because of its central location. It was in no hurry to join the General Synod, voting to do so only as of 1853. Pittsburgh's doctrinal position was still in process of clarification.

General Synod Tensions

In Schmucker's mind, before and after his trip to Europe in 1846, the conviction matured: "Why should there not be an American Lutheran Church as well as any other? There is a German, a Danish, a Swedish Lutheran church, each possessing its distinctive peculiarities." Noting the diversity in civil governments and the different concepts of political life, Schmucker concluded:

> Then why should not American Lutherans be permitted to organize their church, in accordance with the principles of their own glorious civil institutions, in conformity with the dictates of their own consciences and their views of the inspired word of God?[61]

Like some other aspects of life, American Lutheranism had been in the making since the birth of the nation. In time it became a party label. Some upheld it ardently. Others denounced it vehemently. The debate waxed bitter. American Lutherans, as in the columns of *The Lutheran Observer* (1830) in Baltimore, where Benjamin Kurtz had succeeded J. G. Morris as editor, wrote derisively of "symbolists," "confessionalists," or "old Lutherans."

In New York the advocates of American Lutheranism had broken away from the more conservative Ministerium and formed the Hartwick Synod in 1830. For some the new synod was not "sufficiently pious," so the Frankean Synod appeared in 1837. In the words of A. R. Wentz, "this new body abandoned the Augsburg Confession entirely and pressed the 'new measures' to the extreme."[62] Meanwhile conservatism was also growing in the General Synod. In 1853 the Ministerium of Pennsylvania applied for readmission. Since its departure in 1823 it had moved to a more confessional position, giving pre-eminence to the Unaltered Augsburg Confession and Luther's Catechism. The admission of the Pittsburgh, Northern Illinois, and Texas synods also strengthened the conservative elements in the growing General Synod.

As opposition to American Lutheranism mounted from without and even from within the General Synod, Schmucker's brother-in-law, Samuel Sprecher, teaching at the seminary in Springfield, Ohio, pleaded, "A creed we must have." Cautious no longer, Schmucker wrote his mind. Anonymously, in 1855, there appeared "A Definite Synodical Platform." Here it was, an American recension of the Augsburg Confession. It adapted the standard of Lutheranism to the prevailing Reformed Protestantism of the land, with its legacy from the Puritans and Evangelicals. So, for example, the Lutheran doctrine on the sacraments was modified: baptismal regeneration (rebirth) was omitted; the real presence of Christ's Body and Blood in the Lord's Supper was no longer clearly stated. Where the Augsburg Confession made no mention of Sabbath observance, this was now included.

When Schmucker's authorship was disclosed, among his sharpest opponents were his Gettysburg colleagues, like Charles Philip Krauth, the father of the later founder of the General Council, Charles Porterfield Krauth, and others as well.

Even his son, Beale Melanchthon Schmucker (1827-1888), turned against him. There was something anti-climactic about this man's amazing career. He continued to teach, and eventually taught some four hundred theological students. He also busied himself with interdenominational interests like the Evangelical Alliance.

One of the strongest supporters of American Lutheranism, Benjamin Kurtz, editor of the *Observer*, left the General Synod entirely and formed the Melanchthon Synod. It lasted only eleven years. Only three small synods in Ohio, influenced by Sprecher, accepted the "Definite Platform." Most of the synods expressed their disapproval. In the words of A. R. Wentz:

> It was the registered conviction of the great host of Lutherans in America that Lutheranism can live and flourish in this country without giving away its own spirit or adulterating its own original life and character. . . . The Lutheran Church in 1860 was in a position . . . to make steady and rapid progress in the conservation of her faith and the development of her doctrinal resources.[63]

Nevertheless, there followed three decisive and divisive blows, as we shall see in the next chapter. The Muhlenberg legacy was no longer united but separated into several subdivisions. Reuniting it became the goal for many, and the result was the ULCA.

NOTES

1. ULCA *Minutes* 1918: 11-14.
2. Wentz, Abdel Ross, *The Lutheran Church in American History*, 2d ed. (Philadelphia: United Lutheran Publication House, 1933) 3. (Hereafter cited as A. R. Wentz, *Lutheran Church*.) Of course, there were also ongoing influences from Germany and Scandinavia.
3. Ibid. See also *The Lutherans in North America* (by E. Clifford Nelson and associates) (Philadelphia: Fortress Press, 1980 [1975]) (hereafter cited as Nelson, *Lutherans in North America*); *A Basic History of Lutheranism in America* Rev. ed. (Philadelphia: Muhlenberg Press, 1964 [1955] by Abdel Ross Wentz (hereafter cited as A. R. Wentz, *Basic History*); and *Lutheran Churches in the World* (Minneapolis, MN: Augsburg, 1989), by E. Theodore Bachmann and Mercia Brenne Bachmann. (Hereafter cited as Bachmann, *Lutheran Churches*.)
4. See also Evjen, John Olaf, *Scandinavian Immigrants in New York, 1630-1674* (Minneapolis, MN: H. C. Holter Publishing Co., 1916).
5. B. M. Schmucker, "Congregational Constitutions," in *Lutheran Church Review*, vol. 6 (1877), 188-226.
6. Jacobs, Henry Eyster, *A History of the Evangelical Lutheran Church in the United States* (New York: The Christian Literature, 1893), 89. (Hereafter cited as Jacobs, *History*.) and special issue of *Lutheran Quarterly*, new series, vol. 2.1 (1988).
7. Jacobs, *History*, 88.
8. See Sachse, Julius Frederick, *The German Pietists of Provincial Pennsylvania: 1694-1708* (Philadelphia, printed for author, 1895). (Hereafter cited as Sachse, *German Pietists*.)
9. Jacobs, *History*, 111; Glatfelter I, 517-521; II, 375 f.
10. *Kirchenbuch* 331, *CSBH* 202, *Service Book and Hymnal of the Lutheran Church in America* (Minneapolis, MN: Augsburg Publishing House, 1958), Hymn 556. (Hereafter cited as *SBH*). *Lutheran Book of Worship* (Minneapolis, MN: Augsburg Publishing House and Philadelphia: Board of Publication, Lutheran Church in America, 1978), Hymn 182. (Hereafter cited as *LBW*.)
11. Sachse, *German Pietists*, 66.
12. Ibid., 102.
13. Norman C. Witwer, *The Faithful and the Bold: The Story of the First Service of the Zion Evangelical Lutheran Church, Oldwick, NJ* (Oldwick, NJ, 1984), 11-12, 19-42.
14. Bard Thompson, "The Palatine Church Order" in *Church History*, 23 (1954): 339ff.
15. Ibid., 350.
16. Jacobs, *History*, 110-117.
17. Wallace, Paul A. W., *Conrad Weiser, 1696-1760, Friend of Colonist and Mohawk* (Philadelphia: University of Pennsylvania Press, 1945), 3. (Hereafter cited as Wallace, *Weiser*.)
18. Tappert in Nelson, *Lutherans in North America*, 22ff.
19. Ibid., 27.

20. Graebner, August Lawrence, *Geschichte des Lutheranische Kirche in America*, (St. Louis: Concordia Publishing House, 1892) 166.

21. Wallace, *Weiser* 25ff.

22. Wallace, *Weiser*, 17ff, 24-32.

23. Wallace, *Weiser*, 33.

24. Wallace, *Weiser*, 41-46.

25. See Glatfelter, Charles Henry, *Pastors and People: German Lutheran and Reformed Churches in the Pennsylvania Field, 1717-1793* (Breinigsville, PA: Pennsylvania German Society, 1980-1981). Hereafter cited as Glatfelter, *Pastors and People*. Evjen, J. O., "Berkenmeyer" in *Lutheran Church Review*, Vol. 24. (1925), 132-147. Tappert, in Nelson, *Lutherans in North America*, 22ff.

26. See Jacobs, *History* 150-168; and Jones, George Fenwick, *Henry Newman's Salzburger Letterbooks* (Athens, GA: University of Georgia Press, 1966).

27. The standard biography has been *The Life and Times of Henry Melchior Muhlenberg*, by William Julius Mann (Philadelphia: G. W. Frederick, 1888; hereafter cited as Mann, *Muhlenberg*), an engaging narrative published for the centennial of the patriarch's death. Theodore G. Tappert's chapters on the colonial era comprise a brilliant part of the modern volume, Nelson's *The Lutherans in North America*. The three-volume translation by Tappert and John W. Doberstein of *The Journals of Henry Melchior Muhlenberg*, (Philadelphia: Evangelical Lutheran Ministerium of Pennsylvania and Adjacent States, 1942-1958; hereafter cited as Muhlenberg, *Journals*), are an immense resource. Added to these is the newest four-volume complementary work in German as edited by Kurt Aland, *Die Korrespondenz Heinrich Melchior Muehlenbergs* (Berlin; New York: De Gruyter, 1986-1993; hereafter cited as Muhlenberg, *Korrespondenz*).

28. Muhlenburg, *Journals* 1:74.

29. Ibid. 1:73.

30. Glatfelter, *Pastors and People*, 412.

31. Muhlenberg, *Korrespondenz*, 1:49ff.

32. Ibid. 1:78. 80.

33. Mann, *Muhlenberg*, 131.

34. Muhlenberg, *Korrespondenz*, xii; Muhlenberg, *Journals*, 1:vii ff.

35. Schmauk, Theodore Emmanuel, *A History of the Lutheran Church in Pennsylvania (1638-1820): From Original Sources* (Philadelphia: General Council Publishing House, 1903), 159-161.

36. Mann, *Muhlenberg*, 206.

37. Muhlenberg, *Journals*, 1:102.

38. Glatfelter, *Pastors and People*, 23.

39. Muhlenberg, *Journals*, 1:102.

40. Ibid., 1:103.

41. Anna Maria survived Henry by 15 years (d. 1802). Wallace, Paul A. W., *The Muhlenbergs of Pennsylvania* (Philadelphia: University of Pennsylvania Press, 1950), 210-211 (Hereafter cited as Wallace, *The Muhlenbergs*); Mann, Muhlenberg 163.

42. Re: all the above, see Bachmann, E. Theodore, "With Muhlenberg in New Jersey: 1745-1775" (Trenton, NJ: New Jersey Synod of the Evangelical Lutheran Church in America, 1992).

43. *Documentary History of the Evangelical Lutheran Ministerium of Pennsylvania and Adjacent States* (Philadelphia: Board of Publication of the General Council of the Evangelical Lutheran Church in North America, 1898), 3ff.

44. Ibid., 8.

45. Ibid., 9.

46. Glatfelter, *Pastors and People*, 142.

47. Ibid., 165-177.

48. Ibid., 167-68.

49. Wallace, *The Muhlenbergs*; Glatfelter, *Pastors and People*.

50. Tappert, in Nelson *Lutherans in North America*, 62-67.

51. A. R. Wentz, *Basic History*, 73-74.

52. Nelson, *Lutherans in North America*, 97.

53. Nelson, *Lutherans in North America*, 88.

54. A. R. Wentz, *Basic History* 71.

55. Richard C., *Documents of Lutheran Unity in America* (Philadelphia: Fortress Press, 1966), 66-67. (Hereafter cited as R. C. Wolf, *Documents*.)

56. A. R. Wentz, *Basic History*, 80.

57. Bruce Carney, *History of the Allegheny Evangelical Lutheran Synod* (Philadelphia: The Lutheran Publication Society, 1919), 2: 148-192. Gongaware, George J. *History of the First English Evangelical Lutheran Church in Pittsburgh 1837-1909* (Philadelphia: J. B. Lippincott Company, 1909), 10-16.

58. Bachmann, E. Theodore, *They Called Him Father: The Life Story of John Christian Frederick Heyer* (Philadelphia: The Muhlenberg Press, 1942), 99.

59. Ohl, J. F., *The Inner Mission: A Handbook for Christian Workers* (Philadelphia: General Council Publication House, 1911), 98.

60. Bassler's 1st report in *The Missionary*, (Oct. 1849) 78-79.

61. Schmucker, Samuel Simon, *The American Lutheran Church, Historically, Doctrinally, and Practically Delineated*, 3rd Ed. (Philadelphia: E. W. Miller, 1852), 234.

62. A. R. Wentz, *Basic History*, 140-1.

63. Ibid., 143-144.

CHAPTER 3

SCHISMS AND REUNION, 1861-1918

FRAMED BY TWO TERRIBLE WARS, THE FIFTY-SEVEN-YEAR TIME SPAN from the outbreak of the Civil War to the Armistice of the First World War saw the United States growing into its stature as a great power and Canada flourishing as a commonwealth. During these interbellum decades a huge tide of immigration from Europe combined with the natural increase of the native-born. To appreciate this country's unprecedented ethnic diversity, add the emancipated African-Americans, still mainly in the South, the Native Americans, mostly on reservations, and the Asian Americans—Chinese and increasingly Japanese—largely on the Pacific coast. A world of peoples was assembling here.

In religious terms, the majority of the newcomers were, at least nominally, Roman Catholics, Lutherans, Reformed, or Orthodox, depending on the state church in the homeland. Nor should one forget the Jews, coming increasingly from Eastern Europe. At least half the Germans and nearly all the Scandinavians arrived as Lutherans, although many were happy to leave behind an oppressive church-state system. Many remained in the eastern United States but the large majority followed the route of earlier comers to the Midwest, and via the Midwest to Canada's prairie provinces. As a result, those Lutherans who could be retained by their church, and the percentage was not high, gave Lutheranism in America a second center of gravity, this one in the Midwest.

SCHISMS

The decade of the 1860s was hard on the mainly eastern and English-speaking General Synod. For it sustained three blows in a row. The departure (early 1860) of the Scandinavians, the Swedish and Norwegian pastors and congregations from the synod of Northern Illinois, seriously diminished the General Synod's presence in the Midwest, or at that time still the new West. The newly formed Scandinavian Augustana Synod would grow and make its own way. Language barriers, personality clashes, and the confessionally more conservative position of the Scandinavians pointed the way to the departure.

A second blow more political than doctrinal, came with the outbreak of the War between the States, as Southerners called the Civil War. Postponing its 1861 meeting, the General Synod in 1862 (Lancaster, Pa.) passed a resolution not against slavery, which had not been debated, but against secession and "armed rebellion."[1] By 1863 in Concord, North Carolina, the Southerners had organized their own General Synod of the Evangelical Lutheran Church in the Confederate States. Its synods were those of North Carolina, South Carolina, Georgia, Virginia, and Southwest Virginia, none of them large but all English-speaking and descended from colonial forebears. The great immigration of the nineteenth century had hardly affected them. Theologically they tended to be more conservative than most of their brethren in the North. With sad but firm eloquence they severed the ties with their Northern colleagues. "While we have always cheerfully conceded to the Northern Church the right to judge for themselves in matters of conscience, we at the same time have demanded that this privilege be extended to us. But how often it has been denied!" Denouncing the Northern resolution (1862), the Southerners concluded, "it becomes us this day to make our separation from them final and complete."[2] A constitution was forthwith adopted.

In their doggedness the Confederate Lutherans had done something more durable than organize. In contrast to the General Synod which, for all its practical designs, had never spelled out its theological basis, the Southerners now did so. In their constitution they were bound to the Old and New Testaments as "the Word of God, and the only infallible rule of faith and practice." They held that "the Apostles' Creed, the Nicene Creed, and the Augsburg Confession, contain the fundamental doctrines of the Sacred Scriptures" and adopted them "as the exponents of our faith." However, since there was as yet no full agreement as to certain articles of the Augsburg Confession, "private judgment as to those articles" is allowed.[3] This position put the Southern Lutherans, theologically and confessionally, on middle ground between the General Synod on the one hand and the soon-to-emerge General Council on the other. This would be important for the eventual merger.

After the war the separation continued, as both pastors and people felt deeply that their Southern Church had needs and convictions not really understood in the North. By the mid-1880s other synods than those already mentioned, the Mississippi early and then the Holston and the Tennessee, joined in forming the now renamed United Synod in the South (1886). Professor Richard C. Wolf would sum it up decades later, "A general Lutheran body comprising all the synods of the Muhlenberg strand in the South had come into existence."[4] A little later we shall see how this Southern strand would be joined by a scattering of postbellum Northerners and how the progress toward Lutheran union, not simply unity, would be prodded from the South. Yet, in the nineteenth century these North-South divisions of church bodies ran deep, some of them enduring for much of the twentieth century. Prospects for a Lutheran reconciliation of North and South depended on reserves of common faith and worship.

The third, and most damaging, blow to the General Synod was the withdrawal of the Pennsylvania Ministerium (1866) and the ensuing formation of a rival entity in 1867 known as the General Council of the Evangelical Lutheran Church in North America. We have already seen how ambivalent had been the relation of the mother synod, the Ministerium, to the General Synod; how its role varied from that of founder and charter member, to outsider for thirty years (1823-53), back to member, on condition of a closer adherence to the Lutheran Confessions. Although it held fast during the storm over "American Lutheranism," the Ministerium left in protest in 1864 at York, Pennsylvania, when the General Synod received into membership a synod which, according to its own constitution, did not subscribe to the Augsburg Confession, the legal basis of Lutheran identity. The Franckean Synod (formed in New York State in 1837) had distinguished itself as the most outspoken among Lutherans in its demand for the abolition of slavery. Franckean missionary efforts extended even to Wisconsin. But the Franckean issue was only part of the story.

Doctrinal, cultural and personal factors animated the Ministerium's withdrawal from the General Synod. "American Lutheranism" had flowered in the 1840s, made strong claims in the middle 1850s and continued to have its advocates. But their numbers and influence appeared to be diminishing.[5] Its chief protagonist, Samuel Simon Schmucker, had for some time been under attack by confessional conservatives both inside and outside the Ministerium. From the Ministerium especially came the complaint that Gettysburg Seminary was proving inadequate for the training of German-using ministers to meet the challenge posed by the rising tide of immigration. Philadelphia was seen increasingly as a suitable place for a second seminary. Once again, Muhlenberg's initial plan (1749) came to mind. Locating a seminary at Gettysburg (1826) had been a second choice made necessary, ironically, by the 1823 withdrawal of the Ministerium from the General Synod.

The personal factor was at least seen as the occasion, if not the cause, for the formation of a new general body. Schmucker retired from the Gettysburg Seminary presidency in 1864. His successor, James Allen Brown, of Quaker lineage and of Presbyterian upbringing, had become a Lutheran and was ordained by the Maryland Synod. He served as a parish pastor before achieving distinction as a teacher and president of Newberry College, South Carolina, until 1860. Returning to the North because of the war, he was called to Gettysburg Seminary in 1864 as professor of systematic theology and elected successor to President Schmucker.[6] This turn of events deeply disappointed the supporters of Charles Porterfield Krauth, who had himself hoped to teach at Gettysburg and head the seminary. Yet a "Plan B" had already been in the making. The Philadelphia Seminary opened for classes in the autumn of 1864. Located near the center city facilities of the University of Pennsylvania, the Lutheran school began with a strong faculty. Krauth divided his teaching time between the university and the seminary. At the latter his field was systematic theology. His father, Charles Philip Krauth, long a member of the Gettysburg Seminary fac-

ulty and for some years also president of the college, was one of the early proponents of a confessionally oriented Lutheranism and thus had been one of
Schmucker's keen critics.

Most rankling to Gettysburgians, institutionally, was the abruptness and lack
of consultation with which the Philadelphia Seminary was begun. Gettysburg
Seminary had suffered heavy damage during the great battle in 1863.
Enrollment was down. So was morale. Five years earlier (1858) a rival school, for
home missionaries, had been set up farther north at Selinsgrove (the cradle of
Susquehanna University). The one professor provided for Gettysburg Seminary
by the Ministerium (Charles F. Schaeffer, Schmucker's brother-in-law and theological rival) was called back without notice in the summer of 1864. Thereafter
there was between the Gettysburg and Philadelphia seminaries an almost calculated enmity, which carried over into an even larger arena.

Excluded from the 1866 convention of the General Synod at Fort Wayne
(Indiana), the Pennsylvania Ministerium at its Lancaster convention formally
severed its connection from the General Synod. Avowing its desire for a "union
of all true Lutherans in America," the mother synod issued an invitation to all
Lutheran synods for the purpose of forming a new general body. In historic
Trinity Church, Reading (Pennsylvania), the General Council of the Evangelical
Lutheran Church in North America was organized in December 1866. Even the
Missouri Synod sent an observer. Nine articles setting forth basic principles of
faith and church polity, and eleven articles on ecclesiastical church power and
government were fully discussed and then unanimously adopted. Their author,
Charles Porterfield Krauth, became the General Council's recognized theolo-
gian.

At the council's first convention, held deliberately in Fort Wayne in
November 1867, representatives of thirteen synods participated: Pennsylvania,
New York, English District of Ohio, Pittsburgh, Wisconsin, Iowa, Michigan,
Scandinavian Augustana, Minnesota, Canada, Illinois, and the Joint Synod of
Ohio. The latter, an offshoot (1818) of the mother synod, raised questions to
which it received no satisfactory answers and which caused it, along with Iowa,
to remain independent. The questions would live on as the famous "Four
Points": Chiliasm (the return of Christ and his millennial reign), pulpit fellow-
ship, altar fellowship, and membership in secret societies. By the time of the
Council's 1875 meeting at Galesburg (Illinois) two of the Four Points, as framed
by Krauth, had become the so-called Galesburg Rule:

> Lutheran pulpits for Lutheran ministers only. Lutheran altars for Lutheran com-
> municants only. The exceptions to the rule belong to the sphere of privilege, not of
> right. The determination of the exceptions is to be made in consonance with these
> principles, by the conscientious judgment of pastors, as the cases arise.[7]

Like the Joint Ohio, other synods in the Midwest would also withdraw from
the General Council: Wisconsin (1869), Illinois and Minnesota (1871), and
Michigan (1888). The German Iowa Synod adopted a friendly wait-and-see atti-

tude, on the basis of which it remained a participant, but not a member. Other synods joined the council: Texas (1868), Indiana (1872), and the Holston (1874). The last would later be released to join the United Synod in the South, while Texas, by agreement, joined the Iowa Synod. The hopes initially held for a General Council comprising all synods which "accept and acknowledge the Unaltered Augsburg Confession in its original sense as throughout in conformity with the pure truth of which God's word is the only rule," was only partially realized. Other developments had been in the making.

OTHER LUTHERANS

Foremost among these other developments was the creation in 1872 of the Missouri-led . Geographically it was a midwestern achievement. Confessionally it bore the mark of a revitalized seventeenth century Lutheran orthodoxy. Strategically it sought to overcome the Missouri Synod's own sense of disappointment with respect to its opportunities posed by masses of immigrant German Lutherans in eastern states. Carl Ferdinand Wilhelm Walther and his colleagues in mission are said to have prodded each other with the couplet: "Der Osten, der Osten, verlorene Posten." (The East, the East, an outpost lost.)

Walther and the Missourians had initiated Free Conferences, four of them between 1856 and 1859, on the Unaltered Augsburg Confession and in opposition to the Definite Platform of "American Lutheranism." These non-binding discussions among Lutherans of whatever background were intended to lay the basis for mutual understanding and any further developments. Being conducted in German, the Free Conferences made no special impact on a predominantly English-speaking General Synod.

Walther and his partners rose above disappointment. Seeing weaknesses in the General Council's first meeting and noting the Joint Ohio's Four Points, they concluded that the way was open for the Missouri Synod to offer an alternative association. The former free conference option now became the Synodical Conference fellowship. After 1872, some synods, like Illinois, left the General Council and allied themselves with Missouri. Synods like the Minnesota (organized under General Synod auspices in the mid-1850s by "Father" C. F. Heyer) as well as Michigan and Wisconsin synods formed the General Synod of Wisconsin, etc., in 1892. The greater part of the Buffalo Synod was already integrated into the Missouri Synod in the 1860s. Language saved the Norwegian Synod from losing its identity while becoming a significant participant in the synodical conference, until the Norwegian merger. In short, a Lutheran power bloc was now in place in the Midwest. Within little more than a dozen years the General Synod adherents fell from two-thirds to only one-third of America's Lutherans.

All of these general bodies were growing at rates without precedent. There was rivalry, sometimes bitter. Our interest here turns especially to relations between the General Synod and the General Council. Each had sprung from the

same American heritage, the Muhlenberg line, but each had adapted it different-
ly. The General Synod, on the one hand, because of its good relations with the
Reformed, claimed friendship with the biggest Protestant church body in
Europe, the Evangelical Church of the Old Prussian Union. The General
Council, on the other hand, proudly felt itself at one with the recently formed
General Evangelical Lutheran Conference (1868) in Germany. The GELC was
made up of Lutheran territorial churches outside Prussia where the confession-
al renewal, mainly since the tercentenary of the Augsburg Confession (1830),
had given Lutheranism in Germany a new lease on life. To them the Prussian
Union Church (1817) embodied the dire aberration to "unionism," for it placed
a large Lutheran majority into an administrative union with a small but elite
Reformed minority. The tensions in Germany were thus reflected in America.

In light of these developments in the homeland of the Reformation we can
sense an element of pride and pressure in the General Council's espousal of the
Galesburg Rule (1875). In its own eyes the General Council, although young,
stood superior to the General Synod. Conversely, the General Synod saw itself
superior to the General Council not only because of its own returning conservatism but especially for its adaptation of the Lutheran legacy to the American
context and the English-speaking world.

Illustrative of these developments was the history of Gettysburg Seminary.
Even before the 1850s, adherents of the confessional revival in Germany were
challenging the proponents of an "American Lutheranism."[8] Among the leaders
was Charles Philip Krauth; another was Charles Augustus Hay. An alumnus of
the Gettysburg Seminary, Hay had done two years of further study in German
universities (Berlin and Halle). Subsequently, on the Gettysburg Seminary faculty, Hay—assisted for a time by the younger Krauth, an early alumnus of the
Gettysburg Seminary, and then by young Henry Eyster Jacobs of the College faculty—translated the already widely recognized doctrinal work by Heinrich
Schmid of Erlangen. It appeared in 1875 under the title, *Doctrinal Theology of
the Evangelical Lutheran Church*, and soon became standard in American
Lutheran seminaries making the transition to English from whatever mother
tongue. Further, it was at Gettysburg that H. E. Jacobs translated the Book of
Concord (1882). This would become the standard edition, its first volume sup-
plying the Confessions of the Lutheran Church and the second providing supplemental documents and notes. In 1883, the celebrative observance of the four-
hundredth anniversary of Luther's birth, Jacobs accepted the call to the
Philadelphia Seminary, there to become successor to the recently deceased
Krauth.

Relations between the two seminaries, much like those between a well meaning
parent and an assertive child, for some years remained strained. Gettysburg, in
keeping with the purpose of its founding, would always be the Theological
Seminary of the Evangelical Lutheran General Synod. But the founding of the
Philadelphia Seminary, as we have seen, was accomplished with an abruptness that
was traumatic. To develop a positive relationship these two church bodies would
need to look beyond their seminaries.

The creation of the General Council was costly to the General Synod. Nowhere was this more evident than in some of the member bodies like the Pittsburgh Synod—often called the "Missionary Synod" of America's Lutherans—as personified in a leader like William Alfred Passavant, the prime proponent of missions at home and abroad.[9] Surviving the shock, the General Synod next convened in Harrisburg, Pennsylvania (1868), and the following year in Washington, D.C. It was there, as Wentz points out, that the General Synod, reflecting the impulses of big business, "centralized its chief branches of benevolence in the hands of general boards." As a result, "the energies and resources of the entire general body were marshaled for rapid development." And just in time. Not only the newly rising tide of European immigration but also the natural increase of the American population stimulated a missionary spirit in all parts of the church. With determination the General Synod "moved due westward from Ohio, Indiana, and Illinois." Already in 1868 came the Kansas Synod, the Nebraska in 1871, the Rocky Mountain in 1891, and the California that same year. Quite naturally the General Synod was especially attached to the "old American Lutherans who had migrated from the East." But it also did its part on behalf of the new German arrivals. Thus the Wartburg Synod (1872) emerged as an offshoot of the Illinois Synod; and the German Nebraska Synod (1890) became a second synod in the "Corn Husker State."[10]

Efforts to bring the General Synod and the General Council into official theological conversation were for some time unsuccessful, much like the saga of the rival seminaries. An informal stratagem worked better. Under the name diet, denoting a deliberative assembly, a Lutheran Free Diet was held in Philadelphia after Christmas in 1877, and a second one the following year. These gatherings were mainly due to the initiative of John Gottlieb Morris of the General Synod, who enlisted the cooperation of Joseph Augustus Seiss of the General Council. In 1877 Morris was seventy-four, and Seiss fifty-four, both of them Marylanders by birth. Morris' base was Baltimore, where he had long served a parish. In retirement he was active in civic affairs. He had served three terms as president of the Gettysburg Seminary board during the Schmucker era. In 1831 he had founded *The Lutheran Observer*, which became prominently associated with the General Synod. In 1877 he was still (and continued to be) a lecturer at the seminary of which he was an early product.[11] Joseph Seiss, of Moravian parentage and a Gettysburg College graduate, had studied theology privately and been ordained by the Maryland Synod. Called to Philadelphia's St. John's Lutheran Church in 1858, he organized the nearby Church of the Holy Communion in 1875 and remained its pastor until his death in 1904. He was widely known as a powerful preacher and prolific writer. His was a congregation of the Ministerium of Pennsylvania.

The first (1877) diet assembled at St. Matthew's Church, on Broad Street and Mt. Vernon, a Philadelphia congregation of the General Synod. Among the 168 participants, were sixty-one laymen and fifteen theological students (most of them from Gettysburg). The others were pastors and professors, of whom the majority were from the General Synod. The response exceeded expectations. It being a free diet, everyone in attendance had the right to speak. As Chairman Morris said, everyone was familiar with synod conventions and other types of official meetings but "as a free Diet [this one occurs] for the first time for our church in this country."[12] The presentations by thirteen essayists were followed by remarks, often extensive. There was much speaking, much listening and no doubt much pondering. From various angles the faith and life and heritage of the Lutheran church was portrayed, assessed and criticized constructively. The printed program shows how those two days, December 27-28, 1877, were full of eagerness to capture a true assessment of the past in order to follow more confidently the leading of the Spirit into the future.

The opening essay, by Morris, on "The Augsburg Confession and Thirty-nine Articles," linked a European past to the American present. Krauth picked up the theme in terms of ecclesiology, "The relations of the Lutheran Church to the denominations around us." Gettysburg's president James A. Brown ventured to describe the neuralgic subject, "The four General Bodies of the Lutheran Church in the United States," i.e., General Synod, Southern Church, General Council, and . H. E. Jacobs outlined "The history and progress of the Lutheran Church in the United States." William Julius Mann, speaking of the Muhlenberg tradition, offered "Theses on the Lutheranism of the Fathers of our church in this country." Joseph Seiss grappled with the frustrations that spared no one as he dealt with "The misunderstandings and misrepresentations of the Lutheran Church." J. A. Repass, from Salem, Virginia (Roanoke College), reminded the Diet of an omnipresent duty, "The conservation of the Lutheran Church in the United States." On such themes as worship and liturgy, Christian education, church polity and organization, and the characteristics of the Augsburg Confession, other essays rounded out the program and evoked the recorded remarks of forty-seven speakers.

In summing up the proceedings, the two secretaries, H. E. Jacobs and W. M. Baum, host pastor of St. Matthew's, wrote forthrightly:

> May we not cherish the hope that the holding of this Diet will prove at least an occasion which may lead, in due time, to the adoption of such means and measures as shall, with God's blessing, eventually culminate in the organic union of the Lutheran Church in the United States of America.[13]

Who would venture to estimate that another forty years would pass before the hopes of this first Free Lutheran Diet would become a reality? Or that one of these two secretaries, Henry Eyster Jacobs, would be addressing the opening session of the constituting convention of the United Lutheran Church in America; and that he would in 1918 present an enlarged and more challenging version of what he had offered in 1877?

COMMON WORSHIP

Lutherans of the three general bodies pursued various ways to church merger, and found that one way, common worship, was especially productive. After the disruptions of the 1860s and the ensuing will to reconciliation these unitive ways gradually were opened and tried. Some lay in fields of practical service. Others, like the Free Diets of 1877 and 1878, fostered friendship and collegiality while a common ecclesial past (and present) was on the agenda. From our latter day vantage point, however, perhaps nothing was able to stimulate more progress on the way to the 1918 merger than the agreement on worship. Anglicans in England (Oxford), Lutherans in Germany (Neuendettelsau, etc.) and German Reformed in America (Mercersburg) sought renewal for the church not only in retrieving a doctrinal heritage from the Reformation and earlier but also in recovering and adapting historic forms of worship.[14] Where else, Lutherans would argue, or where better than in such historical awareness could one experience the oneness of the body of Christ throughout space and time, and together come before God in penitence and for the sake of Christ receive forgiveness and the Spirit's renewal?

In the Anglo-Protestantism as it prevailed in America and strongly influenced by Calvinism, Lutherans, when they joined the ranks of the English-speaking world, tended also to adapt their ways of worship. Call their worship low church or whatever, it lacked both focus and participation. The minister led, reading the Scriptures and prayers. The congregation usually took part silently, with responses centered on the singing of hymns. Sometimes, as happened in New York, choirs, "arrogant choirs" some called them, usurped the hymn singing.[15] When the Lord's Supper was celebrated it came as a special and solemn occasion, not as an integral part of weekly congregational worship. But a change lay ahead. The 1860 *Liturgy in English*, the 1888 *Common Service*, and the 1917 *Common Service Book with Hymnal* became ULCA-bound stepping stones in the field of worship.

The 1860 *Liturgy in English*, a vast improvement on its predecessor orders of worship in English as well as in German, had been commissioned by the Ministerium of Pennsylvania and was looked upon with favor by many in the General Synod. The youngest member of the commission preparing the liturgy was Beale Melanchthon Schmucker, at that time age thirty-three and pastor at Allentown, Pennsylvania. Son of the famed first president of Gettysburg Seminary, he had broken with the "American Lutheranism" of his father, S. S. Schmucker, and was fully on the side of a resurgent confessional Lutheranism. The young Schmucker's interest in historical research was intense. He appears to have had a Schmuckerian fascination with structures, such as tracing the rise of the congregational constitution in seventeenth century Amsterdam and its transmission via the Lutherans in London to colonial New York.

The younger Schmucker became completely absorbed in the church orders (constitutions) and liturgies of Lutheran territorial churches during the sixteenth century Reformation. In time he would become the foremost American Lutheran authority in liturgics and hymnology. This was made possible by his extensive correspondence with and use of works by contemporaries in Germany. Outstanding among them were Wilhelm Loehe (Neuendettelsau) and Theodor Kliefoth (Schwerin).[16]

Already in 1862 the *Liturgy in English* was back in the shop, so to speak, and subject to substantial remodeling in light of Reformation era precedents. This might have become the new order of worship in the General Synod had not the Southern synods withdrawn in 1863 and the mother synod in 1866. Subsequently, the efforts of B. M. Schmucker and colleagues resulted in the carefully researched and tested *Church Book* of the Ministerium of Pennsylvania. In 1868 it became the official order of worship and hymnal for use in Lutheran congregations affiliated with synods in the newly formed General Council. Behind this achievement stood the work of the Council's chief protagonist, Charles Porterfield Krauth, as well as Beale M. Schmucker. Others like Joseph Augustus Seiss (Philadelphia) and Frederick Mayer Bird contributed much.[17]

As to hymnody, spin-offs of England's Oxford Movement in 1861 led to the publication of *Hymns Ancient and Modern* (1861). This collection included excellent translations of German Lutheran chorales and others of medieval and ancient church origin as well as compositions by contemporary British authors. Thus the hymnal accompanying the *Church Book* opened a new treasury of sacred song. The strong hymns of Isaac Watts, the Wesleys and others continued as favorites in many English Lutheran congregations. A number of American authors, New England Congregationalists and others, were likewise represented in the new hymnal. Successive editions brought more hymns until the last one (1910) offered 650. In retrospect, the *Church Book* of 1868 appears like a coming-of-age for English-speaking Lutheranism. The book was calculated to enshrine a Lutheran identity. It contained Luther's *Small Catechism* as well as the Augsburg Confession, and also a number of occasional services. But the quality of its hymnody marked the *Church Book* as a superb vehicle for enabling Lutherans corporately to become more at home than ever in the world of the English tongue while singing the praises of God. An eminent American hymnologist, Louis Fitzgerald Benson (Presbyterian), is quoted by Luther D. Reed (ULCA) with considerable satisfaction:

> English-speaking Lutheranism had at last expressed itself in a hymnal worthy of its own traditions, and on a plane where no other American denomination could hope to meet it. Beside this Lutheran Hymnal of 1868 the Protestant Episcopal Hymnal of 1872 seems like an amateur performance.[18]

Where war and doctrinal schism left their stubborn imprint, agreement on basic worship forms held out hope for reunion. The continuity of public worship being so pervasive, the *Common Service* of 1888 was unquestionably a strong influence toward the ULCA merger thirty years later. Uplifted by a sense of achievement, Beale M. Schmucker, completing the Preface in Holy Week 1888, envisioned a larger significance:

This Common Service of the Reformers may well be placed by the side of the Confession of Augsburg, the one the Central Service, the other the Central Confession, of the Protestant Churches. We would gladly behold the day when the One, Holy, Catholic, Christian Church shall use one Order of Service, and unite on one Confession of Faith.[19]

Today our curiosity prompts the question: How did this achievement of a Common Service come about? As we saw earlier, did not the General Council's *Church Book* (1868) give any further ventures along this line an indispensable head start? But then we remember the barriers of the 1860s raised by the agonies of war and the traumas of schism.

At this point and on this issue, the South led the way. In 1870, from St. John's Church at Charleston, South Carolina, John Bachman, then eighty and frail but still the ranking Lutheran leader in the South,[20] urged the General Synod in the South to confer with other synods "for the purpose of promoting a greater uniformity in our Books of Worship." His reasoning was twofold. "We cannot fail in the course of time to become one of the largest denominations, in point of membership, on this Continent. . . . We have, however, too many Synods and shades of difference. . . . " Therefore, in unifying Lutheran ways of worship, "our Church would, in my opinion be more respected at home and abroad, and would accomplish a far greater amount of good."[21] The Southern General Synod, while endorsing the proposal, was reluctant to act. But six years later, in 1876, the time seemed ripe. A new Book of Worship in the South had become a priority. Formal proposals went out to the General Synod in the North and to the General Council. The General Council at its 1879 convention accepted the invitation, the General Synod likewise in 1881. Yet both northern bodies did so with qualifications. For its participation the General Council required that the rule be followed that had determined the order of worship in the *Church Book* (1868), namely: "the common consent of the pure Lutheran Liturgies of the Sixteenth Century, and when there is not an entire agreement among them the consent of the largest number of the greatest weight."[22] For its part, the General Synod's reluctance arose from the fact that it had but recently adopted a new book of worship. Nevertheless it would be willing to confer with the southerners "whether an agreement upon any common basis is practicable."[23]

The General Synod South also opened the next stage of common work when, in 1882, it accepted the General Council's rule and authorized "the prosecution of this important work with all the speed compatible with the care and research which its thoroughness and accuracy will require."[24] The following year, the four-hundredth anniversary of Luther's birth, in response to a petition from fifty-five ministers "desiring a Liturgy more in harmony with the historic books of worship," the General Synod itself agreed to proceed with the others on "the generic and well-defined basis of the 'common consent of the pure Lutheran Liturgies of the Sixteenth Century,'"[25]

At this point we should bear in mind the growing conservatism among America's English-speaking Lutherans. The return of confessional commitment

marked not only the more recently formed immigrant Lutheran churches or synods in the Midwest but also a growing number of fully Americanized Lutherans
in the East, for whom a so-called American Lutheranism was not the answer. And
it is from this latter constituency that leaders came forth who championed, for
the sake of the future, a return to and adaptation of historic ways of worship. The
revival of Reformation-era liturgies first occurred in Germany. Recent arrivals
and old timers became attracted by their mutual interest in worship. Illustrative
is the case of Beale Melanchthon Schmucker, a third- generation American, a
Virginian by birth, and son of a famous father. His friendship with Adolph
Spaeth, born and educated in Germany, resulted in summer vacations in the mid-
1880s together in Cape May Point, New Jersey, working together on the
Occasional Services. "In the press of other engagements they had had no time to
devote to the subject [of liturgics]. This was their rare opportunity."[26]

Before the main work of editing began, a half-dozen men—two from each of
the three general bodies—gathered in Charleston, South Carolina. There, in the
study of St. John's, hosted by Bachman's successor, Edward Traill Horn, the
course of a pending Joint Committee of the three General Bodies was envisioned
and a *de facto* trio of officers proposed: Beale M. Schmucker, chair; Edward Traill
Horn, secretary, and George Unangst Wenner, representing the General Synod.
A year later came the first meeting of the Joint Committee on a Common
Service Book. Gathered in the library of the seminary in downtown Philadelphia
were four delegates from the General Synod, six from the General Council and
two from the General Synod South. Schmucker was elected chair, and Horn secretary. Aware of the free worship service loyalties of one like Gettysburg
Seminary's Professor Valentine, the moderator carefully avoided ever mentioning the *Church Book* of the General Council. The Joint Committee adopted
some guiding principles, chief of which was: "We dare make no Service binding
upon the Congregation, and no part of a service should be used any longer than
it serves to edification."[27]

Liturgical terms as such were avoided where possible. Parts of the Service
were described rather than named. The Introit became the psalmody at the
opening of worship. The Collect became the prayer before the reading of the
Epistle and the Gospel. And so on. It was like letting the water into a canal lock
in order to lift the level of discourse gradually. Later H. E. Jacobs would declare
that this 1885 meeting of the Joint Committee was "the first real effort at cooperation since the break at Fort Wayne twenty years before."[28]

The Joint Committee stayed together. Its members disagreed at times, and
some were listeners more than contributors. Contributing mightily to the ongoing progress was the General Council's *Church Book*, the homework well done in
advance. In an eloquent speaker and liturgically oriented thinker like Joseph
Augustus Seiss, the Common Service had a ready advocate.[29] But the consistent
initiative for this unifying dimension came from the Synod of the South, specifically and remarkably from one pulpit, that of St. John's in Charleston, South
Carolina. John Bachman led the way and his successor followed through. "At

length it is possible," wrote Edward Traill Horn in 1881, "that the divisions of our Church in this country may issue in a better unity than her most devoted children had hoped for."[30] Horn was right. The resulting *Common Service Book* of 1888 contributed mightily to the local compatibilities and eventual union of the three groups torn apart in the 1860s and still enduring doctrinal disagreements.

CONVERGENCE

After the 1888 publication of the *Common Service*, the pace toward convergence was quickening, amid ongoing doctrinal disputes. Such disagreements were no longer between the confessionally more relaxed General Synod and the confessionally more conservative General Council. With the steady influx of Lutherans from Germany opposed to "unionism" with the Reformed, the General Synod itself gradually became more conservative on this very point, but not without a struggle or two. Already at its 1864 York convention, the General Synod had repudiated the Definite Platform. In 1869 it affirmed the Augsburg Confession, albeit in wording that still did not satisfy the General Council.[31] Gettysburg Seminary, and even S. S. Schmucker himself, gradually moved toward a more confessional stance.

The new battleground was "out West," in Ohio's Wittenberg College and Seminary, founded in 1845 by Ezra Keller (1812-1848), a Gettysburg Seminary graduate who had served as a traveling missionary in the Midwest for the Pennsylvania Ministerium. Schmucker's "American Lutheranism" found a staunch supporter in Wittenberg's President Samuel Sprecher, a brother-in-law of Schmucker. The Sprecher era, as it embodied also the fervor of Ezra Keller, continued to have ardent supporters long after the Civil War. These persons, occupying positions of responsibility, upheld the spirit which had given Wittenberg distinction. They pitted their "American Lutheranism" against the "symbolists," the champions, including those within the General Synod, of a more rigorous adherence to the Lutheran Confessions and of a return to Orthodox Lutheranism. For these devotees to the old order at Springfield, and for many a supporting congregation, the adoption (also by the General Synod) of the *Common Service* (1888) was viewed with disfavor as an attempt to repristinate seventeenth century Lutheran orthodoxy. A liturgy like the *Common Service* meant not only a retrieving of the Church's historic worship, which was absent from low church American Lutheran worship, but also a revival of orthodox Lutheran theology. For the two belong together; "worship is sung doctrine." Therein lay the dismay of those defending the quite different orientation of the Springfield founding fathers whose Lutheran stance, claimed others, was under Calvinist and Arminian influence.

With the coming of James William Richard to Wittenberg in 1885 the theological climate in the seminary began to change. Although he remained there only three years, later generations would look back and reckon the rise of a new Wittenberg (Hamma Divinity School after 1906) from the time of Richard and his immediate successors. By the end of the nineteenth century, as Willard D. Allbeck has shown, "In the forefront of the conservatives in the General Synod were the theological professors of Wittenberg."[32] Among them Professor Richard gave the Wittenbergers a jump-start in this direction, before going on to Gettysburg in 1888. An alumnus of Gettysburg, Richard, a native Virginian, was ordained by the Synod of Northern Illinois (1871), served a parish, then taught at Carthage College for a decade, and served as secretary of the General Synod's Board of Church Extension (1883-85) before being called to Wittenberg Seminary. Three years later he was back at Gettysburg Seminary where he taught until his death in 1909.[33] There, he was an influential teacher, editor of *The Lutheran Quarterly*, author of several books, including *The Confessional History of the Lutheran Church*. Among his students would be Frederick H. Knubel, later the first president of the ULCA.

A notorious example of the Wittenberg tension of "Americanists" versus "Confessionalists" was the Gotwald heresy trial of 1893. The church press gave it wide publicity and a brief reference to it at this point will help us understand something of the conflict within the General Synod. The trial, briefly, was that of a seminary professor at Wittenberg for being allegedly too conservative. Luther Alexander Gotwald (1833-1900), a Gettysburg graduate and later a pastor in Ohio (1859-88), was elected professor of practical theology. It was the year the *Common Service* was adopted also by the General Synod. Gotwald favored the *Common Service* and the confessional Lutheran theology it represented. To certain ones on the Wittenberg board and faculty, Gotwald's position seemed treasonable. It was seen in sharp contrast to the Wittenberg spirit of earlier times, call it a low church American Lutheranism. Gotwald was acquitted but later retired a broken man. His three chief detractors left the Lutheran church, one of them joining the Presbyterians, another the Methodists, and the third the Congregationalists. In his own way Gotwald was a forerunner of the confessional advance among the General Synodists in Ohio.[34]

General Conferences

Despite such conflicts, or rather, because the conflicts reflected a conservative trend within the General Synod, its relationship with the other two bodies was improving. Two decades after the Free Diets came the first (1898) of eventually three General Conferences. The diets had been attended by concerned individuals but the conferences were official. A core of delegates plus other observers came from the General Synod, the General Council, and the United Synod in the South. Spokesman for the three-member planning committee was Henry Eyster Jacobs, the rising church leader equally at home in Gettysburg and Philadelphia. The aim of the planners, according to Jacobs, "was to secure a fair presentation of the life and spirit, the doctrine and work in each of the Bodies."[35]

The first two conferences, 1898 and 1902, were held at Philadelphia, scene of the Diets and birthplace of organized Lutheranism a century and a half earlier.

The third took place in Pittsburgh whose mission-minded synod had split in 1867. Attendance averaged over 260 per conference, but the printed proceedings reached a far wider audience. One thing in particular gave these conferences an accelerated sense of convergence and that was, as noted above, the fact that, since the time of the diets, each of the three General Bodies had adopted the *Common Service* (1888). There had been the three hundredth anniversary of the *Book of Concord* (1880) complete with a new English translation (1882) by H. E. Jacobs while still teaching at Gettysburg College. And in 1883 the observance of Martin Luther's four-hundredth birthday had rallied laity as well as pastors and had kindled in many a proud sense of identity and of purpose in the New World. Many a new church edifice and academic building was dedicated that year. In the nation's capital a large bronze statue of the Reformer graced the newly named Luther Place and its adjoining church.

There was continuity from the Free Diets to these General Conferences. Philadelphia's eloquent preacher, Joseph Augustus Seiss, one of the planners, with Morris, of the first Free Diet two decades earlier, delivered the 1898 opening sermon. From his lifelong nurture of the liturgy and hymnody of the church—he had a shared role with Beale M. Schmucker in pioneering the General Council's *Church Book*—Seiss struck the scriptural keynote. Where better than in Ephesians 4:1-6 could the worshipers be reminded of the primacy of the Word and the working of the Holy Spirit? Or, given the course of events, who better than this highly gifted man of seventy-five could preach on "The True Unity of the Church" and "What Unity Demands of Us."[36]

Major leadership came from the two leading church historians and recently published authors. The two scholars, Edmund Jacob Wolf of Gettysburg and Henry Eyster Jacobs of Philadelphia, were close friends since their days together at Gettysburg. Wolf's popular portrayal of *The Lutherans in America* had been published in 1889; the foreword was by H. E. Jacobs.[37] In 1893 there appeared the first volume (in the American Church History Series, a prestigious multi-volume set) *A History of the Evangelical Lutheran Church in the United States*, by Henry Eyster Jacobs.[38] Both of these works became much in demand, and their authors as well.

Jacobs, as chair of the 1898 conference, led the assembled from Seiss's opening homily to coordinated praxis, with this reminder: "As the faith of the Church is greater than its organization, questions concerning the faith itself overshadow in importance all that pertains to organization." Toward that end, he added, "We are here to learn to know each other better, to grow more deeply into the faith of the Augsburg Confession we all profess to be the standard of our teaching, and into the love of Christ which is the source of all hopes for this world and the next."[39] Noting that the first real cooperation between the three general bodies had begun "successfully in the work of liturgical reform," Henry Jacobs pointed to similar advances in other fields. Home missions, instead of suffering unresolved disputes, had recently set up, by a three-way agreement among the general bodies, a "Joint Board of Arbitration, [that] will practically unite the several

Bodies into one Confederation of Churches." Likewise, he pointed out, "For some years [since 1896] our representatives in the great work of deaconesses have found an association for mutual encouragement profitable."[40] Moreover, the interchange of official visitors between the three bodies, said Jacobs, had led to a fuller grasp of their differences in church polity.

Then it was Wolf's turn. In his opening address, Gettysburg's professor of history struck the note of familial ties linking the three general bodies in a common legacy derived from the patriarch, Henry Melchior Muhlenberg. Reference to this kinship from colonial times would be made or implied not only by Wolf but also in all three general conferences. In an affirmative sense, one might say today, in looking back, that a Muhlenberg "myth" enlivened the historical record and played its own unifying role. "As children of a common household," implored Wolf, "it behooves us to remember that we are not ecclesiastical foundlings." Referring to the American scene, Wolf went on, "we have one common father, even Muhlenberg, a most eminent and worthy patriarch, from whom we all in direct line trace our lineage." But then Wolf continued with a salutary confession, not of faith but of guilt. While Muhlenberg had striven and hoped for unity "that all the Evangelical Lutheran congregations might be united with one another, . . . our respective Synods have [instead] each in turn neglected their priceless heritage. They have all together deviated further from Muhlenberg than they ever deviated from each other. God forgive us . . . degenerate sons of noble sires!"[41] The courageous essayist then proceeded to show how, in recent years, the synods had been making amends. Not only amid the striving for common worship but in other ways as well "we discover throughout our Church a revival of the spirit of Muhlenberg."[42] The story of a unified past inspired many to overcome the schisms of the 1860s.

The doctrinal agreement reached by the General Council and General Synod resulted not merely from the latter's conservative turn regarding the Lutheran confessions after Schmucker and company, although that development was certainly necessary from the General Council point of view. But the Council also modified its position. Earlier, Krauth's *Fundamental Principles* provided the Council's foundation, with practical corollaries like the Galesburg Rule ("Lutheran pulpits for Lutheran ministers only; Lutheran altars for Lutheran communicants only"). In the early twentieth century, however, with H. E. Jacobs leading, this strict orthodox position was softened somewhat, meeting the General Synod partway by omitting the Galesburg Rule and the claim that the confessional writings were an undifferentiated whole. Even Schmauk, long a critic of the General Synod, recognized its doctrinal basis in 1913 as fully satisfactory.[43]

Federal Council

There were still differences to work out, as when the General Synod, in keeping with Muhlenberg's openness and good working relationship with other denominations, joined the new (1908) Federal Council of Churches, while the General Council, pointedly, did not. This basic decision faced the ULCA as well, along with many other Lutheran bodies, regarding the FCC and its successor, the National Council of Churches (NCC). For years there had been interdenominational agencies—as in foreign missions, home missions, Sunday schools—but these had been formed by societies, agencies or individuals. The FCC blazed a new trail by being a council of churches.[44] Its quadrennial conventions were composed of representatives elected by the churches. The General Synod was represented by ten delegates and five alternates, all male and mainly clergy. One of them, Charles S. Albert, although a General Council seminary (Philadelphia) graduate, had retained his membership in the General Synod and was serving as literary editor of the Lutheran Publication Society in Philadelphia.[45] All told, the General Synod delegation brought men of distinction and achievement to this signal event.

Moving into an already teeming field of organizations that in religion as in humanitarian efforts was alive with the voluntarism that marked American society, the Federal Council chose to place its main thrust into social tasks. Traditionally the denominations had been remiss in confronting these mounting needs together. Therefore it made sense for the new Federal Council to focus attention on the church and labor. Reflecting the thoughtways of liberal theology and the ardor of the rising Social Gospel, the Council adopted a far-sighted "Social Creed of the Churches." It was a statement of social ideals considered to be in keeping with the justice demanded by the kingdom of God.[46]

In the General Synod a new generation of leaders was ready to promote a venture like the Federal Council when its time had come. To name but a few, there was George Unangst Wenner (1844-1934), lifelong pastor of Christ Lutheran Church, New York City. A native of Pennsylvania, he graduated from Yale College and Union Theological Seminary. Active in the Religious Education movement, he also fostered the participation of women in the work of the church. Via his connections with Germany he became a pioneer in the deaconess work of the General Synod and was able to station several of them in New York City parishes, including the one served by Frederick H. Knubel. Another fellow New Yorker was Junius Benjamin Remensnyder (1841-1927). A Virginian by birth, he graduated from the College and Seminary at Gettysburg. A veteran of the Civil War, he later headed the Peace Commission of the Federal Council of Churches, and would also become active in the Faith and Order Movement. A third was John Alden Singmaster (1852-1926). Born in Pennsylvania, he too was a Gettysburg College and Seminary graduate. After pastorates in Allentown and Brooklyn, he joined the Gettysburg Seminary faculty in 1900, and three years later became its president for nearly the rest of his ministry. For many outside the Lutheran fold, like Robert Gardiner, the lawyer from Maine who built up Faith and Order in its early years, Singmaster was a supportive friend and guide through the Lutheran maze.

While the General Synod joined the Federal Council as a manifestation of its commitment to Christian unity, the General Council remained outside the Federal Council because of its interpretation of the Lutheran witness to Christian truth. The Lutheran Church, according to Theodore Emanuel

Schmauk, president of the General Council, "stakes all on bearing witness. Her office is one of Public Proclamation and Confession of the Truth as it is in Christ Jesus."[47] Such different perspectives on the FCC, however, could not prevail against the overall convergences aimed at reunion; they were simply taken in to the ULCA to be worked out there.

CATALYSTS TO REUNION

The basic foundations for a three-way merger, or reunion, were all in place: common worship had been achieved by the *Common Service*, in ever wider use since 1888; doctrinal convergences had been gradually worked out; the common history in H. M. Muhlenberg and his work for Lutheran unity had been promoted in print and in powerful oratory, notably by Gettysburg's Professor Wolf, as quoted above. Further emphasis on this common ancestor was sparked by the anniversary of his birth. The General Council called for a worthy observance of the bicentennial of the birth of Henry Melchior Muhlenberg in 1911. In many places the Patriarch's significance for the Lutheran church in America was duly recognized. In the process the sense of kinship among those of a Muhlenberg tradition tended to grow stronger; while in others it was taken for granted. A permanent reminder is the bronze statue and frieze showing the Patriarch amid a congregation of attentive hearers, placed on the Philadelphia Seminary campus in 1917.[48]

These basic foundations for merger were long in the making, and solid. The conditions were right, but a specific catalyst was needed to trigger the action. In 1917, two events shared this role in the formation of the ULCA, producing the same result, but unrelated to each other: the quadricentennial anniversary of the Reformation and the entry of the United States into the Great War. The joint observance of the former was well-planned and the planning process itself led straight to merger. The latter was a sudden national emergency and the urgency of it all prompted fast and effective cooperation by Lutherans in their joint response.

The Luther Commemoration

The plans to commemorate Luther's posting of the ninety-five theses (October 31, 1517) started early and involved church bodies, organizations and interest groups. The General Council used this opportunity to raise two million dollars for educational and missionary work. This encouraged the laymen to assert their influence through a well-organized Laymen's Conference. The Luther League of America, an inter-synodical organization formed in 1894, commemorated this event in local groups in all parts of the country. The Lutheran Social Union in Philadelphia and the Luther Society in New York stimulated a protracted period of confessional consciousness. The latter had the Quadricentennial Committee organized in 1915.[49] It was an intersynodical venture that had the active support of some five hundred laymen. Its initiator was the Missouri Synod pastor,

William S. Schoenfeld from Immanuel Church, 88th and Lexington. He was an enterprising man already in his seminary days in St. Louis when, in 1890, he championed the introduction of the English language.[50] The New York committee engaged the service of Otto H. Pannkoke as its executive officer and director of its program. Pannkoke, a young Missouri Synod pastor from the Midwest, was serving a small mission congregation in Brooklyn while complementing his seminary education with further work at Union Theological Seminary and Columbia University. While his independent course of action made him *persona non grata* in St. Louis, it made him acceptable to the inter-Lutheran committee in New York. Pannkoke's derring-do and aggressiveness shone brightest in his promotion of public relations, an area in which Lutherans were particularly lacking.[51] Even before the actual observance of Reformation Quadricentennial during the second half of 1917, the entry of the United States into the war on the side of the Allies and against Germany and the Central Powers meant that the need for interpreting the Lutheran churches to the American public was urgent. In this situation lay the beginnings of the later Lutheran Bureau, subsequently named News Bureau, of the National Lutheran Council.[52] We have already seen that this Lutheran Bureau prepared the news releases—in advance!—for the first convention of the ULCA. The efforts under way to form the National Lutheran Council also had a positive impact on the three-way merger.

Most significantly, the General Council invited the General Synod and the United Synod of the South and other Lutheran bodies in the United States to cooperate in a "worthy celebration" of the Reformation Quadricentennial.[53] By 1914 the three General Bodies had appointed the Joint Committee on the Celebration of the Quadri-Centennial of the Reformation. The Joint Committee met in Atlantic City on September 1, 1914, set up its office in Philadelphia, duly called an executive secretary, Howard Gold, and had an immediate agenda. "It was within this committee," as Wentz reminds us, "that the first formal step was taken towards organic union of the three bodies."[54] With the influence of its lay members, especially E. Clarence Miller, the move to reunite the three general bodies became the Committee's consuming concern.[55] The time had come. The tripartite schism of Muhlenberg's heirs had been endured long enough. Local worship was based on the same service, doctrinal differences were less divisive, and shared heroes—Muhlenberg and Luther—inspired all.

The presidents of the three general bodies responded favorably to the laymen by appointing a committee to prepare a constitution for the new organization. By June of 1917 it was ready and a few weeks later was ratified by the General Synod. In October the General Council adopted it and in November the United Synod of the South. The constitution was then submitted to the forty-six synods for their approval. Meanwhile a Ways and Means Committee was appointed to prepare the foundation and set up the practical machinery for the operation of the new church.[56]

Augustana Disappoints

All of this happened with amazing speed, but not everything worked out as hoped. Although all but one synod of the General Council approved of the merger and of the proposed constitution, this lone act of dissent was a major disappointment. The withdrawal of the Augustana Synod from the General Council in 1918 was a traumatic event for all parties. Augustana (when it was the Scandinavian Augustana Synod) had joined the General Synod in 1860. It later withdrew and in 1870 joined the General Council. Unlike other components in the Council, Augustana was a continentwide synod. With a three-fold growth between 1880 and 1910, a time when the United States population increased 83 percent, it had become the largest synod in the General Council. Until 1890 Augustana's relations within the General Council were harmonious, especially in deaconess work, missions in India and the Caribbean, and theological education. But the following year the work of the Council's Committee on English Home Missions led to the organization of the English Lutheran Synod of the Northwest, mainly in Minnesota and Wisconsin. Council policy on the affiliation of new congregations led to a clash between the new Northwest Synod and the Minnesota Conference of the Augustana Synod. Many in Augustana, but not all, feared that English congregations outside the Swedish mother synod would siphon off future growth and leave the support of the church and its institutions to become a responsibility of the old folks. Yet there were others in Augustana who, like many frontier newcomers, had already fought in the Civil War and become Americanized. Through the public schools, and even through intermarriage, the Americanization process advanced. Colleges like Augustana, Rock Island (Illinois), or Bethany, Lindsborg (Kansas), or Gustavus Adolphus, St. Peter (Minnesota), or Uppsala, East Orange (New Jersey), gave their distinctive input for the preservation of a Swedish heritage, even as a new wave of Swedish immigrants arrived. The seminary at Rock Island pulled this legacy together, since the Augustana Synod required that all its ministerial candidates be trained there.

The conflict over home missions, especially in Minnesota, led to repeated calls within Augustana to secede from the General Council. This movement reached its peak at the June 1918 Augustana Convention in Minneapolis. It was to that convention that the General Council sent a quartet of trusted friends of Augustana: H. E. Jacobs, Philadelphia Seminary; William D. C. Keiter (Augustana doctorate), a member of the ULCA Ways and Means Committee; Harvey Americus Weller, president of the Ministerium of Pennsylvania; and E. Clarence Miller, the Philadelphia financier and leading layman among the promoters of the ULCA. The newly elected Augustana president, Gustav A. Brandelle, supported this foursome in their appeal to bring Augustana into the United Church. But at this Minneapolis convention neither he nor the distinguished visitors were able to deliver the vote. The feeling, especially in Minnesota, was that the General Council's Northwest Synod, in its organizing of ever-new English-speaking congregations, was, as one critic put it, "an abomination."[57] Besides, a majority seemed to sense that the time had come for Augustana to develop its own, Swedish-rooted Lutheran identity. The vote against joining the ULCA was nearly unanimous, and Augustana thus withdrew from the General Council.[58] Nevertheless, its Board of Missions was directed to pursue common work. Augustana's cooperation in missions and other areas remained crucial throughout the life of the ULCA, until the reunion in 1962.

The Great War

The second, and shocking, 1917 catalyst for joint Lutheranism was the American entry into the Great War. On Good Friday, April 13, President Woodrow Wilson issued a declaration of war against Germany and the other Central Powers. The churches, particularly the Protestants, saw entry into the war in Wilsonian terms, "to make the world safe for democracy." In this situation Lutherans in the United States were caught in a dilemma. War on the homeland of the Reformation was a political matter, but it cut deeply into the reality of confessional kinship. A minority, Lutherans who had themselves emigrated from Germany to America, tended to be pro-German and, quietly, to remain so for the duration. But the vast majority professed an ardent patriotism. In the eyes of the general public, however, there was a tendency to suspect Lutherans as "pro-German" and as potential spies of the Kaiser. To be downgraded as "foreign," considered with some suspicion or condescension by the "patriots," often put those of German stock on the defensive. Lutherans felt duty bound to reaffirm their solid citizenship and patriotism, some even went "Anglophile." Others prided themselves in having been Americans since colonial times. In fact, it is hard at this later date to recapture the turbulent emotions and propaganda of that wartime era. It was more prolonged and sometimes even more intense in its anti-Germanism in Canada than in the United States. The most decisive result was the abrupt transition from German to English in many congregations.

The declaration of war created emergencies in general. The particular responses of many Lutherans, working together, were the Lutheran Brotherhood and the National Lutheran Commission for Soldier's and Sailor's Welfare.[59] In order to bring spiritual and other assistance to the young men in military service, the Lutheran Laymen created an organization that soon had sixty thousand members. By November of 1917 it had become the Lutheran Brotherhood of America, representing many Lutheran bodies. Its main project was to erect and equip buildings near military camp sites as centers in support of the work of the new commission.

Already in the summer of 1917 steps were taken to coordinate efforts, eliminate confusion and give the Lutherans a united representation with the government. By October of 1917 the Lutheran Commission for Soldiers and Sailors was created. It included all the church bodies except the Synodical Conference, which had its own Army and Navy board. However, the Synodical Conference conference cooperated with the Lutheran Commission at some points. The commission's main thrust was to provide pastoral services at training camps. In order to accomplish this a campaign for funds was directed by Walton H. Greever of South Carolina (editor of the *American Lutheran Survey*) with help from the Lutheran Bureau. By February 1918, $1,350,000 had been raised. Thus pastors and other personnel could be provided for the centers created by Lutheran Brotherhood. The commission also chose chaplains for the Army and Navy and provided them with literature for their work. A woman's committee of the commission enlisted volunteers to knit thousands of garments for soldiers. Service houses were maintained in four eastern cities for military men and their families.

Under the pressures of war, and alongside their shared commemoration of the start of the Reformation in Germany, American Lutherans found they could work together well, and fast. What was to prevent a full merger, at least of the three bodies already sharing a worship book and a common patriarch? Nothing, and perhaps the fast pace of the final steps owed something to a "can-do" attitude of war-time. Furthermore, the president of the Lutheran Commission for Soldiers and Sailors was F. H. Knubel, whose inter-Lutheran visibility in the war crisis contributed to his election as the first ULCA president. Before resuming the narrative of 1918 and onward, we need to meet Knubel himself more fully, in the next chapter.

A POSTSCRIPT

In spite of the war, the Reformation Quadricentennial was duly celebrated, but with modifications. Among the festivities were mass rallies, special worship services, feature articles in church papers, pamphlets and books. Among the latter, Carolus Powel Harry produced a slender but searching volume on Luther that found ready reception among the students and young people for whom it was intended.[60] For pastors, students and alert laity, there had appeared the first two volumes of the *Works of Martin Luther*, the later six-volume Philadelphia Edition. The foreword in the first volume (1915) by H. E. Jacobs voiced the conviction that "Luther can be properly known and estimated only when he is allowed to speak for himself."

For the mass of church members, however, and for the young who were being introduced to their confessional tradition at one of its high moments, there was the Reformation drama. Probably none was more telling on the impressionable, of whom this author was one, than the semi-solemn performance in Philadelphia's august Metropolitan Opera House. The eye of memory still catches a tonsured Luther nailing the ninety-five theses on the Castle Church door. Later, Luther, standing fearlessly before Emperor Charles V and refusing to recant his position on faith alone, grace alone, Scripture alone, Christ alone, confessed boldly, "Here I stand; I can do no other." A bit later a delivery wagon came on stage. Out tumbled some fugitive nuns, ready to be liberated from their vows and to do their part in helping to found the evangelical parsonage and family life.

Even when the festival celebrations of the Reformation Quadricentennial were over, the Joint Committee's larger idea for American Lutheranism was just taking shape. The partners were ready to launch the ULCA.

NOTES

1. R. C. Wolf, *Documents*, 118.

2. R. C. Wolf, *Documents*, 121-24 and Jacobs, *History*, 445 ff.

3. R. C. Wolf, *Documents*, # 51, 123.

4. R. C. Wolf, *Documents*, 125.

5. A. R. Wentz, *Basic History*, 231; pp. 136 f. in 1964 edition.

6. *Lutheran Cyclopedia*, 64.

7. *Lutheran Cyclopedia*, 189.

8. A. R. Wentz, *Basic History*, 167 ff.

9. Burgess, Ellis Beaver, *Memorial History of the Pittsburgh Synod of the Evangelical Lutheran Church: 1748-1845-1924* (Greenville, PA: The Beaver Printing Company, 1925), 103 ff. (Hereafter cited as Burgess, *Pittsburgh Synod*.)

10. A. R. Wentz, *Basic History* 188-89.

11. See Michael J. Kurtz, *John Gottlieb Morris: Man of God, Man of Science* (Baltimore: Maryland Historical Society, 1997). A. R. Wentz, *Basic History*, 461 ff.

12. *First Free Lutheran Diet in America (Philadelphia, December 27-28, 1877): The Essays, Debates, and Proceedings*, Jacobs, Henry Eyster, ed. (Philadelphia: J. Frederick Smith, 1878), 13.

13. Ibid., 335.

14. Hebart, Siegfried, *William Löhes Lehre von der Kirche, ihrem Amt und Regiment: ein Beitrag zur Geschichte der Theologie im 19. Jahrhundert* (Neuendettelsau: Freimund, 1939). Nichols, James Hastings, *Romanticism in American Theology: Nevin & Schaff at Mercersburg* (Chicago: University of Chicago Press, 1961).

15. Kreider, Harry Julius, *The History of United Lutheran Synod of New York and New England* (Philadelphia: Muhlenberg Press, 1954), 176.

16. Reed, Luther Dotterer, *The Lutheran Liturgy: A Study of the Common Service of the Lutheran Church in America* (Philadelphia: Muhlenberg Press, 1947), 9-16. (Hereafter cited as Reed, *Liturgy*.) On Wilhelm Loehe, see *Lutheran Cyclopedia*, 284-285; on Theodore Kliefoth, see *Lutheran Cyclopedia*, 263.

17. Reed, *Liturgy* 175-80.

18. Reed, *Liturgy* 179.

19. *CSBH*, 308.

20. Jacobs, *History*, 505 f.; Wentz, *History* 285.

21. Reed, Luther Dotterer, "Historical Sketch of the Common Service" in *Lutheran Church Review*, Vol. 36 (1917), 501. (Hereafter cited as Reed, "Historical Sketch") *Lutheran Cyclopedia*, 123.

22. Reed, "Historical Sketch," 502.

23. Ibid., 502-3.

24. Ibid., 503.

25. Ibid., 503.

26. *Memoirs of Henry Eyster Jacobs: Notes on a Life of a Churchman*, ed. Henry E. Horn; vol. 2. (Huntington, PA: Distributed by Church Management Service,

1974), 264. (Hereafter cited as Jacobs, *Memoirs*.) *Life of Adolph Spaeth: Told by his own reminiscences, his letters and the recollection of his family and friends*, ed. by Harriet Krauth Spaeth (Philadelphia: General Council Publication House, 1916), 171.

27. Reed, "Historical Sketch," 504.

28. Jacobs, *Memoirs* 2: 268; Reed, *Liturgy*, 185.

29. Jacobs, *Memoirs*, 2: 266.

30. Horn, E. T. "The Feasibility of a Service for all English-speaking Lutherans," in *Quarterly Review*, new series 8 (1881), 176. See also Reed, *Liturgy*, 181-203.

31. Allbeck, *Wittenberg*, 69.

32. Ibid., 83.

33. Solberg, Richard W. *Lutheran Higher Education in North America* (Minneapolis: Augsburg Publishing House, 1985), 168-70. A. R. Wentz, *Gettysburg Seminary Record*, 69-70.

34. Allbeck, *Wittenberg*, 75 and Gotwald, Luther A., Jr., *Gotwald Trial Revisited* (Davidsville, PA: Luther A. Gotwald, Jr., 1992).

35. *Second General Conference of Lutherans in America* (Philadelphia: General Council Publication Board, Lutheran Publication Society, 1903), iv.

36. *First General Conference of Lutherans in America* (Philadelphia: General Council Publication Board, Lutheran Publication Society, 1899), 17-30. (Hereafter cited as *First Conference*).

37. Wolf, Edmund Jacob, *The Lutherans in America: A Story of Struggle, Progress, Influence, and Marvelous Growth*, (New York: J. A. Hill, 1889).

38. See Chapter 2, note 9, for full citation.

39. *First Conference*, 32, 33.

40. Ibid., 34.

41. Ibid., 41.

42. Ibid., 57.

43. R. C. Wolf, *Documents* #117, p. 269.

44. Cavert, Samuel McCrea *The American Churches in the Ecumenical Movement*, (New York: Association Press, 1968), 52-57.

45. Kaufmann, *Philadelphia Seminary Record*, 4.

46. Hopkins, Charles Howard, *The Rise of the Social Gospel in American Protestantism, 1865-1915* (New Haven: Yale University Press, 1967).

47. Schmauk, Theodore Emanuel, *The Confessional Principle and the Confessions of the Luther Church: As Embodying the Evangelical Confession of the Christian Church* (Philadelphia: General Council Publication Board, 1911), xii; see also, 894-900.

48. Tappert, *Philadelphia Seminary History*, 2.

49. *Minutes of the Thirty-second Convention of the General Council of the Evangelical Lutheran Church in America* (Philadelphia: General Council Publication Board, 1909) 13, 198. (Hereafter cited, as in this case, as *General Council Minutes* 1909: 13, 198.) *General Council Minutes* 1917: 64.

50. Meyer, Carl Stamm, *Log Cabin to Luther Tower* (St. Louis: Concordia Publishing House, 1965) 117. (Hereafter cited as Myer, *Log Cabin*.)

51. Pannkoke, O. H. *A Great Church Finds Itself: The Lutheran Church Between Wars* (St. Louis: s.n., 1966), 44ff.

52. See *The Lutheran World Almanac and Annual Encyclopedia for 1921* (New York: The Lutheran Bureau, 1920), 3.

53. A. R. Wentz, *Lutheran Church*, 379.

54. Ibid.

55. ULCA *Minutes* 1918: 37-43. (T. E. Schmauk chair).

56. A. R. Wentz, *Basic History*, 282-283.

57. Stephenson, George Malcolm, *The Religious Aspects of Swedish Immigration: A Study of Immigrant Churches* (Minneapolis: The University of Minnesota Press, 1932), 320.

58. Arden, Gothard Everett, *Augustana Heritage: A History of the Augustana Lutheran Church* (Rock Island, IL: Augustana Press, 1963), 256-257.

59. See also, Wentz, Frederick K., *Lutherans in Concert: The Story of the National Lutheran Council*, 1918-1966 (Minneapolis: Augsburg, 1968). (Hereafter cited as F. K. Wentz, *Lutherans in Concert*.)

60. Harry, Carolus Powell, *Protest and Progress in the Sixteenth Century* (Philadelphia: Joint Lutheran Committee on Celebration of the Quadricentennial of the Reformation, 1917). We will meet C. P. Harry again in chapter 7 where his influence on students is evident.

CHAPTER 4

FREDERICK HERMANN KNUBEL: THE MAKING OF A PRESIDENT

URING ITS ORGANIZED LIFE OF FORTY-FOUR YEARS the United Lutheran Church in America drew together the diverse elements of a common confessional legacy, nurtured their creative coalescing and, when the time came, conveyed the result to a larger unity, the Lutheran Church in America (1962). For its entire duration the ULCA had only two presidents, Frederick Hermann Knubel, from 1918 to 1944, and Franklin Clark Fry, from 1944 to 1962. Both men were extremely able and their leadership inspired confidence, as attested by their repeated reelection for the two-year terms of office.[1] In light of these facts, and also for convenience of designation, the following treatment of the ULCA will be in two parts: the Knubel presidency and the Fry presidency. As the story of the church unfolds in the human dimension, so it seems fitting to begin each of the two parts of the ULCA story with an introductory chapter on the making of a church president.

KNUBEL'S EARLY YEARS

In Manhattan's Greenwich Village the fourth child and first son born to Frederick and Anna Knubel arrived on May 22, 1870. Soon thereafter at the family church—St. John's, 81 Christopher Street—he was baptized and given the name Frederick Hermann Knubel. Thankful for their three daughters, the elder Knubels rightly wondered how this little son might one day carry on the family name and the father's business perhaps. Trim and well-built, the Knubel home on West 11th Street is squeezed between a large apartment house to the left and a warehouse to the right. To history buffs it recalls a bygone era when, before the Civil War, Greenwich Village attracted newcomers from abroad in quest of a quiet yet conveniently located place to begin life in America. Among the numerous Germans attracted to the Village were these parents, Fred and Anna. Her maiden name was also Knubel, but of another family line. They both hailed from Bremerhaven in the City State of Bremen, the huge port on the Weser River where the North German Lloyd shipping company was based. By the 1870s Bremen folk could jest that New York had become their "new suburb" on the far side of the Atlantic.

Young Fred grew up bilingual, and attended the local public schools. As second generation Americans most often did, he made English his language of choice and the culture of an Anglo-Saxon society his own. In his father's footsteps he chose a career in business. After high school he enrolled at the City College of New York and, for a practical supplement, at Packard's Business College. At the age of nineteen, he seemed ready to follow his successful father.[2]

In Greenwich Village the Knubel residence was only a couple of blocks from St. John's German Evangelical Lutheran Church. The interplay of family and congregation is evident. The Rev. August H. M. Held, who baptized Fred, was the founder and first pastor (1855-79) of St. John's. Before coming to New York, Held had already been an ordained minister and teacher in North Germany. In Manhattan, over a "misunderstanding," the independent minded Held and a number of adherents quit the congregation he was serving and founded St. John's in 1855. Two of Held's loyal followers were Dietrich Knubel and his younger brother Frederick. The Knubel brothers served as trustees of the church and exemplified an active laity.[3] In this they were not alone. "A marked feature of St. John's Church," said George U. Wenner, pastor of a neighboring congregation (Christ) and later president of the New York and New Jersey Synod, "is the success with which it has developed congregational life. From the beginning its laymen have taken a leading part in the management of its affairs, with the result that there is no more active self-reliant church among us than St. John's."[4]

The church was also recognized for its strong preachers, beginning with Pastor Held. His successor proved even more effective. The Rev. Augustus C. Wedekind, a graduate of the college and seminary at Gettysburg, served St. John's a dozen years (1879-91), precisely when Fred Knubel went through adolescence. Having come to America as a youth, and being eloquently bilingual, he appears to have been a model churchman, engaging in mission and other enterprises. By 1881 he had persuaded St. John's to join the New York and New Jersey Synod. On Sundays people would attend from as far away as Brooklyn's Williamsburg and from Jersey City across the Hudson. It was this pastor who instructed and confirmed Fred Knubel.

Fred Knubel Sr. was on the building committee in 1881, and in due course donated three stained glass windows in memory of his wife. The Sunday school was also a formative influence. By 1886 the number of its pupils exceeded one thousand, just when Fred was sixteen years old. A strong and loyal teachers' association made a big difference.[5] One of the teachers was Henry Busch, a member of a founding family in St. John's. He taught a postconfirmation class of young men, among them Fred Knubel. Busch, like Pastor Wedekind, had a persuasive way. Decades later, Helen Knubel recalled her father telling how Henry Busch as a layman, had challenged him to reconsider his career plans. Just business? Or God's business? The gifts Fred was already demonstrating gave promise of success like that of his father in a business career. But such gifts, one can hear Busch's reasoning, are sorely needed in the church and its ministry. The challenge was not to abandon these gifts but to build upon them.[6]

At nineteen years of age Fred Knubel made his decision to prepare for the ordained ministry. But where? Pastor Wedekind, although recognizing the close ties between the New York and New Jersey Synod with Hartwick Seminary in Upstate New York, nevertheless proposed Gettysburg. As a trustee of Pennsylvania College (Gettysburg) he was confident in developments there, and in the seminary. Besides, Gettysburg's two educational institutions lay at the center of General Synod history and outreach. Furthermore, Knubel would not be going to Gettysburg alone. Another member of St. John's, the twenty-six-year-old Eugene Edward Neudewitz, had also decided to prepare for the ordained ministry. They were both fruits of a vibrant youth program. The Social Union which the young men at St. John's had formed during Wedekind's pastorate met in the spring of 1887 with the young men's group from St. Peter's Church (54th and Lexington).[7] Their gathering at St. John's resulted in the formation of what would become the Luther League of America. Ernest F. Eilert, four years older than Fred Knubel, chaired these beginnings and would soon be editing a journal, the *Luther League Review*, through whose pages the rising concern of the young generation, including also the young women, could gain a fuller knowledge of the Lutheran heritage and strengthen their commitment to Jesus Christ. One of their challenging aims was Lutheran unity. Knubel and Neudewitz carried this background with them to Gettysburg. The two young men crossed the Hudson and went by train to the center of Pennsylvania. The year was 1889. For both of them a nurturing and vibrant congregation had prepared them thus far.[8]

YEARS OF EDUCATION

Preparation for ministry in those days, particularly in communions descended directly from the Reformation era (Episcopalians, Presbyterians, Reformed, and Lutherans) required four years of college and three years of seminary. Other Protestants, such as Methodists and Baptists, were heading in this direction. This was the seven-year prospect that Fred Knubel faced when he arrived at Gettysburg in September 1889, yet, as it turned out, with an important variation.

College (1889-1893)

From the train station of the Hanover-Gettysburg Line, where President Lincoln had alighted in November 1863 for the National Cemetery dedication, the two New Yorkers headed for the Pennsylvania College campus to the north. The 143-foot tower of the recently completed Recitation (Glatfelter) Hall beckoned its invitation to learning. Elsewhere on the campus renovations and new construction, like the new chapel, were in progress. Earlier alternatives to the contrary, the college was here to stay, as the towering landmark seemed to say. For two urbanites, one born in New York and the other in Berlin, what could Gettysburg offer? It reaffirmed the time-honored choice of educators, especially those of denominational connection, to locate colleges and seminaries away from distractions of the city. Yet the Civil War had given Gettysburg a prominence beyond that of any other small town.

College president Harvey Washington McKnight, a Lutheran clergyman of mixed Scotch-Irish and German stock, was himself an alumnus of both the college and the seminary, as well as a veteran of the Civil War. He was a builder and an educator. From him the students learned and the professors were reminded that the policy at Gettysburg was to strike a balance between "old things we should conserve . . . [and] new things we should adopt." The purpose of the college was "to retain inviolate the spiritual and ethical motive in collegiate education." Its aim in the various disciplines of study was "how to think rather than what to think." Toward that end the traditional liberal arts curriculum counted on "Mathematics and the Classical Languages as constituting its fundamental part, and modern languages, physical and mental science and English as indispensable forces." A college, according to McKnight, requires "opportunity for as much self-government as is consistent with good government." The president knew that, whether in the small town or big city, boredom bred pranks. And young Knubel, as his daughter Helen recalled, could delight in pranks. Speaking as educator and *in loco parentis*, McKnight said Gettysburg rejected "the revolutionary program of no control over students" that some colleges were at that time adopting.[9]

In Knubel's time Pennsylvania College (named Gettysburg College in 1921) had an enrollment of about 160 young men. An occasional young woman prefigured coeducation. Extracurricular activities flourished, such as various literary societies. Gymnastics were the way to physical fitness, and intercollegiate sports were getting under way.[10] The college was by charter non-sectarian; nevertheless, since the days of its founding, it was definitely Lutheran in governance and support. Chapel or assembly gathered the college community almost daily. Biblical literature was part of the curriculum. The campus YMCA, attuned to the religious stirrings widespread among young people, was alert to the challenge of Christian missions at home and abroad, as presented by the Student Volunteer Movement then getting started. Fred Knubel and nearly all his classmates took the traditional liberal arts route leading to the A.B. degree. Knubel was one of the twenty pre-theologicals on the A.B. track whose next move would be up the hill to Seminary Ridge.[11]

As to the faculty, Pennsylvania College in those days had ten, counting the president. For the most part they were luminaries in the liberal arts. They had distinguished themselves by self-directed study as well as by work in other institutions. An example was the college's first dean. The office was introduced in 1889, much to the relief of President McKnight.[12] Dean Philip Melanchthon Bikle, like several of his faculty colleagues, was a graduate of the college and the Seminary. He had taught in the South and spent a year at Dartmouth College in astronomy. Called to Gettysburg in 1874, he taught Latin, physics, and astronomy; was associate editor of the *Lutheran Quarterly*, a theological journal of quality; was founder and editor of the *Pennsylvania College Monthly*; and member of the American Philosophical Association.[13] As dean he represented the convergence of many lines of thought and striving that went into the making of future leaders in society, both lay and clerical. Among their college memories students were not likely to forget the dean's dramatic firsthand account of Lincoln's "Gettysburg Address." In the grand procession to that historic speech, Bikle and his college mates were last in line but by some rerouting wound up in front of the speaker's stand. They were therefore ready to reflect later about the meaning of the speeches and the event.[14]

Seminary (1893-95)

Like no other Lutheran "school of the prophets," the Seminary at Gettysburg is steeped in national as well as ecclesial history. A rare height for contemplation is the cupola atop the storied First Building. There, in July 1863, amid the changes of battle on successive days, military leaders of the North and then of the South surveyed the scene and planned their strategy. The price of preserving the Federal Union and of emancipating the African-American slaves was writ in blood and tears. A generation later the seminary campus had become part of the National Military Park (1895).[15] The new Seminary Avenue ran through it, later named Confederate Avenue. Like his peers and teachers Fred Knubel had learned and could recite the saga of that costliest collision of military forces on American soil. What more powerful reminder of human sin and lofty patriotism could now fix itself in these young men responding to the call of the Redeemer?

The seminary student body in Knubel's time just exceeded seventy. Of them, twenty-five were his classmates. Except for Fred Knubel and Eugene Neudewitz, the others were typically American town and country men, with fourteen from Pennsylvania. Ludwig Rosenberg, a Viennese, had the distinction of having come circuitously via the Preacher's Seminary in Breklum, North Germany, where ordainable men were prepared for the General Synod's work among immigrants. He was Knubel's age, added a traveler's touch, but died early in 1900.[16] Besides Gettysburg, only three other colleges were represented in Knubel's class; two from Roanoke (Virginia), and one each from Dickinson (Carlisle, Pennsylvania) and Millersville (Pennsylvania) Normal School. From the latter, Charles P. Wiles, a Marylander, would later employ his remarkable gifts as writer and teacher, and gain wide recognition in Christian education.

It was an auspicious time when F. H. and his mates entered seminary in September 1893. Enrollment was up. A fourth professor had just been added. Earlier uncertainty as to a possible relocation of the seminary had been quelled. An attractive site in Washington had beckoned, and the Board of Directors had favored the move. But the synods said no. Therefore a major building program was in the offing. The sturdy First Building was overcrowded. Renovated from its scars of war, it still breathed tales of the time it had served as a military hospital. A typical Old Main in design, the ground floor housed the caretaker, kitchen, heating plant, and sundry equipment. Dining hall, chapel, lecture rooms, and library occupied the second, with student rooms on the third and fourth, under the famed cupola. Whether Knubel was among the overflow who rented rooms in town, we do not know. The First Building has since become the home of the Adams County Historical Society.[17]

The major influence in the shaping of men for the ministry came from the seminary faculty of four. Milton Valentine (1825-1906), a Marylander by birth, was professor of doctrinal theology and president. Edmund Jacob Wolf (1840-1905), from central Pennsylvania, taught church history and New Testament. James William Richard (1843-1909), born in Winchester, Virginia, taught preaching and ecclesiastical theology. Thomas Charles Billheimer (1842-1923), a native of eastern Pennsylvania, gave instruction in Hebrew and Old Testament. An adjunct instructor and member of the seminary board was John Gottlieb Morris (1803-95), a resident of Baltimore, and an ardent advocate of Lutheran unity.[18] Faculty Chairman Valentine was a man to match the times. Alert students like Knubel could learn from him as a teacher, observe him as a church leader, respect him as a Christian gentleman, and cherish him as a friend, learned scholar, and author. During their years at the college, pre-theological students had become acquainted with him academically, particularly through his book, *Natural Theology* (1885). Revealed there was the author's sharp mind and literary skill. The doctrine of God being basic, the subject matter ranged from the atom to the universe. A reviewer in Philadelphia lauded the Valentine book as "a credit to any institution."[19]

Concerning "some present demands in theological training," the Valentine emphasis was unequivocal. Doctrinal theology "must be the positive and catholic Lutheranism of the Augsburg Confession." It must recognize "the principle of development in theological statement," and take into account the progress of science and knowledge. Theological students are to learn how to "maintain an evangelical position in the face of Biblical criticism." They are to learn "doctrinal preaching in contrast to preaching about Christianity." They are obliged to learn to instruct the young and evangelize adults. Those who teach are "to open the eyes of students to enterprise of worldwide missionary conquest."[20] A consistent exponent of justification by faith, the central doctrine of the Lutheran Reformation, Valentine upheld the milder confessionalism of the General Synod over against the stricter position of the General Council.[21] Widely influential, Valentine contributed frequently to the *Lutheran Quarterly*, of which he was a co-founder and editor for over thirty years. He was much in demand as a speaker and preacher. As one of his former students and later successor as president of the seminary declared, Valentine "was easily the chief leader of theological thought in the General Synod."[22]

In various ways the other members of the faculty also contributed to Knubel's ministerial formation. All were graduates of the college and seminary at Gettysburg. Any institutional inbreeding was largely forestalled by prior parish ministry or other academic activity. Billheimer and Wolf were also veterans of the Battle of Gettysburg. Thomas Charles Billheimer, assuming his duties in 1893, continued in the Old Testament field until 1911. Students quickly noticed that a zeal for his field made him a drillmaster in the teaching of Hebrew, but he was patient. He made lasting friends also for biblical study.[23]

Of special importance was Edmund Jacob Wolf, who came to the seminary in 1874 and continued teaching in church history and New Testament studies until his death in 1905. Thoroughly at home in his disciplines, he was an inspiring teacher. In terms of his preparation he was a rare bird. Amazingly he had but two years of formal theological education. The sequence is revealing. After his graduation from the college came the great Civil War battle at Gettysburg. In it he participated as a volunteer. His first year at seminary got off to a late and encumbered start. His two professors, Charles Philip Krauth and Charles Augustus Hay, impressed by Wolf's exceptional talents, advised him to take his second year in Germany. While Hay himself, in the early 1840s, had studied at Halle and Berlin, the changing currents in theological study made it preferable for Wolf to spend a semester at two other Lutheran universities, Erlangen and Tübingen.[24] There Wolf learned of the legacy of two developments: the "older Tübingen School" of biblical supernaturalism (on which S. S. Schmucker had drawn), and the New Tübingen School of biblical criticism. Like a man of the Lutheran confessional renaissance, Wolf at an early age had been to the sources. His decade of parish experience attuned him to the practical needs of the church. His widely used book, *The Lutherans in America* (1889), provided Lutherans with an overdue view of their ethnic diversity and of their roots in the Reformation.

James William Richard taught at the seminary for two decades (1889-1909), filling the newly created fourth professorship. His career as pastor and teacher had taken him westward. This included a decade at Carthage College (Illinois), a biennium as a home mission superintendent, and four years at Wittenberg Seminary in Springfield (Ohio), as discussed above. He was known for his strong interest in the Lutheran confessional documents, particularly as these pertained to ministerial education. Already at Carthage he had confidently declared:

> As Lutherans we dare not ignore the great doctrinal system of our own church. Our symbols in general . . . may not be absolutely perfect, but next to the Bible, the *Book of Concord* contains more sound theology, more practical soul-comforting truth, and more reverence of spirit, than any other volume. . . . [25]

At Gettysburg, young Knubel and his mates came under the spell of Richard. His impassioned teaching of the Augsburg Confession set forth the catholicity of Lutheranism. As a basic document, the *Augustana* suffices. By contrast, the other confessions in the *Book of Concord*—if subscription to them be required—limit catholicity and accentuate particularism, especially when their teachings are repristinated along the lines of seventeenth century orthodoxy. According to Richard the General Synod stood for a greater catholicity than the General Council. The General Synod sided with Philipp Melanchthon, author of the

Augustana and its *Apology*, and is more open to the Reformed. Implied, though not named, is the *Augustana*'s 1540 version, the *Variata*, in which Melanchthon, the author, had introduced certain changes to accommodate Reformed teachings, especially on the sacraments. The General Council's emphasis was on the Unaltered Augsburg Confession—the *Invariata*. Richard's position agreed with that of President Valentine, as Knubel and his fellow students were kept aware. Professor Richard periodically traveled to Europe and maintained a considerable correspondence, largely with scholars in the Evangelical Church of the Prussian Union, Germany's largest church body by far. Late in his career, and after Knubel's time as student at Gettysburg, Richard's two solid and complementary works were published: his life of Philipp Melanchthon (1898) and his erudite history of the Lutheran Confessions (1910). However, well before the arrival of the Knubel class, professors Richard and Wolf were engaged in conflict.

In Richard's estimation Wolf was too rigid a Lutheran, while Wolf charged Richard with being too flexible and not Lutheran enough. Worship, ever a neuralgic subject, became the arena of conflict. The Joint Committee on the Common Service had achieved its goal in 1888, and there was now a Common Service in prospect for congregations of the General Synod, General Council and United Synod South (chapter 3). Professor Wolf had been on the committee representing the General Synod, and he favored the Common Service. At the seminary the response was mixed. Some students asked permission to try out the Order of Matins at morning chapel. The faculty, with the exception of Wolf, denied the request. Just prior to the entry of Knubel's class, Richard and his Roanoke College friend, Professor F. V. N. Painter, had published their book, *Christian Worship: Its Principles and Forms* (1892).[26] This included a sharp critique of the Common Service. Moreover, Professor Richard complained that, if Professor Wolf had his way, Gettysburg would be maneuvered into the General Council camp. Then there would be no further need for the seminary.[27] This controversy was symptomatic of the times. At Gettysburg's daughter seminary (Wittenberg, in Springfield, Ohio) even greater tensions had developed. There, factions clashed in 1893 and erupted in the notorious heresy trial of Luther A. Gotwald, as already discussed.

Whatever their differences, professors Richard and Wolf could agree on at least one thing: a qualified Gettysburg Seminary student would benefit from an additional year at an appropriate German university. Frederick Hermann Knubel was their choice. Bilingual, gifted, pleasant yet serious, well-connected, and earnestly committed to his calling, he was at twenty-five years of age a young man of promise. The faculty approved. Leipzig would be the university. Americans in various fields of study were being attracted there. Among Lutherans the theological faculty was recognized as the strongest in the Reich. Besides, the Gettysburg Seminary Library subscribed to the *Allgemeine Evangelisch-Lutherische Kirchenzeitung*, published by Professor Luthardt in Leipzig. The choice of Knubel undoubtedly pleased Wolf. With this change things moved swiftly for F. H.

While the curtain came down on his six years at Gettysburg, a new life beckoned. He was now free to marry Christine Ritscher, the young woman who had been waiting for him. She was of a devout Methodist family in Jersey City. Without loss of time they married in late June, 1895. Amid the well-wishing of friends and relatives on both sides of the Hudson, they set out on what became their "yearlong honeymoon", as F. H. described it. Regrettably, family papers are lacking. Inferentially, however, it appears that Fred Knubel Senior made the young couple's trip to Europe financially possible and for him emotionally satisfying. The deceased mother, whose roots were in Bremen, would also be remembered as the son and his bride set forth. There were others, especially the three sisters, for whom the venture of their younger brother and his wife carried special meaning. St. John's as a congregation was naturally interested. The Rev. John Jacob Young, pastor since 1893, had a European connection of his own. His parents had brought him to America as a three-year old. During the Civil War he served in the Union Army, and subsequently graduated from the college and seminary at Gettysburg. Pastorates in Maryland and India had preceded his call to New York. For Henry Busch, still teaching the men's Bible class at St. John's, the Knubel sendoff could appear like a milestone. Remarkably, as Helen Knubel recalled, Busch had written words of encouragement almost weekly during the formative years of her father at Gettysburg. Likewise, George U. Wenner, leader of the New York and New Jersey synod, and pastor of the nearby Christ Church, was following this son of St. John's with keen interest.

German University

Forty years after the first Knubel had arrived in America, a son was making the return journey. Fred and Christine enjoyed the luxury of a week at sea. In the slogan of a rival line, the Cunard, "Getting there is half the fun." "There," in this case, was Bremerhaven, port of entry for the ancient commercial city of Bremen. This was native turf for the Knubel clan. Eager relatives oriented the young couple in the husband's family lore. From there, with a Baedeker guidebook in hand, the journey unfolded for the young pair. Onward they went by railway to the great capital city, Berlin. Its sights, aside from the Brandenburg Gate, highlighted the more recent past, such as the Reichstag building and the Dom, the cathedral of the Hohenzollerns. Besides the culture, commerce and industry, there was the church, alive with its parishes and its socially oriented Inner Mission agencies.

Leipzig in the 1890s continued to draw like a magnet. After Berlin and Hamburg it was Germany's third largest city. Strategically located, its role as a transportation hub had been dramatized since medieval times by its semi-annual fairs, the famed Leipziger Messe after Easter and Michaelmas. Its modern railroad station, the largest in Europe, was the latest indication of the city's commercial and industrial growth. A few blocks south of the main station, the Hauptbahnhof, at Augustusplatz, stood the University, the largest in the Reich. Among its several faculties the one in theology, a subject once known as Queen of the Sciences, in 1895 registered some 380 students.

Presently Fred Knubel was registered as one "engaged in study." His identifying *Kursbuch* would be signed by professors whose lectures he attended. As to housing, the couple found a small apartment. Before summer's end, Christine's mother had visited the young couple and also experienced some of Fred's prankish ways.[28]

For the culturally interested, Leipzig offered much. In music there was the famed Gewandhaus orchestra and the renowned conservatory founded by Felix Mendelssohn. Admission to cultural events was at student rates, usually half price. In the realm of books, Leipzig ranked foremost among the world's publication centers. Students got a hefty discount on books authored by their professors. Nor would anyone of the younger generation fail to visit that ancient inn, Auerbach's Keller, near the Town Hall, where Goethe's "Faust" was set.[29] Without peer was the musical legacy of St. Thomas Church. Here Johann Sebastian Bach held forth as organist and choirmaster (1723-50). Here too the centuries-old choir of boys and men perpetuated a Lutheran tradition in church music. Here also, the year after Knubel, F. Melius Christiansen began the first of two study periods which were to give rise to the distinctive tone of the St. Olaf College Choir in Northfield, Minnesota.[30] Leipzig was rich in historical perspectives. In 1519 Luther had here debated the Roman Catholic John Eck and turned the tide in favor of the Reformation. In 1631, outside the city, at Breitenfeld, Sweden's king, Gustavus Adolphus, defeated General Tilly's imperial forces. Though Gustavus paid with his life, he saved the Protestant cause in the Thirty Years' War. In 1813 the Battle of the Nations, on the outskirts of Leipzig, ended the French occupation of Germany and opened the way to the final defeat of Napoleon at Waterloo in 1815. To one like Knubel, who had come from a Gettysburg steeped in memories of the battle to save the Union, the military perspectives around Leipzig could enable him to see America in a new light.

Between Leipzig and America there is a more specific connection for Lutherans. In this city in 1739 Henry Melchior Muhlenberg was ordained. His biographer, William Julius Mann, pointed out this fact in his widely read portrait of the patriarch of the Lutheran Church in America. Published in 1888, Mann's book was very likely required reading for students at Gettysburg in Knubel's time. The educational situation at Leipzig as at other German universities was largely determined by its professors. Students commonly journeyed from one university to another in order "to hear" this or that professor. In 1895 the Leipzig theological faculty had two professorial luminaries: Christoph Ernst Luthardt (1823-1902) in dogmatics, and Albert Hauck (1845-1918) in church history. In their respective ways both were proponents of the Erlangen theology, which emphasized Scripture, confessions, and religious experience. A normal procedure would have been a letter from Gettysburg introducing Fred Knubel to Professor Luthardt. Besides his teaching, he was editor of the widely circulated and influential weekly, the *Allgemeine Evangelisch-Lutherische Kirchenzeitung*, which came regularly to Gettysburg Seminary.[31] The distinguished Professor

Luthardt was past seventy when Knubel met him. Besides his teaching and editorial work he was a church leader in other areas: president of the Leipzig Mission Society, promoter of service among the needy through the Inner Mission, and a founder of the General Evangelical Lutheran Conference (1868). The latter had become a rallying point for a united and confessionally sound Lutheranism within the Church catholic. The practical-minded Luthardt on occasion would orient students and many others in his ways of thinking theologically as, for example, in the article, "Introductory Words for the Beginning of a Lecture Course in Dogmatics."[32]

Albert Hauck, at fifty, was at his height as church historian. He was perhaps a little closer to the students than his senior colleague. Hauck's "aim was to a waken a new love for the church. As a teacher he directed his efforts to preparing students for the ministry, and as a writer he sought to further the pastors in theological study."[33] Toward that end he was the chief editor of the twenty-four-volume *Realencyklopaedie für protestantische Theologie und Kirche*. It was from the lectures of Luthardt and Hauck, not to forget those of their colleagues, that an American student like Knubel was introduced to a new kind of thoroughness. In the probing of theological thought or historical inquiry answers would not necessarily suffice. The process leading up to a normally accepted answer had to be examined, and if necessary the answer would have to be modified. By analogy it meant the ability not simply to tell time but also to examine the timepiece and its construction. The seminar method, wherein the German university had been innovative, carried the quest for knowledge and the demand for thoroughness several steps further. The give-and-take between the professor and the dozen or more students dramatized the learning process. A newcomer from abroad, like Knubel, would probably not have been an actual participant but a welcome auditor. Forty years later, when briefing this author on the eve of his year in Europe, the then ULCA president recalled, "When I left Gettysburg, I felt I had the answers. But after a year at Leipzig I had a far deeper appreciation of the questions."[34]

For a young American couple in Leipzig it was a time of sharing, asking and answering questions. Friends and strangers drew them into this informal and informative learning process. While the Knubels thus learned about Germany they also saw their own native land in a new light. The bizarre was often good for starters. Tell us, someone might ask, about the suicide club in New York, called Round Robin. An item in Luthardt's *Kirchenzeitung* (July 5, 1895) told of poor, discouraged German-American youth, banding themselves into groups of thirteen, who decided by roulette which of them would be the next to leave this world. Or, what about the false Christ, a German holding forth on a farm near Rockford, Illinois, who was attracting many followers and engaging in carnal excesses (Ibid., July 15, 1895).

For his part, Knubel's curiosity was plausibly aroused by reports in the *Kirchenzeitung* featuring the eighth gathering of the General Evangelical Lutheran Conference. People had come to Mecklenburg from various parts of

Germany and beyond.[35] As described earlier, this General Conference was of the same age as the Lutheran General Council in North America. These two associations remained in touch with each other, and eventually they had a part, after the First World War, in forming the Lutheran World Convention. For Knubel this on-the-spot introduction was significant. After an academic year of learning and sharing Fred Knubel left Leipzig more deeply rooted in the commitment of the Church of the Augsburg Confession.

Fred and Christine had been able to extend their stay until early autumn 1896. After touring Europe, they returned to New York in time for the annual convention of the synod of New York and New Jersey, meeting in the Knubel family church, St. John's in Greenwich Village. On Saturday, October 17, this well-prepared returnee and his Gettysburg Seminary classmate and fellow member of St. John's, Eugene Neudewitz, were examined by the synodical examining committee, and passed. On Sunday night both men were ordained at the closing service. Their ordination was on the strength of calls by the synod to serve as mission developers, Neudewitz in Jersey City and Knubel in Upper Manhattan.

PASTOR IN MANHATTAN (1896-1918)

As a home mission pastor the (now) Rev. F. H. Knubel proceeded directly to a promising field in Upper Manhattan. Support for this venture came from the young pastor's home congregation downtown, St. John's. Its missionary spirit, which we have observed, focused in this case on families who had moved uptown from Greenwich Village. They were the nucleus who, with their pastor, now formed the Evangelical Lutheran Church of the Atonement in 1896. A continuing influx of residents widened the field of opportunity.[36] Counsel and support for the fledgling pastor came from two elder brethren: John Jacob Young, pastor of St. John's, and George Wenner, pastor of Christ Church, on the Lower East Side. Wenner, a recognized leader among the city's clergy, was also president of the synod. He took a particular interest in Knubel and invited him to join a clergy study group, Koinonia.

The young pastor diligently pursued the duties of his calling: preaching with fervor, teaching various groups, visiting the sick, counseling the troubled, seeking out the unaffiliated, and working with the newly formed auxiliaries for women, men, and youth. The St. John's pattern was evident. Frederick H. Knubel would serve as pastor of Atonement Church for twenty-two years, 1896-1918. It would be his only parish prior to his presidency of the United Lutheran Church in America. His recognition of the central place of the congregation in a united church would remain firm. (For five years after his election in 1918 he maintained his pastoral status at Atonement.) Meanwhile, by the end of its first decade (1907), Atonement congregation claimed a baptized membership of about a thousand. Confirmed members numbered 642, of whom 401 were communicants. The accent was on young people. The recent confirmation class numbered 160. The social situation of Atonement's members ranged from well-off to poor. Many were recent arrivals from Germany. In congregational affairs older Americans took the lead. Worship was in English, with provision also for German services.

As the congregation grew, so also did the Knubel family. A son, Frederick Ritscher, arrived in 1897; and a daughter, Helen, in 1901. It was a busy household, as Helen recalled. Mealtimes were usually relaxed and brightened by the father's gift of storytelling. Looking back on the years before the United States entered the war, Helen Knubel reflected that life in the congregation, as in the community generally, moved at a slower pace. There were fewer distractions. Church growth seemed no real problem. People, said Helen, "wanted their children to go to Sunday school, and to be confirmed." In the overcrowded church facilities, especially where Sunday school classes met, "children at times had to sit on the window sills." In her reminiscing, Helen Knubel cited the important role of businessmen and other lay leaders in advancing a periodic expansion of building and service. Concern for the poor and the unemployed remained a continuing challenge. America at that time, in contrast to Europe, had no public welfare program. There was heavy reliance on charity and private initiative. In Germany the Knubels had been impressed by the Inner Mission, a firmly founded and far-flung undertaking of works of mercy among the needy. In it women, especially deaconesses, played a vital part.

Amid the mounting needs at Atonement Church the pastor prevailed upon the congregation to call a deaconess. Again, Wenner had led the way. In the early 1890s he encouraged the founding of the Deaconess Motherhouse and Training School for Christian Workers in Baltimore, an enterprise governed by a Board of Deaconess Work under the General Synod. Wenner's congregation, Christ Church, in New York City, was the first to call a parish deaconess. St. John's, in Greenwich Village, under Pastor Young, presently followed suit. Now came Atonement's turn. Sister Jennie Christ, a Midwesterner, had received her deaconess training at Baltimore. In 1903 she came to Atonement Church. For the next twenty-two years she personified what in church parlance was esteemed as serving love. Of her it was said that her work with the children and with persons in need helped shape the character of the congregation as a caring community. The teamwork of pastor and deaconess commended itself to other congregations in and beyond metropolitan New York. By the end of its second decade the Lutheran Church of the Atonement reportedly had a baptized membership of thirty-five hundred. In the words of Wenner, synod president, Atonement was "one of our strong congregations, . . . a direct offspring of the venerable yet active congregation," St. John's on Christopher Street.[37]

In the Knubel household, meanwhile, burdens competed with blessings. The vivacious mother, a perfectionist in the role of a pastor's wife, experienced a prolonged illness. Helen remembered her mother Christine as a compassionate and resourceful person, blessed with love and understanding as she raised the two children. The severe polio epidemic of 1916 left Helen herself permanently handicapped. Yet with uncommon wisdom and brilliant resolve, plus a confident faith, Helen devoted a full life to the work of the church. Her brother, Fred, did likewise.

Wider Responsibilities

In guiding the career of Frederick H. Knubel into wider avenues of service, no one exerted a greater influence than Wenner. To members of the rising generation in the church, and to Fred Knubel in particular, he was a mentor and man of vision. Wenner's own career provides us with a commentary on leadership. Born in Bethlehem, Pennsylvania, he was a graduate of Yale University and of Union Theological Seminary, New York. A conservative

FREDERICK HERMANN KNUBEL

member of the Lutheran General Synod, he was ecumenically active in church and community. He saw the Lutheran Church from the outside as well as the inside. Having organized Christ Church on the Lower East Side in 1871, he remained its pastor for over fifty years. The Wenner ministry and manner were outgoing. One example was his advocacy of release time in New York's public schools for religious instruction. Another was his initiative in making the acquaintance of Lutheran pastors of almost endless ethnic and doctrinal variety. During his own half century he saw the number of Lutheran congregations in Metropolitan New York leap forward from nine in 1871 to 261 in 1921. In members the Lutheran constituency as a whole was second only to the Episcopalians.

Much of the Wenner mind appears to have been caught by Knubel. In his book, *Lutherans in New York,* Wenner made his position clear:

> The emphasis which we place upon doctrine has given us a reputation of exclusiveness. The author believes that the spirit of Lutheranism is that of catholicity. He holds that in our relations with the people of this city and with other churches we ought to emphasize the essential and outstanding features of the Lutheran Church rather than the minute distinctions. . . . He [Wenner] is in sympathy with the well-known plea of Rupertus Meldinius, an otherwise unknown Lutheran theologian of the seventeenth century (about 1623), to observe "in essentials unity, in non-essentials liberty, in all things charity."[38]

In order to share this spirit Wenner was instrumental in organizing Koinonia (1896), an intersynodical group of Lutheran pastors. Like a seminar in continuing education, Koinonia offered the discipline of a serious paper presented each time by a designated member, and then discussed. Here lay an opportunity for diverse Lutherans not only to become better acquainted but also to develop mutual trust.

Knubel was bound to benefit from this collegiality. Here were pastors from General Synod and General Council affiliation, also others from Scandinavian lineage—Swedish, Norwegian, Finnish, Danish, and others. Not least in Koinonia were pastors from the Missouri Synod, as well as from independent synods like the Joint Synod of Ohio. Not only was this a proving ground for theological positions but also a place where a closer unity among Lutherans could be tested and tasted. Still prior to 1917 and the Reformation Quadricentennial, one of the best kept secrets, as Helen Knubel recalled her father saying, was that on occasion the members of Koinonia celebrated the Lord's Supper together.[39]

In matters pertaining to church and society, Frederick H. Knubel became a valued member of two churchwide boards of the General Synod. His election to the Deaconess Board and then to the Inner Mission Board gave wider recognition to the ongoing ministries at Atonement. Both of these boards provided him with opportunities for interchange with counterparts in the General Council and in the United Synod in the South. As Koinonia had done for him in the city these two boards now accomplished on a bigger scale; they introduced him to a range of partners churchwide. He was gaining recognition. In 1912, at age forty-two, Frederick Hermann Knubel was awarded an honorary doctor of divinity degree by his alma mater at Gettysburg, still known then as Pennsylvania College.

The Ecumenical Missionary Conference held in New York in 1900 was seen as one of the major forces contributing to the formation of the modern ecumenical movement. Mission interest at St. John's, Greenwich Village, and at Atonement could readily resonate to the global challenge.[40] General Synod participants at the conference included missionaries from India. The culminating World Missionary Conference at Edinburgh (1910) gave rise to the movement soon recognized as Faith and Order. Described as an effort to come to terms with the doctrinal diversity among the communions, a pending worldwide conference was prevented by the outbreak of war in 1914. However, an American regional conference was convened in Garden City, Long Island, in January 1916. Knubel was one of five representatives sent by the General Synod to this regional conference. Other Lutheran bodies did not participate, presumably cautious of "unionism." In their report the General Synod delegates advised against joining Faith and Order at that time. Knubel, however, remained on good terms with Robert H. Gardiner, the Episcopal lawyer and the organizing genius of Faith and Order. By correspondence and otherwise, their sharing of mutual concern would prove significant in the future.[41]

Beside the new ecumenical interest there was the old confessional loyalty that aroused the spiritual heirs of Martin Luther to observe the four-hundredth anniversary of the Reformation in 1917. Knubel appears not to have been directly involved in the preparations, but undoubtedly, as pastor of a prominent congregation, he shared in important aspects of the event. It was during the Quadricentennial's planning stage that Knubel became acquainted with Otto H. Pannkoke, the New York committee's general secretary. To publicize the Reformation observance the

Pannkoke program reached across synodical lines, secured cooperation from major Protestant denominations, and aimed to make the American public aware of the part that Lutherans and the Lutheran Church had played in the life of the nation. This venture marked an entry into public relations beyond anything Lutherans had hitherto attempted. This capability became suddenly important in a new direction when, in April 1917, the United States entered the war, on the side of the Allies and against the homeland of the Reformation. In this startling turn of events, Knubel suddenly had prominence thrust upon him.

The war, as already noted, affected the life of the nation in all aspects. The churches were challenged to rise to the occasion. Lutherans were especially handicapped by their alleged foreignness, a charge that was applied not only to those of German descent or recent immigration but also to those of Scandinavian origin. Finding themselves in a common dilemma stirred in Lutherans a new openness toward each other. Cooperation was necessitated by a common concern for "our boys" drafted into the armed forces. For a large congregation like Atonement in Upper Manhattan, and for its bilingual pastor, the problems generated by the times were acute. Although Lutherans were loyal to God and country, their patriotism was often questioned. This situation encouraged, indeed required, Lutherans all across the country to cooperate in ways hitherto not experienced.

Many energies that would otherwise have gone into the observance of the Reformation's four hundredth were diverted into new forms of service. By October 19, 1917, a National Lutheran Commission for Soldiers' and Sailors' Welfare had been formed. For the National Commission it was advantageous to choose a New Yorker. The one who was elected president was Frederick Hermann Knubel. To the post of executive secretary came the thirty-six-year-old Lauritz Larsen, pastor of Zion Church, Brooklyn, and a member of the Norwegian Lutheran Church of America (formed in that year). Treasurer was E. F. Eilert, of St. John's on Christopher Street. The National Commission became the first of a sequence of Lutheran cooperative enterprises. On November 6, in Des Moines, Iowa, the massive Lutheran Brotherhood of America was organized. Its executive secretary, J. A. O. Stub, a pastor of the Norwegian Lutheran Church of America, also served as a liaison with the National Commission, becoming a helpful friend of Knubel's.[42]

Meanwhile the publicity office created by Otto H. Pannkoke to interpret the Quadricentennial had become by January 1918 the Lutheran Bureau. Adjacent to its offices in the Knabe Building, 39th Street and Fifth Avenue, were those of the National Commission. While New York was thus the center of Lutheran cooperative activity, Lauritz Larsen, frequently in Washington, performed a timely liaison there with the Federal Government.[43] As president of this National Commission, a parish pastor like Knubel rose to a position of national prominence. The wartime situation played remarkably into the making of a modern church president. In the national emergency the congregation generously shared its pastor with the church at large. Paradoxically, when peacetime came, his election as the first ULCA president required of Atonement an even greater sacrifice.

NOTES

1. Gilbert, *Commitment to Unity*, 15, 87, 115 n. 93.
2. Personal visits with daughter Helen Knubel, 1989.
3. John J. Young, ed., *The History of St. John's Evangelical Lutheran Church, 79-83 Christopher Street, New York City 1855-1905* (New York, 1905), 31-35. (Hereafter cited as Young, *History of St. John's*.)
4. *Minutes of the Thirty-Fifth Annual Convention of the Evangelical Lutheran Synod of New York and New Jersey, 1906*, 11.
5. Young, *History of St. John's*, 83.
6. Personal visits with Helen Knubel.
7. Young, *History of St. John's*, 114-17.
8. Wenner, *Lutherans of New York*, 134.
9. Samuel Gring Hefelbower, *The History of Gettysburg College, 1832-1932* (Gettysburg, Pennsylvania: Gettysburg College, 1932), 257 ff. (Hereafter cited as Hefelbower, *Gettysburg College*.)
10. Ibid., 475.
11. Ibid., 246.
12. Ibid., 239.
13. A. R. Wentz, *Gettysburg Seminary Record*, 66.
14. Hefelbower, *Gettysburg College*, 219-20.
15. A. R. Wentz, *Gettysburg Seminary History*, 224-25.
16. A. R. Wentz, *Gettysburg Seminary Record*, 138.
17. Personal conversation with Chas. Glatfelter, historian.
18. A. R. Wentz, *Gettysburg Seminary Record*, 2.
19. Review of *Natural Theology or Rational Theism*, by Milton Valentine, in *The Lutheran Church Review* Vol. 5 (1886): 80.
20. A. R. Wentz, *Gettysburg Seminary History*, 246.
21. Ibid., 402.
22. Ibid., 402. See also his essay "The General Synod," in *Distinctive Doctrines and Usages of the General Bodies of the Evangelical Lutheran Church in the United States*, 1st ed (1893): pp. 34-61.
23. Ibid., 472.
24. Ibid., 388. A. R. Wentz, *Gettysburg Seminary Record*, 17.
25. Allbeck, *Wittenberg*, 70-71. See William A. Kinnison, *An American Seminary: A History of Hamma School of Theology, 1845-1978* (Columbus, Ohio: the Ohio Synod of the Lutheran Church in America, 1980), 76-77. (Hereafter cited as Kinnison, *An American Seminary*.)
26. Richard and George Wenner had exchanged their views of the Common Service in the 1890 issues of *Lutheran Church Review*.
27. A. R. Wentz, *Gettysburg Seminary History*, 292-94.
28. Correspondence between Helen Knubel and the author.
29. *Der Grosse Brockhaus*, 1932 ed., s.v. "Leipzig," esp. p. 282.

30. *The Encyclopedia of the Lutheran Church*, vol. 1 Bodensieck, Julius, ed., (Minneapolis: Augsburg Publishing House, 1965), s.v. "Christiansen, Fredrik Melius," by Gerhard M. Cartford, 471-472. (Hereafter cited as *Encyclopedia of the Lutheran Church.*)

31. Gettysburg Seminary Library has a full set from 1866 ff.

32. "Einleitende Worte zum Beginn einer Vorlesung über Dogmatik," *Allgemeine Evangelisch-Lutherische Kirchenzeitung*, 8 November 1895, 1069-1072.

33. *Encyclopedia of the Lutheran Church*, vol. 2, s.v. "Hauck, Albert," by Ingetraut Ludolphy, 988.

34. Helen Knubel pointed the author to Frederick Knubel's notebook of Luthardt's lectures in Dogmatics and New Testament in Frederick Knubel's personal file in the Archives of Cooperative Lutheranism, ELCA, Chicago.

35. See, for example, "Einladung zur VIII. Allgemeinen lutherischen Konferenz," *Kirchenzeitung*, June 27, 1895, 601-602.

36. *Minutes of the Twenty-Sixth Annual Convention of the Evangelical Lutheran Synod of New York and New Jersey, Held in Trinity Lutheran Church, Amsterdam, New York, September 14-19, 1897, 9, 27.*

37. *Minutes of the Thirty-Fifth Annual Convention of the Evangelical Lutheran Synod of New York and New Jersey, 1906*, 11-12.

38. Wenner, *Lutherans of New York*, IV.

39. Helen Knubel to the author, 1987.

40. Hogg, William Richard, *Ecumenical Foundations* (New York: Harper & Brothers, 1952), 16, 45; (Hereafter cited as Hogg, *Ecumenical Foundations.*) Bachmann, E. Theodore, *The Ecumenical Involvement of the LCA Predecessor Bodies: A Brief History, 1900-1962*, Revised Second Edition (New York: Division for World Mission and Ecumenism of the Lutheran Church in America, 1983), 11. (Hereafter cited as Bachmann, *Ecumenical Involvement.*)

41. See Bergendoff, Conrad, "Lutheran Unity," chap. in *What Lutherans are Thinking*, ed. Fendt, Edward C. (Columbus, Ohio: The Wartburg Press, 1947), 368-90. (Hereafter cited as Bergendoff, "Lutheran Unity"); Flesner, Dorris A., *American Lutherans Help Shape World Council* (Dubuque, Iowa: Wm. C. Brown Company Publishers, 1981), 1-15. (Hereafter cited as Flesner, *World Council*); Knubel-Gardiner correspondence, Archives of the World Council of Churches, Geneva.

42. Hauge, Osborne, *Lutherans Working Together: A History of the National Lutheran Council, 1918-1943*, with a supplementary chapter on 1943-1945 by Ralph H. Long (New York: National Lutheran Council, 1945), 25. (Hereafter cited as Hauge, *Working Together.*)

43. Ibid., 23.

CHAPTER 5

THE FIRST BIENNIUM, 1918-20

BEGINNING WITH THE INITIAL AND CRUCIAL BIENNIUM, we now accompany the United Lutheran Church in America in its forward movement of forty-four years. With the outcome of the war the United States had suddenly become a world power. In the face of great need new ventures were in the making, yet not without the push-pull of participation versus isolation. An example was the emergence of a League of Nations out of the Versailles Peace Treaty. Although President Wilson had proposed it and had ardently supported United States membership in the League, Congress rejected it. Isolationism was to characterize the nation's position in international affairs for some years to come.

In religion, equivalent developments took place. In 1918 the Federal Council of Churches completed its first decade. During the war it had proven its value as a link between the Protestant churches and the federal government. The General Synod had been a charter member in the Federal Council's founding and was alone among Lutheran bodies holding membership in it. However, with the formation of the United Lutheran Church this close connection was transformed into a consultative status. This was in keeping with the General Council's interpretation of the practical implications to be drawn from the ULCA's confessional position and would require further definition. The Federal Council, meanwhile, remained active in addressing problems on the domestic front.[1] Globally, more was required. During this postwar biennium many of America's Protestant churches were moved by practical idealism to render help and to advance world mission. Leading Protestants, including the great missionary statesman, John R. Mott, organized the Interchurch World Movement (IWM) in December 1918. The initial goal was to raise $300 million, and further enthusiasm raised the goal to $1 billion. In 1922 the bubble of good intentions burst. Over-borrowing hurt many a mainline denomination, but the indebtedness was repaid.[2]

In this IWM venture and in other interdenominational endeavors, Lutherans were the isolationists. They had a venturesome agenda of their own. The war emergency had rallied them into partnerships. The National Lutheran Commission for Soldiers' and Sailors' Welfare had called forth generosity and service of a scope hitherto unknown among Lutherans. The ULCA arose as a vital partner in this development. It appeared providential that the National

Lutheran Council and the United Lutheran Church in America came on stage at virtually the same time, the one in September and the other in November of 1918. Their roles were complementary and untried. The NLC represented cooperation, the ULCA unification. Intercommunication was made easy, for their offices were located in the same building, The Knabe, at 437 Fifth Avenue, New York City. Soon the NLC's participants would account for about two-thirds of America's Lutherans, nearly one-half of them from the ULCA and the rest from a diversity of church bodies mainly in the Midwest and of various ethnic origins. The remaining third, the Missouri-led Synodical Conference, stood apart but wielded influence. As in the proverbial triangle, there was no lack of interaction.[3] For the United Lutheran Church this was a crucial time to become acquainted with itself and its ecclesial peers. For the other participants in the NLC this was the time to become familiar with the ULCA and with each other. Before the biennium was over the ULCA therefore developed a "declaration of principles concerning the church and its external relationships" (the Washington Declaration of 1920).[4]

The Three-Day Conference

After the constituting convention came the Three-Day Conference, designed to further the unification process. Called by President Knubel, the conference had been authorized by the convention and referred to the Executive Board for action. The meeting took place February 25-27, 1919, in the Church of the Holy Trinity, New York, where the first convention had opened. In attendance were the presidents of nearly all of the church's forty-five synods, the presidents of thirteen boards, the chairmen of eight elected committees and many of the fourteen standing committees, as well as representatives of the auxiliaries enlisting the women, men, and youth of the church. Underlying the agenda were three basic questions: What are the agencies and interests now to be united? How shall unification be pursued? How shall the respective functions be carried out? It was one thing to declare a merger; these three February days were needed to work out some of the particulars left over from the rapid pace of reunion.[5]

Reports from the synods consumed most of the time. What states were to the federal union, synods were seen as being to the new ULCA, or nearly so. There were problems. In some places General Synod and General Council loyalties had caused divisions, and synods overlapped. This was particularly so in New York, Pennsylvania, and Ohio. The central states felt it also. A spirit of reconciliation prevailed. Before year's end the Pittsburgh Synod, divided for a half-century, would be reunited.[6] By the end of 1920 the synods in Illinois, Michigan, Indiana, and Ohio had followed suit. Soon, too, some southern synods would consolidate. Later in the decade New York would see synodical merger, and more would follow.[7] As the Three-Day Conference made clear, there was something federal about the ULCA. Individual synods had their "states' rights" and responsibilities. This often puzzled observers in other Lutheran church bodies.

Language was no longer a major problem, but linguistic diversity had its representatives. Six smaller synods of more recent immigration still used German and lay scattered among New York, the Midwest, western Canada, and Texas. A churchwide German conference fostered a retention of identity. A Slovak synod was in the making (1919), and a Hungarian conference was not far behind (1920). Official agreements with the Lutheran churches in the new Czechoslovakia and in Hungary were unprecedented.[8]

The boards were next on the agenda of this February orientation. The objects of the ULCA were set forth clearly in the constitution (VI). Efforts to avoid redundancy had preceded the merger, but now it was clear how much remained to be done. Depending on the type of function, special interest units in mission, education, publication, social concern, worship, and support needed consolidation, coordination or restructuring. The aim of the conference was to provide various executives with an overview. The complexity of the impending shakeup was apparent.[9] Polity itself played a part. For decades the General Synod had favored centralization in order to channel help from the synods to places where it was needed most. The General Council, later on the scene, was less centralized and worked through established synods and their agencies in missions and other fields. Both forms of polity had advantages. An example was the deaconess work. The General Synod had its Board of Deaconess Work (1894) and Motherhouse in Baltimore. Most of its Sisters were deployed in parish service, as in New York City. The General Council had close but unofficial ties with the Mary J. Drexel Home and Philadelphia Motherhouse of Deaconesses, older (1884) and larger than Baltimore. Most of its Sisters served in hospitals, welfare agencies and schools. Both institutions were part of the Lutheran Deaconess Motherhouse Conference, linking them with similar houses in Brooklyn, Chicago, Omaha, Milwaukee, Minneapolis, and Brush, Colorado. The deaconess office (not an order) gave women an important role in the church's ministry. Since the deaconess work was an import from the much larger enterprises in Europe, both of the ULCA Houses maintained friendly ties overseas: Baltimore with Kaiserswerth (where modern deaconesses began) and Philadelphia with Neuendettelsau (Bavaria). Such connections proved extremely valuable in facilitating postwar relief work.[10]

Next came missions. For the conferees Home Missions presented an outreach from coast to coast, and from Canada to the Caribbean. Here a number of separate boards awaited consolidation. Mission efforts overseas were heavily concentrated in India (since 1842), and had also been faithfully pursued in Liberia (1860) and Japan (1892). In India's Andhra province the General Synod and General Council were reuniting their work. Liberia was General Synod turf, while Japan had challenged the United Synod South. British Guiana and Argentina had General Synod ventures.[11] Inner Mission, the work of serving love on the home front, faced the conferees with a spectrum of institutions and activities. Hospitals, orphanages, homes for the aged and disabled, and other agencies cared for the needy. All of these depended on voluntary support. The

New York conferees needed no reminder that it was characteristic of Inner Mission to respond to emergencies. Its motives and concerns underlay the formation of the National Lutheran Commission for Soldiers' and Sailors' Welfare and sustained its activity. The National Lutheran Council was a next step.[12]

In the field of learning all three merging bodies had boards of education, overseeing their respective colleges and seminaries. The new ULCA fell heir to an array of a dozen colleges and an equal number of theological seminaries. According to the ULCA constitution it was the synods, not the church body, that owned and supported these institutions. As before, the new Board of Education would oversee and advise. The board would also provide leadership (staff) for work among Lutheran students at non-Lutheran colleges and universities. In the inventory of academic institutions, the United Synod South had four colleges and one seminary; the General Synod, four colleges and four seminaries; the General Council, four colleges and six seminaries. Especially the multiplicity of seminaries, small as most of them were, was a chronic problem.

The Parish and Church School Board, organized the week prior to this conference, was preparing a unified program of Sunday School materials for eventual use in the congregations of the three merged bodies. Its carefully planned biblical orientation had been set largely under the influence of Theodore Emanuel Schmauk over the past quarter century. He now was the board's first president, and was deeply challenged by the fact that one-half of the ULCA baptized membership was enrolled in the Sunday schools.[13]

Publications likewise went through a unifying process. Columbia, Baltimore, and Philadelphia had been publishing centers for the three merging bodies. Now a United Lutheran Publication House continued the work in the City of Brotherly Love. Here would originate the Sunday school literature, hymnals, books, and other materials, as well as the church papers, chief among which was *The Lutheran*. The convention having voted that there be but one church paper for the whole ULCA, the role of *The Lutheran* as a unifying influence was given high recognition. Bearing the name of the paper of the former General Council, it was now also successor to the venerable *Lutheran Observer* (1831) of the General Synod and of the South's *Lutheran Sunday Visitor*. The editor was subject to election by the convention.[14]

By no means least in the sequence were the presentations of the church's auxiliaries, which continued the General Synod tradition. The role of the Women's Missionary Society at home as well as overseas stood out preeminently. For what it had already accomplished in the wartime emergency, the Brotherhood was valued for its further potential. The future of work among young people, especially the Luther League with its unifying influence in the church's life, received emphasis.

When the Three-Day Conference was over, Secretary Scherer seemed to speak for many when he observed, "The conference gave those present and participating such a conception of the bigness of the task of the United Lutheran Church in the fulfillment of its manifold and worldwide mission as could not have been obtained in any other way." Besides,

> it clinched the Merger, disclosed that the larger vision is there for every member
> . . . to behold, inspired all with new purpose and resolution to do and to dare for
> Christ's sake, and set in motion influences which will continue to bless and pros-
> per the work of the Church for years to come.[15]

THE ECCLESIAL CONTEXT

Besides learning about itself from the inside, the process of becoming a United
Church involved considerable give-and-take with fellow Lutherans and others
on the outside. The next of kin, so to speak, were the other church bodies participating in the National Lutheran Council. One of the desirable traits of kinship is candor, and as the United Lutherans soon found out, the NLC offered no
escape; instead it soon became a place of candid exchanges of concern, either
directly or indirectly, as in the church press. The National Lutheran Council had
been formed just two months before the end of the war. Of its nine initial members, three were the bodies about to merge into the United Lutheran Church. We
saw earlier how well-wishers greeted the merger convention. But there were critics as well, spreading sharp judgments in their own church press. "The merger,"
said a German Iowa Synod editor, "was one step forward for the General Synod,
two steps back for the General Council."[16]

As discussed earlier, there was great diversity in the confessional kinship of
Lutherans. In Europe there had seldom been occasion for Lutherans to work
together. The state-church and language differences stood in the way, except in
missions at home or overseas. And, lest we forget, a voluntary General Evangelical
Lutheran Conference had also been in the making since the late 1860s and by
1901 was becoming international. Need we be reminded that in America prior to
the war most Lutheran church bodies tended to stand aloof from each other?
There were indeed splendid exceptions, like the Augustana Synod sharing its
Swedish input in the General Council. Following an initial test in the National
Commission for Soldiers' and Sailors' Welfare, which they passed far beyond
expectation, the participating church bodies were for the first time challenged to
apply their potential over a longer pull in the National Lutheran Council. As at an
extended family reunion, each participating group carried its gamut of loyalties
and range of concerns. The intense wartime public outcry against "hyphenated-
Americans" pressured Lutherans to end their ethnic isolation.

The Norwegian Lutheran Church of America (1917), like a preview of the
ULCA, was in the process of consolidating its three merged parts: the Norwegian
Synod, the Hauge Synod, and the United Church. Its president, Hans G. Stub
(Norwegian Synod), moved with caution; doubly so since he was also the first
president of the National Lutheran Council. The Norse body was second in size
in the council after the ULCA.[17] The Augustana Synod, having declined inclusion in the United Lutheran Church, was now having to make good its decision
to go it alone. The Swedes were still divided over that close decision. The major-

ity had been swayed by pleas to develop a Swedish identity. President Gustaf Albert Brandelle, looking ahead, saw the ULCA as "the church of the future in the entire nation."[18] Numerically Augustana was large, although smaller than the Norwegian. The Joint Synod of Ohio, bearing marks of turbulence among synods in the Buckeye State, was confessionally conscious but at times frustrated. To its roots in the old Ministerium of Pennsylvania (1818) were added successive generations from Germany and a prolonged transition into English. Joint Ohio's mission fervor had carried it to the Old Northwest and on into Canada's prairies. Not the *Standard* so much as the Synod's German *Kirchenzeitung*, edited by German-born Professor R. H. C. Lenski, tore into the United Lutheran Church and into the National Lutheran Council as well.[19] The synod finally ordered him to desist. President of the Joint Ohio Synod was Conrad H. L. Schuette. At age seventy-five in 1918, he was the elder statesman among Lutheran leaders.[20] His proposal for a Lutheran federation of synods (1912) had failed. But he was supportive of the National Lutheran Council and of its president, whom he succeeded.[21]

The German Iowa Synod (1854), proud of its lineage from Wilhelm Loehe and his institutions at Neuendettelsau and survivor of doctrinal bouts with Missouri, had built up strength in Texas as well as the Midwest. Wartburg Seminary's Professor Michael Reu, editor of the *Kirchenblatt*, severely criticized the ULCA constitution not for its doctrine but for its failure to include curbs on confessionally compromising practices, notably: unionism, open communion, sharing pulpits with non-Lutherans, and the toleration of clergy membership in secret societies. Synod President Frederick Richter shared these views but practiced a wait-and-see attitude as to how the ULCA would work out in the NLC.[22]

How the United Lutheran Church would fare in the NLC with these four sizeable synods posed problems. Together these four almost equaled the ULCA in size. But there were still five other bodies, diminutive but not unimportant partners in the extended confessional family. If not charter members, they had become participants before the end of the council's first year. Two of these bodies had their roots in Denmark. The United Danish Church reflected the pietism of the Inner Mission movement begun by Vilhelm Beck, and its members were at times called the "sad Danes."[23] The Danish Lutheran Church proudly perpetuated the heritage of Nicolai F. S. Grundtvig, the towering proponent of a culturally alive Christianity, with emphasis on baptism. The Grundtvigians were the "happy Danes."[24] The Lutheran Free Church (1897) of Norse Background, was founded under the leadership of the brilliant American theologian, George Sverdrup. Though small in numbers, the Frees, through their president O. H. Sletten, played a mediating role in the NLC.[25] The Icelandic Synod (1885) resulted from immigration mainly to Manitoba (Gimle) and Minnesota. The Rev. Bjorn B. Johnson, First Church, Winnipeg, represented that synod on the NLC.[26] The Buffalo Synod (1845), was a remnant. Having left Prussia in protest against the imposed Union of Lutherans and Reformed, they remained archly opposed to "unionism" of all kinds. The Rev. K. A. Hoessel, Milwaukee, represented Buffalo on the NLC.[27]

On the NLC Board the United Lutherans had eight representatives, the others thirteen. The ULCA men were a powerhouse of experienced leaders.[28] Administratively the four offices of the NLC were divided between the two largest participating bodies: president, H. G. Stub, Norwegian Lutheran Church of America; vice president, F. H. Knubel, United Lutheran Church in America; secretary, the Rev. Lauritz Larsen, NLCA; treasurer, E. F. Eilert, ULCA. The eight-member executive committee that governed council affairs between the annual meetings included the above-named officers and four others: G. A. Brandelle (Augustana), the Rev. I. Gersten (United Danish), F. Richter (Iowa), and C. H. L. Schuette (Joint Ohio).[29] Presently we shall return to this decision-making group. But first we need to recognize the role of the Lutheran bodies outside the NLC, and then note the influence of Protestant agencies, such as the Federal Council of Churches. External relationships like these influenced the making of the United Lutheran Church.

Other Lutherans in America, a category of convenience for the remaining one-third of the confessional constituency, were mainly in the Missouri-led Synodical Conference (1872). We already know how deeply the Synod of Missouri, Ohio, and Other States (1847) desired unity among Lutherans, but on its own terms. To many in the extended confessional family it seemed that Missouri preferred to stand alone. And for the Missourians themselves, full agreement in doctrine and practice was prerequisite to Lutheran union. Short of such agreement, any cooperation was allowable only "in externals," like helping to meet physical needs. Feeding the hungry, clothing the cold, housing the homeless came under the category of externals. But visiting the sick was an internal matter; it involved pastoral care and the well-being of the soul. Likewise, gathering the unchurched cooperatively, even with other Lutherans, must be avoided. Cooperation within the scope of the Synodical Conference raised no problem. But with other Lutherans, with whom there was no full agreement in doctrine and practice, such as the ULCA, cooperation would be branded "unionism." According to Missouri and other confessional "exclusivists" such would be in violation of the Scriptures and the Confessions.[30] This Missourian influence extended beyond the Synodical Conference. It found voices in the Joint Ohio Synod and in the Iowa Synod as already noted. It also found a following in the Norwegian Synod, many of whose theological students had earlier been educated at Concordia Seminary, St. Louis. It so happened that Hans Stub was one of them, although he had also studied at Leipzig and elsewhere.

Early in their midwestern beginnings, the Missourians had trained their watchful eye on the East. Wherever possible they looked for a foothold; metropolitan New York City was their strategic outpost. Their home mission strategist, F. C. D. Wyneken, began his ministry in the Ministerium of Pennsylvania, and then switched to Missouri. During and after the war effort it was necessary for Lutherans to maintain a common representation in Washington. Concerns for the welfare of soldiers and sailors evoked cooperation from the Missourians; so also did the protest against those state governments that banned the use of the

German or other foreign languages in parochial schools. Activities such as these were inter-Lutheran cooperation "in externals."

In St. Louis, Synod President Friedrich Pfotenhauer and others kept their eyes on the merger, and then on the United Lutheran Church. Concordia Seminary's faculty, led by Professor Franz Pieper, the erudite systematician, affirmed Missouri's position of separateness. Young Professor Theodore Graebner, with several years of ministry in the former Norwegian Synod, kept track of dubious practices in the United Lutheran Church. Many of these were reported, with comment, in the *Lutheran Witness* as well as in its older partner, *Lehre und Wehre*. Editor of the latter was Professor Friedrich Bente, whose book, *American Lutheranism* (1919) caused a stir. It was the first published account of the new United Lutheran Church. Treating the merger critically and, in the manner of Lenski and Reu, pointing out defects in the constitution, especially its silences and (mal)practice, Bente devoted the most space in these two small volumes to a history of the General Synod, the General Council and the United Synod in the South. He wrote: "The ULCA has much to clear away before Lutherans, to whom Lutheranism in doctrine and practice is an earnest matter, can extend to them . . . the hand of brotherhood."[31] Those with whom the Missouri Synod was not in agreement were dismissed by Graebner as persons willing to concoct a "unionistic brew."[32]

To sum up, those outside the United Lutheran Church, whether in the National Lutheran Council or the Synodical Conference, were at times understandably critical. Criticism on such terms was important for growth. But the spirit of the critics, so it seemed, was prone to self-righteousness and premature judgment. For its part, the United Church, rejoicing in its own achievements, was too preoccupied. The first biennium seemed still too early for self-criticism, and the mood still unready "to see ourselves as others see us."

A strained note sounded on both sides. From the outside it appeared that the General Council had willingly given up its confessional integrity by failing to insist on the practice acknowledged in its own Galesburg Rule: pulpit and altar fellowship among Lutherans only, "any exception being in the realm of privilege and not of right." The General Synod side of the ULCA was judged by outsiders as still being "unionist" and lax in practice, and as having made too little progress toward a sound confessional position. In any case, there remained a larger category of outsiders, the other Protestants and their agencies, many of whom held high hopes for some sort of partnership with the United Lutherans.

Interdenominational relationships raised questions that required the United Lutheran Church to clarify its position. This was not a matter of relations with certain non-Lutheran communions but with various agencies, like the American Bible Society, serving the several denominations. It also involved joint participation in the American Sunday School Union, or in the Foreign Missions Conference of North America, or in a number of other enterprises designed to assist the churches. Chief among these interdenominational agencies was the Federal Council of Churches of Christ in America (1908). In it the General

Synod, as we know, was a charter member. No other Lutheran body was originally in the Federal Council, whose reputation had grown progressively liberal and Social Gospel-oriented. With the formation of the United Lutheran Church all these connections in the interdenominational complex were put on hold, subject to clearance by the Executive Board acting for the church. Article VIII of the constitution, with reference to the powers of the ULCA, was clear, and bears repeating here:

> Section 1. As to External Relations. The United Church in America shall have power to form and dissolve relations with other general bodies, organizations and movements. To secure uniform and consistent practice no Synod, conference or Board, or any official representative thereof, shall have the power of independent affiliation with general organizations and movements.[33]

Before the next convention, Washington in October 1920, this regulation of relations externally would require readjustments internally. But nowhere was this concern for the church and its external relationships tested with more far-reaching consequences than in the National Lutheran Council and the role of the ULCA in it. Practical service was the test. It came when Lutherans together were being challenged by a request from the Federal Council to undertake home mission work among their confessional kin residing in the recently settled war industry areas.

DOCTRINE AND PRACTICE

A self-examination of the National Lutheran Council lay at the heart of the external relationships between the several participating members. How this inquiry started was simple enough, yet its consequences would endure for decades. The invitation from the Federal Council of Churches that Lutherans undertake jointly their portion of the home mission challenge in the war industry centers perplexed the National Lutheran Council. In a number of synodical home mission boards there was willingness to respond. But in the top leadership of the NLC (President Stub) there was hesitation and misgiving. On December 18, 1918, the NLC's Executive Board met in Columbus, Ohio with home mission representatives. It was a moment when, for the future, council policy was being set.

For one thing, there was the enormous challenge to render assistance overseas, to Lutheran churches in wartorn Europe, and to Lutheran missions cut off from their supporting societies in Germany. President Knubel's eloquent plea for the European needy led the National Lutheran Council to vote to send a five-man commission to Europe, with John A. Morehead as chairman. Knubel's words are noteworthy: The Lutheran Church in the United States, now being "the strongest and most orthodox in the world . . . makes our duty to exert as much international influence as possible [all] the greater. . . . There is a great need of material help for the Lutheran Church in many countries. . . ."[34] At that same meeting in Columbus, the Council, seeing the need for publicity on a large scale, took over the Lutheran Bureau, that New York agency which had already gained distinction by its invaluable service not only in connection with the Reformation Quadricentennial but also for the National Lutheran Commission for Soldiers' and Sailors' Welfare.[35]

Success on the home front depended on cooperation. But here among Lutherans of certain types, there was hesitation. Cooperation "in externals" like material aid was no significant problem. But if it meant cooperation "in internals," like home missions, which involved worship and pastoral care, then even among Lutherans—if their respective church bodies had reached no prior agreement in doctrine and practice—cooperation would be "unionism." That would mean a violation of confessional integrity on the part of a church body adhering to a strict definition of internal matters.

This brings us back to the issue of joint Home Missions on the part of the National Lutheran Council, and also to the position of its chief officer, Stub. With administrative caution he wanted to make sure where the several participating bodies stood. While there was agreement that the work should be undertaken, at Stub's insistence "a resolution was passed requesting the presidents of the member churches to constitute a 'Joint Committee to confer on questions of doctrine and practice, with a view to the coordination of their home mission and other work.'" [36] Behind his caution lay Stub's awareness that an important element in his own church body—the part of it comprising the former Norwegian Synod—was opposed to cooperating not only with other Lutherans but also with the National Lutheran Council itself. This made Stub skittish, for he knew the problem.

The result of the NLC Executive Committee's decision in December was a succession of three conferences in Chicago on Doctrine and Practice: March 11-13, 1919; January 27-28, 1920; and a wrap-up, March 11-12, 1920. Whereafter the church presidents agreed to drop this probe. However, its outcome was revealing and long lasting. Of the four papers prepared for the first meeting, representing the positions of Joint Ohio, Iowa, Norwegian, and ULCA (by Henry E. Jacobs), discussion of the Norwegian position outlined by Hans Stub occupied the available time.[37] A fifth paper, by F. H. Knubel, upon the request of the National Lutheran Council, was to "define the essentials of a catholic spirit as viewed by the Lutheran Church." A discussion of it was deferred until the next meeting. However, at this first meeting the Stub statement had found favor with the majority of those present. It was subsequently published and because of its precise organization became known as the "Chicago Theses."[38] The Stub statement, to the author's satisfaction, found high praise in *Lehre und Wehre*, the widely read journal of the Missouri Synod. The Chicago Theses came in two parts: (A) Mutual Declaration Regarding Doctrine, and (B) Regarding Practice. A Preamble stated: "All Lutheran bodies represented in the National Lutheran Council are agreed in the fundamental doctrine that the canonical books of the Old and New Testaments are the inspired and inerrant Word of God, and the only rule of faith, doctrine and practice." Besides, the unaltered Augsburg

Confession and Luther's *Small Catechism* "present a true exposition of doctrines contained in Holy Scripture, and are therefore acknowledged and confessed without reservation."[39] In light of disputes over certain doctrines that "have disturbed our Church more or less, we regard it both as a duty and as a privilege to declare our position in regard to the following doctrines." The eight doctrines, each accompanied by brief descriptions, were: Christ (redemption and reconciliation), the Gospel, Absolution, Holy Baptism and the Gospel, justification, faith, conversion, and election. In conclusion, "We reject all forms of synergism . . . [and] all forms of Calvinism which directly or indirectly would conflict with the order of salvation."[40]

As to practice, the Chicago Theses declare that "The Lutheran Church does not claim that it is the Holy Catholic Church. It believes that true Christians are found in every denomination. But the Lutheran church believes that in all essentials, it is the Apostolic Church, with the Word of God in its purity, and the Sacraments as instituted by our Lord." Therefore, "pulpit and altar fellowship with pastors and people of other confessions are to be avoided, as contrary to a true and consistent Lutheranism." Regarding lodge membership, "any association or society which has religious exercises . . . which teaches salvation by works . . . must according to Holy Scripture be regarded in its very nature incompatible with the faith of the Christian Church, and more especially the Lutheran Church." Therefore "We promise each other . . . [to] do our utmost to place our respective Church bodies in the right Christian position in this matter."[41]

The Chicago Theses have been characterized as representing a repristination theology, a mid-ninteenth century renewal of the seventeenth century dogmatics. Determined to remain faithful to the past, its adherents (according to E. Clifford Nelson) were setting forth an "exclusive confessionalism." Their spokesman in this case was President Stub. Most of the National Lutheran Council participating bodies, having agreed to the Chicago Theses, were thus closer to "Missouri" than to the United Lutheran Church. But the ULCA was still to be heard from, although its position was made more difficult by the succession of events.

Two statements had been prepared by representatives of the United Lutheran Church. The one by Professor Henry E. Jacobs (Philadelphia Seminary) was at the request of the conference on Doctrine and Practice. The one by President F. H. Knubel was by resolution of the National Lutheran Council itself. Again borrowing from the Nelson characterization, the point of view in both of these statements was that of an "ecumenical confessionalism."[42] Lacking the precision of the Chicago Theses, they nevertheless displayed a breadth of vision germane to the very nature of Lutheranism.[43]

Professor Henry E. Jacobs titled his presentation "Constructive Lutheranism." At the time he was seventy-five years of age, an honored teacher of the church, author of the most widely used history of the Lutheran Church in the United States as well as of the doctrinal *Summary of the Christian Faith*, a standard work in Lutheran seminaries. To him the word "constructive" described the task facing Lutherans in America, a task analogous to that facing "our fathers at the time of the Reformation: First to separate the pure Gospel from the corruptions besetting it, and to provide for the perpetuation of an evangelical ministry;" and Second, "to adjust and devise details of ecclesiastical constitution with reference to these ends."[44] In contrast to already traditional European establishments, the American scene required a truly constructive Lutheranism. "By the organizing activity of a great leader," Muhlenberg was implied, a diverse array of forebears were "held together by a certain fundamental fidelity to the Lutheran Confession." He deplored

> the misunderstandings liable to arise because of our unwillingness to recognize such unity as already exists. . . . Is it right to publish whatever faults we can detect among our fellowmen, and at the same time to suppress every recognition of what the spirit of God is doing among them, alongside and in spite of such defects?

To a Henry Jacobs this was an addiction to "theological pathology."[45] The representatives of the United Lutheran Church in America, he continued,

> who have been called to partake in this conference, can state, with devout gratitude to God, that, after many years of painful separation, forty-five synods on this continent have united, with great harmony, in one organization, pledged to the maintenance, defense and diffusion of the Gospel.[46]

Knubel's paper, "Essentials of a Catholic Spirit" (in the Church), was read but not discussed at this first conference on Doctrine and Practice (March 11-13, 1919). But by vote of the conference, it was published in the *Lutheran Church Review* (April, 1919) along with the Jacobs paper on "Constructive Lutheranism." Knubel was assured that his contribution would be discussed at the next meeting (January). Meanwhile, Knubel, Stub, and T. E. Schmauk as a subcommittee would examine the paper. Due to illness, Schmauk was replaced by Henry E. Jacobs' son, Professor Charles M. Jacobs. The change marked a turning point. Knubel's confidence in C. M. Jacobs had earlier been formed when the two were, respectively, president and secretary of the National Lutheran Commission for Soldiers' and Sailors' Welfare. Jacobs, then forty-four, was the brilliant son of a famous father. A graduate of Muhlenberg College and of the Philadelphia Seminary, he had done graduate work at Leipzig and several other universities. After a brief parish ministry he became professor of historical theology at his seminary alma mater in 1913. Now Knubel requested his help in reorganizing and rewriting.[47] The result was the Knubel-Jacobs statement, "The Essentials of the Catholic Spirit in the Church."[48] It was ready before the end of 1919 and in good time for the second conference on Doctrine and Practice (January 27-78, 1920). As Nelson observed, the document that followed placed "the ULCA in the general tradition of the Erlangen School".[49] Jacobs himself presented the paper at the conference. But Stub, according to Nelson, withheld his agreement, giving the following reasons: the statement was too long and involved; the Chicago Theses were clearer and had already won Missouri's praise; the section on "Cooperative Movements" lacked reference to the Bible as the "inerrant Word of God;" catholicity as a concept was contrary to the Norwegian Church's Articles of Union.[50]

A third Doctrine and Practice meeting (March 11-12, 1920), tended to bear out Stub's judgment. The United Lutheran Church appeared to be pressing for a catholicity beyond the interests of Midwest Lutherans. It also had failed, according to critics, to take a clear stand against lodge membership and unionism. No further meetings took place on Doctrine and Practice. Among most Lutherans in the Midwest the Chicago Theses became their standard. For the United Lutheran Church the encounter over doctrine and practice became a valued learning experience. By the time of the October 1920 Second Biennial convention, as discussed below, the Knubel-Jacobs paper had been refined and retitled: "Declaration of Principles Concerning the Church and Its External Relationships."[51]

To say it with Professor Nelson (a lifetime member of the Norwegian Lutheran Church, and by marriage related to a leading family in the United Lutheran Church),

> These papers—Knubel's, Jacobs' and Stub's—proved to be of profound significance in the shaping of American Lutheranism, setting forth two points of view: "ecumenical confessionalism" (Knubel and C. M. Jacobs), and "exclusive confessionalism" (Stub).... The Knubel-Jacobs statement insisted that there is an organic union among all parts of God's truth, but a necessary difference of order and importance.... When it is recognized that the Gospel alone is central and constitutive of the church, there is the foundation for a true catholic spirit in the church.[52]

The National Lutheran Council, meanwhile, in early 1920 had come upon troubled times on the home front. The Iowa Synod had withdrawn; Reu charged the NLC with unionism in its overseas help.[53] The Joint Ohio objected to "catholicity." Augustana was uncertain. And the Norwegians were restive. An anxious Stub confided to Knubel his dilemma in leading the NLC. Ironically his own son, H. A. O. Stub, active in Washington in National Lutheran Brotherhood affairs, "sought earnestly but unsuccessfully to get him to see the Knubel-Jacobs point of view."[54] Although things were precarious at home, the NLC was making gains abroad.

INVOLVEMENTS OVERSEAS

In the postwar biennium familiar movements in overseas relations took on new directions. The east-west migration from Europe became the west-east relief action from America. To give proper direction to the latter, the National Lutheran Council sent five commissioners to survey the need of the confessional kin on the continent. The United Lutheran Church in America played a significant part in setting these new directions.

Knubel had initiated the sending of National Lutheran Council commissioners to Europe. From December 1918 a half year elapsed before the right men could be secured and sent. They represented the five major participating bodies in the NLC. Chairman of the team was John Alfred Morehead (ULCA), then fifty-two and president of Roanoke College (Virginia).[55] Morehead, a Virginian by birth, a Philadelphia Seminary graduate, had studied at Leipzig, served in the parish, and had taught and headed Southern Seminary. Highly qualified, he would be shouldering responsibilities of great magnitude and unpredictable implications. His quiet statement of purpose was "We want to help one another."[56] In December of 1919, Morehead and his fellow commissioners returned and gave first-hand reports to the council and its participating churches.

For America's Lutherans the task had just begun. Morehead resigned his college presidency and in January 1920 was back in Europe. Encouraged by kindred spirits in and beyond the Council, he personified and spread the determination of Lutherans in all lands to work together. In the summer of 1920 Lauritz Larsen (Norwegian Lutheran Church of America), director of the Council, made the rounds with Morehead in Europe. It was then that a plan for a worldwide partnership of Lutherans began taking shape. To look ahead a few years, in the summer of 1923 the epochal Lutheran World Convention became a reality at Eisenach, Germany. Tragically, death had claimed Larsen at forty-one, the previous January. Oscar C. Mees, pastor of a Joint Ohio Synod congregation in New York City, was appointed acting director of the Council until succeeded by Morehead after the Eisenach event.[57]

The interrupted flow in mission support from Germany had placed the United Lutheran and other NLC participants in the role of trustee for a number of Lutheran Mission Societies. To facilitate matters and share the responsibilities, the NLC-related Lutheran Foreign Missions Conference in America had been formed as of July 1919. Its organizer and first chairman was Luther Beniah Wolf, secretary-treasurer of the United Lutheran Church Board of Foreign Missions. A veteran India missionary and educator, he had served twenty-two years as principal of Andhra Lutheran College, Guntur, before returning to the States and heading the General Synod's Foreign Board (1908-18).[58] Luther Wolf's familiarity with the India scene enabled him to grasp the plight of German missions whose support—meaning funds and personnel—from the home base had been cut off. One of these was the Hermannsburg Mission in the coastal region of Andhra Pradesh, north of Madras. It was neighborly for the American-related Andhra Mission to render emergency assistance during and after the war. Then, via negotiations between the Lutheran Foreign Missions Conference in America and the Hermannsburg Mission in Germany, the field was transferred to the Joint Ohio Synod (1923). The ULCA had been a valued mediator.[59]

A second example is that of the transformation of the big Gossner Mission into India's first self-governing and property-owning Protestant church (1919).[60] In age it was about the same as the Andhra Mission, Guntur, but about twice the size. Its base in Ranchi lay considerably west of Calcutta. Wooed by other missions, the Gossner native leaders vowed to remain steadfastly Lutheran, much as Johannes Evangelista Gossner, decades earlier, had vowed in Berlin after his conversion from Rome. What saved the Gossner Mission was not money, but an adapted version of the ULCA Constitution. Through the good offices of Missionary George A. Rupley, going repeatedly from Guntur to Ranchi, the adaptation was accomplished. The National Missionary Council of India and the Provincial Government approved. The valiant Gossner Mission became the Gossner Evangelical Lutheran Church Chotanagpur and Assam. Its indigenous president, the Rev. H. D. Lakra, later sent his son, Joel, to the ULCA Chicago Seminary. After World War II Joel Lakra became president of the Gossner Church.[61] Elsewhere in India, in the hill country of the Eastern Ghats, some six hundred miles southwest of Calcutta, Missionary Ernst Neudoerffer (Canada Synod) supervised during the war the work of the North German (Schleswig-Holstein, Breklum) Mission.[62] For this outreach among the very poor the General Synod and then the ULCA Foreign Board provided frugal support, and later also missionary personnel. Through hard times, including World War II, the work survived. Linkage with Europe has long since been resumed, and today this is the Jeypore Evangelical Lutheran Church, self-governing and nearly self-sup-porting.[63]

Reflections from India on the effect of the first biennium of the ULCA strike a positive note. "The merging of the Lutheran Churches in America," one missionary wrote,

> has led to a more rapid merging here in India than the most sanguine among us had anticipated. In October, 1920, final action was taken bringing Rajahmundry and Guntur into one general organization, known as the Council of the India Mission of the United Lutheran Church in America."[64]

A fuller accounting of the United Lutheran Church's missionary enterprise overseas will appear in the next chapter. All of the developments we have been following here helped to widen the horizon and stimulate the growth of the United Lutheran Church.

A few other aspects of the ULCA involvement in the work of the National Lutheran Council should be noted. First, the flow of reports by the council's commissioners from Europe filled the church press. New insights were gained as to the life and conditions among fellow Lutherans in the Old World. Next, publicity of this kind was essential to awaken and maintain a sense of responsibility for generous giving. Confidence had been inspired by the fact that the appeal of the Commission for Soldiers' and Sailors' Welfare had far exceeded its $750,000 goal and brought in $1.3 million (1918). This appeal had been "for us." Could this kind of response be matched "for others"?[65] The National Lutheran Council's appeal for $600,000 seemed a modest beginning. The amount was collected during the forepart of 1919.[66]

Upon the return of the commissioners from Europe in December, and the knowledge of need being more specific, the NLC, upon recommendation, launched a new appeal for $1.8 million. In addition, a clothing drive for two thousand tons was undertaken and successfully carried out. Publicity for this combined endeavor was entrusted once again to the Lutheran Bureau now part of the Council. The work backstage was in the hands of a tireless troika: Otto H. Pannkoke, Walton H. Greever, and that supreme statistician George L. Kieffer.[67] The latter two, Greever and Kieffer, were a ULCA contribution. For them especially it was paradoxical that the ULCA, although the heaviest contributor because of its size, was per capita one of the lowest in rank.[68]

THE SECOND BIENNIAL CONVENTION, OCTOBER 1920

For its Second Biennial Convention, the United Lutheran Church in America chose to meet in the nation's capital, Washington, D.C. The place was significant. The time (October 19-27, 1920) closely preceded the national election that would end the sway of President Wilson and the Democrats, and bring in Warren Gamaliel Harding (Ohio) and the Republicans, with the slogan of a "return to a normalcy." The hundreds who converged at the Luther Place Memorial Church were treated to an impressive setting. On a triangular site at Thomas Circle stood Washington's noblest Lutheran Church. Its sanctuary and adjacent structure were highlighted by the massive tower and lofty spire over the entrance, and the big bronze statue of Martin Luther. It had been placed there by the New York Lutheran Society to commemorate the four hundredth anniversary of the Reformer's birth (1883).[69] The inspiration for this memorial church—the vision of a Washington pastor, John George Butler—had been evoked by longings for peace as these had welled ever stronger during the latter part of the Civil War. The new church "should be a memorial to God's goodness in delivering the land from slavery and from war." The edifice had been dedicated in June 1874.[70] After a disastrous fire in 1904, Luther Place Memorial was rebuilt within a year. President Theodore Roosevelt delivered an address at the reopening. It was later published and widely distributed by the Board of Education of the General Synod.[71] In terms of roots and reach and a sense of direction, a more appropriate place could not have been found for delegates to deal with the tasks and issues facing the ULCA during its first biennium.

Delegates and visitors assembled here for the opening service on the evening of Tuesday, October 19. President Knubel's sermon, based on Acts 23:27 ("Whose I am and whom I serve") developed a grand theme: "The Catholicity of Lutheranism." In recent months he had given much thought to the subject and set the tone of the convention. World-awareness permeated his message.[72] In view of the massive inventory reported at the Three-Day Conference in February 1919, there was ample reason for curiosity as to how the United Church was faring. A full accounting was now available in the Bulletin of Reports describing the work of the several boards and other units. Not included was the report of the president that he delivered in the first business session.[73] The 529 delegates elected to this convention represented forty-two synods. Consolidations, led by the reuniting of the two Pittsburgh bodies, were under way, thus reducing the number of synods from the forty-five at the 1918 convention.[74] The election of officers was completed during the first business session. All three were re-elected on the second ballot.[75]

In his report, President Knubel confessed that he had undertaken the work "with fear and trembling." He was convinced "that the United Lutheran Church in America exists under Providential will, and therefore a purpose of our Lord is to be fulfilled through its existence." Second, the president sensed a "widespread evidence that the new organization [is] to become something definitely better in principle, purpose and plan than even any one of the three previously existing General Bodies had been."[76] He gladly admitted the supportiveness of partners. The secretary, M. G. G. Scherer, "has been a daily counselor, his quiet influence upon the church is far greater than is known." "The consecrated advice of the treasurer, E. Clarence Miller, has been a light upon the way." While formulating "the financial plans for the Church and personally encouraging such forward movements as that of the Board of Ministerial Relief, he has readily and largely given time and trained thought for all purposes." The twelve-member Executive Board, said Knubel, "has willingly become an able cabinet of advisers." Schmauk, its most distinguished member, had died in March 1920, thus depriving the church and its president of an exceptionally experienced counselor.[77]

In the major part of his report, as required in the bylaws, the president endeavored to summarize briefly "the general situation of the Church" during the biennium. Amid the complex interplay of forces shaping the postwar era, the Knubel emphasis on the task of the church, of congregations and individual Christians, was drawn from the three-fold ministry of Jesus, who went about "preaching, teaching, and healing."[78] Granting that these three parts can be separated in thought but not in life, the Knubel way was to apply them to the organized activity of the United Lutheran Church. Under preaching or the missionary department "belong the Boards of Foreign Missions, Home Missions and Church Extension, Immigrant Missions, West Indies Missions, Northwestern Missions, and the Committee on Jewish Missions."[79] To teaching "belong the Boards of Education, Church and Parish Schools, Publication, the Church Paper and its Committees, the Committee on Boys Work, Common Service Book Committee, the Committees on Church Music and Church Architecture, the Statistical and Church Year Book Committee, and the Publicity Committee."[80] To healing and the task of serving love "belong the Boards of Inner Mission, Deaconess Work, Ministerial Relief, the Committee on Moral and Social Reform." In this as in other areas of life, Knubel cautioned church members against forsaking the knowledge of "evil's deep roots in sin, of sin's ineradicable character without the grace of God in Christ."[81] Let the church, he insisted, "so condemn [evil] as to lead to repentance."[82] In concluding his first report, President Knubel recommended "that this convention shall refer to the

Executive Board the duty of surveying the Church's task, possibly in conference with representatives of boards and other agencies, and of locating upon definite agencies any portions of the whole task not as yet assumed as a responsibility by any agency."[83]

For its part, the Executive Board gladly admitted that its first biennium was a learning process. But then it explained:[84]

> The work of the Board has been directed chiefly to the ends of coordinating and harmonizing the activities of Synod Boards, Committees and other organizations of the Church, and bringing them into accord with the principles and policies of the United Lutheran Church in so far as these have been determined.[85]

The Executive Board held fourteen meetings during the biennium. "While by resolution of the board the offices of President and Secretary were established temporarily in the City of New York, most of the meetings have been held in other cities." The reference here was to the fact that, at this formative stage, boards of the church were located wherever they happened to be before the merger, in such places as Philadelphia, Baltimore, Washington, Pittsburgh, and elsewhere.[86] They would gradually relocate to a pair of sites, Philadelphia and New York, but the ULCA never would have a single "headquarters."

Two major addresses marked the convention's second evening (Wednesday, October 20). Luther B. Wolf, the veteran India missionary now secretary-treasurer of the United Lutheran Foreign Mission Board, held forth on Christian missions in view of current world conditions. He reminded the delegates of the American response to the plight of the "orphaned" German Lutheran missions in Asia and Africa. He showed how the merger in America was having its counterpart at that very time in uniting the missions of the former General Synod and General Council. He also could point with satisfaction to the recent formation of the Lutheran Foreign Missions Conference in America that was even then, through the National Lutheran Council, leading to further partnership in mission. He reported on the progress being made in the formation of a sorely needed International Missionary Council (1921). Finally, he praised the faithfulness of missionaries abroad and their supporters at home, notably the Women's Missionary Society of the ULCA. Not least was the inspiration to be gained by the United Lutherans from the faithful congregations in Asia, Africa, and Latin America with whom they were linked in organization and a common witness.[87]

Ernest F. Bachmann, head of the new Inner Mission Board and pastor of the Deaconess Motherhouse in Philadelphia, told of the religious situation in the war-torn countries of Europe.[88] Familiar with the scene from a previous study trip (1906), he was chosen by President Knubel as a commissioner to look after "interests with which the United Lutheran Church are associated [and] could not be cared for merely by correspondence." The assignment typified the aim to accomplish one specific task, to consolidate the efforts of two rival seminaries that had been preparing pastors for America,[89] and to undertake a number of inquiries on behalf of five different boards of the ULCA: Education, Foreign

Missions, Inner Mission, Deaconess Work, and Northwestern Missions (mainly among German settlers in Western Canada). The two seminaries in North Germany, Kropp and Breklum, had for years been training men for the General Council and the General Synod, respectively. Bachmann described the tension between the two as being "even more difficult than that between the General Synod and the General Council before the Merger." But finally the spirit of the United Lutheran Church prevailed, and a consolidated program was signed.[90] Bachmann's itinerary included England, France, Switzerland, Austria, Germany, the Netherlands. In parts of Germany the Revolution of 1918 was creating hard times for the church, separated now from the state and assailed by "the Reds." Yet even in the worst situation, he observed, the deaconesses of the church went about their tasks undisturbed. "Serving love," a favorite Knubel term, was honored. In Geneva, where plans were shaping the ecumenical movement, Bachmann and Luther Wolf teamed up. And later at Leipzig they met Morehead and Lauritz Larsen in a conference with leaders of the German Lutheran mission societies, where the problem of "orphaned missions" overseas was in the forefront and the need for international cooperation foremost. Bachmann emphasized that the day called for a reconciled evangelical faith among Lutherans of Europe, America, and worldwide, and that by faithfulness in specific tasks, "our United Lutheran Church will then be fulfilling . . . its world-mission."[91]

Amid the reports and business transactions there were personal touches. There was a gripping pause when the convention honored the memory of Theodore Emanuel Schmauk. By a rising vote the convention adopted a permanent memorial to this founding father. At the suggestion of the president, the convention sang "For All The Saints . . . " (no. 250, *Common Service Book),* and was led in prayer by David H. Bauslin (East Ohio Synod). "The moments were profoundly impressive," wrote the secretary, "and will never pass from the memories of those present."[92] Later, on another occasion, a cablegram from John A. Morehead, chairman of the Commission of the National Lutheran Council, brought "Warmest prayerful greetings from your representative serving among European suffering."[93]

Issues great and small crowded the agenda of the Washington Convention. *The Lutheran* and other publications had been giving a play-by-play account of developments during the first biennium. Clearly the ULCA had to come to terms with itself. A prominent issue was the place of women in the church. On the minds of everyone at the time was the newly passed Constitutional Amendment—the nineteenth—granting women the right to vote.[94] Would the ULCA follow suit? A step in that direction was taken. The three-man(!) Committee on Women's Work—Keiter, Kaehler, and Markward—recommended that "the Women's Missionary Society be accorded the privilege of advisory membership on all the Mission Boards of the Church." The convention adopted the report.[95] But the specific resolution, adopted the previous month by the Chicago Convention of the Women's Missionary Society went further, and was presented to the Washington Convention by WMS President, Mrs. J. G. Traver:

Be it Resolved, That the Women's Missionary Society of The United Lutheran Church in America request the United Lutheran Church in America to make such amendment to its Constitution and to the Constitutions of its Boards as is necessary in order to grant full voting membership to the representatives of the Women's Missionary Society who are advisory members of the various Boards of the Church.[96]

This resolution expressed the desire of the Women's Missionary Society to be an auxiliary in the true sense of the word and thus increase its helpfulness to the church. It was referred to the Executive Board.[97] Besides, we should bear in mind that the WMS in the several church bodies prior to the Merger had, to varying degrees, developed contacts and associations with similar organizations of women in other denominations or interdenominationally.

THE WASHINGTON DECLARATION

The main item on the convention agenda was the discussion and adoption of a declaration of "Principles Concerning the Church and Its External Relationships," which came to be known simply as the Washington Declaration. Earlier in this chapter we followed its process of formation under the dual authorship of Knubel and C. M. Jacobs. The declaration had been circulated churchwide well in advance of the convention. Its place on the agenda was Tuesday afternoon, October 26, the last full day of the convention.[98] Prior to its formal presentation Jacobs read a prepared statement, describing how the document was a product of ULCA participation in the new National Lutheran Council. It was not a report to the council but was here being presented "as a new matter arising out of the needs of the United Lutheran Church and introduced by your Executive Board as a declaration necessary to meet these needs."[99] Knubel reaffirmed Jacobs, and explained that in the council "there arose a desire for cooperation, especially in home missions operations, as between the various Lutheran bodies. That is the real origin."[100] Therefore, the president concluded,

the Executive Board places it before you entirely independent of its associations, and is convinced that it gives expression to the truest heart of our Church, and that it holds something of the hope of our Church within it; and unanimously pleads with you that you may find it in your hearts to adopt it.[101]

Saving the preamble until last, Jacobs proceeded to read the five subsections of the declaration. These concerned: the catholic spirit in the church; the relation of the Evangelical Lutheran church bodies to one another; the organic union of Protestant churches; cooperative movements among the Protestant churches; and movements and organizations injurious to the Christian faith.[102] Given its character as an official document, anyone who knew its two authors could detect their interplay of style and thought. But it was Jacobs alone who read it to a hushed audience. If he sounded then as he sounded to many of his students, a dozen or more years later, the lucidity of expression and the calmness of conviction must have generated a quiet, indeed a joyful, confidence in his hearers.[103] Its subsequent importance warrants extensive quotation.

A. *Concerning the Catholic Spirit in the Church.* As the Lutheran Confessions declare (Augustana VII and VIII), "one holy church . . . will continue forever," functioning on earth through groups "who profess to be believers in Jesus Christ. . . ." By the term 'catholic,' therefore, we describe that quality of universality which belongs to the Church as a spiritual reality, or object of faith . . . and raises it above all local and temporal forms of expression in organization, rite and ceremony.[104] . . . It is necessary that . . . any such group of Christians shall define its relationship to other groups which also claim the name of Church, as well as to other groups and organizations which do not bear that name. The definition of relationships should be framed in the spirit of catholicity. . .

> 1. To declare unequivocally what it believes concerning Christ and His Gospel, and to endeavor to show that it has placed the true interpretation upon that Gospel . . . and to testify frankly and definitely against error. 2. To approach others without hostility, jealousy, suspicion or pride, in the sincere and humble desire to give and receive Christian service. 3. To grant cordial recognition of all agreements which are discovered between its own interpretation of the Gospel and that which others hold. 4. To cooperate with other Christians in works of serving love . . . insofar as this can be done without surrender of its interpretation of the Gospel, without denial of conviction, and without suppression of its testimony as to what it holds to be the truth.

B. *Concerning the Relation of the Evangelical Lutheran Church Bodies to One Another.* In the case of those Church Bodies calling themselves Evangelical Lutheran, and subscribing the Confessions which have always been regarded as the standard of Evangelical Lutheran doctrine, The United Lutheran Church in America recognizes no doctrinal reason against complete cooperation and organic union with such bodies.

C. *Concerning the Organic Union of Protestant Churches.*

In view of the widespread discussion concerning the union of Protestant Churches in America, we declare

> I. that we hold the union of Christians in a single organization to be of less importance than the agreement of Christians in the proclamation of the Gospel. Union of organization we hold . . . to be a matter of expediency; agreement in testimony to be a matter of principle.
>
> II. that a clear definition of what is meant by "Gospel" and "Sacrament" must precede any organic union of churches.
>
> III. we believe that the Protestant Church Bodies in America should endeavor to set forth, definitely and positively, the views of Christian truth for which each of them does now stand, in order that . . . the

nature and extent of their agreements and disagreements may become apparent.

    IV. that we recognize the obligation which rests upon us to make a clear and full declaration concerning the truth which we hold and . . . to give . . . our reason for accepting and maintaining the doctrines and principles set forth in the Confessions of the Evangelical Lutheran Church.

    V. that until a more complete unity of confession is attained. . . . The United Lutheran Church in America is bound in duty and in conscience to maintain its separate identity as a witness to the truth which it knows; and its members, its ministers, its pulpits, its fonts and its altars must testify only to that truth.

D. *Concerning Cooperative Movements among the Protestant Churches.*

    I. It is our earnest desire to cooperate with other Church Bodies in all such works which can be regarded as works of serving love . . . provided that such cooperation does not involve surrender of our interpretation of the Gospel, the denial of conviction, or the suppression of our testimony to what we hold to be the truth.

    II. Since we hold that cooperation is not an end in itself . . . our attitude must be determined by a consideration of (a) the purposes . . . , (b) the principles . . . , and (c) the effect which our participation will produce . . .

    III. Holding the following doctrines and principles, derived from the Holy Scriptures, to be fundamental to the Christian message, we propose them as a positive basis of practical cooperation among the Protestant Churches. . . We do not regard them as a summary of Lutheran doctrine, or as an addition to, a substitute for, or a modification of the Confessions of our Church; nor do we propose them as an adequate basis for an organic union of the Churches, but . . . a criterion by which . . . to determine our attitude toward proposed movements of cooperation.[105]

The declaration then cites nine doctrines:

1. The Fatherhood of God revealed in his son Jesus Christ.
2. The true Godhead of Jesus Christ and his redemption of the world.
3. The continuing activity of God the Holy Spirit.
4. The supreme importance of the Word of God and the Sacraments of Baptism and the Lord's Supper (including the Real Presence) as the means through which the Holy Spirit testifies of Christ.
5. The authority of the prophetic and apostolic Scriptures of the Old and New Testaments as the only rule and standard by which all doctrines and teachers are to be judged.
6. The reality and universality of sin.
7. The love and righteousness of God, who for Christ's sake bestows forgiveness and righteousness upon all who believe in Christ.
8. The present existence upon earth of the kingdom of God, founded by his Son Jesus Christ, . . . as a spiritual reality and object of faith.

9. The hope of Christ's second coming, to be the Judge of the living and the dead, and to complete the kingdom of God.[106]

In view of the above statements, the Declaration then qualifies United Lutheran Church participation in cooperative movements among Protestant Churches.

IV. In all cooperative movements we claim the right, and regard it as a duty, to testify freely to the truth as it is set forth in the Confessions of our Church, and we believe that the same right must be granted to every participating Church.

It is clear that this kind of attitude opened the way for ecumenical engagement in the 1920s and beyond. The Declaration further warns that "we cannot enter into cooperative organizations or movements whose activities lie outside the proper sphere of church activities."

V. [However,] the Church may definitely . . . commend to the pastors and members of its congregations . . . movements and organizations for social and political reform, the enforcement of law and order, the settlement of industrial conflict, the improvement of material environments of life, and the like.[107]

E. *Concerning movements and organizations subversive to the Christian faith.*

I. That we solemnly warn all our pastors and the members of our congregations against all teachers, sects, and organizations of any kind whose doctrines and principles contradict the truths set forth in Section D. III of this Declaration, or which limit their adherents or members in a free confession of their Christian faith.

II. That we warn them especially against all teachers, sects and societies whose doctrines and principles deny the reality of sin . . . [and] teach that men can be saved from sin, or can become righteous before God by their own works, or by any other means than the grace and mercy of God in Jesus Christ.

III. We therefore lay it upon the consciences of the pastors and the members of all our congregations to scrutinize with the utmost care the doctrines and principles of all teachers, sects, organizations and societies . . . which seek their adherence and support. In the application of this principle the Church should always appeal to a conscience which it is her sacred duty to enlighten, patiently and persistently, from the Word of God.[108]

Thus was lodge membership left to the individual conscience of the pastor, an openness severely criticized by other Lutheran groups throughout the life of the ULCA.

At the conclusion of the half-hour long reading, Jacobs, as promised, presented the Preamble to the Declaration. It stated:

In order that all misunderstandings and misconstructions of this Declaration, or of any of its parts, may be avoided, The United Lutheran Church in America declares in advance that it does not regard the statements therein contained as altering or amending the Confessions of the Church in any particular, or as changing the doctrinal basis of The United Lutheran Church. On the contrary, it declares this Declaration nothing more than the application to present conditions of doctrines already contained in the Confessions.[109]

The adoption of the declaration as a whole was taken by a rising vote, which was unanimous. While standing, the convention sang two stanzas of Hymn 195, "A Mighty Fortress Is Our God."[110] Lest the implementation of the declaration be left open, Jacobs also submitted the following resolution: "That all Officers, Boards, Committees, and other agencies of the Church be instructed to govern their policies and actions by the principles here adopted." On motion the entire matter of "Relationships on the Basis of the Principles" here adopted was referred to the Executive Board with power.[111]

Despite this seemingly total coverage a problem remained with respect to the fifth section (E) of the declaration. According to the Church's constitution, the matter of discipline was in the hands of the synods. In effect this was a loophole, not easily understood by outsiders, regarding the power of synods vis-a-vis the power of the ULCA concerning the external relations of synods (Declaration, Section D).[112] As for powers, the United Lutheran Church, as defined in the Constitution (Article VIII, 1)

> shall have power to form and dissolve relations with other general bodies, organizations and movements. To secure uniform and consistent practice no synod, conference, or board, or any official representative thereof, shall have power of independent affiliation with general organizations and movements.[113]

This contrast reflected the reality of the United Lutheran Church as a federation, and its developing identity as a single body.

During those October days the reports of the several boards and other units as well as the growing sense of fellowship in shouldering common obligations gave proof of the unifying process at work. Near the end the convention voted "That the United Lutheran Church looks with approval upon the holding of an Ecumenical Lutheran Conference in the year 1922 or 1923.[114] The convention adjourned late Wednesday afternoon, October 27th, one day sooner than planned. More than could immediately become apparent, the United Lutheran Church had set its course. The critical first biennium and the gathered antecedent experience, as well as the wise leadership and a determined constituency, had given the ULCA an encouraging start.[115] There would be twenty more biennial conventions held in cities from coast to coast, but for the life of the ULCA, and beyond, the Washington Declaration, under the leading of the Holy Spirit, would prove an invaluable guide.

NOTES

1. On the Federal Council, Ahlstrom, *Religious History*, 802-804. ULCA *Minutes* 1922: 86.

2. Ahlstrom, *Religious History*, 896-99.

3. This commonplace observation became evident from the formation of the National Lutheran Council and the careful accounting of its statistician, George Linn Kieffer. See *The Lutheran World Almanac for 1921.*

4. Full text in ULCA *Minutes* 1920: 92-100. Slightly abridged in R. C. Wolf, *Documents*, #148, 346-53.

5. Scherer, M. G. G., Executive Board Report, ULCA *Minutes* 1920: 61-62. For a fuller account, see also "Convention of Officials in Holy Trinity, New York," *The Lutheran*, March 6 and 13, 1919.

6. Burgess, *Pittsburgh Synod*, 165-186.

7. A. R. Wentz, *Lutheran Church*, 388-98.

8. ULCA *Minutes* 1920: 6, 68, 101, 488f.; ULCA *Minutes* 1922: 67, 309.

9. R. C. Wolf, *Documents*, #119, p. 276.

10. ULCA *Minutes* 1920: 410-16.

11. Board of Foreign Missions, ULCA *Minutes* 1920: 129-45.

12. Board of Inner Mission, ULCA *Minutes* 1920: 293-403.

13. ULCA *Minutes* 1920: 54-55, 305 ff., 535.

14. The church magazines were important shapers of opinion, often over several generations.

15. ULCA *Minutes* 1920: 62.

16. See Meuser, Fred W., *The Formation of the American Lutheran Church: A Case Study in Lutheran Unity* (Columbus, OH: Wartburg Press, 1958.), (Hereafter cited as Meuser, *Formation of the ALC.*)

17. Nelson, E. Clifford and Eugene Fevold, *The Lutheran Church among Norwegian Americans*, 2 vols. (Minneapolis: Augsburg Publishing House, 1960), 2: 183-225 and 288-89.

18. Arden, Gothard Everett, *Augustana Heritage* (Rock Island, Illinois: Augustana Press, 1963), 256.

19. Meuser, *Formation of the ALC* 234-35, esp. note 17.

20. R. C. Wolf, *Documents*, # 125-129, 285-91.

21. *Encyclopedia of the Lutheran Church*, 3:2136.

22. Meuser, *Formation of the ALC*, 149-50.

23. Nyholm, Paul C., *The Americanization of the Danish Lutheran Churches in America: A Study in Immigrant History*, Studies in Church History (Kirkehistoriske Studier) II:16 (Copenhagen: Institute for Danish Church History, 1963), 62-63, 75-79, 400.

24. Mortensen, Enok, *The Danish Lutheran Church in America: The History and Heritage of the American Evangelical Lutheran Church* (Philadelphia: Board of Publication of the Lutheran Church in America, 1967), 9-16, 45-48, 179-80.

25. Nelson *Lutherans in North America*, 341-44, 404.

26. Eylands, Vladimir, *Lutherans in Canada* (Winnipeg: Icelandic Synod, 1945.) 191-95; *Lutheran Almanac for 1921*, 132-34.

27. *Lutheran Almanac for 1921*, 94-95.

28. *Annual Report of the National Lutheran Council*, 1919-1921 (New York: National Lutheran Council, 1919), 4 (Nov. 6, 1919). (Hereafter cited, as in this case, as *Annual Report of the NLC*, 1919-1921, 4.)

29. F. K. Wentz, *Lutherans in Concert*, 202-206.

30. Nelson, E. Clifford, *Lutheranism in North America 1914-1970* (Minneapolis: Augsburg, 1972), 35, n. 58. (Hereafter cited as Nelson, *Lutheranism*.)

31. Friedrich Bente, "United Synod of the Evangelical Lutheran Church in the South," *Lehre und Wehre* 63 (January 1917): 16.

32. Theodore Graebner, "'Richtungen' in der amerikanisch-lutherischen Kirche," *Lehre und Wehre* 63 (April 1917): 183-84. Both quotations (Bente and Graebner) are translated into English in Meyer, *Log Cabin*, 239.

33. ULCA *Minutes* 1918: 66.

34. Hauge, *Working Together*, 43.

35. Ibid.

36. Nelson, *Lutheranism*, 22, 36 n. 62.

37. Ibid., 24-27.

38. Ibid., 22.

39. F. C. Wolf, *Documents*, #133, p. 298.

40. Ibid., 299-300.

41. Ibid., 301.

42. Nelson, *Lutheranism*, 23.

43. Knubel, Frederick H., "Essentials of a Catholic Spirit," in *Lutheran Church Review* Vol. 38 (1919): 187-97; Jacobs, Henry E., "Constructive Lutheranism," in *Lutheran Church Review* Vol. 38 (1919): 198-212. (Hereafter cited as Jacobs, "Constructive Lutheranism.")

44. Jacobs, "Constructive Lutheranism," 198.

45. Ibid., 204-205.

46. Ibid., 209.

47. Nelson, *Lutheranism*, 22.

48. Wolf, *Documents*, # 134, pp. 301-312.

49. Nelson, *Lutheranism*, 36 n. 71.

50. Ibid., 25, 37 n. 77.

51. Summary of the Washington Declaration in ibid., 24-25.

52. Ibid., 23. Notice the role of Lars W. Boe in reassuring Knubel in regard to Stub.

53. *The Annual Report of the NLC, 1920*, is largely concerned with descriptions of such overseas help.

54. Nelson, *Lutheranism*, 37, notes 79-80.

55. Hauge, *Working Together*, 43.

56. Personal recollections of a classmate at the Philadelphia Seminary regarding Morehead, by Ernest F. Bachmann (the author's father). Nelson, E. Clifford, *The Rise of World Lutheranism, An American Perspective*. (Philadelphia: Fortress,

1982), 87-99 and 186. (Hereafter cited as Nelson, *World Lutheranism.*)

57. F. K. Wentz, *Lutherans in Concert,* 44-66, 206.

58. *Encyclopedia of the Lutheran Church,* 2, s.v. "Missionary Conferences," by Oscar R. Rolander; ULCA *Minutes* 1920: 122-23.

59. E. Theodore Bachmann and Mercia Brenne Bachmann, *Lutheran Churches in the World* (Minneapolis: Augsburg, 1989), 214-15. (Hereafter cited as Bachmann, *Lutheran Churches,* 214-215.)

60. Ibid., 207-208.

61. ULCA *Minutes* 1920: 129-30; Joel Lakra, "The Gossner Evangelical Lutheran Church," ch. 4 in *The Lutheran Enterprise in India 1706-1952,* ed. C. H. Swavely. (Madras: Federation of Evangelical Lutheran Churches in India, 1952), 49-80. Lakra, son of the first president of the Gossner Church, graduated from the Lutheran Theological Seminary at Chicago/Maywood in 1926. He was a delegate to the Lutheran World Federation Assembly in Hannover, 1952. (See *The Proceedings of the Second Assembly of the Lutheran World Federation, Hannover, Germany, July 25-August 3, 1952,* 181. See also ULCA *Minutes* 1924: 163, when Lakra was introduced to the ULCA Chicago Convention.)

62. ULCA *Minutes* 1920: 130.

63. Bachmann, *Lutheran Churches,* 210-11.

64. ULCA *Minutes* 1922: 149.

65. Harvey Americus Weller report, ULCA *Minutes* 1920: 447f.

66. F. K. Wentz, *Lutherans in Concert,* 36-37.

67. Ibid., 36.

68. *Annual Report of the NLC, 1919,* 44-51.

69. Wentz, Abdel Ross, *History of the Evangelical Lutheran Synod of Maryland* (Harrisburg, Pennsylvania: Evangelical Press, 1920), 284.

70. Ibid., 284, 289ff.

71. Ibid., 293.

72. ULCA *Minutes* 1920: 5.

73. Ibid., 26ff.

74. Ibid., 6-15.

75. Ibid., 49, 53.

76. Ibid., 26-27.

77. Ibid., 27, 54-55.

78. Ibid., 32-33.

79. Ibid., 33-36.

80. Ibid., 34, 36-38.

81. Ibid., 40.

82. Ibid.

83. Ibid., 41.

84. Ibid., 54.

85. Ibid., 56.

86. Ibid.

87. Ibid., 105. L. B. Wolf attended the IMC meeting, Mansfield College, Oxford, July

1923. See Wolf, L. B, "The International Missionary Council at Oxford," *The Lutheran*, August 23, 1923.

88. ULCA *Minutes* 1920: 105.

89. Ibid., 28.

90. Ibid., 254.

91. Ibid., 255.

92. ULCA *Minutes* 1920: 108.

93. Ibid., 311-12.

94. The State of Tennessee vote was decisive for passage of the Nineteenth Amendment, August 24, 1920.

95. ULCA *Minutes* 1920: 463, 466.

96. Ibid., 466.

97. ULCA *Minutes* 1920: 466.

98. Ibid., 450-56.

99. Charles M. Jacobs, "The Washington Declaration: An Interpretation," in *Lutheran Church Review*, Vol. 40 (January 1921): 1-21. ULCA *Minutes* 1920: 454.

100. ULCA *Minutes* 1920: 453.

101. Ibid.

102. Declaration text, ULCA *Minutes* 1920: 92-100 (in full but minus small changes as amended by the Convention.) F. C. Wolf, *Documents*, #148, 346-55, slightly abridged.

103. Author's recollection from student days at Philadelphia Seminary, Class of 1937.

104. ULCA *Minutes* 1920: 94.

105. Ibid., 95-99.

106. Ibid., 99.

107. Ibid.

108. Ibid., 100.

109. Ibid., 93. Preamble to the Declaration.

110. Ibid.

111. Ibid, 455.

112. ULCA *Minutes* 1918: 67.

113. The Constitution, ULCA *Minutes* 1918: 66.

114. ULCA *Minutes* 1920: 442.

115. Ibid., 498.

CHAPTER 6

THE EXPANSIVE TWENTIES

FLANKED BY LANDMARK EVENTS—the Versailles Treaty (1919) at one end and the financial crash (1929) at the other—the twenties were like a boisterous overture to the rest of the century. The American people, becoming more urban than rural, saw huge changes in daily life. In transportation, horse-drawn vehicles gave way to trucks and family cars. Airplanes and buses were making their bid to supplant trains and streetcars. At home, women got the vote in 1920. That same year, on January 16, Prohibition clamped down on alcoholic beverages, and the nation went officially dry for the next thirteen years. Radio broadcasting stations were beginning to supplement the newspapers and provide entertainment. In motion pictures, the sound track (1927) opened a new era. Jazz, the lively contribution of African Americans, came into its own in the twenties and soon gave its name to these years as the "jazz decade."

In science, the scene also was alive with change, highlighted by Albert Einstein's theory of relativity (English translation, 1921) in physics. Charles Darwin's theory of evolution became increasingly popularized in education; its collision course with traditional biblical religion was made public in the 1925 trial of John T. Scopes, a young Tennessee high school biology instructor. On the international political scene, communism, by its victory in the Russian revolution of 1917 and the creation of the Soviet Union, was feared and fought in many lands, including the United States. The U.S. refusal to recognize Russia politically fit in with the mood of isolationism.

In terms of religion the twenties were a time of conflict for the churches. The so-called Protestant establishment, the mainline denominations and the Federal Council of Churches, was torn by internal dissent and strife. One of the contending forces was the Social Gospel. Crossing denominational lines, this movement was committed to applying the precepts of Christian concern to an institutional perspective on the plight of the needy and to the furthering of corporate structures for justice in a society too ready to neglect its poor. Yet to achieve its ends, the Social Gospel tended to turn the Good News into law, to give priority to good works, and to becloud the redemptive work of Christ. In effect, its critics saw the Social Gospel as another form of liberalism and of the Federal Council's "Social Creed of the Churches" (1910), while its proponents sought to advance it as tantamount to "bringing in the Kingdom" of God on earth. Throughout the twenties theological liberalism, whether in higher criticism of the biblical texts or in doctrinal formulation, remained ensconced in most of the mainline seminaries.

Akin to the Social Gospel but backed by a more diversified constituency was the temperance movement and its commitment to a "dry Messiah." As noted above, the United States went officially dry during the twenties. Actually, however, this decade saw the rise of bootlegging and an unprecedented trafficking in illicit alcoholic beverages. For the society as a whole the Prohibition era, laudable though its aims might be, tended to foster addiction and to breed hypocrisy. For the churches, Prohibition furthered the use of grape juice in the celebration of the Lord's Supper. But for those continuing the use of wine—and most Lutheran congregations were in this category—there was Form 1412. When cleared through the office of a state prohibition director, "1412" authorized a pastor to purchase communion wine at an officially designated outlet.

Among the ardent supporters of Prohibition were the fundamentalists, mainly among those of a Reformed or Baptist derivation. Fundamentalism, as a term, became a popular designation of a certain pattern of evangelical Christian doctrine. Its basic teachings were set forth in a series of booklets called *The Fundamentals*. Published between 1910 and 1915, they were sent to the pastors of all English-speaking Protestant churches. Financing the venture was Lyman Stewart, an ardent Presbyterian and head of Union Oil Company in southern California. With its traditional evangelical doctrines rigidly and literally read from a verbally inspired Bible, Fundamentalism aimed to erect a wall to protect believers from the threats of "modernism," namely, liberalism and the Social Gospel.

During the 1920s, far more than today, the local congregation was a neighborhood church. But forces were already in evidence that, with the family automobile and extended public transportation, a new form of social mobility was in process. A relocation of families to more outlying parts of the city or into the suburbs would eventually lead also to a relocation of the congregation and a transfer of ownership of the church building. As the old moved out the new moved in, sometimes sectarian groups, sometimes recent immigrant or ethnic groups, and often African Americans who had migrated from the South during and since the war effort.

In contrast to the already mentioned contending forces, Protestants in the mainline churches supported significant and well-established interdenominational work, all of it older than and independent of the Federal Council of Churches, and most of it with international ties. During the twenties organizations and agencies such as the American Bible Society, the Young Men's and Young Women's Christian Associations, the American Sunday School Union, the International Society of Christian Endeavor, and, not least, the Student Volunteer Movement as well as the Foreign Missions Conference of North America and the Home Missions Council of North America were foremost in activating the laity in the life and work of the churches. These and other organizations like the Interseminary Movement, the United Council of Church Women, the United Stewardship Council, the National Protestant Council of Higher Education, the Missionary Education Movement, gave ample proof of the extensive involvement of lay men and women and young persons during a decade when postwar prosperity brought not only new challenges to help but also hazards of indifference.

Amid these interdenominational efforts, the twenties witnessed the unfolding of a movement toward Christian unity—ecumenism, as it would be called— that was to influence the course of church history for the rest of the century. In the summer of 1920, small preparatory meetings in and near Geneva laid the basis for organizations that would one day join in forming the World Council of Churches. Meanwhile, three separate movements of global outreach, each with substantial American participation, held their world conferences in the 1920s: Life and Work, Stockholm 1925; Faith and Order, Lausanne 1927; and the International Missionary Conference, Jerusalem 1928. The ULCA and the Augustana Synod took part, but other American Lutherans treated these developments cautiously. Roman Catholicism, growing rapidly in this decade, was still outside of these ecumenical endeavors.

THE ULCA IN CONFESSIONAL CONTEXT

During its forty-four-year life span the ULCA remained the largest among the self-governing Lutheran church bodies in North America. As the number of these bodies gradually diminished, from twenty-one in 1920 to fifteen in 1962, the appeal to confessional consolidation grew stronger. While the number of church bodies dwindled, membership totals grew. The ULCA in the twenties saw its baptized membership increase by some 27 percent, from 1,114,939 in 1920 to 1,424,386 a decade later. This would be the highest growth rate for the ULCA in any decade. In the twenties the number of congregations rose from 3,775 to 3,942. By the end of the decade the average congregation had about 360 baptized members. The roll of ordained ministers also climbed, from 2,823 to 3,284, an increase of about 15 percent. At the same time, the merger led to a reduction in the number of synods, from thirty-nine in 1920 to thirty-three a decade later.

What set the ULCA apart from the other Lutheran bodies was its heavy concentration in the East, and its longer history in America. In sharp contrast, other Lutherans of all types were concentrated in the Midwest and dominated the Lutheran scene in Texas as well as in the far West. Two-thirds of the ULCA membership being in the Middle Atlantic States, it is not surprising that Pennsylvania accounted for 22 percent of the entire church body. The South, from Virginia to Texas, claimed a bit more than 7 percent, but was influential beyond its numbers. The central Midwest—from Ohio to Illinois, plus Michigan and Wisconsin and easternmost Minnesota—comprised nearly 15 percent. The vast expanse from the Mississippi to the Pacific included only 6 percent of the ULCA. All of

Canada, from the Maritimes to British Columbia, trailed with 3.5 percent.

Given this distribution in 1920, the ULCA rate of growth during the twenties varied significantly by region. The nearly "saturated" East gained less than 10 percent. Elsewhere the growth rate was progressively higher: Canada nearly 19 percent; the central Midwest 29 percent; the South 33 percent; the church west of the Mississippi 60 percent. The greater the growth outside the East and South, the more numerous were the contacts, including points of competition and friction, with the other Lutherans. A churchwide paper like *The Lutheran* was effective at keeping its readers informed about these developments across the continent. There were specific challenges crying out for constructive response, such as the plight of the Pacific Seminary in Seattle and its backers who appealed for help from the church at large already at the first convention of the ULCA.

How the ULCA responded to problems on its own frontier, and how seriously it took these, is nowhere better illustrated than in the top-level study commission that headed for the Northwest, Western Canada, and the Pacific Coast on May 25, 1921. Heading it was President Knubel, accompanied by F. G. Gotwald, executive secretary of the Board of Education, and the Rev. J. F. Seibert, western secretary of the Board of Home Missions and Church Extension. Thanks to foresighted preparatory work, especially by ULCA Secretary Scherer, the survey commission was supplied with an inventory of Lutheran strength (or weakness) west of the Mississippi. From a ULCA point of view the facts must have been sobering. In this far region, including western Canada, the six separate Lutheran bodies— ULCA, Norwegian, Augustana, Joint Ohio, Iowa, and Synodical Conference (mainly Missouri)—had a combined total of 763,029 baptized members. Among these six the ULCA ranked fifth. In terms of the two territories farthest out, the ULCA Manitoba Synod included 5,021 members (12 percent) of the 41,673 Lutherans then in western Canada. On the Pacific coast the ULCA synods, California and Pacific (Oregon and Washington), together counted 7,711 members, of whom three out of four resided in California. Of the 42,234 Lutheran total in these three states the ULCA share was less than 20 percent.

When the team returned in early July, its findings as well as quantities of information on the growing edge of the church were put to good use by various units. *The Lutheran* featured this venture into the far West, and the Executive Board included large parts of the survey in its own report at the 1922 Buffalo convention.[1] The prairie provinces and the Pacific coast posed challenges to mission and ministerial education and competed valiantly for attention. Proportionately, these synods more than those in other parts of the continent made the ULCA responsive to its opportunities across the whole of North America.

Thus ULCA members, especially in the Midwest, needed to cope with the "other Lutherans." There was no escape, for the influence was reciprocal. One of the best examples of this sort of interaction during the 1920s was the movement that led to the formation of the American Lutheran Church in 1930. The story of this merger of the Joint Ohio Synod, the Synod of Iowa and other States, and the Buffalo Synod has been ably researched and told by Fred W. Meuser. Here a brief acknowledgment must suffice. Lutheran church unity was the desire of many, but the Ohio initiative (1914) to create an all-Lutheran federation in anticipation of the Reformation's four hundredth had failed. Instead, the Norwegian Lutheran Church of America was formed that year (1917) and the United Lutheran Church in America in 1918. The rise of the ULCA, as Meuser points out, "removed the final barrier to Iowa-Ohio fellowship and stimulated merger thinking as soon as fellowship had been declared."[2]

The criticism of the ULCA by Lenski in Ohio and Reu in Iowa continued during the twenties. In any case the ULCA was a prod, negatively as well as positively, toward the Iowa-Ohio merger. Besides, in the practical matter of partnership in the National Lutheran Council, the twenties made it increasingly clear that the smaller participating bodies should get together. So it was that during the twenties another new alliance, the American Lutheran Conference, was planned, and successfully launched in 1930. Its members—the new ALC as well as the Norwegians, the Augustana Swedes, the United Danes and the Lutheran Free Church (American all, but most still named by their ethnic roots)—formed a common front equal in size to the ULCA.[3]

At this point a brief notice of the Synodical Conference (1872) and its leading component, the Missouri Synod, will enable us to keep the other one-third of North America's Lutherans in the picture. In the confessional family the Synodical Conference, conservative to the core, stood at the end opposite to the ULCA. The twenties reawakened Missouri's sense of mission in the East. During the 1880s the Missourians had come into possession of St. Matthew's, New York City, the oldest Lutheran congregation in America, dating from the seventeenth century. The Missourian aim was to recover as much of eastern Lutheranism as possible, as well as keep the successive waves of German Lutheran immigrants from error or spiritual neglect. The New York City pastors and laymen of the Missouri Synod who in 1914 organized the American Lutheran Publicity Bureau, provided their synod with tools and materials for urban mission work unsurpassed by other Lutherans. In effect these developments gave the Missouri Synod two focal points: St. Louis and New York. The latter was the more irenic and understanding, taking a less critical view of the ULCA. In general, the Missouri Synod regarded the ULCA as a peculiar contradiction. One of its leading theologians (Professor Theodore Graebner, 1876-1950) thought that the ULCA constitution and official documents made it appear conservative enough, but that in practice (in what it permitted to be published and done by its pastors and others) it was too liberal.[4]

STRUCTURE AND FUNCTIONS

In its constitution the ULCA reminded itself as well as its constituent synods that "congregations are the primary bodies through which power committed by Christ to the church is normally exercised." Congregations needed each other. It was their pastors and lay delegates whose coming together bore the time-honored designation of "synod." Synods were the structural hallmark of the ULCA. From the oldest enduring synod, the Ministerium of Pennsylvania (1748), to the youngest (the West Virginia, 1912), the forty-five synods joining the ULCA in 1918 had each separately debated and voted to accept the constitution of the new general church body. In doing so they transferred limited powers to the national body, notably in external relations; in other respects they retained an ecclesial equivalent to "states rights" over against the national government. In contrast to the centralized authority in most other Lutheran bodies with their districts or conferences, there was a certain decentralization in the ULCA. Granted that the executive branch had a heavy concentration of authority for certain activities,[5] there were still broad areas where the synods were relatively independent. This was particularly noticeable when there was talk of further union among Lutherans. Much as other Lutherans might object to certain practices or writings on the part of ULCA pastors or congregations, and might call for the ULCA to discipline its erring members, such discipline remained the duty of the respective synods. The president of the ULCA might exhort or admonish, but he had no power or authority to intervene directly.

Conventions

The United Lutheran Church in America has been called "a body of synods held together by conventions." Without belaboring the pun, it is a welcome fact that the biennial conventions punctuate the story of the united church and give meaning to its ongoing process of formation. The conventions were designed to be the legislative branch of the church and clearing house for reports. Earlier chapters have relied heavily on the reported proceedings of the formative churchwide assemblies in New York and Washington. In this narrative of the twenties, the punctuation is provided by gatherings in four more cities: 1922, Buffalo, New York, that storied western terminus of the Erie Canal and gateway to the West; 1924, Chicago, America's second largest city and center of gravity for a continent; 1926, Richmond, Virginia, leading city of the Old Dominion and capital of the Confederacy during the Civil War; 1928, Erie, Pennsylvania, the Keystone State's busy port and industrial center on the Great Lakes. Just as it was the intention to acquaint the delegates and the people in the region with each other, so also it is our opportunity to learn something about the Lutheran constituency at that time in various parts of the country. Each of these four cities has its own tale to be told.

Buffalo, 1922. Invitations came from various cities and their churches but the decision lay with the United Church's Executive Board in New York City. Its choice fell upon the city at the opposite end of the Empire State; a city teeming with industry and transportation as well as alive with culture and religion. Roman Catholicism was prominent. Among Protestants, Lutheranism, largely of German immigrant stock, was a considerable force.

Holy Trinity, at 1080 Main Street, was a recognized leader among Buffalo's sixteen United Lutheran congregations.[6] Founded in 1879, it was the first English-using Lutheran church in town. By contrast, St. John's, on Hickory near Broadway, begun in 1833 and for long a German-speaking congregation, stood out as the "Mother Church" of Buffalo's Lutherans. The author's maternal grandfather, John Jacob Brezing, as pastor of St. John's encouraged the formation of English-using congregations, including Concordia, where the author's father was the first pastor. The Rev. Frederick Augustus Kaehler, a native of Erie and graduate of the Philadelphia Seminary, in 1922 was in his thirty-eighth year as pastor of Holy Trinity. His encouragement of younger pastors, his leadership among New York State Lutherans, and his active role in the urban scene provided background for his attractive pastoral ministry. That the Third Biennial Convention of the United Lutheran Church was opened by worshiping in Holy Trinity Church brought recognition to the congregation and its pastor, a member of the far-flung New York and New England Synod.[7]

"The City of Buffalo Is Ready," ran the headline in the church press. Hotel rooms were reserved for the delegates. The spacious parish house of Holy Trinity Church had been refurbished. Its oversized auditorium and available office space were set to receive the business sessions of the Third Biennial Convention.

> Preparatory to the opening of the Third Biennial Convention of the United Lutheran Church in America, delegates-elect from the Constituent Synods, a large number of visitors and many members of the Churches of the Convention City assembled to participate in The Service at Holy Trinity Lutheran Church, Buffalo, N.Y. on Tuesday evening, October 17, 1922, at eight o'clock. The Order of Public Confession was conducted by the Rev. H. A. Weller and the other clerical members of the Executive Board assisted in The Service and the administration of the Sacrament of the Altar.[8]

Thus read the 1922 *Minutes* of the ULCA. Almost the same words, like a liturgy, would be recorded every two years until 1962. The conventions were always in October and began with a worship service, the president preaching and members of the Executive Board administering the Lord's Supper.

"Despite the thorough preparation," according to *The Lutheran*, when the convention opened "there was a noticeable lack of enthusiasm."[9] Instead, there was concern. The president of the church was ill with a reported attack of pneumonia, but was on the mend. At the opening service, the president's sermon was read by Secretary M. G. G. Scherer. Subsequently, by action of the Executive Board, one of its members, Professor Jacob A. Clutz (Gettysburg), an eloquent septuagenarian, presided at the opening of the convention. Then, Ellis B. Burgess, president of the Pittsburgh Synod, was elected Acting Chairman of the convention. Although Knubel was able to arrive on Monday, the 21st, he asked Burgess to continue.[10] With Knubel present and Burgess presiding, the spirit of the convention picked up.

Particularly prominent at the Buffalo Convention were ULCA women, whose missionary spirit contributed greatly to a developing unity of purpose.

On November 9, *The Lutheran* reported:

> Among the hundreds who followed with interest the events and decisions of the
> recent Biennial Convention of the United Lutheran Church in America were many
> of our women. Wives of pastor delegates, missionaries and other leading women
> who figured on the program, women of various capacities, drawn to the conven-
> tion by a real devotion to its purposes, made a noticeable part of the large gather-
> ings of the general sessions.[11]

The Women's Missionary Society had a display of its publications in the main
exhibit room of the convention. This also served as the convention information
center.

By happy foresight, the Women's Missionary Society of the Western
Conference of the New York and New England Synod had arranged to have its
convention at Parkside Lutheran Church in Buffalo during the same days as the
ULCA Convention. By this arrangement, the Conference meeting could draw its
speakers from the "great Convention." Mrs. E. C. Cronk, president of the national WMS was present and spoke several times on the various women's mission
projects, including a new one, a girl's school in Japan. This project was also
endorsed by Mrs. Lippard, a missionary to Japan. Other speakers were the Rev.
F. L. Coleman, missionary in India, and Morehead, the National Lutheran
Council's representative in Europe. The work with students at Cornell
University was presented by Miss Grace Henrich. During the convention period,
families of the Buffalo churches entertained in their homes all the missionaries,
as well as the representatives from the senior classes of all the ULCA seminaries.
On Monday, the hostesses and their guests lunched together at the College Club
in order to "cement their relationship." The friendships formed at conventions
helped to consolidate unity in the new ULCA.

Chicago, 1924. Wicker Park Lutheran Church, at Hoyne and LeMoyne, was
the place of worship and starting point of the Fourth Biennial Convention.
There, on Chicago's West Side, stood the Graystone Neo-Gothic edifice with its
characteristic rose window and, in the corner, its square and massively squat
tower.[12] Its architectural style and sturdy construction looked fully fireproof as if
saying never again to the fiery holocaust that had destroyed so much of the
Windy City in 1871. The pastor of Wicker Park was the inimitable Simon Peter
Long. In 1924, he was sixty-four years of age and rounding out his sixth year at
Wicker Park. He was an Ohioan by birth and education, having received his theological education at Capital University's Seminary. For fifteen years (1903-18),
he had served in Mansfield, Ohio, as a pastor in the General Synod's Wittenberg
Synod.[13] In the year of the ULCA merger, Long accepted a call to Chicago, to a
congregation which, until then, had been a member of the General Council's
Chicago Synod.

In those days, some fifty of Chicago's approximately two hundred Lutheran
congregations were members of the two United Lutheran synods, the Illinois
and the Wartburg. The Missouri Synod claimed about the same number, while

the rest were divided among the Swedish Augustana, the Norwegian Lutheran and the smaller Scandinavian bodies, the Iowa Synod, and others. In this setting, the United Lutherans, in terms of pastors and congregations, were manifestly in a minority, but one that was growing.[14]

After the convention's opening service of worship at Wicker Park, the business sessions and special programs took place at the famed Edgewater Beach Hotel on the shore of Lake Michigan. From there, as from a point on the urban periphery, Chicago could be seen in better perspective. Unlike New York where Lutherans at that time were the second largest Protestant communion (after the Episcopalians), here in Chicago they were the largest, and the most divided. To meet here under the banner of a United Lutheran Church seemed "Eastern" and remote from reality. But the United Lutherans were future-oriented. The establishment of the Chicago Lutheran Theological Seminary (1891)—and its relocation to suburban Maywood in 1910 from the property that soon became famous in the baseball world as Wrigley Field—was a challenge to all Lutherans. This was the one midwestern seminary where Lutherans of all ethnic brands could come and receive their full ministerial preparation in English. By the postwar era, Chicago had become the location of the greatest number of theological schools in the world. From a vantage point on the edge of Lake Michigan, the Chicago Seminary motto gains wider meaning: "The future of the Church will, under God, be determined by our Theological Seminaries."[15] Unfortunately, the Chicago Seminary itself had been plagued with trouble, as covered below.

Richmond, 1926. It was high time for the United Lutheran Church to give specific recognition to the third component of its merger, the South. Its Fifth Biennial Convention held forth in Richmond, Virginia, October 19-27, 1926.[16] First English Church, at Monument Avenue and 16th Street, was filled to overflowing for the service of worship on that opening Tuesday evening. Two massive towers in modern Gothic flanked the double entrance to the sanctuary of First Lutheran. At the time, this was the only Lutheran house of worship in Richmond. The congregation was organized after the end of the War between the States. The permanent edifice, after several relocations, was erected during the years just before 1911. It reflected the leadership of its dynamic and personable young pastor, John Jacob Scherer Jr., recently elected president of the Virginia Synod and younger brother to ULCA Secretary M. G. G. Scherer. He and his elder brother were the family's third generation in the ministry. The grandfather, Jacob Scherer, had come from North Carolina, been influenced by New Market's memorable pioneer pastor, Paul Henkel, to prepare for the ministry, and thereafter served many years in southwest Virginia.[17] Jacob's brother Daniel is remembered as a founding father of the Synod of the West, in Indiana and Illinois, in the 1830s.

Born in 1881, at Marion in southwest Virginia, J. J. Scherer Jr., pastor of the convention's host church, was educated at Roanoke College, graduated from Gettysburg Seminary in 1904, and was ordained by the Maryland Synod.[18] His two years of parish ministry in Fairmont, West Virginia, revealed his talents and readied him for a call to Richmond in 1906. For the next half-century he would be the pastor of First English Lutheran. In 1926, the year of the Convention, he was at his prime. As the Virginia Synod historian, William E. Eisenberg, reviews the Scherer ministry:

> Richmond was his parish. Among his people in congregation and community his stature assumed heroic proportions. He knew people, he loved people. He was ever a pastor at heart. . . . Being something of a politician himself, he became the unofficial spiritual advisor to generations of legislators and governors. He became a veritable institution in the city where he delighted to serve.[19]

The Richmond convention, in the year of the nation's sesquicentennial, was a reminder that already in colonial times the elements of a someday united Lutheran church were in the making also in the South.

Erie, 1928. In the twenties, Pennsylvania could still be called "the industrial titan" of North America, and the city of Erie was the Keystone State's busy port and manufacturing center on the Great Lakes. Commerce and industry had drawn rural folk and immigrants in great numbers. Roman Catholicism was strong. In a divided Protestantism, Lutherans ranked foremost numerically. In 1920, some of their congregations were still bilingual. They were mission-minded, also among non-practicing Romans. In 1922, Holy Trinity Italian Evangelical Lutheran church was organized, the first of its kind in America.[20]

The beginnings of Lutheranism in Erie go back to the year 1808, when twenty children and a mother were baptized. Among the occasional pastors coming this way was a certain Christian Frederick Heyer, later the pioneer American Lutheran missionary to India. As a licensed neophyte on the home front, Heyer served in Erie (1817-18).[21] The congregation later took the name St. John's and became the mother church of Erie's eventually nine Lutheran congregations. In the latter half of the nineteenth century, the big name among the pastors was Benze. Two brothers, Gustave Adolphe and Leopold Otto, natives of Warren, Pennsylvania, were both graduates of the Philadelphia Seminary. The elder was called to St. John's in 1891 and served there for the next fifty-two years. The younger served St. Stephan's, a mission of the Mother Church. Before the 1928 convention, he had moved westward along the Lake to Ashtabula, Ohio. The "Benze Era" being on the wane, the choice of a host church, as determined by local arrangements, went to an earlier offshoot of St. John's, Luther Memorial Evangelical Lutheran Church. It was here at 225 West 10th Street that the delegates elected by the synods opened the sixth convention of the United Lutheran Church in America with worship.

Luther Memorial Evangelical Lutheran Church, until 1887 called "First English Evangelical Lutheran Church of Erie," was founded in 1861. It was the fruit of The Lakeshore Mission, a society initiated under the inspiration of William Alfred Passavant, Pittsburgh's great promoter of Lutheran missionary work. Luther Memorial's first pastor, the brilliant John Henry Willibrandt Stuckenberg, was soon on leave as chaplain in the Civil War. Not long after his return, he gave himself fully to an examination of the role of the church in society. In 1880, his book, *Christian Sociology*, written while he was a professor at Wittenberg College and Seminary in Ohio, coincided with the end of his American career. He became pastor of the non-denominational American Church in Berlin. Spending most of his remaining years in Europe, he published writings on the church and society which led later scholars to regard him as the founder of the science of sociology.[22] After Stuckenberg came a succession of gifted pastors. G. Franklin Gehr later became a president of the Pittsburgh Synod (General Council). But it remained for Ephraim Maclay Gearhart (1880-1963) to lead Luther Memorial Church to new prominence.[23] Gearhart was called to Luther Memorial Church in 1922 and continued there as pastor for the next twenty-nine years. A native of Sunbury, Pennsylvania, he was educated for the ministry at nearby Susquehanna University and its Seminary. Coming to Erie in 1922 at age forty-two, and matured by sixteen years of parish experience in three different places, Gearhart stepped into an auspicious situation. Second in size only to St. John's, Luther Memorial had a building program under way. A favorable location had been acquired from the Young Men's Jewish Club. There was no lack of lay leadership and participation. The Ladies' Aid Society (active since Stuckenberg's pastorate), Women's Missionary Society, Luther League, Martin Luther Brotherhood, and still other societies enlisted the laity. The cornerstone for the new Luther Memorial was laid in June, 1925. A commodious dwelling next door did double duty as parsonage and parish house. For a pastor like E. M. Gearhart, it was right to be on the scene. His appearance in clericals showed a thoughtful visage: deep-set eyes, expansive forehead, receding dark hair, and a mouth poised as if to answer the next question.

Delegates and others attending the Erie Convention could readily be oriented. Luther Memorial, the newest church edifice in town, also had (apparently) the highest spire. Could the church seat a convention of eight hundred? A later pastor, David Mumford, replied, "If they sat close together."[24] Luther Memorial Church, Erie, typified the twenties when the religious scene across the land was being marked by brave new edifices. In light of this situation, and upon recommendation of the United Lutheran Church's recognized authorities, Jeremiah Franklin Ohl and Luther Dotterer Reed, the convention voted to upgrade the church's Committee on Church Architecture and make it a Bureau of Church Architecture. This change was to take effect January 1, 1930.[25] But by that time, as we know, economic conditions had begun to decline.

Officers

President, secretary, treasurer—these three were the top elected officers of the ULCA. The president and secretary were the only salaried officials, devoting full-time to their duties. Serving full-time was a novelty, and reflected the ULCA commitment to thorough administration. These officers were *ex-officio* members of the Executive Board.

President Knubel. During the first biennium, President Knubel had won the respect of the church members, both pastors and laity. Besides the care of all the churches and his special concern for the Atonement congregation where he served as part-time pastor until 1923, there were growing family responsibilities. The chronic and advancing illness of his wife, Christine, increased his fatherly burdens. Late in her life, his daughter Helen recalled that he handled them well. With affection she mentioned her father's sprightly conversation at the dinner table and then his love of playing games, especially word games with her and her brothers. "This would be hilarious, and then we'd each go to our tasks refreshed."[26]

In December, 1923, Christine was relieved of suffering by death. Thereafter, housekeepers were a blessing in the Knubel home, particularly in caring for the needs of Helen who had the stubborn after-effects of polio. First it was a cheerful woman named Minnie, and then the kindly and efficient Valerie Baker (recommended by a pastor in Sunbury, Pennsylvania). Knubel's second marriage was to Jenny Christ, in 1925. For years she had been the faithful and effective deaconess in Atonement parish. As noted earlier, she had been Pastor Knubel's right hand in much of the congregational work. As one of the first to be trained in the Baltimore Deaconess Motherhouse, she was imbued with the spirit of *diakonia*. Throughout his entire ministry Knubel showed his understanding of deaconess work as a specially recognized part of Christian ministry. Like his first, the second marriage was happy and supportive.

The gifts he displayed as church president made Knubel appear as an attractive candidate for other work as well, especially in theological education. He was urged to accept a professorship at Hamma Divinity School in Springfield, Ohio, on the campus of Wittenberg College. Then came a tempting offer from his alma mater, Gettysburg Seminary. Even though these were the best of the old General Synod schools he turned down their overtures graciously and swiftly.[27] From his close friend and theological mentor, Charles M. Jacobs, at the Philadelphia Seminary, the cradle of the former General Council, came a perceptive approach that bears repeating. It was January 1926, and Jacobs was wooing him for the presidency of the seminary. In view of the times—a crucial moment for the Lutheran legacy in the English-speaking world as well as in the world at large—Jacobs challenged Knubel. "There is no single thing that our church needs more than a broadening of its intellectual horizon," he wrote. "We must teach our men to think in large ways, as well as to act with vigor. To do this we must have one or more great institutions. We have the beginnings of such an institution here, but only the beginning." "To guide that development," Jacobs continued:

> we must have a man who possesses a rare combination of qualities—executive ability, deep consecration, knowledge of the church and its largest, often unfelt needs; the confidence of the church in the very fullest measure; a scholar's appreciation of the intellectual development which the future must produce. The church has many men who possess some of these qualities; it has very, very few who possess them all. If you decline to consider the matter, I would not know where to look for such a man.

The letter concluded, "Hopefully but fearfully though always faithfully, Jacobs."[28] A few days later came President Knubel's reply. He had apparently discussed the proposal with ULCA Treasurer, E. Clarence Miller, who was also a member of the Philadelphia Seminary Board. Appealing though it was, Knubel declined the proposal.[29] The Knubel presidency—*Deo favente*—would continue. Jacobs himself became seminary president.

Secretary Scherer. After his election in 1918, Secretary Scherer made the move from Charleston, South Carolina to "457," the Knabe Building on Fifth Avenue, the address of the National Lutheran Council as well. There, in contrast to the church president, the secretary worked in anonymity. Preparing the agenda and editing the *Minutes* of the biennial church conventions were a primary duty. Eventually he would fulfill it seven times. The agenda and minutes of boards and committees were his required reading, as were also the reports of commissions and other units. Synod minutes were likewise subject to the secretary's scrutiny. In every case his duty was to screen all actions or proposals for compatibility with the constitution and bylaws of the church and the principles as set forth in the Washington Declaration. In the twenties, when organizational function and structure were in need of discerning governance, the task of the secretary was of crucial import. And it was Scherer's duty to provide the president, and then the Executive Board, with the basic input for action. To the secretary also fell the task of keeping the clergy roster updated, carrying on a large correspondence with synods and individuals, notarizing official papers, serving notice of special meetings, representing the church at selected synodical and other meetings, and more besides. On occasion Scherer also presented a learned paper, for example, at the first World Conference on Faith and Order, in Lausanne, 1927.

The secretary's location, in proximity to the National Lutheran Council offices, kept him in close contact with the church bodies participating in the NLC. This close physical tie between the ULCA and the NLC at times became a cause of envy or anxiety on the part of the other participating bodies, especially since the total membership of the others about equaled that of the ULCA alone. There was more truth than ready wit to the midwesterners' occasional quip about the "Wise Men from the East."[30]

Treasurer Miller. Completing the trio of elected officers was ULCA treasurer, E. Clarence Miller (1867-1944). Himself a lifelong Philadelphian, he was one of those talented and committed laymen on whom the organized church relies and about whom its membership may know little more than the name, until later. The Miller family had for generations been members of St. John's, Philadelphia, the first all-English-speaking Lutheran congregation (1806) in America. Young Clarence, blessed with a goodly heritage, took up a career in business and finance. A partner in the Bioren Company, a brokerage firm, he eventually became its president and for some years headed the Philadelphia Stock Exchange, a task that frequently took him to New York. One who knew him well had this to say:

To complete the original triumvirate, the most dashing figure of all was the treasurer, Dr. E. Clarence Miller, a man of sparkling intelligence, of flowing generosity,
for many years a benefactor of the church, trim, suave, bright-spoken, a man
equally full of social and spiritual grace.

If the era of the 19th century extended to 1914, as historians agree that it did, E.
Clarence Miller was the first twentieth-century Lutheran. On September 1 of that
year [1914], he shocked everybody at the first meeting of the joint committee for
the approaching quadricentennial of the Reformation by proposing that the forth-
coming celebration three years later should be marked by no less than the union of
the three bodies then beginning what they intended to be only a tentative conversation about a single anniversary.[31]

E. Clarence Miller—the "E" was never omitted, for it distinguished him from
many another namesake—was the only one of the three officers elected on the
first ballot at the outset of the ULCA. He provided not only precise treasurer's
reports but also sage financial counsel and a perceptive policy on apportionment, a matter on which the full cooperation of the synods had to be cultivated
with patience and understanding. Dr. Miller (he had an honorary doctorate),
with many interests inside and outside the church, participated in such activities
as brought clergy and laity together. Among these was Philadelphia's Lutheran
Social Union, an annual event that crossed parochial and synodical lines, fostered sociability through personal acquaintance, and after dinner focused attention on some topic involving church and society.

For many years he was chairman of the board of the Philadelphia Seminary.
Like President Charles M. Jacobs, as well as ULCA President Knubel, E. Clarence
Miller was much concerned for quality theological education. With many others, he was convinced that the future of the church depended heavily on the
quality of its ministers. He contributed unstintingly to the support of the
Philadelphia Seminary, even to a fault when he personally and quietly, covered
its annual deficits.[32] Besides, his interest in the church's seminaries spanned the
continent, as seen in connection with Pacific Seminary.

Under these three officers, the ULCA made two major changes in the 1920s
regarding the headquarters of various operations. The Muhlenberg Building in
Philadelphia, an eight-story office structure built by the church near the city
center, was dedicated in 1924. Thereafter the address, 1228 Spruce Street,
became familiar to countless people. Here was the home base of many boards,
the editorial offices of *The Lutheran* and of other papers, and, doubly significant,
the operations and book store of the Board of Publication. The Lutheran
Church House in New York, a residential-type building of six stories, was purchased in 1928, with the help of a loan of $125,000 from the Board of
Publication.[33] At the new address, 39 East 35th Street, within walking distance of
the two major railroad stations (Pennsylvania and New York Central), the ULCA
became host to the slightly older NLC. A sense of belonging could now replace
the awareness of transiency which persisted at "437" despite all the history that
had been made there.

Boards and Their Functions

The Executive Board. Between the biennial conventions (the legislative body of the ULCA) the Executive Board governed the church. Of the board's twelve convention-elected members, six were clergymen of prominence and six were laymen of stature in their respective fields, three in law and three in business. The board's officers were the three elected officials of the church: the president, the secretary, and the treasurer. We can glimpse the dynamics of the Executive Board through the eyes and report of a relative outsider. Arthur H. Smith, D. D., the fifty-seven-year-old pastor of

E. CLARENCE MILLER

Trinity Church, Ashland, in rural Ohio, came on to the Executive Board in 1924. Ten of his fifteen colleagues were easterners and three were from the South. He had been appointed by President Knubel to fill the unexpired term of V. G. A. Tressler, a fellow Ohioan, a founding father of the ULCA and last president of the General Synod, whose death in September 1923 had removed a mentor of rich experience as well as a prime target of criticism due to his Masonic ties.[34] To someone such as Smith, accustomed to synodical turbulence, the meetings of the ULC Executive Board could appear like a constructive calm. His own Ohio Synod, a merger of four synods in 1920, was proving to be a creative blend from which the ULCA would benefit also.

> My first impression, upon attending my first meeting of the Board, was that of great surprise at the very wide scope of its work, and the great volume of business requiring attention. The activities of the whole Church, are [here] under survey, and it is a revelation of the real bigness of the Lutheran Church and the great variety of its contacts with the Kingdom of God. . . . The meetings begin on time and at once interest is fixed upon the succession of subjects requiring consideration. Often hours are given to the study of questions involving the larger policies and contacts of the Church, such as education, missions, our relation to the Federal Council of Churches, the coming World Conference on Faith and Order, and the Stockholm Conference on Life and Work last year. Not infrequently pause is made for prayer for divine guidance in reaching right decisions.[35]

What further impressed this newer member of the board, who was elected on his own in 1926, was:

> the remarkable spirit of harmony that exists in [it]. . . . The members come from different sections of the Church and represent varied activities, but there are no

factions or divisions, and, though they are men of positive opinions and convictions, they almost invariably after adequate discussion arrive at practically unanimous decisions."[36]

With an implied commendation to the officers and an affirmation of the far-sighted planning that went into the organizational structure, Arthur Smith concluded that

> the United Lutheran Church is functioning with surprising smoothness, considering the short interval since the merger. The congregations, Synods, and boards have adjusted themselves to the new and changed order with willingness and promptness, and the result is seen in the increased efficiency, larger service, and the inspiring vision of usefulness for the Kingdom which God plainly has in store for our beloved Lutheran Church.[37]

The Executive Board, situated at the organizational center, was instrumental in keeping the church body united and in furthering unification. We can observe this on two fronts: the internal, or domestic; the external, or interchurch. The Executive Board's internal agenda was divided into parts corresponding roughly to the functions of the church and then condensed into a sufficiently full report for presentation to the biennial convention. A typical report, like that to the 1922 convention, would contain: I. Sundry items requiring immediate attention; II. Synods, for example, an account of their merging; III. Boards and Elective Committees, some detail of their operation; IV. Coordination of inter-board activities, as in determining whether work in the Caribbean area should be done by the Board of Foreign Missions or that of Home Missions; VIII. Finance, including the Treasurer's report, plus the budget proposed for the next biennium and the apportionment to be laid on the synods, as well as the amounts paid by them; IX. Special items, like the challenge of women seeking better defined opportunities to serve in the church, in addition to deaconesses.

On this internal front, and balancing the powers of the Executive Board, was the Commission of Adjudication. To it, as to a supreme court, the church's synods might refer "all disputed questions of doctrine and practice" for interpretation and decision. Depending on the docket of cases, the nine commissioners convened when necessary. The commission's field was confined to ecclesiastical questions. Moot or debatable questions were beyond its scope. Nor did the commission have jurisdiction in the internal affairs of the church's constituent synods.

The external agenda was equally extensive and considerably more weighty. Again citing the 1922 example, the Executive Board was dealing in the area of "foreign affairs" on behalf and subject to the approval of the church body. The matters included: V. Preparations, in cooperation with the other participating bodies in the National Lutheran Council, for the eagerly anticipated first meeting of the Lutheran World Convention (Eisenach, 1923); VI. Agreements of mutual recognition with certain Lutheran churches in newly constituted European countries, Hungary, Czechoslovakia; VII. External relations with a number of other Lutheran churches in North America as well as with important inter-denominational agencies, notably the Federal Council of Churches. Here the ULCA position had to be spelled out with great care, because other Lutheran bodies had shunned the FCC and the "unionism" it represented. Step-by-step the Executive Board helped to guide and coordinate the church's functions.

As a new ecclesial body the ULCA was setting itself the task of unifying a great deal of diversity while preserving an accustomed evangelical liberty. In spiritual terms this meant preserving and extending the pure teaching of the Gospel; conserving and strengthening unity in the true faith; and expressing outwardly the spiritual unity of Lutheran congregations, seeking also "the unification of all Lutherans in one orthodox faith."[38] In functional terms this meant: awakening, coordinating, and directing the energies of the church into a variety of complementary operations. This was accomplished to a great extent through the work of boards. By analogy, what the synods were to its constituency, the boards were to the ULCA's organizational structure: they were relatively independent components. The number of members on a board, all elected by the church convention, ranged between nine and twenty-one. Each board had its own constitution, elected its own officers, called its own staff, could be separately incorporated (for receiving gifts, for example), yet shaped its policies in accord with those of the church body, submitted its reports and recommendations for action to the church convention for approval, and refrained from raising funds without authorization by the church body. No board had the right to enter upon any official relationship with another board of the church, nor with any other ecclesiastical body, without approval of the church convention. To keep the Executive Board as well as the officers informed, and to exercise an element of supervision, the secretary of the church reviewed the minutes of each board meeting.[39]

The ULCA started out with a dozen boards, accommodating itself to a number of special interests, particularly in missions at home and abroad. It also provided for over sixteen standing committees, appointed to serve in such diverse areas as publicity, ministerial education, or the *Common Service Book*. Everything possible was done to provide continuity for the policies and functions held by the merging bodies.[40] Deserving our attention in this chapter are three boards and theological education.

Home Missions. With the merger, the ULCA inherited no fewer than five boards working in different aspects of home mission. The Board of Home Missions and Church Extension planted and encouraged new congregations all across the country. The West Indian Mission Board concentrated its work in the Virgin Islands and Puerto Rico. It also followed West Indians who migrated to the U.S. and in the 1920s established Transfiguration Church in New York City for their benefit. This board also encouraged the ULCA to be more concerned for African Americans. The Immigrant Mission Board met the needs of thousands of Europeans pouring into American ports during the twenties. It had pastors who could speak the languages and meet the spiritual and cultural needs of Hungarians, Slavs, Italians, and others. The North West Mission Board's work spread from Texas into western Canada, also serving immigrants on the Great

Plains. Like the Immigrant Mission Board it sought pastors who understood the needs of these immigrants. Their best source were Kropp graduates in Germany who were given one or two years of further training in a ULCA seminary.

A committee on Jewish Mission was elected at the organizational convention in 1918. It consisted of fifteen members with the Rev. F. O. Evers as president.[41] At that time there was a Jewish Mission in Pittsburgh founded by the Rev. John Legum. Another mission was developing in Philadelphia with the Rev. Paul I. Morentz as missionary. During the first biennium a station was opened in Baltimore and in 1922 another in Toledo, Ohio. The ULCA was the only Lutheran church body having such a mission within its structure. The biennium reports kept the entire church aware of the work as well as the responsibility of every congregation to share the Gospel with Jewish people, and also to be aware of the difficulties converts faced in being ostracized by their families.[42]

In 1924 the convention in Chicago authorized a merger of these boards. To accomplish this without interrupting the work, each board nominated members for a joint commission of twenty-one to oversee the work until the new Board of American Missions could be legally established. The nominees were elected by the ULCA Executive Board in December of 1924. Convened by the Rev. F. F. Fry in January 1925, the Joint Commission organized and, with the cooperation of the Executive Board, worked out a satisfactory plan for continuing the work of all five agencies. When the charter of the Board of Home Missions and Church Extension (incorporated in 1874 by the General Synod) was legally transferred to the Board of American Missions of the ULCA, the Joint Commission was dissolved. In 1926, the Richmond convention elected a new board to carry on the merged work.[43] The first headquarters for the new board was Chicago, at the insistence of the Richmond convention.[44]

Mission Overseas. Despite the political isolationism in the America of the 1920, the overseas missions of the ULCA gave it the joy of partnership and sense of possession on an intercontinental scale. Granted that among the Norwegian or Swedish Lutherans the intensity of mission interest was higher and the support more generous, the ULCA, merged body that it was, had more diversity, and more with which to become acquainted. The sponsorship of missionaries overseas by scores of congregations cultivated the personal ties and gave evidence of the tireless efforts of the Women's Missionary Society. The zeal of a Virginian like Catherine Scherer Cronk, representative of many another promoter of missionary work, was contagious. In congregations and conferences, retreats or Sunday night hymn sings in the family circle, the forward movement of the Gospel had its theme song, "O Zion Haste, Thy Mission High Fulfilling/ To Tell To All The World That God Is Light." The lift of it all transcended denominational boundaries, and also caught up young people in an unfathomed fellowship. Yet that was but part of the story. Another part was ignorance.

As its president Knubel did not hesitate to take the ULCA membership to task for the "huge amount of indifference to foreign mission endeavor" that he saw prevailing in much of the church. The accompanying ignorance, he charged, "grows out of failure to recognize that foreign mission service is simply a part of the Church's whole work." In too many quarters mission overseas is regarded "as something more than duty requires." In fact, some have "even regarded as an unusual thing that officers of the Church would visit the India work."[45] In a churchwide report of 1928 Knubel glowingly described "Our India Mission." He and E. Clarence Miller, accompanied by their wives, had just returned from an intensive study tour of the Subcontinent and especially of the Andhra Lutheran Church. Only the previous year that mission had acquired the status of a self-governing church. With its two synods, the Guntur and the Rajahmundry, it bore many similarities to the ULCA, which was just then completing its first decade. The missionaries had offered—urged—several practical steps to help dispel ignorance in the ULCA: make full use of missionaries when they are home on furlough; avoid sentimentality; present the objectives of sound educational plans before talking finances; promote serious study of missionary problems (failure to do so belittles the missionary enterprise); present facts; set forth a "settled and sane program of development" and let it "challenge enduring enthusiasm."[46]

Knubel's own enthusiasm, intensified by his India tour, sang forth in thanksgiving for the Andhra Church. After seventy-five years there were now 135,000 baptized members, gathered in 1,400 congregations, touching 1,800 towns and villages. "The schools have 33,000 pupils, including high schools and [Andhra Christian] college. Our hospitals and dispensaries treated 66,000 patients last year. Try to visualize those cold figures as meaning just that many . . . beating human hearts."[47] The Andhra and Rajahmundry Synods were equivalent in size to the ULCA's New York Ministerium (Synod) and Illinois Synod. What kind of Christians are they?

> As here in America they are good, bad, and indifferent." The Indian leaders inspired confidence. "Pastors, catechists, heads and teachers of high schools and grade schools, physicians, nurses, prominent laymen—they are men and women whom to hear and to know commands respect and love, giving confidence for the future when the India Church will need less of our American guidance.[48]

The future, indeed, prefigured increasing conflict among competing forces: the British government, rising nationalism, a resurgent Islam, an all-embracing Hinduism, an aggressive educational development, a rising industrialism, a mounting racial consciousness, and more. All this called for a Christian response of high calibre on the part of indigenous leadership and missionaries. Many things in the Andhra Church could be improved. ULCA Treasurer Miller's close scrutinies recommended improvements in financial matters. The key sentence in the Knubel report, which he repeated twice, bears rereading now. It summarizes how interlinked the life of a church like the ULCA really is; how the church at home needs to take its partners overseas more seriously for the sake of understanding itself better. In Knubel's words, "There is no work our church is doing anywhere, of any kind, which is more prosperous and more promising than our mission work in India."[49]

Not only India but also, on a much smaller scale, Liberia, Japan, British Guiana, and Argentina offered opportunities for the ULCA to practice its own sense of wholeness and knowledge. Whether in an African traditional setting with American connections like Liberia, or in a multiracial colonial convergence like Guiana, there was much that Americans in their missionary enterprise could, and sometimes did, learn. Therefore the plea of the missionaries made sense: that their furloughs back in America be utilized more fully for interpretive deputation work. However, were the people ready to listen?

About the China field, newly acquired, there was curiosity. Terse like a headline the record ran: "On January 1, 1925, the China field was taken over from the Berlin Missionary Society of Germany, as authorized by the Chicago Convention on October 24, 1924."[50] The takeover, for $185,000, was really a relief action, since German mission efforts were largely bankrupt due to ruinous inflation in the homeland. What did the ULCA receive? During its colonial expansion, Germany had acquired from China a fishing port in the Shantung Province and transformed it into the modern city of Tsingtao. The Berlin Missionary Society began work there in 1898. In rapid sequence an impressive church edifice, plus buildings for schools and medical care were erected. The aim was not only to evangelize, but also to impress the Chinese with western culture. From Berlin came an able staff of missionaries. It was their model. During World War I the Mission suffered. But even when the Japanese laid siege to Tsingtao, the Mission survived the hardship mainly due to the Chinese Christians and missionaries who stayed during the trying days of virtually no outside support.

When the ULCA took over, some of the Berlin missionaries were transferred to the Canton Mission. However, five experienced persons remained in Shantung. Among them was the director, the Rev. Carl J. Voskamp, a man of impressive bearing who was regarded as an outstanding China missionary. When in 1926 he addressed the Richmond convention during the Foreign Mission evening, the assembled delegates and friends became more aware than ever of the China mission challenge in which they were now a part. Meanwhile, the first American missionary personnel—three couples, two singles—did their best to cope with the demands of a situation still bearing the marks of its German background but alive with national workers. Two other stations besides Tsingtao—Tsimo and Kiaochow—rounded out the field. By the end of the decade it was still a modest enterprise: missionaries fourteen; national workers 170; congregations seventy-one; baptized members 1,613; number of schools sixty-two; pupils 1,536. Progress toward self-support was evident. For the ULCA even a late start in China was important. In time some of its own missionaries would become veterans and gifted participants in the larger work. Among them were a Tsingtao trio: Paul P. Anspach, L. Grady Cooper, and Charles L. Reinbrecht, aided ably by their spouses.

The clouds on the horizon in the late twenties suggested that time was short. Over against the thousands of Christian missionaries and other outsiders there was a rising nationalism on the one hand, and on the other, communism. The impact of western culture in education drew growing protest. Beginnings of a renewed anti-Christian movement became more evident around the time of the 1922 Peking conference of the World Student Christian Federation. The aim of the WSCF at that time, as voiced by Christian students was "to bring the nations of the world together."[51]

When the ULCA entered China in 1925, specifically the Tsingtao area, it became associated with the Lutheran Church of China. The LCC, formed in 1917 and constituted three years later, fostered a cooperative relationship between the several Lutheran missionary societies and boards in Germany, Scandinavia and America working in China.[52] In light of the magnitude of Christian missions in China, it was important for Lutherans, a diverse minority, to stick together. They had four seats in the seventy-two-member National Christian Council of China.

Inner Mission (Christian Service). During the twenties there was a rapidly growing interest in Christian service, known at the time as Inner Mission. Most of the concern was carried on in institutions and a growing number of them. In 1922, sixty-four institutions from orphanages to hospitals were listed in the board's biennium report. Four years later, there were seventy-eight. However, in the field of child welfare there was a growing trend to place needy children in families rather than institutions. There was also a movement toward cooperation among the various church bodies. With its lines running out to numerous institutions and agencies in many ULCA synods and intertwined with kindred undertakings of other Lutheran constituencies not only at home but also overseas, the Inner Mission Board was active in the North American Inner Mission Conference (1922) and subsequently (with approval) in the International Inner Mission Federation, based in Germany.[53]

ULCA SEMINARIES

In 1918 the newly organized ULCA inherited a dozen theological seminaries. Each of the three merging church bodies contributed: the General Synod six: Hartwick, Gettysburg, Hamma/Wittenberg, Susquehanna, Western (Central), Martin Luther; the General Council five: Philadelphia, Chicago, Pacific, Waterloo, Saskatoon; the United Church South: Columbia. Two years later a thirteenth was added when most of the faculty and many students quit Chicago/Maywood and formed Northwestern, soon to settle in Minneapolis after cooling off in Fargo, North Dakota. The ULCA configuration of seminaries straddled the continent from East to West and from South to Canada. This was regionalism. But the heaviest concentration by far was the quintet along the Atlantic, where the oldest and one of the smallest, Hartwick (1797), lay in upstate New York. Three others—Gettysburg (1826), Susquehanna (1858), and Philadelphia (1864)—competed in the Quaker State. In the South it was Southern (1830), in Columbia, South Carolina.

And the Midwest? Here the number of ULCA seminaries in 1918 was four. Hamma/Wittenberg (1845) in Springfield, Ohio, an offshoot of Gettysburg, was the oldest and pioneered an English-using Lutheranism in the Buckeye State. Chicago/Maywood (1891) was different. It was a seminary of the General Council offering theological education in English to Lutherans of diverse ethnic backgrounds and of recent immigration, a venture of wide influence which peaked before the 1920s. Western (later Central) Seminary (1893) in Fremont, Nebraska, was the General Synod's outreach to the Great Plains and beyond. Martin Luther Seminary (1913-32) in Lincoln was its German language counterpart until the two merged in 1932.

Three seminaries remain to be accounted for on the ULCA perimeter. Ontario, Waterloo, became home in 1911 for the Lutheran College and Seminary, serving the eastern half of the commonwealth. Two years later, the Lutheran College and Seminary in Saskatoon made its frugal start for the prairie provinces. At the same time, Pacific Seminary (1911), as already noted, began its first life in Portland and then Seattle before being closed in 1932, only to rise again twenty years later in Berkeley.

Many observers were convinced that the new ULCA had too many seminaries. But there was no central authority to engineer consolidations. The ULCA followed the practice of the General Synod and General Council whereby institutions of the church, including colleges and seminaries, were the responsibility of the territorial synods. To be sure, the founders of the General Synod had intended otherwise. They designated Gettysburg as the Theological Seminary of the [Lutheran] General Synod. And in 1826 it could hardly have been other than that.[54] Practical considerations such as geography presently gave rise to a seminary in the south (1830), and another in Ohio (1845). And so on. A similar reliance on synodical support was necessarily followed in the less centralized General Council. In the United Synod South the seminary was under the general body's control. Reflecting on this part of the ULCA merger, Muhlenberg College President J. A. W. Haas reminisced that "one outstanding reservation was agreed upon. All institutions were to remain unaffected by the merger." Specifically:

> The synods which owned and controlled different institutions were to remain sole masters of their colleges and seminaries. They alone could determine and fix the policies. . . . The United Lutheran Church had only an advisory place in matters educational.[55]

With synods overlapping and seminaries competing, the ULCA thus inherited a chronic problem. Its ramifications extended to congregations and individuals. How would the problem be tackled, and specifically, what could the Board of Education do?

The new Northwestern Seminary became a test case, with a history. Midyear in 1920 trouble erupted in Chicago. The self-perpetuating board of the Chicago Seminary called the institution's promotional agent to the professorship of

English Bible, without prior consultation with the faculty. This arbitrary act was not the sole cause but rather the occasion that ignited an accumulation of resentments on the Maywood campus. Most of the faculty walked out and so did many of the students. Whether it was the seminary board's paternalism, or whatever else, the local feud shook the normally poised ULCA leadership. Significantly, the Chicago Seminary president, Elmer F. Krauss, a Philadelphia Seminary alumnus and a respected churchman, was the western representative on the first ULCA Executive Board. In the ensuing exchanges it remained for the president of the church to initiate negotiations leading ultimately to a seminary board made up of representatives elected by the supporting synods.[56]

Where would the excluded, or self-exiled, faculty of the Chicago Seminary go? And, more importantly for our larger question of polity, who should decide on the location? The English Evangelical Lutheran Synod of the Northwest provided a way out. The academic refugees first found a welcome in Fargo, North Dakota, where G. H. Gerberding had been a parish pastor. Indeed, the orders from the ULCA topside had been for the migrant faculty to remain west of the Mississippi. Honoring its patron synod, the school took the name Northwestern. But for the synod itself, whose headquarters were in Minneapolis, the city of Fargo was inconveniently far away. The Twin Cities were at the hub of Minnesota Lutheranism, and the Northwest Synod, so its leaders argued, was at the center of a rapidly expanding English-using Lutheran constituency. By mid-1922 the Northwest Synod voted to relocate the seminary from Fargo to Minneapolis. It did so contrary to the express admonition of the ULCA administration and the special committee of fifteen, which the 1920 convention had appointed to investigate the entire matter.[57]

The debate highlights the problem of the ULCA versus its synods in the matter of seminaries. The ULCA Constitution (VIII. Powers. Section 4) declares: "Each synod retains every power, right and jurisdiction in its own internal affairs not expressly delegated to the United Lutheran Church in America."[58] Consequently the Special ULCA Committee on Northwestern Seminary concluded:

> We recognize the constitutional right of a constituent synod to decide its internal affairs. . . . In deciding to remove the Seminary to Minneapolis . . . the Synod of the Northwest was acting under its constitutional right . . . but we deplore the fact that the Synod has seen fit to act contrary to the judgment of the Survey Commission, of the Executive Board and of the Board of Education of the United Lutheran Church in America.[59]

The Washington convention in 1920 had authorized a thorough survey of the ULCA situation in the Northwest, in western Canada, and on the entire United States Pacific coast. The challenge raised by the Pacific Seminary lay at the heart of the matter, but the rumblings in Chicago, and the likely consequences, provided a sense of urgency. The Survey Commission, headed by President Knubel, had a timely stopover with leaders of the Northwest Synod. This enabled Knubel to express his firm disapproval of relocating the errant seminary from Fargo to Minneapolis. Despite the president's stand, the educational plans of the Northwest Synod proceeded according to synodical wishes.[60]

The meeting of the commission in Seattle with Pacific President Bussard, Seminary President Kunzmann, and others became another point of encounter over synodical versus ULCA powers, specifically over the location of the young Pacific Seminary.[61] The Survey Commissioners did their best to persuade their hosts in favor of relocating Pacific Seminary to Berkeley, California. But the Pacific Synodists were adamant. The seminary campus was about a mile from the University of Washington. Since the fledgling seminary's 1914 move to Seattle, including the lean war years, the synod had worked hard to build up "our lone little Sem in the West." Even ULCA Treasurer E. Clarence Miller and other individuals back East had been helping financially. A summer camp for boys possibly electing the ministry as a career was beginning to flourish. Besides, it was argued, Seattle is at a midpoint on the Pacific coast, when taking Alaska into account! Synod President Bussard's correspondence with President Knubel had some harsh words for some persons back East who, in a few minutes in a valley in Pennsylvania (he meant Gotwald in Harrisburg), can decide what we need out here; as if years of striving here in the Northwest had not taught us what we need.[62] Bussard was complaining of the skimpiness of the grant received from the office of the Board of Education.

All of this was part of the struggle in the ULCA between the general body and its synods over seminaries, with the synods victorious. Northwestern Seminary was moved according to the preference of the Northwest Synod. Pacific Seminary did not move, also according to the preference of Pacific Synod. The responsibility for support as well as ownership and governance lay with the respective synods, while the church body itself remained deeply concerned. In the course of the Great Depression of the 1930s, Pacific Seminary would close in 1932, a decade after the Survey Commissioners had urged its relocation to Berkeley.

Dissatisfied with the status quo, successive ULCA conventions, in concert with and at times apart from the Board of Education, projected remedial action. The 1924 convention in Chicago authorized the appointment of a Commission on Theological Education. Already in 1922 a memorial from the Pittsburgh Synod, the first to have merged its two separate parts after the formation of the ULCA, called for a consolidation of the theological seminaries in the Northeast; meaning Hartwick, Philadelphia, Gettysburg, and Susquehanna.[63] A large order indeed. But it raised the issue of multiplicity of seminaries in the Midwest as well. As President Knubel reported, an informal conference in April, 1923, in Cleveland concerning the Chicago Seminary "was constantly found to be entering upon consideration of the whole theological problem of The United Lutheran Church in America."[64] The ten-member Commission on Theological Education (1924) included four seminary professors, four prominent pastors, and two highly regarded laymen (one a judge, the other a banker).[65] When this commission reported to the 1926 convention (Richmond, Virginia), its detailed presentation bore all the marks of a document seeking to teach the seminaries and their supporting synods as well as the church at large the basics of a full-orbed program. It read like a concerted effort to make up for any past remissness in policy and also as an attempt to apply what had been learned during the early years of a United church. Annual conferences of seminary professors not only cultivated mutual acquaintance but also a sharing of common concerns.[66] This was a necessary step.

Progress of sorts, surprising to some, was reported by the commission when the church convention assembled in Erie in 1928. The most touchy subject on the recent agenda had been the consolidation of seminaries in the Northeast. By and large, Gettysburg, Susquehanna, and Philadelphia expressed willingness and entertained a large vision of what a united effort could promise. But Hartwick Seminary, the oldest and smallest of the schools, marched to a different drummer. It envisioned its own task, though still discharged in remote upstate New York, as unfolding in relation to the greatest metropolis on the continent. Much as Wagner College had relocated from Rochester to Staten Island, Hartwick entertained hopes of a comparable strategic leap. Besides, some observers could detect similarities between Pacific Seminary's immovability on the West Coast and Hartwick's hold-out position on the East Coast. In 1930 Hartwick would indeed move, first to Brooklyn and then to Manhattan, and would eventually conclude a dozen years of life in the Metropolis before it too would close its doors in 1942.

The Wall Street "crash" of October 1929 and the ensuing Great Depression ushered in a different phase in virtually all aspects of national life. In ULCA seminary education, financial pressures contributed to some merging and closures, but the big question was still Philadelphia and Gettysburg. Increasingly cordial relations between the two major seminaries in the East reflected the spirit of the 1918 church merger. In 1919 the faculties of the two schools met and explored the possibilities of a possible merger. Among the leading proponents were the two church historians, Professor Abdel Ross Wentz, at Gettysburg, and Professor Charles M. Jacobs, at Philadelphia. Merger attempts were resumed in earnest between 1926 and 1928. In his history of the Philadelphia Seminary, Professor Theodore G. Tappert shows how the initial four-way merger plan soon became three-way when the Hartwick Seminary board demurred. Then the three Pennsylvania seminaries, including Susquehanna, worked out a mutually acceptable plan. This included Gettysburg providing the charter, while the site of the new campus would be in the Philadelphia area, within twenty miles of center city. Professors would be elected by the several supporting synods.[67]

As already noted, Professor C. M. Jacobs wrote his close friend, President Knubel, early in 1926 challenging him to consider the presidency of the Philadelphia Seminary, anticipating its expanded importance.[68] But Knubel declined. Then the supporting synods split over the project as such. The visionary venture failed.[69] Nevertheless, three other seminaries—Pacific, Martin

Luther, and Susquehanna—either closed or merged. Although these developments saddened some, the demise of these institutions as separate entities fit into a ready plan. The latter had grown out of the work of the Commission on Theological Education, the commission itself having been discharged after having made its last report in 1930.[70] One of its recommendations urged closer ties between the ULCA and its seminaries, a proposal that seemed to reflect the mood and mind of the majority in the church.

THE ULCA AND ITS EXTERNAL RELATIONSHIPS

Amid the manifold changes of the 1920s, the ULCA benefited greatly from having at hand the 1920 Washington "Declaration of Principles Concerning the Church and Its Relationships."

Inter-Lutheran

It became clear that the ULCA had pushed the "United" potential about as far as it would go. Despite the invitation to further union in the preamble of its constitution, the response was modest. Not many congregations and only one synod, the Slovak Zion (1919), joined the ULCA. Joining, on ULCA terms, required no statements of faith or practice in addition to those in the Lutheran Confessions. It was not ULCA doctrinal position that stifled further uniting but the perceived aberrations like unionism or lodge membership by individual pastors and others.

Yet even standing alone, the ULCA's numerical size played an important part in its external relationships. The National Lutheran Council was the common ground for a disparate group of participants, but numerically the ULCA was larger than all the rest combined. Lauritz Larsen, the first director of the NLC, came from the second largest group in the council, the Norwegian Lutheran Church of America. His Norse background, of the former Norwegian Synod, endowed him with a sense of churchliness and confessional conservatism. Even so, his church president, Hans Stub, feared that Larsen had come under the influence of Eastern Lutherans, meaning the ULCA. Like Knubel, Larsen had found Professor Charles Michael Jacobs of the Philadelphia Seminary not only a staunch support and theological mentor but also a valued friend. The National Lutheran Council was committed to the challenge of relief and reconstruction in Europe, particularly because of ULCA ties to Germany, but the funds were slow coming in.[71] Furthermore, the NLC followed the ULCA lead in fostering some outward manifestation of the worldwide fellowship of Lutherans. Leadership here came from Professor Jacobs and Lauritz Larsen, before his death in 1923.

The Washington convention of the ULCA in 1920 had voted "That the United Lutheran Church looks with approval upon the holding of an Ecumenical Lutheran Conference in Europe in the year 1922 or 1923."[72] Similar action came from other participating bodies in the National Lutheran Council. John A.

Morehead, chair of the NLC commissioners overseas, had learned firsthand how Lutheran churches in newly independent countries like Czechoslovakia, Poland, or Hungary felt themselves cut off.[73] The Austro-Hungarian empire was no more and the prewar ties between Germany and the Lutheran dispersion in eastern Europe were down. Ethnic German Lutheran communities struggled desperately in revolution-wracked Russia and the Ukraine. Wherever he traveled in Germany, but even more so outside it in the "Diaspora"" of dispersed Lutherans, Morehead came as a mediator of help. Not much, for the funds were low. Not at once, for communication and transportation were crippled. But it came, none the less.

So the idea of an internationally inclusive fellowship grew. The war had prevented the European General Lutheran Conference from meeting in Philadelphia in 1917. Now, with a war-weary Europe, it remained for American Lutherans to take the initiative. There was no precedent for a worldwide organization of Lutherans. The Augsburg Confession and Luther's *Small Catechism* provided the bond of a confessing faith, which was far more durable than any formal structure. But the times demanded an organized effort. Fortunately, Larsen and Jacobs had drafted a plan. The organization would be an association of churches, loosely linked, and bearing the tentative title: International Lutheran Conference; later changed to Lutheran World Convention.[74]

The initial negotiations had been undertaken by Morehead. At times he was the only American Lutheran in Europe. But he and Bishop Ludwig Ihmels of Saxony, president of the General Lutheran Conference, were the key members of an international (transatlantic) arrangements committee. Despite bouts of illness Morehead carried on. A near deadlock arose over the choice of location for the convention. The Americans, Jacobs and Larsen, had suggested a neutral country. The Hague was rejected by the Germans; Budapest likewise. When Jacobs learned that the Germans insisted on Eisenach, he wrote to Larsen:

> If we go to Eisenach it will seem that the Lutheran church of the world is . . . making [the church in Germany] the center of Lutheran work . . . . We will appear again as the branches and twigs of the great vine whose roots are in the soil of Saxony. At the present time I would give up the project.[75]

In spite of such frustration, Jacobs and many other American Lutherans, including President Knubel, did not give up their determination to further the ties engendered by postwar assistance. The importance of this aid, which, coupled with personal contacts in many countries, had awakened and nurtured the bond of confessional kinship, cannot be overestimated. In America the NLC and in Germany the General Conference created a joint General Committee on Arrangements. After some tension, the meeting place was agreed upon. It would be Eisenach. The wisdom of this decision was justified by the economic situation in central Europe. On the day the convention opened, August 19th, 1923, the German mark was selling at three million for one dollar. If the convention had been held in Holland or Switzerland, as Americans initially preferred, one day's expense for a German delegate would have consumed a month's salary or more.[76]

For the participants at Eisenach, it was history in the making. A little over one-half of the 147 delegates were from the host country. The next largest group was the North American, with eighteen from the United States and one from Canada. Of the seventeen European countries, recently freed nations like Finland (seven delegates) or Estonia (four), and restored nations like Poland (four), or a created nation like Czechoslovakia (five), were proportionately better represented than the almost homogeneously Lutheran Scandinavian countries, including Sweden (five), Denmark (three), and Norway (two). From Asia, India had three representatives (two nationals), and China one. Russia, now under Communism, had one, Theophil Meyer, Bishop from Moscow. Neither Africa nor Latin America had representation.

Reporting on the convention in *The Lutheran*, C. M. Jacobs noted the importance of John Morehead, who is "personally known to more of those present than any other man" and whose appearance "marked him as the most important figure in world Lutheranism."[77] The next was the scholarly and saintly Bishop Ihmels of the Church of Saxony. As president of the convention Ihmels opened the gathering with an address of welcome, then Morehead gave his address, which set the tone of the convention, "Let us help one another." *The Lutheran* gave detailed reports of the convention and highlighted the prominence of ULCA delegates. President Knubel gave a major address in English (all the others had been in German) on his assigned theme, "That they may all be one." Professor A. R. Wentz of Gettysburg Seminary was one of several who summarized the convention on the last day. In his analysis, the "First Ecumenical Council of the Lutheran Church has been a distinct success." There prevailed "a general spirit of brotherly love and Christian spirit" as well as "unity" in Lutheran essentials among a "diverse gathering from many lands with many tongues—varied as the nations of earth themselves." The convention "did not rest with a consideration of abstract themes but definitely "addressed itself to practical problems . . . directed its eyes to the future, and gave assurance that the first Lutheran World Convention shall not be the last one."[78]

Before the decade ended, a second Lutheran World Convention took place in Copenhagen, Denmark (June 26-July 4, 1929). An executive committee, chosen at Eisenach to plan a second convention, had continued to work for Lutheran unity. Deputations had been sent to minority churches in Hungary, Yugoslavia, Austria, and France. Concern was shown for the church in Russia and for the new church bodies in Asia. In an attempt to include these churches in the program at Copenhagen, there were some misunderstandings reviving the tensions between Americans and Germans. Thanks to the skillful and diplomatic leadership of Morehead and others, preparations were completed and an inspiring and successful convention brought new hopes for Lutheran unity. Americans were less conspicuous and the Scandinavians moreso, including the wonderful hospitality of the Danes. The convention closed with a general agreement that the

Lutheran World Convention had established itself as an ongoing institution, that the executive committee would be the focal point of administrative affairs, that there would be national committees; and that the office of president would "as a rule" be rotated among German, Scandinavian, and American church leaders.[79]

Interconfessional

Inter-Lutheran, inter-Protestant, or interconfessional, the fact that the new church body possessed a "Declaration of Principles concerning the Church and Its Relationships" helped to keep it on course. President Knubel and the Executive Board found it so; likewise the synodical presidents and their governing units, as well as the boards of the church and their staffs. There was no escaping external relationships. In inter-Lutheran relations there was a recognized common confessional base. Inter-denominational cooperation—as in a council of churches, local or national—was determined by a principle called "evangelical and representative." In ULCA terms this meant trinitarian faith and churchly (not individual) participation.

An early example of how this principle was applied occurred in 1922 when the United Lutheran Church defined its relation to the Federal Council of Churches as a consultative relationship. In this manner it struck a compromise. On the one hand, on a limited basis the ULCA continued the earlier relationship of the General Synod as a full member of the Federal Council. On the other hand, the ULCA showed that it too was critical of the Federal Council at certain points. Unlike the other Lutheran bodies, however, it chose to participate without fear of "unionism." The report of the ULCA's three-member delegation to the Federal Council's Executive Committee meeting (Columbus, Ohio, 1923), illustrates the point: "Many things were said . . . that met with the hearty approval of your delegation; many other things only served to deepen the conviction that our United Lutheran Church was wise in sharply defining her relations to the Council."[80]

The Federal Council's manifest policy to gloss over doctrinal substance for the sake of practical cooperation and social action prompted the United Lutheran Church to take its cautious position. A survey of the situation at the Federal Council's 1920 assembly in Boston led to this judgment:

> The United Lutheran Church cannot authorize any relationship on the part of Synods, Boards, pastors, congregations or societies which would compromise loyalty to its confessional position or imply any abatement of its jealous guardianship of the faith. The Executive Board believes that to cooperate in good faith with others in any organization which purposely works with eyes closed to confessional differences, would necessarily involve it in practice that would amount to the surrender of our interpretation of the Gospel, the denial of conviction, or the suppression of our testimony to what we hold to be the truth.[81]

In taking this position the United Lutheran Church was defining its relationship not outside but within America's Protestant establishment. The consultative relationship would continue for three decades. Meanwhile, the Federal Council, despite the caveats of outsiders like the Lutherans, remained a way to express faith in action.

The ULCA maintained a guarded yet often fruitful relationship with a range of societies and agencies specializing in various functions of the several denominations. This was true in the field of home missions, Christian education, stewardship, higher education, women's missionary enterprises, youth work, and the like. Safest for Lutherans was the American Bible Society, of which in its modest way the ULCA was a supporting member. The list could go on, but there was also the lure, or challenge, of Christian unity overseas.

The missionary movement in the nineteenth century had fostered international Christian unity when external relations among the denominations became directed toward unity in the Gospel. In three areas the United Lutherans responded, and in three different ways. First, in foreign missions. We have noted the involvement of the National Lutheran Council in the care of German overseas missions orphaned by the war and the creation in 1920 of the Lutheran Foreign Missions Conference of America. This paralleled larger and older developments like the Foreign Missions Conference of North America (1892) and the epoch making World Missionary Conference at Edinburgh (1910).[82] With the International Missionary Council (IMC), organized in 1921 at Lake Mohonk, north of New York City, a new era in partnership began. The 1928 Jerusalem meeting of the IMC took place at the Augusta-Victoria Foundation, a German orphaned mission property built atop the Mount of Olives for the refreshment and renewal of missionaries. President and Mrs. Knubel attended on their way home from India and the celebrations on the Andhra field.

A second area of response concerned relations to the 1925 Stockholm Universal Christian Conference on Life and Work, of which Sweden's Archbishop Nathan Söderblom was the prime mover. A four-member delegation from the ULCA included: Secretary M. G. G. Scherer, E. P. Pfatteicher, Jacob A. Clutz, and J. B. Franke. In the observer category were E. E. Fischer and Frank H. Clutz.[83] The other American Lutheran was J. C. K. Preus (Norwegian Lutheran Church). The Swedish Augustana Synod sent no one, apparently in protest to the alleged liberalism of Söderblom. Recognizing the enormity of evil and sin corrupting the postwar world, the Stockholm conference aimed to stimulate direct Christian action for more rapid results. The invitation assured the participating churches that nothing would be done at this sixteen hundredth anniversary of the Council of Nicaea that would invade the teachings or structures of the churches.

In reporting on Stockholm the ULCA delegates expressed admiration for the city, the "Venice of the North," as well as appreciation of the earnestness with which the conferees treated major issues on the agenda: the church's obligation in view of God's purpose for the world; the church and economic and industri-

al problems; . . . social and moral problems (drink, and other issues); . . . international relations . . . the church and Christian education; and finally, methods
of cooperative efforts by the Christian communions. However, the ULCA delegates expressed their disappointment over the failure of Stockholm "to give us
the solution of at least some one of the problems that were discussed."
Nevertheless, they were pleased to hear that "the mission of the Church above all
is to state principles and to assert the ideal."[84] Tragedy, however, struck the
ULCA delegation. Its oldest member, Professor Jacob Clutz (seventy-eight), died
from the effects of a traffic accident sustained during the conference.[85]

A third area of response, the Faith and Order movement, bore more promise
than the other two. It appealed to the Lutheran emphasis on doctrine and took
into account the diversities of polity. Forms of church government such as the
Episcopal, Presbyterian, or Congregational were present in Lutheranism in various forms and were thus regarded as being of secondary importance. That fact,
however, was quite subordinate to the confessional concern for the substance of
the Christian faith as expressed in doctrine, what is taught about faith in Christ
and a true understanding of the Word of God. So it was that for American
Lutherans generally and for the United Lutheran church in particular, a respon-
siveness and then a commitment to Faith and Order became the major route
into the ecumenical movement. General Synod Lutherans were among the early
responders to the Faith and Order movement. Young Pastor Knubel was one of
those representing the General Synod at the first American gathering at Garden
City, Long Island, in 1916; yet at that time these Lutherans favored delaying further involvement with Faith and Order.

Faith and Order laid emphasis on the church, and participation in it, in contrast to Life and Work and the International Missionary Council. Not long after
the United Lutheran Church was formed, Robert H. Gardiner, a lawyer and Faith
and Order's persistent promoter of Christian unity, urged President Knubel to
bring the ULCA into the movement. Again there was delay. The movement
required interpretation. Most of the other Lutheran bodies had responded negatively to Gardiner's invitation.[86] Involvement in Faith and Order would easily
evoke the charge of "Unionism" from confessional zealots. The ULCA Executive
Board was mindful of the principles stated in the Washington Declaration. It
favored efforts by churches to strive for Christian unity. But, as of 1922, there
was preoccupation among Lutherans as they were preparing for their own pending affirmation of confessional unity at Eisenach. Meanwhile both world conferences—Life and Work as well as Faith and Order—remained on the Executive
Board agenda. A full explication was drawn up by Secretary Scherer.[87] If the participation of the ULCA delegation in the Stockholm conference was rather pas-
sive, a comparison with the Lausanne gathering is more encouraging.

The first World Conference on Faith and Order convened at Lausanne, on
Lake Geneva, August 3-21, 1927. Episcopal Bishop Charles H. Brent was the
chair. The assembled delegates, some 435 representing more than seventy
church bodies, included four from the United Lutheran Church and one each

from the Lutheran Free Church (Norse), and the Norwegian Lutheran Church in America.[88] Besides these six there were more than sixty other Lutherans from churches mainly in Europe. Recognized leader among them was Sweden's Archbishop Söderblom. The ULCA delegates were led by Secretary M. G. G. Scherer and included Holmes Dysinger (professor, Western Seminary, Fremont, Nebraska); Walton H. Greever (professor, Southern Seminary, Columbia, South Carolina), and Augustus Steimle (pastor, Church of the Advent, New York City). The last-named was appointed to draft the report. The four were distributed among several commissions: Dysinger on the Message; Scherer and Steimle on the Nature of the Church; Greever on the Confessions of the Church. As English-speaking Lutherans they were a novelty, a new presence, on the ecumenical scene. To become better acquainted with their fellow Lutherans, like resourceful Americans they invited the others to an evening meal.

At the opening plenary, held in the medieval Gothic cathedral, the subject was "The Call to Unity." After a resolution to the memory of the recently deceased Robert H. Gardiner, the first presentation was by Lutheran Professor Werner Elert of Erlangen. Nine days after Elert came the first and only ULCA presentation. Secretary Scherer, following the Bishop of Bombay, made his presentation under Subject V, "The Church's Ministry." His paper launched the United Lutherans into an early stage of the ecumenical discourse. His was a good example of Faith and Order in its stage of comparative symbolics, when distinctions were drawn and positions made clear. At Söderblom's initiative the Lutheran delegates, like the Orthodox, presented a declaration expressing the position of their communion on the unity of Christendom and the relation thereto of existing churches.

As the late Professor Dorris Flesner has pointed out, the American Lutherans succeeded in having the conference "receive" reports rather than "adopt" them.[89] Thereafter in ecumenical gatherings and procedure, to "receive" has allowed for flexibility and growth, while to "adopt" has been reserved for goals achieved. In this way Lausanne was an important beginning. It marked, in its own way, an entry of the United Lutheran Church into the ecumenical movement. Under President Knubel's leadership, it was an engrafting of a new dimension into the external relations of the ULCA, and eventually into other parts of the Lutheran communion in North America and the English speaking world.

In general the 1920s were a major installment in the unfolding story of the ULCA, blessed as it was with the dedication and leadership of many gifted individuals, especially its president. The strengths and momentum gained in this decade would be sorely needed in the hard years to follow.

NOTES

1. ULCA *Minutes* 1922: 44-56.

2. Meuser, *Formation of the ALC,* 142.

3. Ibid., 235ff.

4. Graebner, Theodore, *The Problem of Lutheran Union and Other Essays.* (St. Louis: Concordia Publishing House, 1935), 1-44.

5. Wentz, *History,* 274f.

6. Kopenhaver, W. M., comp. and ed., *United Lutheran Church Year Book for 1923* (Philadelphia: The United Lutheran Publication House, 1923), 108. (Hereafter cited as ULCA *Year Book,* 1923.)

7. Reed, Luther D., ed., *The Philadelphia Seminary Biographical Record, 1864-1923* (Philadelphia: Lutheran Theological Seminary and the Alumni Association, 1923), 81. (Hereafter cited as Reed, *Philadelphia Seminary Record.*)

8. ULCA *Minutes* 1922:5.

9. *The Lutheran* November 2, 1922, 5.

10. ULCA *Minutes* 1922: 509.

11. "Lutheran Women's Activities," *The Lutheran,* November 9, 1922, 12.

12. Wagner, Martin L., *The Chicago Synod and Its Antecedents* (Waverly, Iowa: Wartburg Publishing House Press, 1909), photo following page 152.

13. *Lutheran Cyclopedia,* 591.

14. Kieffer, George L., comp., and Ellis B. Burgess, ed., *The Lutheran Church Year Book for 1920* (Philadelphia: The United Lutheran Publication House, 1920), 205-206.

15. Frequently on the cover of the Catalogs of the Chicago (Maywood) Seminary.

16. ULCA *Minutes* 1926: 5.

17. Eisenberg, William E., *The Lutheran Church in Virginia, 1717-1962* (Roanoke, Virginia: The Trustees of the Virginia Synod, Lutheran Church in America, 1967), 96. (Hereafter cited as Eisenberg, *Virginia.*)

18. A. R. Wentz, *Gettysburg Seminary Record,* 162.

19. Eisenberg, *Virginia,* 283-84.

20. Burgess, *Pittsburgh Synod,* 508-509.

21. Ibid., 483-89; E. Theodore Bachmann, *They Called Him Father: The Life Story of John Christian Frederick Heyer* (Philadelphia: The Muhlenberg Press, 1942), 35.

22. Hopkins, Charles H., *Rise of the Social Gospel in American Protestantism, 1865-1915* (New Haven: Yale University Press, and London: Oxford University Press, 1940), 111-12, 136, 205, 268; Evjen, John O. *The Life of J. H. W. Stuckenberg, Theologian-Philosopher-Sociologist* (Minneapolis: The Lutheran Free Church Publishing Company, 1938), chapters 8-19; Allbeck, *Wittenberg,* 60-63, 109-10.

23. *Proceedings of the Third Convention of the Western Pennsylvania-West Virginia Synod, Lutheran Church in America, 1964,* 76-77; Burgess, *Pittsburgh Synod,* 494-95.

24. Burgess, *Pittsburgh Synod,* 502.

25. ULCA *Minutes* 1928: 537-41; Cf. ULCA *Minutes* 1918: 77-78 (provided in Bylaws, ULCA Constitution.)

26. Helen Knubel to the author.
27. Victor G. A. Tressler, Springfield, Ohio, to Frederick H. Knubel; John A. Singmaster, Gettysburg, to Frederick H. Knubel, mid-1920s, Knubel Correspondence, ELCA Archives, Chicago.
28. Charles M. Jacobs, Philadelphia, to Frederick H. Knubel, January 29, 1926, Knubel Correspondence, ELCA Archives, Chicago.
29. Charles M. Jacobs, Philadelphia, to Frederick H. Knubel, February 11, 1926, Knubel Correspondence, ELCA Archives, Chicago.
30. W. P. Gerberding, to E. Theodore Bachmann, 1940.
31. President Franklin C. Fry, in his farewell address to the ULCA, Detroit, June 26, 1962 in the *Minutes of the Adjourned Meeting of the Twenty-second Biennial Convention of the United Lutheran Church in America, Detroit, Michigan, June 25-27, 1962,* 663.
32. Ibid.; Edward T. Horn III to E. Theodore Bachmann, February 14, 1991; and personal recollections.
33. ULCA *Minutes* 1928: 68-70.
34. ULCA *Minutes* 1924: 45-46.
35. ULCA *Year Book* 1926: 21.
36. Ibid., 22.
37. Ibid.
38. ULCA Constitution, Article VI, 1, 2, 3 in ULCA *Minutes* 1918: 65.
39. Bylaws, Article V, C, in ULCA *Minutes* 1918: 75-76. Cf. Revised Constitution, Article XIII and Bylaws, Section VIII in ULCA *Minutes* 1956: 1283 and 1290-1292 (See the Report of the Commission on Organizational Structure in ULCA *Minutes* 1954: 546-645.)
40. Bylaws, Section VII, B in ULCA *Minutes* 1918: 77-78.
41. ULCA *Minutes* 1918: 52.
42. ULCA *Minutes* 1924: 177. *Minutes* 1926: 308.
43. ULCA *Minutes* 1926: 92 and 473.
44. ULCA *Minutes* 1924: 152.
45. ULCA *Minutes* 1928: 195-96.
46. ULCA *Minutes* 1928: 196.
47. ULCA *Minutes* 1928: 198-99.
48. ULCA *Minutes* 1928: 199.
49. ULCA *Minutes* 1928: 198, 204.
50. ULCA *Minutes* 1924: 160; Hogg, *Ecumenical Foundations,* 210-12, 226-30; *Annual Report of the NLC, 1919-1921,* 30 (1919), 30ff. (1920) 29-30 (1921); Drach, George, "The Return of German Missionaries," *The Lutheran Church Review* 40 (1921): 267-71.
51. Rouse, Ruth, *The World's Student Christian Federation: A History of the First Thirty Years* (London: SCM Press, 1948), 226.
52. Bachmann, *Lutheran Churches,* 160; ULCA *Minutes* 1924: 139-41.
53. ULCA *Minutes* 1930: 37.
54. The Constitution of the ULCA, in ULCA *Minutes* 1918: 62-71, and the

Constitution of the Board of Education, in ULCA *Minutes* 1920: 257-59. See also Fortenbaugh, Robert, *The Development of the Synodical Polity of the Lutheran Church in America to 1829* (Ph.D. diss., University of Pennsylvania, 1926), (Philadelphia, 1926), especially pages 114-30.

55. Haas, J. A. W. "Our Educational Problem," in "Open Letters," *The Lutheran*, August 25, 1927, 21.
56. ULCA *Minutes*, 1922, 39-44, regarding the promise to do so by 1924.
57. Ibid., 107.
58. ULCA *Minutes*, 1918: 67.
59. ULCA *Minutes* 1922: 470-71. The Survey Commission of 1921, consisting of Knubel, Gotwald and Seibert, is referred to in ULCA *Minutes* 1922: 44ff.
60. Ibid., 45, 49.
61. Ibid., 50ff.
62. F. W. Bussard to F. H. Knubel, January 15, 1925; ELCA Archives.
63. Ibid., 424, 457.
64. ULCA *Minutes* 1924:96.
65. Ibid., 558; ULCA *Minutes* 1926:519-43.
66. ULCA *Minutes* 1926: 543.
67. Tappert, *Philadelphia Seminary History*, 86-88.
68. Charles M. Jacobs, Philadelphia, to Frederick H. Knubel, 1926, Knubel Correspondence, ELCA Archives, Chicago.
69. Tappert, *Philadelphia Seminary History*, 88.
70. ULCA *Minutes* 1930: 377-80.
71. ULCA *Minutes* 1922: 320; F. K. Wentz, *Lutherans in Concert*, 41.
72. ULCA *Minutes* 1920: 442; reaffirmed in 1922: ULCA *Minutes* 1922: 315-23.
73. *Annual Report of the NLC, 1919-1921*, 35-72 (1920).
74. Nelson, *World Lutheranism*, 101ff.
75. Ibid., 109.
76. Jacobs, Charles M., "The Lutheran World Convention: A Retrospect," *The Lutheran Church Review*, 42 (1923): 288-89.
77. Ibid., 291.
78. Abdel Ross Wentz, "The Convention at Eisenach Was a Success," *The Lutheran*, September 27, 1923, 6.
79. Nelson, *World Lutheranism*, chapters 7-8.
80. ULCA *Minutes* 1924: 95.
81. ULCA *Minutes* 1922: 85. See also the "Washington Declaration," D, 1 in ULCA *Minutes* 1920: 97-99 and the ULCA Constitution, Article II in ULCA *Minutes* 1918: 63.
82. Hogg, *Ecumenical Foundations*, chapter 5, pages 202-43.
83. ULCA *Minutes* 1926: 50.
84. ULCA *Minutes* 1926: 59-60.
85. ULCA *Minutes* 1926: 50, 63.
86. Bergendoff, "Lutheran Unity," 368-90.
87. ULCA *Minutes* 1922: 88-94.

88. ULCA *Minutes* 1928: 74; T. O. Burntvedt from the Lutheran Free Church of America and S. O. Sigmond from the Norwegian Lutheran Church of America. See Bate, H. N., ed., *Proceedings of the World Conference on Faith and Order, Lausanne, August 3-21, 1927* (New York: George H. Doran Company, 1927), 511, 522. (Hereafter cited as *Faith and Order Proceedings* (1927).)

89. Flesner, *World Council*, 38.

CHAPTER 7

THE THRIFTY THIRTIES

L IKE FLASH CARDS OF MEMORY, a few key phrases will recall for us the domestic and global context of the 1930s, the second decade of the ULCA—the financial crash of October 1929, the ensuing years of economic depression in America and worldwide, mounting totalitarianism, international unrest, anti-Semitism, race prejudice, resurgence of the gospel, Christian unity as manifested ecumenically, and not least, fear and foreboding about the future—then, as the decade ended, the beginning of World War II. The stock market crash of October 1929 and the outbreak of Europe's war in August of 1939 framed the span like cataclysmic bookends.

For American church bodies, the "thrifty thirties" were years of depression and yet growth. Despite the financial pressures, the ULCA experienced considerable expansion, both in terms of sheer numbers and also in relationships with other Lutheran bodies and various ecumenical endeavors. For example, in 1934 Paul W. Koller, executive of the Board of Foreign Missions, reported to the biennial convention a disturbing paradox: "On the one hand growing interest and developing churches on the mission fields and [on the other hand] the spirit of missions considered critically or indifferently at home, with depression and its sometimes selfish fears cutting missionary giving."[1]

The 1932 convention in Philadelphia expressed its grief over the loss of M. G. G. Scherer, secretary of the church who had passed into eternal life on March 4th. Scherer had been a member of the Ways and Means Committee for the ULCA merger and had been elected secretary at the organization meeting in 1918. He had not only kept accurate records for the church, but had also helped to lay out the programs and shape policies which gave direction to the life and mission of the newly formed church. He had been a delegate to the Universal Conference on Life and Work in Stockholm (1925) and to the World Conference of Faith and Order in Lausanne in 1927. There his clear and scholarly lecture won for the Lutheran Church "fresh ecumenical recognition and prestige."[2]

Compared with Philadelphia in 1932, the Savannah convention of 1934 was upbeat. A money-saver, for one thing, had been the group-rate, fifteen-car Pennsylvania and Seaboard railroad train to Georgia. Some two hundred delegates, clerical and lay, enjoyed a rare opportunity for fellowship, plus a stopover in Columbia, South Carolina, to become acquainted with Southern Seminary, an important center of the ULCA in the South. In terms of its own spiritual legacy the Savannah convention honored a double anniversary: two hundred years since the arrival of the refugee Lutherans from Salzburg, Austria, and their settlement in Savannah and Ebenezer, Georgia; and four hundred years since the publication of Luther's translation of the entire Bible in German in 1534. Indeed, had the Salzburgers not been such ardent devotees of the Scriptures, they would not have been expelled for their evangelical faith by Firmian, the Roman Catholic Archbishop of Salzburg. Besides, it was here in Georgia that Henry Melchior Muhlenberg in 1742 received his initial orientation before proceeding northward to Philadelphia and six years later forming the first permanent Lutheran church body in North America, to which the ULCA traced its organizational roots. "Is it not clear," said Professor Abdel Ross Wentz to the hundreds assembled in Savannah's Civic Auditorium on Sunday, October 21,

> that there is a continuous unbroken line of history from Luther's Bible in 1534 to the Salzburger settlement in Georgia in 1734 and on down to this convention in 1934? . . . Let us trace that line and gather its scattered strands together. Perhaps we can weave it into a sturdy rope for the anchor of our faith today.[3]

Among the convention's high points was the discussion and passage of what became known as the Savannah Declaration, a formal bid for closer accord among America's Lutherans.[4] It made clear that the ULCA requires no other tests of authentic Lutheranism than the historic Lutheran Confessions. Basic was the mutual acceptance of the Holy Scriptures as the only rule and standard for faith and life, by which all doctrines are to be judged. Indeed, this position of no-other-tests would in the future as in the past mark the steadfast stance of the ULCA. Ecumenically as well as among other Lutheran bodies internationally, "Savannah" made clear where the ULCA stood.

Four years later, the Baltimore convention in 1938 observed the twentieth anniversary of the ULCA. "I appeal for the unanimous will to unity among us," said President Knubel in his opening sermon. With an eye to the times, to the world situation, and to the promotion of oneness in the ULCA itself, Knubel concluded, "There never was a time when our unity was more needed than now, unity furthermore in the purest Lutheranism conceivable; and that means unity in the Gospel, in its truth and spirit."[5] Toward that end, the Baltimore "Declaration on the Word of God and the Scriptures," as adopted by this convention, was to mark still another step on the way toward Lutheran accord as well as to ecumenical witness.[6] This Declaration set forth the position of the ULCA on the authority of Scripture, the meaning of the "Word of God," and the inspiration of Scripture. This forthright document, as did the Washington and Savannah declarations, placed the ULCA on the side of neo-Lutheranism, that is, the kind which reflected the nineteenth century dynamic Erlangen theology, and the Luther renaissance of the earlier twentieth century. It contrasted sharply with the "old Lutheranism" of seventeenth century dogmatic orthodoxy.

Meanwhile, against the background of the thirties, we shall follow the ULCA story of ecclesial growth in the face of difficulties of stewardship (and pensions) in a depressed decade, especially regarding theological education.

FISCAL CHALLENGES FOR VARIOUS BOARDS

Churchwide statistics compiled from an aggregate of parochial reports give us some idea of how an ecclesial body like the ULCA was faring during its second decade. In the number of members it grew by about 18 percent, or twice the U.S. growth rate. Other "mainline" Protestant denominations as well as the Roman Catholic Church could report similar gains. Specifically, the ULCA baptized membership rose from 1.4 million in 1930 to 1.7 million in 1940. (This total includes 160,000 in the mission congregations of India and Japan.) The communing membership (a minimum of once a year) went from 682,000 in 1930 to 817,000 in 1940; in both cases it was about 48 percent of the baptized membership. In a related category, the Sunday school enrollment was about 640,000 in 1930, and up only to 662,000 in 1940, showing a proportionate weakness when compared with the other categories and an early indication of the coming decline of the Sunday church school. The ULCA membership in the United States and Canada was dispersed into 3,942 congregations in 1930, rising modestly to 4,039 in 1940. But the size of the average congregation had increased more significantly, from 361 to 419, perhaps because tight funds led to few new mission starts in the 1930s. The ULCA congregations—plus academic and specialized interests—were served by a total of 3,284 ordained ministers (counting the retired) in 1930, and by 3,613 ten years later.

The Baltimore convention provided for the periodic holding of a school for statisticians. The first one convened in 1939. A major contributor was Edward Traill Horn III, then campus pastor at Cornell University. His "Pastor's Manual on Statistics" helped clear the way for other standardizing helps for the keeping of the "Parish Register," the preparation by the ULCA of uniform report forms, and the like. The introduction to Horn's manual offers a good supplement to this statistical section:

> The importance of accurate and complete statistics for the ULCA is being emphasized as never before by the uses made of them today: (1) By the ULCA leaders in their efforts to induce the Church to see itself as it is; (2) By other Lutheran bodies, who make comparisons; (3) By other denominations; (4) By the U.S. Government (with increasing significance, necessitating documentary accuracy); and (5) By the enemies of the Church, who seek in every way to discredit the Church.[7]

Behind this periodic school or workshop for church statisticians lies a story easily missed. Call it the story of the two Georges: George Henry Schnur Jr., and George Lynn Kieffer. Both were Gettysburg Seminary graduates, Schnur in 1886, and Kieffer in 1912. Schnur, a native of Illinois, served congregations in the

Midwest and later in western Pennsylvania. As editor of *Luther League Topics* 1898-1917, he remained attuned to the church's rising generation as well as to the church's growing edge. For his last twenty-three years—most of them spent as pastor of Grace Church, Erie, Pennsylvania—he served as statistician of the Pittsburgh Synod. And for seven years (1927-34) he edited ably the ULCA *Year Book.* Schnur had a fine sense of history and balance in his choice of background materials that helped to make ecclesial data come alive. Nor was he unappreciative of the long continuity that linked his work to that of T. Newton Kurtz, of Baltimore, who had compiled and published the *Lutheran Almanac* in 1849.

The other George, George Lynn Kieffer, in his foreshortened life became America's leading Lutheran statistician. He was general church statistician for the *Christian Herald,* and served as consultant for the U.S. Census Bureau in the preparation of the nation's decennial Religious Census, an invaluable resource book that last appeared in 1936. His decade of pastoral ministry (Rosedale, Long Island, 1916-26), as well as graduate study at Union Theological Seminary and Columbia University, sharpened his lifelong fascination for an accurate and informed grasp of his Lutheran confessional kin locally and worldwide. Kieffer was stimulated and encouraged by older men of kindred spirit, the noted O. M. Norlie, of the Norwegian Lutheran Church of America and a tireless gatherer and compiler of ecclesial data, or the maverick Missourian, Otto H. Pannkoke, a mover and shaker for cooperation leading to the joint observance of the Reformation's four hundredth anniversary and to the cooperatively run Lutheran Bureau. Kieffer did yeoman's work in compiling and largely editing the first *Lutheran World Almanac* (1921) and subsequent editions.

The Executive Board

In the depressed thirties just about everyone was striving to do more with less, an exercise in which the officers of the ULCA and its Executive Board shared concerns not unlike those in the synods, the congregations and the households of the church members. Only the scale was different. For example, at the 1932 Philadelphia convention, the budget proposed for 1933 was up for discussion. This involved apportionment and drew attention to two points in particular: the amount asked of the synods, and the actual amount received from them. Some delegates, brave souls, argued for keeping the apportionment where it had been pegged in the late twenties namely, at $2.4 million. Of course everyone knew from the Bulletin of Reports that receipts were falling off. In 1930 (ending the fiscal year on June 30, 1930) the ULCA receipts from the apportionment had reached their high at $1,422,919. By 1932 they had slipped to $1,166,992, a loss of 18 percent. Therefore the church officers and the Executive Board proposed that, for the sake of realism, the apportionment be cut back to $2 million, and that every effort be made to reach this lofty goal.[8] Despite the plea by the defenders of the higher $2.4 million apportionment, the convention voted for this reduction. The amount actually paid during the depressed fiscal year 1932-33, however, sank drastically to $866,538. This would be the low point for the 1930s, and 39 percent below that of the banner year, 1929-30.

For the rest of the thirties the apportionment figure remained at $2 million while the actual receipts from the synods gradually climbed up to 50 percent of that sum. Such a poor showing was sobering, and led to further action. Already at the Milwaukee convention (1930) memorials submitted by several ULCA synods requested that adjustments germane to the changed economic situation be developed under auspices of the Executive Board.[9] Accordingly, President Knubel appointed a "special committee on plan of apportionment." This committee of nine was headed by the astute Ellis B. Burgess, until 1930 president of the Pittsburgh Synod and a former member of the Executive Board. Presented to the Philadelphia convention in 1932, the report recommended a fairer basis for the distribution of the apportionment among the synods, 75 percent based on communing membership and 25 percent on allocation. This was referred to the synods for their study and response. In due course the plan of apportionment committee received replies: nine synods approved, three disapproved, ten took no action, seven were continuing to study the plan, and four were working on a new plan of their own. The committee's second report was referred to the Executive Board by the 1934 convention.[10]

Meanwhile, outside events intervened. In general, the economic crisis in the United States was decisive for many church budgets. And there were specific needs as well. On March 10, 1933, an earthquake hit Long Beach, California. The dead numbered 117. Destruction of property was extensive, including the California Synod's Trinity Church. There were appeals for help. A month later, in the wake of the Roosevelt inauguration, came the nationwide "Bank Holiday," to help get the disarrayed financial institutions back on course. Again came appeals from pastors and congregations in critical need. Added thereto was the disparity of support for mission activities of the ULCA. Financially it was a case of Have-nots versus Haves. Both the Board of Foreign Missions and the Board of American Missions were in a bind. Furloughed missionaries could not be returned to their overseas fields: no money. Home mission pastors took drastic cuts in salary. Yet at the same time, the Women's Missionary Society was flourishing, and its projects and supported personnel, mainly female missionaries, apparently had a decided advantage.

To address the problems and to respond to complaints of pastors over the multiplicity of appeals, President Knubel drew on his earlier experience and formed a Special Committee on the Present Emergency. As might be expected from the historically minded, this 1933 appeal was linked to two anniversaries: the 450th of Luther's birth, and the fifteenth of the ULCA. A precondition to supporting this appeal, or any other special giving, was that each congregation and synod should first pay its benevolence (apportionment). Coming at year's end, this suggestion was not out of line. For it was to follow two other activities: the Every Member Visitation of the congregations, and the follow-up endeavors of the Lutheran Laymen's League for Stewardship, under the indefatigable Washington lawyer, Arthur P. Black. This well-named Jubilee Offering netted nearly $45,000, a modest sum, yet in those days a little went farther.[11]

For the Knubel presidency in the thirties, support (not only financial) for the churchwide functions, as in mission and education, and also the nurture of those functions in coordination with the work of the synods, became matters of major importance. The depressed state of the economy generated a struggle for survival that expressed itself in the church. For many parishioners, there was a ranking of priorities that placed the needs of the congregation first, those of the synod second and those of the church at large third. An example of this is the course of congregational giving; after the low of 1933, it was by 1939 back to within 3.5 percent of what it had been in 1931. Yet within that scale of total expenditures, congregational giving for benevolence in 1939 was still 17.5 percent behind what it had been in 1931.[12] In many ways 1933 marked the low point in support for the ULCA. President Knubel reported to the 1934 convention that the preceding two years were "the most critical biennium since the first one in our history." Those were days of "severe strain on all leaders" in the church: synod presidents and staffs expressing awareness "of their human weakness before seemingly hopeless situations." Board secretaries and other officials, in seeking help, "came constantly with their real distresses." Locally, "all sincere pastors and their best lay helpers were at their wits' end." Besides, "the officers of the Church have never before conferred so often nor so intensely."[13]

Surely the gravest specific crisis was the loss of pension funds tied up in failed banks. The 1926 Richmond convention had authorized a $4 million general funding campaign for the pension funds and President Knubel had exerted forceful leadership. The Pension Board, he said, "should not ask cooperation, but commandeer every individual in the Church for service" in raising this money.[14] The money was raised, invested and then lost, shaking the confidence of all. The Pension Board's treasurer was a top officer at Philadelphia's Oak Lane Bank, which invested the money in scores of mortgages destined for default. The bank itself was merged, then liquidated and closed. The whole sorry tale was laid out to the 1934 convention,[15] and spelled the end of the non-contributory pension plan. After a difficult transition, a contributory pension linked congregations, participants and beneficiaries together in mutual support.

Given this situation, President Knubel added confidently, "I believe we have passed the crisis." There was a tone of approval in his remark that "the voices of some of the most thoughtful men within the ULCA . . . have been pressing for more centralized authority in the Church."[16] A round of discussions in the Executive Board led to a number of propositions, four of which the president treated in his report. Summarized, they dealt with: strengthening the spiritual life in the church; a stepped up promotion of educational concerns; a better distribution by synods of the funds received from the congregations; and an improved coordination of the work of the Women's Missionary Society (as well as other auxiliary societies) with the work of the church as a whole. Most critical of all, the central Executive Board decided how the tight ULCA budget would be apportioned to the other boards.

First came the two major units: Foreign Missions and American (Home) Missions; then those in (Higher) Education, and in Parish and Church School work; and last but not least, those in Inner (Social) Missions, Deaconess Work, and Pensions. The one self-supporting or non-apportionment board was Publications, the profitable standby. Biennially, the Executive Board divided up the authorized budget—$2 million, although only less than half of that amount could be expected—into allocations or, as nicely said, a percentage of the synodical dollar. The 1934 division was as follows: Foreign Missions, 30 percent; American Missions, 38.57 percent; Education (colleges, seminaries, and campus ministry), 9 percent; and Ministerial Pensions and Relief, 11.75 percent. Parish and Church School, Inner Mission (Social Ministry), Deaconess Work, and National Lutheran Council each received between 1 and 2 percent, with the rest for reserves and miscellaneous.[17] This distribution key remained fairly constant during the thirties.

The Board of Foreign Missions

The work of Foreign Missions was always placed first among the reports from the apportionment boards. Headed by Paul Koller and then Edwin Moll, its advancement in personnel and projects was aided by the ULCA Women's Missionary Society, especially regarding women missionaries. Contributions from the latter (in 1938) increased by about 35 percent the money received by the Foreign Board from the apportionment of the ULCA.[18] In addition a fair amount came from the investments and special funds of the board. Besides, some forty congregations and individuals were supporting missionaries overseas under BFM auspices and another seven supported designated women missionaries under the WMS program.[19] From these various sources the ULCA could do more missions even when its own depressed budget had less.

Annually the Epiphany Season, first in the ULCA Calendar of Causes, was a time for promoting interest in and support for missioning overseas. Scores of congregations visited by furloughed missionaries found this a welcome way of linking the story of Jesus' epiphany or manifestation of his Lordship to the challenge of bringing the gospel to specific places in distant lands. Toward the end of the decade the ULCA counted 155 missionary personnel (including wives and retirees).[20] Well over one-half of them were stationed in India, the country where C. F. (Father) Heyer, the first American Lutheran overseas missionary, had commenced the work in 1842.

While plans were being readied for the centennial observance of this event, immediate interest centered on the meeting of the International Missionary Council (IMC) in Madras/Tambaram in December 1938. The ULCA delegate to this ecumenical gathering was Abdel Ross Wentz, Gettysburg Seminary's professor of history. The then fifty-five-year old churchman and his wife, Edna, along with Mrs. O. A. Sardeson (Chicago), in behalf of the Women's Missionary Society, also visited the centers of ULCA mission work not only in India but also in China and Japan. The war already in progress between China and Japan intensified the importance of the visitation. In fact, Japan's invasion and occupation of Manchuria in 1931 was unofficially the beginning of an Asian conflict, the violent side of Japan extending its Co-Prosperity Sphere over East Asia. Amazingly, at the Madras International Missions Conference in late 1938, despite the war, Japanese and Chinese delegates not only participated but also prayed together for peace.

India's Andhra Evangelical Lutheran Church (self-governing since 1927) and the Japan Evangelical Lutheran Church (mission begun in 1892 and self-governing since 1922) were both recognized as synods of the ULCA, with voice but no vote at the biennial conventions. In India, against a background of agitation for independence, the church continued to grow, exceeding one hundred thousand baptized members before 1940. In Japan, amid government curbs on religious liberty and pressures to unite all Protestants into one church (the Kyodan), the JELC continued to make modest gains. The newly acquired China mission gradually became a favorite in ULCA circles. When the Lutheran Church of China was organized in 1928, the ULCA-related constituency became part of it. The 1930s tested this venture in mission and unity. Despite manifest hardships the number of communicants by 1940 well exceeded five thousand in the Shantung field.

The work in India, Japan, and China would prove highly significant in cultivating ecumenical relations overseas even more so than at home; this was also true, though to a far lesser extent for the ULCA, in Africa and South America. Work initiated in Liberia in 1860 by the General Synod made slow but steady progress under the ULCA. Closer to home, in South America and the Caribbean, the missionary vision pressed for definition. Work in the Caribbean—in Spanish-speaking Puerto Rico and the English-speaking Virgin Islands—came under the ULCA Board of American Missions. The work in South America— English-speaking British Guiana (later Guyana) and Spanish-speaking Argentina—was under the Board of Foreign Missions. While the venture into Argentina began in 1909, and developed laboriously, that in British Guiana went back to a Dutch Lutheran congregation in 1743. Dutch lands became British, and slaves from Africa and especially workers from India swelled the local population. Thanks to the initiative of John Robert Mittelholzer (an African-Guianian trained by the London Missionary Society), the Lutheran heritage was recovered and a tie formed with the Lutheran General Synod in North America in 1890.[21] Cooperation among the several Lutheran congregations grew under the ULCA, leading by 1943 to the formation of the Lutheran Church in Guyana.

The Board of American Missions

The home missions board, already mentioned as the product of a five-way merger of mission units in 1926, was the agency through which the ULCA carried out the domestic part of its missionary task in the United States and Canada. Its executive secretary, Franklin Foster Fry, told the 1930 Milwaukee convention:

The Board of American Missions has been doing big business in Kingdom building during another biennium. It helped to establish eighty-seven new missions—
one for every eight days. A Church Extension loan was granted every two weeks.
These new missions are distributed through twenty Synods, and minister to different linguistic groups: English, German, Italian, Hungarian, Siebenbuerger
[Transylvania Saxons from Romania], Slovak, and Finnish.[22]

The early thirties curtailed this progress, but Fry's commitment was contagious. His death late in 1933 was a severe blow, particularly to those counting
on his leadership during the deepening Depression. Zenan Corbe, building on
his experience with the West Indies Mission Board, then served faithfully and
long as BAM executive secretary, from 1934 to 1948. During the thirties the
ULCA gained almost a hundred new congregations. The apportionment
received by the Board of American Missions in 1940 remained 23 percent less
than the amount in 1929. Here, too, bequests and other resources helped soft-
en the impact. By means of its church extension fund and other resources, the
BAM assisted over four hundred congregations in 1930. By 1940 the number
had risen to nearly 570. Many of these were young congregations with debts
threatening foreclosure. Others were older congregations in changing urban
settings. Rural congregations were usually solid fiscally, but also frugal in their
broader stewardship.

Everywhere churches and their members were making do with less. Perhaps
western Canada, where drought and depression converged, was hardest hit.
Founded in 1891, the Manitoba Synod owed its formation to the Ontario-based
Canada Synod and to the mission outreach of the old General Council. Prior to
the Great War, German as well as Scandinavian and other Lutheran immigrants
had begun coming into the country in large numbers. But after about 1920 the
influx became impressively large. The newcomers remained predominantly
rural. The home missionary challenge in western Canada loomed larger than
almost anywhere else on the continent, especially for Lutherans. According to
the Canadian religious census in 1931 the inhabitants of the four western
provinces—Manitoba, Saskatchewan, Alberta, British Columbia—totaled
279,546 who indicated a Lutheran preference. Of this number only 82,700 had
joined a Lutheran congregation. And of that baptized membership some 23,000
had been gathered by the Missouri Synod and about 46,000 by the Scandinavian
synods; leaving the ULCA synod with just under 14,000, or under 20 percent of
the churched Lutherans.

This poor showing can in some respects be blamed on the heavily eastern
character of the ULCA, and on a corresponding tardiness in responding to a cry
for help. Already in 1921 (see above, chapter 6), a top survey commission—
President Knubel, Education Secretary Gotwald, and Western Mission Secretary
Seibert—had included western Canada in their swing across the Northwest
Synod and down the Pacific coast. Awareness of the prairie provinces was kept
alive in the church press and by other channels as well. It remained, however, for

the double jeopardy of drought and depression as well as for the general tendency in the United States to take its northern neighbor for granted, to make the Canadians request the ULCA to survey their synods, this time from the Maritimes to British Columbia. The published results, out in time for the 1932 convention in Philadelphia, took into account not only the congregations but also educational institutions—especially the theological seminaries in Waterloo (Ontario) and Saskatoon (Saskatchewan)—and inter-Lutheran relations as well.

In 1940 some 134 congregations in the sprawling Manitoba Synod were receiving BAM support. E. A. Tappert, Board Secretary for Linguistic Interests,[23] reported in 1932 that:

> All our field men and missionaries have worked with great zeal and efficiency, and in consequence the Manitoba Synod has an increase in membership of more than 20 percent during the biennium. No section in our Church equals the Canadian Northwest in low cost and missionary service. None of this year's graduates, nor most of last year's, receive a salary in excess of $600 a year. The living conditions are most primitive. One of our youngest missionaries who had come from Kropp Seminary and spent a year in Saskatoon [Seminary] went into a parsonage built of sod, with walls two feet thick, warm in winter and cool in summer, yet a strange kind of parsonage. We attended his final examination. In all our experience as a member of examining committees for years we have never met a young man so well versed in all branches of theology.[24]

In 1932 the transition to the use of English was already under way in Canada, and with the end of a supply of home missioners from overseas, the training of native-born Canadians was progressing at Saskatoon Seminary.

Striving to do more with less, the ULCA Board of American Missions paralleled the energetic optimism of Roosevelt's New Deal with creative initiatives of its own. With the approval of the Executive Board and the biennial convention the Board launched a churchwide funding campaign, marking the twentieth anniversary of the ULCA.[25] Besides the printed materials the home missionary challenge was depicted in a film entitled "The Thunder of the Sea," the closing phrase of Justus Falckner's stirring hymn, "Rise, Ye Children Of Salvation."[26] By mid-1940 the Anniversary Appeal had brought the BAM $384,499.[27] The late thirties saw several other BAM initiatives. Lent, 1936, included the appearance of *Ecclesia Plantanda*, a house organ of the BAM for the information and encouragement of its missioners. ULCA Treasurer E. Clarence Miller introduced the first number with a realistic note: "An 'appeal' for funds is wrong—the money for our work is sure to come when men who know the truth as it is in Christ Jesus and believe it, will tell it to all the people."[28] The summer of 1936 also marked the beginning of an annual, week-long School for Home Mission Pastors. Aiding the BAM staff were three summer faculty members, including a thirty-six-year-old parish pastor from Akron, Ohio, named Franklin Clark Fry, who soon became dean of this summertime school. Elected to the BAM in 1934, not long after the death of his father, the board's late executive, he continued on it until 1942, at which time he was elected to the ULCA Executive Board and then in 1944 to the ULCA presidency as narrated shortly.

Finally, in striving to accomplish the maximum with modest funding, the BAM, on authorization of the 1936 convention, set up a Division of Research and Survey. Heading it was the layman, H. Torrey Walker. A former colonel in the Army, he was now working for the church militant. A New Jerseyan from Moorestown, he was active in the Laymen's Movement and able to give a persuasive account of his Christian faith. Later on he would become manager of the Lutheran Publication House. But in 1936 he and his fellow staffers introduced a new "stewardship of spending," as they called it. During the 1936 biennium they undertook 162 surveys of potential missions, recommended thirty-five for starting, put thirty on hold, and rejected the rest. The Colonel presented the 1938 ULCA Convention with this strategic assessment:

> This Division has produced facts that powerfully confirm what was formerly only a conviction of home mission leaders; namely, that at the present time there are opportunities for the inauguration of successful missions such as would require resources in men and money four times greater than are now available.[29]

The quip had not yet been coined, but before the end of the thirties the BAM was indeed getting a "bigger bang for the buck." The dollars may have been tight but churches were planted, and growing. And the challenge to the church at large had intensified.

The Board of Social Missions

During the thirties, the Executive Board considered the proposal that the Board of Inner Mission, the Deaconess Board, and the committees on Evangelism and Moral and Social Welfare be combined into one unit.[30] After careful study, the Executive Board in 1939 recommended that all but the Deaconess Board be joined into one board.[31] The term "social missions" had been suggested for the title as a more adequate term to describe the work being done than "Inner Mission." After heated discussion, the term was accepted and the new board approved. The new Board of Social Missions was organized into three divisions to carry on the work that had been done by the three units.

Also in 1939 the National Lutheran Council added the Department of Welfare after a broad survey indicated the need for an agency to coordinate and assist the numerous inner mission agencies. Chosen to head this department was Clarence E. Krumbholz, a ULCA pastor who had already served the church exceedingly well in this field. He would also be remembered by many young women as the one who encouraged them to prepare in graduate schools for service in Lutheran agencies. During the thirties, especially in the Midwest, new statewide Lutheran welfare agencies were being formed with the support of all church bodies of the NLC. They followed the pattern already set by Minnesota in the twenties. The Department of Welfare took over the work of the National Lutheran Inner Mission Conference and planned biennial Lutheran welfare conferences.[32]

The Board of Education

The ULCA stake in academia, like Caesar's Gaul, was divided into three parts: campus ministries, church colleges, and theological seminaries. Ranked third in the funds received from the central treasury, this board worked with a modest amount, down from a high of $135,000 in 1929 to a low of $78,000 four years later and then, by early 1940, climbing back to $90,000. These funds were over and above the synodical support sent directly to the church's colleges and seminaries in the United States and Canada. According to ULCA church polity, the synods bore the structural responsibility for supporting and governing the colleges and seminaries of the church. The campus ministries to Lutheran students at non-Lutheran colleges and universities were even more decentralized, often depending upon a local Lutheran congregation. They found earnest advocates, however, as well as modest funding, in the Board of Education.

Executive Secretary (Norman Jay) Gould Wickey served this board throughout the thirties, indeed into the late 1950s. A Harvard Ph.D., Wickey brought to his post the right experience (pastor, college professor, then president of Carthage College) and the relentless energy of a benevolent bantam.[33] After his first biennium as an executive he explained how he had been using his time: half of it visiting colleges, seminaries and student centers; one-fourth of it in promotion and research; and one fourth in administration. Not confined to Lutheranism, Wickey served thirteen years as executive secretary of the Council of Church Boards of Education, was general secretary of the National Conference of Church Related Colleges, and edited the interdenominational journal, *Christian Education.* His long tenure was matched, even exceeded, by the trio of extraordinary staff members who welcomed him in 1929: Mary E. Markley, the first woman on the ULCA staff back in 1919; Mildred E. Winston, whose bachelor of divinity degree from the Biblical Seminary in New York also made her a pioneer; and Carolus P. ("C. P.") Harry, a Pennsylvania pastor who was particularly influential in the formation of the Lutheran Student Association of America, inspiring many toward inter-Lutheran and ecumenical cooperation.

All three of these spent the major part of their time in student work. Theirs was a ceaseless yet ever changing round of campus visits, study groups, student conferences, personal counseling, correspondence, as well as meeting with professors and academic administrators. They called on the growing number, actually many scores, of parish pastors of congregations conveniently near the local college or university or professional school, the contact pastors for student work, as they were called. And when these three staffers were at the board's home base in Washington, they assisted the executive secretary in research and other projects. Mary Markley, after 1935, was editor of the *News Bulletin* of the National Lutheran Educational Conference. Mildred Winston had special connections with the Deaconess Community. Both she and Miss Markley also cultivated other professional women's groups and associations as well as the ubiqui-

tous Women's Missionary Society. In more ways than can now still be pinpoint-
ed but that are well remembered, these two staff women worked valiantly in setting forth the task of women in the church amid the changing times and new
opportunities. Mildred Winston, for example, studied at the Biblical Seminary,
New York, at a time when there were no female students attending Lutheran theological seminaries.

Mary Markley became acquainted with the outreach of the ULCA, and of
other churches in India, China, and Japan. Her first acquaintance with church
work came during the Great War when, in Washington, she helped conduct one
of the Hospitality Centers run by the National Lutheran Commission for
Soldiers' and Sailors' Welfare. Thus Miss Markley—she was never addressed
without the "Miss"—was won for a lifetime of service in the church. A person of
extraordinary gifts and keen perceptivity, she was concerned and compassionate, ever gracious and dignified.

C. P. Harry was a man of ideas, clear in expressing them, and patient in hearing others out. Theologically he appears to have been soundly rooted, while at
the same time being open to the religious loyalties of people in other parts of the
world. An example of this surfaced in 1934. To leaders of the then still young
Lutheran Student Association of America he proposed that their desire to convene a national conference sometime in the summer of 1935 be given the name
"Ashram," the word used in India to denote a place of retreat for a religious band
of disciples. The Board of Education report to the Columbus, Ohio ULCA convention in 1936 indicated that the Lutheran Student Association of America
(LSAA) was nationwide with no official affiliation to any synod or church
leader.[34] It was directed by the Lutheran Student Council of America made up of
student delegates from various regions. Harry, who had annually been elected by
the Council as one of its advisors, was in 1935 made a councilor for life. He
helped organize and conduct the first national Ashram held in Oconomowoc,
Wisconsin in August of 1935. This was limited to one hundred delegates, many
of whom were from other Lutheran church bodies. Also in 1935, Miss Markley
and Harry met with the Student Commission of the American Lutheran
Conference to explore areas of cooperation which in time developed into the
Commission of Student Service in the National Lutheran Council (1945).
Beginning in 1938 the Board of Education reports were changed to Board of
Higher Education.

As the decade closed, the 1939 Ashram on the Lenoir-Rhyne campus in
Hickory, North Carolina, welcomed the news that the Lutheran Student
Association of America had been received into membership by the World
Student Christian Federation (Geneva-based). The LSAA was said to be the first
confessional organization to be so received. The World Conference of Christian
Youth, still in July, had met in Amsterdam. Carl Lund-Quist, Norman Goehring
(University Lutheran, Cambridge), and Stewart Herman had been among the
American Lutheran participants. Lund-Quist was one of those who, back in
1934, had been among the planners with C. P. Harry of that first Ashram.

The student work of the ULCA Board of Education, and its campus ministries as well as contact pastors and supportive congregations in the United States and Canada, undoubtedly played a highly significant part in furthering lay leadership in church and society as well as the aims of unity among Lutherans, a striving that bore ecumenical promise as well. Led by the efforts of University Lutheran Church near Harvard, the Lutheran Association near Cornell (William M. Horn) and Luther Memorial Church at the University of Wisconsin (Howard Gold), ULCA student work influenced countless women and men for all sorts of lay vocations, in addition to those who went on to seminary. As an inter-Lutheran endeavor, especially in the American Lutheran Conference, it paved the way for further cooperation and even union among North American Lutherans. Even the later ecumenical movement showed the legacy of these campus ministries.

The Board of Education and its executive, also spoke up for the church colleges. At the head of his 1936 convention report, Wickey quoted with approval the warning of an unnamed layman:

> It is not a question so much of churches and preachers as it is of colleges that will make leaders who will create a world in which churches can thrive.... If American churchmen fail to support the kind of colleges that turn out Christian leaders, American life under another leadership soon will close the churches.[35]

The church colleges, said Wickey, provide education not primarily to leaders within the church but "to those who will exercise an intelligent Christian influence whatever their occupation."[36] The church-related colleges "present the relationship of Christian principles to our social and economic life." The fourteen ULCA colleges were usually modest operations, especially in the frugal 1930s, set in smaller cities or towns. Only one (Wagner College, Staten Island) was in a major metropolis. Six of the fourteen were in the Northeast: four in Pennsylvania (Gettysburg, Muhlenberg, Susquehanna, Thiel) and two in New York (Wagner and Hartwick). Four were in the South: two in Virginia (Roanoke and Marion, a junior college), and one each in North Carolina (Lenoir-Rhyne) and South Carolina (Newberry). Three were in the Midwest: in Ohio (Wittenberg), Illinois (Carthage), and Nebraska (Midland).[37] This geographical distribution was paralleled by a remarkable denominational diversity. Only 50 percent of the students, on average, were Lutheran, from a low of 40 percent in 1934 to a high of 56 percent in 1940.[38] Most ULCA pastors, however, were alumni of Lutheran colleges: 87 percent of the ULCA seminary students in 1930 and 73 percent in 1940.[39]

The third arena of work for the Board of Education was the theological seminaries. As noted in chapter 6, the last report of the Commission on Theological Education during the twenties (1924-1930) recommended and urged closer ties between the ULCA and the seminaries. So it was that the Executive Board, in consultation with the Board of Education and Committee of Synod Presidents, came up with a churchwide plan, reported in 1932 and 1934.[40] The plan proposed just four theological seminaries: one in the South, one in the East, one in the Central region, and a fourth in the near West. Each of the four seminaries was assigned its own group of supporting synods by region, thus doing away with instances of overlapping. The six synods in the South were to continue their support of Southern. Nine synods in the East would provide a coordinated support of the merged Eastern seminary, meaning Gettysburg and Philadelphia combined. Five synods would support the Midwest seminary, a merger of Hamma and Chicago. Seven synods would support a Western seminary, a merger of Western, Martin Luther, and Northwestern. Furthermore, two synods could make possible a relocated Pacific Seminary. Or so it was hoped, if and when the problem of too many seminaries could be solved. Yet neither the Executive Board nor even a ULCA convention had the constitutional authority to merge or move any seminary. That prerogative remained constitutionally with the synods, and they guarded it and their seminaries jealously.

A change was proposed by the recently merged United Synod of New York (1929), where impatience had been growing. In 1936 this body, aware of its own divided stand on Hartwick Seminary, voted to request the ULCA to amend its constitution so as to relate theological seminaries directly to the general church body. The establishment, control and maintenance of seminaries would thus be directly in the hands of the ULCA. Raising the hopes of those seeking a constitutional change, the 1938 Convention created the new Commission on Theological Education.[41] Chaired by President Knubel's son, F. R. Knubel, it consisted of seven members, including two parish pastors, three college presidents, a lawyer, and the executive secretary of the Board of Education (Gould Wickey) as secretary of the commission. Its assigned task was to "seek ways and means of realizing the principle of control." This commission reported to the 1940 convention in Omaha (see chapter 8).

The world of theological education can provide us with a final glimpse of the impact of the Great Depression on church life, especially at the grassroots level of congregations and prospective pastors. As local churches tried to do more with less during the depressed thirties, fewer full-time pastoral salaries were available. Staffs were reduced, parishes yoked or merged to share a pastor. Nevertheless, seminary enrollments were still strong, resulting in more candidates than calls. In a nutshell, according to a 1936 report, "God calls. Our youth respond. But our church has no plan for placement."[42] A seminarian's life was full of uncertainties, like America in general in this decade. The Augustana Synod made a pedagogical virtue out of this same predicament of oversupply by delaying a class of graduates with an added year of supervised internship, but the ULCA made no such adjustment. Ironically, the opposite problem, undersupply, loomed in the early 1940's as many young men chose military service instead of seminary and many pastors left congregational life for army or navy chaplaincy. Seminary enrollments boomed after the war, almost doubling from 1945 to 1950,[43] as did church life in general, but no one could see that far into the prosperous fifties during the thrifty thirties, especially when the decade ended amid such ominous global developments. In 1939, the guns of August roared the beginning of what would become the Second World War.

NOTES

1. ULCA *Minutes* 1934: 117-118.
2. ULCA *Minutes* 1932: 34-35.
3. Wentz, Abdel Ross, "The Salt that Kept Its Savor," *Lutheran Church Quarterly* 8 (1935): 27, 13.
4. R. C. Wolf, *Documents* # 149, pages 355-57; the full text in ULCA *Minutes* 1934: 415-417.
5. Greever, Walter H., ed., *Year Book of the United Lutheran Church in America for 1939* (Philadelphia: The United Lutheran Publication House, 1939), 5.
6. Wolf, *Documents* # 150, 357-59; the full text in ULCA *Minutes* 1938: 473-474.
7. ULCA *Minutes* 1940: 582.
8. G. Morris Smith, president of Susquehanna University, argued "that the budget of $2 million be accepted not as a retreat but as an advance to be actually secured by synods and conferences and congregations stimulated by the delegates here assembled" ULCA *Minutes* 1932: 86.
9. ULCA *Minutes* 1930: 140.
10. ULCA *Minutes* 1934: 115ff.
11. Ibid., 62.
12. ULCA *Minutes* 1932: 500; ULCA *Minutes* 1934: 545; ULCA *Minutes* 1940: 590.
13. ULCA *Minutes* 1932: 176
14. Ibid.
15. ULCA *Minutes* 1934: 83-99.
16. Ibid, 24.
17. Ibid., 99-100.
18. *Minutes of the Eleventh Biennial Convention of the United Lutheran Church in America, Baltimore, Maryland, October 5-12, 1938*, 40 and 449. (Hereafter cited as ULCA *Minutes* 1938.)
19. Ibid., 124f.
20. Ibid., 146.
21. Bachmann, *Lutheran Churches*, 510.
22. ULCA *Minutes* 1930: 210.
23. Ernst August Tappert (formerly pastor in Johnstown, Pennsylvania) was himself a product of the Kropp home mission seminary in Schleswig-Holstein, Germany. A native of Hanover, Tappert arrived in America in 1891 at the age of 17. Ordained four years later, his dedication and diversity of gifts enabled him to be the ideal person to welcome newcomers. His duties with the BAM (during the thirties) included the supportive oversight of some 270 bilingual congregations, and the supplemental training of seminarians for bilingual preaching and pastoral care. Already in 1931, under ULCA sponsorship, he visited the Lutheran Synod and others in Brazil; a journey that he would repeat, including Argentina, after World War II. Tappert's gift for winning the confidence of others was demonstrated in his rapport not only with Germans but also with other ethnic groups, including Finns, Icelanders Slovaks, Hungarians, Romanians (the Siebenbuerger Saxons),

Poles, and others. In western Canada, with its rich mixture of immigrants, he could be at home, and then tell others about these hardworking people.

24. ULCA *Minutes* 1932: 323.

25. ULCA *Minutes* 1930: 264, 302; ULCA *Minutes* 1932: 323.

26. *CSBH*, no. 202; *LBW*, no. 182.

27. ULCA *Minutes* 1940: 250, 255.

28. E. Clarence Miller, *Ecclesia Plantanda*, Lenten Number, 1936, 1.

29. ULCA *Minutes* 1938: 185ff.

30. ULCA *Minutes* 1938: 78-79.

31. ULCA *Year Book* 1939, page 15.

32. F. K. Wentz, *Lutherans in Concert*, 88, 96, 97.

33. A. R. Wentz, *Gettysburg Seminary Record*, 191.

34. ULCA *Minutes* 1936: 229.

35. ULCA *Minutes* 1936: 196.

36. Ibid., 205.

37. Ibid., 209.

38. ULCA *Minutes*, 1934: 251; ULCA *Minutes* 1940: 491.

39. ULCA *Minutes* 1940: 513.

40. ULCA *Minutes* 1932: 453-54; ULCA *Minutes* 1934: 233-45.

41. ULCA *Minutes* 1938: 483-84.

42. ULCA *Minutes* 1936: 202-204.

43. There were 287 students enrolled in seminaries in 1945 (ULCA *Minutes* 1951: 92). There were over five hundred in 1950 (F. Eppling Reinartz, *1951 Year Book of the United Lutheran Church in America* (Philadelphia: The United Lutheran Publication House, 1951), 92.

CHAPTER 8

THE TRANSITIONAL WAR YEARS, 1940-45

THE WAR YEARS OF 1940-45 MARKED THE ULCA'S ONLY SUCCESSION of presidents and its greatest transition in overall leadership and administrative location. For the membership, for all church bodies, indeed for all Americans, this half-decade was a traumatic sequence of apprehension, then self-sacrifice and commitment, and finally jubilation and new hopes for the future.

The year 1940 unfolded from eerie calm to violent storm. Hitler's Germany and Hirohito's Japan campaigned in Europe and Asia, and, along with Mussolini's Italy, formed an open military alliance. A profound apprehensiveness troubled thoughtful people everywhere. The flight of refugees from Nazi anti-Semitism and political intolerance revealed the sinister power of totalitarianism. For Roman Catholicism, and to a lesser extent for Protestantism, international connections were invaluable but increasingly in jeopardy. In totalitarian eyes religious ties were suspect, like a nervous system linking nations and posing a threat. By ethnic derivation and confessional kinship, Lutherans in America were the most international among the Protestants. And nowhere did they follow the course of events from 1940 onward more keenly than in New York. The single Manhattan address—39 East 35th Street—said it all, so far as cooperative efforts went. Here, in the Lutheran Church House, were lodged the headquarters of the ULCA and the National Lutheran Council.

Perhaps no one individual traced this unfolding drama with more personal and vocational concern than ULCA President Frederick Hermann Knubel, a German-American who had traveled and studied in his ancestral and confessional fatherland. But the German Church was being corrupted by the ideological encroachments of the Nazis, who had also occupied Denmark and Norway in late April of 1940. The Lutheran World Convention was paralyzed except for the American Section, which he led. Many overseas missions, begun and once funded by Europeans, were now "orphaned" and looking to American Lutheranism for help. Refugees were arriving in ever greater numbers and Americans everywhere were increasingly affected by the distant conflicts. Knubel's report to the

1940 ULCA Convention in Omaha reflected this crisis, especially for worldwide Lutheranism.

> Humanly speaking, the Lutheran Church of the whole world has never before been threatened as it is today. We in America are, so to speak, the last human help for Lutheranism. It would seem that our God wishes to use us, and we must not fail him.[1]

A man of three score and ten was speaking. Soon he would weaken and reduce his schedule, including the many necessary and normal contacts with synods and their heads. He would lead his church through the increasing trauma of 1941 and full-scale war, with all of its financial pressures, deployment of young parishioners along with many of their pastors, tragic injuries, and too many casualties. But he would not lead the ULCA through to the end of the global conflict. By the end of 1945, the new ULCA president, from new headquarters with new staff, would preach at Knubel's funeral, and mark the end of the first half of the ULCA.

OMAHA (1940) AND THEOLOGICAL EDUCATION

The 1940 convention at Omaha was the first ULCA churchwide gathering west of the Mississippi. Of the eleven preceding biennial conventions six had been in the East, two in the South and three west of Pennsylvania, in Ohio, Illinois, and Wisconsin. In one way the thrust into the Midwest was to make Lutherans in that part of the country better aware of the ULCA. Even more deliberate with respect to location was the effort to lift easterners out of their own provincialism. Hence the special significance in 1940 of meeting in Nebraska.[2] In Omaha, moreover, the Kountze Memorial Church in which the convention opened was at that time with its sixty-four hundred baptized members, the largest congregation in the ULCA. While churchwide conventions might thus foster a kind of wholesale awareness of the Lutheran Midwest, the church press—especially *The Lutheran*—kept easterners alert to the ULCA minority in that part of the continent. It remained for individual contacts and connections, countless numbers of them, to cultivate an ongoing westward interest and understanding. N. J. Gould Wickey personified the easterner who spent nearly the first decade of his career among various brands of Lutherans in the Midwest.

Illustrative, even though not typical, of easterners becoming acquainted with their midwestern peers was the case of this author. At age twenty-nine, with his eastern education supplemented by study in Europe and the Middle East, this curious cleric lacked an acquaintance with Lutherans west of Pennsylvania. Bent on correcting this deficiency and encouraged by Knubel and leaders in the National Lutheran Council, he used the spring of 1940 to meet Lutherans in the Midwest and to learn of their history as well as current attitudes. Focal points of the journey were seven theological seminaries in Ohio, Illinois, Missouri, Iowa, and Minnesota, two of them ULCA schools. Sample congregations, including Omaha's Kountze Memorial, as well as a number of church colleges and Inner

Mission institutions, rounded out the picture. He spent the most time in St. Louis delving into the history and ways of the church body he knew least, eventually doing a doctoral dissertation on the rise of Missouri Lutheranism. In Illinois and Minnesota the data gathered in home mission pioneering later became part of an interpretative biography of "Father" Heyer, the first American Lutheran missionary in India.

Seminaries drawing students from an entire church body—Concordia, St. Louis; Augustana, Rock Island; Luther, St. Paul (Norse)—impressed him for their ample vision of a whole continent, though not necessarily for their awareness of Lutherans in the East. A curious visitor from "back East," he was warmly received and his curiosity was reciprocated in part. But there was more to it than that, the cleric learned. Except for Augustana (Rock Island) the non-ULCA seminaries seemed to regard the United Lutheran Church with benevolent suspicion. This was true among students as well as faculty. In professors and students he often sensed a certain type of unease over first-hand contact with someone from the ULCA. What did this visitor, this recently ordained young man, intend? For him it was not like visiting in a foreign country, where the curiosity of hosts was directed toward learning about the visitor's homeland. Rather, in these non-ULCA seminaries it seemed more like a restrained and already informed curiosity. They, the faculty and students, already knew about the ULCA. They had read about the ULCA in their church papers and had talked about it, critically, much of the time. However, the cleric also realized that he was visiting strong seminaries. Their strength, quite apart from academic standard, unfolded in a unified church body with wide horizons but one seminary.

Our "curious cleric" was not alone in the discontent he felt over the diverse theological education in the ULCA. In response to "persistent unrest in the Church in relation to the control of theological education" the seven-member commission, appointed two years earlier, reported to the Omaha convention in 1940.[3] Board of Education executive, Gould Wickey, was the official link to the seminaries and the commission's secretary. In 1932, the church convention had been presented with a relatively drastic plan which proposed to merge the then twelve ULCA seminaries and reduce their number to five. What the regional interests of the synods prevented from happening, the Depression and the Board of Education had accomplished in part. In 1940 there were still seven in the United States: Gettysburg and Philadelphia in Pennsylvania; Southern at Columbia, South Carolina; Hamma, at Springfield, Ohio; Chicago at Maywood; Western, at Fremont, Nebraska, and Northwestern, at Minneapolis. Owned and operated by their supporting synods, the seminaries treasured their locations and school spirit, which predated the ULCA.

But there was a problem peculiar to the ULCA, chronic and nagging enough to require the help of a commission. We have noted earlier how its constitution committed the church at large to "the training of ministers and teachers to be witnesses of the Word".[4] Yet the federal structure of the ULCA left this commitment to the respective synods. It thus raised the problem of control. Would its exercise be central or regional? The compromise agreed upon at the Baltimore convention, as proposed by Charles B. Foelsch, gave the new commission its directive:

> to seek ways and means of realizing the principle of control, but interpreting the word 'control' as applying in the field of theological education and curriculum content, academic standards and kindred matters, but specifically not in the field of seminary ownership and maintenance.[5]

Agreeing "that our Church has not been completely satisfied with the products of theological education," the commission spelled out and recommended a range of improvements. In doing so it built on the earlier report but this time avoided any reference to seminary mergers or relocations, matters of synodical jurisdiction. And the outcome? The Omaha convention adopted recommendations that would exercise ULCA control of seminaries in terms of: academic standards, supplemental financial grants, information gathering and surveys, periodic conferences of faculty and seminary boards, and holding before the church and its seminaries the need for and tasks of an educated and committed ministry.

But the convention voted down any centralized control, such as the ULCA exercising advisory powers with synods and congregations with respect to theological education, or introducing a churchwide examination of all candidates for ordination, or approving the nominations to seminary professorships. Likewise lost was the proposal that there be a standing commission on theological education. Such overall functions would in future be assigned to the Board of Education, which thus increased its impact. Besides, given the wartime emergency and its impact also on education, the Board of Education's location in the nation's capital proved advantageous. Secretary Wickey, with characteristic energy and enterprise, ably served the interests also of the American Association of Theological Schools. Standards proposed for ULCA seminaries by the Board of Education thus reflected the interdenominational situation in theological education and enabled even the weaker of our schools to strive higher. In looking back one can see positive developments during these wartime years.

What happened at the Chicago Seminary-Maywood is illustrative. For two decades it had lived with problems that, as we have seen, ranged from the split that in 1920 led to the creation of still another seminary, Northwestern in the Twin Cities, and erupted in the later 1930s into a variety of intrafaculty feuds. With the death of Chicago Seminary President L. Franklin Gruber in 1941, a learned scholar and bibliophile, came a signal for change.

With encouragement from the ULCA Board of Education the self-perpetuating seminary board at last became a board fully elected by the supporting synods. The faculty members were given opportunity to resign. One of them, H. Grady Davis, was retained. A new president was called; none other than Foelsch from Washington. A new faculty was assembled. The students of the two upper classes had the best seats from which to observe the contrast between "before" and "after." One of them, Robert J. Marshall, would later become professor of Old Testament, then president of the Illinois Synod, and later, as successor to Franklin Clark Fry, president of the Lutheran Church in America. Besides, the incoming junior class, a small but talented group (a majority of them from Carthage College), by the example of their decision to come, proved an encouragement to the new faculty. (The writer of these lines was one of the latter.)

There is more to the illustration. For some years the consolidation of seminaries (Philadelphia Report, 1932) had been proposed, including a merger of Hamma Divinity School (Springfield, Ohio) and Chicago Seminary-Maywood. A growing number of Ohioans favored relocating Hamma to Chicago. In fact, with its many seminaries representing a spectrum of denominations, Chicago was billed as the "biggest theological center in America." The vote of the Ohio Synod convention in 1942 failed by one vote to bring Hamma to Chicago. The one whose vote would have made the difference was on that occasion unavoidably absent from the convention. A year later, however, it was that man, Joseph Sittler Jr., who accepted the call to Maywood. "If Hamma couldn't come, I felt obliged to accept the call and come."[6]

Like the seminaries across the land in wartime their students were on deferred status as to military service. But their numbers nevertheless diminished. Besides, by 1944 all seminaries were on an accelerated program and for the first time in history there was also a summer quarter. ULCA synods struggled hard and kept their seminaries in the running. Some benefited from special wartime programs, like the Philadelphia Seminary with its V-12 offering, a program for prospective Navy chaplains. It was inter-Lutheran. Among the enrollees was Carl H. Mau Jr., an ALC man from Washington state, who would later be serving in postwar Germany and eventually become general secretary of the Lutheran World Federation.

The accelerated curriculum during the war years brought some new departures. At times the smaller ULCA seminaries, like the smaller English vessels against the impressive Spanish Armada, proved more maneuverable and given to see things whole. As in one seminary, for example, a professor of church history might also be teaching a course in the Lutheran Confessions in their historic interpretation. He might also treat the mission of the church, past and present, as one, including the outreach at home and overseas as well as amid various aspects of contemporary society. All the while he would seek to show his students the inter-relatedness of the several fields of theology—the biblical, the doctrinal, the functional as well as the historical—and then try to help students see how, even under the pressure of time, it was important to link academic learning and real life situations by going on carefully planned field trips. Was it worthwhile?

Years later a student who had gone through this accelerated process and had made a career in the Navy, Ross H. Trower (eventually Navy Chief of Chaplains), showed his former professor around his aircraft carrier. "Do you know why I have done this?" he asked. "Because when we were your students in the accelerated program you nevertheless insisted on taking us on field trips. We could in those days imagine no more crazy waste of time. But when we got into our jobs we found that our field trip learnings were what we needed most to get started." This was his way of saying thank-you.

These war years, so it now seems, provided incentives in seminary or in parish to see the work of the church through new eyes. There was impatience, especially among seminary students, and at times a feeling of guilt that theological students were deferred while their friends were in military service. The pressure of preparation for ministry also placed the variety of the church's tasks into closer relatedness.

INTER-LUTHERAN DIALOGUE AND COOPERATION

The biennium 1940-42 provides us with worthy examples of the process and problems of unification and inter-Lutheran dialogue: its modest success when the Icelandic Synod was received into the ULCA, and its embarrassment when the laboriously wrought Pittsburgh Agreement failed to bring the ULCA and the American Lutheran Church (1930) beyond the latter's "selective fellowship." As failures are often more instructive than successes, the Pittsburgh Agreement merits special attention. Both the history of the ULCA and the later years of Knubel's presidency can be grasped better by examining, as in a case study, this particular search for closer fellowship and, according to the ULCA intentions, possible union.

From its outset the United Lutheran Church in America, by the accent on *United*, was open-ended toward union with other Lutherans. On the basis of the Lutheran Confessions mutually held, it nurtured unity and was ready for organic church union, be it by the reception of a single synod such as the Icelandic, or a local congregation, or merger with another body like the America Lutheran Church, formed in 1930 by the merger of four churches. The Savannah Declaration (1934) invited any and all Lutheran church bodies in America to consider closer relations of fellowship or union with the ULCA. This declaration, based on the Lutheran Confessions and in line with the ULCA Washington Declaration (1920), deemed no additional "standards and tests" as requisite to "true Lutheran unity and union."[7] The Baltimore Declaration" (1938) on the Word of God and the Scriptures made clear the ULCA position with regard to the authority of Scripture, the meaning of "Word of God," and the inspiration of Scripture. In fact, this unambiguous declaration was in part the product of conversations begun with representatives of the American Lutheran Church already in 1936.[8] It was the outcome of these conversations that led in 1940 to a prospective agreement.

Pittsburgh Agreement

The so-called Pittsburgh Agreement (1940, 1942) was between the two principals already mentioned, with other Lutheran church bodies looking on. It consisted of three articles. These had been proposed by the ALC when it accepted the invitation. They represented moot points on which not only the ALC but also other Lutherans, mainly in the Midwest, had raised doubts about the ULCA since 1918 and even before that big merger. The three Articles of Agreement thus dealt with neuralgic points in the perceived life and faith of the ULCA: (1) the membership of pastors (and laymen) in secret societies like the Masonic Order; (2) indiscriminate pulpit and altar fellowship as practiced by certain pastors; and (3) the highly charged issue of the verbal inspiration of the Scriptures. The latter was closely guarded by the Missouri Synod and its Synodical Conference as well as some other bodies but held especially in ULCA circles as being un-Lutheran. In short, the agenda for the ULCA-ALC conversations touched the profession of evangelically held faith in terms of practice as well as doctrine. This turned out to be a testing of the ULCA by an approach (invited, to be sure) from without. And it complemented the already prolonged testing from within, which, as no one knew better than the president, was the ULCA's own self-examination.

The conversation, or dialogue, was entrusted to two commissions of nine members each. The ULCA Commission on Relationships to American Lutheran Church Bodies included four laymen (two bankers, a contractor, and a lawyer) and five clergymen (two ministers of large congregations, two seminary professors, and the president of the church). The ALC had a similar team. On the ULCA side President Knubel served as chair, and Professor Charles M. Jacobs as secretary until his sudden death in early 1938. These two men, we recall, had drafted the Washington Declaration. Jacobs, moreover, had written most of the Baltimore Declaration before his death. Another Philadelphia Seminary scholar, Professor Henry Offermann, followed Jacobs as secretary of the ULCA team. For the ALC the leading participant was the Wartburg (Dubuque) Seminary president, Michael J. Reu, known not only for his biblical scholarship but also as the one who, already in 1917, at the fiftieth anniversary and final meeting of the General Council had spoken against the ULCA merger. His reason was that the council should not sell out its sound confessional position by joining with a "unionistic" body like the General Synod.[9]

For a time in the later 1930s the Missouri Synod had also taken part in the dialogue.[10] In fact, the so-called Brief Statement (1932) that it had drawn up for the Synodical Conference would also serve later on to guide a rapprochement between Missouri and the ALC. Thus, to look ahead, after 1940 the ALC would find itself torn between the unfinished Pittsburgh Agreement and the Brief Statement, both of which it had some reason to respect. In this triangular affair the Missouri Synod was not about to relinquish its interest in the ALC and thus strengthen the ULCA. From whichever angle, Michael Reu was the focal point. Word was out that Missouri counted Reu as the foremost Lutheran theologian in America. The triangle could also be lopsided; at a joint meeting of the commissioners and the Missourians there would be opening prayers, the Missourians in one room and the ULCA-ALC commissioners in another. Yet it was not long before the Missourians and the ALC representatives held their own meetings, the ULCA and the ALC having completed, as far as they could go, the Pittsburgh Agreement.

The three Articles of Agreement—named for Pittsburgh, the city where the two commissions first met (February 1936)—appeared in the Bulletin of Reports, circulated a month in advance of the Omaha convention (October 9-16, 1940). The Executive Board's comprehensive report on activities during the past biennium also printed resolutions from the 1938 convention of the ALC urging that the two commissions complete their joint endeavor that had enjoyed a promising beginning. With this corporate resolution came a personal greeting to President Knubel from his counterpart in the ALC, Em. Poppen, who wrote:

> Your visit and your greetings [to our Convention at Sandusky] have done much to strengthen the desire in our hearts for a closer relationship to the United Lutheran Church. I wish to thank you again . . . for a message that was both frank and heart-warming.[11]

Pleasantries aside, at least two items could give a careful ULCA reader pause to reflect. At the first meeting of the commissions at Pittsburgh they discovered, first of all, that they were operating under different instructions. The ULCA goal was for organic church union.[12] The ALC, more cautiously, would work for pulpit and altar fellowship. It was agreed that fellowship would not rule out eventual organic union.[13] Secondly, the two commissions could not agree on the character of the Scriptures. The ALC version declared that the books of the Bible "taken together, constitute one organic whole without contradiction and error (John 10:35)."[14] The ULCA version provided the whole with a center, declaring that the books of the Bible "taken together, constitute a complete, perfect, unbreakable whole of which Christ is the center (John 10:35)." We note the similarity. In both cases the reference to the Gospel according to John contains the word of Jesus, "scripture cannot be broken" (*RSV*). But the ULCA version, with Offermann's touch, not only omits the ALC reference to error but inserts Luther's emphasis on Scripture as centered on Christ.

In their final form, the Articles of Agreement, as presented by the ULCA commission and its ALC counterpart, were a compromise. The third article stated: "The books of the Bible . . . taken together constitute a complete, errorless, unbreakable whole of which Christ is the center (John 10:35)."[15]

At the Omaha convention an impasse lay ahead. "Errorless," for example, was a term regarding verbal inspiration denoting the correctness of all biblical statements also in the field of history, geography, and numerical data. Objections resounded from followers of even a moderate higher criticism of the Scriptures, as taught in most ULCA seminaries. One hour was given over to debate, and three commission members spoke for the Articles of Agreement. Leading those who spoke against the articles was a young pastor from Ohio, Franklin Clark Fry, and the Chicago Seminary professor, H. Grady Davis.[16] While most of the debate turned on the third of the Articles of Agreement, the first two articles likewise came in for discussion. The first article, that persons (pastors mainly) "be admonished" to sever connections with "organizations injurious to the Christian faith" (lodges), was seen as an unwarranted curbing of private judgment. The second article, against indiscriminate pulpit and altar fellowship, was the least criticized. Those taking exception to it were reminded that the substance of this article, like that of the first, was already embodied in the Washington Declaration. Knubel left the chair in order to express himself with deep feeling and in broad perspective prior to the vote on the agreement. At some length he pointed out the linkage between the Articles of Agreement and the ULCA Constitution as well as the succession of declarations: the Washington, the Savannah, the Baltimore. In no way, he insisted, did the new articles depart from this identifiable and confessional character of the ULCA.

Even though dissent among the delegates remained unresolved, the Articles of Agreement were approved by the Convention (Saturday morning, October 12). The resolution declared the readiness of the ULCA "to establish pulpit and altar fellowship with the American Lutheran Church" as soon as the ALC reciprocates with "a resolution of like effect."[17] Moreover, the ULCA hereby requested that the ALC "authorize its commission . . . to negotiate with our commission with a view to the organic union of our two Church bodies."

Time was of the essence. President Knubel was instructed, by further resolution, to convey the news of the Omaha convention to the ALC convention in Detroit, then in session. Notice of these actions in the form of a resolution "reached the American Lutheran Church in convention at Detroit in ample time for it to act upon them," according to Commissioner Edward Rinderknecht, a lawyer.[18] In its reply the ALC convention greeted the ULCA, and recognized the latter's adoption of the Pittsburgh Agreement as "evidence of the strength of conservative Lutheranism in the ULCA." Nevertheless, the ALC rejoinder contended that as of now "circumstances do not make it possible to enter into pulpit and altar fellowship." Instead, the ALC resolved that "our commission continue to work constructively toward full unity and ultimate pulpit and altar fellowship."[19]

Why this sudden reversal? Why was this, in Franklin Fry's words later, an "ill-starred Pittsburgh Agreement"? President Knubel, for one, felt it as the second of a double blow. The first had been the dissent from within the Omaha convention. The second was the ALC Detroit convention's decision to postpone adoption of the agreement. The protest within the ULCA convention was itself twofold. There was dissent, as already noted, during the debate before the adoption of the Articles of Agreement. Then, before the convention adjourned, as a delayed reaction, came what President Knubel especially must have felt as a severe blow not only to his own lifelong striving for Lutheran unity and union but also to those hopes of the ULCA itself.

Although the Pittsburgh Agreement had been approved, nevertheless four days later smoldering dissent and protest flamed forth in the closing session. First, three members of the ULCA Commission—H. H. Bagger (Lancaster) and Paul H. Krauss (Fort Wayne) as well as ULCA Treasurer E. Clarence Miller—presented a statement asking,

the privilege of recording our present dissent from the report because of its implications. Though fearing it from the beginning, we are now more than ever convinced that neither truth nor the cause of unity can be served by the ambiguity of
the report in question, particularly as regards the third Article of the Agreement.[20]

From another quarter a "protest" was formally presented by Central
Pennsylvania, the second largest of the ULCA Synods. Of its seventy-eight delegates, seventy-one had signed. They alleged that (1) the agreement was presented with too little advance notice or time for discussion; (2) the commission had
no guidance from the church "with respect to the first two Articles" (lodge and
indiscriminate fellowship), and (3) Article III is "a departure from the Baltimore
Declaration in that it presents an exclusive view of the mode of inspiration and
thereby reverses the Baltimore Declaration."[21] The convention closed with these
two public and formal dissents by key segments of the ULCA.

Nevertheless, the Pittsburgh Agreement was not dead, not yet. Two years
later, in October 1942, the two church bodies again assembled in convention; the
ALC in Mendota (Illinois), and the ULCA in Louisville. This time the ALC acted
on the agreement, yet with resolutions that proved ambiguous. To some ALC
leaders, including Ralph H. Long, director of the National Lutheran Council, it
appeared that indeed the ALC and the ULCA were now in "pulpit and altar fellowship." Yet when ALC President Poppen addressed the ULCA convention, he
said not a word about such fellowship. The silence was evocative. It turned out
that the ALC, as before, would continue to practice "selective fellowship" with
the ULCA. This presumably meant with those parts of the ULCA of General
Council or Southern background. Over against the General Synod element in
the ULCA there remained the old taboo, chiefly because of the General Synod's
past record on lodge membership and unionism. Admittedly, according to
Knubel, the president of the ULCA could do nothing directly to enforce discipline in the synods.

To his undoubted disappointment, President Knubel also learned from
President Poppen the backstage reason for the ambiguity in the ALC resolutions
on the Pittsburgh Agreement. Reu, said Poppen, had advised against adopting
the agreement. Why? Lest the ALC be accused by other Lutheran bodies, such as
Missouri, of practicing unionism.[22] In his own opinion, at least, Reu was consistent. Just as we noted earlier, the Reu voice that was raised in 1917 against the
ULCA merger was heard again off-stage and heeded for its cautioning against
the Pittsburgh Agreement.

Yet not all ALC members were of one mind in this matter. One of those who
respected and cherished the friendship of the ULCA was the rising theologian,
Edward C. Fendt. Professor and then dean of the ALC seminary at Columbus,
Ohio, he was a representative of his church body in intersynodical and interchurch unity negotiations for over thirty years. Several decades later, he reflected:

The sentences adopted [by the ALC] . . . do not contain an offer of pulpit and altar fellowship with the ULCA. They contain some preachments, savoring of criticism of past performances and expecting better 'behavior' in the future on the part of the ULC. The general idea communicated was that the ULC would have to qualify further before fellowship could be established.

Many of us in the ALC were embarrassed and chagrined when we compared the 1940 [and 1942] resolutions of both churches on the 'Pittsburgh Agreement.' There was a lack of trust in both camps.[23]

Under another president the ULCA would later again try to promote Lutheran union, for there must surely be a more trusting way. And trust was being built up by the lessons of cooperation in Texas and Canada, especially during the war years.

Texas and Canada

A comity arrangement between the ALC and the ULCA had been attained in the Lone Star State in home mission and related matters. The ALC Texas District had the size, the little ULCA Texas Synod the history (1851). This was no ordinary comity. The presence of a large Texas District of the Missouri Synod may have prodded comity between the other two judicatories. Before 1918 the original Texas Synod (it had been founded with the help of Pittsburgh's William Alfred Passavant) was a member first of the General Synod and then of the General Council. To be sure, it had early enjoyed close ties with the Iowa Synod, but it considered itself independent of Iowa. When the ULCA began, only a part of the original Texas Synod joined the merger. The rest, according to its own testimony, remained independent until in 1930 it was the fourth of the synods forming the American Lutheran Church. We can understand why Knubel, with his sense of history and love of unity, could address the Omaha delegates glowingly about the newly achieved comity in Texas. It was like a homecoming, for those who knew their history.

As for Canada, a war emergency and cooperation go together. During the first half of the forties this estimate fit America's Lutherans especially well. As the outbreak of war involved Canada before it did the United States, the three Canadian synods of the ULCA—the Canada (1861), the Manitoba (1897), the Nova Scotia (1903)—along with the respective judicatories of the Augustana, Norwegian, American Lutheran, and other United States-based general bodies, formed a Canadian Lutheran Commission, doing so with the help of the National Lutheran council. The Missouri Synod's Canadian districts were observers. Here some would see the "calamity theory of progress" at work. Ever since its merger the ULCA synods, accounting for nearly one-half of the Lutherans in Canada and being strongest in the East, seemed almost dissociated from the other constituencies which were strong in the prairie provinces. In background the ULCA synods, were of General Council affiliation, so that one spoke not so much of doctrine or practice as a dividing factor as of geography.

Even so, with the formation of the American Lutheran Conference stateside in 1930, in the following year the constituents across the border proposed a Lutheran Commission on Canadian Affairs.[24] The National Lutheran Council's action in 1939 could thus bring into a working partnership the commission and the ULCA Canada Section. Cooperation among them was easier than in the United States. So, for example, the Norwegian Lutherans in 1939 opened their own Luther Seminary on the campus of the ULCA's Lutheran College and Seminary in Saskatoon. Ethnic differences, though plentiful, were not insurmountable. The Canadian Lutheran Commission for War Service, as it emerged in 1939, became in effect a commission of the National Lutheran Council.

Many Canadians worked ardently for Lutheran convergence, but none more than the father-figure of the ULCA in Canada: Nils Willison.[25] A teacher and a pastor as well as a poet at heart, Willison early on envisioned a grand unity and union of Lutherans in Canada. Toward that end he saw an indigenous ministry, trained in Canadian Lutheran seminaries, as a basic necessity. By 1940, only half of the 168 pastors serving in the three ULCA Canadian synods were graduates of Canada's two Lutheran theological schools, Waterloo Seminary (Ontario), and Saskatoon Seminary (Saskatchewan). The other half were from the States or had come from the seminary at Kropp (Schleswig-Holstein) to serve the German-using congregations, mainly in western Canada. Willison himself was an immigrant from southern Sweden. Settling with his parents in Ontario, he was confirmed in a Norwegian congregation, and became the first graduate of Waterloo Lutheran Seminary in 1914. After four years in a parish, he was called to Waterloo College and Seminary, where he taught for the next ten years. Called as president and dean of the Lutheran College and Seminary, he spent the next thirteen years in Saskatoon. From that base and bearing in mind the needs of the church in Canada East and West, Willison had a vision of Lutheran unity which could gradually take shape in the vast dominion. The Willison vision extended beyond the ULCA. To him it made sense to invite the Norwegians to open their new seminary on the Saskatoon campus. It also made sense to look beyond the war service of the new Canadian Lutheran Commission. In 1942, Willison, saw one of his former students, Helmut T. Lehmann, called from Trinity Church, Winnipeg (Manitoba) back east to the presidency of the college and seminary at Waterloo. Bit by bit the ULCA was contributing its share to what would years later (1985) become the Evangelical Lutheran Church in Canada.

THE NATIONAL LUTHERAN COUNCIL IN WARTIME

As war years the early 1940s accentuated the necessity for Lutherans and others to cooperate more so than ever before. What was being done by some had to keep others in mind. The ULCA motif of seeking an enlarged united church had been put on hold. The failure of the Pittsburgh Agreement to achieve organic ecclesial union with the American Lutheran Church was a strong reminder that some unity, selectively pursued, was possible, but union, as merger, would have to wait. Happily this wartime era of cooperation, as noted above, greatly increased the significance of an agency like the National Lutheran Council. As participants in it, the Lutheran bodies were learning to trust each other by working together. It was a matter of learning by doing. Learning by saying, as in documents like Articles of Agreement (Pittsburgh) was a vulnerable exercise. To repeat with Edward Fendt (ALC), agreement failed for lack of trust.

By 1944, however, another man of the ALC, Ralph H. Long, director of the National Lutheran Council, expressed solid joy over the fact that, at long last, the NLC had a constitution. The participating bodies in their respective conventions had approved it. And there were even advocates that the Council should become a federation. As an agency of the churches, the Council did what was requested of it, and thus developed certain services further during the war. As the working arm of the American Section it also did what was entrusted to it by the Lutheran World Convention. Knubel, Long, and A. R. Wentz were the key figures in this dual outreach at home and overseas. By mid-1940 the recently formed NLC Department of Welfare, led by Clarence E. Krumbholz, had more than six hundred refugee cases on file, and had made 243 placements representing 441 individuals. E. A. Tappert, secretary for linguistic interests of the ULCA Board of American Missions, was looking after the refugee clergy.[26]

The war curtailed some inter-Lutheran activities and accelerated others. Preparations for a big gathering of the Lutheran World Convention at Philadelphia in 1940, the first official international meeting of Lutherans in the New World, were postponed indefinitely.[27] On the other hand, war's end, presuming victory, would require the cooperative sending of massive help abroad. Lutheran World Action (LWA) was launched in 1940 as a coordinated appeal for funds in support of the several emergency activities of the NLC and the American Section. It grew out of an initial drive in 1939 that included aid to Finland after the attack by the Soviet Union. Oscar C. Mees, the dynamic ALC pastor in New York led the way, soon aided, then succeeded by Paul C. Empie, the Ministerium of Pennsylvania's Director of Benevolence (to 1944), and later followed by Rollin Shaffer (ULCA), 1950-66. Among Lutherans, nothing surpassed the annual funding of LWA as its interpretive materials kept the manifold outreach of America's Lutherans ever in view and on their heart. Orphaned missions, refugees, service centers, defense area missions, and more, were included, as was the prospect of peace, the enormous challenge of relief and reconstruction in Europe. "Love's Working Arm," the strong outstretched arm holding the Cross, became the well-known symbol worth more than the proverbial "thousand words."[28]

The NLC Service Commission of 1941 was the Lutheran response to the U.S. Government's imposition of the draft in 1940. Its mood was patriotic and its aim was to attend to the well-being of men and women drawn into the armed forces. Like its predecessor, the National Lutheran Commission for Soldiers' and Sailors' Welfare, the Service Commission located centers near training camps and at other convenient places. By 1943 there were fifty-six service centers, complementing the famed USO centers, and another thirty-seven so-called parish centers.[29] A budget of more than $250,000 (LWA money) supported the work. Headquartered in Minneapolis, with the main branch in Washington, the commission employed forty-four pastors by 1944, plus other staff, and countless helpers and hosts from local congregations. Total annual attendance at these service centers, according to Frederick K. Wentz, approached 3.5 million. Director N. M. Ylvisaker's other, and perhaps major, task was the recruiting and screening of Lutheran candidates for the military chaplaincy, and of upholding them in the subsequent discharge of their duties. Almost overnight the commission sprang into life. Adapted to changing needs, it continued its work until 1966.[30]

The Commission of American Missions was another of the National Lutheran Council's bright achievements, dating from 1942 and renamed a Division in 1944. Its origins lay in the American Lutheran Home Missions Council (1931, Chicago). The imaginative and enterprising director, H. Conrad Hoyer, an Augustana pastor, took on the task at age thirty-five and continued in it for the next eighteen years. The sound policy underlying this emergency service laid the basis for much needed trust between the ULCA and the other participating church bodies. The mutual recognition accorded all the parties soon led to comity arrangements that would prove highly significant in future cooperation among Lutherans. On the Pacific coast the commission's work proved to be especially important for future growth of the church and continuing cooperation among Lutherans.

The Lutheran Commission for Prisoners of War was based on an agreement in 1943 between the Missouri Synod and the National Lutheran Council.[31] As Frederick Wentz reminds us, by 1944 there were some four hundred thousand POWs in the United States. "Most of them were Germans and half the Germans were in some sense Lutheran.... For the NLC, the Department of Welfare carried this responsibility."[32] It cooperated with the War Prisoners' Aid of the International YMCA (Geneva) and maintained an executive and two field representatives. Their task was to locate and authenticate Lutheran clergy among the prisoners, supporting their ministry among the men, providing worship materials religious books, and other helps. By mid-1946 the commission's work was completed. An estimated "million and a half prisoners of war had been reached by this ministry, the spiritual blessings of which are beyond computation."[33]

In light of the council's rapid growth, in 1944 proposals came from various sides for its reorganization. Most influential was the National Lutheran Editors' and Managers' Association. As recipients of news releases and other materials, editors like Nathan R. Melhorn of *The Lutheran* and his colleagues on the Augustana *Lutheran Companion,* the Norwegian *Lutheran Herald,* and the ALC's *Lutheran Standard* were best able to appreciate the value of the NLC's little-noted but widely-influential departments, namely, publicity and information and statistics. Through these sources the public press had also been able to channel news about Lutherans to media in many localities. As to reorganization, the near explosive growth of the National Lutheran Council during the war years had over-taxed the regulations governing it. To be sure, the regulations had been updated. But, as the editors urged, the council now required a constitution. Drafted in the main by Gould Wickey (ULCA Board of Education and a Washington "pro"), a constitution was ready before the end of 1944, and so were the bylaws. The ULCA convention approved and so did the other participating church bodies. Indeed, there was talk of going even further, of federating. But the time was not yet, although the incentive, so it seemed to devotees of unity, lay in the example of a well functioning American Section of the Lutheran World Convention. Had not Knubel, and especially the NLC director, Long, spoken repeatedly of the need for a unified Lutheran Church in America to face the postwar challenge?

Student work, by its very nature, held a central place in the Lutheran future. In fact, when the American Lutheran Conference was formed in 1930 as a non-ULCA association, the main task that bound its partners together was student work. Therefore, indicative of the mood of grander partnership being learned during the war years, the ULCA was ready to make common cause with the conference. At its 1944 convention (Minneapolis) the ULCA opened the way to a next step. It resolved

> that the United Lutheran Church in America authorize the Executive Board and the Board of Education, at their discretion, to prepare a plan and to effect the transfer of student work, in whole or in part, to the National Lutheran Council, when said council sets up a Department of Student Work.[34]

Thus did the war years accelerate various aspects of inter-Lutheran activity, especially within the National Lutheran Council.

ULCA LIFE DURING THE WAR

The 1942 ULCA convention in Louisville illustrated concretely how local church life was changed when the United States found itself fully at war. President Knubel's report on the "horribly tortured world of war" indicated several dimensions of the situation, including the "emergency powers" granted to him by the Executive Board but rarely needed.[35] Throughout the reports of boards and agencies, the urgencies of war pressed in on church life: pastors needed special authorization for automobiles and gasoline, seminarians and pre-seminarians needed draft deferments, conscientious objectors were extended support in prayer and financial aid.[36] The military needed chaplains, of course, and the ULCA supplied 126 of them, thirty-four taken from the precious ranks of mission pastors.[37] Overseas missions were disrupted everywhere, but especially in Japan and China; a special message of support went to Norway.[38]

Vast amounts of relief were needed worldwide for the displaced, the injured, the orphaned and other casualties of war, and yet the Lutheran World Convention was now dependent upon United States Lutherans alone, with small help only from Sweden.[39] The 1942 convention took in stride the visit and greetings by United States Vice President Henry Wallace,[40] and devoted considerable time to a major statement on the war. "The Church and a World at War" called for repentance, re-dedication and renewal, a diligent search for peace and yet avoidance of revenge, and generous support of relief programs. In a patriotic amendment from the convention floor, a concluding paragraph was added:

> The Church is praying that God may swiftly send His victory and His peace to suffering mankind:
> Therefore, be it resolved that we pledge to our leaders and to the men and women in the armed services of our country, at home and abroad, whatever their need, the church's wholehearted help; and that we call upon our own people and all other Christians to give their fullest measure of support, under God, and in the light of their consciences, to our country in this critical hour.[41]

As the Board of Deaconess Work put it at the outset of its report, "we face a new world order."[42] In 1942, however, no one yet knew how the war would turn out and what that new order would be. The accent in wartime fell on steadfastness amid change; on worship and the nurture of the spiritual life while coping with transitions. It was a faith active in love, from the home congregation to the service centers for the military and the chaplains far and wide. It was outreach to the workers and their families in war industry areas. And it exercised identity amid cooperation with other Christians, with the community, and with the government.

Quantified, during these war years the ULCA was hard-pressed for pastors. Their number grew by less than one hundred, reaching 3,710 in 1944, and many of them were needed as chaplains. New congregations increased by twenty-three, to a total of 4,062. Up by almost one hundred thousand, the baptized membership stood at nearly 1.8 million. But during that same period Sunday School enrollment dropped by one-seventh, to 574,000. Financially, the usually lagging support for ULCA boards reached 80 percent of the $2 million goal. During the war years the work of the church through these units bore various signs of the times. The "apportionment boards," those depending on the synods paying their apportioned benevolence, found their normal routines altered by new priorities or highlighted by noteworthy events.

Board of American Missions

The Board of American Missions, largest recipient of the synodical dollar, reported seventy-one of its mission pastors as having entered the military chaplaincy. Of the 762 mission congregations assisted by the BAM, seventy were shepherdless.[43] These constituted the most serious problem, but received provisional care. The greatest gain operationally had come through the cooperative program mentioned earlier, developed through the Division of American Missions under the National Lutheran Council. Operative especially in war industry areas, it had grown into a venture second only, in size, to the NLC-sponsored Service Commission to military personnel. Besides the linguistic ministries in seven languages there was now also the large and welcoming hostel for the *nisei* (first generation Japanese Americans) in Minneapolis. Conducted by Martha Akard, a repatriated ULCA missionary from Japan, the hostel program aided in the resettlement of hundreds of families en route from wartime camps to a new beginning.[44] An inter-denominational undertaking, it was aided by the Women's Missionary Society of the ULCA and by other sources as well.

Board of Foreign Missions

For the Board of Foreign Missions World War II really hit home. Work in Japan and China was suspended, with nationals maintaining their congregations as best they could.[45] Missionary personnel (thirteen from China and twenty-nine from Japan) were repatriated, but some were detained.[46] Stateside they also rendered significant linguistic service, living reminders of a continuing mission. One year after the Japanese attack on Pearl Harbor the last meeting of the Japan Evangelical Lutheran Church took place. While there was still time, before the Kyodan would absorb the JELC along with the other Protestant bodies, the native church historian recorded: "Our JELC is gathered today, December 5, 6, 1942 in our Lutheran convention in Tokyo to celebrate the fiftieth anniversary of the first preaching service in the city of Saga, Kyushu, in 1893. Through the many years our [JEL] Church has grown to seven thousand members."[47] While the connections with China and Japan hung in suspense, the JELC remained an associate synod of the ULCA. The work in China was more dispersed and inter-Lutheran. While the Japanese occupied vast regions, the capital of China was relocated to the west. In Chungking, as the representative of the American Section of the Lutheran World Convention, Daniel Nelson (Norwegian Lutheran Church of America) directed a remarkable interdenominational service. The link between Chungking and the outside world was via the famed Burma Road and on to the Indian subcontinent. But Nelson, born in China of pioneer missionary parents and trained for the gospel ministry in America, was the ideal living link.[48] For he administered LWA relief funds to orphaned missions in China, be they of German, Norwegian, Finnish, Danish, American, or other origin.

India was a completely different story, less directly affected by the war yet not without frustrations. The Andhra Evangelical Lutheran Church, an associated synod of the ULCA, celebrated its centennial in 1942 with a festive sequence of events observed by a baptized membership now numbering some two hundred thousand. Missing, however, were the ULCA visitors from America, since wartime conditions prevented their journey. But the Louisville convention in 1942 approved full self-governance for the Andhra Church. The AELC thus became a self-governing church body during the war, except that it still requested and received missionary personnel from America, from the Augustana Synod as well as the ULCA, and continued to receive grants-in-aid from the Foreign Board and from the Women's Missionary Society. Besides, individual ULCA congregations shared in sponsoring or aiding a number of individual American workers as well as native congregations. Largest of the nine Lutheran bodies on the subcontinent, the Andhra Church was a leading member of the Federation of Evangelical Lutheran churches in India. Concentrated in the Telugu-speaking Andhra country, this church had acquired its share of institutions: Andhra Christian College in Guntur, a theological seminary in Rajahmundry, a hospital at Guntur (Kugler Hospital today), besides several hundred elementary and Sunday schools. Over the generations hundreds of devoted men and women had been sent from America. In 1942, fifty-nine of them were actively serving, with still others on furlough.[49]

This brief look at the formation of young churches in wartime conditions is important for the ULCA story in several ways: it reveals the mission process in transition; it notes the rise of young churches that are indigenous and self-governing (though not yet fully self-supporting); and it suggests something of the part played by the ULCA in the global outreach of the Lutheran communion within the church evangelical and catholic. The latter course was becoming increasingly evident as World War II was approaching its end, particularly as the ULCA, through President Knubel and others, pursued participation in the Faith and Order Movement as a confessionally sound route into the World Council of Churches. In short, the ULCA story, precisely in these war years, needs to be seen in global as well as local terms.

The Board of Social Missions

A small unit with wide responsibilities, the Board of Social Missions had a three-fold churchwide task: evangelism, welfare services, and social action. The Board of Deaconess Work was closely akin to the BSM. These two units gave expression in their special ways to what President Knubel and the Washington Declaration called "works of serving love," an expression of the Church. Perhaps better than any other unit, the BSM was in a position to know what was happening to people at the grassroots. Besides, it dealt on a small scale in those diaconal services which, at the war's end, would be required on a massive scale in postwar reconstruction and rehabilitation in Europe and elsewhere. The largest involvement of the board was in welfare services. Dealing with human need from infancy to old age, these services easily spilled over synodical boundaries and became interlinked with like services in other Lutheran church bodies as well as with similar services rendered in the local community by public as well as private agencies. In this way, the Board of Social Missions, more than nearly any other board, attended to individual needs while keeping the wider social context in view. In 1944 the Board's Inner Mission constituency included twenty children's homes, twenty homes for the aged, thirteen general and special hospitals, eight hospices (residences for young persons coming to the city for work), seven settlement houses in neighborhoods of poverty or new Americans, two Deaconess Motherhouses (Baltimore and Philadelphia), as well as twenty-seven Inner Mission societies and service agencies.[50] This ULCA array was well represented in the National Lutheran Inner Mission conference, whose executive was the ULCA's Clarence E. Krumbholz, also director of the National Lutheran Council's Division of Welfare.

Wartime services of this board included such specialties as assistance to lay readers for congregations bereft of pastors gone into the military chaplaincy, and similarly concern for conscientious objectors to war. The reduced flow of refugees was handled in cooperation with the National Lutheran Council. Social action, continuing the work of the former Committee on Moral and Social Welfare, was promoted as feasible in the synods through visitations and institutes, through seminars and study grants, as well as through published materials on temperance, and family life. Seminary courses on social missions (as introduced at the Chicago Seminary-Maywood in 1944) were encouraged.[51]

By 1940, in the new Board of Social Missions, evangelism had "arrived" and took its place in the organizational structure. Oscar W. Carlson became the ULCA's first director of evangelism. The visitation evangelism he conducted was concentrated in selected cities across the continent. In addition, institutes and schools of evangelism as well as preaching-teaching missions accentuated the program. Everywhere the participation of the laity, men and women, was seen as complementing the evangelizing task of the pastor. Compared with what had been, the war years brought a new day.[52]

Deaconesses during the war years attracted attention to the role of women in the life and outreaching service of the church. Although they were few in number (150), their garb was a symbol that gave identity, and in many places won ready acceptance. The ULCA deaconesses in the 1940s had two communities, the older and larger (1884) in Philadelphia, the other in Baltimore (1894). Those in Philadelphia continued actively serving in institutions, agencies and schools, as well as in parishes. Those in Baltimore, although also diverse in their placement, concentrated on service in congregations. Sister Nora McCombs was a 2nd Lieutenant, stationed with the United States Army in the Far East as a psychiatric nurse. Two others, Sisters Margaret Fry and Margaret Schueder, rendered timely service in one of the major war industry centers in Michigan.[53] Though deaconesses were much in demand, in wartime especially the recruits were too few; even as the jobs for women boomed. By 1944 the Deaconess Board elected its first field secretary. Sister Mildred Winter, a persuasive and brilliant young woman, thus became the roving representative of *diakonia* as she visited congregations far and wide. For her as for others the deaconess motto rang true: "The love of Christ constrains me."[54] The diversity of its tasks linked the Board of Deaconess Work not only to other ULCA boards and auxiliaries but also to deaconess houses in other church bodies around the world. Since 1896 the Conference of Lutheran Deaconess Motherhouses had been fostering inter-Lutheran cooperation. Until 1944 the president of the conference was always a pastor. But then came sister Anna Ebert, Philadelphia's directing sister. A calm, confident and gracious leader, she personified the women's diaconate in the new (postwar) day. In 1943 and 1944 the Philadelphia Motherhouse hosted the first two meetings of a "Council of Women in Full-Time Service in the Church."[55] In light of later developments one can see in the deaconess work and its friends a beginning of a more aggressive women's movement in the ULCA.

Particularly supportive of wartime deaconess work was the Women's Missionary Society. This auxiliary's support of women missionaries overseas was in effect a mission-oriented *diakonia* that helped to emphasize the oneness of mission as such and of women's service in the church at home and overseas. Furloughed women missionaries continued to find a welcome and to share their experiences with the Motherhouse community in Philadelphia or Baltimore. Likewise refugees and others were welcome. In fact, a deaconess community at any time, but especially in the war years, was alive with contacts worldwide, an unparalleled place in the church.

The year 1944 was also E. F. Bachmann's last full year as pastor of the Philadelphia Motherhouse. At war's end, the following year, he retired after thirty-nine years as a deaconess pastor. Both of his predecessors, Rector Cordes and Pastor Goedel, had come from and returned to Germany. In 1906 Bachmann, a Philadelphia Seminary graduate and promising pastor of English-speaking Concordia Church in Buffalo, New York, was called. Fluent in English as well as German, and active in youth work, he expedited the deaconess community's transition from German to English. During both World Wars, and especially after the first one, he and the Sisters maintained ties with the Kaiserswerth International Conference of Deaconess Motherhouses, and helped to handle postwar relief shipments. As mentioned earlier, Bachmann was elected first president of the ULCA Inner Mission Board. Twice the church sent him to Europe (1920, 1926) on special assignment. A close friend of Knubel's (both men were born in 1870), and a seminary classmate of Morehead's, Bachmann had a gift for making and keeping friendships in America and Europe, and with missionaries overseas. A recognized leader in the Conference of Deaconess Motherhouses, he was able to adapt an established way to ever changing needs. His successor, Richard C. Klick, (1945-50) could build on the groundwork already laid by the veteran pastor and others as well as by the deaconesses themselves. The consistency and commitment of the Bachmann career may be seen in the fact that his fellow pastors elected him delegate to every one of the ULCA conventions from 1918 to 1944.

Secretary for Promotion

The Board of Publication in 1938 called F. Eppling Reinartz as a consulting secretary of promotion. His service became so valuable that by 1942 he became Secretary of Promotion and his report followed that of the president. After Louisville in 1942, post-convention meetings were held for the first time. Their aim was to bring to the congregations a closer awareness and comprehension of the work of the church. The visiting speakers had been delegates to the convention, who numbered some eight hundred. Of the more than four thousand ULCA congregations an estimated eighteen hundred had been reached. Happily the 1942 convention theme, as we have seen earlier, had a missionary theme and a personal dimension of forthright appeal: Muhlenberg's phrase, "The Church must be planted," and Father Heyer's self-starter, "I am ready now" [to return to India].[56]

If this proved a good way to nurture unity within the ULCA, then in terms of promotion the observance of the church's twenty-fifth anniversary in November 1943 could be called a hit. The anniversary theme "Toward God's Golden Goals" was forward-looking, over the next twenty-five years. Most pastors, it was said, used the anniversary text from Joshua 13:18, "There remaineth yet very much land to be possessed." And on that Sunday, November 14, nationwide over the Columbia Broadcasting "Church of the Air," President Knubel preached the sermon and the Wittenberg College choir sang. Special contributions to the Pension Board flowed in (more than $42,000). A painting, to be hung in the new Lutheran Church House, and now in the ELCA Archives, depicted Jesus gathering a group of modern-day followers en route to a big city on the horizon. A Knubel-Miller Foundation Fund was launched to support an annual lecture series, honoring the matched twenty-five years of service given the ULCA by its first president and treasurer.[57]

The Office for Promotion, in retrospect, appeared as a welcome and, in the hands of its incumbent, innovative way of nurturing a growing sense of wholeness in the church at large. The many diverse functions were reminded of, and assisted in, their interrelatedness. The Reinartz outreach was in effect the extended and helping hand of the church president. It not only included the thirty-two synods but also touched congregations and their pastors. His own parish experience in Ohio provided input for the *Pastor's Plan Book*. Devised with the help of professors of practical theology, the book became widely used, also by students in their seminary years. Outside the ULCA it compared favorably with similar publications. The Practical Theology Department of Yale Divinity School adopted it for the course in Church Administration.

As the president's right hand the secretary for promotion worked closely with the Committee of Executive Secretaries, a cabinet equivalent in the church's structure. The agreed emphasis on promotion was fourfold: Be Christian, Search the Scriptures, Live Helpfully, Win Others. For an informed promotion like that entrusted to Reinartz a wise mentor like Secretary Greever was essential. Only then, and with access to the many resources of the secretariat, could a Reinartz be called the "right hand" of an intensely busy president. Indeed, it would come as no surprise when, a few years later, Reinartz would be elected Secretary Greever's successor.[58]

TRANSITION

Morgan House

An opportune change during the war years was the acquisition of the new Lutheran Church House in New York. The six-story former private dwelling at 39 East 35th Street had become increasingly cramped. Both the ULCA and the National Lutheran Council required more room. The searches of Secretary Greever and some informed laymen led to a "find" less than three blocks away, to a historic brownstone residence at 231 Madison Avenue, on the southeast corner at 37th Street. There, in the still residential area called Murray Hill and in a section once dubbed "Bankers' Row," stood the last mansion of the banking House of Morgan. Adjacent, at 36th Street, was the Pierpont Morgan Research Library. Upon the death of the younger John Pierpont Morgan in 1943, the family, active Episcopalians, sold "231" to the Lutherans for $265,000. The price was a bargain: 60 percent less than the assessed valuation of $672,000.

Although the sale was firm in September of 1943, the title was not cleared until January of 1944. By June 15, the alterations were sufficiently advanced to allow the offices of the ULCA and the NLC to move in. The Executive Board Advisory Committee had coped successfully with such wartime authorities as New York City's Zoning Board, the War Production Board (for materials), and the Tax Commission (for exemption). Centerpiece of the extensive remodeling was the chapel. The well-known church architect T. Norman Mansell altered the large ballroom-library into an exquisite place of worship: altar of white Italian marble with retable , including mosaic insignia of Christ, atop which stood an intricate wrought-iron polychromed cross, flanked by matching candlesticks and vases. The lectern and pews (white, with mahogany trim) suggested Georgian colonial style. An alcove to the right of the chancel provided space for a small pipe organ (acquired later).[59] Exclusive of the chapel (the gift of an anonymous donor), the cost of the other alterations came to some $70,000, with the furnishings for the offices another $25,000. Precisely during a time of war it was felt that those engaged in the far-flung work of the church should have a place where, in the beauty of holiness, daily worship should be an uplifting experience.

The ULCA offices occupied the first three floors, while the National Lutheran Council spread out over the top floor where house lore claimed that the Morgans' servants lived, trusted housemaids from Lutheran Sweden. Yet on this top floor there now converged the life and death issues of relief and reconstruction as the end of World War began to draw near. For President Knubel, however, the move to the new Church House gave a touch of climax to his twenty-six years at the helm of the church body he loved.

Minneapolis Convention

From October 11-17, 1944, Minneapolis was host to the fourteenth biennial convention of the United Lutheran Church in America and the last of the twenty-six-year Knubel presidency. To this still young flour milling capital of the continent came 554 of the 559 elected delegates as well as others complying with the restrictions of wartime travel. From the opening service on the evening of the eleventh to adjournment six days later, all sessions took place in Central Lutheran Church, the spacious neo-gothic showpiece of the Norwegian Lutheran Church in the heart of downtown Minneapolis. Here at Central the stated conventions of the Norse-descended church body regularly took place. And here the heads of the several bodies based in this other half of the Twin Cities—the (Swedish) Augustana, the Lutheran Free Church as well as the

Norwegian Lutheran Church—extended their welcome.

The ULCA's Synod of the Northwest (1891), known for its pioneering of English-using Lutheranism in the Upper Midwest, was the convention's ecclesial host. Nearby, the big Curtis Hotel, accustomed to large-scale church patronage, combined dignity with a congenial atmosphere. Besides the headquarters of the three named Scandinavian bodies, Minneapolis was also home to an array of church institutions, starting with the ULCA's own Northwestern Seminary and including Augsburg College and Seminary of the (Norwegian) Lutheran Free Church. Across the river in St. Paul, the capital of the North Star State and the older of the "Twins," was Luther Seminary, the mind-shaping powerhouse of the Norse Lutherans. Not far away was Concordia College, one of the feeders to Concordia Seminary, St. Louis, and a stronghold of the Missouri Synod in the Upper Midwest.

For discerning members of the ULCA, about half of whom were from the East, the journey itself had the effect of a field trip into the nearest thing to a "Lutheran establishment," a world apart from Pennsylvania and yet a homeland of confessional kin. It remained for a man of imagination like the Rev. William Passavant Christy, pastor of the then little Lake of the Isles Church, Minneapolis, to create a symbol of the dream of Lutherans united. Following the address of welcome to the convention by Minnesota's Governor Thye, a Lutheran of Norse descent, Christy presented President Knubel with a gavel. As Christy explained, his crafted gavel

> has been prepared for your use during this convention. It is made of wood from the first Lutheran churches in this city [as begun by] Iowa, Ohio, Missouri, Norwegian, Free, Augustana and the Synod of the Northwest. It demonstrates that these elements can be united so perfectly that they cannot possibly be hammered apart.

Then came Christy's clincher, "It has been my purpose to identify the pieces for you, but the identity disappeared in the process of making. Now I am really glad that it has and I hope this too is prophetic as well as symbolic."[60]

It was Columbus Day, Thursday, October 12, 1944, when the familiar voice of President Knubel led the convention in the traditional versicle and response for the opening of synods. Before noon, that Thursday was already the day of greatest transition in the history of the ULCA. Not only was there the customary round of reports from the top officials and from the Executive Board but there was also the election of officers. At age seventy-four (there being no mandatory retirement) Knubel appeared willing to continue, "as long as they elect me." But his presiding over the first quarter century of the ULCA seemed ready for rounding off. Remarkably, Knubel's election in 1918 launched a succession of twelve reelections by the church's biennial conventions. Every two years the Knubel presidency was up for review. And each time the vote of confidence reaffirmed him in office by a high margin on an early ballot. His willpower was iron, but his health at times showed the strain. From the personal standpoint he had outlived many an old friend and trusted colleague. There was the death of his theological mentor, Charles M. Jacobs, in 1937. Later that same year, Paul W. Koller, executive of the Foreign Board and former mainstay of Knubel policies in Ohio, departed this life. A quartet of Knubel supporters among the laity died in the early 1940s: Jesse L. Clark (Lutheran Laymen's Movement for Stewardship) in 1942; Ernest F. Eilert (twenty-one years as treasurer of the National Lutheran Council, and pioneer of the Luther League) in 1943; Arthur P. Black (tireless promoter of stewardship for fifteen years) in 1944; and, in March of 1944, E. Clarence Miller (in his twenty-sixth year as ULCA treasurer) succumbed to a heart attack. Their loss was felt churchwide, especially Miller, and especially by a president who had unfailingly encouraged and counted on them during long years of service.

Before the Minneapolis convention various names were mentioned as possible successors in the ULCA presidency. Among them Henry H. Bagger (Lancaster, Pennsylvania), F. Eppling Reinartz (New York), and others. Most prominently named, yet also encumbered with reservations, was Franklin Clark Fry of Akron, Ohio. If the balloting began with a sense of change in the air, this atmosphere must have intensified when Knubel was not elected on the first or second ballot, or the third. Before noon on October 12, the fourth ballot was held and President Knubel declared the Rev. Franklin Clark Fry president of the United Lutheran Church in America for the biennium beginning January 1, 1945.[61] He had received 358 votes out of 517 cast.

> Dr. Fry addressed the convention briefly and with deep feeling in announcing his acceptance of the election. In acceptance of the results of the election, President Knubel spoke to the deep satisfaction and edification of the convention concerning his retirement from official responsibilities in accordance with his interpretation of the will of the Lord.[62]

By mid-afternoon the other top offices were also elected for the next biennium, both on the first ballot. Walton Harlowe Greever, the genial southerner and alert master of matters backstage, was re-elected secretary. In more ways than could be anticipated he would personify the administrative continuity of the ULCA: convention minutes, Executive Board actions, the annual *Year Book* with its rosters, memberships and statistics, a reviewing of the minutes of each of the thirty-two synods, keeping an eye on any matters requiring follow-up or clarification, and much more besides. The Office of ULCA Secretary was indeed a point where the ongoing life of the church converged. And its incumbent, so rich in experience as Greever, then seventy-four (the same age as Knubel) would be ideally suited to assist and counsel the new church president who was thirty years younger and bore the character of a postwar take-over generation. Likewise that afternoon the delegates elected Henry Beisler treasurer of the ULCA. Beisler, a successful businessman in northern New Jersey, was already interim treasurer after the late and lamented E. Clarence Miller.[63] A generous and committed layman, he was president of the council of St. John Lutheran

Church, Jersey City. At the Minneapolis convention the two newly elected officers firmed up what would become a durable friendship, aided by the move of the treasurer's office from Philadelphia to the new Church House in New York. By a remarkable providence, the veteran Knubel-Miller duo of president and treasurer (1918-44) would be succeeded as of January 1, 1945 by the new one of Fry and Beisler.

Knubel's New Life

After the Minneapolis convention, President Knubel served out the calendar year, but in declining health. Church Secretary Greever and the knowledgeable staff, especially the president's secretary, Sigrid Wilson, kept the agenda moving and made ready for the coming of Knubel's successor. Meanwhile Knubel also continued as president of the American Section of the Lutheran World Convention. His nearest partner and the actual administrator of these duties was Ralph H. Long, director of the National Lutheran Council, whose office on the top floor of the Church House was conveniently near.

Over the Christmas holidays and into 1945, the Battle of the Bulge raged as a reminder that war is hell. Back in New Rochelle three generations of Knubels gathered during the Christmas holidays in 1944. Nearly fifty years later, Fred, one of the three grandchildren, recalled how Grandfather was ailing but Grandmother Jennie in her customary way enlivened the party. The former parish deaconess, since 1925 the second Mrs. Knubel, had a special way with children. On this occasion she entered the room as "Mrs. Box," the name given her by the children because of the large corrugated carton inside which she stood and, Santa-like, distributed gifts.[64]

New Year's Eve—St. Sylvester, December 31, 1944—marked the official end of the Knubel presidency. In retirement he was granted an annual pension of $3,300, which was a bit over 40 percent of his former salary.[65] On January 11, he received a glowing "Testimonial of Esteem to the President Emeritus." Finding himself with a new title, an appreciative Knubel, ever the seeker for clarity, asked for a "definition of the term 'president emeritus' as applied to the president emeritus of the United Lutheran Church." The inquiry was referred to the Board's Legal Committee.[66] Meanwhile, as the war in Europe was in its final throes, he was grateful when Ralph Long and his two fellow fact finders, P. O. Bersell (Augustana president) and Lorenz Meyer (Missouri administrator), had returned safely from their six-week wartime investigation in Europe. But, as Knubel and others learned, "the present status of the Lutheran World Convention is chaotic." Even so "the functions of the Convention are being performed as fully as circumstances permit through the leadership of American representatives."[67]

Knubel's seventy-fifth birthday came on May 22, a fortnight after Victory in Europe (V-E) Day. His birthday was a quiet affair, yet alive with expressions of love and esteem and intercessions for his well-being. As the summer advanced so did Knubel's progressive illness. "At the meeting of the Executive Board, October

10-11," so runs the record, "President Fry announced the critical illness of Dr. Knubel, and he was especially remembered in the devotions of the Board."[68] And what was going on in the world at large as Frederick Hermann Knubel lay dying? Into two great harbors, San Francisco and New York, naval units of the Pacific Fleet were coming home. The return of these tested vessels gave proof of the end of World War II. A new era was beginning. New duties were being imposed, the scope of which was as yet unfathomable. Over it all hovered the awesome image of the mushroom cloud, symbol of the Nuclear Age. Not long before his death, Knubel could still catch this portent, and thank God he was going home. For his successor the possibility of a man-made doom was a challenge to live and preach the Good News of salvation.

On October 16, "The United Lutheran Church in America suffered its saddest bereavement."[69] *The New York Times*, on the 17th, ran a one-column obituary, plus photograph. The native New Yorker who had prepared for a career in business had instead been redirected to use his exceptional gifts in the ordained ministry. "He did not engage in Modernist-Fundamentalist controversies. In general he was conservative in his theology, in line with the general policy of his church," said *The Times*. It added that during his twenty-six years as president the ULCA had grown by six hundred thousand new members. Besides:

> Dr. Knubel, an orator and an expert parliamentarian, wielded a strong influence over the body he headed. It was due largely to his diplomacy and executive ability that divergent elements in his organization were invariably reconciled.[70]

The funeral service at Our Savior's Atonement Church in Upper Manhattan, his home congregation, included sermons by President Fry and Secretary Greever. The large gathering and people throughout and beyond the United States and Canada gave thanks for the life and ministry of this servant of the Lord. In the words of President Fry:

> God gave our father a marvelous degree of wisdom. . . . By his gracious Christian churchmanship, loving and shepherding men of various views, many a breach was prevented and many a wound never occurred. This is what has made our Church strong. Indeed, it has gone far to make it possible. . . . There need be no turning back for the United Lutheran Church, there can be a steady going forward into the future. It will be a natural outgrowth of our late president's judgment and his vision.[71]

As it turned out, the eulogist was the only successor to President Knubel, whose leadership had already led the ULCA past its halfway point.

After Fry's eulogy, a member of the Executive Board, Oscar C. Blackwelder, noted preacher and pastor of Washington's Church of the Reformation, helped many to recall and countless others of a later time to imagine this first president of the ULCA, when he wrote:

> We remember [Dr. Knubel's] distinguished personal appearance. . . . He looked the bishop's role. His face seemed to mold like bronze as his responsibilities increased.

We remember his voice, filled with diapason tones and minor chords,
capable of peculiarly moving others into his way of thought and policy.

We remember his power of friendship. Who among us will forget the warm, radi-
ant letters we received from him.

We remember his genius at parliamentary procedure, his kindly handling of convention delegates, his firm but fair rulings upon sharp differences among honest
men.

We remember his fidelity to administrative details, his faithfulness to
presidential details in the guiding of boards, commissions, committees and
individuals into comprehensive churchmanship.

We remember his evangelical convictions in the larger Christian relationships. He
firmly held to the total of revealed truth. He appeared to keep the cosmopolitan
spirit of the city he served as pastor and which seemed to help fit him for his later
ecumenical and international responsibilities.

In the United Lutheran Church in America he will be remembered, honored and
revered as long as our history endures.[72]

NOTES

1. ULCA *Minutes* 1940: 26f.

2. Naus, Alford R., *West of the Mississippi, A Picture Story of the United Lutheran Church in America* (The Omaha Committee for the 12th Biennial Convention of the ULCA, 1940).

3. ULCA *Minutes* 1938: 483-4. ULCA *Minutes* 1940: 479-87.

4. VI/4a. (ULCA *Minutes* 1918: 60ff.)

5. ULCA *Minutes* 1938: 484. ULCA *Minutes* 1940: 479.

6. Also quoted by Louis Voigt, "History," (unpublished manuscript) hereafter, Voigt "Ohio Synod."

7. R. C. Wolf, *Documents*, page 345; see the earlier discussions in chapters 5 and 7.

8. ULCA *Minutes* 1936: 398-401.

9. Meuser, *Formation of the ALC*, 150-55.

10. With Missouri, a first, at Detroit, November 1936. ULCA *Minutes* 1938: 467.

11. ULCA *Minutes* 1940: 106.

12. ULCA *Minutes* 1936: 400.

13. Ibid.

14. ULCA *Minutes* 1938: 468-9.

15. ULCA *Minutes* 1940: 264.

16. ULCA *Minutes* 1940: 266.

17. ULCA *Minutes* 1940: 278.

18. Rinderknecht, Edward, "Lutheran Unity and Union from the Point of View of the United Lutheran Church," *Lutheran Church Quarterly* 19 (1946):18. (Hereafter cited as Rinderknecht, "Lutheran Unity.")

19. Rinderknecht, "Lutheran Unity," 18-19.

20. ULCA *Minutes* 1940: 566.

21. ULCA *Minutes* 1940: 567.

22. Rinderknecht "Lutheran Unity," 19: 20.

23. Fendt, Edward D., *The Struggle for Lutheran Unity and Consolidation in the U.S.A. from the Late 1930s to the Early 1970s* (Minneapolis: Augsburg Publishing House, 1980), 35.

24. Threinen, Norman J., *Fifty Years of Lutheran Convergence: The Canadian Case-Study,* Lutheran Historical Conference 3 (Dubuque, Iowa: Wm. C. Brown Company Publishers, 1983), 19-21.

25. Ibid., 40-41, 45, 57, 70, 79, 81-82.

26. ULCA *Minutes* 1940: 444.

27. ULCA *Minutes* 1940: 443-44.

28. Shaffer, Rollin G., "LWA: A Quarter Century of Christian Compassion," *The National Lutheran*, December 1965, 11-13, and January 1966, 8-10, 17; F. K. Wentz, *Lutherans in Concert*, 107, 111, 125-29, 207 n. 197.

29. F. K. Wentz, *Lutherans in Concert* 100-103.

30. Ibid., 100-102, 208.

31. ULCA *Minutes* 1944: 220, 229.

32. F. K. Wentz, *Lutherans in Concert*, 108-109.

33. ULCA *Minutes* 1946: 635.

34. ULCA *Minutes* 1946: 191.

35. ULCA *Minutes* 1942: 26, 28-29.

36. Ibid., 85, 409, 443.

37. Ibid., 103-105, 151-56, 180.

38. Ibid., 143, 237.

39. Ibid., 273.

40. Ibid., 319f.

41. Ibid., 144-146 (proposed statement), 545-46 (action), 617-19 (final statement).

42. Ibid., 454.

43. ULCA *Minutes* 1944: 139, 142.

44. ULCA *Minutes* 1944: 151-52. Cf. ULCA *Minutes* 1946:367-8. Akard was the first Lutheran woman missionary allowed back to Japan in June of 1946.

45. ULCA *Minutes* 1942: 218.

46. ULCA *Year Book* 1945: 105.

47. Knudten, Arthur C. and A. P. Stauderman, *The Forgotten Years and Beyond*, Philadelphia: Fortress Press, 1972), 5; ULCA *Year Book* 1945, 36.

48. On Daniel Nelson, see Nelson, *Lutheranism*, 151.

49. ULCA *Year Book* 1945, 105.

50. ULCA *Minutes* 1944: 342.

51. ULCA *Minutes* 1944: 340-45.

52. ULCA *Minutes* 1944: 344.

53. ULCA *Year Book* 1944: 121; ULCA *Minutes* 1942: 461.

54. ULCA *Minutes* 1944: 404.

55. ULCA *Minutes* 1944: 402-3.

56. ULCA *Minutes* 1944: 25. For this occasion, Muhlenberg press published the author's *They Called Him Father*.

57. ULCA *Minutes* 1944: 26-27.

58. ULCA *Minutes* 1946: 255 on 3d ballot.

59. ULCA *Minutes* 1944: 104-108; Strodach, Paul Z., *A Manual on Worship: Venite Adoremus*, revised edition (Philadelphia: Muhlenberg Press, 1946), drawing of the Church House cross, candlestick, vase, on page 68.

60. ULCA *Minutes* 1944: 31.

61. ULCA *Minutes* 1944: 135.

62. Ibid.

63. ULCA *Minutes* 1944: 136; on Henry Beisler, see ULCA *Minutes* 1952: 73, "New Jersey Synod of the Lutheran Church in America," in *New York Ministerium Legacy* (Two Hundredth Anniversary Committee, 1986) 48-49.

64. Fred Knubel, telephone conversation with E. Theodore Bachmann, November 30, 1993.

65. ULCA *Minutes* 1944: 47.

66. Ibid., 55.

67. The Report of the Committee on Interdenominational Relationships, April 12, 1945, cited in ULCA *Minutes* 1946: 216.

68. ULCA *Minutes* 1946: 55.

69. Ibid.

70. *The New York Times*, October 17, 1945, 19.

71. ULCA *Minutes* 1946: 56.

72. Ibid.

CHAPTER 9

FRANKLIN CLARK FRY:
THE MAKING OF A PRESIDENT

N O ONE AMONG TWENTIETH CENTURY American Lutheran church leaders achieved greater distinction either within or beyond his own communion than Franklin Clark Fry. As successor to Knubel, he headed the United Lutheran Church in America for eighteen years, from January 1, 1945 to December 31, 1962. His presidential tenure did not end there but continued in the larger union of the Lutheran Church in America, which Fry headed until his death on June 6, 1968.[1] During the Fry presidency the ULCA baptized membership grew by more than 50 percent, from 1.7 million in 1945 to 2.5 million in 1961.[2] Gains like these complicated the life of a church body like the ULCA and yet, with his penchant for clear-cut governing documents and parliamentary procedure, Fry made of it a rather tightly run ecclesiastical ship.

It was during the fifties (chapter 11) that President Fry attained his wide recognition within and beyond the Lutheran ranks. Some examples to be treated later include the following: his pivotal role in turning the constitution of the nascent National Council of Churches of Christ in the United States of America in an explicitly church-oriented direction (1950); his guiding hand in the development of Lutheran World Relief (1946); his gradually attained place of "first among equals" heading Lutheran church bodies in America; his rescuing of a common confessional stance among European as well as American Lutherans with respect to the postwar formation of the Lutheran World Federation (1947) as well as of the World Council of Churches (1948); his key position on the WCC Central Committee (vice chair, 1948-54, chair, 1954-68); his confessionally firm yet ecumenically oriented term as LWF president (1957-63); and his many other involvements at home and overseas in the cultural as well as ecclesial spectrum. These were the sorts of duties which drew on his talents and which, in his wide-ranging yet orderly mind, never became confused but benefited from his sharply focused attention. While his presidential office thus became a crossroads of responsibilities, and while he developed a rare rapport with Eastern Orthodox, Anglican, Protestant, and also Roman Catholic leaders, he did not overlook his primary responsibilities in the ULCA. To the ULCA constituency he was fully accountable. In reporting, for example, to the biennial conventions he helped raise the sights of the members to a grander and profounder grasp of the church catholic and evangelical. To journalists, as when *Time* magazine in 1958 ran his portrait on the front cover and made his career the week's feature story, he personified "Mr. Protestant."[3] But at heart, and by faith active in love, he knew himself a forgiven sinner and a dutiful servant of Jesus Christ.

EARLY YEARS

The child was born in Bethlehem (Pennsylvania) on a Thursday, August 30, 1900. He was the only child of his parents, Franklin Foster Fry, pastor of Grace Lutheran Church, and Minnie Clark Fry. Baptized "Franklin Clark," the little boy thus bore the names of both parents. In lineage the paternal roots ran back to colonial times, when a certain Heinrich Frey and his family lived in Trappe, a little northwest of Philadelphia, and had Henry Melchior Muhlenberg as neighbor and pastor.[4] In their distinctive way the Frys (the spelling was Anglicized) have been a Trappe family. The ancestral burial ground remains to this day a well-groomed part of the Augustus Church in Trappe. A grandson of Heinrich was Jacob Fry, for a time serving in the U.S. House of Representatives. The son of Jacob, bearing the same name, became a Lutheran pastor. It was during the pastorate of this Jacob Fry, in Trinity Church, Reading, that the General Council was organized in 1867. Later, Jacob Fry became professor of preaching on the Philadelphia Seminary faculty (1892-1920). As the father of Franklin Foster Fry he delighted in the arrival of a grandson in the year of the double zero, 1900.

We have already met Franklin Foster Fry as the first executive secretary of the ULCA Board of American Missions, and prior to that as pastor in Rochester, New York. But at this point, in 1900, Franklin Foster's decade in the Moravian-founded town of Bethlehem would soon be up. Minnie Clark Fry had Scotch-Irish forebears. A woman of superior talents and boundless energy, she was described by a family friend as "the firebrand, outspoken, with strong likes and dislikes, and unfortunately some personal prejudices." Yet "her basically motherly nature encompassed the congregation and a host of friends. Her pride in her child was immense."[5] Minnie Clark, married earlier to a man named Stormfeltz, was a young widow when Franklin Foster Fry proposed to her. As American Lutheran history has shown at times, the mingling of German and Scotch-Irish stock—as in the case of Charles Porterfield Krauth, or John Alfred Morehead—can produce particularly gifted leaders. When Franklin Clark was born, his mother was thirty-two years of age, and his father thirty-four.

Resettled in Rochester in 1901, the three Frys occupied the parsonage adjacent to the Church of the Reformation. Franklin, or "Buster" as his parents called him admiringly, appears to have been a born explorer, or prankster, in the jargon of grown-ups. His mother seemed to relish talking about what her son had been up to.[6] Once, dressed in a spanking white sailor suit, he was left in the care of a sitter. When the parents returned they found their Buster black from head to foot. He had escaped the vigilance of the sitter and, noiselessly, spent a good part of the afternoon playing in the basement coal bin.[7]

Educated in the Rochester schools, young Frank early displayed the gifts that would later be dedicated to serious pursuits. Physically he headed rapidly toward his eventual height of nearly six feet two inches. Yet, as contemporaries recall, he lacked the fine coordination required for success in athletics, a lack that (analogous to Einstein's deficient sense of rhythm when playing in a string quartet) may have turned him early into an avid reader. With a twinkle his mother would admit that the lad read everything he could lay his hands on, even synodical minutes.[8]

Perhaps from his father he acquired a sense of duty and self-discipline that were later to mark his ministry and administration. Meanwhile his venture into higher education began at age seventeen with his entry at Hamilton College, a noted liberal arts college in Clinton, New York. Previewing some key vocational skills, Fry not only took the required four years of courses in public speaking, a particular emphasis of Hamilton, but also served as the captain of the intercollegiate debate team.[9] Frank Fry earned his bachelor's degree in 1921. He achieved academic distinction, and was elected to Phi Beta Kappa. How did Frank get on with his classmates? In his own bent toward exaggeration (suggesting St. Paul's "chief of sinners" motif), Frank later claimed that he may have been "the most cordially detested member of his class." A close friend reflected years later, "Hamilton put more than a little iron into Franklin's blood, and, yoked up with the other gifts and influences . . . made him a person of adequacy in everybody's eyes, his own not least."[10] And what would he be? Had he made up his mind fully to prepare for the ordained ministry? Perhaps nearly so. But his proficiency in the classics opened the way for him after graduation to head for the storied Aegean. His year at the American School of Classical Studies in Athens was no doubt a liberating experience, a plunge into the Greek mystique. As Helen Knubel reminisced,

> I first met Franklin in 1922 at his home in Rochester. [He] had just returned from Greece after his year of graduate study. As we sat on the porch, Franklin, ebullient and enthusiastic, told of his days in Greece. He was never an antiquarian and I believe his great attachment to Greece was his joy in the intellectualism, the classic beauty.[11]

Then came the three years at Mount Airy, the name by which The Lutheran Theological Seminary at Philadelphia was known. There Franklin prepared for the gospel ministry. Sixteen of the twenty-four entering students were graduates of Lutheran colleges. Three were fresh from Europe: two from Germany and one from the new Czechoslovakia. Four came from universities: Cornell, Purdue, Washington, and Rochester. The latter was the alma mater of Harry J. Kreider, Fry's assigned roommate. Like Clarence Krumbholz earlier, and Robert W. Stackel later, young Fry was the occasional man from Hamilton College. Fry's preseminary education, supercharged in Athens and the Mediterranean scene, made it no easier to get started at Mt. Airy. The name of the place might indeed conjure up tales going back to Revolutionary times, when the Battle of Germantown began on the rise in front of the subsequently erected Gowen Mansion, the airy summer retreat for escapees from Philadelphia's humidity and then the landmark of the seminary campus. For the twenty-two-year-old Fry the name Mt. Airy denoted a three-generational family connection: Grandfather Jacob, the professor; Father Franklin Foster, the Seminary board member; and now, Franklin Clark, the student. He got on well with his peers and, according to roommate Kreider, he diligently attended classes, even though he was bored by most of the lectures. Professor Reed recalled later, with admiration more than chagrin, "He soon detected weaknesses in the curriculum and in the faculty and openly showed his scorn of both, while meticulously meeting all requirements of the institution."[12]

As a result young Frank at times felt, even more so than some of the other bright students, that the vital process of ministerial preparation was being short-changed. The church, he lamented, was being cheated, and not only the students. It may be that his privileged start in life, intellectually speaking, intensified the great expectations common among entering seminarians. Some have claimed that Frank Fry's dim view of his own seminary education later made him all the more convinced as a champion of top quality seminaries and teachers for the church.[13] At the time, the prospects for seminary cooperation and even merger were bright. The Lutheran seminaries at Philadelphia and Gettysburg were the earliest in their communion to take part in the new American Association of Theological Schools. More specific and even exciting was the envisioned merger of these two Lutheran schools on the Philadelphia Seminary campus. By 1923, early in Fry's years at Mt. Airy, the architect's plans showed what could be done. Whatever the potential, however, eventually nothing was done; the onset of the Depression and other factors preserved the status quo for the remainder of the ULCA.[14]

Of the faculty in Frank Fry's time, Henry Eyster Jacobs was the gray eminence.[15] An erudite scholar, but with no love for biblical criticism, "H. E." was alert, but slowing down. Beyond old Dr. Jacobs, the brightest of the seven-man faculty was the younger Jacobs, Charles Michael, who was introduced above regarding the path-breaking "Washington Declaration" of ULCA principles and policy (chapter 5). His collaboration with a recognized scholar like Professor Preserved Smith at Cornell (on the *Letters of Martin Luther*, 2 vols.), his substantial contribution to the eventual six-volume edition of *Luther's Works*, as well as his wit and pastoral understanding, made him a favorite among students.[16] There were others, less than electrifying yet solid teachers in their assigned fields. Henry Offermann, Professor of New Testament, combined his German study of Erlangen theology with his Philadelphia experience as a parish pastor; he collaborated with C. M. Jacobs on the Washington Declaration discussed above and the Baltimore Declaration on scriptural authority and interpretation, paving the way for his students, like Fry, to adapt to higher criticism in biblical studies.[17] The relative newcomer to the faculty was Emil E. Fischer, who taught Christian ethics as well as Hebrew and Apologetics.[18] C. Theodore Benze taught Old Testament and Missions out of his linguistic virtuosity and international experience.[19] Luther D. Reed taught liturgics, directly from his influential role as secretary for the committee that completed the *Common Service Book and Hymnal* (1917).[20] John Conrad Seegers taught homiletics and chaired the ULCA Committee on Evangelism from its founding in 1920 until 1932. Beyond the standard curriculum, life at Mt. Airy during Fry's seminary years included special dimensions, such as C. M. Jacobs' participation in the 1923 Lutheran World Convention in Eisenach[21] and Nathan Söderblom's visit and lecture in late 1923 in anticipation of the Life and Work Conference in Stockholm in 1925.[22]

For Frank Fry as for most other students the seminary years were not simply a curricular routine but also a time of spiritual formation. More than anyone could ascertain, the 1920s, with their new tempo and secular abandon, were a time when, by way of contrast, preparation for the Christian ministry required a committed and disciplined life. Not all students understood it that way. But many of them did. And Frank Fry was one who did. In a possible overstatement, Frank's roommate, Kreider, later wrote:

> How Fry ever endured those three years at the seminary heaven only knows. It could only have been because the good Lord had such a big place for him in His church and kept his "strong hand" upon him until the three nightmarish years were over.[23]

Most of his classmates expected that the faculty would elect Frank Fry to the position of Junior Fellow. This would have kept him on campus another year or two, teaching New Testament Greek and pursuing graduate studies. The latter would have enabled him to write a modest dissertation as required for the B.D. degree. In those days seminary graduation carried simply a diploma and additional work was required for the bachelor of divinity. The faculty choice, however, fell to another, Russell W. Stine, who later wound up as an able professor on the faculty of his alma mater, Muhlenberg College. If Fry was in any way disappointed, as some students thought he might justifiably be, he never showed it. Whither now?

THE YOUNG PASTOR

In 1925, Redeemer Lutheran Church of Yonkers, New York, extended a call to Franklin Clark Fry, and the New York and New England Synod Examining Committee approved him for ordination. Like the unnumbered succession of ordinands before him, he pledged fidelity to Christ and His Church and set his signature to the Lutheran Confessions as contained in the *Book of Concord* (1580). The president of the synod, Samuel Geiss Trexler, performed the ordination on June 10, 1925, at the synod convention in Ithaca, New York.[24] A man of dignity and discernment, Trexler knew his synod from Buffalo to Boston, had been a pioneer in student ministry, and showed concern for young pastors starting out.

A congregation of the General Council, Redeemer was formed in 1902, the same year as the General Council's English-speaking New York and New England Synod. The membership of Redeemer before 1925 seems never to have exceeded four hundred baptized, if that many. The Sunday School, before 1917, was surprisingly small, hovering around 120 children.[25] Redeemer, however, was not the only Lutheran church in town. There were two small Slovak Lutheran congregations, one affiliated with the ULCA, the other with Missouri. Indeed, Missouri Lutherans far outnumbered those of the ULCA as represented by Redeemer. Missouri's "Mother Church" in Yonkers, St. John's, had a history going back to 1860 and represented one of those critical instances when a congregation, momentarily vacant and caught up in internal debate, quit the New York Ministerium and opted for Missouri. In 1911 two other Missouri Synod congregations were organized in Yonkers.

It is probably safe to say that young Frank Fry, when accepting the call to Redeemer, was not acquainted with much about his predecessors in the pulpit. But the members, depending on their generation, surely remembered them, and would presently be drawing comparisons. Their responses to his ministry among them, and the working of the Holy Spirit, would from the summer of 1925 pick up the young man's educational process and lead it into those "practical channels" that ever escape academia but are complementary to it. To Frank Fry this would be nothing new. From his father, and from his home church he knew that the local congregation was the proving ground. Now he would experience it at first hand, and alone. But not for long.

Yonkers would be Frank Fry's pastoral apprenticeship. In the middle 1920s, the city was growing. The big Otis Elevator Company had long since earned its worldwide reputation, and the rug mills of Alexander Smith were the city's second largest employer. Various schools and educational institutions had found Yonkers a favorable location. Dunwoodie, the seminary of the Archdiocese of New York, was here, and Sarah Lawrence, a women's college, opened in 1926. Above all Yonkers possessed an attractive and convenient residential area. The population was ethnically diverse and still vastly white.

Churches at the time were located near the center of town: Episcopalian, Roman Catholic, Presbyterian, Methodist, Baptist, Congregational, Lutheran, and others. By comparison, Redeemer Lutheran was a midget. Its neat white stucco edifice on Elliot Avenue, near Post, a busy street, was situated in the middle of the block. Its sanctuary seated about two hundred, and it had rooms for Sunday school and other activities. The value of the church property was $16,000 before the war. According to available records, Redeemer was no longer on "mission" status but stood on its own financial feet and was debt free.[26]

Into this setting came the new pastor. Tall, buoyant, friendly, and resourceful, Frank Fry soon found his way around. From his call it was clear: the congregation had sought him; not he, the congregation. Further, as with one newly ordained, the remembered personal promise required fidelity in the gamut of ministerial duties "to preach and teach the pure Word of God in accordance with the Confessions of the Evangelical Lutheran Church." And the church council was itself pledged "to discharge its duties faithfully, in the fear of God, and in accordance with the Constitution of this Congregation, and the principles and usages of the Church."[27] Mutual supportiveness was the way.

This is not the place, nor are the sources readily available, to elaborate on Pastor Fry's ministry in his first parish. But old-timers recall a few interesting things. A later pastor, Otto Reimherr, remembers how still in the mid-1940s the Redeemer choir maintained its admirable reputation.[28] The *Common Service Book and Hymnal* (1918) had done much to bring fresh life into congregational worship. In this respect the 1920s were a heyday. And a not unrelated happening at Redeemer would happily shape the young pastor's career. In the choir was a young woman, Hilda Adrianna Drewes, whom the pastor found irresistible. During his seminary days he had spoken "about his invincibility with respect to the female sex."[29] Here was the daughter of one of the charter families of Redeemer Church, who moved from St. John's in Manhattan to help start the new congregation in Yonkers. She had proven her talent in the business world as an accomplished secretary and office administrator. During the twenty-fifth anniversary year of Redeemer—on Tuesday, May 17, 1927—Franklin and Hilda were married. On March 13, the following year, Franklin Drewes Fry was born.

In 1929, after four years in Yonkers, Frank Fry accepted a call to Akron, Ohio. Holy Trinity Lutheran Church, on North Prospect Street, was about six blocks from the city center and a world away from Redeemer Church, Yonkers. Its revered pastor, Emor W. Simon, had retired after a ministry of twenty-six years, firmly anchored in the General Synod. With dignity he wore the designation "emeritus." Sundays he continued to attend the main service, occupying a red plush chair provided especially for him and located in front of the pulpit.[30] There he listened to his successors for the next twenty years, starting with the newcomer from the East, Franklin Clark Fry, age twenty-nine. For the next fifteen years this personalized polarity would continue, the old man listening and the young man striving. This perhaps prodded Pastor Fry to accentuate his ministry in two main areas: preaching and calling on members and prospects.[31] These at least are two activities of his that have been best remembered, and about which more will be said in a moment. But first a word about the local church and its urban context.

Akron, Greek for "the highest point," lies prominently on the old Ohio-Erie Canal in the northeastern part of the state and gained fame in the earlier part of the twentieth century as the center of North America's rubber industry. By 1917 its spectrum of churches included seven Lutheran congregations: one Augustana (Swedish), affiliated with the General Council; one Joint Synod of Ohio; three Missouri Synod (one of them Slovak); and two English-speaking congregations of the East Ohio Synod, affiliated with the former General Synod.[32] The English language denoted upward mobility, sometimes up and out of Lutheranism. The Seiberling family, accumulating a fortune in rubber manufacturing, included members who remained steadfastly Lutheran. In Gertrude Seiberling, along with others like the Pflueger family (fishing tackle manufacturers), Holy Trinity Lutheran Church in Akron provides a striking exception to the up-and-leave theme. It is not clear what, if anything, Emor W. Simon may have had to do with this. But during his pastorate from 1903 to 1929 Holy Trinity Lutheran Church, organized in 1868, was relocated from South Prospect to North Prospect and Park Avenue.[33] Not that the move as such would be unusual, but what took place on the new site had few parallels in Lutheran experience.

In 1914 the new church edifice was dedicated; a Lutheran congregation gathered in a French Gothic sanctuary. Funds had made possible the retaining of Le Corbusier (Charles-Édouard Jeanneret) as architect on the eve of his later famous departure from traditional to radical design.[34] It was a time when others like Ralph Adams Cram and later Norman Mansell were bringing Gothic back into church construction. For the congregation and for the pastor this kind of sanctuary with a seating capacity of seven hundred may well have generated a feeling of having "arrived," not to overlook the profounder joy of worshiping God in the "beauty of holiness." Adjacent stood the capacious facility for Christian education. True to the city that gave its name to the design, it was an Akron Plan Sunday school structure: an assembly area with stage surrounded on three sides by two floors of classrooms. The entire design fostered the notion of Sunday school as a virtually separate enterprise and, as in other congregations of various communions, recalled an earlier time when Christian nurture was enthusiastically pushed by the laity. This was particularly true of General Synod congregations like Holy Trinity which moved in the vanguard of Lutheran Americanization.

Looking back to the year 1929 and the onset of the Depression, young Pastor Fry was destined for no easy time. Success, in pastoral terms, seemed locked in the era just ended. Nevertheless, the Council of Holy Trinity Church had extended the call, very likely on recommendation of Synod President Joseph Andrew Sittler Sr. Sittler, president of the Ohio Synod for thirteen years (1928-41), was originally a pastor in the Joint Synod of Ohio before coming into the ULCA Ohio Synod, and a few years later being elected its president. He knew Franklin Foster Fry and welcomed him, then in his third year as executive secretary of the ULCA Board of American Mission, as a featured speaker at the thriving synodical summer conference at Lakeside, Ohio. Perhaps between them, they saw the benefits of having a young pastor of General Council stock called to an established congregation from the General Synod. In any case the benefits were substantial, not least to the younger Fry's growing familiarity with the whole ULCA.

If Yonkers was Frank Fry's proving ground, Akron became his elimination tournament. By its combination of forces Holy Trinity congregation challenged and nurtured his talents. They would develop along two major lines, one in the congregation itself, the other in the church at large. As to the congregation, the call had made clear that he was the new pastor of Holy Trinity. He was wanted there, but even after a lapse of time he was not sure that he was accepted. The "Old Guard" and the pastor emeritus made Fry feel observed through critical eyes. Simon, a widower, was staunchly supported by his daughter, Ruth, who served as housekeeper and hostess.[35]

In this situation the new pastor's two-tiered approach (visiting and preaching) paid off. He called on the members diligently in their homes, visited them when in the hospital, counseled them amid their problems, especially as the Depression multiplied unemployment, and otherwise exercised pastoral care. In the process he learned to know the wider community and its enveloping problems. He was outgoing. He could be sharp. But, make no mistake, here was a pastor who cared. The other tier was his preaching. He took care to make his sermons scriptural and to relate the Word to the needs of his hearers. He took utmost pains to prepare thoroughly. Then, Saturday mornings, he would pace the church office area, committing the contents to memory and checking out his emphases and nuances in delivery. Very early Sunday morning, so several reliable sources attest, he would pace the sidewalk in front of his suburban home and rehearse his delivery aloud once again.[36] Why, then, would he take his manuscript into the pulpit? Just to be sure, may be the simplest answer. But the awareness of the pastor emeritus seated directly in front of the pulpit may have had something to do with it. To some at times his sermons seemed flamboyant.[37] But in substance they were sound, and in style elegant.

Neither the worship life nor the round of visitation can here be noted without reference to the Fry mind for organization. It went down "to the last inch," as Thomas B. Kline, an assistant pastor, observed.[38] Monday morning staff meetings included the pastor, the assistant, the deaconess, and others. The week's visitation assignments were determined, Pastor Fry keeping the most difficult for himself. The parish districts were systematically covered. Much of the visitation, shared by a larger team as well, concerned evangelism and follow-up of visitors in church. Even in the darkest years of the Depression, as Charles M. Cooper, Fry's first assistant, observed, Holy Trinity never received less than a hundred new adult members per year.[39] What working of the Spirit lay behind such outreach? As Kline observed, "In making evangelism calls [the Pastor] seems to sense to an uncanny degree the most fruitful type of approach to use and the right person to send on a particular case."[40]

Holy Trinity's pastor attended the monthly meetings, on Monday mornings, of the interdenominational ministers' association. But he was averse to pronouncements that did not come out of a properly organized council of churches. Herein one can see beginnings, as Charles Cooper did, of Frank Fry's later insistence on evangelical and representative principles as basic to all councils of churches with which the ULCA affiliated. Besides, his interests then were "far from ecumenical."[41] In this field of interest lay a challenge close at hand: the organizational pattern of Holy Trinity Church. It affronted Frank Fry's perception of ecclesial order that the Sunday school was separate from the church and was governed by its own constitution and bylaws. Actually this was not an uncommon arrangement, but it was a holdover from the days in various denominations when the Sunday school movement was at its height. Adults as well as children were often accustomed to attend Sunday school but not church. In that way the practice of Christian nurture created its own power bloc. In his carefully laid strategy Pastor Fry was bent upon consolidating the church and the Sunday school. Making sure of his support for the change, he then proceeded to rewrite Holy Trinity's constitution. It turned out to be a first-rate exercise in congregational polity. From whatever source his interest in the subject arose, his skill in drafting constitutions and bylaws became immediately evident. It was undoubtedly aided by the revised model constitution for ULCA congregations as prepared by the Committee on Constituent Synods of the ULCA Executive Board (and available on request from the Publication House in Philadelphia).[42]

The important point, however, was not that Frank Fry rewrote the constitution of the church where he was pastor but that this action of his disclosed a centralizing concept of the church. His later career would reveal how centralization advanced during his presidency of the ULCA and became an actuality when he headed the enlarged successor body, the Lutheran Church in America, after 1962. That later period takes us beyond the scope of this account, but the Fry recasting of Holy Trinity's governing document was a discernible first step. It revealed the man's will, if not to power, then at least to a benevolently guided orderliness, the bounds of which only time would tell.[43]

In the meanwhile, the Fry family circle in the parsonage was growing. After Franklin Drewes came a second son, Robert Charles, and then a daughter, Constance Hilda. It was a vivacious household, with the give-and-take of growth in grace, as well as patience in suffering. Franklin Foster Fry died in 1933. In 1939 began Hilda's siege with cancer; gravely ill, she was miraculously restored to her caring role.[44]

WIDENING RESPONSIBILITIES

Franklin Clark Fry's extra-parochial duties unfolded in fields that had also absorbed his father's energies. Appointed to the ULCA Standing Committee on Evangelism in 1930, he became its secretary and held the post for the next eight years.[45] His election to the board of Wittenberg College and Hamma Divinity School in 1934 took him regularly to Springfield until he resigned in 1940.[46] Likewise in 1934 he was elected to the ULCA Board of American Missions, where he continued for two terms until 1942. In that year the Louisville convention elected him to the church's Executive Board, a position from which he resigned at the end of 1944 because he had been elected the successor to Knubel in the presidency of the church.[47] In 1939 Muhlenberg College awarded him the D.D., his first of honorary doctorates.[48]

A closer look at these involvements reveals a leader in the making, with rough spots and sharp edges to boot. Ever since 1920 the ULCA had the Committee on

Evangelism. The word itself was admittedly more common among other com-munions than among Lutherans at that time. Initially the committee of twelve included three lay members. By 1930 it had shrunk to ten members with only one layman. Its continuing chairman for a dozen years (1920-32) was John Conrad Seegers, professor of homiletics at the Philadelphia Seminary, also dur-ing Frank Fry's student days. Already in 1926 the committee pleaded for a staff member of its own, for an executive secretary able to carry the concerns of evan-gelism to the synods. Nothing happened. Occasional articles in *The Lutheran*, biennial reports to the church, brochures, summer institutes by one or several synods indicated the limitations within which the committee could pursue its task. It was a lackluster situation.

Beginning in 1930 the committee initiated a survey of the state of evangelism in the several synods. The task of reviewing and assessing the returned ques-tionnaires fell mainly to the committee's secretary, Frank Fry. In the committee's report to the 1932 convention (Philadelphia), Fry made the presentation. A few excerpts reveal the tone as well as substance. The Committee on Evangelism "confronted its task to stimulate the Church to achieve its prime, undergirding purpose, which is to conquer lives with the Gospel of eternal salvation in the abundant might of the Holy Spirit." The emphasis was at this time on a single phase of Evangelism: "recruiting for Christ."[49] The scope of the task, quoting from a ringing paragraph in a recent number of *The Lutheran*, was enormous and called for a new orientation:

> It is time for us to cease making the ingathering of our scattered Lutherans the chief objective of our work of evangelizing. We must clearly see the foe that is in front of us rather than the laggards at the sides and in the rear of the Church Militant. It is of far less concern that we should have so many thousands of Lutheran ancestry than that there are forty of fifty million unbelievers in the United States and Canada as well as hundreds of millions in the world.[50]

Recognizing that in this sense evangelism is a duty no congregation and no pastor dare evade, the committee's survey of the thirty-three synods brought signs of encouragement. Twenty-four of them had their own committees on evangelism. Three combined it with adjunct fields like inner mission or stew-ardship. But "six apparently and, we believe, censurably, have made no organized provision for this essential interest."[51] Given the worsening times, the report concluded, the Depression "has not brought spiritual revival of itself. It has merely furrowed the ground for the seed . . . the Word of God. . . . We should be much in prayer. We must articulate our forces. . . . Then may the Spirit of God set us aflame!"[52]

The committee had met but twice during the biennium, leaving the drafting of the report to Chairman Seegers and Secretary Fry. Members had then an opportunity to suggest changes. In three of the four biennial conventions from 1932 to 1938, Frank Fry was asked to present the report. It was a sure way to gain visibility. The committee's separate existence ended in 1938 when evangelism was one of several tasks merged into the newly created Board of Social Missions. More than "a tinge of regret" was manifest in the final report, as the committee's secretary lamented that frustration over the absence of funding had been its abiding burden. "Even in those days of financial flood tide [1926 and following] it did not commend itself to our superiors in the church, [and so] it has never become effective."[53] President Knubel had expressed hope that Frank Fry would consent to be nominated to the new Board of Social Missions. Instead, Fry preferred to remain with the Board of American Missions. In addition he was much involved in Ohio, notably in the affairs of Hamma Divinity School.

Elected to the board of Wittenberg College/Hamma Divinity School in 1934, Franklin Clark Fry's participation over the next six years made a difference. This dual academic institution was the jewel of the Synod of Ohio. From the time of its founding in 1845 as the first English-using Lutheran educational enterprise in the Buckeye State, it had come a long way. In fact it had been in the forefront of Ohio proponents seeking concerted action in behalf of higher standards, retirement pensions for professors, and the like. It had early qualified for a Carnegie grant by indicating that its college was open to students of whatever religious denomination. And what was formerly Wittenberg Seminary, preparing young men for the Lutheran ministry, became in 1904 Hamma Divinity School, named in memory of the first wife, Elvira Crothers, of Michael Wolfe Hamma, pastor of First Lutheran Church, Springfield.[54] An alumnus and an esteemed pastor, Michael Hamma personified the qualities cherished for the Gospel ministry.

When Frank Fry came on the Wittenberg/Hamma board the institution was coping with the burdens of the Depression. Old timers like his predecessor, Emor W. Simon, would fondly recall the bright days before the Great War. Others never forgot the tide of "hate the Germans" that engulfed even an institution like Wittenberg because of its Germanic implications. Still others recount those half-dozen years, 1924 to 1930, when Hamma took a chance with John Oluf Evjen as he rocked the academic boat with his Leipzig-imbued demands for excellence. Evjen, whom people later looked back upon as "the Prophet," was a second generation American of Norse parentage. His theological acumen, akin to that of George Sverdrup (leader of the Norwegian Lutheran Free Church) under whom he had studied theology in Minneapolis before going on to earn his doctorate in Germany, was accompanied by a propensity to criticize. Admiring students at Hamma, such as Joseph A. Sittler Jr., son of the synod president, became an Evjenite clique.[55] All of which created difficulties for the academic president, Rees Edgar Tulloss. A Wittenberg/Hamma alumnus, Tulloss broke out of his native Ohio and earned a Harvard doctorate, which diminished neither his commitment to the church nor his business acumen. Installed in 1920, Tulloss would be president of Wittenberg/Hamma for the next twenty-nine years and also exert much influence in the church at large in behalf of Christian higher education.

For President Tulloss in mid-career the election of Frank Fry to the board of directors, an election by the Synod of Ohio, spurred new tensions. To keepers of the status quo the newcomer appeared as "a brash, young Lutheran pastor in Akron, whose relationships with Ohio became strained over the seminary and other issues." His reputation had preceded him to Springfield and, at least to the wary, pictured him as one

> engaged with his congregation over Sunday School, and showed himself as opposed to church camps and deaconess schools. . . . Many in the synod considered him autocratic, egotistical, and unwilling to submerge his own dominant will to allow cooperative efforts among other Lutherans to emerge peaceably.[56]

For openers (it was typical of Frank Fry to pick up some item that others might have let pass as a small matter) he objected to the ordination of a young person on the strength of a call from Wittenberg/Hamma. Institutions, insisted Fry, do not call with an authority to ordain to the Gospel ministry, only a congregation or a synod (as church) is empowered to do that. His protest was appealed, finally reaching the ULCA Commission of Adjudication, where it was dismissed. Even so, Frank Fry had made his point, a point for which he would become known: a strictly ordered doctrine of the church.

Fry's accompanying concern, for which he was undoubtedly pleased to be on the Wittenberg/Hamma board, was for improved ministerial education in the church's theological seminaries. Frank Fry was not the only one deploring the excessive number of seminaries to which the ULCA, by its merger, had fallen heir. In the twenties a demand for studying the number and location of ULCA seminaries gained support. Critical as Frank Fry was said to be of all ULCA seminaries, including his own, it was to be expected—and certainly many loyal Ohioans did more than suspect—that Fry strongly favored the relocation of Hamma to Chicago. Most people knew, however, that the Hamma faculty in the 1930s, even without Evjen, was considerably superior to Chicago's. It was mainly Chicago's superior location (even though the seminary lay in suburban Maywood) that was attractive, an attraction born of reasonable proximity to great universities and to the western world's largest assemblage of theological schools of all communions.

Yet the signals were mixed as they came from the field. Between October, 1932, and June, 1933, under the ULCA Board of Education, the seminaries (faculty and board members) and synods of the church went through an exercise called, "Re-Thinking Theological Education." In light of developments in Ohio decades later—when Hamma and its traditional rival, the Evangelical Lutheran Theological Seminary at Columbus, actually consolidated (1978)—the Hamma statement of 1933 was prophetic, and bears repeating here:

> In view of the above [position] we raise the question whether for the years immediately ahead, the needs of the United Lutheran Church in this territory in the field of theological education may not best be met by the continuance and strengthen-

ing of Hamma Divinity School in the present location; and whether for the more distant future, sound considerations may not call for the permanent location of a theological seminary within or near the borders of the state of Ohio.[57]

During the thirties the issue of Hamma's possible relocation to Chicago was hotly debated. Those favoring relocation found leadership among the former students of Professor John Evjen, young pastors such as D. Bruce Young, John W. Rilling, Joseph Sittler Jr., and others. The pro-Chicagoans tended to reflect the old General Council line; the pro-Springfielders reflected General Synod and local loyalties. When the issue came to a showdown at the Ohio Synod's 1942 convention in Toledo, the vote was almost a tie: 106 to remain in Springfield, 105 to go to Chicago, as noted in chapter 8 above.[58]

There was indeed more at stake, so far as Frank Fry saw it, than the relocation of a seminary. It was the strengthening of the ULCA's preparation of its future ministers and, linked thereto, the firming up of the ULCA's structure as a church body. Upon looking back, this comes out more clearly than would have been apparent at the time. To borrow a political example, just as in the 1920s Franklin Delano Roosevelt made use of New York State as a laboratory for developing an eventually stronger federal government, so his fellow Democrat, Franklin Clark Fry, made use of the Synod of Ohio for devising ways of centralizing the basically federal structure of the ULCA.[59]

For the church at large Frank Fry's extraparochial activities during his years in Ohio require at least this brief run-down. He was fortunate to have the supportiveness of two synod presidents: Joseph A. Sittler Sr. (1928-41) and George W. Miley (1941-57). Neither of them was a Hamma graduate, Sittler's alma mater being Capital in Columbus (Ohio Synod), and Miley's Chicago (General Council).[60] Frank Fry's position on the ULCA Commission on Evangelism made him a logical choice to chair the synodical Committee on Evangelism (1935). Soon thereafter his expressed concern about the structure of the synod led him to chair the synod's Committee on Constitution. By 1937 the Synod of Ohio had a revised constitution and new bylaws. This set of documents was so designed as to bring the synod into closer conformity with the Constitution and Bylaws of the ULCA. Some members were wary of this manifestation of centralization. But on its second reading the Fry-made version was adopted.[61] What he had achieved in his congregation in Akron he now saw applied to the synod. What Frank Lloyd Wright had made axiomatic in architecture, Franklin Clark Fry found equally apt in structuring the organized church: form follows function. Later on Fry would have ample opportunity to share his organizational talents with the church at large. But they began to unfold in Ohio.

One thing more on the extraparochial side: when the ULCA convention in 1938 (Baltimore) authorized the consolidation of three separate units into a new Board of Social Missions, the change was speedily followed in the Synod of Ohio, if not even anticipated there. From then on evangelism, inner mission (mainly institutional service), as well as moral and social welfare concerns came under the single Committee on Social Missions.[62] But the up-and-coming pastor in Akron preferred to continue on the Board of American Missions. Like his late father, Franklin Clark Fry manifested a passion for mission. Elected to the Board of American Missions in 1934, he remained with it until 1942, when the Louisville convention voted him on to the church's Executive Board.[63]

While reference has already been made to some aspects of the BAM during the 1930s (see above, chapter 7) the coming of Frank Fry to the board is reason enough to note its personnel. Like other major boards of the ULCA the one for American Missions had twenty-one members, twelve clergymen and nine laymen. Each was elected for a six-year term, making possible a rotational membership with seven newcomers every two years. Among the four clergymen elected in 1934, one was from Virginia (J. J. Scherer Jr.), another from Maryland (J. E. Harms), a third from Illinois (O. G. Beckstrand), and the fourth from Ohio (Fry). The three laymen new to the board were Easterners and experienced in business. A curious observer might note that the four new clergymen also represented what, numerically, would be called success. The baptized membership of their respective congregations ranged between fifteen hundred and four thousand, the latter being in Rockford, Illinois, a kind of beacon for mission-minded outreach.[64]

President of the board during Frank Fry's first biennium was Henry W. A. Hanson, president of Gettysburg College and formerly a pastor in Harrisburg. Hanson had played a key role in merging the several units that in 1926 had formed the BAM. His own interest had been in Latin American (Hispanic) missions, and this seems to have guided him in shaping a mission strategy for a multi-lingual home mission policy for the board.[65] For the next six years (1936-42) Henry J. Pflum, pastor of Holy Trinity (the pioneer English-using) Church in Buffalo, presided. He maintained rapport with President Knubel as well as with his fellow board members and the BAM staff. Despite the departure of a number of valued veteran members, under Pflum's leadership the board reorganized successfully. Even though, as he reported, "church finances still continue at the deadly level of 1933,"[66] resourcefulness was alive. And so was the missionary challenge that extended from the Caribbean to western Canada and from New England to the Pacific coast.

For Franklin Clark Fry this was the place to be, on a mission board with continent-wide concerns. Already in 1934 a unit in the BAM tackled the task of survey and research, an activity with which Fry became closely associated. In response to the frequent appeals from home mission pastors—many of them mission developers—for more task-oriented education, the first of annual schools for home missionaries was launched in July, 1936.[67] Here again Frank Fry chaired the BAM subcommittee and took part in the teaching. In the process he learned important things about the problems of young pastors and new congregations at the church's growing edge, input that contrasted illuminatingly with his own ministry in Akron.

Then came the long-deferred funding campaign for the work of the Board of American Missions. Known as the "Anniversary Appeal", its launching in 1938 marked the twenty years since the organization of the ULCA. Authorized by the Columbus convention (1936), the Appeal was widely publicized.[68] It was inaugurated on January 1, 1938, by President Knubel speaking over the coast-to-coast facilities of the National Broadcasting Company free of charge.[69] Fry was among the thirty-five selected speakers deployed across the United States and Canada. A specially prepared film, "The Thunder of the Sea"[70]—said to have been "the first sound motion picture presentation to be prepared by any branch of the Christian Church"—was viewed in over three thousand congregations by an estimated combined audience of over 350,000. In various synods anniversary rallies highlighted the work of the ULCA over the past score of years and traced its American antecedents back to early colonial times. Justus Falckner's hymn, "Rise, Ye Children Of Salvation," —composed while Falckner was still a student in Halle, Germany, in 1697, and before he became the first Lutheran pastor to be ordained in America—provided the motion picture's title by its concluding line. The funding campaign was deliberately "low pressure." With all the effort put into it, the total response brought in a bit more than $482,500. Deducting expenses (disbursements), which slightly exceeded $125,000, the net cash receipts for the Anniversary Appeal Fund totaled a modest $357,117.[71] In light of the magnitude of the missionary challenge, one could conclude that the habits of frugality prevailed, although many family budgets were still suffering the effects of the Depression.

During Frank Fry's fourth (and last) biennium on the BAM, the board reported in 1942 that twenty-six new mission congregations were organized. "The great majority of these congregations," noted Board President Pflum, "started with many more than the minimum requirement of fifty charter members."[72] An additional twenty-four congregations received grants to tide them over financially. Besides, with the coming of Elwood Bowman in 1940 as divisional secretary for Church Extension, the board had acquired an expert and dedicated layman to handle its fiscal affairs and to save money by refinancing "unfortunate debt situations that involved $2,329,910."[73] This figure was exclusive of the regular renewal of Church Extension Loans.

These excerpts from the BAM story throw light on what could be called the in-service training of a coming church leader like Frank Fry. But his extra-parochial responsibilities had one more stage to go. Elected to the Executive Board in 1942 by the Louisville convention, Fry was then forty-two years of age and the board's junior member. Since the main work of the Executive Board has already been described in connection with the Knubel presidency (see chapter 8), it suffices here to focus briefly on a few aspects of Frank Fry's participation. Inevitable stories about this likely *enfant terrible* began circulating here and there, especially in Ohio.[74] Yet the level-headed judge from Allentown, Pennsylvania, James F. Henninger, declared:

> As a fellow member of the executive board, I did not find Dr. Fry a disturber of the peace that many people believed him to be. Forthright and fearless, yes; intransigent and trouble-making, no.[75]

It appears that three friends in particular helped with some advance orientation: Paul H. Krauss, pastor of the big Trinity Church, Fort Wayne; Charles B. Foelsch, president since 1942 of the Chicago Seminary-Maywood and former pastor of Luther Place Memorial Church, Washington, D.C.; and Henry H. Bagger of Holy Trinity in Lancaster, Pennsylvania, and until 1940 president of the Pittsburgh Synod. Along with Frank Fry (some years younger than the rest) they called themselves the Four Horsemen.[76] For whatever it meant, two (Bagger and Fry) were Mt. Airy Seminary graduates, and two (Foelsch and Krauss) were Chicago Seminary men. Their respective alma maters bore the old General Council stamp. Anyone (like this writer) who became fairly well acquainted with them learned to respect the Four Horsemen for their knowledge and wisdom and to relish their wit and humor. Aspects of these qualities sparkle in the story Paul Krauss told about the initiation of Frank Fry into the work of the Executive Board. Fry had been assigned to the three-member Committee on Constituent Synods, of which Bagger was chairman. Foelsch was on the three-member Committee on Boards and Committees. The four of them together were thus in a position to share a comprehensive view of the ULCA.

There was, however, another connecting factor: the Pennsylvania Railroad. To attend an Executive Board meeting in New York, Foelsch, after 1942, could board the Broadway Limited in Chicago. Paul Krauss would get on at Fort Wayne, and Bagger at Lancaster. The first time around, Krauss invited Fry to travel the short distance to Canton, and there catch the same train. On that first occasion (Bagger having boarded early in the morning at Lancaster) at breakfast in the diner, according to Krauss,

> we organized the schedule for our committee activities. It was Dr. Fry's first meeting as an executive board member, and on that occasion two of his most striking qualities revealed themselves: (1) a sharp, swift comprehension of issues and (2) his magnificent sense of humor.

In New York, as Krauss recalled, "we got to the hotel and continued our meeting as a committee . . . to study and certify to the executive board the constitutionality of the proposed new constitution of the Andhra Lutheran Church of India." As always, when it came to constitutional language, Fry took a keen interest and distinguished himself.[77] He was also given the assignment to negotiate sounder terms with the United States Navy Chief of Chaplains for the accelerated V-12 wartime training program for Lutherans, for which purpose the government had selected the Philadelphia Seminary (Mt. Airy). Happily, the new terms were a considerable improvement. "For two years," reminisced Judge Henninger, "Dr. Fry sat at Dr. Knubel's feet in the executive board. He and his older friends and associates [especially Krauss and Bagger] . . . did not hesitate to speak up or to show their displeasure with reactionary actions" such as those bearing on the advancement of Lutheran unity.[78]

FROM PARISH TO PRESIDENCY

In the early 1940s President Knubel appeared to show his age; in 1944 he turned seventy-four. True, he had repeatedly said that he would continue in the presidency "as long as they elect me." Moreover, in the eloquent and energetic Reinartz, the church's secretary for promotion, many believed that Knubel had been grooming an heir apparent. But there were alternative choices. One of these was Frank Fry. At the Minneapolis convention, in October 1944, Knubel's "they" were no longer in the majority. A first ballot victory, given the ecclesiastical ballot's openness to all comers, was out of the question. Many sensed this. Not least among those sensing a change in the making, although not herself a delegate, was Minnie Clark Fry. Far from outright electioneering, for which she was much too proper, she encouraged certain wives of delegates (including this writer's mother) to remind their husbands that her son, Franklin, would be an excellent choice. As already recounted, Franklin Clark Fry was elected president of the United Lutheran Church in America on the fourth ballot.[79]

The end of the Fry parish ministry was at hand. The year 1944 saw the Lutheran Church of the Holy Trinity, Akron, reach its peak in membership. It counted 2,821 baptized members and had a Sunday school that was on the rise again. In May the congregation (as its historian, Ruth I. Simon, has recorded) "honored Dr. Fry for fifteen years of service with a gala reception." Fry's first associate pastor, Professor Charles Muhlenberg Cooper—he was teaching Old Testament and Hebrew at Mt. Airy Seminary—came back "to preach on anniversary Sunday." Likewise that year, Trinity Church "made the largest contribution, $3,035, to Lutheran World Action of any congregation in the Ohio Synod."[80]

The "most eventful event of all" was what had happened to the congregation's deeply cherished pastor at the ULCA convention. In the words of Ruth Simon, "Reaction at Trinity was twofold. First, there was pride that their pastor of more than fifteen years should be selected for the highest office of the national church. Second, there was keen sadness at his leaving."[81]

Fry submitted his resignation on October 22, 1944. Including his wife, Hilda, and the three children in his sentiments, he wrote:

> Today with a heavy heart I am faced with one of the most painful and difficult duties of my life. By action of the United Lutheran Church in America which has elected me its president, I must resign as pastor of Trinity Church. My ministry, my labors, my very being have been so intertwined with this congregation after more than fifteen years of intimate, blessed fellowship that it means a deep wrench for us all.[82]

He arranged no farewell service, wrote the local historian. "He asked only for continued faithfulness. The two thousand members of Trinity congregation would merge into the two million throughout the church who would be his constant spiritual concern."[83]

Nearly a score of years later in Princeton, New Jersey, Fry was the American anchorman on a CBS-sponsored ecumenical "Town Meeting of the World" that included corresponding participants in London and Rome. On the return trip to New York, he confided to this writer that he longed for a return to the parish ministry. In that longing perhaps lay Fry's fitness and durability as a Christian leader.

NOTES

1. Fry's leadership (unlike Knubel's) has been heavily documented, as seen through-out the sources cited here. On his LCA presidency, see Gilbert, *Commitment*, especially pages 87, 128-31, 182.

2. ULCA *Year Book* 1946: 52; LCA *Year Book 1963*: 186.

3. "The New Lutheran," *Time*, 7 April 1958, 58-60 +, reprinted in *Mr. Protestant: An Informal Biography of Franklin Clark Fry* (Philadelphia: The Board of Publication of the United Lutheran Church in America, 1960), 58-72. (Hereafter cited as *Mr. Protestant.*)

4. Muhlenberg, *Journals*, I:594 (February 4, 1763).

5. Helen Knubel, ch. 9 in *Franklin Clark Fry: A Palette for a Portrait*, ed. Robert H. Fischer, Supplementary Number of *The Lutheran Quarterly* 24 (1972): 52. (Hereafter cited as *Palette.*)

6. Ibid.

7. Winnefred Young's experience as a sitter. She was later my Aunt Win, wife of Uncle George W. Bachmann.

8. Helen Knubel, in *Palette*, 52.

9. Frank K. Loreng, Curator of Special Collections, Hamilton College, to E. Theodore Bachmann, June 8, 1995.

10. Charles B. Foelsch, ch 8. in *Palette*, 46.

11. Helen's brother Fred, was Franklin Foster Fry's assistant at Reformation Church, having come in 1921. Helen Knubel in *Palette*, 51.

12. Reed, in *Palette*, 10.

13. Harry J. Freider, "At the Philadelphia Seminary," in *Mr. Protestant*, 8-10.

14. Tappert, *Philadelphia Seminary History*, 85.

15. H. E. Jacobs' teaching of systematic theology, as set forth in his book, *Summary of the Christian Faith* (Philadelphia: General Council Publication House, 1905), was a question and answer adaptation of seventeenth century dogmatics to the contemporary English-speaking world. See also Kreider, in *Mr. Protestant*, 10; chapter 1 above.

16. Enough has already been said about "C. M." as a scholar, with university graduate study in America and Germany to suggest that he was a profound thinker and dynamic teacher to whom a brain like Fry's would resonate. In C. M., moreover, a theological stance like that of his father was updated, at least in terms of the faith-and-experience orientation of an "Erlangen theology." He became Mt. Airy president in 1927.

17. A graduate of the Kropp Seminar in North Germany, and of Immanuel in South Philadelphia, Offermann was also thoroughly conversant in the Old Testament.

18. A graduate of Rutgers University and Mt. Airy ('07), Fischer had served parishes in Brooklyn and Allentown. Tappert, *Philadelphia Seminary History*, 101-102. See also "Professor Fischer's Inaugural," in "Addresses at the Inauguration of Emil E. Fischer at the Philadelphia Seminary," *Lutheran Church Review* 39 (1920): 463-67.

19. Called in 1915 to teach Old Testament, Benze had an unusual background.

Educated by tutors, he never attended college. When he graduated from the Chicago Lutheran Seminary, he was astir with the spirit of mission as that associated with the great missionary pioneer, Passavant. Tappert, *Philadelphia Seminary History*, 101 and 159 notes 78-80.

20. Called to the Philadelphia Seminary in 1911, Reed was responsible for the construction of the Krauth Memorial Library (until 1945 he served as its head librarian) and for the daily worship services in the seminary church (Ascension). Tappert, *Philadelphia Seminary History*, 98-99.

21. When seen in the wake of the Great War and in light of what was happening to the churches of the Reformation in Europe, the Lutheran World Convention was hailed as an epochal event, rallying Lutherans to a new awareness of their confessional unity. With Mt. Airy participants at Eisenach like C. M. Jacobs, and an alumnus like John A. Morehead the most prominent American, there remained little excuse for not conveying to the students like Fry a global awareness of confessional kin.

22. The visit by Söderblom, Archbishop of Uppsala, could have had special significance for the students who might later become ecumenically involved. Convened in the summer of 1925, the Life and Work Conference observed the 1600th anniversary of the Council of Nicea, brought together Eastern Orthodox and Protestant church leaders for the first time, co-opted leading lay as well as clerical representatives from the churches, and seated a small delegation from the ULCA in which Prof. Emil Fischer was a keen observer. See, for example, Sandt, George W., "Across the Desk," *The Lutheran*, November 22, 1923, 3; and "Editorial," *The Lutheran*, November 29, 1923. See also Bengt Sundkler, *Nathan Söderblom: His Life and His Work* (Lund: Gleerup, 1968), and Fischer, Emil E., "The Stockholm Conference," *The Lutheran Church Review* 44 (1925): 281-95.

23. Kreider, in *Mr. Protestant*, 10.

24. *Minutes of the Twenty-Fourth Annual Convention of the Evangelical Lutheran Synod of New York and New England, June 9-11, 1925*, 17, 98. See also "Only the Facts," in *Mr. Protestant*, 74.

25. See, for example, *Minutes of the Twenty-Third Annual Convention of the Evangelical Lutheran Synod of New York and New England, 1924*, 110; *General Council Minutes* 1915: 343.

26. General Council *Minutes* 1917: 193-94.

27. *CSBH*, "Order for Ordination," 272 and "Order for the Installation of a Church Council," 289.

28. Otto Reimherr, telephone conversation with E. Theodore Bachmann, March 15, 1991.

29. Roommate Kreider, in *Mr. Protestant*, 12.

30. Jan Walker, telephone conversation with E. Theodore Bachmann, March 18, 1991.

31. Charles M. Cooper, ch. 4; Walter E. DeBruin, ch. 5; B. Evangeline Witzeman, ch. 7 in *Palette*. See also Kline, Thomas B., "In the Pastorate," in *Mr. Protestant*, 14-20.

32. W. M. Kopenhaver and Grace M. Sheeleigh, comps. and eds., *The Lutheran Church Annual for 1917* (Philadelphia: The Lutheran Publication Society and The General

Council Publication Board, 1917), 174.

33. DeBruin, in *Palette*, 34.

34. *Columbia Encyclopedia*, 1993 ed., s.v. "Le Corbusier".

35. Ruth Simon (d. 1991) authored the congregational history *A Centennial History: 1868-1968.* (Hereafter cited as Simon, *Centennial History.*)

36. Kline, in *Mr. Protestant*, 17.

37. Charles M. Cooper, ch. 4, in *Palette*, 29.

38. Kline, in *Mr. Protestant*, 15.

39. Cooper, in *Palette*, 29.

40. Kline, in *Mr. Protestant*, 16.

41. Walter E. DeBruin, ch. 5, in *Palette*, 35, and Cooper, in *Palette*, 29.

42. ULCA *Minutes* 1928: 50.

43. Abdel Ross Wentz, ch. 25, in *Palette*, 99-106.

44. Franklin D. Fry, "At Home," in *Mr. Protestant*, 1-6; and "Only the Facts," 76.

45. ULCA *Minutes* 1930: 615.

46. Kinnison, *An American Seminary*, 164; ULCA *Minutes* 1934: 566; ULCA *Minutes* 1940: 609.

47. "Only the Facts," in *Mr. Protestant*, 74.

48. Kaufmann, *Philadelphia Seminary Record*, 119. (The list of honorary doctorates is incomplete, since it extends only to 1962.)

49. ULCA *Minutes* 1932: 272

50. Ibid., 373.

51. Ibid., 374.

52. Ibid., 376.

53. ULCA *Minutes* 1938: 228.

54. Kinnison, *An American Seminary*, 115 ff.

55. Joseph Sittler, Maywood, Illinois, conversation with E. Theodore Bachmann, 1943.

56. Kinnison, *An American Seminary*, 163.

57. ULCA *Minutes* 1934: 238; "Re-thinking Theological Education," in ULCA *Minutes* 1934: 233-49.

58. Voigt, "Ohio Synod," 101.

59. A. R. Wentz, in *Palette*, 105. Voigt, "Ohio Synod" supplies some data, pp. 75-108 passim.

60. Chicago Seminary *Alumni Record*. '14.

61. Voigt, "Ohio Synod," 80, 84.

62. Ibid, 86-87.

63. ULCA *Minutes* 1934: 566; ULCA *Minutes* 1942: 593.

64. ULCA *Minutes* 1934: 331, 382.

65. ULCA *Minutes* 1936: 147.

66. Ibid., 144.

67. ULCA *Minutes* 1938: 197-98.

68. ULCA *Minutes* 1936: 185.

69. ULCA *Minutes* 1938: 206.

70. Ibid., 205.

71. ULCA *Minutes* 1940: 236-37.

72. ULCA *Minutes* 1942: 162.

73. Ibid.,181.

74. Kinnison, *An American Seminary*, 164-65.

75. James F. Henninger, ch. 5, in *Palette*, 68.

76. Paul H. Krauss, ch. 16, in *Palette*, 73.

77. Ibid.

78. Henninger, in *Palette*, 68.

79. ULCA *Minutes* 1944: 135.

80. Simon, *Centennial History*, 33.

81. Ibid.

82. Ibid.

83. Ibid.

CHAPTER 10

THE POSTWAR YEARS, 1945-1950

IMMEDIATELY AFTER WORLD WAR II, countries and churches found themselves in new alignments. Indeed, the whole world was changing, and quickly. For the ULCA the half-decade saw momentous cooperative involvements, first in post-war relief efforts and then in inter-Lutheran negotiations and ecumenical ventures. Through it all, post-war energies fueled growth on several fronts, and, among many gifted ULCA leaders like O. Frederick Nolde, Paul C. Empie, A. R. Wentz, and others, Franklin Clark Fry emerged as a singular force of ecclesial leadership in worldwide Lutheranism and in North American Protestantism.

In the early days of 1945, while costly military campaigns were running unabated, a shimmer of hope on far horizons gave promise that this year the global war would end. On Wednesday, January 10, the newspapers and radio reported U.S. forces landing massively on Luzon, ready to retake the Philippines. That same day the Battle of the Bulge in eastern France found the Americans poised to penetrate into Germany. On the Eastern Front, the Russian advance engaged the *Wehrmacht* in Budapest.

That same Wednesday evening, January 10, 1945, the Rev. Franklin Clark Fry was inducted as the second president of the ULCA. In this very place, New York's Lutheran Church of the Holy Trinity, the euphoria of armistice had permeated the first session of the newly formed United Lutheran Church in America back in November of 1918. That the ULCA over all those years had been under the presidency of but one man, Hermann Frederick Knubel, must have struck home like some undeserved gift of providence. In January of 1945 it was too soon for euphoria, but not too soon for hope—hope for the global scene and hope for the ULCA under its new president.

Following the sermon by Paul Hartzell Krauss, a former stalwart on the Executive Board and one of the ULCA's staunchest supporters in the Midwest (Trinity Church, Fort Wayne, Indiana), came the Order of Induction of a President. Walton Harlow Greever, venerable secretary of the church, declared:

The Office of President of the United Lutheran Church in America is committed to you, In the Name of the Father, and of the Son, and of the Holy Ghost. Amen.

Upon which, among the collects, was this traditional prayer:

Direct him, O Lord, in all his doings, with Thy most gracious favor, and further him with Thy continual help; that in all his works, begun, continued, and ended in Thee, he may glorify Thy Holy Name, and administer his office to the good of Thy Church.[1]

Despite the sobering times and the uncertainties ahead, there was hope and confidence in the new man. Franklin Clark Fry had appropriate experience, and he emerged as the new leader for new times. In fact, the time span between the Fry induction on that winter night in 1945 and Fry's presiding in 1950 at the constituting session of the National Council of Churches appears from our later vantage point as perhaps the most crucial and formative half-decade of twentieth century church history. Various singular dynamics converged: the challenge of relief and reconstruction in postwar Europe and of orphaned missions in Asia and Africa, the return of thousands from military service and war-related industries, the reaffirmations of confessional kinship leading to the rise of the Lutheran World Federation in 1947, and the summons to Christian unity in the World Council of Churches in 1948.

In all these matters, the ULCA clearly played a leading part; yet it was acting in concert with the other participating bodies in the National Lutheran Council, and where possible with the re-named (1947) Lutheran Church Missouri Synod. These were the years when hopes and proposals to unite or at least to federate the participating bodies in the National Lutheran Council were first expressed with a confident contagion. Today the Evangelical Lutheran Church in America (1987), as well as its Canadian counterpart (ELCIC, 1986), stands as the deferred outcome of that process, with the American Lutheran Church (1960), the Lutheran Church in America (1962) and the Association of Evangelical Churches (1976, ex-Missourians) marking the way stations.

POSTWAR RELIEF, THE LWF, AND THE WCC

War and Peace

In May of 1945, on the soon memorable eighth day, came Nazi Germany's unconditional surrender to the Allied forces. Meanwhile the flood of refugees and expellees from the East continued unabated. By the hundreds of thousands, soldiers of the *Wehrmacht* had been taken as prisoners and were held in Russian as well as British and American camps. The relentless Allied bombing from the air had wrought destruction on the German home front on a scale beyond belief. Suffering and privation were everywhere. Aside from the displaced persons (D.P.) from the Baltic countries, the number of ethnic Germans as well as the German nationals expelled from the new western parts of Poland (including most of Silesia and East Prussia) was estimated at twelve million. Of these it was claimed that perhaps one-half were Evangelical Lutherans. Under the circumstances, church-initiated relief work was the spearhead of self-help in occupied Germany. Outstanding in its resourcefulness and organization was the Evangelical *Hilfswerk*. Its prime organizer was the clergyman Eugen Gerstenmaier, assisted by scores of able members of the Confessing Church, the designation of those Christians who had opposed the formerly pro-Nazi German Christians. The courageous Theophil Wurm, Bishop of the Evangelical Church of Wuerttemberg, had emerged from the war years as the Protestant church leader.

Winning the war was one thing. But winning the peace? America's churches were not idle. Early in 1942, at a conference convened at Delaware, Ohio, under sponsorship of the Federal Council of Churches, efforts were made to find the way to "a Just and Durable Peace." At that time the ULCA was represented by Philadelphia Seminary's Professor O. Frederick Nolde. He would later become prominent as director of the World Council of Churches' Commission of the Churches on International Affairs, and as an associate general secretary. In the meantime, however, he participated, usually as secretary, at the Princeton Roundtable (1943) on international affairs. Likewise, at the Cleveland Conference (January 16-19, 1945), his services as a perceptive summarizer and reconciler of varying views, made him much in demand. For Nolde, all this came to a peak during the organizational period of the United Nations in San Francisco in April 1945. Chair of the Protestant churches' delegation was the Presbyterian layman, John Foster Dulles. Dulles played a part in the framing of the United Nations Charter. The proposals of the churches for better ways than war for settling international disputes were taken seriously. Nolde's proposed international bill of rights was accepted, pledging nations "to secure for their inhabitants without discriminations such fundamental rights as freedom of religion, speech, assembly and communications, and to a fair trial under just laws."[2]

Postwar Relief

Gratifying as it was for representatives of the churches to be heard in the international political realm, there were problems of immediate urgency in the realm of refugees, relief, and reconstruction. Even while the war was still on, relief and reconstruction became issues of utmost urgency. From his office in the Church House newly acquired from the Morgans, President Fry kept track of developments abroad and at home. Above him, on the third floor, were lodged the Board of Foreign Missions and the Board of Social Missions. On the spacious fourth floor was that honored tenant: the National Lutheran Council. From that top level, symbolically one might say the vision extended out across the continent and, indeed, around the world. For the NLC dealt with service centers for the military, and the emergency fund-raising called Lutheran World Action. As the administrative agency for the American Section of the Lutheran World Convention, the NLC channeled aid to German and various Scandinavian overseas missions that had been orphaned by the war.

At this crucial moment of postwar transition a man of experience readily stood by Fry, Abdel Ross Wentz from Gettysburg. Some seventeen years Fry's senior, he was thoroughly conversant with the European scene. With Knubel, Wentz had formulated the principles for the Lutheran World Convention (1936), which guided Lutheran participation in ecumenical affairs. In 1944 he became head of the Foreign Missions Board.[3] A year later, upon the death of President emeritus Knubel, Wentz was elected president of the Lutheran World Convention's American section. As the year 1945 opened he shared his perceptive and prophetic vision with the church at large.

> It is true that the situation in international politics just now presents the greatest difficulty for any undertaking of worldwide scope. [But] the horizons of the world have drawn so close together during the past five years that the whole globe has become a neighborhood. There is great promise in the new spirit that has come over the entire missionary enterprise in our day. It calls for a new type of missionary. [Overseas] it aims at an autonomous Church, or at least an indigenous Church. It eliminates the word "foreign" with all its implications. On the home front there are indications that a new surge of interest in overseas missions is on the way. All this discussion about the postwar world and all these plans for enduring peace have required many thousands of minds to apply themselves for the first time to a worldwide view of things.
>
> The United Lutheran Church seems to be about to renew her youth. There are many indications that the agencies of the Church are preparing to attack their work with new vigor and aggressiveness . . . in nobler undertakings . . . for the Kingdom of God.[4]

With such sentiments penned before the end of the war, Wentz was indeed prophetic, and later contributed much to the realities here foreseen.

Although Wentz and Fry had been elected to the LWC American Section's Executive Committee, it remained for others to make the first wartime trip to liberated parts of Europe. In the spring of 1945 President P. O. Bersell (Augustana Lutheran Church) and Ralph H. Long, executive director of the NLC and the American section, accompanied by Lawrence B. Meyer, executive director of the Missouri Synod, spent more than a month on a European fact-finding trip, notably in Sweden and Switzerland. This proved of immense value in charting the next steps in relief and reconstruction. Especially significant was the visit to Geneva. There the trio met with those who were forming the World Council of Churches, including General Secretary Visser 't Hooft and the director of the incipient Reconstruction Department, James Hutchison Cockburn, a former moderator of the Church of Scotland. Of great significance for the future was the agreement that "all Lutheran reconstruction, interchurch aid, and relief for the stricken churches of Europe should be coordinated with the new [WCC] department."[5] Also agreed was that a Lutheran representative "should be invited to establish an office in Geneva." By July this arrangement was happily staffed by two Americans. Stewart W. Herman Jr., of the ULCA, formerly pastor of the American Church in Berlin (until America's entry into the war), joined Cockburn as assistant director. Sylvester C. Michelfelder, an ALC pastor on a year's leave from his congregation (St. Paul, Toledo, Ohio), accompanied by Mrs. Michelfelder, set up the Lutheran office, in behalf of the American Section of the LWF, in the WCC Gatehouse. From there on events developed rapidly. Michelfelder soon became coordinator of Material Relief, thus avoiding needless duplication by the Lutherans and the WCC partner churches. In the United States and Canada, meanwhile, funds were being raised and supplies gathered.

At this point ULCA President Fry entered the international scene, making an indelible impression. In light of the urgent need for foodstuffs and clothing in Europe, Lutheran World Relief (LWR) was organized in October of 1945, building on the momentum of Lutheran World Action as led by Ralph Long and Paul Empie of the NLC, which raised a million dollars for orphaned missions, refugees, and military personnel. Franklin Clark Fry was named president of LWR and remained so for the rest of his life. Fry gave LWR strong and personally committed leadership; LWR gave Fry visibility and prominence among Lutherans in North America and then worldwide. In contrast to the fund-raising task of Lutheran World Action, LWR was designed to deal not in cash but in kind. In this respect LWR could also cooperate with the United States and exemplify a working relationship between church and state. Then, in November of 1945, President Fry headed for Europe, with a heavy agenda. In the words of the Executive Board the trip was "for the purpose of planning relief and strengthening the bonds which unite the Lutheran Churches of the world."[6] Other members of the party were President J. A. Aasgaard, Norwegian Lutheran Church of America, two leaders of the Missouri Synod (President John W. Behnken and Executive Director Lawrence B. Meyer) as well as Ralph H. Long, executive secretary of the National Lutheran Council. In Fry's absence the duties of the president's office were covered by Charles B. Foelsch, a member of the Executive Board and president of the Chicago Lutheran Seminary. Foelsch spent alternate weeks in New York during November and December.

In addition to Fry's involvement in this Lutheran delegation, he was also one of a three-member team of American Protestant churchmen delegated by the Federal Council to visit the churches in Germany. North American Protestantism had not normally included a Lutheran in such small and elite circles, especially since no Lutheran church body was a member of the Federal Council at this time, but post-war dynamics suggested the inclusion of the ULCA and therefore President Fry. Their purpose, as Episcopal Bishop Henry Knox Sherrill explained, was "to hold out the hand of friendship to the leaders of the German churches."[7] The third member was Bishop G. Bromley Oxnam of the Methodist Church and a member of the Provisional Committee of the World Council. Tour guide for this trio was the now Geneva-based Stewart W. Herman Jr. The simultaneous sending of these two teams gave emphasis to the high importance American Protestants attached to re-establishing good relations with the German Protestants, particularly in light of Christian unity as sought by the ecumenical movement on the threshold of a new beginning. The ULCA representatives provided an ethnic and confessional point of contact with the Germans, and some expert guidance into the complexities of the German church struggle and postwar developments. It was also Fry's opportunity to strengthen his friendships and his stature among North American Protestants.

The WCC and the LWF

As if participation in these two delegations were not enough for one brief trip (November 12 to shortly before Christmas 1945), President Fry also carried a momentous responsibility to represent a growing Lutheran concern about the emerging World Council of Churches. In mid-July of 1945, the ULCA Executive Board had directed President Fry to invite the other participating bodies in the National Lutheran Council as well as the Missouri Synod to join with the ULCA representatives in shaping a common policy toward future cooperation with the World Council. At the ensuing meeting of Lutheran representatives (September 6) in Columbus, Ohio, Fry's main argument was that "before an approach to European Lutherans could be made there must first be as united a front as possible among the Lutheran churches in America."[8]

By virtue of their Faith and Order membership the ULCA, Augustana, and the ALC had already received invitations to join the World Council. Lutherans would accept the invitation only if certain conditions were met, mainly "that the provisional constitution of the World Council be amended so as to provide for Lutheran representation in both the Assembly and the Central Committee on a confessional basis."[9] The Columbus gathering further stated the goal of achieving agreement on this point among all Lutheran churches in America and in the whole world.

As the Columbus resolution made clear, confessional representation was not seen as something for Lutherans only but for the sake of the Church as a whole, within which the Lutheran witness has its time-honored place. Indeed, a precedent had already been set in the World Council's provisional constitution that allocated a given block of seats to the Eastern Orthodox. Interestingly the Baptist World Alliance, as it turned out, would also ally itself with the Lutheran position on representation. But the provisional constitution leaned heavily on representation by nation. There would be so many seats in the General Assembly or the Central Committee allotted to France, Britain, the United States, Sweden, India, and so on. This geographic approach to the church and to the striving for Christian unity had generally found favor, in America as well as in Europe, including European Lutherans.

Much, therefore, depended upon the success of Wentz and Fry in presenting the American Lutheran concern not only to the WCC's General Secretary Visser 't Hooft and Samuel Cavert of the United States Federal Council of Churches, but also to the European Lutheran representatives who favored national representation rather than confessional. In addition to meetings in London, Berlin, and

Hanover, Fry and company met with WCC representatives in Geneva and then with fellow Lutherans in Copenhagen (December 16-17). Only later on, after the Americans appealed to Lutherans worldwide, was the issue of confessional representation ready for resolution.

The decisive moment came in July of 1946, at the Uppsala meeting of the Lutheran World Convention's Executive Committee. We miss the drama of Uppsala if we simply mark the outcome of its actions without fathoming its meaning for the external relations of the ULCA. According to President Fry's report:

> July 25, 1946, was one of those pivots on which history is swung. A momentous issue was in the balance at Uppsala. Should the Lutheran Churches of the world adopt a common stand in relation to an emerging World Council of Churches? A more powerful Lutheran unity or a pivotal cleavage waited on the choice. The verdict on that day would affect the future decisively. If the article of the World Council's constitution about representation were not altered, the Scandinavians would be *in* and the Americans would *stay out*. The glory of the achievement in Uppsala was that Lutheran solidarity was not only preserved, it was mightily buttressed and extended. The thrilling conclusion was that the convictions of the American Lutherans prevailed.
>
> To the last day of my life I shall still tingle to the magnanimous reply of Archbishop Eidem. "We of the northern countries are willing to recommend this proposal with gladness to our brethren and our churches. This is not just a gesture of compliance. We agreed because it is right and expedient." Without any hesitance Doctor Jørgensen of Denmark, Professor Moe of Norway, and Bishop von Bonnsdorf of Finland concurred.[10]

Representatives of the ULCA had succeeded in uniting the Lutheran church worldwide on the principle of confessional representation in the World Council of Churches. The question now was how the emerging WCC would respond to this major condition for Lutheran participation.

On the last day of July and the first day of August in 1946, in historic Horsham, south of London, the WCC Committee on Arrangements was planning the first assembly. The pending event at Amsterdam, a first in church history as a gathering of churches, would take place in a mere two years' time. Between Horsham and Amsterdam there would be one more meeting of the Provisional Committee, this one in April of 1947, at Buck Hill Falls in Pennsylvania. From a Lutheran standpoint any action taken at Horsham and Buck Hill Falls with regard to confessional representation would have immense bearing upon the agenda and ecumenical disposition of the churches anticipating the formation of the Lutheran World Federation at Lund in the early summer of 1947 as well as of the World Council a year later.

The debate at Horsham, told in some detail in the already cited work by Dorris Flesner, found leaders like General Secretary Visser 't Hooft, New York's Union Theological Seminary President Van Dusen, and others opposing any modification of the proposed constitution. Initially, as presenter, Professor

WALTON HARLOWE GREEVER, FRANKLIN CLARK FRY, HENRY BEISLER, 1946

Wentz raised the lone voice in advocating the acceptance of an alternate form of representation. Presently others voiced their support. It remained for Samuel McCrea Cavert, the Arrangements Committee chair, to serve once again as bridgebuilder and to propose the amendment which was adopted. It stated that seats in the Assembly and the Central Committee "shall be allocated [with] due regard being given to such factors as numerical size, adequate confessional representation and geographical distribution."[11]

At its Cleveland convention, in October 1946, the ULCA at last voted to join the World Council.[12] Until now it had held firmly to the principle that its membership in the World Conference on Faith and Order sufficed. However, with the favorable course of recent developments, especially at Horsham, the time had come for the ULCA to accept the WCC invitation. There remained one comparatively low hurdle: the Provisional Committee's acceptance, in April 1947, of the amendment as already adopted at Horsham. To this writer, in Geneva at the time, Visser 't Hooft expressed full awareness that influential voices like Van Dusen's still opposed confessional representation. Then, looking at the agenda for Buck Hill Falls, he commented, "It will be best for Wentz to speak once again for the Lutherans." Wentz did. The amendment was adopted. As a recommendation to amend Article V of the WCC it was transmitted for inclusion in the agenda of the 1948 Amsterdam Assembly, which would bring Lutherans, including the ULCA, into deeper ecumenical commitments.

When the Lutheran World Convention gathered in Lund, Sweden, in late June and early July 1947, its demise made way for the Lutheran World Federation. The detailed account of this restructuring, as told ably by E. Clifford

Nelson in *The Rise of World Lutheranism,* need not detain us here, except for one item pertinent to the WCC and ecumenism in general. Early in the session the constitution proposed for the LWF was up for adoption. Wentz , in large part the author of that constitution, was presiding. Few exceptions were taken to the document. One item, however, upon motion from the floor, was amended. Among the Federation's stated purposes, ecumenical participation was given its own line, thus setting it off from a mingling with common efforts in education and missions. The change was proposed and seconded by two Geneva-based ULCA members, and read that the Federation is "To foster Lutheran participation in ecumenical movements."[13]

It remains simply to relate that a year later, at Amsterdam, the World Council Assembly adopted unanimously the amendment to the council's constitution guaranteeing the Lutheran proposal: confessional representation. For the historically minded the WCC Assembly action marked a continuous line of development in ULCA external relations, from the Washington Declaration of 1920 to the actual participation in a World Council of Churches some twenty-eight years later. The ULCA not only participated in the WCC, its president became one of the major leaders. From among the members of the assembly-elected Central Committee one of them stood out preeminently as the desired chair, namely, George K. A. Bell, bishop of Chichester. But the one proposed to serve as vice chair of the Central Committee for the next six years came as a surprise to many, even to Lutherans. Visser 't Hooft years later told this writer that he wanted Fry's talents and energy inside the WCC leadership rather than outside and potentially critical. Franklin Clark Fry proved to be a superb choice. Under the Bishop of Chichester he served his ecumenical apprenticeship. He declined the proposal that he and the bishop take turns in chairing the meetings. Fry's own parliamentary style in an ecumenical context would become evident later. Indeed, this president of the ULCA, and after 1962 president of the Lutheran Church in America, would grace the WCC Central Committee as chairman for an unprecedented two terms, from 1954 until his death fourteen years later.

POSTWAR DEVELOPMENTS WITHIN THE ULCA

For the ULCA, these postwar years hastened an important maturing process. The distant synods of the ULCA in Japan and in India entered upon a new stage toward becoming indigenous churches, open in their respective situations to ecumenical influences. Comparable developments were under way in Africa (Liberia) and in Latin America (Argentina and British Guiana).

On the home front, the mission possibilities curbed by wartime conditions began to flower. By the first half of the year 1950 the Board of American Missions reported organizing one new congregation each week.[14] The BAM was also giving a new twist to its linguistic concerns, reporting in 1950 that no fewer than thirty-four pastors of recent displaced persons origin were under the board's clinical program, meaning that they were learning under supervision the essentials of parish practice as applied to Latvian, Estonian, and other DP congregations in America. In those days the resettlement of the displaced from the Baltic countries and elsewhere was a major service of the Lutheran World Federation and its North American counterparts in Canada and the United States. The award-winning film, "Answer for Anne"(1949), made under the auspices of the National Lutheran Council, opened untold numbers of doors in congregations and communities for sponsoring the newcomers.[15]

The return of peace, meanwhile, had unleashed varieties of energy and mobility all across the continent: from military service to civilian life, from farm to factory, city to suburb, South to North, East to West. The lure of California outdid the rest. Even for the ULCA, outdistanced in the West by Missouri Lutherans and the other participants in the NLC, its California Synod added some seventeen new congregations during this postwar span. Their total number rose from forty-two to fifty-nine, and the total baptized membership jumped from 17,561 to 27,102 or 54 percent.[16] In fact, the entire Pacific coast exerted a magnetism far exceeding that after World War I. So, for example, the far-sighted James Prince Beasom, president of the California Synod, annually visited ULCA seminaries where he challenged the best students to come to California to develop new congregations. He also laid plans to revive the defunct Pacific Theological Seminary (closed in 1932) and thus to train mission-minded pastors "in the West and for the West."[17]

In the field of church and society, the Board of Social Missions exercised a three-fold form of outreach: Inner Mission, with foci on institutions and agencies and personnel; Social Action, including concerns for family life, race relations, peace and world order amid the new Cold War; and Evangelism, directed toward aiding the church and its members in witnessing to the gospel. During 1949-1950 the Commission on Evangelism was organized by the participating members of the National Lutheran Council.[18] The purpose was to engage in a churchwide and nationwide program of evangelism to deepen the spiritual life of every congregation by establishing the family altar, reviving the indifferent and winning the unchurched. This laid stress on training lay visitors. By studies, surveys, and allied services the board sought to help the church and individuals to remain on course in an era of postwar readjustment and rapid social change. Likewise, the board joined a successful protest against the exclusion of employees of religious institutions and agencies from the Social Security program.

With interests closely allied with those of Social Missions, the Board of Deaconess Work entered upon a new era during these postwar years. On behalf of the church this board was entrusted with the task of recruiting, training, providing, and placing committed women in the office of deaconess. A backlog of 180 requests for deaconess services showed how the demand churchwide exceeded the existing total of 156 deaconesses (including the retired) who comprised the two Motherhouse communities: Baltimore sixty, Philadelphia ninety-six.[19] Their fields of service were fairly divided among institutions, agencies, and parishes. Their placements were scattered across the continent. But there was much searching for improvement, as the postwar years encouraged. Was the traditional format of the diaconate, including its garb, ready to be modified? Was the community life too strict? Should deaconesses be permitted to marry and still serve as deaconess? Ought they be salaried and free to live on their own? Should more of them go to college? To theological seminaries? To graduate study? And when a church like the Andhra Lutheran in India requested that the women's diaconate be introduced in its midst, what might result from the exploratory venture (1948-50) of two ULCA deaconesses, Sisters Margaret Fry and Edna Hill? The answer remained with the Foreign Board and was deferred. The women's diaconate as an office and the much larger Women's Missionary Society helped to advance the role of women in the church. In their way the two deaconess communities became focal points of a fellowship including women in various occupations and professions. Meanwhile during this postwar span the vastly greater number of Lutheran and other non-Roman deaconesses in Europe, recognized for their unsurpassed services during and after the war, laid the basis for a new international association called Diakonia. Leading ULCA deaconesses like Sister Anna Ebert, Sister Martha Hansen, and Sister Mildred Winter would play a part in these international developments.[20]

President Fry helped to invigorate several internal expansions. For example, the educational responsibilities of the ULCA, as carried out by its Parish and Church School Board, should be shouldered more aggressively, said Fry at the 1946 Convention (Cleveland) in his first presidential report, and "no longer at its leisurely, faltering, pre-war gait."[21] Accordingly, programs and curriculum materials appeared in short order, such as the Christian Growth Series (in concert with the Augustana Church). Also born of the Fry initiative came the report of the Committee on Faith and Life. Like an inwardly directed Washington Declaration, this document, prepared by a team of fifteen, addressed "the individual member's faith and life." The Philadelphia convention's approval of Part I (1948) opened the way for subsequent follow-up.[22]

Despite war's end one could not speak of higher education, and the ULCA stake in it, as a return to normal. Church colleges and seminaries, like educational institutions everywhere, experienced an influx, especially of young men. The G.I. Bill of Rights (1944) opened the way to higher learning, covering expenses in theological seminaries as well as in church-related colleges. The ULCA Board of Education, led by Gould Wickey, was itself deep in change. Already in 1945 its well established campus ministry was turned over by the ULCA to become a major component, along with the more recent work of the American Lutheran Conference (1938), in the newly formed Division of Student Service of the National Lutheran Council. The advantage here was that henceforth there would be, except for the Missouri-related bodies, a coordinated outreach to Lutheran students and faculty at non-church institutions. As elsewhere, a rising tide of students rolled onto ULCA college campuses. The total enrollment swelled from less than 4,500 in 1945 to more than 14,000 in 1950, a jump of over 350 percent. Yet the proportion of Lutheran students in ULCA colleges waned from 36 percent in 1945 to 32 percent in 1950. During the same period the total number of faculty virtually doubled, and expenditures of the fourteen colleges increased by 45 percent.[23]

The ULCA theological seminaries, with college graduation a prerequisite, initially showed a less dramatic increase. Their total enrollment reached five hundred in 1950, up by 32 percent.[24] The total number of faculty, part-time and full-time, remained the same. Yet operating expenses rose by some 25 percent. Changes lay ahead. More faculty and future faculty were doing advanced graduate study and earning doctorates in recognized universities. The standard-setting American Association of Theological Schools (Wickey, in Washington, was its wartime executive) encouraged such training. Likewise the whole climate of theological education, including inter-denomination relations and intellectual horizons, was being broadened by the rapidly advancing ecumenical movement. Lutheranism was becoming an increasingly recognized partner in the American movements toward Christian unity.

Given these changes in college and seminary education and responding to the challenge of the future, the ULCA authorized in 1946 a campaign that unfolded in 1950 as the Christian Higher Education Year (CHEY). Meanwhile the plans for an Inter-Lutheran Post-Graduate Theological Seminary (a venture voted by the 1944 convention in Minneapolis) failed to materialize. It would have involved those church bodies participating in the National Lutheran Council.[25] While most of them appeared to favor the venture, a major potential participant like the Norwegian (after 1947 the Evangelical) Lutheran Church of America abstained. These were still years when, more than in any other place, a theological seminary was prized as the guarantor of a church body's identity.

These early postwar years proved intensely stimulating to spreading the gospel not only in print but also by audio-visual aids. The Board of Publication generated a flow of materials from its base in Philadelphia.[26] For the wider circulation of *The Lutheran*, an eventually standard plan was initiated whereby Ohio and the Canada synods congregations took out blanket subscriptions for their member families. This assurance of a wider readership gained popularity. By 1950 "literally hundreds of congregations" were benefiting from a far more informed membership than before. Reports each week of the "surging life of the Church" still had a long way to go. While one in ten ULCA communicants thus received their church paper, in another, the more closely knit Norse ELC, the ratio was one in three communicants.[27]

Since few persons can match the influence of the editor of a church body's official paper, such a post is filled by the biennial convention. The ULCA was fortunate in this respect. George Elson Ruff began as editor in 1945 and would be reelected as a vote of confidence until the termination of the ULCA in 1962, and beyond that into the Lutheran Church in America. A native of Dunkirk, on the shores of Lake Erie, a graduate of Thiel College and of the Philadelphia Seminary, he was a parish pastor in Schuylkill Haven (in Pennsylvania's anthracite coal region) when called to *The Lutheran*. The church bulletin service that he had initiated in 1938 had given him visibility. A voracious reader with a retentive and analytical mind, he also had the forthrightness and friendliness that made him ideally suited for the job. Like President Fry, Elson Ruff rapidly grew into the stature of one whose gifts bore him easily from the local to the global, and from reporting to interpreting and motivating.[28] In the work of his predecessors—Nathan Raymond Melhorn, editor from 1928 to 1945; and earlier George Washington Sandt, to 1927—Elson Ruff had a firm foundation upon which to build.

During these years the church publishing house, Muhlenberg Press, issued a tide of new titles. Among the scholarly works of enduring value were *The Journals of Henry Melchior Muhlenberg*, vol. II (1945), translated by Theodore G. Tappert and John W. Doberstein. (The third and final volume appeared in 1958, complete with an invaluable index.) Historians of the colonial era and genealogists as well as probers of the Muhlenberg tradition have been returning to these three volumes of source material without pause ever since the first one appeared in 1942 for the bicentennial of the patriarch's arrival in America. Among the other substantial works was *A History of Christian Thought*, Volume II, by Otto W. Heick (1946), with contributions by J. N. Neve. In doctrinal theology there came *The Resurgence of the Gospel*, by Taito Almar Kantonen (1948), a Religious Book Club Selection for September. Gustaf Aulen's *Faith of the Christian Church* was translated from the Swedish by Eric H. Wahlstrom and G. Everett Arden (1948) and became widely used also in non-Lutheran seminaries as contributing toward an ecumenical theology. Other important titles included solid works on Lutheran liturgy by Luther D. Reed, and the *Manual on Worship*, by Paul Z. Strodach; also a biography of Justus Falckner (first Lutheran pastor ordained in America) by the historian, Delbert W. Clark. The twenty-five titles published in the biennium 1948-50 exceeded in number those of any previous biennium.[29]

In a class by itself stood the matter of pensions. We have already noted the beginnings of a ULCA pension fund and its harrowing course during the Great Depression (chapter 7). The endowment, or non-contributory, plan survived the 1930s and into the 1940s. Retired pastors during those latter times were promised a pension of $300 per year, and widows $200. The situation was unsatisfactory. Pastors bought as much insurance as they could on their own. Congregations chipped in. By 1942, however, a full-scale Contributory Pension Plan had been drawn up and presented to the ULCA convention in Louisville. It went into effect when five hundred pastors and the same number of congregations or church agencies applied for admission, which did not happen until 1948.[30] A Lay Pension Plan for church employees, first proposed in 1944, was subsequently adopted by the Executive Board in 1946, and then by the church convention.[31] The investment policy of the Board of Pensions and Relief, as explained in 1950, disclosed a sound conservatism. Its portfolio included Government bonds, corporate bonds, preferred stocks, real estate, with a cautious eye toward the rising favor being shown common stocks. While the board's caution reflected past experience, its policy was in line with that of the insurance industry and of pension plans as a whole.

In contrast to the standby character of pensions and the cautions of fiscal policy, the field of Christian stewardship, seldom a strong point on the Lutheran agenda, surged ahead in these early postwar years. Encouraged by President Fry, some visionary laymen took the lead. With little debate, the 1946 convention voted that the ULCA "call upon its congregations to aim for the attainment of 200 percent of the apportionment" in 1948. The resolution, presented by Paul C. Empie, associate director of the National Lutheran Council, was motivated by "the growing needs of our day, and as a special token of thanksgiving to God in connection with our thirtieth anniversary."[32]

Laudable though its aim, a doubling of the apportionment in terms of benevolence receipts fell short. Even so, the designated Part II of the ULCA budget, over and above the basic allocations in Part I, provided timely assistance especially to the church's missionary tasks at home and overseas. The real story behind the story concerns the specific leaders in the stewardship field, especially the laymen. Call it a convergence of talent. On the clergy side Paul Empie was secretary for stewardship of the Ministerium of Pennsylvania before coming to New York City in 1944 as associate director of the National Lutheran Council. In that capacity he long remained a skilled and persuasive advocate of Lutheran World Action (LWA) and generous giving in concert with other Lutherans.

On the laity side there was the remarkable team of Stoughton and Endress. On January 11, 1945, the day after Fry's induction as president, the Executive Board voted to establish the office of stewardship secretary, "separate from the present promotional efforts of the Church" and "elected Clarence C. Stoughton, LL.D., as stewardship secretary 'to serve under the Executive Board.'"[33] Stoughton's role from here on was twofold. He continued as executive director of the Lutheran Laymen's Movement for Stewardship, having succeeded the doggedly diligent Arthur P. Black who had died in 1944. He closely coordinated its tasks, such as Every Member Visitation, with his new office of ULCA stewardship secretary. His associate in both of these positions, as of January 1, 1946, was Henry Endress.[34]

Stoughton had come from the presidency of Wagner College, Staten Island, to the LLM. He had been in real estate before becoming registrar, then dean, and then president of the college. During his nearly five years at ULCA headquarters, during which time his field staff grew to more than thirty, he proved himself an innovative leader.[35] In 1949 he returned to education, capping his career with fourteen years as president of Wittenberg University (Springfield, Ohio). "Dr. Fry took his chances with the laity, and won," reminisced Henry Endress, who became Stoughton's associate in 1946 and his successor in stewardship in 1949. Indeed when Stoughton and Endress spearheaded the proposal for a double apportionment, in concert with Empie, "Fry was surprised, but went along."[36]

If Stoughton had the flair, Endress had the imaginative persistence. Although he was handicapped from infancy by polio, his limp was disarming. The Endress mind was as keen as his approach was engaging. As a lad Endress showed up in a Sunday school class taught by "Prof" Stoughton at Trinity Church, Staten Island. A lifelong friendship began. President Fry encouraged these two lay colleagues to "teach the concept of stewardship. Raise the sights of the people, have them learn about tithing and sacrificial giving."[37] An initial four-page pamphlet was mailed to all ULCA church councilmen. That in itself, recalled Endress, was an innovation. The idea took root: laity teaching laity in the congregations while being supportive of the pastors, too. A little later the stewardship idea was beamed to children, via cartoons. With a touch of the comic "Dennis the Menace," came the pitch of "Stewart the Steward" to visualize, motivate, and mobilize the young. Henry Endress found his niche in the ULCA administrative structure and remained at the head of the stewardship enterprise until early into the consolidated Lutheran Church in America in 1962.

It was an imaginative application of a "stewardship of lives" that led Paul Empie, Clarence Stoughton, Henry Endress and others to initiate the first of a sequence of significant Lutheran-sponsored motion pictures. The already mentioned film "Answer for Anne," on understanding resettlement of refugees, set the pace. Out of this venture emerged the acclaimed film, "Martin Luther" (1953), the first in the Lutheran Church Productions line.

THREE AUXILIARIES

A church body benefits from its auxiliaries more than it realizes. In return a body like the ULCA seeks to nurture the faith and life of its members who comprise the auxiliaries: the Women's Missionary Society, the Brotherhood, and the Luther League. While their aims and programs differed and each had a keen sense of identity and purpose, all three were linked to one or more of the church boards, while the Executive Board exercised a benevolent oversight. Fry and others gave these auxiliaries their ready encouragement.

The Women's Missionary Society

Society membership rose during these years from sixty-four thousand in 1945 to more than eighty-three thousand five years later. During that time WMS contribution doubled from $722,000 to $1,464,000. Some of these funds supported women missionary personnel at home as well as in overseas missions. Their number reached eighty-nine in 1950.[38] While an increasing support went toward new mission congregations at home, through the Board of American Missions, the largest share by far went to the Board of Foreign Missions and the rehabilitation of church work in Japan and China as well as toward projects in India that had been deferred by the war. Nor were Liberia, Guiana, Argentina, the Caribbean, and other places overlooked. The magazine, *Lutheran Woman's Work*, continued to be well edited and widely used by the local study groups. Under Nona Diehl, its executive secretary, the WMS nurtured its members and reached out to new ones. Organizationally the WMS added a thirty-first to its array of synodical societies when it welcomed in 1950 that of the newly formed

New Jersey Synod. In that year, as in a moment of reckoning, the purpose of the WMS was reaffirmed by these words lifted from the charter:

"To disseminate information, to promote missionary education, and financially to aid the missionary operations of the church through its regularly established boards."[39]

Lutheran Brotherhood

Compared with the Women's Missionary Society, the Lutheran Brotherhood was the far younger and lesser sibling. Yet it too flourished in the post-war years. For the year 1945-46 this ULCA auxiliary reported "the largest number of new congregational units and financial support in the history of the Brotherhood."[40] Already in 1942 it had determined to support the churchwide appeal for funds and adopted the slogan, "Lutheran World Action is OUR Action." Brotherhood contributions thus augmented the already much larger ones from the church which, during the war and after, helped to maintain Lutheran Service Centers at home and abroad for military personnel.

The Brotherhood's quarterly, *Lutheran Men*, was designed to facilitate lay programs in the local congregation "without the necessity of having to draw upon outside speakers." Admirable in terms of self-help, this intention also proved self-limiting. There were other limitations as well, particularly in terms of leadership. When compared with the Lutheran Laymen's Movement for Stewardship and its manifested purpose as well as financial requirement for membership, the Brotherhood offered a modest "everyman's" version of the layman in the church. Encouragement came when in 1946 by action of the Federal Council of Churches the third Sunday in October was designated churchwide as "Laymen's Sunday." Packets provided for the pastors were to help the good cause along. Even so, it was common to hear men complain to the effect that the women have their missionary societies but the men are simply recruited to be brothers.

It was a puny report to the church that came from the Brotherhood in 1948, except for one thing, and that spelled the difference. The Brotherhood had been restructured and enlisted a new cadre of clerical as well as lay leaders. A joint committee of Executive Board representatives as well as Brotherhood officers and staff had fixed upon a four-point plan: (1) to adopt the ten objectives of the Federation of Lutheran Brotherhoods; (2) to become an auxiliary of the various ULCA boards and agencies; (3) to channel its study and promotional materials through the Parish and Church School Board; and (4) to locate its headquarters in Philadelphia or New York, adjacent to other units of the church, all of which would presumably enhance the Brotherhood's effectiveness.[41]

The report a biennium later declared that there had been "visible progress in every phase of Brotherhood work."[42] Reorganization was working. The journal, *Lutheran Men*, had an able editor in Amos John Traver, professor of practical theology at Hamma Divinity School in Ohio. The deficit that had been mounting for years was nearly wiped out. Participation in funding drives like CHEY as well as LWA cast the Brotherhood in a welcome role. The promotion of Lutheran unity with other counterparts in the Federation of Lutheran Brotherhoods was giving voice to aims of the laity. Not least was the Brotherhood's commitment to the gospel. Its motto was designed to say it all: "Evangelize. Educate. Energize!"[43]

Luther League of America

The Luther League of America, the youth auxiliary of the ULCA, reached its fiftieth anniversary in 1945. Because of wartime travel restrictions the convention signaling this event was postponed a year, whereupon it could be held in Pittsburgh, the city where this continent-wide organization was formed. A sixty-four-page booklet recounted the aims and historical development of the league.[44] Like other denominations, the ULCA had found the youth movement a challenge to spiritual nurture at a crucial time in life as well as a proving ground for future leadership in the church. As there was no upper age limit, some young men and young women stayed active into their twenties and sometimes beyond. LLA presidents, excellent lay leaders, changed each biennium. The executive director, a clergyman, served a number of years, as in the case of Joseph W. Frease, the Ohioan, and one of his associates, William J. Ducker, the Southerner (1940-50).[45]

Clearly the aim of the church was to retain its members through the critical years of adolescence. In 1945 the Luther League program served three age-groups: intermediate (junior high), age twelve to fourteen; senior (high school), age fifteen to seventeen; and young people, age eighteen and older.[46] Nevertheless the dropout rate after confirmation remained high. Confirmation was often regarded as a rite of passage into young adulthood, especially since the usual age for it was at that time about fifteen or sixteen years. By 1950 the thirty-three synodical or state groups of the LLA totaled 1,884 and counted a membership of 30,302.[47] League membership in Canada ranked eighth in this listing of thirty-three, an example of their care for the future.

The war effort had thrust responsibility on younger age groups and they had responded with remarkable evidence of leadership. Now the postwar years saw growth in all six of the League's major objectives: Program, Organization, Christian faith, Church loyalty, Usefulness, and Witnessing for Christ.[48] During these half-dozen years one can trace a strengthening of the LLA in structure and performance, and concern for the most precious asset of church and community, the youth. There was cooperation with selected boards: Education, Deaconess, Foreign Mission, Parish and Church School; plus coordination with the Women's Missionary Society and the Brotherhood. In addition to the *Luther League Review*, other publications were directed toward the LLA's three age categories. Helps in the choice of a career were usually less prominent than encouragement for Christian living, in whatever the situation.[49]

Concern for wider horizons and the need of seeing the wholeness of the church in its faith and life became more evident as President Fry or Secretary

Greever attended the annual meetings of the LLA's executive committee. A further step in this direction was the initiation of promotional conferences that brought together synod and state heads of the LLA. At the first such meeting, in Springfield, Ohio, (November 1947), Fry, Henry Endress, and Wittenberg's President Tulloss set a high standard for guest speakers.[50] Inter-Lutheran relationships in youth work scored a breakthrough in August 1948, when an all-Lutheran youth leaders' conference, including a contingent from the Missouri Synod's Walther League, convened at Valparaiso University (Indiana).[51] The crossing of lines was in the air. There were all kinds of spin-offs from the previous year when the epochal World Conference of Christian Youth had met in Oslo, Norway, and shortly before that the Lutheran World Federation had had its first assembly in Lund, Sweden. In light of the great prominence which totalitarianism—Nazi, fascist, communist, or whatever—had given its work among the young, youth work in the churches was gaining a fresh seriousness.

In the adjacent field of Student Service, at the college and university level, there was an equal, if not more intense, concern for Christian life and action in a rapidly changing world. On the LLA side by 1948 the League of Young Adult Lutherans (LOYAL) was under way. Its study topics ranged from local to global issues, from personal faith to Christian doctrine, from the local congregation to the worldwide church.[52] A new spirit seemed to be blowing. An example was the League's fifty-fourth anniversary convention, held at Roanoke, Virginia, in August, 1949. It drew an attendance of some 1,250, marking the largest number ever in the history of the ULCA's Luther League. What mattered most was the content of the program and the joyful spirit of fellowship, all of it gathered up in the theme, "We Follow Christ."[53]

INTER-LUTHERAN STANDSTILL AND NCC BREAKTHROUGH

Besides the international scene and internal developments, post-war alignments also occupied the ULCA on two domestic fronts: inter-Lutheran dialogue and the emergence of the National Council of Churches. In 1945, the former seemed more promising, while the latter seemed unlikely, at least with respect to any central role for the ULCA. By 1950, however, the actual course of events showed that history again, as so often before, could confound and surprise mortal expectations.

Inter-Lutheran Relations

During his last years as president Knubel reminded the ULCA and America's Lutherans as a whole that the world situation after the war would challenge of them a unified response. The National Lutheran council, acting also for the American Section of the Lutheran World Convention, was proving itself an increasingly welcome and effective instrument toward that end. The ULCA Commission on Relations to American Lutheran Church Bodies, with President

Fry as chair, reported to the 1946 convention that progress had been made "showing solid advance in some areas and new and bold ventures in others."[54] Under Ralph H. Long (ALC), the participating bodies in the National Lutheran Council had a director of vision and integrity. His sudden death in February 1948 was a severe loss. But his successor, Paul C. Empie (ULCA), advanced the cooperative work in this same spirit.

Meanwhile sentiment had been growing that for its participants the council was showing the way either toward federation or union. Two strong voices raising this promising option came from the Augustana Synod and its president, P. O. Bersell, and from the American Lutheran Church and its president, Em. Poppen. The ULCA, moreover, at its 1948 convention voiced sentiments already heard in 1918. In high resolve it spoke out:

> In the conviction that this is God's day for Lutheran union in America, and
> In order to present to a troubled world a more united front for Christ in the proclamation of His gospel, The United Lutheran Church in America hereby declares to all bodies now constituting the National Lutheran Council its desire to merge with any and all of them in organic union. . . . [55]

Toward that end committees were appointed, meetings held, concerns shared and hopes raised. Even the Lutheran Church Missouri Synod, through its College of Presidents, made overtures. The times, Missouri agreed, caused distress over "Lutheran disunity."[56] Therefore, in typical fashion, Missouri proposed the holding of free conferences. Equally typical, the ULCA response (1940 and again in 1949) was that "no further definitions of doctrine are necessary in dealing with the problems of relationships of American Lutherans to each other."[57]

Backstage among the National Lutheran Council participants the year 1949 saw sides being formed. Progress that had seemed so promising began to slow down. To the 1950 Convention, the Commission on Relations reported that, as of mid-June, five of the NLC participating bodies had taken action. Augustana approved either merger or federation. Three favored federation only—United (Danish) Evangelical Lutheran, Lutheran Free (Norse), and Finnish Suomi—all of them small bodies. But the biggest, the (Norse) Evangelical Lutheran Church of America, opposed both union and federation. The ULCA and two other bodies still had to vote. The American Lutheran Church, similar to Augustana in size, and the American Evangelical Lutheran Church, the small Grundtvigian Danish body, were already exploring closer ties with the ULCA. In October 1950 the ULCA convention thus voted the creation of a commission of eight, with President Fry the chair, "to continue to strive for the goals . . . of Lutheran unity and union."[58] All of this may seem like progress, but the full story showed otherwise.

As E. Clifford Nelson pointed out, developments taking shape in the late 1940s would take center stage in the 1950s.[59] The realignments would eventually lead to the formation of the American Lutheran Church (1960), replacing its earlier and smaller namesake. The new ALC would include the (Norse) Evangelical Lutheran and the (Danish) United Evangelical Lutheran as well as the former American Lutheran Church. On the other side, Augustana Lutheran Church decided not to go along with the American Lutheran Conference, in which it had been a partner since the formation of it in 1930. Instead, Augustana threw its lot with the ULCA and, with the American (Danish) Lutherans and the Finnish Suomi Synod, formed the Lutheran Church in America (1962).

In its 1948 convention Augustana also issued an invitation to all participating bodies in the National Lutheran Council to discuss under NLC auspices organic merger or federation as an immediate step. In November 1948 the American Lutheran Conference, a conveniently loose and largely anti-ULCA entity, went along with the Augustana proposal. Two meetings were scheduled for early January of 1949. The one on January 4th found the heads of the National Lutheran Council bodies convened at the Augustana headquarters in Minneapolis. The next day, on January 5th, the heads of the bodies in the American Lutheran Conference gathered at the ELC (Norse) headquarters also in Minneapolis. At the meeting on the 4th the ULCA was represented by its president. Fry spoke strongly in favor of federation. The ALC representative, Henry F. Schuh, likewise urged federation if not union. "What are we waiting for?" he challenged. At the same meeting the two ELC representatives, President Aasgaard and Luther Seminary President T. F. Gullixson, sat as observers, claiming that their church body had given them no official authorization.[60] On the next day, at ELC headquarters, the conference leaders met. There being no ULCA representation, the outside presence was provided by the Missouri Synod. Concordia Seminary's noted professor, Theodore Graebner, had been invited from St. Louis, but no one knew who had done the inviting. Graebner was editor of the *Lutheran Witness* and, having a nose for news as this writer had learned firsthand in 1940, he may well have invited himself.

Given the situation, Gullixson, an eloquent speaker and a man of known Missouri sympathies despite his reputation for fairness, launched out at length against the ULCA. Others like the "Inner Mission Danes" of the UELC might score the ULCA for its laxness in disciplining its membership, but a man like Gullixson dug deeper. His target was the recently published book by Joseph Sittler Jr., entitled, *The Doctrine of the Word*. Sittler had attacked assertions on verbal inspiration of the Scriptures: "to assert the inerrancy of the text of scripture is to elevate to a normative position an arbitrary theological construction ... which represents a departure from the central principle of Lutheranism"[61] As indicated by its full title, *The Doctrine of the Word in the Structure of Lutheran Theology* concerned the whole theological framework and the place therein for Christ, the Gospel and the scriptures, as recently interpreted in several studies of Luther and his teaching on the Word. In this view, a centrality for Christ, the gospel, and faith meant that formal theories of verbal inspiration or the inerrancy of scripture were not central to a doctrine of the Word. This issue, as it turned out, was the fulcrum on which most twentieth century Lutheran alignments turned.

It may seem overly precise for Gullixson or for us to single out Sittler's book for such a pivotal role. But the book was not merely a professor's opinion, it was the third in the sponsored Knubel-Miller lecture series. These lectures were invited and funded by the ULCA Executive Board, delivered in multiple locations *and* distributed to all ULCA pastors, compliments of their leadership. Thus semiofficial, Sittler's position was also supported by a generation of ULCA seminary teaching, including Philadelphia's Offermann who had taught Franklin Clark Fry. Further, Hamma's T. A. Kantonen had just published *The Resurgence of the Gospel*, which paralleled Sittler's position and reinforced Gullixson's doubts about the ULCA.[62]

Future alignments were also previewed at this stage by the Augustana position of Conrad Bergendorff (*Christ as Authority*, 1947) and Edgar Carlson (*The Re-Interpretation of Luther*, 1948). As 1949 wore on, Gullixson's position united the ELC with the ALC and the Danish UELC, pointing toward their merger in 1960. The postwar realignments of these Lutheran bodies in North America thus pivoted on the doctrine of Scripture, as represented by Gullixson's critique of Sittler's book. Since the immediate effect was to dampen all merger prospects for the ULCA, President Fry bluntly reported to the 1950 ULCA convention that "inter-Lutheran relations [are] at such a disappointing standstill."[63]

The National Council of Churches of Christ

The postwar years also meant changes for the Federal Council of Churches and its successor, the National Council of Churches, and especially for its relationship with the ULCA. From its beginnings, the ULCA maintained a carefully limited consultative relationship with the Federal Council. The oldest of the ULCA antecedent bodies, the General Synod, had been a founding member of the Federal Council. Yet it was the liberalism in some of the Federal Council's policies and practices that had kept the ULCA itself from joining. Instead the ULCA maintained a cordial but not close relationship with the council. Most other Lutherans judged the Federal Council as the embodiment of ecclesial unionism and as an association to be avoided. ULCA relations with the Federal Council were thus subject to frequent fire from other Lutherans and not only from the Missouri Synod. In this critical conclave, the Augustana Synod was usually the exception, and that was supportive.

Yet the ULCA was firmly positioned to take part in interdenominational relations on the home front. Its Declaration of Principles, the Washington Declaration of 1920, governed the church and its external relations. Implicit in that Washington Declaration were two basic elements of relations between churches. One of these, the "evangelical principle," emphasized the Christocentric and Trinitarian character of the church. The other, the "representative principle," made sure that associated churches work together as churches through their chosen representatives and not by randomly co-opted persons. We are already familiar with this kind of ecclesiology from the earlier account detailing the ULCA and the successful quest for confessional representation in the World Council of Churches. But would it apply to the domestic scene?

During World War II, when there was a premium on cooperative effort, far-sighted church leaders envisioned a grand National Council of Churches. Besides the Federal Council it would include seven other interdenominational agencies, in mission at home and overseas, Christian education, publication, stewardship, women's work, and the like. Initial enthusiasms after the war lay becalmed while other challenges beckoned, like the preparations for the coming World Council of Churches. Promoters of the National Council idea operated with a dual concern: to unify the agencies, and to gain the support of the largest number of denominations. Plausibly the major backers, being themselves administrators of agencies, were preoccupied with functional unification. Among the denominations, however, the most glaring absence was that of the Lutherans and the Orthodox.

World War II had changed the North American Protestant scene in several respects, and the catalyst for one particular change with respect to Lutherans was Samuel McCrea Cavert, sole general secretary of the Federal Council of Churches after 1930. As recorded in his biography, *Architect of Unity*, Cavert was deeply interested in the German church struggle of the 1930s and in reaching out to Germans after the war.[64] As noted earlier in this chapter, an American Protestant delegation of only three would not likely have included a Lutheran before the war, but the post-war outreach to Germany suggested such representation. Cavert saw to it that the ULCA was included in this triumvirate, and the newly installed President Fry was the man. From there on, Fry's own abilities impressed Cavert directly, and the Federal Council took special note of the ULCA.

With its headquarters in New York City, and its consultative links not only with the Federal Council but also with most of the other agencies, the ULCA was approached about a new structure. As Cavert recalled,

> All who were committed to an advance in cooperative unity through the proposed National Council were greatly concerned about the policy which the United Lutheran Church would adopt with reference to the new interdenominational structure.[65]

They soon found out. Fry chose not to meet with committees or to take part in formal conferences. Instead, he engaged the chair of the planning committee, its secretary, and Cavert in extended conversations. Precise constitutional language was a Fry specialty, whether congregational, synodical or otherwise; so naturally, the subject was the proposed constitution of the nascent council. The test that Fry applied to it—and so likewise did Reinartz, the new ULCA secretary —was that of the two declared principles: the evangelical and the representative. Or, to put it another way: the proper place of the churches in a council of churches. What caught the attention of Fry as well as Reinartz and others was the emphasis in the proposed constitution for agencies, and the apparent eclipsing of the churches to be served by the council. The chair of the planning committee, Luther A. Weigle, dean of Yale Divinity School and himself once a student of Gettysburg Seminary, was eager to include the Lutherans; he and his colleagues agreed to call a meeting of denominational heads. This kind of gathering was a first in American church history.

It was February 24, 1949. At the meeting most major Protestant church bodies were represented by their heads. One other Lutheran body, Augustana, was present. Only the Methodist and American Baptist leaders were absent. The administrative heads of six of the eight merging agencies were on hand, as were Dean Weigle and others of the Planning Committee. After the ULCA Executive Board had carefully reviewed their work, Fry and Reinartz presented some fifty amendments to the proposed NCCC constitution. Never had there been such a meticulous presentation of evangelical and representative principles set forth in such an august company of Protestant leaders. As some of the participants observed (to put it mildly), the amendments were "discouragingly numerous." Nevertheless, in the end, nearly all of them were adopted. Theologically the most important amendment was in the preamble. Christology and ecclesiology were brought into proper perspective. The original draft spoke of "the essential oneness of the Christian churches of the United States of America in Jesus Christ as their divine Lord and Savior. . . . " The ULCA amendments adjusted the emphasis from a humanly created to a God-given reality. The change, as adopted, reads:

> In the Providence of God the time has come when it seems fitting more fully to manifest oneness in Jesus Christ as divine Lord and Saviour, by the creation of an inclusive co-operative agency of the Christian Churches of the United States of America.[66]

The evangelical and representative principles thus applied not only to the new National Council but also to "local and state councils of churches, if they were to be recognized as in association with the National Council." As Cavert later pointed out "this raised a serious administrative question as to how far the National Council could properly go in a centralized control over local structures of cooperation." There were those, said Cavert, who felt that "Dr. Fry's stand involved the imposing of too much ecclesiastical authority 'from the top.'"[67] Further, the representative principle, from Fry's standpoint, "was a way of insuring complete denominational authority and control while meeting the practical need for established contacts with state and local councils."[68]

It remained for Henry Knox Sherill, presiding bishop of the Episcopal Church, to leave us this vivid description of Fry backstage. With a lawyer's mind and a theologian's comprehension, Fry was a formidable participant. His friend Sherrill recalled:

> Along about 1948-49 we were both members of committees considering the work of the overall Planning Committee. I have no taste for details of constitution and

by-laws. But for Frank it was a different matter. At the sight of such documents his eyes sparkle like those of a bird dog who flushes a quail. He moves into the legal underbrush with a certainty and an eagerness which is truly amazing. I am not saying by any means that Frank Fry has missed his calling, but he could have been a brilliant and successful member of the bar. In our meetings no detail escaped him, he questioned, he probed. I recall his saying once, "I do not mean to be 'picky.'" There were some members of the committee who thought Frank too meticulous and too cautious. But as I look back I am confident that his careful study and discussion added greatly to the later strength and stability of the constitution of the National Council.[69]

In any case, the NCC bore many marks of Fry's hand, as the 1950 ULCA Convention soon learned.

The president's report to the 1950 convention (Des Moines, Iowa) focused on "the interchurch relationships of the United Lutheran Church in America." The officers, the Executive Board, the Committees on Inter-Lutheran Interests and Interdenominational Relationships (the latter two were formed only in 1946) have expended more time and vitality "in negotiations on all the frontiers of our Church in 1949-1950 than has ever been demanded before."[70] Delegates were challenged by their president to examine seriously the recommendations of the Executive Board concerning the proposed membership of the ULCA in the new National Council of Churches. To the question as to whether this proposed joining with other evangelical Christians represents a broadening or even a departure from past policies, the president's reply was, "None at all."

> The significant change from the past is to be found in a new willingness on the part of our fellow-evangelical Christians to recognize the principles of the United Lutheran Church even to the extent of remolding almost every article of the constitution of the National Council of Churches in accordance with them, rather than any abandonment of our principles by our Church itself.[71]

People were asking whether the ULCA was inconsistent by joining the World Council and still showing "hesitancy about membership in the National Council." "That is not so," said Fry, and continued:

> The truth is that our Church's principles are much more congenial to the churches in Europe than to our nearer neighbors. The whole body of world Protestantism and Orthodoxy feels much more of an immediate and natural affinity with our position than its North American segment does. The logic and conviction which persuaded the United Lutheran Church to enter the World Council of Churches will extend validly to national, state and local councils only when the resemblance is convincing and close.[72]

Under these circumstances, and with guidelines still intact regarding ULCA principles and policies, the recommendation of the Executive Board was presented by Frederick R. Knubel, son of the first president, and moved by him. Extensive discussion followed. The vote to join, a rising vote, was "almost unanimous."[73] In commenting on the action taken, President Fry reaffirmed what he had stated in his report, saying, "Had not others accepted the principles for which the ULCA stands . . . he himself would have been bound in conscience to oppose the recommendation."[74]

Inter-Lutheran relationships, once promising, had stalled; ULCA participation with other Protestants, once minimal, were increasing dramatically. President Fry summed up the surprising realignment of relationships:

> By a strange historical coincidence, the biennium 1948-1950, which ends with the United Lutheran Church's inter-Lutheran relationships at such a disappointing standstill, has simultaneously been marked with notable developments in the wider field of our dealings with other evangelical Christians.[75]

On the morning of Wednesday, November 29, 1950, in the city of Cleveland, the National Council of Churches was assembled for the first time. This constituting assembly had perhaps no more conscientious or eager delegation than that from the ULCA, twenty-four delegates and twenty-four alternates, all present.[76] They met together before the assembly, became better acquainted with each other, received briefings from President Fry, Secretary Reinartz, and others, and together became more aware of the significance of their involvement, and of the leadership which their officers, Fry and Reinartz, had provided in shaping the NCCC constitution. Presiding at the constituting session was none other than Franklin Clark Fry. Upon reading the act of constitution he concluded: "As your presiding officer, I declare that the National Council of the Churches of Christ in the United States of America is officially constituted. Let us now dedicate it to the glory of God and to the service of mankind."[77]

The featured address for Thursday night, the 30th, was to be given by the British ambassador, Sir Oliver Franks. However, emergency duties kept him in Washington. His place was taken by O. Frederick Nolde. As we have already noted, the credentials of this dean-on-leave from the Graduate School of the Lutheran Theological Seminary at Philadelphia were by now impressive. On twenty-four hour notice Nolde prepared a characteristically clear and moving statement on "A Christian View of the International Crisis." In light of the pervasive fear of a possible third world war, the speaker calmly cautioned his hearers to guard against hysteria, self-righteousness, unilateral action, and the like. Nolde premised his statement on his "conviction that God in his goodness makes available strength in proportion to the needs of the hour."

> [I do] not presume to say that these [guarded] steps will prove effective. I recognize that full catastrophe may break upon the world at any time. Nevertheless I make bold to contend for my fundamental thesis. . . . The struggle for peace must go forward unremittingly. . . . In these trying days and always, we pray God through Jesus Christ our Lord, for the faith that will enable us to stand in the face of principalities and powers of darkness. From Him alone can come strength . . . adequate for the needs of our day. [78]

Fry may have retained his reservations about the NCC: "the first convention of the NCCCUSA was staff-dominated and agency-directed."[79] Nevertheless, the wholehearted participation of the United Lutheran Church in America in the new National Council of Churches was a culmination of thirty years of growing together of three branches of a common Lutheran heritage. At the merger in 1918, a decision to join the former Federal Council of Churches had to be sidetracked. The General Synod had been one of the founding members in 1908 and had contributed the service of influential churchmen in order to fulfill the Synod's commitment to Christian unity as guided by its Lutheran heritage and Muhlenberg tradition. The General Council and the United Synod of the South remained outside the Federal Council for the sake of a Lutheran Witness to Christian truth. In 1918 a compromise was reached that enabled the new ULCA to have a friendly relationship with the Federal Council.

By 1948 both principles had been achieved. Knubel of General Synod background was admired and respected for his relentless striving for Christian unity during his years as president. Fry of General Council background built on Knubel's preparation and with support from colleagues skillfully convinced the planners of the National Council of Churches of certain basic principles.

As the 1940s were ending, a more united church body was better prepared to strengthen the work of service and mission in the 1950s.

NOTES

1. *The Occasional Services, from the Common Service Book of the Lutheran Church* (Philadelphia: The Board of Publication of the United Lutheran Church in America, [1918, 1930] 1943), 139-140; Reed, *Liturgy,* 615.
2. *The Lutheran,* (Dec 26, 1945), 20.
3. ULCA *Minutes* 1946:654 ff.
4. *The Lutheran* (January 3, 1945), 2, 11.
5. Solberg, Richard W., *As Between Brothers.* (Minneapolis: Augsburg Publishing House, 1957), 25.
6. ULCA *Minutes* 1946: 53.
7. *Palette,* 296. *The World Council of Churches, Its Process of Formation; Minutes and Reports of the Meeting of the Provisional Committee of the World Council of Churches Held at Geneva from February 21st to 23rd, 1946.* (Geneva, 1946), 193.
8. Flesner, *World Council,* 98.
9. Flesner, *World Council,* 99; ULCA *Minutes* 1946: 221-2.
10. Bachmann, *Ecumenical Involvement,* 78-79. Cf. Flesner, *World Council,* and Nelson, *World Lutheranism,* 376.
11. Flesner, *World Council,* 118-122.
12. ULCA *Minutes* 1946: 230, 266.
13. Bachmann, *Ecumenical Involvement,* 84; LWF *Proceedings,* Lund 1947, 100.
14. ULCA *Minutes* 1952.
15. Re-released in 1989 on the occasion of its fortieth anniversary by Lutheran Film Associates (Lutheran Immigration and Refugee Services, Washington, DC).
16. ULCA *Year Book* 1946: 120-121; 1951: 156-57.
17. Hidy, Ross F., and Richard M. Bennett, Eds., *Beasom the Builder* (Berkeley, CA: Lutheran History Center of the West, 1996) ch. 20.
18. ULCA *Minutes* 1950: 623-24.
19. ULCA *Year Book* 1951: 102.
20. ULCA *Minutes* 1952: 889.
21. ULCA *Minutes* 1946: 24.
22. ULCA *Minutes* 1948: 300-308, 39.
23. ULCA *Year Book* 1946: 59, 1951: 93.
24. ULCA *Year Book* 1951: 58, 92.
25. ULCA *Minutes* 1946: 419ff.
26. ULCA *Minutes* 1950: 1021-22; 1948: 566.
27. ULCA *Minutes* 1950: 858, re: *The Lutheran Herald.*
28. Ibid., 1022.
29. Ibid., 566-67.
30. ULCA *Minutes* 1942: 607-35 (Appendix).
31. ULCA *Minutes* 1946: 94-99, 1948: 104-105.
32. ULCA *Minutes* 1946: 602.
33. Ibid., 62

34. ULCA *Minutes* 1944: 355-57;1946: 59-61. ULCA *Year Book* 1948: 33,37.

35. NOTES 365: 57f.

36. NOTES 365:60.

37. NOTES 365:60

38. ULCA *Minutes* 1946: 568; 1950: 728, 741.

39. ULCA *Minutes* 1950: 733.

40. ULCA *Minutes* 1946: 584.

41. ULCA *Minutes* 1948: 696-97.

42. ULCA *Minutes* 1950: 1023.

43. Ibid., 1024.

44. ULCA *Minutes* 1946: 603. *Lutheran Cyclopedia*, 295-96.

45. ULCA *Minutes* 1946: 607, 1950: 818.

46. ULCA *Minutes* 1946: 603.

47. ULCA *Minutes* 1950: 817-18.

48. ULCA *Minutes* 1946: 603; *Minutes* 1948: 527.

49. ULCA *Minutes* 1946: 604-5.

50. ULCA *Minutes* 1948: 527.

51. Ibid., 529.

52. ULCA *Minutes* 1948: 532-33.

53. ULCA *Minutes* 1950: 815.

54. ULCA *Minutes* 1948: 532-33.

55. ULCA *Minutes* 1948: 653.

56. ULCA *Minutes* 1950: 401.

57. ULCA *Minutes* 1950: 402.

58. ULCA *Minutes* 1950: 925.

59. Nelson, *Lutheranism*, 174-79.

60. Ibid., 174-176.

61. Sittler, Joseph, *The Doctrine of the Word in the Structure of Lutheran Theology* (Philadelphia: Muhlenberg Press, 1948), 68.

62. Nevertheless at this same time Gullixson was showing interest in "Pan-American Lutheranism" by thoroughly investigating the possibility of engaging a ULCA Lutheran who would "truly represent the old General Council" to fill a temporary need. He remembered a young Eastern historian who in 1940 was showing interest in midwestern Lutherans including the Missouri Synod (chapter 8).

63. ULCA *Minutes* 1950: 31; see also E. C. Fendt, *The Struggle for Lutheran Unity* (Minneapolis: Augsburg, 1980).

64. Schmidt, William J., *Architect of Unity* (NY: Friendship Press 1978), 119.

65. *Palette*, 282.

66. ULCA *Minutes* 1950: 471. These minutes present eighteen pages of constitutional text, before and after the ULCA amendments.

67. *Palette* 282.

68. Ibid., 283.

69. *Mr. Protestant*, 32-34.

70. ULCA *Minutes* 1950: 26.

71. Ibid., 34.

72. Ibid., 34-35.

73. Ibid., 605-6.

74. Ibid., 606.

75. Ibid., 31.

76. National Council of Christian Churches of Christ in the United States of America, *Christian Faith in Action* (New York: Central Department of Publication and Distribution of the National Council of Christian Churches of Christ in the United States of America, 1951), 52. (Hereafter cited as NCC, *Faith in Action*.

77. *ULCA Pastor's Desk Book* (Philadelphia: United Lutheran Publication House, 1947-1962), January 1951, NE 217f. (Hereafter abbreviated as *Pastor's Desk Book*; the "State of the Church" section bears code letters NE, with pages numbered consecutively from 1947 to 1962.)

78. NCC, *Faith in Action*, 111-112.

79. *Pastor's Desk Book* January 1951, NE 217f.

CHAPTER 11

THE FORMATIVE FIFTIES

A S THE DRAMA OF THE 1950S DEMANDED A WORLD STAGE, so too the outreach of the ULCA was inter-continental. The war in Korea was like an aftershock of World War II and came at a time when former colonies were evolving into independent nations. Great expectations had their price and growing pains their accompanying misery. A political ice age of fear crept over the human family as the two superpowers plied the ways of the Cold War. China had gone communist. Where, people asked, would communism stop? America had the bomb. But presently the Soviet Union had it too. The arms race between the superpowers and the Red Scare articulated by McCarthyism fanned America's fears.

In this setting the decade of the fifties began with a dramatic ecumenical and global exposure. In 1951, President Fry, accompanied by the director of the Protestant Radio Commission, flew around the world in thirty-four days. They were gathering input for an upcoming interchurch campaign for overseas relief. Entitled "One Great Hour For Sharing," the venture was under National Council of Churches sponsorship, and came at a time when Fry was deploring the dwindling ULCA response to Lutheran World Action. Upon his return to New York, he was interviewed at length over NBC's National Radio Vespers. In a sequence of word-pictures Fry set forth vividly what he had seen and heard in Japan, in war-torn Korea, as well as in Hong Kong, Burma, India, Pakistan, several countries in the Arab world, Israel, Greece, Switzerland, and Germany.[1] Listeners would find it hard not to respond. Thus Fry, as the head of Lutheran World Relief (the material complement to Lutheran World Action), assisted Church World Service, now under the new National Council of Churches, in launching the "One Great Hour of Sharing."

There were global signs of confidence, as well as need. In India, despite the cost of new nationhood, one could celebrate the end of a colonial past and call it the "end of the Vasco da Gama era." The United Nations was just getting started. Its imposing slender slab of glass and concrete, a new landmark on Manhattan's East Side, was dedicated in 1950. The Methodists built the Church Center for the United Nations across the street. Internationally, especially in Africa and Asia, colonial powers lowered their flags. Joining the United Nations became the badge of identity. In western Europe, especially in West Germany, the Marshall plan turned rubbled remains into an economic miracle. Similarly in Japan, under United States occupation, a determined people defied depression, laid out new infrastructures and set an industry in motion which, by the end of the fifties, was challenging America for a share in the world markets. While Britain went into decline with dignity, the United States and Canada gained new prominence and responsibilities.

In North America, agriculture and industry, having been redirected during the prolonged struggle of the war years, expanded to new heights of productivity in order to meet postponed demands. With its worldwide dispersion of military bases and alliances the goal of the "American century," as many called it, was to keep communism in check. At home the benefits of the GI Bill of Rights enabled the hundreds of thousands discharged from military service to get on with their lives, notably in higher education. Federal loans provided for home building and upheld the institution of marriage and the family.

The ULCA also gained recognition by its national and international ecumenical involvement, as noted in chapter 10. Abroad and at home Lutherans became better known. The ULCA and Franklin Clark Fry emerged in the American public press. *Newsweek* previewed such attention in 1951 with an item entitled "Big Fry" and in 1957 called him "Protestantism's Busy Lutheran." *Life* dubbed Fry the World's Leading Protestant and *Time* not only anointed him "Mr. Protestant" but also ran a feature story on him for Easter of 1958.[2]

In the 1950s there were three ecumenical firsts for North America. In Toronto in 1950 the first North American meeting of the World Council of Churches' Central Committee convened. The statement on "The Church, the Churches and the World Council of Churches" adopted at Toronto would clarify the ecclesiological interrelatedness of the "Oikoumene." Then, in 1954 came the Second Assembly of the World Council of Churches at Evanston, Illinois, north of Chicago. Three years later, for the first time in America, the World Conference on Faith and Order (its third) convened at Oberlin, Ohio, near Lake Erie. In its way it marked the "coming of age" for North America as a meeting ground for modern ecumenical internationalism. Fry, representing the World Council, also attended the 1957 Ghana Assembly of the International Missionary Council, the last big gathering of the IMC prior to its integration with the World Council.[3] To his "Dear Partner" in his own church he made a mainly unexciting meeting interesting, despite the equatorial heat. He indicated the serious crisis he observed in the mission enterprise worldwide.

We should not leave the religious climate without mentioning another sphere of interaction. In the fifties, theological discourse between Europeans and Americans became more fruitful. At Princeton Theological Seminary Otto Piper, himself an emigree scholar of Lutheran background, drew many future Lutheran scholars especially from the Midwest. Similarly, Wilhelm Pauck, at the University of Chicago, attracted future Lutheran scholars of ecumenical import, among them Joseph Sittler Jr., Jaroslav Pelikan, and others whose work began to flower in the fifties. Lutheran scholars and professors, especially from Europe, were in demand. Also, an increasing number of Lutheran seminarians of scholarly bent enrolled in topflight non-denominational divinity schools. All of which brings us back to the practical role of Lutherans in the ecumenical realm at this time.

INTER-LUTHERAN RELATIONSHIPS

The Lutheran World Federation

During the fifties, the Lutheran World Federation had two assemblies, one in Germany (1952) and one in the United States (1957). To prepare delegates and visitors for the assembly in Hannover, the National Lutheran Council published a ninety-page booklet, *Epic of Faith*, on the history, work, and membership of the LWF. It was distributed to some eight thousand pastors of the cooperating churches. With a foreword by A. R. Wentz, it was written by E. Theodore Bachmann, at that time guest professor at Luther Seminary in St. Paul, Minnesota.[4] He had the assistance of a few students, including some who had served the LWF in refugee camps in Europe under the direction of Howard Hong of St. Olaf College. According to the report of the ULCA delegates to the Seattle Convention, the Hannover Assembly lifted Lutherans of the world "to a new height of solidarity and fellowship." On Sunday, August 3rd, 1952, sixty-five thousand people worshiped in the Hindenburg Stadium, among them 250 ULCA delegates and visitors. The 1952 assembly authorized three permanent departments for its work: Theology, World Service, and Mission. The delegates of the ULCA were actively engaged in the proceedings. Stewart Herman gave the assembled delegates a vivid report on the Federation's service to refugees. Fry and Judge James F. Henninger were elected to the twenty-two member Executive Committee and A. R. Wentz, the retiring vice president, was declared an "honorary member."[5]

For the third assembly of the Lutheran World Federation held in Minneapolis in the summer of 1957, two kinds of preparation were required. First, the twenty-two delegates and twenty-two official visitors of the ULCA, as well as those of the other church bodies belonging to the LWF, needed an update on world Lutheranism. This was provided by *Lutheran Churches of the World* published by Augsburg Publishing House in Minneapolis under the auspices of the Federation. The authors of the three hundred pages were "seven renowned clergymen . . . each an authority" on his own geographic area. Central Europe was covered by Bishop Hans Lilje, Scandinavia by Dean Ragnar Askmark, Europe's minority churches by Pastor Lasslo Terray, Asia by Bishop Rajah B. Manikam, and Africa by Fridtjov Birkeli. Two ULCA churchmen covered Latin America and North America: Stewart Herman and E. Theodore Bachmann. The foreword was written by Carl E. Lund-Quist, executive secretary of the LWF.

Second, as hosts the Lutherans in America had to be ready to receive the 240 delegates and many more official and unofficial guests representing sixty-one member churches from thirty-two countries. The American Section of the LWF and the National Lutheran Council recognized their responsibility and worked with the local committee under the direction of E. Clifford Nelson to be ready with meeting places, housing, and much much more. Hospitality by American Lutherans was demonstrated in many and various ways. At the suggestion of President Fry the ULCA Committee on German Interests hosted the German-speaking guests at a delightful party after an evening session.

"Christ Frees and Unites" was the theme of the assembly that led to the "Minneapolis Theses" on freedom and unity in Christ. It "dominated all the devotional life, the corporate life and the business," according to the lengthy report of the delegates to the 1958 ULCA Convention in Dayton, Ohio. Their enthusiastic first paragraph deserves repeating here:

> "For those who participated in it, the Lutheran World Federation Assembly will go down in memory as one of the great experiences of a lifetime." This exclamation of joy and appreciation, written by a professional newspaperman, finds a resounding echo in the hearts and minds of all of us who had the honor to represent the ULCA at the great event in Minneapolis on August 15-25, 1957. The Federation's third assembly was historic on many counts. It was the first international congress of Lutherans to be held in North America, a fact of which we, as citizens of the United States and Canada, were vividly and gratefully aware in every waking moment. By far the largest throngs of Lutherans flowed together at Minneapolis during the eventful assembly days that have ever gathered at any one place and time in American Lutheran history, culminating in a congregation numbering up to one hundred thousand attendants at the closing rally in St. Paul on the grounds of the State Capitol of Minnesota. Worship, pageantry, sparkling theological lectures, the pressing affairs of the kingdom, dynamic group discussions, overflowing public events, a youth parade and outdoor rally, exhibits—all of a high quality—filled the days and nights with unforgettable experiences.[6]

Following a precedent established at Lund, the new President of LWF was chosen from the host country. As the prominent American Lutheran leader, Fry was elected president, to serve until the next Assembly of the LWF. He commented on the sequence of assemblies: "At Lund we learned to walk together; at Hannover we learned to pray together; at Minneapolis we learned to think together."[7]

The ULCA and the National Lutheran Council

From its very beginning (1918), the National Lutheran Council had support and leadership from the ULCA. Its work, although administratively separate, was an essential part of the United Lutheran Church. In the fifties, as in other decades, the ULCA Biennial Convention Minutes included a report from the Commission to the National Lutheran Council. The commissioners were always named, headed now by President Fry. Included were items of activity and concern in the various departments of the NLC.[8]

During these years the NLC executive director (since 1948) was a ULCA pastor, the Rev. Paul C. Empie. He was a man of unusual ability and compassion who could identify needs and arouse the churches to respond. Already in the 1940s he was working with Secretary Long to establish Lutheran World Action in the National Lutheran Council. His task then was to gather information and human interest stories for the promotion of LWA. For three cold weeks in 1946 he traveled in Austria and Germany, visiting the needy amid the ruins and acquainting himself with the persons and agencies engaged in relief and reconstruction. His first published article, admitting the feelings of an "innocent abroad," disclosed his own gifts. In time he developed a mastery not only in the use of the media but also in speaking factually and movingly about the suffering and the victims of injustice and racial discrimination. The fifties were his finest decade.

Division of College and University Work. The head of this division, which replaced the Commission on Student Services in 1948, was Executive Secretary Donald Heiges (ULCA). Some 550 pastors, counselors, interns and assistants continued the ULCA tradition of serving students. In most places they were organized into Lutheran Student Associations. Regional conferences and national Ashrams retained their popularity and impact. An increasing number of students were declaring their intention to enter the ministry or other forms of Christian service. During the fifties more and more foreign students were coming to America for advanced education. In places where there was a large concentration, the division provided specialized personnel, as in Berkeley, California and New York City, with funds provided by United Lutheran Church Women. The importance of student centers became increasingly evident, and this inter-Lutheran experience on the student level contributed directly to the various mergers later on.

As an educator, Heiges had another concern. Which colleges and universities were including religion as an academic subject? And, what was being taught? To answer these questions, the National Lutheran Council, with the Missouri Synod cooperating, engaged the services of the Rev. George Forell, a ULCA scholar teaching at Gustavus Adolphus College, to explore the situation. He spent a year visiting universities and colleges and gave a detailed report of his findings. As a result a plan was worked out with the University of Iowa in Iowa City. Here the School of Religion had Chairs supported by Jews, Catholics and Protestants. The school would welcome a Lutheran Chair. The NLC engaged Forell to fill this position on an experimental basis. Being at the center of a strong Lutheran state, it was so well received that at the end of the 1956-57 school year it was continued on a permanent basis. Forell as Lutheran chair was made associate professor in the School of Religion. As such he had the opportunity and obligation to teach students working for higher degrees, some of whom became professors at Lutheran seminaries. In 1958, Forell accepted a call to the Chicago Lutheran Seminary. But three years later he was back at Iowa as full Professor in the School of Religion.

Division of Lutheran Cooperation in Latin America. The ULCA made repeated proposals to the NLC for a cooperative partnership with Latin American Lutherans. Finally in 1951, the NLC formed the Division of Lutheran Cooperation in Latin America. This served as an incentive to the Lutheran World Federation to create a Committee on Latin America in 1952. Both had the same executive secretary, Stewart Herman, who now was working from Geneva, Switzerland, as the Lutheran World Federation's Director of Services to Refugees. As such he had become acquainted with and well accepted by the established Lutherans in Latin America. The recent refugees also trusted him. The Division also had the enthusiastic support of the NLC's executive, Paul Empie, who skillfully kept up the interest and support of the churches involved. This joint arrangement enabled the LWF to care for the spiritual needs of European refugees finding new homes in the welcoming Latin American countries. Here only one of the many similar projects is recounted.

Already in 1952 there were numbers of German, Hungarian, and Latvian Lutheran refugees in and around Caracas, Venezuela. The LWF soon organized a congregation with three chapters or groups under one constitution and arranged for three pastors who could meet the language needs. The ULCA became directly involved when one of its pastors serving the First Hungarian congregation in Cleveland, Ohio, accepted the NLC's call to serve the congregation's Hungarians. George Posfay, educated in Hungary, Sweden, and the United States, served there until 1961 when he became LWF Latin American secretary, following in the footsteps of Stewart Herman.

The division also had the mandate to begin Spanish Missions in Uruguay and to encourage other Spanish work. Support for work in Uruguay was promised by both Augustana and the ULCA. Already in the 1940s, a ULCA missionary, the Rev. Herman D. Hammer, had been gathering a congregation in Montevideo. On his own initiative, he commuted monthly from Buenos Aires. This work in Montevideo was continued and then extended to Rivera. By 1956 the Augustana Church assumed full responsibility. The ULCA continued to assist by producing Spanish materials for worship and theological education.

The NLC also extended help to the largest Lutheran Church in Latin America, in the southern part of Brazil. Already in 1947, the United States National Committee of the Lutheran World Federation provided funds to assist the far-sighted President, Herman Dohms, who had in 1946 established a one-man seminary, the Faculdade de Teologia. He had faced the present with a look at the past. The German settlers in Brazil, arriving back in the 1820s, maintained a strong relationship and loyalty to Germany. Pastors were sent from Germany by the church and missionary societies. Young men who felt called to be pastors were sent to Germany for education. This encouraged dependence. World War II caused great havoc for the Lutherans in Brazil. German pastors were detained, and congregations left without care. Young pre-theological students, not yet twenty years of age, were sent out to baptize and bury. And among the young there was a growing surge of Brazilian nationalism.

At war's end, again a few pastors arrived from Germany. Then, beginning in 1953, three well-educated German professors came to bolster the seminary. In 1954, the four synods joined in forming the Evangelical Church of the Lutheran Confession with a strong determination to support the seminary in Sao Leopoldo. Aware of this history and situation, Herman encouraged the NLC to contribute funds. In 1957, $20,000 was given as a revolving fund. Repayment on loans would remain in Brazil for other needs. An additional $100,000 of Lutheran World Action funds were given to help in the construction of a seminary building. This aid was gratefully accepted and inspired the Brazilian Lutheran laity to blaze a trail in self-support.[9] The NLC also sent two visitors to Brazil. The Rev. Ernst Schmidt, a ULCA pastor in Philadelphia, spent three months in Brazil acquainting pastors and congregations with American stewardship and evangelism methods. Otto A. Piper of Princeton Theological Seminary lectured at the seminary.

Then in 1959, Herman, with Lutheran World Federation funds and encouragement, arranged with the young Pacific Seminary to permit their History and Mission professor to spend an academic year at the Faculdade de Teologia. Although lectures had to be in German, it was a great opportunity to strengthen American identity. It was also an opportunity and obligation to open the eyes of students and pastors to the vast mission opportunities in Portuguese-speaking Brazil. Before the year ended, a modest gift from Pacific Lutheran Seminary was used to bring the professors from the ULCA-supported seminary in Argentina and the professors from the two Missouri-related seminaries in Brazil to the Faculdade for a conference on theological education in Latin America. This proved so beneficial that annual conferences have continued at their own expense. During the year, the new seminary building was dedicated to the joy of the entire church. The professor was also able to welcome and help interpret the Brazilian church to a group of ELC pastors who had been sent to Brazil to begin mission work among Portuguese-speaking Brazilians. Their arrival also had to be interpreted to the German church. In time, their work was appreciated and combined.

ULCA GROWTH AND GLOBAL AWARENESS

For the ULCA the fifties were a time of growth and maturing in its internal life, its ecumenical stature, and its global involvements. Quantified, the growth during this decade in baptized membership rose from 2 million to almost 2.5 million. The confirmed membership topped 1.25 million. The number of communicants grew by some 140,000 and the number of congregations totaled 4,591 in 1959, an increase of 430 during the fifties. In some years more than fifty new congregations were organized. While the average size of a congregation in 1951 was 480 baptized members, in 1959 it was 543. The number of ordained ministers, three-fourths of them serving congregations, reached 4,872, an increase of 884 since 1951. Furthermore, ULCA related churches in Asia, Africa, and Latin

America accounted for an additional quarter million baptized. The valuation of church property during the decade more than doubled, surpassing $650 million. Congregational indebtedness quadrupled, exceeding $80 million in 1959. Many were the new edifices and renovations. By the end of the decade the grand total of expenses paid by congregations had doubled, reaching nearly $89 million. Meanwhile the total benevolence—"For Others" as the weekly envelopes reminded—neared $25 million, almost twice what it had been in 1951.[10] This sizable growth included major ULCA contributions to overseas missions as well as to Lutheran World Action.

By virtue of his diversified duties Franklin Clark Fry in the fifties became more than ever the traveling church leader, experiencing global missions first-hand and sharing his experience with the whole ULCA. The Church House on New York's Madison Avenue was unceasingly his point of departure and, thankfully, of his safe return. His encompassing mind and ready recall, plus his gifts of observation, analysis, and narration, gave productivity to his times in transit. In his characteristically small script, he penned notes from the plane, like one to a bishop in South India whose wife was stricken with a heart attack.[11] On a vaster scale he remembered his fellow pastors each month with his "Dear Partner" letters. His intention was to take his ordained colleagues into confidence a step ahead of the published news.

A strong supporting cast kept the store while he was away. F. Eppling Reinartz, whom we met earlier as director of promotion during the Knubel presidency (chapter 8) was now secretary of the ULCA, and by the constitution second in command. In the president's office George F. Harkins served as chief assistant (1949-60), and was joined in the widening work in 1956 by Raymond H. Tiemeyer. In her quiet way, the bilingual Margaret Duhme was office administrator and secretary to the president. On the fiscal side was the Office of the Treasurer—first Henry Beisler, and after 1953 Edmund F. Wagner, a New York banker—with Carl A. Warden, the eagle-eyed comptroller throughout the decade.

In the discharge of other functions of the church as well, the fifties accentuated mobility. Travel by air, moreover, brought the "ends of the earth" within reach. Nothing brought this out more clearly than the travel diaries of President Fry. As part of taking his "Dear Partner" into his confidence, Fry allowed glimpses of his travel schedule. The strenuous pace with which he had begun in 1945 continued through the fifties. With his gift of narration he covered a gamut of subjects germane to the life of the church near or far. The Fry accounts had the effect of creating in many parts of the ULCA a greater sense of belonging in the worldwide church. Spaced across the decade, his itinerary was determined by events of more than usual import. Japan in 1952, India in 1953. Because there were "so many flatterers about the journals of my Japan and India tours . . . you are in for it again", Fry wrote as he focused on Europe in 1955. Later in the year (November) he introduced ULCA partners to Liberia, and gave a preview of the first All-Africa Lutheran Conference in Marangu, Tanzania, which became a trailblazing event. Input in 1956 was about Malaya's new Lutheran mission.

Mission is one, a oneness in diversity of outreach whether overseas, at home or in society. The ULCA in the 1950s relied heavily, yet not exclusively, on its trio of mission-related boards: Foreign Missions, American Missions, and Social Missions. They were not operating alone but in concert with others in the National Lutheran Council and, in the case of the ULCA, in cooperation with the National Council of Churches. Internationally the net was spread to all continents via the Lutheran World Federation (Geneva), and aided by Lutheran World Action (in funds) and by Lutheran World Relief (in material aid).

Before taking up the ULCA mission work in the fifties, we do well to note what had been happening in the wider setting of global missions. Since the late 1930s and especially during the war years, with the growth of the ecumenical movement among the churches and the care of "orphaned missions," there had grown a keener realization of a "worldwide Christian family." Amid the darkest days of the war, Anglican Archbishop William Temple called this global family the "great new fact of our time."[12] After the war and in the early fifties, moreover, in 1947 and 1952, gatherings under the International Missionary Council in Whitby (Canada) and Willingen (Germany) helped the emerging churches in Asia and Africa and Latin America see themselves side-by-side with the churches in Europe and North America as "partners in obedience," meaning the obedience of faith. ULCA mission staff as well as other Lutherans were fully engaged in this sense of partnership, this oneness.

FOREIGN MISSIONS

Through its half-dozen affiliated churches overseas—in Asia, Africa and Latin America—the ULCA in the 1950s and up to the formation of the LCA in 1962 maintained lively ties. Indeed these ties provided the give-and-take for support and personnel "over there" and for input from familiar parts of the world scene "over here." Church publications like *The Lutheran*, but especially *The Foreign Missionary* and *Lutheran Woman's Work* nurtured an informed readership. Besides, one-third of the budget of the Board of Foreign Missions was raised by the Women's Missionary Society of the ULCA. In addition, the continuing partnership in mission with the Augustana Church, particularly in missionary personnel, ably complemented the ULCA work in India and, after the 1949 revolution in China, the inter-Lutheran and ecumenical efforts in Hong Kong. In addition Augustana and ULCA partnership in Malaya (Malaysia later) in 1953, and in Uruguay in 1952 gave added dimension to their missioning enterprise.

"I rejoice to express my complete solidarity with the work of the Board of Foreign Missions," said President Fry to the 1956 convention at Harrisburg. On stage were fifty-six missionaries, about one fifth of the number maintained in the eight countries where the ULCA was at work. There were also three retirees, women who had served with distinction as medical missionaries in India. Add to these the board's executive secretary, Earl S. Erb, his eight field secretaries and staff associates, as well as the board's vice president, Ralph W. Loew (Holy Trinity Church, Buffalo, New York) and the cast of characters interpreting the church's overseas outreach was virtually complete. Fry's concluding observations placed the evening's presentation in perspective when he reflected: "As I travel to many lands across the world I am impressed and also oppressed by certain evidences which I meet." The three that he lifted up bear remembering also at a later time.

1. On every hand are unbelievable revolutions. There have been no such revolutions in European or American history.
2. The forces of Christianity, though making up a gallant company, are a very small minority. . . . It is our clear obligation to fortify the brave and tenacious national churches.
3. A dominant impression is that the little we are doing in world missions is significant only as part of the total Christian enterprise. I covet for our own church that its contribution to that total may be a worthy one. Our voice is only one in a grand chorus.[13]

Considered individually and in their context the spiritual pilgrimage of the affiliated churches and mission fields in the fifties is a commentary on the times. Alphabetically, as the Foreign Board habitually listed them, there were eight: Argentina, British Guiana, China, India, Japan, Liberia, Malaya, and Uruguay.

Argentina

The United Evangelical Lutheran Church ("Unida") in Argentina began in the early decades of the century, with leadership and support from the East Pennsylvania Synod, especially missionary Edward H. Mueller. After World War II it attained its maturity, and was self-governing since 1948. With postwar immigration at its high—there were said to be some 165,000 of German, Scandinavian, and central European stock—the "Unida" grew, as did other Lutheran bodies. Old Lutheran congregations were being enlarged and new ones founded, as immigrants from Europe, notably Displaced Persons, were beginning a new life. During the fifties the Unida's membership nearly doubled, well exceeding four thousand by 1960 and including a Spanish-speaking Lutheranism.[14]

Midway through the decade the founding of the Lutheran Theological Seminary (1955) in Jose C. Paz, a Buenos Aires suburb, gave the United Evangelical Lutheran Church in Argentina a new lease on life and actualized the dream of Edward Mueller. The smartly structured new institution, in its pleasant setting, was to prepare ministers for all of South America except Brazil. The Seminary was multilingual. Its faculty included men of Argentine, German, Hungarian, Swedish, and American background. Among the first students the ethnic background was equally diverse, even as the countries from which they came included Peru, Venezuela, Chile, Argentina, and other lands.

The ULCA Foreign Board plus the widespread response generated by the first All-Latin America Lutheran Conference (Curitiba, Brazil 1951) led to the formation in 1952 of the Lutheran World Federation-linked Latin America Committee. Stewart W. Herman Jr., (ULCA) was the far-sighted promoter as he executed the tasks of the Latin America Committee, as noted above.

British Guiana

The Evangelical Lutheran Church in British Guiana, self-governing after 1943, doubled its baptized membership in the 1950s and was approaching ten thousand. Its ethnic composition included African, European, Amerindian, East Asian (India), Chinese, and combinations thereof. Since slavery was abolished in 1834, the British in 1903 began bringing in East Asians, Chinese, and Portuguese as indentured servants for the sugar plantations and other tasks. How an eventually ULCA-related body of believers arose in "B.G." and has antecedents nearly as old as the Dutch Lutheran presence on the Hudson in North America requires a brief explanation.

Since 1743, when its first congregation was formed by Dutch lay people on the Berbice River, a Lutheran presence has continued in the land. But its existence was tenuous. Had it not been for John Robert Mittelholzer (1840 1913), a civil engineer of African and German ancestry, Ebenezer congregation would have vanished for lack of a pastor. Challenged and prepared by the London Missionary Society, he was ordained and retained his inherited Lutheran connection. He transformed Ebenezer into a lively missionary enterprise. For further assistance he turned to the East Pennsylvania Synod (General Synod). In 1890 he and Ebenezer congregation were received into the synodical membership.[15] The missionary enterprise expanded its ethnic diversity, fostered education, and became a recognized influence in the colony. By 1920 the "B.G." field came under the ULCA Board of Foreign Missions.[16] At bicentennial time in 1943, this diversified body of faithful became self-governing. Its history and postwar growth linked Europe, Africa, and Asia to the Americas North and South uniquely.

China

Given the 1949 revolution and rise of the People's Republic of China, the work of ULCA missionaries under the Foreign Board on the mainland was ended by 1952. Charles Reinbrecht and his partners from overseas had relocated from Tsingtao and its outposts in Shantung Province to southern China in the Canton region in 1951. But they soon had to move on to Hong Kong along with thousands of Chinese refugees, the majority of whom continued on to Taiwan (formerly Formosa).

In Tsingtao, however, one ULCA missionary had elected to stay on. Paul Johannes Mackensen Jr., a recent Philadelphia Seminary graduate, had arrived on the scene in 1948. The following June, Tsingtao was taken over. The Communist government requisitioned the mission schools and took other steps to liberate the people from "foreign imperialism." Mackensen stayed at his post, seeking perhaps to be a bridge between conflicting parties. On March 7, 1952 he was imprisoned. For the next five years to the outside world Paul Mackensen was a powerful symbol of faith—"Address Unknown." When he was released in 1957, Mackensen decided to stay and learn more about China. The equivalent of the Red Cross in China lent a hand. He moved to Shanghai and for the next three years (1957-60) taught English in a high school. Finally, he made his way to Canton (the British kept him out of Hong Kong). There he booked a freighter heading for the United States' West Coast and then via Panama to New York where his family met him. No story of Paul Mackensen's China experience has been published, but he is fondly remembered by the hundreds of ULCA members who prayed for him during his exile.

Reinbrecht and fellow Lutherans from the mainland, while lamenting the course of events, made the most of a new opportunity. Although the revolution had virtually driven the United Lutheran Church of China underground, the several missions—German, Swiss, Scandinavian, American (Augustana, Norwegian, ULCA)—had learned to work together. Only Missouri, a paradoxical term in China, stood alone. In Hong Kong the United Lutheran Theological Seminary, relocated already in 1948 from its base outside Hankow, occupied the lofty height of Tao Fong Shan in Shatin, a meeting place where the Norwegian missionary Karl Ludwig Reichelt had welcomed Buddhist monks.[17]

Hong Kong in the fifties had become a welter of Christian denominations, some fifty in all. By 1954 the Hong Kong Christian Council was giving this diverse concentration, actually only about 10 percent of the population, a semblance of order. Already in 1953 the Hong Kong Lutheran Mission was formed. It comprised representatives of the various missions that had support from overseas for the work of the Lutheran Church of China (LCC). The LCC had been a dispersed church body claiming some one hundred thousand baptized members: worshiping in about twelve hundred congregations, maintaining scores of schools from elementary to higher education, rendering health and welfare services through hospitals, clinics, and agencies, publishing Christian literature from pamphlets to books to catechisms and hymnals. At the end of World War II and the Japanese occupation, many LCC members found refuge in Hong Kong. A permanent church body was formed in 1955, the Evangelical Lutheran Church of Hong Kong. It elected Peng Fu president, inasmuch as he had headed the LCC earlier. ELCHK was, in effect, a continuation of the Lutheran Church of China. Among others it included the ULCA missionary enterprise in Tsingtao. A close working partnership developed between Reinbrecht and President Peng Fu. Not surprisingly, under the unusual circumstances the baptized membership of the ELCHK by 1960 approached ten thousand, an increase of over 260 percent during the decade.[18]

India

Dating back to Father Heyer in 1842, the Andhra Evangelical Lutheran Church was India's largest Lutheran church body, with more than 265,000 baptized members in 1960. Self-governing since 1927, it had been prominent in forming the Federation of Evangelical Lutheran Churches in India, which was a charter member of the World Council of Churches (1948). As further testimony to its maturity, the Andhra Church in 1947—like the Tamil Lutheran Church (linked to the Church of Sweden Mission) and four other Lutheran bodies related to German and Norse missionary societies—had become a charter member of the Lutheran World Federation.[19]

Illustrative of the linkage between the ULCA and India during the fifties are the careers of three leaders. Luther A. Gotwald II, executive of the ULCA Foreign Board (1947-52) was a veteran of twenty-five years as missionary in India. After his period with the ULCA he spent his last decade (1953-63) heading the Division for Foreign Missions of the National Council of Churches. Another was Earl S. Erb, a Pennsylvanian. Co-opting him to succeed Gotwald as its executive, the Foreign Board sent Erb to India in 1951 for four months. His trip appears to have fostered "a better spirit of partnership" between the national church leaders and the missionaries who together made up the church's executive committee. Erb's role as executive inspired confidence at home and abroad. He continued in that position for a decade, and then for another five years as director of the LCA Division of World Mission. Third, among Erb's able staffers none was more suited to his task than the India-born and Canada-educated J. Fred Neudoerffer. The son of missionary parents, J. Fred spoke Telugu like a native, knew the ways of Indian life and the aims of Christian ecumenism. After a parish ministry in Montreal he served on the Foreign Board as Asia secretary from 1954 to the 1962 merger, and then for another twenty-two years in that capacity for the LCA Division of World Mission.

In this ULCA connection with the mission work in India an indigenous leader should be named. Rajah Bushnahan Manikam (1895-1972), born in the land of the Tamils in south India, became in 1951 the first East Asia secretary jointly for the International Missionary Council and the World Council of Churches. It was a position of great responsibility and at times of demanding diplomacy in places closed to Westerners, such as conferring in 1956 with Communist China's Premier Chou En Lai. That same year was also the 250th anniversary of the beginning of Protestant (Lutheran) missions in India, at Tranquebar, Tamil Nadu (then in Danish India). On that commemorative occasion Manikam, having been duly elected, was consecrated as the fourth bishop, and the first Indian national of the Tamil Evangelical Lutheran church. The ties of this church were with Sweden since the first World War, and continued older German ties with the Leipzig Mission, as well as some more recent ones with Augustana in North America. But in training and earlier service, Manikam was a ULCA man. His theological education was completed at the Philadelphia Seminary (1927), and by 1929 he had earned his doctorate at Columbia University. His wife, Ruby, meanwhile had studied public health and social work at Douglass College, Rutgers University. Returning to India, Manikam taught for eight years at Andhra Christian College, in Guntur, the scene where Father Heyer began his labors. Under the National Christian Council of India

Manikam served in Nagpur as secretary of the Central Board of Christian Education (1937-51). In America the Manikams remained well-known especially throughout the ULCA. Rajah Manikam's book, *Christianity and the Asian Revolution* (1954), rang like a trumpet reveille, calling the church to the new day in mission.[20] The India relationship was the oldest, strongest, and most influential bond between the ULCA and Asia.

Japan

In 1952, the Japan Evangelical Lutheran Church (JELC) observed its sixtieth anniversary. It was in 1892 that the United Synod of the South sent two missionaries, James A. B. Shaner and Rufus Benton Perry, to Japan to begin Christian work there. After language study in Tokyo, the missionaries went south to the Kyushu island to the small city of Saga. In 1898, in behalf of the Danish Lutherans in America, J. M. T. Winter of the West Schleswig Missionary Society in Denmark visited these missionaries on his way to China, and stayed for the rest of his ninety-five years! Two years later, in 1900, the first emissaries from the Lutheran Evangelical Association of Finland arrived. They worked separately until 1940 when they joined forces with the JELC. Early in the century, work in Saga expanded to the more promising city of Kumamoto. Here schools were opened for boys and girls as well as a small seminary for the training of Japanese pastors (1909). In 1925 the seminary was moved to Tokyo.[21]

Evangelism, education, and service went hand in hand in the JELC. The founding of Jiai-En (Colony of Mercy) in 1921 in Kumamoto underscored the church's concern for people and introduced modern social work into Japan. It grew into one of the largest and most respected agencies in the country. In 1949, the resourceful director, Maud Paulos, and Jiai-En were honored by a visit from the emperor.

World War II brought severe setbacks. The church was compelled by the government to become a part of the United Church of Christ (Kyodan) along with other Japanese Protestants. Missionaries were expelled and Japanese pastors forced into war employment. There was great loss of life and property. The first postwar figures listed 2,050 baptized members of JELC, a loss of 60 percent of prewar membership. In 1947, the JELC withdrew from the Kyodan, received back its seminary and was officially established. Once again the ULCA along with the Lutheran Evangelical Association of Finland joined their Japanese fellow believers in the task of reconstruction and outreach. Already by 1950 the two high schools in Kumamoto, the Bethany Home, the seminary and nineteen kindergartens had been repaired or reconstructed.

Now to the sixtieth celebration in 1952. President Fry accepted the invitation of the JELC and the ULCA Foreign Mission Board to visit the church. Accompanied by his wife Hilda, Fry spent a month in Japan. The highlight of his visit included attendance at the anniversary convention where he preached the sermon and conveyed "the official greetings of the Mother church." He also preached a dedicatory sermon for a new church building in Saga where the first

Lutheran baptism occurred in 1893 and where the first congregation was subsequently organized. The Frys also had an extensive twelve-day tour of the churches, institutions of mercy, schools, and kindergartens. They met with the Japan Lutheran Missionaries Association. The president was also honored by the United Lutheran Chaplains by being the guest preacher at the largest United States Navy and Air Force bases in Japan. His sermon at a base hospital chapel in Tokyo was broadcast over the Far East Network.[22]

During this anniversary year, plans were made for a Student Center in Tokyo. Under the direction of a ULCA missionary, the Rev. Norman Nuding, and an influential Japanese pastor, Atsumi Tasaka, this became a reality two years later. Centrally located, it served students from many universities and other schools of higher education. Here the pastors and helpers ministered to student needs: housing for a few, recreation, counseling, Bible study and church services. The Center attracted many non-Christian young people, a number of whom became interested in the Christian faith and were baptized. In time they formed a congregation. In 1956, the JELC took active part in a Lutheran Unity Committee composed of representatives of the twelve Lutheran bodies in Japan in the hope of forming one Lutheran Church. Chitose Kishi, president of the seminary who also became president of the church that year, assured the committee of the JELC's total support.[23]

Liberia

In 1950 the ULCA also remembered the work begun in Liberia in 1860 when Morris Officer, commissioned by the General Synod, opened the Muhlenberg Mission station twenty-five miles up the St. Paul River from Monrovia. Since the American Baptists and Methodists were already serving the returned American freed slaves along the coast, Officer decided to penetrate into the interior "where Africa was still primitive and untouched."[24] The work was difficult and remains so due to the climate. David A. Day, a physician and pastor who served from 1874 to 1897, was the first to survive the difficult climate for any length of time.

Due to industrial development during the post-war years, Liberia in the 1950s was in a prosperous mood looking forward to more development and an extensive road building program. This had an effect on the Lutheran Church in Liberia (LCL). A Mission House in Monrovia was built as a business center for the church. Here supplies purchased in the city or imported from abroad could be stored and prepared for shipment into the interior. It also served as the home of the treasurer of the church and it could accommodate missionaries arriving or leaving. In the interior, buildings of mud and sticks were now replaced by permanent cement block buildings even at the farthest station. Here the Curran Memorial Hospital, joined for a time by the Phoebe hospital, became a reality in stone and mortar. This greatly strengthened the medical program as well as evangelistic efforts. Some towns that had earlier rejected Christian workers now welcomed them because of the physical benefits they had received from a surgeon.

In 1957 an accelerated building program provided the Lutheran Training Institute and High School at Salayea a permanent building. This school was intended for the intensive training of national leaders to serve in the church as evangelists, Bible women, teachers, nurses, and pastors. By 1952, two small classes had graduated and each year the enrollment increased. There were eighty-four students in the High School Department in the late fifties.[25]

By 1958 the LCL was ready to relocate its Phoebe hospital to land adjacent to Cuttingham College, an Episcopal institution where there were already twelve Lutheran students sponsored by the Church and Mission. The location enabled the hospital to become a Nurses Training Center. The project was endorsed and funded by the ULCA Board of Foreign Missions and the United Lutheran Church Women. The ULCA Foundation agreed to encourage private grants. The Liberian government pledged seventy-five thousand dollars. The entire cost of the new hospital was estimated at one million dollars.

The literacy program of the Church under the direction of missionary Norma Bloomquist acquired new zeal with the visit of Frank Laubach who trained her in his method of "each one teach one." Wesley Sadler, a linguistic expert of the board, worked with a team of evangelists to encourage literacy. He translated the Gospel of John into their language. This work was also a great encouragement for the missionaries to learn the native language well enough to teach and preach.[26]

Malaya

In 1952 the Commission of World Mission of the Lutheran World Federation sent out a call for some church to establish work in Malaya among the thousands of Chinese finding refuge there in "New Villages." Upon the recommendation of the Foreign Board, the ULCA Seattle Convention of 1952 gave approval and pledged support for what became an international undertaking with ULCA leadership.[27] Paul P. Anspach, a staff secretary and a former missionary in China, was given the responsibility of directing the undertaking. He arrived in Malaya in September of 1954 and was followed soon by five missionaries. All had worked in China except one, Deaconess Gladys Reidenouer of the Philadelphia Mother House. By 1956, an international staff of thirty-eight was working well as a team. Plans were under way to extend the outreach to Singapore where thousands of Chinese refugees were crowded into a huge housing complex.[28] The first pastor to be ordained in Malaya was a graduate of the Lutheran Seminary in Hong Kong. The honor of ordaining him fell, naturally enough, to President Fry.

Malaya received her independence in August of 1957 and became Malaysia. Although Islam was the state religion, the country recognized the freedom of all religions, so the missionary work was not jeopardized. Rather, there was a new challenge for Christian work among the now three million Chinese in the land. As yet no congregations had been organized, but twenty-seven preaching points were maintained, and an increasing number of adults were attending evening Bible classes.[29]

Uruguay

In 1956 the work in Uruguay became Augustana's responsibility with the coop-eration of the ULCA, as discussed above.

AMERICAN MISSIONS

As we have seen in chapter 9, Fry had a keen concern for American Missions. He was not alone. During the fifties American Missions were fortunate in having a steady and aggressive board of twenty-one members. As to chairman, the period was divided between three churchmen of stature: the Rev. W. C. Schaeffer Jr., D.D., of Allentown, Pennsylvania; the Rev. Charles B. Foelsch, Ph.D., president of the Pacific Lutheran Seminary; and the Rev. Fred C. Wiegman, D.D., of Columbus, Ohio. The Rev. R. H. Gerberding served as executive director from 1940 until his retirement in 1958 when the Rev. Donald Houser, English secre-tary, took over the responsibilities. The office was in the Church House in New York, but a branch office in Chicago continued the insistence of the Richmond Convention (1926). Organizationally, there were four departments: English Missions, Church Extension, Latin America, Special Missions, and a fifth added in 1952 for Survey and Research. The board received the largest share of the ULCA budget, $1,262,000 in 1950 and $3,725,000 in 1959. But it was never enough for the manifold responsibilities from Newfoundland to Hawaii.

English Missions and Church Extension

In the fifties there was a realization that much more should be done in American Missions, for the opportunities for outreach were greater than ever. The mobil-ity of the population was tremendous. The 1954 report of the board stated, "more people in the USA and Canada have moved within the past two years than have been moved by all the enforced shifts in Europe since World War II."[30] Would these transplants find a church near their new home? If not, could they become a nucleus for starting a new one? Besides, the fifties were also prosper-ous years. Raising of funds was comparatively easier. Yet most home mission activities were accomplished by the synods with encouragement and assistance by the board. Some synods raised substantial funds for this work within their domain, while other areas were sometimes undeveloped for lack of funds. A churchwide strategy was needed.

In 1956 the Harrisburg Convention adopted a plan that would change the funding patterns. Instead of multiple local and synodical mission bases, changes were made that would create a unified national plan: "relative needs rather than relative resources." Synods were discouraged from separate fund-raising efforts and encouraged to increase their benevolent giving to the ULCA. Synodical funds for home missions were to be used "only in fields approved by the Board of American Missions and under its supervision."[31] Thus, if funds increased, a mission could be planted where the need and opportunities for growth were greatest and even in the territory of a small synod short of funds.

The 1958 biennium report revealed that the new policy (along with the major evangelism effort discussed shortly) had helped the church in its planting. One hundred forty-one new congregations had been started, compared to fifty-eight ten years earlier. A new mission was being formed every five days and a first unit erected every twelve days. In addition, twenty-five established congregations were granted mission status for a building program. Nevertheless, because the funds still fell short of the opportunities, the Dayton Convention (1958) adopted a resolution that allowed the board to borrow up to eight million dollars for church extension purposes.[32]

It was and always had been the policy of the board to encourage and expect every newly organized congregation to participate in the whole program of the church through the benevolence offerings. Thus the financial return from these congregations often quickly exceeded the amounts given to them for salary aids.[33] Generous giving on the part of mission congregations often served as an example for older churches to follow. Mission congregations were also encouraged to refinance their mortgages as soon as possible so that the money returned could be used for another mission. Increased support also came from the Women's Missionary Society, renamed the United Lutheran Church Women.

In the fifties, the ULCA came to a new awareness of its rural churches and endeavored to find ways of strengthening them. In spite of the trend to the large cities, 55 percent of the church membership was still in open country or in communities of less than twenty-five hundred people. Synods as well as the American Board held institutes and convocations so that pastors and laity could discuss subjects that would lead to an increased understanding of the impact of the Gospel of Jesus Christ on rural life. Large and multiple parishes were studied in an effort to increase their effectiveness. At times dividing, regrouping, combining or even relocating seemed appropriate. Emphasis was placed on the importance of weekly worship no matter how small or remote the church might be. The rural pastor gained dignity by recognition and appointments to the boards and agencies of the church. Leadership training increased the involvement of the laity in the work, including evangelism. The 1951 *Year Book* devoted pages of pictures, statistics, and an article to the rural church.[34]

The work of the board in the Caribbean Islands required a bilingual secretary in order to meet the needs of Spanish-speaking Puerto Ricans and English-speaking Virgin Islanders. Even when the two areas joined into a Caribbean Synod in 1952, Board Secretary Wm. G. Arbaugh remained in the field for a time in order to help the new synod assume the normal responsibilities. However, in 1956, Arbaugh moved the office to New York where he worked on editing a Spanish Hymnal in addition to his work with the Caribbean Synod.

Special Missions

Included in this category were Linguistic congregations, the Rocky Boy Mission, and Mountain missions.

Linguistic congregations. In 1949 the Board of American Missions created the Division of Special Missions to encompass several linguistic groups, some of them of long-standing concern such as German, and some of more recent postwar concern such as Latvian. In the early fifties the Board of American Missions continued to serve pastors who along with their flocks had become refugees in the United States and Canada. Some had come on secular assurances and were called to the attention of the Board by employees or local pastors. As mentioned in chapter 10, six months' training in an established congregation under a ULCA pastor was required for recognition as clergy in the ULCA. Altogether, more than fifty pastors were given this opportunity. Some were then called to English-speaking congregations.[35] Others were used in bilingual situations to care for the thousands of Lutheran refugees from Latvia, Estonia, Lithuania, Czechoslovakia, Poland, Finland, and Rumania. To serve these, ten new congregations were organized, three Estonian and seven Latvian, all affiliated with ULCA synods. Linguistic or immigration work had been and continued to be an important part of the board's work. In 1954, there were eighty-four congregations and fifty-three preaching points using languages other than English.[36] For new Americans it was a blessing to hear the gospel in their mother tongue. Nevertheless, it was the policy of the board to help prepare them for a time when English should and would be used.

Rocky Boy Mission. The year 1954 saw an anniversary of a particularly interesting mission program. Concern and respect for American Indians had been an important aspect of Lutheran missions early on in the "New World." After a careful study of all the facts and possibilities, the Board of American Missions in 1928 "resolved to take over Rocky Boy Mission in the name of the United Lutheran Church in America."[37] Here in Montana 550 Indians representing 125 families had been living for 11 years on an 80-acre tract. Its supervision had been entrusted to the National Indian Association who agreed to transfer the rights to the United Lutheran Church. By 1930 there was already an enthusiastic progress report at the Milwaukee convention. Missionary William H. Gable and his family adjusted to a new way of life and were cordially accepted by the Indians. Paul Mitchell, a native who served as an interpreter of the Cree language, was a devout Christian who did much to strengthen the Christian program of worship and instruction. His son, who wanted to become a missionary to his people, was enrolled as a freshman at Midland College. This mission became a favorite of Women's Missionary Societies and Luther Leagues, who donated bundles of clothing and other supplies. With an increasing number of Indians asking for baptism, the future looked bright for the new mission.[38] In 1954, the mission celebrated its twenty-fifth anniversary by rededicating the original log chapel that had been reconditioned.[39]

Mountain Missions. The closing of a mission reflected success, of a sort. The mountain work in southwestern Virginia and western North Carolina became the responsibility of the Board of American Missions in 1936 by action of the Executive Board of the ULCA. Until then part of the work of administering the school and health center had been under the Inner Mission Board.[40] The Konnarock School for Girls was founded in 1925 by the Women's Missionary Society, which continued its support. The Iron Mountain School for Boys, also in Konnarock, was founded by the Brotherhood in 1930, but later had to be closed for lack of support. Both schools provided excellent education through high school (home management for girls and farming for boys) plus additional Christian education. A medical center under the competent direction of H. C. Meyer and Sister Sophia Moeller provided medical care for a vast area.[41]

In this area were a number of small congregations most of which had American Mission support. They benefited greatly from the training the students received in music and Christian education as well as their skills that raised standards of living. Nevertheless, "special work of this nature, if it is successful, must come to an end," stated the 1958 report of the Board.[42] Consolidated schools and good roads were now common in this once depressed area. Medical doctors had established private practices in the surrounding communities where the Lutheran Medical Center had raised health standards in general. Therefore, the "Mountain Work" was discontinued at the end of the 1958-59 school year with grateful thanks to the Women's Missionary Society and others who had made this work possible. The preaching missions and congregations continued.

SOCIAL MISSIONS

The Board of Social Missions began each biennium report during the fifties with words such as the following: "The Central dynamic of the Board is to bring people into such a vital relationship with Jesus Christ that He will become a transforming power within them."[43] To carry out this commitment, the work was divided into three areas: Evangelism, Inner Mission, and Social Action, with secretaries in charge of each. All work came under the careful eye of the executive secretary, C. Franklin Koch, who assumed this responsibility in 1940 shortly after the board was formed by combining three boards. Koch served until 1958 when the Rev. Harold Haas, Ph.D., assumed responsibility.

Department of Evangelism

Evangelism was given high priority in the ULCA, under department directors Oscar Carlson and Royal Lesher. In the early fifties it profited from the Lutheran Evangelism Council of the National Lutheran Council that sponsored "Preaching, Teaching, and Reaching" Missions. There were also efforts of the Joint Department of Evangelism of the National Council of Churches of Christ to reach the unchurched in the United States. Already in 1948 the ULCA convention in Philadelphia stated, "Evangelism is the first thing, the central thing and the last thing in the life of the Church."

Four years later (1952) at Seattle, the convention requested the Board of Social Mission to "study and prepare an intensive churchwide program of Evangelism including the cost of executing it" to be presented to the 1954 convention. There followed a year of intensive study using surveys and population analysis. These revealed that as a church the ULCA was "not making disciples on a scale commensurate with either our responsibility or opportunity." Thus the board prepared a plan for the church to consider. The purpose would be "to quicken the United Lutheran Church in America to all its responsibilities, resources and potentialities for bringing the Gospel of Jesus Christ to the people in Canada and the U.S.A."[44] The plan called for a series of Lutheran Evangelism Missions (LEM) to be held across the continent until "every congregation has had an opportunity to participate." It would involve careful training of lay leaders, pastors, guest preachers, special services, and year-round programs. The plan was adopted at the Toronto convention with the understanding that it be presented to all synodical conventions to enlist their full cooperation and that it be the chief emphasis during 1956 and 1957. This Convention also reaffirmed the action of 1940 "that a carefully selected and well organized committee on Social Missions be established in every congregation of the ULCA."[45]

By 1956 the Lutheran Evangelism Mission was in full action. An administrative committee of sixteen had selected a director, the Rev. Robert Stackel. He had the full support of President Fry, Executive Secretary Koch and the three associates assigned to this work, Clifton M. Weihe, E. Dale Click and Gordon C. Lund. On the field were directors for each of the eight areas into which the country was divided. In October the Board gave a glowing report to the convention:

> The United Lutheran Church in America has never been so stirred to its depths by any previous undertaking as by the Lutheran Evangelism Mission. In every quarter of the church observers testify to the transformation that comes over congregations engaged wholeheartedly in this Mission. . . . A vast unused potential is being released throughout the church. A recovery of lay witnessing with apostolic power is unfolding. The Holy Spirit, who is the sole author of all these good things, is astounding His people with what he can do through them when they yield themselves to Him in trust.[46]

In 1958 the board reconfirmed the above and added that the missions evidenced a "growing maturity." Never before had the whole church taken so seriously the stewardship of the gospel. It was long overdue. Yet no other denomination in America had engaged in such a comprehensive evangelistic effort. Lay people became involved as witnesses as never before. One out of every fourteen confirmed members made pre-mission visits on prospective members.[47] The selected preachers for these missions events stressed the importance of personal commitment to Jesus Christ.

The missions had the effect of strengthening teamwork among ULCA congregations as well as synodical leadership. In some areas they also brought about a closer friendship with congregations of other Lutheran Church bodies. Successful as the missions were, the board recognized some weaknesses. Of the 4,447 congregations, 865 did not participate. The follow-through of year-round evangelism was spotty. The young people and children were not involved as much as they could have been. At the end of the two years the Board of Social Missions came to the conclusion that "in the long run evangelism would be best stimulated by synodical staff rather than by a large field staff." To encourage this, conferences for synodical evangelism chairpersons were held in 1957 and 1958. During the same period, 195 lay schools in evangelism were conducted across the country. More than twenty thousand congregational evangelism committee members, pastors, and council members attended one of these. Lay people were used to lead discussion groups.[48]

Department of Inner Mission

During the fifties the Department of Inner Mission, under the direction of the Rev. Francis Shearer, continued to work closely with the Division of Welfare of the National Lutheran Council in many areas of concern including the resettlement of refugees and much more. In this relationship, progress was made in establishing standards of care for older people, as had been done for children's agencies earlier. With an increasing use of case work and the wise admission policies of institutions, the individual's welfare was protected.

Standards for chaplaincy service—including the qualifications of the chaplain, the work involved and his relationship to the institution—were also reviewed by the Division of Welfare of the NLC. The ULCA was involved and showed its concern. The 1952 convention requested the Board of Social Missions to cooperate with the theological seminaries in locating hospitals and institutions for clinical pastoral training. The 1956 report indicated that both Chicago and Northwestern seminaries had courses in this field. Besides, several ULCA pastors became qualified to serve as supervisors in two non-denominational agencies with high standards: the Council for Clinical Training and the Institute for Pastoral Care. Director Shearer served on the personnel Committee of the Department of Pastoral Services of the NCC which supplied names to be considered for chaplaincy in federal prisons and Veterans' hospitals. ULCA pastors serving in such positions were to be called by their Synod.[49]

The department increased its concern and service to the blind, deaf, and mentally limited. Braille devotional materials, "Message for the Day," went to 169 persons. Luther's *Small Catechism* and the new *Service Book and Hymnal* were made available in Braille. The board commended Our Savior's congregation in Tucson, Arizona for ministering to children attending the Arizona State School for the Blind. For the deaf, the board conducted a course at Gettysburg Seminary in 1955 for eight pastors actively engaged in ministering to the deaf. The instructor was from Gallaudet College, Washington, D.C., the only college for the deaf in the world. Courses in sign language were conducted at Gettysburg, Philadelphia, and Southern seminaries.[50] For the mentally limited a churchwide survey was conducted. It revealed that there were 1,203 of them in the ULCA parishes and 515 others living in institutions away from the local congregation. This survey was in response to the 1952 Convention's request that the Board of Social Mission, in cooperation with child care institutions, study trends in child care, "including the need for sheltered care for mentally deficient children and possibly development of a program for such care."[51] The 1954 convention heard a detailed report on child care services provided by the institutions and agencies affiliated with the ULCA, as well as other services available such as given by the National Association of Retarded Children. As requested, it included current trends in such care.[52]

Immigrant Mission was most needed in eastern Canada where many immigrants were welcomed. More than one hundred thousand arrived in the postwar years. Yet even in 1954, another fifty-four thousand were expected. The board served these people in cooperation with the Canada Synod. Social workers met boats, planes, and trains in an effort to help these people who desperately needed jobs, housing, and guidance for the new life in Canada. In the United States the main work was at New York's Ellis Island where all the people who had some defect in their status with the Bureau of Immigration and Naturalization were sent. These were people in trouble and in need of help from a social worker sent by the Church.[53]

Two important social welfare conferences in the fifties highlighted the board's work and concerns. On November 1-4, 1955, the NCCCUSA sponsored the National Conference on the Churches and Social Welfare in Cleveland, Ohio. This was largely planned and directed by the Rev. William Villaume, a ULCA pastor. *The Activating Concern*, one of three books prepared for the conference, was edited by E. Theodore Bachmann, then professor at the Pacific Lutheran Seminary. The other important conference was the First World Inner Mission Conference held at Wittenberg College, July 1957, preceding the Lutheran World Assembly in Minneapolis.[54]

Department of Social Action

The constitution of the Board of Social Missions mandated that the Department of Social Action "study the moral and social welfare of humanity in the light of Christian principles and counsel the church in the Christian solution to the problems of society."[55] In the fifties, the board took this responsibility very seriously and for the first time added full-time staff leadership, i.e., the Secretary for Social Action: first the Rev. Harold C. Letts and later the Rev. Rufus Cornelsen. Many serious concerns were confronted.

One of the most valuable studies was that on *Christian Social Responsibility*. This was triggered by the "Report of the Committee on Faith and Life" which assigned to the board a "scholarly study" to "school Lutherans on the Scriptural and Confessional grounds of social action." The Committee on Christian Responsibility was informally organized. Functioning under the guidance of Secretary Letts it met two or three times a year for discussion of basic concepts. Topics assigned to competent authors were reviewed and refined. This process resulted in a three-volume study, *Christian Social Responsibility*. It was published by Muhlenberg Press and released in August of 1957. The fourteen authors all contributed their scholarly work without compensation. In order that there would be a churchwide emphasis on Christian responsibility, the board's staff arranged a meeting with synodical committees during the fall of 1958. In January 1959 a congregational study guide appeared.[56]

Another important subject for study was marriage and family life. A vital force for this study was the School on Marriage and Family Life held at the Hamma Divinity School in Wittenberg, Ohio, in June of 1951. Representatives of twenty synods participated and a program for action developed out of the discussions. The 175 participants urged the board to restudy the 1930 statement on marriage and divorce with a view to issuing a new statement. A preliminary survey by a theological professor at a ULCA seminary, a local pastor and the Secretary for Social Action agreed that the request was warranted. The Committee on Marriage and Divorce, appointed by the board in 1952, submitted its study and recommendations to the 1956 convention. This covered a multitude of related subjects, biblical and theological as well as current practices and deviations from the will of God. The report of fifteen pages in the 1956 *Minutes* was followed by a "summary statement" for discussion at the Harrisburg Convention. And discussion there was! The convention then adopted it "as a guide to its congregations."

In order to help people relate the Christian faith "to the practical issues of daily work and public life," Faith and Life Institutes were conducted in the late fifties. In part they were stimulated by the 1950 convention that recommended that the Board of Social Missions explore a program of group discussion and fellowship similar to the evangelical academies in Germany. The participants of these academies came chiefly from the professions, the educated business leaders and industrial workers, groups that often were lost to the church. Held in a retreat-like center the informal discussions usually centered on some aspects of a political, social, or intellectual problem.

The board tested the principles of this German type of academy in five pilot projects. The first was held on Pigeon Lake in Ontario and was programmed by the board's staff for "the average layman." The theme, "Outreach of the Christian Life," used the recently published *Christian Social Responsibility* as resource. There were Bible studies also. For many of the eighty-two participants it was their first serious examination of the implications of the Christian faith for their daily lives. The participants agreed that they went home to face serious questions. The second institute, using the theme "The Farmer under the Impact of Technology," was held in Des Moines, Iowa. The third in Santa Barbara, California, was planned for middle and upper level managers and had the theme, "The Company Man." A copy of William H. Whyte's book, *The Company Man*, was sent to each participant for orientation. The fourth institute was for women. Held in Washington, D.C., its theme was "The Changing Role of Women in Public Life." The final pilot institute meant for physicians was in March 1957, at the Columbia University Conference Center in Harriman, New York. "Science of Man and the Practice of Medicine" was the topic. When these pilot institutes were reviewed by the Board's staff it was agreed that further experimentation should continue with no less than ten each year for the next biennium.[57] The 1958 convention adopted a recommendation that the institutes continue.

CONVENTIONS AND KEY DOCUMENTS

During the fifties the United Lutheran Church in America held four biennial conventions in cities spread across the country: Seattle, Washington, 1952; Toronto, Canada, 1954; Harrisburg, Pennsylvania, 1956; Dayton, Ohio, 1958. As in prior years, they were all in October and were week-long in duration. They were days of review of the past two years and an expression of hope and vision for the future. The books of minutes and reports of each convention contain more than a thousand pages. Here we condense the highlights of four documents: Ministry, Structure, Christian Unity, and Joint Efforts.

The tone of each convention was set by the president's report. In Seattle, in 1952, it centered on "How does the ULCA serve its congregations?" This convention adopted with minor amendments the Report of the Commission on the Doctrine of Ministry as a guide to the church. In 1954, at Toronto, the president's report was a "preface to the report of the Commission on Organizational Structure". The COS undertaking is best seen as initiating a form of self-examination that became, in effect, the important opening phase of a decade-long preparation for partnership in the LCA. With its organizational structure updated, the ULCA was ready at its 1956 convention in Harrisburg for something more basic: the theme of Christian unity and its implications for a Lutheran understanding of ecclesiology and the church.[58] What Fry set forth in 1956 on unity, a classic statement from a confessional position, became the first of three biennial reports whereby he prepared the ULCA constituency for Lutheran unity. In 1958, at Dayton, the president reported on "merger developments" with a "lucid interpretation to our church of where we stand at this juncture . . . a companion piece to the report on the Joint Commission on Lutheran Unity."[59]

Ordained Ministry (1952)

For Lutherans in the 1950s "the" ministry meant the ordained. The definite article took care of the meaning. And, "the ministry" meant men. Confessional kin in some parts of Europe, beginning in Denmark, had begun to ordain women, under pressure from the state in behalf of fair employment opportunity. In ecumenical circles references to ministry without the definite article were becoming common. In any case, and in contrast to Anglicans, Roman Catholics, and Orthodox, Lutherans understood the ordained ministry not as an order, like holy orders, but as an office (*Amt* in German). As such the ministry is a function, duly designated, for which those discharging it are duly prepared and set apart. The central and entrusted task of this office is, according to the Augsburg Confession, the preaching of the Word and the administration of the Sacraments.

However, the situation in the church in the early fifties reflected tendencies that required special awareness. As the report of the Commission on the Doctrine of the Ministry (1952) noted: first, the parish ministry was thought by many a minister simply as a stepping stone to something supposedly better; second, there was a tendency among many to exalt the ministry at the expense of other legitimate callings; and third, there was a tendency to downgrade the ministry as such so as to make of it just one among many functions. According to a 1938 document ("Call to the Ministry") every ULCA clergy was required to have a valid call unless retired. This was not uniformly enforced by the various synods, and there were pastors who accepted secular work without turning in their ordination papers.[60] In an effort to "balance these tendencies . . . and to give positive guidance in matters of the call, ordination, and the determination of the ministerial roll" the seven drafters of the report determined to present "a clear definition of the doctrine of the ministry." It was after all the "holy ministry" to which the minister was ordained.[61] The document on the "Doctrine of the Ministry" was considered by Fry as one of the "four ULCA theological documents that will outlive all the rest."[62] With eloquence and precision the document did three things. It presented an historical review of the emergence of ordination from New Testament times, its treatment by Luther and the Confessions, and its contemporary emphasis. Secondly, it defined the doctrine of the ministry for today. Thirdly, it concluded with some practical implications, leading to a list of recommendations.[63] Some excerpts from these implications show us how the church and its ministry expected, in the obedience of faith, to face the fifties. To say it with the historic confessions:

> The church is where Christ is—not in a hierarchy, not in a Bible merely, but the living Word of God in Christ, present, speaking and acting in Word and Sacrament. This gave Luther his criterion of continuity, legitimacy, and authority, and enabled him to avoid both extremes—that of the hierarchy, from which he had been excluded, and that of the enthusiasts who did not see the necessity of the continuity with the past and the inseparability of believers from the Word.[64]

In this context, according to the document, "ordination is an ecclesiastical rite by which the call is ratified and the office of the ministry is publicly committed to the one called. It confers no permanent rank or indelible character."[65] And the implication of this? In the words of the document:

> Since the Word and the Sacraments are the congregation-building aspect of the church, 'through which as by instruments the Holy Ghost is given,' the minister of Word and Sacraments must in his work be contributing toward this building of the church. He must be making a constructive contribution to the church as the body of Christ in the world, not just as a believer, but through the exercise of his office.[66]

For ULCA ordinands as for those in other Lutheran bodies their signing of the Augsburg Confession—indeed their subscribing to the whole *Book of*

Concord—perpetuated a tradition from the time of the reformation and affirmed the unity of the church catholic and evangelical. The text was adopted as a guide to the church.[67] The commission presenting this statement consisted of: Voigt R. Cromer, H. Grady Davis, Jonas H. Dressler, J. Frank Fife, Martin J. Heinecken, T. A. Kantonen and Emil E. Fischer.

Structure (1954)

In organizational structure the ULCA remained basically the same throughout its forty-four years. At the same time it grew together and developed a distinctive identity. Built on a secular model, the federal government of the United States, the ULCA structure had a durability which should come as no surprise.[68] As church organizations go, that of the ULCA has been called unique in Lutheran history. Others have taken their lead from it, like the United Lutheran Church in Germany (VELKD, 1948). The founders of the ULCA, as we have already seen (chapter 3), were gifted in the art of compromise. In terms of polity, they made the united church a federal union of autonomous synods. The branches of church government were legislative, executive, and judicial. The biennial conventions were the church's congress; the Commission of Adjudication, its court; the Executive Board and the three officers of the church, its loosely operative executive branch.

Over the years, especially in the beginning stages, modifications and structural improvements were introduced. Yet thirty-four years passed before a "fresh look at the bony skeleton of the ULCA" was ventured. In 1952 the Seattle convention directed the Executive Board to appoint a "Commission of sixteen members, eight clerical, eight lay, to study the organizational structure of the United Lutheran Church in America and to report its findings and recommendations to the 1954 convention of the church."[69] Continuous growth and an expanding program were a matter of record: baptized membership nearly doubled, size of average congregation rose to five hundred (up by 58 percent), number of ordained pastors, including retirees, exceeded four thousand (up by 43 percent), all of this between 1919 and 1952.[70]

The Commission on Organizational Structure, promptly called the COS, worked rapidly and thoroughly, and reported to the Toronto convention in October, 1954. President Fry's own report to the convention held up a mirror of things as they are and also a picture of how they might work better. The to-and-fro of ties—the ULCA and the congregations, the ULCA and the synods, the ULCA and its boards, the synods and the boards, the boards and the congregations, and more besides—came under presidential scrutiny, and stimulated discussion.[71] Could one speak of the ULCA as being really a church? Or was it a federation? There were those outside as well as inside who thought of the ULCA as a federation. If not in America then in Europe the ULCA was challenged on this point. Already in 1946, while the World Council of Churches was in formation, Visser't Hooft made President Fry prove that the ULCA was a church, in contrast to the Evangelical Church in Germany, which called itself a federation and thus raised questions as to the proper components or partners in a world council of churches.

As an exercise in practical ecclesiology, the COS report recommended some 150 modifications or changes in the ULCA constitution. The effect was not as drastic as the number might suggest. The duties of the president were clarified and strengthened somewhat. The size of the Executive Board was tripled (from three clergy to nine, from three lay to nine). The Commission of Adjudication became the Court for Adjudication and Interpretation. Church boards were brought under closer coordination and supervision. Auxiliaries—Women's, Men's and Young People's—had no change. Synods were brought closer to each other through a Council of Synodical Presidents. Meeting at least annually, the council's presider was the church president, and its functions consultative and advisory.[72] The COS report thus represented an advance toward better inter-linked organizational structure. By 1958 most of the suggested changes had been put into effect, including clearer provisions in the church's constitution and bylaws. The latter were timely changes, particularly in light of the current step forward in inter-Lutheran relations. Since the Joint Commission on Lutheran Unity (JCLU) first met in December 1956, in Chicago, and laid the groundwork of the anticipated Lutheran Church in America,[73] it was the right moment for the ULCA to have put its house in good structural order.

Christian Unity (1956)

"The growth of Christian partnership," declared Franklin Clark Fry in his 1956 presidential report, "is in many ways the most conspicuous development in church life today, and we have our share in it." Delegates to the Harrisburg convention were reminded that "our own church belongs to the World Council of Churches, the National Council of the Churches of Christ in the United States of America, the Lutheran World Federation, the National Lutheran Council, the Canadian Lutheran Council, and is in friendly association with the Canadian Council of Churches."[74]

That was enough involvement. Some confessional kin thought it was too much. But President Fry was a consummate churchman who represented the ULCA in all the partnership agencies. He was the adroit chair of the World Council's Central Committee, after having served his apprenticeship as vice-chair (1948-54). He had been foremost in giving the National Council of Churches (1950) its specific ecclesiological accent on the church instead of being satisfied with a merging of agencies (see chapter 10). Manifestly Fry was not act-ing alone. But an acceptance of these conditions by the council was prerequisite to ULCA membership in the new organization. Besides, ULCA boards, synods and congregations—when considering participation in national, state or local councils interdenominationally—were bound by the same principles. The old way of interdenominational agencies co-opting the talent of their choice thus yielded to the participating churches doing the choosing. Despite opposition, the line was held.

The ULCA involvement interdenominationally was suspect to most other Lutherans, Augustana being the exception. Not only the Missouri-led Synodical Conference but also the other bodies in the American Lutheran Conference continued to harbor the suspicions held earlier against the former Federal Council of Churches. There had been a surging sentiment for Lutheran unity and even union, so much so in the postwar years that it appeared for a time as though the National Lutheran Council could be the vehicle at least for a federation of the participating bodies. Nevertheless, the old tensions persisted. The ULCA was on the one side, the American Lutheran Conference members on the other.

FRANKLIN CLARK FRY

Overcoming its own reservations, the Augustana church, mindful of its earlier partnership in the General Council, precipitated a "truly historic event." In Fry's words, "to our joy and gratitude, the Augustana Church has joined our ULCA in inviting all the Lutherans of America to enter into organic union as an act of loyalty to the Christ whom we confess with one voice. Our hearts leap at the prospect."[75] Thus began a sequence of events that in six years would lead to the formation of a new church body consolidating the ULCA, Augustana, Suomi, and the Grundtvigian Danes, the four together bearing the name: Lutheran Church in America. Moreover, the Fry report of 1956 became the first of a trilogy—with 1958 and 1960— shedding light on merger developments.

Disappointed though Fry was with the polarizing of the American Lutheran scene, as articulated in no uncertain terms in his monthly letter to ULCA pastors, his words to the Harrisburg convention were confident, incisive, and inclusive. Admittedly he wrote with an eye on 1957 when two events of global outreach would be highlighting the year, and their themes would be complementary: the Lutheran World Federation Assembly (Minneapolis), on the theme "Christ Frees and Unites," and the World Conference on Faith and Order (Oberlin, Ohio), on "The Nature of the Unity We Seek."

> Lutherans unanimously affirm that a wide and deep consensus of doctrine must underlie church union. For our own ULCA, this includes not only the Word of God and the ecumenical creeds but also the confessions which have always been regarded as the standards of Evangelical Lutheran doctrine. The one and only purpose of all my introspection has been to hold a mirror up before our eyes as we go forward—if this convention so decides—in search of a wider unity.[76]

The reception of the president's report by the convention was highly appreciative. It acted to make the report on Christian unity the basis for further study in the congregations and conferences of synods. The report also drew attention outside the ULCA, in ecumenical as well as confessional circles. Eventually it was included in a widely used book of readings in American church history as expressive of ecumenical stirrings within the communions.[77]

Merger Developments

Also at the 1956 convention in Dayton, Ohio, the Commission for Relations to American Lutheran Church bodies reported on its work for unity. On March 28, 1955, in Chicago, the commission met first with the ALC Committee on Church Union and then with the Augustana Committee on Ecumenical Relations. The meeting with the American Lutheran Church resulted mainly in an exchange of information. Fry responded to the request for information on the structural and constitutional changes made in 1954 (COS). President Schuh reported on their proposed merger with the ELC, the UELC, and the ALC. Pulpit and altar fellowship was discussed. But since the ULCA had "consistently declared itself in fellowship with other Lutheran Bodies in America," the next move was, "clearly up to the American Lutheran Church."

The following meeting, at the invitation of Augustana, had a different tone. After a brief discussion of relevant issues, Fry, the ULCA chair, repeated the declaration of 1948 (and earlier), that the ULCA "desires to merge with any or all Lutherans in America" and that the commission was authorized "to participate in drafting a constitution and in devising such organizational procedures as may seem wise in effecting union." The commission then invited Augustana to appoint a commission of equal members. In September, President Fry was notified by President Benson that at their June convention the Augustana church accepted the proposal and had authorized the Commission on Ecumenical Relations to "enter into conversation looking toward organic union with the ULCA and any other Lutheran Church accepting the invitation."[78]

At the first meeting of the two commissions on December 18, 1955, letters of invitation, with signatures of the two presidents of the churches, were sent to fourteen church bodies requesting that they designate authorized representatives to meet with the two commissions to "consider such organic union as will give real evidence of our unity of faith."[79] The American Evangelical Lutheran Church (Danish background) and the Finnish Evangelical Lutheran Church (Suomi Synod) answered affirmatively. Then, forty-six commissioners representing the four churches met on December 12, 1956, and formed the Joint Commission on Lutheran Unity (JCLU).[80] By all accounts, the key document for the early work of the JCLU was Fry's statement on Lutheran unity first delivered at the ULCA convention of 1956. It "was immediately recognized as an unofficial charter for the new church and as a guide to the joint commission."[81]

JCLU Report (1958)

During 1957, the JCLU met four times as a whole, and much of the work was furthered by seventeen subcommittees. Although there were many aspects still to be determined, the JCLU presented a progress report to the conventions of the four churches in 1958. The ULCA convention in Dayton spent considerable time in contemplating the lengthy report printed in the convention bulletin. President Fry used his entire report to "shed all the illumination that is possible on the merger developments, and give a lucid interpretation to our church of where we stand at this juncture." As such it was a "companion piece to, and a commentary" on the report of the JCLU. His report was full of contagious enthusiasm for the work that had been done in drafting a *new* church, one that would be more church than federation.

In great detail President Fry described the process that enabled the commission to carve out a consensus on matters of disagreement, such as lodge membership for pastors. A statement proposed by Augustana that pleased the other two churches read:

> If the church shall be free to advise and admonish concerning association and affiliation with organizations which claim to possess in their teachings and ceremonies that which the Lord has given solely to His church, its ministry must not be compromised by pastors who belong to such organizations. Provisions shall be made in the constitution of the church whereby ministers ordained by the new church shall agree to refrain from membership in such organizations or be subject to discipline.[82]

The ULCA commissioners attempted to inject an "evangelical approach that by counsel and persuasions in the light of the Gospel" would be "preferable to a legalistic one." When they lost (twenty-three to ten) for a third time, the ULCA commissioners withdrew for "private consultation" and prayer. Ten minutes later they returned, and President Fry as chairman read a statement.

> As a concession in love to the living tradition of our sister churches, the commissioners of the United Lutheran Church in America acquiesce unanimously in the vote just taken.[83]

The conflict was resolved and merger plans could continue.

Considerable time was allowed at the convention for commission members to report on various aspects of the new structure. This also gave the delegates an opportunity to recognize some of the commissioners. T. A. Kantonen indicated that the doctrinal statements represented the consensus of the four churches expressed in their constitutions. The statements also tried to reflect the best biblical scholarship in a fresh spirit. He also reported that the Baltimore Declaration had been very helpful. The Rev. Charles M. Cooper stated that the congregation and the church at large would be the two foci of the new church, yet unnamed. Six names were being considered. Paul H. Krauss stated that there would be thirty-two synods with congregations in every state of the union and in eight provinces of Canada plus a mission development in Newfoundland. Gilbert E. Olson made clear that the conventions of the new church would be like those of the ULCA. The commissioners favored representations by synods. James F. Henninger assured the conventioners that the Board of Publications would continue much as usual since the three churches were willing to accommodate in large measure to the ULCA plan. World Mission would be the new name for Foreign Mission and would more accurately describe the response of the church to the "worldwide proclamation of the gospel." In Home Missions, there would be regional directors working under a church board of American Missions. The Rev. Dwight F. Putnam said "each congregation of the new church is to be a member of the general body, but will be received by 'a constituent unit.' Every congregation is to 'covenant' to abide loyally to the decisions of the general body." The Rev. Frank P. Madsen explained that ministers would be members of the general body "which would set the standard for ordination and retention of pastors."

Plenty of time was given for delegates to ask questions and make comments. Occasionally Fry left the chair and gave his opinion on various matters. The Board of Higher Education would be two boards: one on college and church vocations which would include deaconess work and the other a board of theological education. In the latter a compromise had to be made that would satisfy both the three bodies whose theological schools were part of the churchwide structure and also the ULCA with its numerous schools owned and controlled by synods. The new Theological Board would set standards as well as increase the possibilities for the continuing education of pastors.

The convention was informed that the other three bodies had expressed appreciation for the work of the JCLU and the opportunity given to request changes. Augustana summed up its report with this sentence: "the proposal now in process represents in general a happy line between a highly centralized church and a loose federation of autonomous synods."[84]

Fry himself liked certain aspects of Augustana's more centralized polity[85] and took a leading role in writing the new constitution accordingly, even during a hospitalization. His whole career—parish, synod, and churchwide—was marked by detailed attention to constituting documents, especially on the occasions of writing new ones and usually with an eye to a clearer role for the central authority. Thus it was no surprise that the chairman of the JCLU Committee on Constitutions was Franklin Clark Fry.

ANOTHER COMMON LITURGY

As the 1888 *Common Service* prepared the grassroots for the reunion of the tri-furcated Muhlenberg tradition in 1918, so too the 1958 *Service Book and Hymnal* facilitated further Lutheran merger, several of them. A proposal initiated by the ULCA Common Service Book Committee in 1938, but subsequently delayed by the war, nevertheless led to the formation (June 23, 1945) of the Joint Commission on a Common Hymnal. All the National Lutheran Council church bodies joined, which meant that the result would tap several ethnic traditions as well as American music. Included on the agenda was a revision of The Service. Among the revisions: the Kyrie ("Lord, have mercy") was elaborated according to Eastern Orthodox usage; the Prayer of the Church interspersed with responses ("We beseech Thee to hear us good Lord"); a Eucharistic Prayer introduced, to considerable controversy. Among the hymns fifty-two were omitted, twenty-nine inserted.[86] As finally published in 1958 this "Red Book" became a common bond among most of the congregations of the eight participating church bodies of the NLC. Two settings of the liturgy provided a choice either of chant or of a more melodic style (as arranged by Regina H. Fryxell, Augustana). A third setting, separately published, was in the style of ancient plainsong. To help familiarize interested parties, a recording of the Second Setting by the Augustana College Choir (Rock Island) provided a pre-hearing.

Earlier in the decade President Fry's widely read article, "Sursum Corda: on adoring God through the Liturgy," rang across the church, a vibrant reminder to capture or recapture the meaning of worship. It quoted the *Formula of Concord* (1577), whose intention had been to bring harmony to churches of the Lutheran confessions: "we cheerfully maintain the old traditions for the sake of usefulness and tranquility." Liturgy, according to Fry, "must be a citadel of culture to the glory of God." Liturgy "is the most potent unifying force in Lutheranism . . . a puissant evangelistic force."[87] He concluded,

> Every basic and distinctive doctrine of the evangel, from that of the Trinity in the Invocation to a mystical apprehension of Christ in the Holy Communion, reverberates in the liturgy. . . . For us, the worship of our fathers becomes a portal of splendor into the eternal, invincible church of God. Our consecration should be to conserve and transmit this heritage of rapture. Lift up your hearts![88]

The *Service Book and Hymnal* took shape in 1958 and was adopted by eight Lutheran bodies. In spite of the tensions generated during the later fifties by the separation of these eight bodies into two separate mergers, The American Lutheran Church (1960), and the Lutheran Church in America (1962), the bonds of common worship held fast, and prepared for further revisions and further merger in 1987.

EXCURSUS:

REMEMBERING THE ULCA IN BERKELEY

BERKELEY, CALIFORNIA IN THE 1950s experienced not only a "calm before the storm" of the sixties, but also the power of the Holy Spirit working in the lives of ordinary people. The same could and should be said of many a city or community, but the authors remember Berkeley, for they were there.

In the center of the city sprawled the University of California with its learned professors and learning students. There a Nobel Prize physicist, Ernest O. Lawrence, was producing radioactive elements and neutrons useful in nuclear, chemical and biological research in the cyclotron he invented.[1] His equally famous brother, John, was the father of medical imaging. While they worked in their labs, a few blocks away their aging mother was receiving loving concern and pastoral care at St. Michael's Lutheran Church where she worshiped regularly. Her late husband had been president of the State Teacher's College in Aberdeen, South Dakota, where he, as a devout Lutheran, encouraged the young Lutheran Student Association in the thirties.[2]

In the spirit of the times, St. Michael's had in 1952 moved from a small edifice in the middle of a side street in nearby Oakland to a large former Methodist church one block from the University. Under the leadership of an energetic pastor, Ross Hidy,[3] the congregation was ready to reach out more effectively to the University and community. President Fry was there on the Sunday the congregation moved to the new location. He brought greetings from the entire church and added his blessing.[4]

Among the members of St. Michael's were two missionary families who had been forced out of China in the forties and had opted to retire in the United States rather than Germany. They were "interest" on the investment the ULCA made in 1924 when it purchased the Berlin Missionary Society's Shantung field. Lottie Kohls, younger than her retired pastor husband, George, was soon serving as parish visitor for St. Michael's, showing concern for the hundreds of foreign students at the University. Close by to St. Michael's was the Lutheran Student Center, one of the many being built by the National Lutheran Council in the fifties. There she shared her concern with Ruth C. Wick, at that time executive director of the NLC's Division of Student Work, who was making her rounds. Wick encouraged Lottie to begin work as a volunteer at the center. Invitations were sent out to Chinese students to come to the center for tea. Beginning with eight students, each invitation brought a few more. Meanwhile, the division, with encouragement and funds from Lutheran Church Women, was able to engage Lottie as a full-time foreign student counselor. Soon contacts were made with students from twelve different countries. They met at the center in three groups: Chinese, European, and Indian-Pakistani. In time the Lutheran Welfare Society of Northern California purchased a building that could be used for a

Berkeley office with living space for a few needy students. St. Michael's warmly welcomed both Christian students and other seekers after the truth.[5]

Lutherans on the West Coast had for some time been hoping for the revival of the Pacific Lutheran Seminary that had aroused interest and concern at the organizing convention of the ULCA in 1918.[6] Since seminaries, according to ULCA polity, were the responsibility of synods, the small Pacific Synod, in spite of heroic efforts, had to close its seminary during the Depression. Now, thirty years later at the 1948 San Diego Convention of the California Synod, two young pastors, recruited from the East by the ever mission-minded President Beasom,[7] took bold action. They moved and seconded that "in view of the shortage of men in the Gospel ministry, the California Synod in cooperation with the Pacific Synod, establish a seminary on the territory, preferably in the Bay Area." With enthusiasm the motion passed. The Pacific Synod agreed and a joint board began working with the Board of Education to establish the Seminary in Berkeley, near the University and the several established theological schools. Soon Gould Wickey was guiding the seminary board that would be responsible for the purchase of property and selection of faculty.[8] CHEY funds, gathered by the California Synod, were matched by the carefully guarded funds of the original school of the Pacific Synod.[9]

Property in Berkeley was at a premium. Pastor Hidy and William Scheehl, a seminary board member living in Berkeley, were asked to search for a suitable location. A prize was found in 1951 when two adjoining estates with beautiful large homes and formal gardens became available. The July 1951 issue of *The Lutheran* announced their purchase at a cost of $144,500. The article included photographs showing the handsome library in one home and other rooms that could readily be converted into classrooms and chapel.[10]

In September 1952, the seminary opened with twenty-five brave students willing to take a chance on an untried school. Four professors were on hand: Charles Behrend Foelsch, an experienced pastor, a member of the ULCA Executive Board and one-time president of the Chicago Lutheran Seminary, would teach New Testament. Harry Joachim Mumm, an alumnus of Central Lutheran Theological Seminary in Fremont, Nebraska, and a recent Ph.D. graduate of Hartford Seminary in Connecticut, would cover the Old Testament and English Bible. Gerhard Lenski, D.D., a recently retired pastor of an American Lutheran Church in Washington, D.C., was the professor of systematic theology and ethics. E. Theodore Bachmann, having been a guest professor at Luther Seminary after a period of postwar service in Germany, would cover church history and missions. All would share the functional fields.[11] After a month of getting acquainted with each other and the work required, two of the professors and a number of students made a pilgrimage to Seattle, Washington, to attend the ULCA convention, the first on the West Coast and an unusual privilege for seminary students. At this convention the new Professor of Missions was elected to the Board of Deaconess Work, an interest and concern of long standing.

After the convention, President Fry visited the seminary and took part in the inauguration of the president and installation of the other faculty. The joyous service was at St. Michael's where a renovation of the sanctuary was still in process. The church was packed not only with ULCA members, but also with clergy and members of other church bodies who expected to use and be blessed by the institution. President Fry preached the sermon. He focused on the importance of sound theological training for the future pastor.

> No fake humility allowed, such as claiming "I'm not a theologian!" It is the pastor's business to be one, as people rightly expect of an ordained ministry in the Lutheran tradition.[12]

The first field trip and festivities over, it was back to the lectures and books on the Hill. But the students soon learned that future pastors were to learn from other helping professions and para-professionals. Field trips were an essential part of the learning process and the Bay Area was rich in resources: the School of Social Work at the University, the Berkeley Police Department (then ranked among the nation's best), San Quentin Prison, the Saint Vincent de Paul Society, and the Catholic Charities enterprise in San Francisco, the Jewish Family Welfare Agency, the Alameda County Public Welfare Agency, plus hospitals, medical schools, and the Lutheran Welfare Society of Northern California. On weekends the students were assigned to area churches to be of assistance where needed. Pacific Seminary was also the first ULCA seminary to require a year of internship, usually in a congregation, between the second and last year of study.

The half dozen seminaries in the city cordially welcomed the new school and extended courtesies to both students and faculty.[13] Relations were arranged so that students from one seminary could take courses of approved professors at another. Professors of various fields met together for mutual enlightenment and support, the history professors more than the others. These discussions as well as those of the students who participated in the Interseminary Movement, and encouragement from the American Association of Theological Schools, laid the basis for the later Graduate Theological Union.

As the student body grew, coming not only from the West Coast but also from the East and several from Germany, so did the faculty. Funds were scarce, so part-time instructors from the area were added. The Rev. Toivo Harjunpaa was the first. He had been sent to Berkeley by the Board of American Missions and the mission-minded Beasom to be the pastor at a promising mission in the Berkeley Hills that used the seminary chapel for worship. He was one of the many refugee pastors from the Baltics and Germany who in the late forties were given special training in American church life and then six months of internship under an experienced ULCA pastor. He had been assigned to Holy Trinity Church in New York City where Foelsch was the pastor.[14] His talents in liturgics and his solid theological grounding gained from good education and experience in Finland and England were appreciated and remembered. In time Harjunpaa became a full professor with a Ph.D. from the University of California. Another was the Rev. Paul Morentz, M.D., a Philadelphia Seminary graduate with a medical degree in psychiatry, who assisted with pastoral care courses while employed in a veterans' hospital. The Rev. George Muedeking, serving a nearby American Lutheran congregation, taught Christian education courses and worked for a Ph.D. at the University.

President Föelsch was a hard-working man of vision, and expected the same from his faculty. Already in the school's second semester graduate courses were offered to pastors in the Bay Area and also in Los Angeles. An overnight trip on the train made this possible. The ideal weather in Berkeley was conducive to the summer courses, usually with guest professors. Most graduate courses were in the biblical, theological, or historical fields, but one course on "The Urban Church—the Nature and Scope of its Mission" was geared to a current study of the Bay Area conducted by the Lutheran churches in cooperation with the Urban Church Planning program of the National Lutheran Council. Under the supervision of the professor of missions, who also had responsibility for graduate work, lectures were given by specialists, among them some University professors. Topics such as the church and economic life, population trends, social problems, education, government, urban research, were considered. After the lectures, the Executive of Lutheran Social Services in Northern California, the Rev. A. E. Syverud, led the discussions. The last two lectures were delivered by the Rev. Walter Kloetzli Jr. (ULCA), secretary of the National Lutheran Council's Urban Church Planning program. Since this course broke new ground in Lutheran seminaries, it was given publicity in the NLC's News Releases and also in the *Christian Century*.[15]

From its beginning the Pacific Lutheran Seminary was blessed with an active auxiliary, with enthusiastic support of the women of both synods, and especially those in the Bay Area. Their contribution to the physical well-being of the students in general and to the encouragement of the early female students cannot be overestimated. The first female student, accepted as a "special," had a desire to increase her effectiveness in Christian education. Others followed. By 1957, a two-year M.A. in Christian Education was introduced, with a B.A. as an entrance requirement. Sister Ruth V. Harper, a deaconess from the Philadelphia Motherhouse, was the first graduate in 1959.

The very nature of the seminary as a pioneer venture stimulated historical inquiry. In one respect, this interest extended eastward and sought to pick up the westward movement of the churches. This put Lutherans in context continentally. In a second way, this interest looked southward, to the vast Latin American scene with its massive Roman Catholicism so different from the Reformation. Thus there was a ready-made challenge to accentuate Lutheran substance in the teaching not only of church history but also of the Lutheran Confessions. Yet the confessions, in turn, were part of a now ecumenically oriented "comparative symbolics," endeavoring to show how and why Lutherans have a future not in isolation but in participation with others in the quest for Christian unity.

The view from the PLTS hilltop campus on clear days revealed the majestic beauty of San Francisco Bay. Beyond the city there rolled the vast Pacific. So the third direction was westward, to Asia and Australia and the islands of the sea. Some missionaries en route to Japan, Hong Kong, or Malaysia, among other places, put in briefly at PLTS.[16] Intercession for those serving beyond the distant horizon became charged with meaning. From distant India came the first foreign student in the graduate program. He was Devanesan Rajarigam, from near Tranquebar, South India, where—with Ziegenbalg and Pluetschau (1706)— Protestant world mission had its Lutheran forerunners. He had the guidance of the history and missions professor and the stimulation of the others. His research culminated in a study of Christian poetry (actually hymnody) as a mark of the indigenization of the gospel in a Hindu setting. The advisor learned a lot from Rajarigam; and the student learned the importance of documenting his sources. At first he resisted documentation as if it meant distrusting him. "At Serampore," he complained, "when Rajarigam writes something, people trust Rajarigam." When he at last saw that by documentation he could also win others to his side in a greater undertaking, his dark Tamil face glowed. His short dissertation was later translated from English into German (by Professor Hans Werner Gensichen, Heidelberg), and into Swedish (Church of Sweden Mission), as well as into his native Tamil. Later, Rajarigam—a nephew of Bishop Rajah Manikam, the first Indian to lead the Tamil Evangelical Lutheran Church)—wrote a history of the Christian Church in India. Before he died, he had virtually completed a revised Tamil edition of the New Testament.

As in all America in the fifties there was much coming and going in Berkeley. Students came and went: some to distant places, some to unexpected opportunities for service, some with the joy of a new found Christian faith. The National Lutheran Council sent fresh counselors for the student center. Lottie Kohls stayed on to receive new groups of foreign students. Pastor Hidy answered the call of the Board of Social Missions to become western director of the Evangelism Mission that the ULCA featured in 1956-57. A new pastor came to serve St. Michael's. At the seminary new students from near and far continued to come. Others graduated and after receiving calls were ordained to proclaim the gospel and serve where needed. Melvin Langeland and his wife went to Liberia to serve a ULCA-related church whose members were in the remote areas, the bush. The history and missions professor left early in 1959 with his family for an academic year of teaching at the new seminary in Brazil.[17] The arrangements had been made by the Lutheran World Federation through its Latin America secretary, Stewart Herman. The professor returned before the fifties ended with an ever fresh understanding of church history, how the gospel fares among us and among our neighbors in Latin America. He looked forward to another year of teaching curious and able students at Pacific Lutheran Seminary. The fifties in Berkeley anticipated the multicultural, ecumenical, and international shape of church life to come.

NOTES

1. *Pastor's Desk Book* March 1951 NE 229ff.

2. *Newsweek*, February 19, 1951, 76 and *Newsweek*, September 2, 1957, 36. *Life*, September 2, 1957, 100. *Time*, September 2, 1957, 36 and April 7, 1958, 58-60.

3. Orchard, Ronald K., Ed., *The Ghana Assembly of the International Missionary Council, 28th December, 1957 to 8th January, 1959: Selected Papers* (London: Edinburgh House Press, 1958), 9-22.

4. *Epic of Faith: The Background of the Second Assembly of the Lutheran World Federation, 1952* (New York: The National Lutheran Council, 1952).

5. ULCA *Minutes* 1952: 368-370.

6. ULCA *Minutes* 1958: 446.

7. Nelson, *Lutherans*, 512.

8. Ibid., 831ff. For a detailed account of the various NLC activities see F. K. Wentz's *Lutherans in Concert*.

9. ULCA *Minutes* 1958: 851.

10. For these statistics and more, see ULCA *Minutes* 1950: 642. ULCA *Year Book* 1951. 5; 1952: 98; 1962: 186f.

11. As R. B. Manikam recalled in *Palette*, 248.

12. Fey, Howard Edward, Ed., *The Ecumenical Advance: A History of the Ecumenical Movement*, Vol. 2. (Geneva: World Council of Churches, 1986), 176-177.

13. ULCA *Minutes* 1956: 866-8.

14. Bachmann, *Lutheran Churches*, 534-40.

15. Regarding Mittelholzer, see J. N. Lenker, *Lutherans in All Lands*, 2 vols. (Milwaukee: J. A. Hill 1894), 731-4; Bachmann, *Lutheran Churches*, 507-11; S. W. Herman, *Lutheran Churches of the World* (Minneapolis, MN: Augsburg 1957), 279-80.

16. ULCA *Minutes* 1926: 143-44.

17. Bachmann, *Lutheran Churches*, 159-66.

18. ULCA *Year Book* 1952: 98. ULCA *Yearbook* 1962: 188.

19. Bachmann, *Lutheran Churches*, 167-68.

20. Madras: Christian Literary Society, 1954. See also Carl Gustav Diehl and E. T. Bachmann, *Rajah Bushanam Manikam* (Madras: Christian Literary Society, 1975).

21. Bachmann, *Lutheran Churches*, 182.

22. ULCA *Minutes* 1952: 632.

23. ULCA *Minutes* 1956: 842.

24. *Lutheran Encyclopedia*, 21; see also Bachmann, *Lutheran Churches*, 137.

25. ULCA *Minutes* 1956: 843.

26. ULCA *Minutes* 1950: 894.

27. ULCA *Minutes* 1952: 633; see also Bachmann, *Lutheran Churches*, 245.

28. ULCA *Minutes* 1956: 844.

29. ULCA *Minutes* 1958: 977.

30. ULCA *Minutes* 1954: 825.

31. ULCA *Minutes* 1956: 917 and 957.

32. ULCA *Minutes* 1958: 888, 904, and 927.

33. ULCA *Minutes* 1952: 666.

34. ULCA *Year Book* 1951: 7-11.

35. ULCA *Minutes* 1950: 647; 1952: 662.

36. ULCA *Minutes* 1954: 833.

37. ULCA *Minutes* 1928: 215.

38. ULCA *Minutes* 1930: 251.

39. ULCA *Minutes* 1954: 824.

40. ULCA *Minutes* 1936: 150.

41. ULCA *Minutes* 1954: 824.

42. ULCA *Minutes* 1958: 884.

43. ULCA *Minutes* 1956: 1112.

44. ULCA *Minutes* 1954: 742.

45. Ibid., 743.

46. ULCA *Minutes* 1956: 1113.

47. ULCA *Minutes* 1958: 733.

48. Ibid., 741.

49. ULCA *Minutes* 1956: 1148-50.

50. ULCA *Minutes* 1952: 774. ULCA *Minutes* 1956:1149-50.

51. ULCA *Minutes* 1954: 425.

52. Ibid., 727.

53. Ibid., 727-28.

54. ULCA *Minutes* 1956: 1147.

55. ULCA *Minutes* 1954: 710.

56. ULCA *Minutes* 1958: 758ff.

57. Ibid., 760-765.

58. ULCA *Minutes* 1956: 29-38.

59. ULCA *Minutes* 1958: 29-72 and 1960: 19-66.

60. ULCA *Minutes* 1938: 65-72.

61. ULCA *Minutes* 1952: 543.

62. *Pastor's Desk Book* January 1959, NE 997.

63. ULCA *Minutes* 1952: 544-51.

64. Ibid., 548.

65. bid., 552.

66. Ibid., 554.

67. ULCA *Minutes* 1958: 556.

68. ULCA *Minutes* 1954: 28.

69. ULCA *Minutes* 1952: 994.

70. ULCA *Yearbook* 1962: 186-7.

71. ULCA *Minutes* 1954: 27-40.

72. Ibid., 624-25.

73. Knudsen, Johannes, *The Formation of the Lutheran Church in America* (Philadelphia: Fortress Press, 1978), 22. (Hereafter cited as Knudsen, *Formation.*)

74. ULCA *Minutes* 1956: 29; see also Gilbert, *Commitment to Unity*, 99-101.

75. Ibid., see also pp. 1057-59.

76. Ibid., 37.

77. Ibid., 1956: 1104-5; *American Christianity: An Historical Interpretation with Representative Documents* by H. Shelton Smith, Robert T. Hendy and Lefferts A. Loestcher (New York: Charles Scribner's Sons, 1963) vol II, pp. 593-599.

78. ULCA *Minutes* 1956: 1056.

79. Gilbert, *Commitment to Unity*, 99-101. Wolf, *Documents*, #225, 546 ff.

80. ULCA *Minutes* 1958: 669.

81. Nelson, *Lutherans in North America*, 506. Gilbert, *Commitment to Unity*, 102. The text of Fry's statement is in ULCA *Minutes* 1956: 29-38.

82. JCLU Report in ULCA *Minutes* 1958: 690.

83. Gilbert, *Commitment to Unity*, 104.

84. ULCA *Minutes* 1958: 690.

85. *Palette*, 101-105.

86. ULCA *Minutes* 1958: 429-440.

87. ULCA *Year Book* 1952: 5.

88. Ibid., 92.

NOTES TO EXCURSUS

1. *The Columbia Encyclopedia,* (New York: Columbia University Press, 1967), 1543.

2. Remembered by Mercia Brenne Bachmann, student advisor at Aberdeen State College in 1935.

3. Ross Hidy, graduate of Philadelphia Theological Seminary in 1942. His first call was as assistant to his uncle, the Rev. Ross Stover of Messiah Lutheran Church in Philadelphia. From 1943 to 1948 he served the wartime Harbor Gate Housing Project sponsored by the NLC. Then he spent some time in Europe with a photographer in preparing the movie "Answer for Ann" which helped Americans understand the refugee resettlement program. He served St. Michael's in Berkeley from 1949 to 1955.

4. *The Lutheran,* April 30, 1952.

5. *Lutheran Women's Work,* April 1951.

6. Already in 1906, when the Rev. Revere Franklin Weidner, then president of the Chicago (later Maywood) Seminary, requested facilities for a summer program for Lutheran pastors on the West Coast, the Pacific School of Religion faculty granted his request. Apparently, nothing came of this overture at the time. But soon West Coast pastors and lay folk of California (General Synod) and Oregon and Washington (General Council) began planning a joint Lutheran Seminary, but Lutheran unity was not yet that far. Finally, the first Pacific Lutheran Seminary was opened in Portland, Oregon, by the Pacific Synod. Soon the seminary was relocated to Seattle, near the University of Washington where it remained until closed (see chapter 7).

7. James P. Beasom, one of the seminary's graduates, was California Synod's president in the fifties who planted churches as Muhlenberg had done. He visited seminaries and attracted some of the most able seniors to accept calls to California. See *Beasom the Builder* by Richard M. Bennett and Ross F. Hidy (Berkeley, CA: Lutheran History Center of the West, 1986) for more on Beasom and on the seminary. A Committee to Conserve the Assets of the Pacific Seminary functioned conscientiously and, when the time came, turned over these assets as an initial nest egg for the new PLTS in Berkeley.

8. ULCA *Minutes* 1950: 767; California and Pacific Synod elected a board that approved a constitution. ULCA *Minutes* 1952: 705; Berkeley Seminary incorporated on May 10, 1950, and opened its session in September, 1952.

9. Christian Higher Education Year (CHEY) appeal was approved by the Church in 1948 (ULCA *Minutes* 1950: 757). It was for buildings at colleges and seminaries.

10. *The Lutheran,* July 4, 1951.

11. ULCA *Minutes* 1952: 705.

12. ETB personal papers.

13. Pacific School of Religion, the Church Divinity School of the Pacific, Berkeley Baptist Divinity School, Starr King School for the Ministry (Unitarian), and, across the Bay in San Anselmo, San Francisco Theological Seminary; while in Oakland there was the Dominican Seminary.

14. ULCA *Minutes* 1950: 214-217, Report of Board of American Missions.
15. NLC's News Release (9-19-55)
16. David Hoh, Luther Theological Seminary graduate, was sent by the Board of Foreign Missions to Japan in 1953. Sister Gladys Reidenouer of the Philadelphia Motherhouse was sent to Malaya in 1956.
17. Already in 1947 the USA National Committee of the LWF had provided funds for an assistant to the farsighted President of the Lutheran Church in Brazil who had established a small seminary, the "Faculade de Teologia" in 1946. The church needed an American to help encourage the transition to the Brazilian language (Portuguese) and culture and to recognize its immense mission opportunities in its vast country. See the fuller discussion earlier in chapter 11.

CHAPTER 12

TOWARD MERGER, 1960-1962

WITH THE NATIONAL ELECTION OF 1960, the presidency of the United States changed, from Eisenhower to Kennedy, from age to youth, and from Protestant to Roman Catholic for the first time. A nuclear-powered Navy submarine, like a latter-day Magellan, circled the globe under water without surfacing even once. In 1960 two men in a bathysphere descended in the Pacific to a point more than one mile deeper than Mt. Everest is high. The first weather satellite was launched by the U.S. to transmit images of cloud cover around the world. A Nobel prize went to the scientist perfecting the measurement of time by the use of radioactive carbon 14. That year, too, scientists harnessed the power of light by means of a laser device: Light Amplification by Stimulated Emission of Radiation. In general, science and technology were picking up speed and changing the world.

Tension between the two superpowers was mounting as the United States and the Soviet Union held most of the human family hostage. But there was also hope and determination, especially among young people. North of the border, meanwhile, Canadians had the benefit of a different perspective, a side view that made Canada a potentially strong "middle power" of distinctive culture and independent policies, welcomed in the Third World.

On the world scene, United States Secretary of State Christian M. Herter, seeing no real changes in the Soviet position, cautioned the West to maintain its defense. General Maxwell Taylor, former commander of United States Armed Forces in Germany, in his book *The Uncertain Trumpet*, not only observed the waning of American strength in a world of rising tension but also warned against reliance upon a policy of "massive retaliation." With the construction of the Berlin Wall, the alignment of the USSR with Cuba, the failure of attempts to control nuclear arms, the Chinese Communist invasion of northeastern India, and the expulsion of ten thousand Chinese refugees needing food from Hong Kong, fear gripped many nations.

In the realm of religion, preparations were under way in 1960 for the Second Vatican Council and the Roman Catholic venture into ecumenism. In 1961 at New Delhi the Third Assembly of the World Council of Churches welcomed the Russian, the Rumanian, the Bulgarian, and other Orthodox churches not yet members of the UCC. It also completed the merger with the International Missionary Council. This event in India's capital, New Delhi, in some ways marked the high point of ULCA participation in the ecumenical movement. Franklin Clark Fry was elected to an unprecedented second term as chairman (moderator) of the WCC Central Committee. A ULCA delegate, the Chicago theologian Joseph A. Sittler Jr., delivered his acclaimed and controversial keynote address on "Cosmic Christology." Stateside the National Council of Churches at San Francisco in 1960 observed its first decade of Protestant and Orthodox cooperation. The ULCA was represented by twenty-eight delegates.[1]

Vicariously the ULCA was represented in apartheid-torn South Africa when its president chaired a crucial meeting between an invited six-member delegation from the World Council of Churches and a group of top representatives of the Dutch Reformed Church. As chairman of the WCC Central Committee, Fry handled a difficult situation with great understanding and kindly firmness.[2] That this meeting failed of its intended objective became clear when the rank and file of the South African Dutch Reformed Church refused to accept the outcome and voted to withdraw from the World Council.

ATLANTIC CITY (1960)

In Atlantic City, a magnet for conventions in its pre-casino days, the ULCA gathered in October 1960 for its twenty-second and last biennial convention. It did so by design. For it was in Atlantic City in 1914 that E. Clarence Miller, a Philadelphia businessman, proposed a merger of the three general bodies to a committee preparing for the 1917 observance of the Reformation Quadricentennial (see chapter 3). Now after forty-two years of growing together, the ULCA was ready for the next step.

For the hosting New Jersey Synod, organized only in 1950, the ULCA convention marked the synod's coming of age, out from under its "adjacent state" category between New York and Pennsylvania and into its own identity. After much negotiating by the New Jersey Synod, the ULCA secured the Atlantic City Auditorium for a week of sessions (October 13-20) while the refurbished Ambassador served as convention hotel. St. Andrews-by-the-Sea, the local Lutheran church, became the hospitality center. St. Andrews-by-the-Sea was initiated in 1889 by the Rev. William Ashmead Schaeffer, then a teacher at the Philadelphia Seminary and later Home Mission director for the Ministerium of Pennsylvania. He saw the need and opportunity for a Lutheran congregation in the famed resort and convention city. It was the first of a succession of Lutheran congregations along the Jersey shore. During its seventieth anniversary year, St. Andrews, led by its pastor, Christian Schenck, was deep in a building program.

A smartly modern church edifice was completed just in time to serve the ULCA conventioneers as a quiet place of refreshment and informal meeting. Its role, on behalf of the host synod of New Jersey, turned it into "an almost twenty-four hour 'open house' from October 10 to several days after the convention closed."[3] Michigan and Pacific streets became a welcome rendezvous. Among the talented members of the congregation was Sister Maude Behrman. A deaconess of the Philadelphia Motherhouse and a published authority on the dietary care of diabetics, she came to Atlantic City in 1955 as director of Mercer Memorial House, popular among church people from Philadelphia and elsewhere. Sister Maude's contribution to the 1960 convention was the careful selection of refreshments for the delegates.

Merger

As to the business of the convention, the big item was merger. Great expectations animated the Lutheran scene in the early sixties. In the Midwest a three-way merger during Easter Week 1960 formed The American Lutheran Church. Now in the United Lutheran Church in America, the eagerness to get on with consolidation was shared by the Augustana Church, the American (Danish) Evangelical Lutheran Church, and the Finnish Evangelical Lutheran Church of America (Suomi). Each of them played a role in the merger, as documented elsewhere; the perspective here is necessarily that of the ULCA.

JCLU. The Joint Commission on Lutheran Unity (JCLU), at work since 1956, was nearing the completion of its task. Some complications remained, but confidence was high. As Johannes Knudsen, assistant secretary and treasurer of the JCLU during its entire six years, made clear, the chosen leaders of the four church bodies and their colleagues on the commission had achieved a mutual trust and creative confidence, also among their constituencies, for the task ahead. The name of the new body had finally been adopted: The Lutheran Church in America.

Much else was also in progress for this penultimate gathering of the ULCA. In the *Bulletin of Reports* sent to the delegates and others during the month before the convention, the program was presented in full. As usual there was the opening act of divine worship, with sermon by the president, "Father and Brethren," and the celebration of Holy Communion. This was the second time that the convention would be using the *Service Book and Hymnal,* the "Red Book."[4] A sense of anticipation animated the delegates. They were eager to hear the president's report on the coming shape of the consolidated church. They would thus prepare themselves to examine and then vote on the basic document: The Agreement of Consolidation. But there were also other matters to review and act upon, such as statements on the Problem of Nuclear Weapons, the Sacrament of the Altar and Its Implications, as well as other items of reference.

The president's report to the Atlantic City convention and to the church at large reads today, as it did in 1960, like an expertly conducted tour of the anticipated (and now remembered) Lutheran Church in America. The report was part three of a trilogy. In the two previous conventions—Harrisburg (1956) and Dayton (1958)—the Fry report dealt masterfully with the theme of Christian unity, and with "the governing principles of the polity of the church-to-be." Then as now these reports pulsated with the authenticity of a church leader who was not only president of the ULCA but also chair of the World Council of Churches Central Committee and, since 1957, president of the Lutheran World Federation.

The 1960 report, its author confessed, has "a far more menial although still indispensable assignment." Its thirty-eight pages delineated meticulously a vision to be shared and acted upon. For openers Fry, anticipating what delegates might ask, came with ten general questions and ten remarkably instructive responses. The catechetical style made for ready communication of the contents subsequently to the congregations. Next came his leading the hearer, or reader, on a peripatetic examination of "the completed mechanism of our church of the future."[5] Back and forth he led, showing the function and interrelatedness of the components: boards, commissions, auxiliaries, and so on. Nothing of consequence seemed left out. The third and concluding part brought out the Fry credo, his conviction that "the manifested unity of the church is the will of God."[6]

This returned him to where he began, to "the evangelical basis of our seeking this union . . . [to] Christ's yearnings for the oneness of His people in confession, in their stance in the presence of a hostile world, and in their common life within a reunited church." With the Holy Spirit guiding, "good faith is the quality, humanly speaking, on which everything will stand or fall." In his words, "When Christians are one in faith, they ought to become visibly one before God, before each other, and before the world."[7]

The Atlantic City delegates had been well-prepared to vote on merger. To all ministers and secretaries of congregations of the ULCA as well as of the three other merging church bodies a basic booklet had been sent out. Entitled, "Official Documents of the Lutheran Church in America 1960," it contained four documents in their final form: the Constitution and By-Laws of the new church, the Approved Constitution for Synods and the Approved Constitution for Congregations. This reflected the four years of labor by the Joint Commission on Lutheran Unity. Franklin Clark Fry had played a decisive part in the drafting of these documents. Others like Augustana's Conrad Bergendoff had made significant contributions.

Doctrinal Agreement. Nowhere was a consensus expressed more joyously than in the Doctrinal Article (II) of the Constitution. Already on December 12, 1956, in Chicago, the basic resolution to proceed toward union was adopted by the JCLU.

> After hearing the reading and interpretation of the doctrinal statements of the four churches here represented, the Commission [JCLU] rejoiced to note that we have among us sufficient ground of agreement in the common confession of our faith, as witnessed in the Lutheran confessions, to justify further procedure in seeking a basis for organic union of our churches, including the formulation of a proposed constitution for a united church having in it articles on doctrine and practical matters of organization.[8]

The central place and far-reaching import of the doctrinal article was spelled out by the JCLU Committee on Doctrine and Living Tradition (1957) in order to bring the ULCA and its partners into concert. The key here was an affirmation of doctrine regarding the center of the faith, as shared by the partners, rather than explicit written agreements on all doctrinal details. "For us the doctrinal article has become a confession of faith." Specifically, "it is first of all a ringing challenge and a joyful affirmation of the blessings we share in our Christian and Lutheran fellowship." Furthermore, "the article must be interpreted as an affirmation pointing to the fountain from which all the life and activities of the church flow." And also "as a flag under which all those of like faith may gather." The article "seeks to relate the practical life of the church to its doctrinal subscription . . . [and] to affirm and to preserve the evangelical character of the church."[9]

Here let it suffice to quote but two of the seven sections of the Doctrinal Article II.

> Section 2. This church holds that the Gospel is the revelation of God's sovereign and saving grace in Jesus Christ. In Him, the Word Incarnate, God imparts Himself to men.

> Section 7. This church affirms that the Gospel transmitted by the Holy Scriptures, to which the creeds and confessions bear witness, is the true treasure of the Church, the substance of its proclamation, and the basis of its unity and continuity. The Holy Spirit uses the proclamation of the Gospel and the administration of the Sacraments to create and sustain Christian fellowship. As this occurs the church fulfills its divine mission and purpose.[10]

Incorporation. There remained the matter of incorporation, a point at which, in a free society guaranteeing separation of church and state, the state recognizes a given church body as a legal entity. In order to provide continuity from the four merging bodies to the coming consolidated body, it was required that there be a legally binding document called an "Agreement of Consolidation," accompanied by a copy of the Constitution and By-Laws governing the new church body. To accomplish this, much legal work was involved. Reliable legal counsel was essential. No one, as Fry admitted, worked with greater vision, acumen, or commitment than the Philadelphia attorney H. Ober Hess. Both he and the astute Allentown judge, James F. Henninger, were delegates from the Ministerium of Pennsylvania.

As to the Agreement of Consolidation itself, its contents opened with the names of the incorporators, forty-six of them, of the new church body. It provided a verbal description of the boundaries of the thirty projected synods. It made provision for eight operational boards, three auxiliaries, as well as for the discharge of fiduciary responsibility and the continuation of a common investing fund. After formal action by each of the four consolidating churches, "the Church [LCA] will begin corporate existence on June 1, 1962, and the incorporated boards of the Church will begin corporate existence on July 1, 1962."[11]

The Agreement of Consolidation was the main item on the convention agenda on Thursday morning, October 14. Judge Henninger was called upon to present the proposed action on the Agreement. He explained "that a purpose of the Agreement of Consolidation is to guarantee that every body which is a party to it will be carried forward in the new church." To him union could be likened "to the confluence of four rivers which, produced by four streams, holds all four of its tributaries."[12]

Judge Henninger explained that Minnesota had been chosen as the state for incorporation because of the generous provision in its laws for non-profit corporations. He admitted that a vote to postpone action at this time was a possibility but, in his judgment that would "be tantamount to the rejection of this merger for ten to twenty years." In his estimation, and no doubt mindful of the substantial authorship of the ULCA president, "we will have a constitution which is entitled not to adoration, awe or reverence, but to respect."[13]

The judge thereupon moved the adoption of a resolution (drafted by H. Ober Hess) on the Agreement of Consolidation by the ULCA; that this resolution be submitted for ratification by the several synods of the ULCA; that when at least two thirds of the synods have ratified it the "president and secretary of this church be authorized to execute the Agreement forthwith." If this procedure is met, an adjourned meeting of the ULCA would follow in June 1962. "Whereupon the Agreement shall be deemed approved by this Church." Failure of a two-thirds ratification by May 31, 1962, shall deem the Agreement rejected by the ULCA. With parliamentary precision Chairman Fry alerted the delegates, saying: "This is the decisive motion."[14] It had already been adopted by the Augustana Church and was in process in the American Evangelical Lutheran Church and the Suomi Synod.

No one spoke against the resolution. Some requested clarification, which Judge Henninger or the chairman supplied. Yes, there would be an opportunity for hearings if the realigned synodical boundaries worked hardships. Discussion took less than a half hour. Whereupon John G. Simmons, pastor in North Hollywood and a politically active transplant from Minnesota, moved the previous question. It was at 10:55 on the morning of Thursday, October 14, 1960, that the Atlantic City convention delegates voted that the ULCA consolidate with three other church bodies and with them form the Lutheran Church in America. The convention vote at that moment was 640 to one.

On request, President Fry offered prayer. Blessing God for the presence of the Holy Spirit, "so palpably and manifestly felt among us this day," he went on.

> We commend ourselves and the United Lutheran Church in America, which we have loved with all our hearts, into thy hand and entreat thee to lead us forward . . . . We beseech thee never to allow us to take our eyes from the goal which thou thyself erected before us, that thy Church may be one, that men may see it and be enabled to believe that Jesus Christ is Lord, to the glory of God the Father. In His name we pray. Amen.[15]

In summary, Oscar W. Carlson, the Baltimore pastor who had served on the JCLU from its beginning in 1956, reminded the convention of "the poetry and romance that go along with this merger." He recalled how forty-two years earlier, in a sermon at the merger convention of the ULCA in November 1918, Henry Eyster Jacobs had exulted: "I look forward to the day when the Lutheran Churches in America will be one indeed and will bring Lutheranism to its finest flowering on the American continent."[16] That was then, but Carlson concentrated on the present and on what would be expected of the members of this new church body:

> We are to be doctrinally creative and correct . . . give loving obedience to the general church . . . and unflagging devotion to the local congregation. . . . To be sincerely ecumenical but strongly loyal to our evangelical Lutheran traditions. . . . To be evangelically sound and socially dynamic.

"How are we as individuals going to feel about this new church?" Carlson asked. And then he concluded that although recent years may have familiarized Lutherans of different origins with each other, the sense of newness is kept alive "in Christ, rising daily to serve. . . ."[17]

As a first postscript Fry introduced attorney H. Ober Hess, counsel to the JCLU. "He has accomplished great tasks in incredibly short time." An hour later the lone dissenter, a lawyer from North Carolina who was apprehensive over the future of his synod's cherished home mission fund, begged leave to change his negative vote into a positive. As a wag later suggested, there was more joy at the Church House over the one Tar Heel who repented than over the 640 who needed no repentance.

The Atomic Era

Even as the convention was moving the ULCA into a new ecclesial future, it also found itself grappling with the anxieties of the atomic era and the complex problem of nuclear weapons. A number of synods had requested the Board of Social Missions to initiate a statement representing the position of the ULCA, a statement that might then be channeled through individuals to their representatives in the government.

In light of the Cold War and the build-up of tensions between the two superpowers and their respective allies or hangers-on, it soon became clear that any statement from a widely connected church body such as the ULCA would see nuclear weapons as part of the global picture of international relations in which justice and peace require the supportiveness of Christians. The statement as presented by the Social Action Department of the Social Missions Board was inclusive in scope and to the point. Rufus Cornelsen and other staff members as well as recognized outside consultants—William H. Lazareth (Philadelphia Seminary), Kenneth W. Thompson (Rockefeller Foundation) and others—had made it a corporate effort.[18] Yet that was no guarantee of ready acceptance. The new era was confusing.

Recognizing the great technological advances of the nuclear space-age for good or ill of the human family, the statement declared "that these new dimensions of knowledge and power have developed under the sovereignty of God who continues to rule over men and nations."[19] And more:

> In light of His redeeming act in Jesus Christ we hold that it is His loving will that this new potential be used in the service of justice, freedom and peace, and that it is the responsibility of Christians to make every effort to guard against its destructive employment and to harness it for the general enhancement of the life of all mankind.

"The pervasiveness of sin," the statement went on, makes "war always a threat." Therefore "we urge the governments of the United States and Canada to wage peace," to support and strengthen the United Nations, to recognize the validity of conscientious objection but not to endorse it.

The statement saw armaments as "a basic element in international diplomacy. Their possession in peace may serve to deter aggression. Their use in war for purposes of defense may be justified as a necessary evil in a sinful world. Under no circumstances can aggression or preventive wars be sanctioned." Moreover, "The dangers inherent in the nuclear-space age will be decreased in proportion to the effectiveness of agreements for the cessation of nuclear weapons testing and the reduction of national armaments under international inspection and control."

The third paragraph of this statement, focusing as it did on a dynamic policy in international relations, became the subject of debate, at times impassioned. President Fry, seeing the impasse develop and the time running out had an informal group work out the sharpest disagreements. With the assistance of O. Frederick Nolde, director of the WCC Commission of the Churches on International Affairs, a compromise was achieved. As debated by the convention and then adopted, paragraph three read:

> We urge the governments of the United States and Canada to wage peace and seek the prevention of war simultaneously by (a) assisting the economically underprivileged nations of the world to attain higher standards of living; (b) consolidating and extending their ties with free nations; (c) engaging with other governments in peaceful competition where important differences exist and in peaceful cooperation where fundamental principle is not compromised.[20]

Perceptive parliamentarian that he was, President Fry reminded the delegates of the gravity of the subject and its context.

The Sacrament of the Altar

After the joyful affirmation of the Agreement of Consolidation and the heated debate over a statement on nuclear weapons, there now came a quiet time to ponder and approve a document dealing with the very heart of the church's life. In the estimation of President Fry, this statement on the Lord's Supper would rank with three others as the most enduring and significant in the history of the ULCA. The Washington Declaration (1920), the Baltimore Declaration (1938), the Doctrine of the Ministry (1952), these three had set forth principles concerning the church and its external relations, had stated the church's position on the Word of God and the Scriptures, and spelled out the ULCA understanding of the doctrine of the ministry. Now came, fittingly, the statement on the Sacrament of the Altar and Its Implications. It was actually an incourse change of an earlier pronouncement, authored by the Executive Board and adopted by the 1940 convention, regarding corporate communions, namely, communion services at conventions or camps not directly within a congregation's worship life.[21] As we have already paid attention to the first three documents, this fourth one, linked to the initiative of auxiliaries, has a tale to tell.

Some church-related auxiliaries in the 1930s tended to add corporate communions to their annual conventions or other significant programs. Not only the synodically grouped organizations for women, men and youth were involved but also student associations, summer camps, chaplaincy programs and others. Brought to the attention of the 1938 convention, the matter was referred to the Executive Board for study.[22] Two years later, at Omaha, came the pronouncement limiting communion. As adopted it was an official statement based on Articles VII and XIII of the Augsburg Confession wherein "the Church is the congregation of saints in which the Gospel is rightly taught and the Sacraments rightly administered."[23] The key word was congregation, and the concern was to avoid the impression of loose practice, for which the ULCA, as we know, was at times criticized.

The 1940 pronouncement interpreted Article VII of the Augsburg Confession administratively when noting that the authorization of Holy Communion "is either by the local congregation or by the church-at-large as the congregation of congregations." Therefore:

> Permission to hold a Communion Service must be secured a) from the pastor and church council for the congregational [auxiliary] communions, and b) from the President of the United Lutheran Church in America or the President of a Constituent Synod for all other communions.[24]

As we have seen earlier (chapter 7) the 1930s were a time when the ULCA, aware of being watched by other church bodies, was eager to avoid their criticism as it sought to advance Lutheran unity, particularly as sought by President Knubel at the Omaha convention (1940). The 1940 statement was a self-consciously strict interpretation.

Generally the pronouncement gained dutiful compliance, but the arrangement was cumbersome and open to questioning. College and seminary communities, not being recognized congregations, in their way became foci for the practice of corporate communions. Theological students, especially, might find their course in the Lutheran Confessions evoking questions about the pronouncement. For example, when Article VII says "the Church is the congregation of saints" (in German "the assembly of all believers") does this imply a narrow (denominational) or a catholic (ecumenical) view of the church?[25] And how does this provide the context for a right preaching of the gospel and a right administration of the Sacraments in keeping with the gospel?

While the first decade showed little unrest over the 1940 pronouncement, the second came alive with a quest for a better way. In 1951 the New York Synod requested the Executive Board to restudy this issue of "corporate communions." In 1952, the year in which the Doctrine of the Ministry statement cleared the Seattle convention, a commission to study the Statement [Pronouncement] on Corporate Communions was appointed. Two years later the commission's report was referred back for further study. At Harrisburg in 1956, the commission, seemingly at an impasse, requested help, namely, more theological professors. Instead, Edward Traill Horn III proposed the naming of a new commission to approach the issue from a different perspective. The outcome was a fifteen-member Commission on the Sacrament of the Altar and Its Implications. Nine members were from theological academia, and six from parish or synodical work.[26]

Chaired by the Rev. Horn, a Philadelphia parish pastor and strong liturgical scholar, the commission organized into working parties, sent out questionnaires, assessed the present as it probed the past and anticipated the morrow. They drew upon an impressive array of resources. The commission members were ever reminded of their assignment as initially worded: "To make an extended study of the Sacrament of the Altar in all its implications as they relate to the life of the church."[27] With characteristic foresight, Indiana Synod President Walter Wick, a member of the commission, cautioned the 1958 convention that the coming report "might cast on the church the first faint shadow of canon law." Instead, what was in the making was intended to serve as a guide for the "broad base of congregational life."[28]

"The Sacrament of the Altar and Its Implications" appeared in the preconvention Bulletin of Reports. As the title suggested, the commission's report had two main parts: Basic Affirmations, and The Shaping of Practice. Not only its more than ten thousand words but also its weighty content made it a formidable teaching document.

The document's basic affirmations limited its forty-three paragraphs to "the kind of questions which occasioned this commission" (Section 1). It presents the sacrament in the context of the church "as this church was constituted by the resurrected, living Lord, Jesus Christ, and as it continues to be constituted and nourished by this same Lord, who is present and active wherever and whenever the good news of God's gracious action in him is proclaimed." (Section 2). From there on the alert reader would alternately be reminded or informed of profound yet simple theological affirmations. The Word of God and the Scriptures, the awesome sweep of Christology—the living Christ—in Word and Sacrament, the Lord's Supper as memorial and presence and anticipation of Christ, the Words of Institution, the place of liturgy, and distracting matters such as the "how" of Christ's being in the elements of bread and wine, and other matters are set forth lucidly. Commended is the emphasis on the gift of the forgiveness of sins; condemned is the "covert Pelagianism" inherent in language of sacrifice (sections 27, 35). A quotation from Luther ends this part: "Reform of impious rites will come of itself when what is fundamental in our teaching, being effectively presented, has taken root in pious hearts."[29]

The second part, The Shaping of Practice, endeavors to draw guidelines from the aforementioned "description of the Lutheran understanding of the Lord's Supper." The report reminds the reader that in worship "we should be doing nothing at all had not God done a huge deliverance." (C. 2) For "the Lord's Supper is, in one respect, the glad acceptance over and over again of the merriment bestowed upon the human condition by God's forgiveness of sins, and his incarnated dwelling with men." (C. 3) This combination of joy and gratitude will not have itself confined—certainly not to even benevolently contrived ecclesial structures, or to venerable terms like congregation when interpreted too narrowly. Indeed, congregation as mentioned at the outset of this description, received an inclusive treatment on this report. When the Augsburg Confession in Articles VII and VIII asserts "that the church is the *congregatio sanctorum* in which the gospel is preached in its purity and sacraments are administered according to the gospel, the expression 'congregation of believers' does not mean a legally organized local group of Christians." (D. 2a) The context of these articles as well as Luther's explanation to the Third Article of the Apostles' Creed "make it abundantly clear that the reference is to the assembly of Christians, the flock of Christ, the community of God which exists wherever people are gathered by the Holy Spirit through the gospel."[30]

From this it is clear that "it is not the existence of a particular ecclesiastical polity but trust and confidence in God's saving deed in Christ which provides the essential context for the celebration of the sacrament. . . . The legally organized congregation may well provide the context within which the sacrament is normally celebrated, but as an institution it has no sacramental monopoly." (D. 2b)

In treating the occasion that initially led to the action requested of the Executive Board in 1938, the report discussed still another term besides "congregation." It declared,

> The phrase 'corporate communion' is a redundancy which betrays a misunderstanding of the Lord's Supper. The sacrament is by nature a participation in the Body of Christ. The communion in the sacrament is a fellowship of the church with its living Lord and, simultaneously a fellowship of each member with the whole church. (E. 1a)

So, for example, the private communion offered a sick person in the hospital or one who is house-bound transcends the isolation and unites that person with all the people of God. (E. 1a)

In drawing some practical conclusions the report had this to say about the church's ordering of its ministry locally:

It is the obligation of the local congregation to cherish, guard and provide for the celebration of the sacrament within its own membership. Provision may also properly be made for the celebration of the sacrament in special groups within the congregation when the general edification of the entire congregation is sought thereby. This responsibility is not to be delegated to the synod or the church at large. (E. 2a)

It had this to say beyond the local scene:

It is proper for the synod or the church at large to guard, cherish and provide for the celebration of the holy communion in assemblies which are gathered in the name of and for the purpose of the church. (E. 3a)

It is also proper for the synod or the church at large, through ministers called by these bodies, such as chaplains in institutions and in military service, to provide for communion services among groups or for individuals who desire to receive the sacrament. Similarly, the synod or the church at large may make provision for the sacrament within conventions of auxiliaries, or assemblies at youth camps, laymen's conferences and such other organizations and groups which are constituted by individuals who are communing members of their home congregations.[31]

Thus the position taken by the Executive Board and approved by the ULCA in 1940 was reversed. Moreover, intercommunion among Lutheran bodies in North America and beyond was seen as progressing and to be encouraged. Confidently the report added: "The time is ripe for Lutherans to initiate theological discussion with other Christian bodies in North America regarding intercommunion."[32]

Although the ecumenical movement had been making significant progress during the 1950s, with the ULCA a prominent participant, the report declared: "No blanket ruling may be made about the celebration of the sacrament in interdenominational assemblies. The decision in each instance will have to be arrived at in the light of whether the proclamation of the church is compromised or enhanced. Indiscriminate participation in such services of communion should be discouraged." (E. 4c)

As to access—open and closed communion—the Order for Public Confession (*Service Book and Hymnal*, 249-52) states the conditions. The sacrament is "for those who humbly confess their sins and who hunger and thirst after righteousness." The essential components were: self-examination, confession of sins, remembrance of Christ—"that he was 'delivered for our offences and raised again for our justification'"—and thankfulness "for his saving death and resurrection;" as well as love toward one another, and the obligation "to take up one's cross and follow him."

Such matters as the frequency of celebration and reception of the sacrament and aspects of liturgical practice came in for consideration. One perennial question, puzzling particularly to parents with young children and of no little concern to pastors, was the relation of the age of confirmation to admission to the sacrament of the altar. The commission's report recommended that the church "engage in a re-examination of the theology of confirmation and the age for admission to communion." By action of the convention, this paragraph (E) was deleted in favor of a joint study to be undertaken in cooperation with the Augustana Church.[33]

The commission's report stirred up only mild discussion. The part on Basic Affirmations by definition was unlikely to arouse disagreement. The first twenty-three paragraphs sailed through unchallenged. Only minor points of clarification marked the remaining twenty paragraphs. The second part of the commission report that dealt with the shaping of practice tempted persons of experience to speak up. Even so nothing was basically changed while some things were clarified.

All told, the commission had done its work well and had filled a felt need, although the report came very late in the life of the ULCA and was challenged early on in the LCA. The positive side was expressed well by one of the youngest members of the commission. James R. Crumley, pastor in Oak Ridge, Tennessee, was just five years in the ministry when appointed to the commission. His congregation included some top scientists in the atomic energy program. He told the convention,

> As a parish pastor, I look upon the report as an important theological resource. In this sense it is the foundation of the church's view of the Sacrament in biblical and confessional theology. Further, since the statement is not unaware of the contemporary situation, it assists me in making such theology relevant to my congregation and to the needs of my people.[34]

As recommendations go, those of the Commission on the Sacrament of the Altar and Its Implications were unusual and brief:

> 1. That the 1940 "pronouncement" on Corporate Communion be rescinded. (The summary text of the 1940 "pronouncement" was reprinted for the sake of the record.)
> 2. That the report of the Commission on the Sacrament of the Altar and Its Implications be adopted by the church as a guide.
> 3. That the Commission be discharged.[35]

These recommendations were adopted by the convention.

A Convention Highlight

A highlight was provided the convention on Sunday night, when the auditorium of the Atlantic City High School held a crowd of seventeen hundred. The oratorio type presentation, "The Time Is Now," linked the Lutheran liturgy and daily life, the church in the struggling inner city and the church in suburbia, and by implication the church at home and the church worldwide. Imaginatively composed by an editor of *The Lutheran*, Robert Huldschiner, and given its musical setting by Philadelphia Seminary's Professor Bornemann, this presentation left the audience, as someone observed, with a sense of wholeness that transcended not only the components of the diversified agenda but also the brokenness of human existence from which Christians were not immune.

Recess Arranged

With a merger imminent, would the 1960 Atlantic City convention be the last? It should not end without a solution. Charles Muhlenberg Cooper had the answer. He presented and moved the adoption of the following:

> Resolved: that the convention now adjourn to such time as the President of the United Lutheran Church may call it to reconvene;
> that such call shall be promulgated by notice of the time and place for reconvening published in *The Lutheran* not fewer than sixty days in advance; and
> that if such a call is not issued for reconvening prior to October 1962, this convention shall be deemed adjourned *sine die*.[36]

The motion passed. The Atlantic City Convention adjourned at 11:25 A.M. on Thursday, October 20, 1960.

THE ULCA FINALE

After due notice the adjourned convention reconvened at 10:00 A.M. Monday, June 25, 1962, in Cobo Hall, Detroit, Michigan.[37] At the same time the other three bodies in the merger were having their final conventions. During the first three days of the 1962 convention final decisions and reports were made. Special consideration was given to matters that did not fit into the JCLU pattern of organization. Memorials were adopted to accomplish smooth transitions for exceptional cases. As agreed, the reports of the various boards, departments, commissions, committees, and auxiliaries were summaries of their work during the lifetime of the ULCA (see the postscript, page 324). Together they comprised a history of the church's functions. They were in the Convention *Bulletin of Reports*, so the delegates had been well-informed. As each report was scheduled, only highlights could be given orally. However, there was always time given for questions and comments. Fry, as chair, was most gracious in recognizing and thanking the people responsible for the reports and introducing new people on the staffs.

One report, that of the Board of Deaconess Work, demanded special attention. The president of the board, the Rev. Donald C. Heft, after acknowledging the dedication of the deaconesses, announced the merger plans of the Baltimore and Philadelphia Motherhouses to be consummated already in the fall of 1962. He then introduced Sister Mildred Winter, executive of the board and the three field secretaries: sisters Louise Burroughs, Marian Mauer, and Sally Tschumi. Then Sister Mildred, using slides, showed the various ways deaconesses serve, combining the skills of nurses, teachers, parish workers, and social workers. Embodying the motto "the love of Christ constraineth me," one hundred deaconesses then appeared and walked across the stage and around the auditorium.

On the last day, Earl S. Erb, executive secretary of the Board of Foreign Missions, also had some good news for the convention. In 1920 the ULCA had 116 missionaries working in British Guiana, India, Japan, and Liberia; in 1962 there were 310 missionaries in these fields and in four additional countries: Argentina, Hong Kong, Malaya, and Uruguay. He also announced that, with the approval of the Executive Board, work would begin in Chile in cooperation with the Evangelical Lutheran Church of Chile.

At the opening of the last session, in the Cobo Hall Ballroom, on Wednesday, June 27, 1962, the Committee on Reference and Counsel added a human touch. The Committee chairman was Charles Shearer Jacobs, son of the ULCA trail-blazing president of the Philadelphia Seminary, Charles M. Jacobs. The son, a Philadelphia lawyer, recommended "that the President request all persons who are here present and were present at the 1918 convention of the Church to rise and be recognized." Eighteen persons arose. The one woman among them was Helen Knubel, daughter of the church's first president. The other seventeen, nearly all clergymen, had since risen to positions of prominence. The convention greeted them with a standing ovation.[38]

This last convention was not a funeral for the United Lutheran Church in America. It was new life with the American Evangelical Lutheran Church, the Augustana Evangelical Lutheran Church and the Finnish Evangelical Lutheran Church. The rebirth took place on the morning of Thursday, June 28, in Detroit when these four Lutheran Churches became one. Malvin Lundeen, Chairman of the Joint Commission on Lutheran Unity and president of the Augustana Lutheran Church, called to order the assembled delegates of the four churches. Then the four presidents, the Rev. A. E. Farstrup, Malvin Lundeen, Raymond W. Wargelin and Franklin Clark Fry, each testified that his church body had approved the "Agreement of Consolidation" which provided the legal basis for the merger.[39] The formation of the LCA was then symbolized as four acolytes lit separate quarters of a massive candle. When the four sections were pushed together, the four lights became one, brightly burning to symbolize the fusion of the four church bodies into one.[40]

Valedictory

It is fitting that this account of the ULCA should close with the valedictory address of Franklin Clark Fry, given to a hushed audience on the Tuesday evening of the final ULCA Convention. He began by expressing appreciation for the summaries of the work already presented by the boards and agencies of the ULCA. That historical survey having been accomplished by others, he wanted his contribution to be one of gratitude, contrition, acknowledgment, and dedication.[41]

Gratitude to "God because he has chosen to make the United Lutheran Church a part of his holy church. . . . He has been the wellspring of its life, the fountain of its being. . . . He is the all in all, the alpha and omega of the United Lutheran Church, from its birth until its end. By his fire it has been kindled. By his breath it has lived." Gratitude that "our worship has grown during these years, that in more and more of our churches our worship has been touched with these coals from the fire of his altar as we behold our King."

Gratitude for "the clarity and consistency of the faith with which the United Lutheran Church in America has been endowed, for the deepening of theology, for the measure of 'unity,' the growth of churchmanship." Fry credited the Lutheran Evangelism Mission for providing a "feeling that we are members one of another, because we have simultaneously been discovering the church, the whole body of Christ in which we are one" instead of seeing ourselves as "merely descendants of our ancestors with a tribal loyalty." He expressed gratitude for "open doors of ecumenicity" and for the "role that God has permitted the United Lutheran Church to play in it." Fry reminded his hearers that "until recently we lived to ourselves and within ourselves." But "it was His act . . . that has suddenly and spectacularly thrown open a whole array of doors to the United Lutheran Church and has given to it influence almost grotesquely out of proportion to any that we could expect to have." He also expressed gratitude for the "degree of flexibility which the United Lutheran Church has had with which to match the changes in this fluid age, of which the readiness of our church to enter into the coming merger is the best and most conclusive evidence." "When God unhinges history, he expects his church to move. I praise him that we are ready and on our way."

Contrition. Quoting the words of the seventeenth chapter of St. Luke, "So likewise you, when you have done all those things that were commanded you, say, we are unprofitable servants, we have done only that which was our duty to do," Fry mentioned a few of his deep regrets: "Too often we have taken our standards from society instead of imposing the higher one. Instead of being a conscience and pioneer in the towns and cities of America, we have been content to be their echo. How sadly slow we have been to welcome . . . to our churches every one who is God's child . . . and to extend out beyond the natural borders of our own constituencies." The president ended his contritions with words of admonition. "Our reason for contrition needs to be that we have scarcely begun to utilize the resources of God, to give free scope to the light that the Spirit has so graciously kindled in our hearts."

Acknowledgment. Fry began his acknowledgments by paying tribute to the first president, Frederick H. Knubel.

> I loved him as a father. He was the symbol and focus of our unity, irenic and firm, unforgettably expert as a presiding officer and equally skilled as a shepherd of souls either together in a flock or one by one. He lived with a vivid awareness of God's voice and no one in the length and breadth of the ULCA ever had the slightest doubt that he had also been God's choice.

Tribute was also paid to the first secretary, M. G. G. Scherer. "He was the first to invoke the blessing of God" upon the ULCA "convening it in the name of the Father and the Son and the Holy Ghost." "He infused into our church in its earliest days the calm, temperate and steadfast spirit of his heritage."

In acknowledging the first treasurer, E. Clarence Miller, Fry reminded the delegates that it was Miller who shocked everybody at the first meeting of the joint committee for the approaching Reformation Quadricentennial by proposing that the celebration be a union of the three bodies. Miller was also the only officer "elected on the first ballot at the outset of the church."

Turning to his own colleagues, Fry took special pleasure in giving honor to the "beloved Dr. Walton H. Greever" who at age ninety-two was present at the convention and "whose ministry spans both halves of the history of the ULCA." "An apostle of unity far ahead of most of us, he was editor of the all-synodical and non-synodical *American Lutheran Survey*, a long, long generation ago, and while he rejoices to see the union that we are achieving, he must be disappointed that it is so much more meager than he had dreamed."

The next in "the gallery of honor" was Henry Beisler whose "life is as full as any of the noblest of all virtues, the virtue of gratitude." Fry mentioned that Beisler, in anticipation of the merger, had joined an Augustana congregation that was anticipating building a "costly new sanctuary, where he could help."

F. Eppling Reinartz, president of the Southern Seminary and one-time secretary of the church, was beautifully described and honored as a "poetic spirit" who never held himself back from the prosaic tasks. While immersed in the papers that were inseparable from his office, he never failed to see faces and behind them the souls of men." The last and present treasurer, Edmund F. Wagner, was described as a "competent business man, with only one face and that a face of honor . . . a manifestation of what the church lives to produce and a justification of what it is."

George F. Harkins was the last to be acknowledged. Fry referred to him "as my brother and my own closest colleague. . . . No one has meant more to me or has looked more deeply into my very soul. For thirteen years he has been trusted, tactful, all but indispensable, a good genius to me as to all his other companions, always a stabilizing spirit, a rare blend of serenity and action. . . . For one and all, and not the least for the last, I say, thank God."

Then without naming individuals, Fry paid tribute to the Executive Board, the executive secretaries of the various boards, the departments and all who served on their staffs, "men and women too who had in them the salt that has not lost its savor." He also remembered the editors of *The Lutheran*, the leaders of the auxiliaries, the presidents of the synods, "varied as they can be and yet all of them alike in being conscientious, dedicated undershepherds for their Lord."

Fry was not finished acknowledging partners. "But my widest appreciation has not yet been mentioned. It is to my brother pastors in the thousands and to the loyal laity of the ULCA behind them." He reminded the convention that Knubel at the 1938 convention called attention to the fact that "the strength of the church in any generation—and it is certainly true of the long one through which ULCA has lived—is in its vigorous and vital parishes." Then back to the pastor who leads the congregation.

The man, the parson, is still the man with the word in his mouth and the sacraments in his hands, the instructor of the young, the counselor of the grieved, the one who is called to be the spokesman, the visible representative of the Most High God. I salute my seniors, I link my arms with my contemporaries, I exult in those who come after me as a living proof of Christ's unfailing promise that he will never leave us nor forsake us, that he will build his church."

Fry had more to say about the laity. "The most heartening development in the ULCA has been not only the volunteering of laymen to elevate stewardship in life, but of men from every calling and rank in society who are eager to serve their Lord in every way in our share of his church.

Dedication. President Fry's parting words expressed the long-standing ULCA commitment to fuller Lutheran unity, now finally being realized:

Now, overdue, it is time for a parting word of dedication. Facing the future, with the ULCA trailing behind us, we face Christ. It is his voice that we hear; in his obedience we go forward.

It is for him that we seek unity, not for the sake of prestige, but for the amplification of our human resources, certainly not in a spirit of rivalry toward any of our other brethren, not even because those with whom we are merging are congenial and attractive people. All such motives are prudential and are foreign to the Lord of us all. It is all tremendously simple. He wills that his followers who are one in confession should manifest that oneness before men. Anything less is false witness to the One in whom we all believe.

Him the new church will exist to serve. He will continue to be the one Lord in whom there is one faith and one ransom for sins. He is the one shepherd and bishop of our souls. As he leads us through new corridors on the way toward mansions in the Father's house, we follow Christ.

By him we reverently believe the ULCA was brought into being. At his call we strike our tents. To the only wise God our Savior be glory and majesty, dominion and power, our love and our obedience now and forever.

Notes

1. ULCA *Minutes* 1962: 360.
2. See William Adolf Visser 't Hooft, *Memoirs* (London: SCM Press; Philadelphia: Westminster, 1973), 282-86. *Pastor's Desk Book* 1960 NE-1176.
3. Franklin W. Kemp, St. Andrews-by-the-Sea (eightieth), 1970, 107.
4. ULCA *Minutes* 1960: 362.
5. ULCA *Minutes* 1960: 1037.
6. ULCA *Minutes* 1960: 65, 1038.
7. Ibid., 1037.
8. Ibid., 632.
9. Ibid.
10. Ibid., 442-443.
11. LCA Constituting Convention June 28-July 1, 1962 "Bulletin of Reports" 18. The complete text of Articles of Consolidation are found on pges 7-21. Also, see ULCA *Minutes* 1960.
12. ULCA *Minutes* 1960: 657.
13. ULCA *Minutes* 1960: 658.
14. ULCA *Minutes* 1960: 659.
15. Ibid., 661.
16. See above, Ch. 1. ULCA *Minutes* 1960: 669.
17. Ibid. 670.
18. Ibid., 89.
19. Ibid., 593f.
20. Ibid., 1026-27.
21. ULCA *Minutes* 1940: 63, 145.
22. The Executive Board Committee was composed of three members: Ernst P. Pfatteicher, Henry H. Bagger, and Ellis B. Burgess.
23. Augsburg Confession, Article VII, in the 1911 translation by H. E. Jacobs: *The Book of Concord: or, The Symbolical books of the Evangelical Lutheran Church.* (Philadelphia: United Lutheran Publication House, 1911, [1916 printing].) In the Latin: "congregatio."
24. ULCA *Minutes* 1940: 63; 1960: 934.
25. See T. Tappert, ed.: *The Book of Concord: The Confessions of the Evangelical Lutheran Church* (Philadelphia: Fortress Press), 32. See also *Der Bekenntnisschriften der evangelisch-lutherische* Kirche (Gottingen: Vandenhoeck und Ruprecht, 1930) 1: 50; and Schlink, Edmund, *Thelogie der Lutheranischen bekenntnisschriften* (Munchen: Evangelischerverlag Albert Lamp, 1940), translated into English as *Theology of the Lutheran Confessions* (Philadelphia: Fortress Press, 1985, 1961) 256-258.
26. ULCA *Minutes* 1958: 1012.
27. ULCA *Minutes* 1956: 1184.
28. ULCA *Minutes* 1958: 1012-13.
29. ULCA *Minutes* 1960: 926.

30. Ibid., 929.

31. Ibid., 930.

32. Ibid., 931.

33. Ibid., 932, 1066.

34. Ibid., 637.

35. Ibid., 933-34. By 1964, however, the LCA revised this statement; see Gilbert, *Commitment*, 151 f.

36. ULCA *Minutes* 1960, 1115-6.

37. Ibid., 19.

38. ULCA *Minutes* 1962: 703-04.

39. Lutheran Church in America *Yearbook* 1963, 4.

40. Ibid., 5.

41. The complete text of Fry's speech can be found in ULCA *Minutes* 1962: 659-665, and in the *Pastor's Desk Book*, September 1962.

Postscript:

Retrospectives

THE FINAL REPORTS TO THE 1962 ULCA CONVENTION allow us to look back over various structures, offices, boards, departments, committees, and auxiliaries of the ULCA. Some of them have received extensive treatment in previous chapters, but others should now receive their due. The order is that of the ULCA constitution: congregations, synods, churchwide conventions, officers, boards, departments, and committees.

Congregations

The relationship between the ULCA structure and its congregations was both basic and confused. At the very outset, as stated in the preamble of the 1918 constitution, "We members of Evangelical Lutheran congregations invite all Evangelical Lutheran congregations and synods in America . . . to unite with us . . . in the United Lutheran Church in America."[1] Thereafter, however, reference to congregations goes into eclipse. They remain implied, as shown in the duty of the ULCA "to protect and enforce its Doctrinal Basis,"[2] as cited above. But, as both presidents Knubel and Fry wrestled with the problem in their time, how was this enforcement of "pure preaching and right administration of the sacraments in all its Synods and congregations"[3] to be accomplished? At best it was done indirectly, the synods cooperating. At worst, it was bypassed, leaving the ULCA itself exposed to its ever ready critics. Neither before nor after the Commission on Organizational Structure was the gulf between the ULCA and its congregations effectively bridged.[4]

Synods

Although synods were the structural hallmark of the United Lutheran Church in America, forty-five of them were too much of a good thing. The merger of the three general bodies in 1918 set the stage for the merger of overlapping and often competing synods, as well as the merging of small synods adjacent to one another. All but one of the mergers took place between 1919 and 1929. The other came in 1938 when the Central Pennsylvania Synod was created by the merger of four synods. New synods continued to form. The Slovak Zion (in 1919) was an ethnic non-geographic body formed by recent immigrants who had come prior to World War I from the then Austro-Hungarian Empire in the area later known as Czechoslovakia. The Florida Synod joined in 1929.

In Canada, a 1925 merger had joined two synods into the Central Canada Synod. Together with the Nova Scotia (1903) and Manitoba (1891) synods, hope was growing for a united Lutheran church in Canada that would include other Lutheran church bodies.

The 1950s saw the formation of two new synods, beginning with that of New Jersey (June 20, 1950). At long last the congregations in the Garden State—hitherto divided between the United Synod of New York and New England, the Pennsylvania Ministerium, and the Central (formerly East) Pennsylvania judicatories—now became one synod, with the difficult task of consolidating their own history. Then, in an unusual convergence offshore, the Caribbean Synod, organized May 30, 1952, brought together the once Afro-Danish congregations in the Virgin Islands and the Hispanic congregations of the Missionary Conference in Puerto Rico. All of them had been under the supervision of the Board of American Missions almost since the formation of the ULCA.

The Evangelical Lutheran Synod in the Central States, organized June 8, 1954, brought together the former synods of Kansas (1868), Nebraska (1871), and Midwest (1890, the German Nebraska).[5] In Pennsylvania there was a realignment of the historic but outmoded boundaries between the Ministerium and the Central Pennsylvania Synod. As of 1954 the number of ULCA synods stood at thirty two and remained at that figure until 1962, when extensive rearrangements of synodical structures and functions were occasioned by the formation of the Lutheran Church in America.

Constituent Synods

Listed in the order of their founding, as in the ULCA *Minutes;* see also the list of synod mergers below

1. Ministerium of Pennsylvania (Aug. 15, 1748)
2. United Synod of New York and New England (Oct. 23, 1786)
3. United Synod of North Carolina (May 2, 1803)
4. Maryland Synod (Oct. 11, 1820)
5. Synod of South Carolina (Jan. 14, 1824)
6. Central Pennsylvania Synod (Sept. 5, 1825)
7. Synod of Virginia (Aug. 10, 1829)
8. Synod of Ohio (Nov. 7, 1836)
9. Pittsburgh Synod (Jan. 15, 1845)
10. Indiana Synod (Oct. 28, 1848)
11. Illinois Synod (Sept. 8, 1851; first org. 1856)
12. Synod of Texas and Louisiana (Nov. 10, 1851)
13. Synod of Iowa (Feb. 10, 1854)
14. Mississippi Synod (July 25, 1855)
15. Michigan Synod (Oct. 27, 1855)
16. Georgia-Alabama Synod (July 20, 1860)

17. Synod of Canada (July 21, 1861)
18. Central States Synod (Nov. 5, 1868)
19. Wartburg Synod (1875)
20. Icelandic Synod (June 25, 1885)
21. Synod of the Pacific Southwest (April 5, 1891)
22. Rocky Mountain Synod (May 6, 1891)
23. Synod of the Northwest (Sept. 23, 1891)
24. Synod of Western Canada (July 16, 1897)
25. Pacific Synod (Sept. 26, 1901)
26. Nova Scotia Synod (July 10, 1903)
27. Synod of West Virginia (April 17, 1912)
28. Slovak Lutheran Zion Synod (June 10, 1919)
29. Synod of Florida (Sept. 24, 1928)
30. Kentucky-Tennessee Synod (June 6, 1934)
31. Synod of New Jersey (June 20, 1950)
32. Caribbean Synod (May 30, 1952)

The synod mergers, at a glance, were these:

Pittsburgh Synod	Nov. 18, 1919	reunited the two Pittsburgh Synods
Illinois Synod	June 10, 1920	united Synods of Northern Illinois (1851) GS Central Illinois (1862) GS Southern Illinois (1901) GS part of Chicago (1896) GC
Michigan Synod	June 10, 1920	united congregations in Michigan plus part of Chicago GC part of Indiana (1896) GS
Indiana Synod	June 24, 1920	united Olive Branch (1848) GS plus part of Chicago GC
Ohio Synod	Nov. 3, 1920	united Synods of East Ohio(1836) GS Miami (1844) GS Wittenberg (1847) GS Ohio (1861) GC
No. Carolina Synod	March 2, 1921	united North Carolina (1903) and part of Tennessee(1820) USS
Virginia Synod	March 17, 1922	united Synods of Virginia (1829) Southwestern Virginia (1842) Holston (1860) USS

Susquehanna Synod	Sept. 5, 1923	united Synods of Central Pennsylvania(1855) and Susquehanna (1867) GS
Canada Synod	June 12, 1925	united Synods of Canada (1861) and Central Canada (1908) GC
United Synod of New York	June 5, 1929	united NY Ministerium (1786) GC NY & New England (1902) GC NY Synod (1908), comprising three former synods: Hartwick (1830), Franckean (1837), NY and NJ (1872) GS
Central Pennsylvania Synod	June 8, 1938	united four bodies of GS origin: Allegheny Synod (1842) East Pennsylvania (1842) Susquehanna Synod (1867) including Central Pennsylvania Synod itself (1855) West Pennsylvania Synod (1825)
Central States Synod	June 8, 1954	United Kansas (1868) and Midwest Nebraska (1871)

CONVENTIONS

The convention, like the United States Congress, was the highest legislative authority, depending on informed lay and clerical participants. The constitution does not explain the significance of the convention, but it defines and determines the membership of it, indicates its legislative function, and provides for equitable representation. Throughout its history, however, the twenty-two biennial conventions have contributed enormously to the ULCA becoming mutually acquainted with itself beyond the transaction of the church's business.

A reading of the meticulous minutes even at this latter day recalls the manifold human dimension that lent joy and inspiration—and at times tedium and frustration—to the business at hand. The volumes of these printed proceedings grew in size, from under six hundred pages in 1920 to more than thirteen hundred pages in 1956. Missing from them, with rare exception, is the local color of the meeting place. Yet each of the cities, from coast to coast and in Canada, was chosen for the purpose of manifesting a ULCA presence; and, conversely, for informing the ULCA itself about the nature of its continental outreach.

The ULCA conventions were all-male until 1948. In that year, of the 582 elected delegates, two synods, United of New York and California, each included a woman in its delegation. Four years later, there were seven women. The last convention, (Detroit, 1962) included twenty-seven women among its 681 delegates. This was a slow, small beginning, but an accelerating change was in the offing with the new Lutheran Church in America.

Convention Sites and Dates

1918	New York City, Nov. 18
1920	Washington, D. C., Oct. 19-27
1922	Buffalo, New York, Oct. 17-25
1924	Chicago, Illinois, Oct. 21-29
1926	Richmond, Virginia, Oct. 19-27
1928	Erie, Pennsylvania, Oct. 9-16
1930	Milwaukee, Wisconsin, Oct. 7-14
1932	Philadelphia, Pennsylvania, Oct. 12-19
1934	Savannah, Georgia, Oct. 17-24
1936	Columbus, Ohio, Oct. 14-21
1938	Baltimore, Maryland, Oct. 5-12
1940	Omaha, Nebraska, Oct. 9-16
1942	Louisville, Kentucky, Oct. 14-21
1944	Minneapolis, Minnesota, Oct. 11-17
1946	Cleveland, Ohio, Oct. 5-11
1948	Philadelphia, Pennsylvania, Oct. 6-14
1950	Des Moines, Iowa, Oct. 4-12
1952	Seattle, Washington, Oct. 8-15
1954	Toronto, Canada, Oct. 6-12
1956	Harrisburg, Pennsylvania, Oct. 10-17
1958	Dayton, Ohio, Oct. 8-15
1960	Atlantic City, New Jersey, Oct. 13-20
1962	Detroit, Michigan, June 25-27

OFFICERS

President, secretary, treasurer—these three, and no more, were the top elected officers of the ULCA. The president and secretary are salaried officials, devoting full-time to their tasks. They were *ex-officio* members of the Executive Board. Before 1918 few church bodies had full-time officers. Among the Lutherans (so far as this author has determined) the ULCA president and secretary were the first to serve full-time in their respective offices.

President

In addition to what has already been said about the Knubel presidency and the Fry presidency, it suffices here to emphasize that the ULCA was fortunate in the comparatively long terms of service of its presidents.

Secretary

Nowhere was information about the ULCA more heavily concentrated, and nowhere was the work performed in greater anonymity, than in the Office of the Secretary. In 1960 the Rev. George Frederick Harkins was moved from the position (since 1949) of assistant to the president to that of secretary of the ULCA by election. He succeeded F. Eppling Reinartz who had served as secretary for thirteen years (1947-60). The practice of near anonymity was introduced by M. G. G. Sherer (1918-1932) and subsequently maintained by his successor, Walton Harlow Greever (1932-1946). The outsider inclines to take the actual work for granted.

From the secretary's office the *Year Book* appeared annually and on time. Few persons realize the painstaking efforts that go into this kind of product or fathom the sustained accuracy required. Manifestly the secretary has helpers, but where do their names appear that they may be thanked? The Office of the Secretary served the ULCA as statistician, archivist, and necrologist. Evidence of these and many other duties culminate in the biennial conventions of the church: the preparation, the gathering and publication of the "Bulletin of Reports," the taking of the convention protocol and finally the publication of the completed *Minutes*.

To this author, George Harkins became the *de facto* historian of the ULCA. Acquaintance with his work raised to new heights this regard and also for Harkins' predecessors, all but the first of whom he counted as friend. The complete set of ULCA *Minutes*, indispensable in writing this book, stem from his father's library and were then continued on his own.

The final volume (*Minutes of the Adjourned Meeting of the Twenty-second Biennial Convention of the United Lutheran Church in America, Detroit, Michigan, June 25-27, 1962*) arouses a distinctive tug of remembrance. It depicts a church body at full strength, yet throttled down for a joyfully awaited consolidation.

Treasurer

The United Lutheran Church was served by three devout and efficient treasurers during its forty-four years. All were capable and successful businessmen who kept the Lord's business in good order.

E. Clarence Miller	1918-1944
Henry Beisler	1944-1952
Edmund F. Wagner	1952-1962

Executive Board

The Executive Board as well as eight other boards were elected by the biennial convention of delegates. These units, along with a dozen or more appointive commissions or standing committees, carried out the executive functions of the church. Together they comprised the ULCA bureaucracy, in the positive sense. Its center piece was the Executive Board, whose initial membership of twelve was increased to eighteen in 1954. The church's three officers were *ex-officio* members. The Executive Board's duties ranged widely. It carried out the resolutions of the church convention; filled vacancies not otherwise provided for; received reports from the other boards, regulated their funding, and coordinated their work; prepared a budget for the biennium, proposed its apportionment among the synods; represented the ULCA, and otherwise attended the church's business between conventions.[6]

Considering the ULCA as a federation of autonomous synods, the Executive Board represented an impressive concentration of power. As might be expected, such power was not left unchallenged, certainly not by other boards. It remained for the Commission of Adjudication to render a decisive opinion on an appeal on behalf of one of the boards from the Maryland Synod. "The authority of the Executive Board," according to Adjudication,

> is in various respects different from that of the departmental Boards. The other boards are charged with the administration of certain departments of work, not further described in the Constitution and Bylaws than as the name and designation of the respective Board indicates. . . . The Executive Board, on the other hand, is charged with a number of duties more or less distinctly specified in the Constitution, all of which may be comprehended under the idea of general administration... [that] inevitably includes a certain degree of supervision of the work of the other Boards.[7]

It was not surprising that the Executive Board, in time, found its supervisory role expanding. Among the appointive standing committees were some whose functions became increasingly germane to the ongoing life of the church. At the 1954 recommendation of the Commission on Organizational Structure (COS) several committees were consolidated into departments administered by the Executive Board: Church Architecture; Worship; Stewardship; and Press, Radio, and Television.

In practice, the Executive Board epitomized the ULCA. Its members received the impact of presidential leadership and, in return, they helped keep a president attuned to the needs and mind of the church. To the church at-large, this select circle appeared at times to radiate an aura of dignity and wisdom, and at other times a penchant for legalism or even triviality. Whatever the case, the Executive Board was an indispensable partner with the president in the administration of the church.

COURT OF ADJUDICATION

The Court of Adjudication and Interpretation, like the United States Supreme Court, had the "power and duty to decide all disputed questions of doctrine, principle and practice" that might arise in the ULCA and were properly referred. In 1958 it replaced the little-used Commission of Adjudication and then acquired the power to give opinions on "moot questions." The nine members of the court consisted of "six ministers and three laymen, learned in the doctrine, the law and the practice of the church, who shall be appointed by the President of the church for a term of six years each, subject to confirmation by the convention."[8] Over the years the members, representing various areas of the continent as well as the three merged traditions, had fulfilled the church's expectation for fairness and clarity. According to the Rev. Robbin B. Wolf, its president in 1961, the paucity of the court's business was "a good indication of the fundamental strengths of the ULCA."[9]

BOARDS

Like the synods, the boards were relatively autonomous components. There were initially twelve departmental boards, mostly taken over from the merging bodies. Not surprisingly, each had its vested interests, programs and methods. In the early years of the ULCA, much energy had to be devoted to achieve a more rational and efficient pattern. Their membership, elected by the biennial convention, ranged from nine to twenty-one. Each board elected its own officers, called its own staff, was separately incorporated (to meet legal requirements), shaped its policies and programs in accord with those of the church body, submitted its minutes and financial records to the Executive Board, presented its report and recommendations to the biennial convention for approval and action, and refrained from soliciting funds without church approval. No board had the right to enter upon any official relationship with another board of the church, or with any other ecclesiastical body or agency, without the approval of the Executive Board. By the mid 1920s the number of boards had been consolidated to eight.

Board of Foreign Missions

Executive Secretary: The Rev. E. S. Erb; Board President: The Rev. Paul L. Graf.

In its lengthy 1962 report the Board of Foreign Missions did not dwell on history but gave a vivid account of the present situation. After paying tribute to a fine working relationship with Augustana, and the generous support from United Lutheran Church Women, the report recognized its relations with inter-Lutheran and ecumenical mission agencies, introduced new missionaries, and paid tribute to the retiring and those departed. The present state of the work was then expounded.

The School of Missions, located on the campus of the Chicago Lutheran

Theological Seminary, had completed five years of training missionaries for overseas service. During the biennium, twenty-nine ULCA missionaries, including eleven wives, were given pre-field orientation. Among the missionaries there were eight pastors, two nurses, one seminary professor, one agriculturist, one industrialist, and two business administrators.

Argentina established several new congregations, one being multilingual (Spanish, German, Slovak). Currently there are twenty-two congregations with a baptized membership of 4,193. The seminary has begun an ambitious task of translating Luther's Works into Spanish. The church was honored by a visit of the Rev. and Mrs. Fry and the executive secretary, Rev. Erb.

British Guiana. The most significant event was the ordination of three theological candidates and the reception of one from Ohio, bringing the number of Guiana pastors to seven. Three more, completing studies at Waterloo, Canada, were to be ordained in 1962. An emphasis on stewardship has been very successful. Every congregation desiring a new chapel must first raise 10 percent of the cost. The church now has eighteen primary schools, fourteen aided by the government. The church also had visits from President Fry, Erb, and Bishop Manikam from India.

Hong Kong. The Rev. Peng Fu, president of the Lutheran Church of Hong Kong since its organization in 1957 and before that the president of the Lutheran Church in China, retired in 1961 and was succeeded by the Rev. Wu Ming-Chieh. He was pastor of the Un Long congregation of fifteen hundred members. Truth Lutheran Church on the Lutheran Center site was dedicated by Erb in December 1961. A Lutheran middle school in rented quarters has an enrollment of 808 students and fifty-seven teachers. The ULCA three-year missionaries serve as English instructors. Sponsored by LWF-DWM, a conference on theological education for the Chinese of the South East Area was held in Hong Kong in 1960. It seems that Hong Kong, Taiwan, and Malaya will have to develop separate institutions for education of pastors. Through the efforts of LWF, a China Advisory Committee has been formed to serve as a liaison agency between the Lutheran church of Hong Kong and the various overseas groups supporting the work.

India. The New Delhi Assembly of the WCC afforded the opportunity for President and Mrs. Fry, Rev. and Mrs. Erb, as well as President and Mrs. Lundeen, and Rev. P. O. Bersell of Augustana to visit Andhra Evangelical Church in 1961. The Rev. J. F. Neudoerffer, field secretary, spent eight months in India. A new relationship was established with the Tamil Lutheran Church when the ULCA sent an Augustana missionary for work in an industrial school. Inter-Lutheran and inter-denominational work is progressing, including the formation of a united seminary at Luthergiri. Students in bachelor of divinity and master of theology degrees at Gurukul Seminary are bringing increased attention to the school. The need for new missionaries is a priority.

Japan. A study of the work of the church by representatives of both the ULCA and the Japan Evangelical Lutheran Church in November 1961 produced valuable insight. Board members, the Rev. Ralph Loew, the Rev. Samuel Kidd, the Rev. Carl Tambert, and Josephine Darmstaetter, secretary of Lutheran Church Women, represented the ULCA. On Reformation Day 1962, the thirty-year-old Japan Evangelical Lutheran Church (an affiliate of the ULCA) was expanded to include nine synods stretching from Sapporo to Kagoshima. This was the outcome of ten years of negotiating with eight overseas Lutheran groups with whom the JELC will continue to have cooperative relations. JELC has sent a missionary to Brazil to work among the Japanese who have settled there. Erb and David Vikner visited the church in 1960 and 1961.

Liberia. Four graduates of the three-year theological course at the Lutheran Training Center were ordained at a special service where the Rev. Paul Graf, president of the board, preached the sermon. By 1965, the Lutheran Church and the Mission will begin to operate as one. A number of Liberian students have gained post graduate degrees in the United States. Plans have been made for a new Phoebe Hospital that will then become a nursing school. The Rev. H. L. Gilbert, staff secretary for Liberia, visited the mission in 1961 and 1962.

Malaya. In 1961, efforts of the ULCA missionaries and those of Tamil-related workers from Sweden have resulted in a joint committee for the organization of a single Lutheran Church in Malaya with three language sections: English, Tamil, and Chinese. In order to prepare qualified clergymen there will be a cooperative arrangement with the inter-denominational Trinity College in Singapore. The Bible Training Institute graduated its first nine students in June 1962. President and Mrs. Fry and Rev. and Mrs. Erb visited Malaya in November 1961. Vikner visited several times.

Uruguay. The work begun in 1945 by the ULCA came under NLC administration in 1952, and since 1957 is under the direction of the Augustana Board with the ULCA board cooperating. Work is mainly in Montevideo and Rivera where a new church has been completed. Erb visited in 1962.

Chile. New work has begun among Spanish-speaking people at the invitation of and cooperation with the Evangelical Lutheran Church in Chile. It will be to carry on evangelism among Spanish-speaking people who are not affiliated with the ELCC.

Board of American Missions

Executive Secretary: The Rev. Donald L. Houser; Board President: H. T. Rasmussen.

Through the years since the Board of American Missions was formed in 1926, 1,298 congregations were organized. There had been years of salvaging congregations due to economic conditions; other years when people were moving to the cities, and town and country congregations needed special attention. During the war years housing projects demanded attention so that disrupted families could have the support of the gospel. There were years of caring for "displaced persons" and the need for organizing bilingual congregations. There were postwar years when the "nation became alive with moving people," and there was a new sense of urgency to follow the people and plant the church. Then there were the years when the church became awake to what was happening in the city and the changes taking place around congregations with disappearing numbers. Would they welcome their new neighbors? There were plenty of opportunities for mission, but never enough money to support the need of buying parsonages and building first units. The convention of 1958 allowed the board to borrow $8 million for working capital, which proved to be a good investment.

In addition to church extension the board assumed other responsibilities over its forty-four years: Mission to the American Indians in Rocky Boy, Montana, in 1926; Southern Mountain work in Konnarock, Virginia, in 1939; Canadian work among the Finns and Icelanders in 1946. Work in Hawaii began during the war years. Meanwhile the work in Puerto Rico and the Virgin Islands was strengthened, all in an effort to bring the Gospel to people of various ethnic and racial strains.[10]

Board of Social Missions

Executive Secretary: The Rev. Harold Haas; Board President: The Rev. Alfred H. Stone.

The Board of Social Missions founded in 1938 by the eleventh biennial convention gave a lengthy report to the twenty-second adjourned convention in 1962.[11] The report reminded the Church that it had been formed by combining the Inner Mission Board, the Committee on Evangelism, and the Committee on Moral and Social Welfare. All three had been in existence since the early days of the ULCA. To carry on the work of the three merged entities, the Board maintained three departments: Evangelism, Inner Mission and Social Action. Over the years all three departments became intertwined with other ULCA boards and units as well as with the National Lutheran Council and the National Council of Churches. During the last biennium of its existence, the Board of Social Missions became more involved in and controlled by the coming merger. Although the BSM had announced to the 1960 convention that it had appointed a commission to study the "Role of the Church in Social Welfare," the merger approval suggested that Augustana be asked to join in the study. With Augustana's consent a thirteen-member joint commission continued the study begun by the ULCA Commission. It was the hope that a finished report would "serve as a foundation for policy formulation in the Lutheran Church in America." Another study on the "Causes of Crime" requested by the 1960 convention was considered by the board to be so involved that it would continue far beyond the time of the merger. Therefore, six prominent and competent people in this field were requested to write brief articles on various aspects of the subject. These were distributed through the *Pastor's Desk Book*, and also combined and printed in a pamphlet form.

Out of many informal as well as planned meetings came a "common understanding of concepts" as well as a "proposal for the development of policies and program materials that might be helpful in the future." These were forwarded to the Joint Commission on Lutheran Unity.

Board of Deaconess Work

Executive Secretary: Sister Mildred I. Winter; Board President: The Rev. C. Donald Heft.

The 1962 report of the Board of Deaconess Work began with a tribute to the Rev. J. L. Deaton who had served on the board since 1952 and was the president at the time of his death on November 8, 1960. He had also served on the Board of Trustees of the Philadelphia Motherhouse and the Board of Management of the Baltimore Motherhouse. Prior to his election to the Board of Deaconess Work he had been president of the Board of Higher Education for eight years. With this background he helped prepare the way for the deaconess work to be consolidated with the proposed Board of Education and Church Vocations of the new church.

A step in this direction occurred in 1961 when the deaconesses themselves proposed that the Baltimore and Philadelphia sisterhoods and motherhouses be combined. A study committee composed of the two directing sisters (Anna Ebert and Anna Melville), legal counsel, representatives of the Executive Board of the ULCA, of the two institutions and of the Deaconess Board explored the situation and found it feasible. When both sisterhoods voted in favor of the merger, the Board of Deaconess Work assigned a special committee of the Board to work out a specific plan. First the Baltimore Motherhouse and School had to be incorporated. Then it and the corporation of the Philadelphia Motherhouse could enter into an agreement to function as a single deaconess house and school, and the two sisterhoods could combine into one with one motherhouse and one retirement center. At the time of the merger, the total number of sisters, including the retired, was 165. They were all listed in the 1962 report. The plan indicated that in the fall of 1962 there should be one deaconess school conducted by two houses, temporarily on the Baltimore campus. It would continue to be a specialized college (two years) devoted to the concentrated preparations of church workers. It would be affiliated with church related colleges and universities which would confer the bachelor degrees. A program of graduate study with several theological seminaries was expected. These plans were approved by the Executive Board of the ULCA.

In anticipation of the seventieth anniversary of the Baltimore Motherhouse and the seventy-fifth of the Philadelphia Motherhouse in 1959, the Board of Deaconess Work reviewed its history and development for the 1958 convention. With an upcoming merger in 1962, the final report highlighted other aspects.

Beginnings. The General Synod in 1889 appointed a twelve-man Board of Deaconess Work. Its purpose was to establish within the church the office of deaconess. By 1893 there were six young women ready for training. Four were sent to Kaiserwerth Motherhouse in Germany and two to the Deaconess Motherhouse in Philadelphia. They were consecrated on October 23, 1895, by the General Synod. This was significant, for rarely since early Christianity had a church body taken action to bring the diaconate into its organic structure. A rented house in Baltimore served as the first Motherhouse and training school for Deaconesses and also for other women intending to become foreign missionaries or parish workers. This, too, was a significant first step that led to others. Within the first decade there were so many women inquiring about opportunities to prepare for service in church institutions that the Board reviewed its training program and in 1910 opened a specialized school to prepare women for full-time church work. "For almost a half century it was the only ULCA institution where women other than deaconesses could secure training for varied types of church service."[12]

In 1911, a new motherhouse was built modeled after the Augsburg Motherhouse in Germany. It served until 1952 when the state of Maryland purchased it for a State Teacher's College for Negroes. Fortunately the twenty-eight-acre campus of a former girls' school was available; it was providing excellent facilities for the Motherhouse and school at the time of the merger.

When the ULCA was formed in 1918 the work of the General Synod became the responsibility of the Board of Deaconess Work of the new church body. This Board was instructed to "awaken a general interest in the office of deaconess," to "maintain a Lutheran Deaconess Motherhouse in Baltimore;" and to cooperate with the other two Motherhouses conducted by self-perpetuating boards, the Philadelphia Motherhouse and the Milwaukee Motherhouse.[13] The latter, founded in 1893, was an offshoot of work begun in 1849 when Theodore Fliedner brought four deaconesses to Pittsburgh to assist Passavant in his Infirmary (later Passavant Hospital) and the other inner mission agencies he founded. The Motherhouse was supported by an autonomous association, the "Institute of Protestant Deaconesses." Its directing pastor, H. L. Fritschel, was a member of the German Iowa Synod. The sisters served in many General Council institutions. Nevertheless, since the deaconesses came largely from the Midwest church bodies, the Motherhouse chose to be an inter-synodical institution. The last report from Milwaukee was in 1926.[14] Friendly relations were maintained through the Lutheran Deaconess Conference, the oldest inter-Lutheran organization in America (1894) to which nine Lutheran deaconess groups were related. In June 1961 the conference met at the Baltimore Motherhouse.

Cooperation with Philadelphia continued and over the years grew stronger. This Motherhouse was not founded by a church but by an individual. John D. Lankenau, president of the board of the German Hospital (later named for him), had in 1884 persuaded seven sisters from Iserlahn, Germany, to come to Philadelphia to manage the hospital. The sisters also came with a desire to establish a center for preparing young women to serve their church "in every avenue of ministering love."[15] Three years later (1887) a charter was granted to a new corporation known as the Mary J. Drexel Home and Philadelphia Motherhouse of Deaconesses. It was to be managed by a self-perpetuating Board of Trustees "of Lutheran faith." The Board was responsible for a Home for the Aged and the Motherhouse. Within a year Lankenau had provided such a commodious home that there was adequate space for the sisters, the new recruits, a home for the aged and also a children's hospital and a girls' school. From the very beginning a training program was established that prepared teachers for Christian kindergartens and schools as well as nurses for hospitals and other institutions.

Cooperation and Growth. During the early years of the ULCA, both Motherhouses under the guidance of the Board of Deaconess Work expanded their range of service. There were always more requests for deaconesses than could be filled. Educational standards continued to advance. In 1943 the board inaugurated specialized courses for health and welfare services at Philadelphia and for parish work and related fields at Baltimore. (By 1958, these two schools had trained 1,195 deaconesses and lay workers.)[16] A year later, arrangements were made with ULCA colleges so that bachelor degrees could be granted to female church personnel. The most capable women, including deaconesses, were encouraged to continue their education in fields of special need. As noted in chapter 8, the 1940s were years when women were asserting their rights and showing their leadership, also in the church. In 1947 a closer organizational relationship between the United Lutheran Church and the Philadelphia Motherhouse was achieved.

There were also organizational changes within the Philadelphia Motherhouse Corporation. In 1942 the Lankenau Girls' School moved to the Germantown section of Philadelphia and became separately incorporated. The Children's Hospital became the Mary J. Drexel Department of the Lankenau Hospital which moved to the Overbrook area of Philadelphia in 1953. In the same year the Home for the Aged moved to Bala Cynwyd. The Motherhouse and School moved into a magnificent home in Gladwyne, Pennsylvania, a gift of the Pew Memorial Foundation.

The innovative fifties saw the deaconesses entering ever new fields of service and also new geographic areas. In 1950, Sister Mildred Winter, who had served the board as promotional and field secretary, was elected by the Board of Deaconess Work to be its executive secretary. She was the only woman to serve the ULCA in such an important position. The first deaconess trained as an occupational therapist was soon using her skills in a Lutheran home for the aging. Another deaconess developed a school for severely retarded children. Another was sent to Alaska to supervise the nursing in a hospital sponsored by the Pacific Synod. The demand for deaconesses was far greater than could be supplied.

In an attempt to ease the situation, the board in 1956 submitted a plan to the Harrisburg convention. It was a challenge to women to give one year of their life to the service of the church. They would work without pay, but would receive maintenance and a small cash allowance. The board decided to call these short-term workers Associates in Deaconess Service. The church readily accepted the plan and it was given wide publicity. The board secretaries visited nineteen synods, *The Lutheran* gave it visibility, and the *Desk Book* brought it to the attention of all pastors. The first year thirty women responded. They ranged in age from twenty-one to sixty-four years, in education from one year of high school to graduate study and advanced degrees. They were homemakers and professional women of all types. They came from seventeen synods in all parts of the U.S. and Canada. They had two things in common: a joyous Christian faith and a desire to serve their church. Each group was given a three-week orientation and then sent to the place that needed their skills. The first year was so successful that a continuation of the program had the support of the Board and the entire ULCA. In 1960 the convention adopted a recommendation that the Deaconess Year Program be continued as a responsibility of the Board of Deaconess Work. August 1961 provided the eighth opportunity for women to begin a year of loving service. By the 1962 convention, seventy-five Associates in Deaconess Service had served in forty-two agencies. About a third of them remained in church service.

Two important books on the diaconate were brought to the attention of the 1962 convention. *On Call—Deaconesses Across the World*, by Catherine Herzel, a twelve-year member of the Board of Deaconess Work, was for young women choosing a vocation. The other, *Love's Response, A Story of Lutheran Deaconesses in America* by Frederick S. Weiser, was written at the request of the board. It is a well-researched and readable book that traces the biblical, theological and sociological aspects of the deaconess movement. A doctoral thesis by the Rev. Paul John Kirsch, "Deaconesses in the United States Since 1918," is interdenominational in its scope.[17] For the seventy-fifth anniversary of the Philadelphia Motherhouse, a booklet on the women's diaconate in historical perspective was written by the son of E. F. Bachmann who had served as pastor from 1906 to 1945 and then as pastor emeritus until his death in 1954. The anniversary celebration in June 1959 featured President Fry as preacher.

Since 1943, the Board of Deaconess Work, with permission from the church, had called eleven councils of women, informal gatherings of those serving as lay workers, missionaries and deaconesses. Besides the camaraderie, they were helpful in compiling for the board a list of all full-time church workers in the ULCA, in locating positions for women wishing to serve in the church, and improving personnel practices in church agencies. The eleventh council on December 2, 1961, was at the Philadelphia Motherhouse. The board's report to the last ULCA Convention closed with a detailed account of its material assets ready to be turned over to the new church and also a statement expressing its other gifts (Koinonia):

> Inherent in the diaconate are tremendous strengths: its common purpose, its unity of spirit, the feeling of equality in work, the family spirit and special cohesiveness pervading the deaconess houses, the joy of close spiritual fellowship, a service that can be wholehearted because its members are free from economic worries, the continuity of service that lends stability to the whole, and the joy of self-giving, self-sacrificing, self-oblation in living service of our Lord.[18]

As its last act, the board urged the merged church to restudy its structure and to consider the creation of the Board of Church Vocations with a department for the diaconate.

Board of Parish Education

Executive Secretary: S. White Rhyne; Board President: The Rev. Walter B. Freed.

"Parish Education from Merger to Merger" were the words the Board of Parish Education used to begin its final report to the 1962 convention.[19] Although none of the three merging bodies in 1918 had a board as such, yet the interest and concern were strong. The General Synod prepared the *Augsburg Uniform Series* for its Sunday schools. The General Council used a pioneer graded series of lessons for children and youth. The United Synod of the South to a large extent used the materials prepared by the synod and council. When plans for merger were in the making, sentiment was so strong for more and better education methods that the Committee on Ways and Means, chaired by the Rev. Theodore E. Schmauk recommended to the organizing convention "that the United Lutheran Church in America elect a Sunday School Board of twelve." It did, choosing Schmauk to be the first president of the board. Under his guidance, the first two meetings set the pattern of the work of the board. The members wrote a charter, a constitution and bylaws, which guided the course of the board through the entire forty-four years of its life. The pattern of operation involved five steps: (1) Study and Evaluation (2) Planning (3) Expansion (4) Production, and (5) Promotion. These steps form a cycle that needed repeating through the years.

Unfortunately, Schmauk died before the third meeting, but other gifted leaders carried on. They realized that the Sunday School Board was not able to meet all the demands. The second convention therefore adopted a plan for the Parish and Church School Board. The object of this board was to develop

a system or systems of literature for use in the home, the parish, and the church schools; to organize schools for weekly Christian training; to plan methods of school administration; to recommend books for the library; to outline programs for summer assemblies, Sunday School conventions and all festive occasions of the church; to prepare hymnals; to have oversight over and control of whatever pertains to the best interest of the parish and church school. It shall carry on its work in the name of the United Lutheran Church in America, and in accordance with the doctrinal bases, constituted acts, and rulings of said United Lutheran Church in America.[20]

During the first decade, 1921-1930, the demands were so great and the resources so few that "revision" was the way, namely, the improved *Augsburg Uniform Series of Sunday School Lessons* and a continuation of the *Lutheran Graded Series* with some revision. During the years 1931-1938 the emphasis was on reorganization and coordination. S. White Rhyne was called as the board's first executive secretary and remained in that position until the formation of the Lutheran Church in America in 1962. The board was divided into three standing committees: Field Work, Literature, and Finance. The staff was reorganized along the same lines and job analysis prepared for each staff member. *The*

Christian Life Course was completed and the *Lutheran Leadership Course* was launched in cooperation with the Augustana Lutheran Church. Working with the Luther League, the Women's Missionary Society, and the Executive Board, a merged plan was known as the "Program for the Children of the Church."

During the years 1939-1951 the board introduced new programs, new curricular and promotional materials, refined its organization, increased its staff and expanded its relationship with other units. The new *Christian Growth Series* was introduced and promoted. A better working relationship with the Board of Publication was achieved by having the executive secretaries attend each other's meetings. Curriculum editors, who had been employed by the Board of Publication, were placed administratively under the Parish and Church School Board.

In 1952 the board's name was changed to the Board of Parish Education, a title being used increasingly among Lutheran bodies. The board also began discussion of a philosophy of Christian education. This led to a unified study program, which had the board's attention during 1952-1955. It was a self-study under the direction of an outside specialist, Paul Vieth, professor at the Yale Divinity School. It resulted in *Parish Education—a Statement of Basic Principles and a Program of Christian Education.* It was sent to a large and varied group of church leaders for their comments and suggestions. With these in mind, the document was revised and distributed widely in the church. The final report suggested more study that would lead to the development of a long-range program of parish education for the church.

One of the problems that had surfaced during the unified study was that there was lack of coordination and overlapping among such agencies as the Sunday School, Vacation Church School, the Weekday Church School and Leadership Education since their curricular materials had been developed at different times. The long-range program strategy called for a completely coordinated program and curriculum from one age level to another and across agency lines to include the Sunday School, Weekday School, Vacation School, leadership education, catechetics, church camps and family life education. Such an ambitious effort had never been contemplated before by any denomination.

During the transition period of 1956-1962, the board undertook to expedite the strategy for the long-range program. Within a year cooperation came from eight Lutheran church bodies. However, the four that withdrew became the ALC, leaving Augustana, Suomi, and the American Evangelical Lutheran Church (Danish) to continue with the ULCA. The plan called for the Joint Board Committee made up of representatives of each cooperating board of parish education. The ULCA had fourteen, Augustana five, Suomi and AELC each one. W. Kent Gilbert, a ULCA editor, was named director of the program; gradually a staff of forty was assembled, including specialists in research, department-field services, and editors.

After developing detailed age-level and functional objectives, a complete curriculum design describing every course was adopted in 1960. After writing and editing, each course was produced in a field test edition and tried in sixty-two laboratory congregations that had been carefully selected to reflect a cross section of the parishes to be served in the new Lutheran Church in America. The courses were then revised and readied for publication in time for an intensive, two-year training program of 250,000 leaders when the new church was born.

Board of Higher Education

Executive Secretary: Robert Mortvedt, Ph.D.; Board President: the Rev. Lawrence D. Folkemer, Ph.D.

The UCLA's three-prong commitment to higher education included the Church's fourteen colleges, the ten theological seminaries, and a ministry to students at public institutions as well as to those in other institutions not related to the church. For the excitement of expansion no field provided more than that of higher education. During one generation, from 1930 to 1960, the enrollment in collegiate education tripled. However, the proportion of students in privately supported institutions fell from 51 percent to 42 percent. Even so, public education left an enormous share of students to the private colleges and universities.

The decade of the fifties had opened with a financial appeal, Christian Higher Education Year (CHEY), which was unprecedented in size in the ULCA. The 1962 report of the board was very positive. Some of the colleges were facing for the first time an overabundance of applications. This posed problems and opportunities. It enabled the colleges to raise standards of admission as well as tuition. With help from CHEY funds and federal loans, a number of the colleges were in building programs.

During the 1950s the opening of the Pacific Lutheran Theological Seminary in Berkeley (1952)—aided by CHEY funds gathered by the California Synod—was paired at the end of the decade by the founding of California Lutheran College (today, University). An inter-Lutheran undertaking, its opening in September 1961 foreshadowed the partnership of the already formed American Lutheran Church and the soon-to-be-consolidated ULCA, Augustana, AELC, and Suomi. With the new seminary on the West Coast plus a long overdue college in the Los Angeles area, balancing the Pacific Lutheran University in Tacoma, the ULCA connections in higher education now spanned the continent, even as the ULCA ventures in Canada, east and west, spelled out a continental commitment.

As a separate board for theological education in the Lutheran Church in America was being anticipated, still another change was in the making. It began with the recognized need for fuller attention on a churchwide basis for the education of the church's future ministers and for their continuing education. Pastoral institutes, as then called, received church authorization in 1958. Hopes ran high when early in 1960 Reginald W. Deitz, the young and gifted professor at Gettysburg Seminary became the BHE's first associate secretary for theological studies. His sudden death in early March left the church poorer for his passing. The search was on for a replacement. In the spirit of the inscription, "God buries

His workmen but carries on His work," a successor was soon found. To the Atlantic City convention BHE President Lawrence D. Folkemer (Gettysburg), after paying tribute to Deitz, announced "that the Rev. E. Theodore Bachmann of the faculty of Pacific Lutheran Seminary, Berkeley, California, had accepted the Board's call . . . and will begin his service on March 16, 1961."[21]

The long-anticipated pastors' institutes got under way in June, the first at Wagner College, Staten Island, New York, the second at Southern Seminary, Columbia, South Carolina, and the third at Northwestern Seminary, Minneapolis. On a pilot basis two parallel institutes were held at Gettysburg Seminary and Hamma Divinity School. With more attention to the needs of pastors in mid-career, and greater effort to nurture their growth in ministry, important input was contributed to the programming of the anticipated Board of Theological Education in the LCA. More important was the recognition that pastors should be given more opportunity for ongoing growth in their ministerial careers. The work offered at these institutes was intended to be of graduate-study quality without credit. It was hoped that they would be an encouragement for the pastors to continue work in the graduate programs of the seminaries.

Under the direction of the new associate director, faculty field consultations got under way in 1962. This enabled professors in the major fields—functional theology; historical and doctrinal theology; and biblical theology—to convene in a series of consultation early in 1962 in Chicago. Clinical training (a year of internship) for theological students was being encouraged, but as yet only the Pacific Lutheran Seminary required it for graduation. Psychological services under the direction of the Rev. Victor Benson included testing, counseling and therapy if needed.

Services in church vocations were being expanded. This involved recruitment on campuses and through synodical activities. A summer service program placed college students in church agencies. A lay placement service registered people seeking church work and also registered positions that were available. This program was developing in close cooperation with the synods. Mildred Winston served as director.

Both within this field of higher education and reaching far beyond it had been the leadership of one person in particularly: Gould Wickey. His retirement in late 1959 marked the end of an era; but after three decades it also signaled time for a change. His successor, Robert Mortvedt, already headed the Augustana Board of Christian Higher Education. Mortvedt's feat of wearing two hats and shuttling between Chicago (at times Minneapolis) and New York began in late '59 and presaged the consolidated church and its administration.

Board of Pensions

Executive Secretary: The Rev. George H. Berkheimer, D.D; Board President: William G. Semisch.

Even before the organization of the ULCA, a concern was shown for the welfare of retired pastors and widows. However, only one of the three bodies, the

General Synod, had a "pastors fund" from which grants of $250 a year were made. The Board of Ministerial Relief of the ULCA , the official title, decided to have the "most liberal policy possible" and raised the annual grant to $300. Since the only means of financing this expenditure was through the uncertain source of the budget, the 1920 convention approved the raising of an endowment fund of two million, later raised to four million. Efforts during the years 1927 and 1928 culminated in pledges totaling $4,176,135. By 1932, $3,198,305 had been received. Then due to the economic depression and ineffective investing, the market value of the fund reached the alarming low of $2,500,000 in 1938. With careful service and decisions regarding investment policies, the tide turned. Gradually pensions increased. In 1947, ministers received $450 a year and widows $225. A minimum pension of $900 a year became effective in January 1954. Then under a revised plan adopted by the 1956 convention, all eligible retired ministers and missionaries were to have a minimum pension of $1,200 in 1957 and $1,500 by 1961. This non-contributory plan was gradually phased out by limiting the entrance of new pastors, 1950 being the demarcation.[22]

Meanwhile the Contributory Pension Plan, in the making since 1934, went through various stages of acceptance, rejection and revision. Finally in 1945 a plan that had been recommended by the Executive Board in 1942 was activated when five hundred ministers and congregations agreed to the conditions: contribution of 4 percent of total salary by the member and an equal amount by the congregation or salary-paying organization. By 1952 it was necessary to raise the congregation's contribution to 8 percent. When Social Security became available to ministers in 1956, adjustments were made so that ministers could obtain coverage under both plans. In 1960, deaconesses were declared eligible for the Contributory Pension. A weakness in the Contributory Plan soon became apparent. It provided no funds at the time of death for funeral and other expenses. At the board's recommendation, the 1950 convention adopted a plan at a cost of $36 a year for the member. The amount distributed at death depended on the age of the member. The highest, $3,000, went to those pastors who were younger than sixty-one years. The lowest, $500, for those over seventy-one years. The board also had an emergency assistance fund that was used to help pastors with unusual medical or other expenses. For these benefits the approval of the synodical president was required.

From 1945 on, a pension plan was also available to lay employees with five or more years of service. Since the Board of Publication already had a pension plan for its employees, this was managed and administered by the Pension Board. At the closing convention in 1962, the board announced that the endowment fund's book value of $4,536,900 had a market value of $5,264,576.

Board of Publication

Executive Secretary: H. Torrey Walker, L.H.D.; Board President: Bertram M. Wilde.[23]

The charter of the Board of Publication granted already in January 1919 indicated its purpose: "To give material support for the benevolent, charitable, educational and missionary operations of the United Lutheran Church in America." With these goals in mind, the board claimed "parity with all other boards." Besides, on more than one occasion the board kept the church finances "on even keel."

Publishing books, its main task, was done under the trade name of Muhlenberg Press. Already in 1923 the Muhlenberg Building was constructed on 1228 Spruce Street in inner-city Philadelphia. Here an untold number of books for pastors and seminaries was published at a reasonable price and with discount to pastors. Other books of biblical and theological content reached far beyond denominational borders. The board continued to translate and publish such books as were needed to keep Americans abreast of new European developments. Other services for pastors and congregations included a pastor's "desk book" for organizing and planning work and the annual appointment book, all free to pastors and deaconesses. A church bulletin service introduced by the Rev. G. Elson Ruff was assumed by the board in 1940. The Department of Ecclesiastical Arts, established in 1941, was a source of "appropriately designed vestments, paraments, furnishings and clerical clothing." Many of these articles were made in the board's own shop. Branch stores were opened in cities across the United States and Canada to accommodate customers. In 1958, the Journal of Music was established to make selected new choral works available to church choir directors and organists. Parish education material as well as those of the auxiliaries were published and distributed by the board.

Ever since the merger, *The Lutheran* was published and distributed by the publication house, often at a deficit borne by the board. It was through *The Lutheran*, the official organ of the ULCA, that the two hundred thousand subscribers (1960) were kept informed and nurtured. The indefatigable journalist and thoughtful churchman, G. Elson Ruff, had by 1960 completed twenty-five years as editor of *The Lutheran,* and was ready for more, as the Atlantic City convention reelected him once again. Ruff's top associate was Albert P. Stauderman, plus a trio of assistants.

One of the most appreciated services of the Board of Publication was that of providing housing under one roof for the ULCA's boards and auxiliaries stationed in Philadelphia. It also provided funds for the first United Lutheran Church headquarters in New York City on 35th Street and helped finance the move to 231 Madison Avenue.

By 1958 the Philadelphia Spruce Street building was cramped for office space and the publication services needed expansion. A new Muhlenberg Building was constructed at 2900 Queen Lane where it was surrounded by beautiful open space with plenty of room for parking. Here again units such as Parish Education, Pensions, Deaconess Work, United Lutheran Church Women and others would have improved and enlarged office space and the benefits of a cafeteria. The board's printing press, workshops and warehouse were located five blocks away at a former lithographing company. The head man was H. Torrey

Walker with Frank G. Rhodes as associate executive director.

A memorable quotation from Martin Luther headed the Board of Publication's 1960 biennial report:

> Printing is the last and also the greatest gift of God. By it He wanted to have the cause of the true religion become known and spread in all languages at the end of the world to all the countries of the earth.[24]

Appropriately, the 55-volume edition of *Luther's Works*—launched jointly in 1955 by the Missouri Synod's Concordia Publishing House and the ULCA's Muhlenberg Press—was beginning to take shape. In this notable inter-Lutheran agreement, Concordia would bring out translations of Luther's writings on the Scriptures (31 volumes), and Muhlenberg would bring out his so-called Reformation writings and occasional pieces (23 volumes). Volume 55 would be the index. Taken as a whole, this extensive edition in English, although still offering only a generous selection of his complete writings in the Weimar Edition (in Latin and German), promised to give Luther a wider audience than ever among people able to use English. Thus, the significance of this edition was worldwide. During the biennium (1959-60) five volumes from Muhlenberg Press (v. 32, 34, 35, 36, and 51), treated mainly the career of the reformer, and a section on Word and Sacrament, as well as some of Luther's sermons.

Among those who envisioned and designed this massive project were seminary professors Theodore G. Tappert and John W. Doberstein (Philadelphia), as well as others in St. Louis. But the heaviest share of the credit goes to the two enterprising editors: Jaroslav Pelikan and Helmut T. Lehmann (Muhlenberg's book editor and a former president of the ULCA's Waterloo College and Seminary in Ontario). With this and other instances of theological scholarship the ULCA's Muhlenberg Press bequeathed a strong tradition to the LCA's Fortress Press.

DEPARTMENTS

Since 1918 the ULCA had its Committee on **Church Architecture**. Its consultative services were available to individual congregations and especially to the Board of American Missions. The guiding principle was the achievement of a harmonious relationship between the enclosed space and liturgical worship. In this field contacts were interdenominational and the influences often Anglican, whose ways of worship were akin to Lutheran. In 1948 the committee became the Bureau of Church Architecture, and two years later a department.[25]

Although the Department of **Press, Radio, and Television (PRT)** was established only in 1948, its antecedents (minus TV) go back to the News Bureau of the National Lutheran Council (1918) and to the Lutheran Bureau that handled the publicity of the first ULCA convention. A cooperative arrangement with the NLC News Bureau provided that the ULCA's PRT limit its releases to ULCA matters.[26]

Stewardship, approved as a department already in 1920, was a field in that Lutherans could learn much from other American denominations.[27] The Lutheran Laymen's Movement for Stewardship, of pre-ULCA origin (General Synod) in time became a power in the church and also exercised a strong influence in postwar Europe among the German and Scandinavian Churches. It also organized Lutheran Church Productions in connection with the "Martin Luther" film (1952).

The United Lutheran Church Foundation was authorized by the Harrisburg convention in 1956 and began its work in November of 1957 with Chester A. Myrom as its director. Expenses of the Foundation were covered by the ULCA budget so that all gifts could be channeled to the appropriate board, agency, institution, or auxiliary of the church, according to the designation of the donor. The foundation encouraged "the making of wills, trust agreements, insurance contracts, and gift annuity agreements under which the church or its parts may become the actual or contingent beneficiary." A committee of twelve supervised and encouraged the endeavor. By May 15, 1962, Foundation receipts had passed the one million dollar mark and had received gifts for ninety-four designated beneficiaries. Roland C. Matthies (Ohio), chair of the Foundation's directing committee, told the 1962 convention: "It can be fun to open the eyes and hearts of people who have not yet learned to give."[28]

The Department of **Worship** was created by action of the Toronto Convention in 1954.[29] It combined the work of the Committee on the *Common Service Book* and the Church Music Committee. This new Department was activated in 1956 when the Rev. Edgar S. Brown Jr. became Executive Secretary. The immediate responsibilities were with the Inter-Lutheran Joint Commission on the Hymnal and the Joint Commission on the Liturgy in introducing the new *Service Book and Hymnal* and the setting up of synodical committees on worship within the ULCA. During its short life, the department prepared forms and manuals of worship and devotional material. It gave approval to all matters pertaining to the formal worship of the church that bore the imprint of the ULCA or any of its boards or auxiliaries. It organized conferences on worship to serve synods, congregations, pastors, and church members in promoting good liturgical practice and the best types and forms of church music. It adopted and revised the Spanish Hymnal *Culto Cristiano*. The Inter-Lutheran Commission on the Liturgy and Hymnal, a twenty-six-member force chaired by ULCA's Edward T. Horn III, by 1962 had proven itself a strong unifying influence.[30]

COMMITTEES AND COMMISSIONS

The Committee on **German Interests** began in 1924 as a replacement for the Committee of Conferences on Special Linguistic Interests. As a committee of the church it was to "arrange with the Executive Council" of the ULCA for meetings of the General German Conference, and to "counsel any agency of the church with concerns for the German-speaking portion." The committee also had the "privilege of approaching any agency of the church concerning these interests." Thus each time the conference planned to meet, usually biennially, the committee had to secure permission to include Communion from the Executive Council,[31] until the change of policy in 1960. Since most of the fourteen members of the committee were from the eastern United States, the presidents of the Manitoba, Midwest, Texas, and Wartburg synods were "correspondence" members.[32] Thus concern was shown for all the bilingual congregations. In 1954 there were 240, and twenty-eight of them without pastors, in spite of the efforts that had been made to have the seminaries prepare bilingual students. About this same time, there were twenty-seven students in the ULCA seminaries that could qualify as German-English preachers. With assistance from the Board of Higher Education one Gettysburg graduate took another year of training at the Inner Mission Society of Bremen in order to serve better the needs of a bilingual congregation of new Americans who longed to hear the gospel in their mother tongue. The committee kept the church aware of the need for devotional and worship materials. In cooperation with the Board of Publication and the Committee on Worship, the German *Liederbuch* came out in 1959 and the "Handbuch" of Ministerial Acts was waiting approval from the Joint Commission on Liturgy. The ULCA budget subsidized the *Kirchliches Monatsblatt*, a magazine that reached more than two thousand subscribers. It was given free to the new immigrants who were the constant concern of the Committee.[33]

The Consultative Committee on **Church Statistics** in 1956 replaced the former Committee on Statistics. This culminated a process of centralizing statistical concerns and interpretation in the secretary's office. New committees would be appointed biennially by the secretary, usually with ten members. Over the years the ULCA had been a leader in developing and simplifying parochial reports for the synods and congregations. In response, there was excellent cooperation so that it was possible to integrate annual reports of the church. The ULCA in this field had the benefits of some outstanding statisticians. (See chapter 7.)

The five-member Consulting Committee on the **Military Chaplaincy** had antecedents going back to World War I and the formation of the National Lutheran Commission on Soldiers' and Sailors' Welfare (1917). With its roster of some 285 chaplains of various categories the ULCA in 1962 had over one-half of the total who were endorsed by the participating church bodies in the National Lutheran Council. President Fry's personal letters to each of the ULCA chaplains during the biennium as well as other correspondence helped keep alive a sense of fellowship and identity. A feature of significance in the area of care for military personnel and their family members is the Central Church of Military Membership. As a repository for the records of pastoral acts by chaplains, it receives and maintains the records of personnel who have no active relationship to ULCA congregations "back home." Historic Luther Place Memorial Church in Washington, D.C., served as a continuity of reference until these individuals could be received into a more permanent membership than their military service often allows. By 1962, this Central Church had grown to 487 baptized members.

The Consulting Committee on **Scholarships and Fellowship** was an aid to the Board of Higher Education, which administered the scholarship and fellowship fund. The Committee included staff representatives from the boards of Deaconess Work, Foreign Missions, American Missions, Higher Education, Social Missions, and the United Lutheran Church Women. The purpose of the program was "to assist worthy and needy men and women to pursue such studies as will prepare them for positions under the direction of a board, agency and institution or parish." During the last biennium, 157 grants totaling $120,861 were approved for 142 individuals.

On the financial side, there was the ULCA **Investment Commission** and Board of Directors of the Common Investing Fund. The membership of the Commission is identical with that of the fund. Presiding over this dual entity was the treasurer of the ULCA, Edmund F. Wagner. The two tasks performed by this nine-member unit included overseeing all securities purchased or sold in connection with the Contributory Pension Plan of the Church, and periodically reviewing the investments of the United Lutheran Church Foundation.[34]

The **Commission to the National Lutheran Council**, comprised of sixteen members, reported to the 1962 convention that the NLC's budget for 1962 was $2,210,752, of which $496,540 was the ULCA's share.[35] Another $110,802 was due for the third phase of the Lutheran Student Center Fund of the Division of College and University Work and another $7,795 for the core budget of the Department for the Christian Approach to the Jewish People of the Division of American Missions. President Fry was an ex-officio member of this Commission.

The **Commission to the Canadian Lutheran Council** consisting of eight members reported to the 1962 convention that the "Council is filling an increasingly important place in Canadian Lutheranism." The American Lutheran Church had been recognized as a participating Body in the CLC in January 1961. The others were the Augustana Lutheran Church and the Lutheran Free Church. The executive director of the CLC, Earl J. Treusch, was elected for another three-year term.

The **Special Commission on Relations to American Lutheran Church Bodies** succeeded the one that in 1956 had recommended that the ULCA "declare to all Lutheran bodies in America its desire to merge with any or all of them." The Executive Council elected twelve members, and reported the same to the 1962 convention.

The ULCA **Representatives to the National Council of Churches of Christ in the USA** were, since the NCC organization in 1950, elected by the Executive Board of the Church. They reported to the board that had responsibility for interdenominational work. In 1962 the representatives reported on the NCC's biennial Assembly in December 4-9, 1960, held in San Francisco with three thousand in attendance. Secretary Harkins substituted for President Fry, who chaired the twenty-four representatives.

The ULCA **Representative on the Advisory Council of the American Bible Society** served as President Fry's deputy. The Rev. Harold S. Miller, by action of the 1954 convention, reported annually to the president instead of biennially as the constitution required. In the 1962 report, called the "Cold War Emergency," he indicated that the Bible has now been outsold by the writings of Nikita Krushchev, a claim well substantiated. Representatives of other Lutheran bodies took active part in the program of the 1962 meeting and the ULCA's Miller presided.

President Fry headed the team of **delegates to the World Council of Churches** assembly in New Delhi, India in late 1961. At the January 1962 Executive Board meeting, Paul H. Rhodes, at the request of the other nine, gave a comprehensive and enthusiastic report. The theme of the assembly was "Jesus Christ the Light of the World."[36]

At the instigation of the Maryland Synod a memorial was presented to the 1958 convention in Dayton that the Executive Board appoint a committee to study the field of **anointing and healing**, a subject of interest and concern.[37] The appointed committee of ten included both theological and medical scholars. Although there was no consensus within the committee, a lengthy report was ready for the 1962 January meeting of the Executive Board. The committee was "commended for its diligence, thoughtful and spiritual insight." The board recommended that it be passed on to the "adjourned convention."

The commission on the **Sacrament of the Altar** was asked by the 1960 convention to continue the study of confirmation and the age for first communion with the Augustana Church. With the approval for merger, President Fry requested that the other two churches be included.[38]

The commission on **Liturgy and Hymnal** comprised members from the participating bodies of the National Lutheran Council. The ULCA had ten members including the executive secretary of the Worship Committee, the Rev. Edgar S. Brown. In 1962 the commission reported on the number of copies of the *Service Book and Hymnal* that had been printed and announced that the manuscript for the new *Occasional Service Book* was ready for publication.[39]

The committee on **Church Papers**, appointed by the president, worked closely with the Board of Publication. Originated in 1918, over the years it oversaw a mixed field. In 1928, it aided in creating the *Lutheran Church Quarterly*, a merger of two hitherto separate journals, Lutheran Quarterly, based at Gettysburg Seminary, and *Lutheran Church Review*, based at Philadelphia Seminary. The committee's chief concern over its entire duration, however, was *The Lutheran*. As the 1962 summary revealed, circulation of this "official organ" began in 1918 with some forty thousand subscribers, gradually declined to seventeen thousand in 1934 (Depression), then steadily picked up. In 1944, with G. Elson Ruff as editor, *The Lutheran* was subtitled as "The Weekly News Magazine" of the ULCA. By 1960 its circulation topped two hundred thousand. No written history of Lutheranism in North America would be true to its subject without drawing upon *The Lutheran.* No wonder that its editors have been held accountable to the church at-large and been reelected biennially by the church convention.

AUXILIARIES

The Luther League of America

This auxiliary came to the closing biennium of the ULCA with a firm sense of accomplishment. We have already seen its influence in connection with the formative years of Frederick H. Knubel (chapter 4). Since its founding in Pittsburgh (1895), the LLA had been attracting young people of many backgrounds and fostering their sense of purpose in light of a common spiritual heritage. In 1920 the LLA became the official youth organization of the ULCA. Not narrowly denominational the LLA was alertly evangelical in its programs and projects. The benefit of this kind of youth work over successive generations for the church at large as well as for its young people would be hard to specify but also hard to overestimate.

During the later 1950s, as the final (1962) report indicates, the scope of LLA benefited from good leadership, linking local and churchwide activities. Some twenty-one hundred young people gathered in 1961 at the LLA biennial convention at the University of Illinois (Urbana). Outstanding speakers from other continents as well as America, and youth-led discussion groups gave the gathering high marks. There was in the League a concern for nurturing the "depth dimension" of the Christian faith and for youth to participate more fully in the life of the church. The potential power of the League's seventy-five thousand members lay open to the Spirit's leading.[40]

Youth-to-youth summer caravaning, league training schools, youth worker's institutes, conferences for professional youth workers, plus exchange programs overseas (under the LWF) as well as at home, and much besides, gave emphasis to the league's routines in the local church. Since 1953 a five-fold program had been gaining in acceptance. It linked the LLA to a number of the church's boards by means of its emphases: Christian Vocation, Evangelism, Missions, Social Action, Recreation. All of them culminated in the common theme for 1962: "The People of God."[41]

Fiscally the LLA accomplished much with little. Receipts, including an appropriation from the ULCA, totaled only $170,000. Contributions from the synodical Luther Leagues were highest from Ohio, and next among the top five: North Carolina, Central Pennsylvania, Ministerium of Pennsylvania, South Carolina.[42] As to the LLA publication, the time-honored *Luther League Review* in 1951 became *Luther Life*, only to change again in 1961 to *Time Out.* Herein and in the LLA *Minutes* and Biennial Reports lies the story, as yet insufficiently told, of the ULCA and its young people.

United Lutheran Church Men

Known as the Brotherhood of the ULCA until 1957, the ULCM had endeavored to live up to its role as an auxiliary of the church. As its 1962 report shows, the ULCM anticipated that the coming consolidation of the four church bodies would breathe new life into its own auxiliary function. Here we need but recall an earlier era of men's work in the churches (chapters 1 and 3). During World War I, initially in the Midwest, an inter-synodical Lutheran Brotherhood aided immeasurably the work of the National Lutheran Commission on Soldiers' and Sailors' Welfare. And earlier still in the East laymen took a leading role in bringing Lutherans together.

Now, after more than four decades of ULCA life, the ULCM was cooperating with a number of boards of the church. Social Missions, notably evangelism and social action, had ULCM support. In select ways so also did Higher Education, Parish Education, Foreign Missions, the Department of Stewardship, of Press, Radio, and Television, and the ULCA Foundation. ULCM endeavored to help the Board of Deaconess Work by reminding fathers of a possible service career for their daughters. And ULCM cooperated with ULC Women in leadership workshops. Not least was ULCM's service to military personnel under direction of the National Lutheran Council. Organizationally ULCM, as inherited from Brotherhood days, had its basic group in the congregation, its larger fellowship in the synod, and its loose bonds through a churchwide structure, including a paper, *Lutheran Men*. ULCM's most prominent activity was with the Boy Scouts of America. The National Lutheran Committee on Scouting reported that in 1961 Lutherans received 1,267 *Pro Deo et Patria* awards, of which number 491 went to ULCA boys.[43]

In recognition of his concern for the youth of the church and for his supportiveness of scouting, President Fry was given the organization's highest honor, the Gold Lamb Award at its fiftieth anniversary in 1960. Over the years Lamb Awards for community service and leadership had gone to 147 ULCA men.[44] To conclude, men's work in the ULCA strove for high ideals with mixed results. Unlike the time-honored mission motif of ULC Women, which provided challenges at home and abroad, men's work was more confined to the congregation. Finally, with the formation of the ULCA Lutheran Laymen's Movement for Stewardship there was the feeling among some men that the LLM was elitist. Nevertheless, in its reports the Brotherhood and lastly the ULCM in 1962 professed cordial and cooperative relations with the other organizations for men. A subtle question remained, even as hinted in 1939 by Henry H. Bagger in his rousing booklet, *Forty Thousand Strong*. The success of men's work in the parish depended in some ways upon the local pastor.

The ULCA Women

Over the years the auxiliaries of the ULCA had become more closely drawn into the church's structures, cooperating with the several boards. The Women's

Missionary Society, the oldest of the three, in 1955 had become United Lutheran Church Women.[45] The Women's Missionary Society of the ULCA was organized simultaneously with the ULCA itself (chapter 1). In its final report (1962), the ULCW reported a total membership of nearly 185,000. During the fiscal year 1961 ULCW had contributed over $975,000 to the work of the church: nearly $610,000 to the Board of Foreign Missions (about one-third of that board's budget); nearly $290,000 to the Board of American Missions; and the rest to four other boards: Deaconess Work, Higher Education, Parish Education, Social Missions, as well as to Pensions.[46] As a wrap-up these figures appear small compared to the cumulative effect of women's work over the years - and indeed back to the last third of the nineteenth century (especially in the General Synod). Many a congregation owed its founding and/or survival to this kind of auxiliary help; so too did many a pastor, and all the single women missionaries overseas and at home who were engaged in the missionary outreach of the ULCA.

AFFILIATED CHURCHES

According to the 1948 *Minutes*, an amendment to the Constitution provided for Affiliated Churches: those who had been "fostered by the Board of Foreign Missions of the ULCA" had accepted "this Constitution with its Doctrinal Basis as set forth in Article II" and whose Constitution had "been approved by the Executive Board." Affiliated churches were entitled to representatives at ULCA Conventions with seat and voice but no vote. There churches were expected to "welcome and receive counsel" from the ULCA in Convention and in turn the ULCA was to "manifest interest and solicitude in the life and development of the Affiliated Churches."[47]

United Evangelical Lutheran Church in Argentina (org. 1948)
Evangelical Lutheran Church in (British) Guyana (org. 1943)
Andhra Evangelical Lutheran Church in India (org. 1927)
Evangelical Lutheran Church in Japan (org. 1922)
Evangelical Lutheran Church in Liberia (org. 1948).

In Conclusion

These 1962 reports, here concluding our history of the United Lutheran Church in America, were a summary of the countless ways and means the church had to carry out its great commission. Behind each report are men and women, young and old, clergy and laity, who gave endless hours of thought, prayer and work in order to accomplish their part in this mission. We thank God that the Holy Spirit called, gathered, and enlightened them to serve the church of Jesus Christ, our Lord. To Him be all honor and glory now and forever. Amen.

NOTES

1. ULCA *Minutes* 1918: 62-63.
2. Ibid., 67.
3. ULCA *Minutes* 1918: 67; 1954: 28-29.
4. See chapter 11 on this Commission.
5. ULCA *Minutes* 1954: 196.
6. ULCA *Minutes* 1918: 68-9, and 1958: 1104-5.
7. ULCA *Minutes* 1922: 119-120.
8. ULCA *Minutes* 1958: 72.
9. ULCA *Minutes* 1960: 596.
10. ULCA *Minutes* 1962: 617-625.
11. Ibid., 428-459.
12. ULCA *Minutes* 1958: 790-1.
13. ULCA *Minutes* 1962: 587, 589f.
14. ULCA *Minutes* 1926: 416, 513; thereafter it affiliated with the German Iowa Synod.
15. ULCA *Minutes* 1958: 794; 1962: 589.
16. Ibid., 791.
17. ULCA *Minutes* 1962: 583.
18. Ibid., 594.
19. Ibid., 542-559.
20. ULCA *Minutes* 1920: 308.
21. ULCA *Minutes* 1960: 1020; 1962: 674.
22. ULCA *Minutes* 1962: 497-503.
23. ULCA *Minutes* 1962: 485-7.
24. ULCA *Minutes* 1960: 545.
25. ULCA *Minutes* 1918: 78; 1926: 635-6; 1946: 171; 1948: 322.
26. ULCA *Minutes* 1948: 290.
27. ULCA *Minutes* 1920: 85, 108, 352; 1962: 608-610.
28. ULCA *Minutes* 1962: 666.
29. ULCA *Minutes* 1954: 806.
30. ULCA *Minutes* 1962: 258-267, 658; ULCA *Yearbook* 1962: 61.
31. ULCA *Minutes* 1924: 111.
32. ULCA *Year Book 1939*, 35.
33. ULCA *Minutes* 1954: 1129; 1958: 1052-53.
34. ULCA *Minutes* 1962: 213.
35. Ibid., 308-9.
36. Ibid., 386-393.
37. ULCA *Minutes* 1958: 82 and 923.
38. ULCA *Minutes* 1962: 230.
39. Ibid., 274- 276.
40. Ibid., 643-650.
41. Ibid., 643.
42. Ibid., 651-656.

43. Ibid., 478.
44. ULCA *Minutes* 1960: 593-594.
45. ULCA *Minutes* 1956: 444-445.
46. ULCA *Minutes* 1962: 568-570, 576.
47. ULCA *Minutes* 1948: 112.

BIBLIOGRAPHY

Ahlstrom, Sydney E. *A Religious History of the American People.* New Haven and London: Yale University Press, 1972.

Aland, Kurt, ed. *Die Korrespondenz Heinrich Melchior Muhlenberg.* Berlin; New York: De Gruyter, 1986-1993.

Allbeck, Willard D. *Theology at Wittenberg, 1845-1945.* Springfield, Ohio: Wittenberg Press, 1945.

Allgemeine Evangelisch-Lutherische Kirchenzeitung.

Annual Report of the National Lutheran Council, 1919-1921. New York: National Lutheran Council, 1919.

Arden, Gothard Everett. *Augustana Heritage: A History of the Augustana Lutheran Church.* Rock Island, Illinois: Augustana Press, 1963.

Bachmann, E. Theodore and Mercia Brenne Bachmann. *Lutheran Churches in the World.* Minneapolis, Minnesota: Augsburg, 1989.

Bachmann, E. Theodore. *The Ecumenical Involvement of the LCA Predecessor Bodies: A Brief History, 1900-1962,* rev. 2nd ed. New York: Division for World Mission and Ecumenism of the Lutheran Church in America, 1983.

Bachmann, E. Theodore. *The Personal Notebooks of E. Theodore Bachmann.* To be deposited in the Archives of the Evangelical Lutheran Church in America. Chicago, Illinois.

Bachmann, E. Theodore. *The Personal Correspondence of the Rev. Dr. E. Theodore Bachmann.* To be deposited in the Archives of the Evangelical Lutheran Church in America. Chicago, Illinois.

Bachmann, E. Theodore. *They Called Him Father: The Life Story of John Christian Frederick Heyer.* Philadelphia: The Muhlenberg Press, 1942.

Bachmann, E. Theodore. "With Muhlenberg in New Jersey." Trenton, New Jersey: New Jersey Synod of the Evangelical Lutheran Church in America, 1992.

Bate, H. N., ed. *Proceedings of the World Conference on Faith and Order, Lausanne, August 3-21,* 1927. New York: George H. Doran Company, 1927.

Bente, Friedrich. "United Synod of the Evangelical Lutheran Church in the South," *Lehre und Wehre* 63 (January 1917).

Bergendoff, Conrad. "Lutheran Unity," in *What Lutherans are Thinking*, ed. Fendt, Edward C. Columbus, Ohio: The Wartburg Press, 1947.

Bracher, Edwin. *The First Fifty Years of the Pacific Synod, 1901-1951.* Seattle: The Pacific Synod of the United Lutheran Church in America, 1951.

Brown, William Adams. *The Church in America: A Study of the Present Condition and Future Prospects of American Protestantism.* New York: Macmillan, 1922.

Burgess, Ellis Beaver. *Memorial History of the Pittsburgh Synod of the Evangelical Lutheran Church: 1748-1845-1924.* Greenville, Pennsylvania: The Beaver Printing Company, 1925.

Canup, M. Luther. "Merger Mass Meeting at the Hippodrome," in *The Lutheran*, November 28, 1918.

Carney, Bruce. *History of the Allegheny Evangelical Lutheran Synod.* Philadelphia: The Lutheran Publication Society, 1919.

Cavert, Samuel McCrea. *The American Churches in the Ecumenical Movement.* New York: Association Press, 1968.

Christian Faith in Action. New York: Central Department of Publication and Distribution of the National Council of Christian Churches of Christ in the United States of America, 1951.

The Columbia Encyclopedia. New York: Macmillan Company, 1932.

Common Service Book of the Lutheran Church with Hymnal. Philadelphia: Board of Publication of the United Lutheran Church in America, 1918.

"Convention of Officials in Holy Trinity," in *The Lutheran*, March 6 and 13, 1919.

Der Bekenntnisschriften der evangelisch-lutherische Kirche. Gottingen: Dandelwed und Ruprecht, 1930.

Der Grosse Brockhaus. 1932 ed.

Diehl, Gustav, and E. T. Bachmann. *Rajah Bushanam Manikam.* Madras: Christian Literary Society, 1975.

Documentary History of the Evangelical Lutheran Ministerium of Pennsylvania and Adjacent States. Philadelphia: Board of Publication of the General Council of the Evangelical Lutheran Church in North America, 1898.

Eisenberg, William E. *The Lutheran Church in Virginia, 1717-1962.* Roanoke, Virginia: The Trustees of the Virginia Synod, Lutheran Church in America, 1967.

The Encyclopedia of the Lutheran Church, vol. 1, ed. by Julius Bodensieck. Minneapolis, Minnesota: Augsburg Publishing House, 1965.

Evjen, John Olaf. "Berkenmeyer," in *Lutheran Church Review,* vol. 24 (1925).

Evjen, John Olaf. *The Life of J. H. W. Stuckenberg, Theologian-Philosopher-Sociologist.* Minneapolis: The Lutheran Free Church Publishing Company, 1938.

Evjen, John Olaf. *Scandinavian Immigrants in New York, 1630-1674.* Minneapolis Minnesota: H. C. Holter Publishing Co., 1916.

Eylands, Vladimir. *Lutherans in Canada.* Winnipeg: Icelandic Synod, 1945.

Fendt, Edward D. *The Struggle for Lutheran Unity and Consolidation in the U.S.A. from the Late 1930s to the Early 1970s.* Minneapolis, Minnesota: Augsburg Publishing House, 1980.

Fey, Howard Edward, ed. *The Ecumenical Advance: A History of the Ecumenical Movement,* vol. 2. Geneva: World Council of Churches, 1986.

First General Conference of Lutherans in America. Philadelphia: General Council Publication Board, Lutheran Publication Society, 1899.

Fischer, Emil E. "Professor Fischer's Inaugural," in "Addresses at the Inauguration of Emil E. Fischer at the Philadelphia Seminary," *Lutheran Church Review,* vol. 39 (1920).

Flesner, Dorris A. *American Lutherans Help Shape World Council.* Dubuque, Iowa: Wm. C. Brown Company Publishers, 1981.

Fortenbaugh, Robert. *The Development of the Synodical Polity of the Lutheran Church in America to 1829.* Philadelphia: Ph.D. diss., University of Pennsylvania, 1926.

Franklin Clark Fry: A Palette for a Portrait, ed. Robert H. Fischer, Supplementary Number of *Lutheran Quarterly,* vol. 24 (1972).

Gilbert, W. Kent. *Commitment to Unity: A History of the Lutheran Church in America*. Philadelphia: Fortress Press, 1988.

Glatfelter, Charles Henry. *Pastors and People: German Lutheran and Reformed Churches in the Pennsylvania Field, 1717-1793*. Breinigsville, Pennsylvania: Pennsylvania German Society, 1980-1981.

Gongaware, George J. *History of the First English Evangelical Lutheran Church in Pittsburgh 1837-1909*. Philadelphia: J. B. Lippincott Company, 1909.

Gotwald, Luther A., Jr. *Gotwald Trial Revisited*. Davidsville, Pennsylvania: Luther A. Gotwald, Jr., 1992.

Graebner, August Lawrence. *Geschichte des Lutheranische Kirche in America*. St. Louis: Concordia Publishing House, 1892.

Graebner, Theodore. "'Richtungen' in der amerikanisch-lutherischen Kirche," *Lehre und Wehre* 63 (April 1917)

Graebner, Theodore. *The Problem of Lutheran Union and Other Essays*. St. Louis: Concordia Publishing House, 1935.

"The Great Auditorium Meeting," in *The Lutheran*, November 21, 1918.

Greever, Walter H., ed. *Yearbook of the United Lutheran Church in America for 1939*. Philadelphia: The United Lutheran Publication House, 1939.

Haas, J. A. W. "Our Educational Problem," in "Open Letters," in *The Lutheran*, August 25, 1927.

Harry, Carolus Powell. *Protest and Progress in the Sixteenth Century*. Philadelphia: Joint Lutheran Committee on Celebration of the Quadricentennial of the Reformation, 1917.

Hauge, Osborne. *Lutherans Working Together: A History of the National Lutheran Council, 1918-1943*, with a supplementary chapter on 1943-1945 by Ralph H. Long. New York: National Lutheran Council, 1945.

Hebart, Siegfried. *William Loehes Lehre von der Kirche, ihrem Amt und Regiment: ein Beitrag zur Geschichte der Theologie im 19. Jahrhundert*. Neuendettelsau: Freimund, 1939.

Hefelbower, Samuel Gring. *The History of Gettysburg College, 1832-1932*. Gettysburg, Pennsylvania: Gettysburg College, 1932.

Herman, S. W. *Lutheran Churches of the World*. Minneapolis, Minnesota: Augsburg, 1957.

Hidy, Ross F., and Richard M. Bennett, eds. *Beasom the Builder*. Berkeley, California: Lutheran History Center of the West, 1996.

A History of the Lutheran Church in South Carolina. Columbia, South Carolina: The South Carolina Synod of the Lutheran Church in America, 1971.

Hogg, William Richard. *Ecumenical Foundations*. New York: Harper & Brothers, 1952.

Hopkins, Charles Howard. *The Rise of the Social Gospel in American Protestantism*, 1865-1915. New Haven: Yale University Press, 1967.

Horn, E. T. "The Feasibility of a Service for all English-speaking Lutherans," in *Quarterly Review*, new series 8 (1881).

Jacobs, Charles M. "The Washington Declaration: An Interpretation," in *Lutheran Church Review*, vol. 40 (January 1921).

Jacobs, Charles M. "The Lutheran World Convention: A Retrospect," in *Lutheran Church Review*, vol. 42 (1923).

Jacobs, Henry Eyster. *First Free Lutheran Diet in America*, Philadelphia: J. Frederick Smith, 1878.

Jacobs, Henry Eyster. *A History of the Evangelical Lutheran Church in the United States*. New York: The Christian Literature, 1893.

Jacobs, Henry Eyster. *The Book of Concord: or, The Symbolical Books of the Evangelical Lutheran Church*. Philadelphia: United Lutheran Publication House, 1911 [1916 printing].

Jacobs, Henry Eyster. "Constructive Lutheranism," in *Lutheran Church Review* vol. 38 (1919).

Jacobs, Henry Eyster. *Summary of the Christian Faith*. Philadelphia: General Council Publication House, 1905.

Jones, George Fenwick. *Henry Newman's Salzburger Letterbooks*. Athens, Georgia: University of Georgia Press, 1966.

Kaufmann, John A., ed. *Biographical Record of the Lutheran Theological Seminary at Philadelphia, 1864-1962.* Philadelphia: The Lutheran Theological Seminary, 1964.

Kieffer, George L., comp. and Ellis B. Burgess, ed. *The Lutheran Church Yearbook for 1920.* Philadelphia: The United Lutheran Publication House, 1920.

Kinnison, William A. *An American Seminary: A History of Hamma School of Theology, 1845-1978.* Columbus, Ohio: The Ohio Synod of the Lutheran Church in America, 1980.

Kirchenbuch.

Knubel, Frederick H. "Essentials of a Catholic Spirit," in *Lutheran Church Review,* vol. 38 (1919).

"Knubel Correspondence," in the Archives of the Evangelical Lutheran Church in America.

"Knubel-Gardiner Correspondence," in the Archives of the World Council of Churches, Geneva.

Knudsen, Johannes. *The Formation of the Lutheran Church in America.* Philadelphia: Fortress Press, 1978.

Knudten, Arthur C. and A. P. Stauderman. *The Forgotten Years and Beyond.* Philadelphia: Fortress Press, 1972.

Kopenhaver, W. M., comp. and ed. *United Lutheran Church Yearbook for 1923.* Philadelphia: The United Lutheran Publication House, 1923.

Kopenhaver, W. M., and Grace M. Sheeleigh, comps. and eds. *The Lutheran Church Annual for 1917.* Philadelphia: The Lutheran Publication Society and The General Council Publication Board, 1917.

Kreider, Harry Julius. *The History of the United Lutheran Synod of New York and New England.* Philadelphia: Muhlenberg Press, 1954.

Kurtz, Michael J. *John Gottlieb Morris: Man of God, Man of Science.* Baltimore, Maryland: The Maryland Historical Society, 1997.

Lakra, Joel. "The Gossner Evangelical Lutheran Church," ch. 4 in *The Lutheran Enterprise in India 1706-1952,* ed. C. H. Swavely. Madras: Federation of Evangelical Lutheran Churches in India, 1952.

"Leading Features of the Merger Convention," in *The Lutheran*, November 21, 1918.

Lenker, John N. *Lutherans in All Lands*, 2 vols. Milwaukee: J. A. Hill, 1894.

Life of Adolph Spaeth: Told by his own reminiscences, his letters and the recollection of his family and friends, ed. by Harriet Krauth Spaeth. Philadelphia: General Council Publication House, 1916.

The Lutheran Book of Worship. Minneapolis, Minnesota: Augsburg Publishing House and Philadelphia: Board of Publication, Lutheran Church in America, 1978.

Lutheran Church in America Yearbook.

The Lutheran Cyclopedia, ed. by Henry Eyster Jacobs and John A. W. Haas. New York: Charles Scribner's Sons, 1899.

Lutheran Women's Work.

The Lutheran World Almanac and Annual Encyclopedia for 1921. New York: The Lutheran Bureau, 1920.

Manikam, Rajah. *Christianity and the Asian Revolution*. Madras: Christian Literary Society, 1954.

Mann, William Julius. *Life and Times of Henry Melchior Muhlenberg*. Philadelphia: G. W. Frederick, 1888.

Memoirs of Henry Eyster Jacobs: Notes on a Life of a Churchman, ed. by Henry E. Horn, vol. 2. Huntington, Pennsylvania: Distributed by Church Management Service, 1974.

Meuser, Fred W. *The Formation of the American Lutheran Church: A Case Study in Lutheran Unity*. Columbus, Ohio: Wartburg Press, 1958.

Miller, E. Clarence. *Ecclesia Plantanda*. Lenten Number, 1936.

Minutes of the Thirty-Second Convention of the General Council of the Evangelical Lutheran Church in North America. Philadelphia: General Council Publication Board, 1909.

Minutes of the Thirty-Fifth Convention of the General Council of the Evangelical Lutheran Church in North America, Held in Zion Lutheran Church, Rock Island,

Illinois and First Lutheran Church, Moline, Illinois, September 9-14, 1915.

Minutes of the Thirty-Sixth Convention of the General Council of the Evangelical Lutheran Church in North America, Held in Zion Lutheran Church, Witherspoon Hall, and Holy Communion Church, Philadelphia, Pennsylvania, October 24-29, 1917.

Minutes of the Twenty-Third Annual Convention of the Evangelical Lutheran Synod of New York and New England, June 17-191924, Holy Trinity Church, New York, N.Y.

Minutes of the Twenty-Fourth Annual Convention of the Evangelical Lutheran Synod of New York and New England, June 9-11, 1925.

Minutes of the Twenty-Sixth Annual Convention of the Evangelical Lutheran Synod of New York and New Jersey, Held in Trinity Lutheran Church, Amsterdam, New York, September 14-19, 1897.

Minutes of the Thirty-Fifth Annual Convention of the Evangelical Lutheran Synod of New York and New Jersey, Held in St. Peter's Lutheran Church, Berlin, Ontario, Canada, September 11-14, 1906.

Minutes of the First Convention of the United Lutheran Church in America together with Minutes of the Conventions of the General Synod, the General Council and the United Synod Held in Connection with the Merger, November 10-18, 1918.

Minutes of the Second Biennial Convention of the United Lutheran Church in America, Washington D.C., October 19-27, 1920.

Minutes of the Third Biennial Convention of the United Lutheran Church in America, Buffalo, N.Y., October 17-25, 1922.

Minutes of the Fourth Biennial Convention of the United Lutheran Church in America, Chicago, Illinois, October 21-29, 1924.

Minutes of the Fifth Biennial Convention of the United Lutheran Church in America, Richmond, Virginia, October 19-27, 1926.

Minutes of the Sixth Biennial Convention of the United Lutheran Church in America, Erie, Pennsylvania, October 9-16, 1928.

Minutes of the Seventh Biennial Convention of the United Lutheran Church in America, Milwaukee, Wisconsin, October 7-14, 1930.

Minutes of the Eighth Biennial Convention of the United Lutheran Church in America, Philadelphia, Pennsylvania, October 12-19, 1932.

Minutes of the Ninth Biennial Convention of the United Lutheran Church in America, Savannah, Georgia, October 17-24, 1934.

Minutes of the Tenth Biennial Convention of the United Lutheran Church in America, Columbus, Ohio, October 14-21, 1936.

Minutes of the Eleventh Biennial Convention of the United Lutheran Church in America, Baltimore, Maryland, October 5-12, 1938.

Minutes of the Twelfth Biennial Convention of the United Lutheran Church in America, Omaha, Nebraska, October 9-16, 1940.

Minutes of the Thirteenth Biennial Convention of the United Lutheran Church in America, Louisville, Kentucky, October 14-21, 1942.

Minutes of the Fourteenth Biennial Convention of the United Lutheran Church in America, Minneapolis, Minnesota, October 11-17, 1944.

Minutes of the Fifteenth Biennial Convention of the United Lutheran Church in America, Cleveland, Ohio, October 5-11, 1946.

Minutes of the Sixteenth Biennial Convention of the United Lutheran Church in America, Philadelphia, Pennsylvania, October 6-14, 1948.

Minutes of the Seventeenth Biennial Convention of the United Lutheran Church in America, Des Moines, Iowa, October 4-12, 1950.

Minutes of the Eighteenth Biennial Convention of the United Lutheran Church in America, Seattle, Washington, October 8-15, 1952.

Minutes of the Nineteenth Biennial Convention of the United Lutheran Church in America, Toronto, Canada, October 6-13, 1954.

Minutes of the Twentieth Biennial Convention of the United Lutheran Church in America, Harrisburg, Pennsylvania, October 10-17, 1956.

Minutes of the Twenty-first Biennial Convention of the United Lutheran Church in America, Dayton, Ohio, October 8-15, 1958.

Minutes of the Twenty-second Biennial Convention of the United Lutheran Church in America, Atlantic City, New Jersey, October 13-20, 1960.

Minutes of the Adjourned Meeting of the Twenty-second Biennial Convention of the United Lutheran Church in America, Detroit, Michigan, June 25-27, 1962.

Mortensen, Enok. *The Danish Lutheran Church in America: The History and Heritage of the American Evangelical Lutheran Church.* Philadelphia: Board of Publication of the Lutheran Church in America, 1967.

Mr. Protestant: An Informal Biography of Franklin Clark Fry. Philadelphia: The Board of Publication of the United Lutheran Church in America, 1960.

Myer, Carl Stamm. *Log Cabin to Luther Tower.* St. Louis: Concordia Publishing House, 1965.

Naus, Alford R. *West of the Mississippi: A Picture Story of the United Lutheran Church in America.* The Omaha Committee for the 12th Biennial Convention of the ULCA, 1940.

Nelson, E. Clifford. *Lutheranism in North America 1914-1970.* Minneapolis, Minnesota: Augsburg, 1972.

Nelson, E. Clifford. *The Rise of World Lutheranism: An American Perspective.* Philadelphia: Fortress Press, 1982.

Nelson, E. Clifford, and associates. *The Lutherans in North America.* Philadelphia: Fortress Press, 1980 [1975].

Nelson, E. Clifford and Eugene Fevold. *The Lutheran Church Among Norwegian Americans,* 2 vols. Minneapolis, Minnesota: Augsburg Publishing House, 1960.

"New Jersey Synod of the Lutheran Church in America," in *New York Ministerium Legacy.* Two hundredth Anniversary Committee, 1986.

"The New Lutheran," in *Time,* April 7, 1958.

The New York Times, November 11, 1918.

Nichols, James Hastings. *Romanticism in American Theology: Nevin & Schaff at Mercersburg.* Chicago: University of Chicago Press, 1961.

Nyholm, Paul C. *The Americanization of the Danish Lutheran Church in America: A Study in Immigrant History,* Studies in Church History (Kirchehisstoriske

Studier) II:16. Copenhagen: Institute for Danish Church History, 1963.

The Occasional Services, from the Common Service Book of the Lutheran Church. Philadelphia: The Board of Publication of the United Lutheran Church in America, [1918, 1930] 1943.

Ohl, J. F. *The Inner Mission: A Handbook for Christian Workers.* Philadelphia: General Council Publication House, 1911.

Orchard, Ronald K., ed. *The Ghana Assembly of the International Missionary Council, 28th December, 1957 to 8th January, 1959: Selected Papers.* London: Edinburgh House Press, 1958.

Pannkoke, Otto H. *Great Church Finds Itself: The Lutheran Church Between Wars.* St. Louis: s.n., 1966.

Pannkoke, Otto H. and Walton H. Greever, eds. "News Releases" of The Lutheran Bureau, New York. Archives of Cooperative Lutheranism, The Evangelical Lutheran Church in America, Chicago.

The Proceedings of the Second Assembly of the Lutheran World Federation, Hannover, Germany, July 25-August 3, 1952.

Proceedings of the Third Convention of the Western Pennsylvania-West Virginia Synod, Lutheran Church in America, 1964.

Reed, Luther Dotterer. "Historical Sketch of the Common Service," in *Lutheran Church Review,* vol. 36 (1917).

Reed, Luther Dotterer. *The Lutheran Liturgy: A Study of the Common Service of the Lutheran Church in America.* Philadelphia: Muhlenberg Press, 1947.

Reed, Luther Dotterer. *The Philadelphia Seminary Biographical Record, 1864-1923.* Philadelphia: Lutheran Theological Seminary and the Alumni Association, 1923.

Reinartz, F. Eppling. *1951 Year Book of the United Lutheran Church in America.* Philadelphia: The United Lutheran Publication House, 1951.

Rinderknecht, Edward. "Lutheran Unity and Union from the Point of View of the United Lutheran Church," in *Lutheran Church Quarterly,* vol. 19 (1946).

Rolander, Oscar R. "Missionary Conferences," in *The Encyclopedia of the Lutheran Church,* vol, 2, ed. by Julius Bodensieck. Minneapolis, Minnesota:

Augsburg Publishing House, 1965.

Rouse, Ruth. *The World's Student Christian Federation: A History of the First Thirty Years.* London: SCM Press, 1948.

Sandt, George, W. *Theodore Emanuel Schmauk.* Philadelphia: United Lutheran Publication House, 1921.

Sachse, Julius Frederick. *The German Pietists of Provincial Pennsylvania: 1694-1708.* Philadelphia: printed for author, 1895.

Schlink, Edmund. *Theologie der Lutheranischen bekenntnisschriften.* Munchen: Evangelischerverlag Albert Lamp, 1940.

Schlink, Edmund. *Theology of the Lutheran Confessions.* Philadelphia: Fortress Press, 1985 [c. 1961].

Schmauk, Theodore Emanuel. *The Confessional Principle and the Confessions of the Lutheran Church: As Embodying the Evangelical Confession of the Christian Church.* Philadelphia: General Council Publication Board, 1911.

Schmauk, Theodore Emanuel. *A History of the Lutheran Church in Pennsylvania (1638-1820): From Original Sources.* Philadelphia: General Council Publishing House, 1903.

Schmidt, William J. *Architect of Unity.* New York: Friendship Press, 1978.

Schmucker, B. M. "Congregational Constitutions," in *Lutheran Church Review,* vol. 6 (1877).

Schmucker, Samuel Simon. *The American Lutheran Church, Historically, Doctrinally, and Practically Delineated,* 3rd ed. Philadelphia: E. W. Miller, 1852.

Second General Conference of Lutherans in America. Philadelphia: General Council Publication Board, Lutheran Publication Society, 1903.

Service Book and Hymnal of the Lutheran Church in America. Minneapolis, Minnesota: Augsburg Publishing House, 1958.

Shaffer, Rollin G. "LWA—A Quarter Century of Christian Compassion," in *The National Lutheran,* December 1965.
Simon, Ruth. *A Centennial History: 1868-1968.*

Sittler, Joseph. *The Doctrine of the Word in the Structure of Lutheran Theology.* Philadelphia: Muhlenberg Press, 1948.

Solberg, Richard W. *As Between Brothers.* Minneapolis, Minnesota: Augsburg Publishing House, 1957.

Solberg, Richard W. *Lutheran Higher Education in North America.* Minneapolis, Minnesota: Augsburg Publishing House, 1985.

Stephenson, George Malcolm, *The Religious Aspects of Swedish Immigration: A Study of Immigrant Churches.* Minneapolis, Minnesota: The University of Minnesota Press, 1932.

"A Stirring Address," in *The Lutheran,* November 21, 1918.

Strodach, Paul Z. *A Manual on Worship: Venite Adoremus,* rev. ed. Philadelphia: Muhlenberg Press, 1946.

Stulken, Marilyn Kay. *Hymnal Companion to the Lutheran Book of Worship.* Philadelphia: Fortress Press, 1980.

Sundkler, Bengt. *Nathan Söderblom: His Life and His Work.* Lund: Gleerup, 1968.

Swanson, Byran E. "Conrad Bergendoff, The Making of a Lutheran Ecumenist." Ph.D. dissertation at Princeton Theological Seminary, 1980.

Tappert, Theodore G., *History of the Lutheran Theological Seminary at Philadelphia, 1864-1964.* Philadelphia: The Lutheran Theological Seminary at Philadelphia, 1964.

Tappert, Theodore G., ed. *The Book of Concord: The Confessions of the Evangelical Lutheran Church.* Philadelphia: Fortress Press, 1959.

Tappert, Theodore G. and John W. Doberstein, trans. and eds. *The Journals of Henry Melchior Muhlenberg.* Philadelphia: Evangelical Ministerium of Pennsylvania and Adjacent States and Philadelphia: Muhlenberg Press, 1942-1958.

Thompson, Bard. "The Palatine Church Order" in *Church History,* 23 (1954).

Threinen, Norman J. *Fifty Years of Lutheran Convergence: The Canadian Case-Study,* Lutheran Historical Conference 3. Dubuque, Iowa: Wm. C. Brown Company Publishers, 1983.

ULCA *Pastor's Desk Book*. Philadelphia: United Lutheran Publication, 1947-1962.

United Lutheran Church in America Yearbooks. Philadelphia: The United Lutheran Church Publication House, 1918-1962.

Valentine, Milton, "Review of *Natural Theology or Rational Theism*," in *The Lutheran Church Review*, vol. 5 (1886).

Visser 't Hooft, William Adolf. *Memoirs*. London: SCM Press; Philadelphia: Westminster, 1973.

Voigt, Louis. "Ohio Synod History" (unpublished manuscript).

Wagner, Martin L. *The Chicago Synod and Its Antecedents*. Waverly, Iowa: Wartburg Publishing House Press, 1909.

Wallace, Paul A. W. *Conrad Weiser, 1696-1760, Friend of Colonist and Mohawk*. Philadelphia: University of Pennsylvania Press, 1945.

Wallace, Paul A. W. *The Muhlenbergs of Pennsylvania*. Philadelphia: University of Pennsylvania Press, 1950.

Waters, M. S. "The Jersey City Merger Meeting," in *The Lutheran*, November 28, 1918.

Wenner, George U. *The Lutherans of New York, 1648-1918*. New York: The Petersfield Press, 1918.

Wentz, Abdel Ross. *A Basic History of Lutheranism in America*, Rev. ed. Philadelphia: Muhlenberg Press, 1964 [1955].

Wentz, Abdel Ross. "The Convention in Eisenach was a Success," in *The Lutheran*, September 27, 1963.

Wentz, Abdel Ross. "The General Synod," in *Distinctive Doctrines and Usages of the General Bodies of the Evangelical Lutheran Church in the United States*, 1st ed., 1893.

Wentz, Abdel Ross, ed. *Gettysburg Lutheran Theological Seminary*, 2 Vols. Harrisburg, Pennsylvania: Evangelical Press, 1964.

Wentz, Abdel Ross. *History of the Evangelical Lutheran Synod of Maryland*. Harrisburg, Pennsylvania: Evangelical Press, 1920.

Wentz, Abdel Ross. *The Lutheran Church in American History*, 2nd ed. Philadelphia: United Lutheran Publication House, 1933.

Wentz, Abdel Ross. "The Salt that Kept Its Savor," in *Lutheran Church Quarterly*, vol. 8 (1935).

Wentz, Frederick K. *Lutherans in Concert: The Story of the National Lutheran Council, 1918-1966*. Minneapolis, Minnesota: Augsburg, 1968.

Witwer, Norman C. *The Faithful and the Bold: The Story of the First Service of the Zion Evangelical Lutheran Church, Oldwick, NJ*. Oldwick, New Jersey, 1984.

Wolf, Edmund Jacob. *The Lutheran in America: A Story of Struggle, Progress, Influence, and Marvelous Growth*. New York: J. A. Hill, 1889.

Wolf, L. B. "The International Missionary Council at Oxford," in *The Lutheran*, August 23, 1923.

Wolf, Richard C. *Documents in Lutheran Unity in America*. Philadelphia: Fortress Press, 1966.

The World Council of Churches, Its Process of Formation; Minutes and Reports of the Meeting of the Provisional Committee of the World Council of Churches Held at Geneva from February 21st to 23rd, 1946. Geneva, 1946.

Young, John J., ed. *The History of St. John's Evangelical Lutheran Church, 79-83 Christopher Street, New York City: 1855-1905*. New York, 1905.

PUBLISHED WRITINGS
OF E. THEODORE BACHMANN
Compiled by David J. Lose

Books

The Ecumenical Involvement of the LCA Predecessor Bodies: A Brief History,
1900-1962, rev. 2nd ed. New York: Division for World Mission and Ecumenism
of the Lutheran Church in America, 1983.

Epic of Faith: The Background of the Second Assembly of the Lutheran World
Federation, 1952. New York: The National Lutheran Council, 1952.

Lutheran Churches in the World, with Mercia Brenne Bachmann. Minneapolis,
Minnesota: Augsburg, 1989.

Lutherans in Brazil: A Story of Emerging Ecumenism. Minneapolis: Augsburg
Publishing House, 1970.

Raja Bushanan Manikam: A Biography, with Carl Gustav Diehl. Madras, India:
The Christian Literature Society, 1975.

The Rise of "Missouri Lutheranism." A Dissertation Submitted to the Faculty of
the Divinity School in Candidacy for the Degree of Doctor of Philosophy.
Chicago, Illinois, 1946 (Unpublished).

They Called Him Father: The Life Story of John Christian Frederick Heyer.
Philadelphia: The Muhlenberg Press, 1942.

Edited Volumes

The Activating Concern: Historical and Theological Bases. National Council of
Churches, 1955.

The Emerging Perspective: Response and Prospect. Proceedings of the First
Conference on the Churches and Social Welfare. National Council of the Churches
of Christ in the U.S.A., 1956.

Luther's Works, Volume 35: Word and Sacrament I. Philadelphia: Muhlenberg
Press, 1960.

Lutheran World, 1973-1977

Chapters in Books

"Canada's Lutherans in a Mediating Role?" in *Festschrift: A Tribute to Dr. William Hordern*, ed. by Walter Freitag. Saskatoon, Saskatchewan: University of Saskatchewan, 1985. Pp. 194-215.

"Der Clown als Erloser: Ernste Gedanken zur Pfarrerausbildung in den USA," in *Solidaritat + Spiritualitat = Diakonie: Gottesdienst als Menschendienst Ein okumenisches Symposion*. Stuttgart: Evangelisches Verlagswerk Stuttgart. Pp. 152-160.

"The Church and the Rise of Modern Society, 1830-1914," in *The Lutheran Heritage: Christian Social Responsibility*, Vol 2, ed. by Harold C. Letts. Philadelphia: Muhlenberg Press, 1957. Pp. 89-137.

"Churches of North America," in *Lutheran Churches of the World*, ed. by S.W. Herman. Minneapolis, Minnesota: Augsburg Publishing House, 1957. Pp. 133-181.
    —*also published as*
"Luthertum in Nordamerika," in *Die Lutherischen Kirchen in der Welt: Herausgegeben vom Lutherischen Weltbund*, Berlin: Lutherisches Verlagshaus, 1957. Pp. 97-134.

"Ecumenical Movement," in *The Encyclopedia of the Lutheran Church*, vol. 1, ed. by Julius Bodensieck. Minneapolis, Minnesota: Augsburg Fortress Publishing House, 1965. Pp. 750-764.

"Formaçâo Teológica: Relato histórico para o Brasil," in *Sementeira E Ceifa: Publiçâcao comemorativa por ocasiâo da inauguraçâo do Prédio Principal da Faculdade de Teologia em Sâo Leopoldo, October 4, 1959*. Pp. 15-22.
    —*also published as*
"Theologische Ausbildung: Eine Vorgeschichte für Brasilien," in *Saat und Ernte: Festschrift zur Einweihung des Hauptgebäudes der Theologischen Hochschule in Sâo Leopoldo, October 4, 1959*. Pp. 16-23.

"The Function of the Lutheran World Federation," in *The Lutheran Church Past and Present*, ed. by Vilmos Vajta. Minneapolis, Minnesota: Augsburg Publishing House, 1977. Pp. 352-366.
    —*also published as*
"Die Funktion des Lutherischen Weltbundes," in *Die Kirchen Der Welt, Band XV: Die Evangelisch-Lutherische Kirche*, Herausgegeben von Vilmos Vajta. Stuttgart: Evangelisches Verlagswerk Stuttgart, 1977. Pp. 384-400.

"Kenneth Scott Latourette: Historian and Friend," in *Frontiers of the Christian World Mission Since 1938: Essays in Honor of Kenneth Scott Latourette*, ed. by

Wilber C. Harr. New York: Harper & Brother Publishers, 1962. Pp. 231-280.

"Man," in *What Lutherans are Thinking: A Symposium on Lutheran Faith and Life,* ed. by E. C. Fendt. Columbus, Ohio: The Wartburg Press, 1947. Pp. 148-173. "Penn's 'Holy Experiment' in Context: Some Aspects of a Nascent Ecumenism in the Lutheran Involvement (1638-1762)," in *Quest for Faith, Quest for Freedom: Aspects of Pennsylvania's Religious Experience,* ed. by Otto Reimherr. Selingsgrove: Susquehanna University Press / London, Associated University Press, 1987. Pp. 41-69.

"Samuel Simon Schmucker (1799-1873)," in *Sons of the Prophets: Leaders in Protestantism from Princeton Seminary,* ed. by Hugh T. Kerr. Princeton, New Jersey: Princeton University Press, 1963. Pp. 39-68.

"Walther, Schaff, and Krauth on Luther," in *Interpreters of Luther: Essays in Honor of Wilhelm Pauck,* ed. by Jaroslav Pelikan. Philadelphia: Fortress Press, 1968. Pp. 187-230.

Articles

"A Bishop on Sabbatical—Eduard Lohse of Hanover" in *Partners,* Vol. 4.2, April, 1982. Pp. 20-22.

A Year of Impressions, for *The Lutheran,* Vols. 19-20, 1937-1938
"God's Word is Not Bound: Despite Adverse Conditions the Basel Missionary Society Makes Progress," August 11, 1937, p. 2.
"Seminarian In Europe," August 18, 1937, p. 25.
"The Faith and Order Conference: Impressions of its Proceedings upon a Visitor," September 8, 1937, p. 2.
"Finland, A Lutheran Frontier," October 20, 1937, pp. 19-20.
"Dying: Monastery in Finland Continues Rites but Declines in Attendance," December 1, 1937, pp. 8-9.
"A Morning At El-Ashar," May 4, 1938, pp. 18-19.
"And Thou, Capernaum," May 11, 1938, pp. 6-7.
"Easter Rites in Jerusalem," May 25, 1938, pp 8-9, 27.
"Philadelphia, the First," July 27, 1938, pp. 3, 30.
"Outline of Tragedy," November 9, 1938, pp. 3-4.
"Outline of Tragedy-II," November 16, 1938, pp. 3-4.

"American Lutheran Studies: A Career as Historian to 1948," in *American Lutheranism: Crisis in Historical Consciousness?,* the Essays and Reports of the 1988 Lutheran Historical Conference (Vol. 13) held at Valparaiso University, Valparaiso, Indiana, October 27-29, 1988. St. Louis: The Lutheran Historical Conference, 1990. Pp. 100-119.

"Confessional Kin Worldwide," in *Concordia Historical Institute Quarterly*, Vol. 64, no. 1, Spring, 1991. Pp. 7-17.

"Curricular Offerings on the History of Lutheranism," in *Concordia Historical Institute Quarterly*, Vol. 38, no. 4, January, 1996. Pp. 197-203.

"Deaconesses on Skis," in *The Bond*, Vol. 16, no. 12, April, 1940. P. 2.

"Inventory of Fields of Deaconess Service," in *The Thirtieth Lutheran Deaconess Conference in America*. Philadelphia, 1951. Pp. 40-51.

"Lutheranism on the Pacific Perimeter: A Synopsis of Beginnings," in *Lutherans on the Pacific Rim*, Essays and Reports of the 1986 Lutheran Historical Conference (Vol. 12) held at St. Mark's Lutheran Church, San Francisco, California, November 5-8, 1986. St. Louis: The Lutheran Historical Conference, 1988. Pp. 1-35.

"Mission Frontier in Palestine," in *The Moslem World*, vol 29, July, 1939. Pp. 3-12.

"Missouri and its Relations to other Lutherans: Some Observations on the Shaping and Exercise of Conscience," in *Concordia Historical Institute Quarterly*, Vol. 45, no. 2, May, 1972. Pp. 159-170.

"Protestantism in the Nazi State," in *The Lutheran Church Quarterly*, Vol. 8, no. 1, January, 1935. Pp. 1-12.

"Religion in a Reformatory," in *The Lutheran Church Quarterly*, Vol. 10, no. 2, April, 1937. Pp.133-142.

"They Plan for Service," in The Lutheran, Vol. 32, July 17, 1940. Pp. 28-29.

"Why Not Deacons," in *The Chicago Lutheran Seminary Record*, Vol. 49, no. 4 (October, 1944). Pp. 3-9.

Translations

I Will Tell You About God, by Hans Froer. Philadelphia: Fortress Press, 1970.

Luther in Mid-Career: 1521-1530, by Heinrich Bornkamm. Philadelphia: Fortress Press, 1983.

From *Luther's Works, Volume 35: Word and Sacrament I*. Philadelphia: Muhlenberg Press, 1960.
    "A Brief Instruction on What to Look for and Expect in the Gospels."

"Defense of the Translation of the Psalms."
"How Christians Should Regard Moses."
"Prefaces to the Apocrypha."
"The Sacrament of Penance."

Tracts and Devotionals

"With Muhlenberg in New Jersey." Trenton, New Jersey: New Jersey Synod of the Evangelical Lutheran Church in America, 1992.

"Light for Today: Advent-Christmas, 1939" (Vol. 5, #1). Philadelphia: The United Lutheran Publication House, 1939.

"Light for Today: July-August, 1957" (Vol. 22, #4; August 25-31). Philadelphia: Muhlenberg Press, 1957.

INDEX OF PERSONS